NORTH FROM THE HOOK

150 YEARS OF THE GEOLOGICAL SURVEY OF IRELAND

The National Gallery of Ireland viewed from Merrion Square during the summer of 1995. The Gallery was then commemorating the sesquicentennial of the Geological Survey of Ireland by staging an exhibition devoted to the artistic work of George Victor Du Noyer, an officer of the Survey from 1847 until his death in 1869. It was an apposite setting for such an event. The Gallery stands upon the site of Dublin's Great Industrial Exhibition of 1853, where Richard Griffith, 'the Father of Irish Geology', had on display his pioneering geological map of Ireland. Shortly thereafter, Griffith played a leading role in the planning of the National Gallery itself, and during the 1860s there was a proposal that the fossil, mineral, and rock collections of the Geological Survey should be placed upon permanent exhibition within the Gallery. The 1995 exhibition was sponsored by Bord Gáis Éireann, the body which makes available to the people of Ireland the natural gas from the Kinsale Head Gas Field. The discovery of that field in 1974 was one of the events which inspired a revitalisation of the Geological Survey of Ireland during the years following 1968. Photograph by Roy Hewson, reproduced by courtesy of the Director of the National Gallery of Ireland.

NORTH FROM THE HOOK

150 YEARS OF THE GEOLOGICAL SURVEY OF IRELAND

Gordon L. Herries Davies

GEOLOGICAL SURVEY OF IRELAND
1995

First published 1995
Geological Survey of Ireland

ISBN 1 899702 00 8

The image for the end papers is taken from a watercolour by George Victor Du Noyer.
The watercolour shows the unconformity between the Old Red Sandstone
and the Lower Palaeozoic rocks at Waterford Harbour.
The original is in the archives of the Geological Survey of Ireland.

Design, typesetting and origination by Printset & Design Ltd.
Printed by Criterion Press Ltd, Dublin, Ireland.

FOREWORD

The Geological Survey of Ireland (GSI) celebrates 150 years in existence this year. Founded in 1845, the first year of the Great Famine, it has evolved over the years in response to the changing needs of the community it serves. Its story is abundantly laced with success and failure - and it demonstrates that geologists are as well endowed with eccentricity, humour, intrigue and sadness as any other part of humanity. Anyone who believes that geology, particularly as conducted within the Civil Service, is an altogether respectable but rather dull discipline is invited - challenged! - to open these pages.

GSI commissioned this historical study because it believes it will form a significant and entertaining story that will be of interest beyond the limits of the geological community. It is a study which draws heavily on GSI archives and unashamedly tells its story from the perspective of the organisation itself. Indeed we deliberately gave the author a free hand so that he could tell his story without looking over his shoulder. This is an historian's reflective view of the place of GSI in Irish society.

Professor Gordon L. Herries Davies is the foremost historian of the earth sciences in Ireland, and his reputation extends far beyond the coastline of this country. We asked Gordon to attempt something very difficult - to write a history that was both entertaining and authoritative; one that might enthral the general reader while still catering for those with specialist interests in the growth of the geological sciences in Ireland. I believe that readers of these pages will find he has succeeded to an extraordinary degree.

Gordon has tackled many of the social aspects of the Survey's history which a less courageous writer might have chosen to ignore. This has greatly enhanced the value of the work and, I believe, makes it a valuable source book on the development of science in Ireland since the mid-nineteenth century. I congratulate Gordon on producing this fascinating story.

I want to thank all the persons and organisations who have assisted the author in his work; the names of all these are recorded in the text. For my own part, I wish to thank my two predecessors, Mr M.V. O Brien and Dr C.E. Williams, for facilitating the author in many ways.

Dr Peadar McArdle
Director
Geological Survey of Ireland

3 October 1995

PREFACE

This volume is possessed of roots which extend back over more than forty years - back to the time when I was a young academic in Trinity College Dublin. My own Department was that of Geography, and we were located within the College's magnificent Museum Building. Adjacent to us there lay the Geology Department, and in the basement of the Building my friends the geologists maintained a library which, though small, was well stocked with long runs of the British geological periodicals. These periodicals fascinated me then; they continue to fascinate me today. Their fascination lies not at the level of the individual papers which the volumes contain, but rather in the character of entire volumes as a reflection of geological communities existing at particular moments in time past. To take down volume 10 (1910-15) of the *Transactions of the Edinburgh Geological Society,* or volume 8 (1883-84) of the *Proceedings of the Geologists' Association,* is to become a time-traveller in science. It is to enjoy the privilege of looking in upon a long-since extinguished community as its members acted and interacted. Each volume of the journals is like an historical goldfish-bowl in which there still swim the ghostly forms of the bowl's former occupants.

Among all the periodicals, I have my unquestioned favourite: the *Geological Magazine,* founded in July 1864 and still going strong. In its earlier decades the journal was such a wonderful potpourri of scientific papers, reviews, news, letters, and obituaries. It was through the pages of the *Geol. Mag.* that I first began to gaze upon the ghosts within the goldfish-bowl of the Geological Survey of Ireland.

Within the green covers of the *Geol. Mag.* I made the acquaintance of such Survey figures as Tim Hallissy, Grenville Cole, Will Wright, Edward Hull, Henry Kinahan, Beete Jukes, and Thomas Oldham. I became enthralled. These were the men who had made the geological maps which I was using for my own field-study. These were the men who had explored the recesses of Ireland which were now attracting my own attention. These were the men whose writings I found myself able to purchase for just a few pence in the Dublin second-hand bookshops. These were the men who had spiced the pages of the *Geol. Mag.* with their acrimony. Clearly, they had not always co-existed in a happy state of fraternal scientific companionship. I desperately wanted to know them better, to relive their achievements, to discover their problems, and to understand their failures.

I see from the pages of the Survey's visitors' book that I first entered the Survey rather later than I would have expected - on 5 May 1958 to be exact. By 1965 I was being allowed to borrow some of the Survey's Victorian letter-books for study - a service which, very properly, would be denied to me today - and I employed much of the material I had unearthed in the writing of my 1983 history of Irish geological cartography over the period between 1750 and 1890. But that volume told only one part of the Survey's story. The Survey has lived on for a further hundred years since 1890, and, in any case, geological cartography has never been both the alpha and the omega of the Survey's existence.

With the approach of the Survey's 1995 sesquicentennial, I was delighted to receive from Ralph Horne, the Assistant Director, a letter dated 7 February 1992. He invited me to write a full-scale history of the Survey, in all its many facets, for publication in 1995. This task I was delighted to undertake. This volume is the result.

In conclusion, just one word of apologetic explanation. The volume had to be kept within a reasonable compass, and it was just not possible to give the source for each and every statement made in the pages that follow.

Gordon L. Herries Davies
30 September 1995

26 Trinity College Dublin

ACKNOWLEDGEMENTS

The birth of this volume has been assisted by many a physician, midwife, accoucheur, and apothecary. To all of them I now express my heartfelt appreciation and gratitude.

In further itemising the help I have received, there is but one location in which to commence - in the Geological Survey's headquarters at Beggars Bush in Dublin. There, throughout my writing of the work, I have been received as an honorary member of the Survey. I have been allowed to go where I pleased, to search as I pleased, and to see what I pleased. Most important of all, I have been allowed to write what I pleased. No author of an institutional history could have been accorded more freedom than that so willingly granted to me.

Throughout the last three years, the Director, Peadar McArdle, the Assistant Director, Ralph Horne, and the Principal Officer, Eddie Mortimer, have all been extremely supportive. They have read my chapters as they were completed, and they have been able to tender to me many an enlightening insight. To Ralph Horne I owe a very special vote of thanks. He was in charge of the Survey at the time of the conception of this historical study, and during its gestation he effectively responded to all my appeals for guidance and help.

Tony Glackin has served for me as a consul within the Survey during my periods of absence, and I am extremely grateful to him for the care and enthusiasm with which he has executed tasks undertaken on my behalf. I have also enjoyed - especially during the project's earlier stages - the assistance of Tony's colleague Liam O'Brien. Likewise within the Survey's General Office there are two ladies to be mentioned: Madeline Loughlin and Suzanne Lyons. It was their skill which put a substantial part of the volume onto disk.

Among the remainder of the Survey's staff it becomes almost invidious to mention names. Virtually everybody has helped me in some way or other. Something of the extent of my probing inquiries, and of the co-operation which I have received, is revealed in the Staff List which constitutes Appendix Two.

There are, nevertheless, six other inhabitants of Beggars Bush whose contribution was such as to merit particular personal mention. Loreto Farrell went to immense trouble to recapture memories of the premises which accommodated the Survey during the early 1970s. Aubrey Flegg put into my hands the Survey's most venerable man-made relic (see p.10), and he volunteered a cycle ride down Dublin's Hume Street upon my behalf. Piers Gardiner has been helpful in so many ways, from guidance through the Law of the Sea conferences to memories of 4 Kildare Street. We must all be grateful to him for having persuaded both Mark Cunningham and Mike O'Meara to allow some of their memories to be recorded upon paper. Matthew Parkes took the trouble to search the Survey's collections for the set of superb fossils featured in Plate XII. John Pyne was of great service in looking out for me the records pertaining to the issue of prospecting licences during the years around the time of the rich discovery at Tynagh.

It is an odd coincidence that of the five individuals just mentioned, three are now members of their Department's Exploration and Mining Division rather than of the Survey itself, while the name of Parkes is absent from my Staff List because he is a geologist present in Beggars Bush on contract rather than as a permanent member of the Survey's staff. The sixth inhabitant of Beggars Bush to be named I shall for the moment leave aside.

Two of the major figures in my story are two former Directors of the Survey: Murrogh O Brien and Cyril Williams. Both are in retirement, both have given me freely of their time, and both have kindly read my words relating to their periods of office. Chapter Seven has benefitted enormously from their stimulating comments. Murrogh inhabits a small island, and most of our conversations have therefore contributed handsomely to the budget of Telecom Eireann. One Sunday morning we allowed ourselves three telephone conversations, and with Murrogh I enjoyed what, by several hours, was the longest telephone call of my life. Geographically speaking, Cyril is far more accessible. Many are the occasions upon which I have talked with him about the Survey while enjoying his own, and his wife's, splendid hospitality in a memento-filled setting redolent of years in Africa.

Many a former member of the Survey has answered my queries and allowed me to tap their memories. I may only hope that the following bald listing will in some measure serve as an expression of my gratitude: Joan Barragry (Mrs Brück); Professor Peter Brück; Timothy Downing; John Duffy; Dilys Jones; Professor Tom Murphy; Dave Naylor; Tom Reilly; Keith Robinson; Jean Wilkinson (Mrs Stanley).

Two other former, and now deceased, officers over the years regaled me with Survey tales of yore: Tony Farrington and Mike O'Meara. Tony's experience went back to the days of Grenville Cole in the aftermath of World War I; Mike had stories to tell of Tim Hallissy and Douglas Bishopp. How I wish now that we had Tony and Mike upon tape.

In a few cases I have been able to establish contact with the relatives or the descendants of former Survey officers. In this category I wish to thank the following: Janet Bishopp Harding, of Marnhull, Dorset; Henry Cruise, of Killiney, Co. Dublin; Alyn Jones, of Ashby de la Zouch; Glascott J. R. Symes, of Dublin; and Margaret Synge, of Dublin. Here I must express a particularly deep debt of gratitude to Barbara, Lady Dainton. She has provided me with an immense amount of material relating to her father, the eminent Pleistocene geologist W.B. Wright, and to her mother, who was a Survey supernumerary.

Away from the Survey, many people have helped in a variety of ways. Perhaps most of them will never see this acknowledgement of their contribution, but I nevertheless mention their names: Tom Bain (British Geological Survey, Edinburgh); Mike Boland (Ennex International PLC); Proinsias Brinkley (Electricity Supply Board); Norman Butcher (Edinburgh); Timothy Collins (University College Galway); Mairead Dunlevy (The Hunt Museum, Limerick); Terence Dunne (Trinity College Dublin); David Fitzgerald (Ennex International PLC); Eamonn Grennan (Sligo); J.M. Hammond (Tonbridge School, Kent); Roy Hewson (National Gallery of Ireland); Patrick Hill (Worthing and Ottawa); Leonard Hynes (Ordnance Survey, Dublin); Marie McFeely (National Gallery of Ireland); Bob McIntosh (British Geological Survey, Edinburgh); Bill Maxwell (National Gallery of Ireland); Frank Mitchell (Townley Hall, Co. Louth); Nigel Monaghan (National Museum of Ireland); P. Stainthorpe (Commonwealth War Graves Commission); Nicholas Stephens (Emsworth, Hampshire); John Thackray (Natural History Museum, London); Hugh Torrens (University of Keele); T. K. Whitaker (formerly Secretary, the Department of Finance); Patricia Woodward (School of Geography, University of Oxford).

A very special word of thanks is due to Graham McKenna, the Chief Librarian at the British Geological Survey in Keyworth. He made very pleasant my 1993 visit to Keyworth and he even located for me a copy of the elusive 1900 confidential report of the Wharton Committee.

All the typing not carried out in the Survey was done for me in Nenagh, Co. Tipperary, by Deirdre O'Dowd under the watchful eye of the dog Misty. I enjoyed meeting both of them.

The majority of the photographic work was executed by David Davison and his son Edwin. It was, as always, a pleasure to work with them. I express the same sentiments in relation to Bill Deevy of the Criterion Press, our printers. It was pleasant to find myself working with somebody who already had an appreciation of the charm of The Hook.

And that brings me to three final but rather special acknowledgements. The first two are to former colleagues in Trinity College Dublin who, like myself, have now retired from the bustle of the university scene: John Andrews and Charles Holland. Over the years, John has read much of what I have written in advance of its publication. On this occasion he has again afforded me the benefit of his wide literary expertise, his incisive thinking, and his critical judgement. Charles used to demonstrate to me when I was a first-year undergraduate, and after we became Dublin colleagues I regularly turned to him for geological and other guidance. I turned to him again while preparing many of the chapters which follow. That John and Charles were not asked to review all of the chapters was entirely due to the pressures of a tight publication schedule. I am sure it is my loss - and that of my readers.

My very last acknowledgement, appropriately, takes me back to Beggars Bush - back to an officer of the Survey. I owe to Jean Archer a particularly deep debt of gratitude. For twenty years she has taken a keen interest in the history of the Survey, and her knowledge of its archives is unrivalled. In so many respects she has been to me an assistant throughout this project. She has searched the Library for obscure pieces of literature. She has spent hours leafing through six-inch field-sheets in search of specimens worthy of illustration. She has ferried archival material to and from the Davison's studio. She has even positioned herself to lend human scale to some of the photographs which I was taking for use in the book. Without her help, so readily given, this volume would never have been published within the Survey's sesquicentennial year.

TABLE OF CONTENTS

LIST OF COLOUR PLATES

A knowledge of what lies below the surface of the ground in any locality is so obviously a useful knowledge that no words need be expended on the enforcement of its truth.

> Professor J. Beete Jukes, Local Director of the Geological Survey of Ireland, in the notes to an address delivered at the Museum of 63.472 mmIrish Industry on 21 December 1866.

The Geological Survey of Ireland is the national earth science agency whose mandate is the provision of earth science information and advice as they relate to Ireland and the acquisition of data for this purpose.

> From the Final Report of the Department of Energy *Review of the Geological Survey of Ireland and the Minerals Exploration and Development Division,* 31 January 1992.

CHAPTER ONE

ANCESTRY

In his opinion it would be for the advantage of the kingdom if a proper and accurate chart of all the lands in Ireland was made, so as to point out the lands where there were mines and minerals, or where such were most likely to be found, which would be of infinite benefit to the nation to know the substrata of the kingdom.

From the report of a speech delivered in the Irish House of Commons on 8 February 1786 by Charles O'Hara, one of the Members for the County of Sligo.

White breeches, a dark blue coat decorated with gold-embroidered oak-leaves, a red, white, and blue sash, and a bicorn hat with a red, white, and blue cockade. That, I presume, was the uniform which the youthful French general Amable Humbert brought with him when he landed his troops at Killala, County Mayo, in the August of 1798. What he cannot have brought with him was an accurate map of Ireland. Such a map simply did not exist. The nineteenth century was almost into its fifth decade before the activities of the Ordnance Survey made available the first accurate topographical map of the whole of Ireland. Such maps - maps depicting Ireland's rivers and mountains, roads and towns - are today thoroughly commonplace. We buy them in our local newsagent's shop, we see them upon our TV screens, the Irish Tourist Board gives them to our visitors, and our children pore over them in the classroom. Topographical maps have become a part of our everyday existence.

Rather different is the case of the geological map. Such a map - a map depicting the areal distribution of the various types of rock from which Ireland has been shaped - is far less generally familiar. Virtually everybody understands the topographical map, but the geological map is today seen as a specialised document capable of being understood only by the expert. This is unfortunate. The user of a geological map really faces problems little more taxing than those faced by the user of a topographical map. All it behoves us to know is that a splash of blue represents an area of limestone upon the geological map and a lake upon the topographical map; that a black line indicates a geological fault upon one map and a railway upon the other; or that a splatter of a black symbol depicts in one case a mantle of glacial drift and in the other a forest or an area of rough grazing. Such parallels are hardly surprising because throughout much of the first half of the nineteenth century the story of the geological map of Ireland is closely intertwined with the story of Ireland's topographical map.

My story begins with Richard Kirwan during the 1790s. Kirwan is one of history's unfortunate victims. Posterity has delighted in chuckling over his many eccentricities, but few have chosen to remember that in the years around 1800 he enjoyed an international scholarly reputation. The title page of one of his works, published in 1796, advertises his membership of the Royal Society, the Royal Irish Academy, and 'the academies of Stockholm, Upsal, Berlin, Manchester, Philadelphia, &c.' Publications in chemistry, geology, meteorology, mineralogy, philology, and philosophy streamed from his pen. In 1799 he was an obvious choice as the successor to Lord Charlemont in the presidency of the Royal Irish Academy. His Dublin contemporaries even founded a Kirwanian Society in his honour, and when he died, in June 1812, he was accorded what is said to have been the largest funeral that Dublin had ever seen.

Late in the 1790s Kirwan issued for official consideration a document entitled *A plan, for the introduction and establishment of the most advantageous management of mines in the Kingdom of Ireland.* His scheme envisaged the establishment of an Irish Mining Board consisting of twelve expert and salaried members, all of them required to be resident in Dublin. The Board was to meet twice weekly, and it was to be charged with the general oversight of all Irish mining enterprises. In order to be eligible for service upon the Board, candidates were to have studied for two years at the famed Freiberg Mining Academy in Saxony, and they were then to have spent a further two years acquiring a practical knowledge of mining in both Germany and the British Isles. They were to be proficient in Latin, French, arithmetic, geometry, trigonometry, surveying, subterraneous geometry, drawing, mineralogy, chemistry, assaying, and the working of ores; their mathematical skills were to be tested by

FIGURE 1.1. *Richard Kirwan (1733-1812), Ireland's most famed scientist in the years around 1800.* (Reproduced from a plate in the *Proceedings of the Royal Irish Academy,* volume 4, 1847-50.)

the Provost and Fellows of Trinity College Dublin; and their chemical expertise was to be assessed by the professors of chemistry in Trinity College and the Dublin Society. These highly trained members of the Board, Kirwan proposed, should in addition be made responsible for a mineralogical survey of Ireland. His idea was that each summer two or more members of the Board should visit one of the Irish counties to conduct a mineralogical survey, the work proceeding year by year until the entire country had been examined.

In offering his proposal Kirwan was probably influenced by news of the mineralogical developments that were taking place in Sweden and among the German states. Nonetheless, Kirwan's was a progressive, imaginative, and even startling proposal. Had it been implemented, Ireland would have been among the first nations in the world to benefit from the existence of a national geological survey, and we would today be about to celebrate not the sesquicentennial of our Geological Survey, but rather its bicentenary. In fact Kirwan's suggestions came to naught. He was living long before the age of state interference and planned economies, and it was suspected that a Mining Board such as he proposed might violate the constitutional rights of individual mine owners.

Kirwan was the Dublin Society's *éminence grise,* and the Society was sufficiently interested in his proposals to accord them a place within the pages of its *Transactions*. Such interest needs evoke within us little surprise because since 1786 the Society had itself been conducting a rudimentary mineralogical survey of Ireland. In the June of that year the Society had commissioned a Scotsman named Donald Stewart to be the Society's Itinerant Mineralogist at a wage of one guinea per week. His first assignments were to investigate the geology of County Wicklow and to study the exposures revealed along the line of the Grand Canal in the Irish Midlands. Other commissions followed, and down to his death in 1811 Stewart visited most parts of Ireland on behalf of the Society. He is reputed to have made many geological discoveries of economic significance, and his published report, dated 1800, describes in sketchy outline the economic geology of twenty-five of Ireland's thirty-two counties.

Useful though Stewart's work may have been, the Dublin Society recognised that any comprehensive survey of Ireland's geological resources was a task far beyond the capabilities of a single individual. Stewart could hardly be left to plough his mineralogical furrow alone. In the opening years of the nineteenth century the Society therefore placed two other geological irons squarely into the fire.

First, from the shortly to be extinguished Irish parliament, the Society in 1800 obtained permission to expend a portion of its annual government grant upon the commissioning of a series of statistical surveys of the Irish counties. Kirwan was one of the leading figures involved in the project, and the first of the surveys was published in 1801. The other county volumes followed somewhat fitfully, and the series finally fizzled out in 1832 with only twenty-three of the thirty-two counties having been covered. The surveys were designed to assist appraisal of the economic potential of each county, and although the volumes are primarily concerned with agriculture, they do broach many another issue. The Society's *Suggestions of enquiry for gentlemen who shall undertake the forming of agricultural surveys* (the *Suggestions* is reprinted in each of the published surveys) recommends that prospective authors should devote attention to 'soil and surface' and to 'minerals', and this advice was well heeded. Indeed, four of the authors - Robert Fraser in Wicklow, William Tighe in Kilkenny, George Vaughan Sampson in Londonderry, and Horatio Townsend in Cork - all went so far as to offer a comprehensive account of their county's geology accompanied by a detailed, hand-coloured geological map. Those four Irish maps are all deserving of honourable mention in any international history of geological cartography. Even the youngest of them predates William Smith's renowned pioneering geological map of England and Wales by five years, and it is to be regretted that the four maps are not better known. Presumably their want of international recognition arises from the fact that the Dublin Society's county statistical surveys were mostly published in small editions of either 150 or 250 copies. In consequence the volumes are now rare even within Ireland itself.

Second, the Dublin Society brought into its employ a young man whose name will feature many times in the pages which follow. He was Richard John Griffith, a figure who in his later years was to be hailed as 'the father of Irish geology'. Born in Dublin's Hume Street in 1784, the son of the owner of the Millicent estate in County Kildare, Griffith had studied geology and mineralogy in their theoretical aspects under William Nicholson in London and Robert Jameson in Edinburgh, and in their practical aspects amidst the mining districts of England and Wales. In 1808, with his profession now at his finger-tips, he decided to return home to try his fortune in Ireland, and on 11 May 1809 he was commissioned by the Dublin Society to undertake an investigation of the Leinster Coalfield. In November 1812 his talents were recognised by his formal election to the newly-created post of Mining Engineer to the Dublin Society, a post which gave to him both surveying responsibilities in the field and teaching duties in the Society's lecture-theatre. His investigations in the Leinster Coalfield were now crowned by the publication in 1814 of a report accompanied by a geological map and several geological cross-sections, and between 1814 and 1828 he conducted for the Society similar surveys of the coalfields of Connaught, Ulster, and Munster, and of the metallic mines of Leinster.

Kirwan had seen his Mining Board as the medium through which Ireland's mineral resources might better be exploited. Stewart had been sent out by the Dublin Society to identify hitherto unknown mineral riches. In their county statistical surveys that same Society had encouraged its authors to draw attention to exploitable mineral resources. Griffith had been employed by the Society specifically to investigate all the Irish coalfields and metallic mines. This all reveals the existence, around 1800, of a profound Irish interest in the nation's subterranean riches. Indeed, after 1786 the Dublin Society was conducting an organised programme of mineral exploration which was entirely without precedent anywhere within the British Isles. Kirwan, Griffith, and the members of the Dublin Society were all figures belonging to the Irish ascendancy. Now why, in those years around 1800, should that ascendancy have been so anxious to develop Ireland's mineral resources? A comprehensive answer to that question must await further research amidst the documents of the period, but there are a few relevant points which may with confidence be made. We must remember the social and political background of the day.

Ireland was a poor country with a fast-growing population. Its many ill-fed, ill-clad, ill-housed, underemployed or unemployed people constituted a grievous potential threat to the established social order. The massive but old bolts and bars inside the hall door of many a Georgian house in central Dublin serve as very tangible evidence of the fact that the former ascendancy occupants did not always sleep easily in their beds. William Hamilton, a geologist and well-known member of the Irish intelligentsia, had been murdered by a mob in County Donegal in 1797, and the rising of 1798 had only served to remind the ascendancy of the fragility of the established order. Griffith's family had felt it prudent to withdraw from their home at Millicent for the duration of the rebellion, and young Griffith himself had twice come within a hair's-breadth of becoming one of the rising's victims, first at the hands of the rebels and then at the hands of some dragoons who mistook him for an insurgent. His schoolmaster (Griffith at the time was in school at Rathangan) was less fortunate. He was murdered by the rebels, and to his dying day Griffith carried the gruesome memory of

FIGURE 1.2. *The marble bust of Sir Richard Griffith, Bart, (1784-1878) by Sir Thomas Farrell (1827-1900), sometime President of the Royal Hibernian Academy. The bust was presented to the Royal Dublin Society by Griffith's son in the year of his father's death. It is a powerful work which amply conveys an impression of Griffith's commanding character.* (From a photograph by Terry Dunne of Trinity College Dublin, reproduced by kind permission of the Royal Dublin Society.)

discovering his preceptor's body lying in a ditch, the face horribly mutilated by musket shot. In 1805 Griffith visited Birmingham to see its mines and its factories. While there he was perhaps regaled with stories of the 'Church and King Riots' of July 1791. If that be so, then his informants will surely have found him impossible to shock. At home in Ireland he had lived through an episode which made Birmingham's troubles look like a Sunday afternoon picnic party.

The Birmingham riots were just a part of the British reaction to the French Revolution, and France's Reign of Terror was shortly to evoke a sense of outraged horror throughout the British Isles. The chemist Antoine Lavoisier was loaded into a tumbrel and taken to the guillotine on 8 May 1794. He had been one of Kirwan's scientific correspondents. By 1800 there was every reason for Francophobic sentiments to be deeply and uniquely entrenched among members of the Irish ascendancy. Ireland had suffered as no other part of the British Isles had suffered. In 1798 French troops had actually marched upon Irish roads. They had actually fought Irish battles with the intention of overthrowing the established Irish order. Their very leader was a symbol of social upheaval. Humbert was a citizen general. Before the Revolution he had been a horse-trader and rabbit-skin dealer, and he owed his elevation from the ranks to votes cast by his erstwhile comrades on the barrack-square.

The French Revolution was to be deplored, but much closer to home there was occurring another revolution which the Irish ascendancy could view with far greater equanimity. This was that revolution in Britain which a later generation was to know as the Industrial Revolution. In Irish ascendancy circles it was well-known that the new machines and the new factories were together both transforming British society and creating an immense new wealth. During his tours in Britain before 1808 Griffith had with his own eyes seen the developments which were taking place, and he had actually visited that industrial wonder of the age, Boulton and Watt's famed manufactory at Soho, near Birmingham. All this was happening in Britain, but why should Ireland not benefit from its own equivalent revolution? Why should Birr not become an Irish Birmingham, Manorhamilton an Irish Manchester, or New Ross an Irish Newcastle? The essential keys to Britain's success were human inventiveness combined with minerals extracted from the earth. Surely the Irish must possess a similar streak of inventiveness. All that was necessary to effect transformation of the Irish economy was therefore the discovery of a native mineral wealth. And that wealth, it seemed, must exist. There appeared to be excellent grounds for optimism. Had gold, that queen of minerals, not recently been found in County Wicklow, and in 1795 had there not resulted a local gold-rush? Who knew what other subterranean riches might await the skilled prospector? That is why Kirwan wanted his Irish Mining Board. That is why the Dublin Society employed Stewart to tramp the Irish countryside between 1786 and 1811. That is why the Society adjured the writers of its county statistical surveys to devote particular attention to mineral potential.

The mineral most needed was coal. If Ireland was to have its own throbbing centres of manufacturing industry, then there had to be coal in abundance to feed the boilers which would be powering the bourgeoning steam-engines. And that is why the Dublin Society commissioned Griffith to survey in turn each of the known Irish coal districts between 1809 and 1829. If coal could be found in quantity, then the discovery must bring in its wake a flood of new Irish employment opportunities. Idle Irish hands which might once have been tempted to reach again for the pikes and muskets of '98, would now be gainfully employed in foundries and lathe-shops. Mining and manufacturing populations might be well regimented populations, their daily round strictly controlled by the mine's whistle and the factory's hooter. Mineral discoveries amidst Ireland's geological stratification might thus serve to ensure the survival of Ireland's existing social stratification.

There is one other point to be made about the Irish search for minerals during the decades around 1800. It is a point which is patently obvious. The location of hitherto unknown Irish mineral deposits would bring wealth tumbling into the somewhat depleted coffers of the Irish ascendancy. More especially, landlords whose Irish estates proved to be mineraliferous were likely to reap a rich financial harvest. The ascendancy in general, and the landlords in particular, were in control of the Dublin Society (it assumed the title 'Royal' in June 1820), and the Society's programme of mineral investigations was in so many respects an exercise in enlightened self-interest upon the part of the dominant Irish social group. In Ireland during those decades around 1800, a mineralogical report or a geological map were, hopefully, steps towards the stabilisation of the existing social order and the financial enrichment of the ascendancy.

These were the political and economic reasons behind the geological surveys carried out in Ireland during the decades around 1800. But early in the nineteenth century there developed another set of factors which reinforced the attractiveness of all such surveys. In Ireland, in Britain, throughout much of Western Europe, and in North America, geology suddenly began to command wide public attention. To some extent this was simply because the construction of the 'navigations' during the canal age, and the mining and quarrying associated with the Industrial Revolution, had for the first time laid bare the bones of the earth upon a grand scale. That, however, was only the beginning of the story. Those canal-cuts, mines, and quarries posed innumerable silent questions about the nature and origin of the earth's surface. As a result geologists were soon adding a completely fresh dimension to the human experience. They were discovering the earth's past. They were exploring the vast, new, and hitherto undreamed of continent of geohistory. They were bringing to light a story of stunning complexity and breathtaking grandeur. Lands had been converted into seas and seas into lands. Mountains had been raised only to be removed by Nature's engines of destruction. Immense spreads of rock had been bent, twisted, and broken. Fiery volcanoes had once belched forth their lavas where today all is placid and serene. And all those ancient landscapes had been populated by creatures utterly different from those familiar to us in the modern world. Among those bygone creatures were the members of that group which in 1841 was christened with the name Dinosauria, or 'fearfully great lizards', and from that date to this the dinosaurs have exerted their peculiar fascination upon the human mind.

The early nineteenth-century discovery that our earth was no pristine maiden but a vastly experienced hag was analogous in its intellectual repercussions to the sixteenth-century realisation that our earth is not the cynosure of the universe but just one of the smaller planets encircling our sun. The point has often been made that sixteenth-century astronomy discovered universal space, whereas nineteenth-century geology discovered terrestrial time. To many it seemed that the new geohistory being assembled by the early nineteenth-century geologists flew in the face of the old and respected story of the Creation as presented in *Genesis*. This gave to geology a certain spice - a certain piquancy - among those of the age who, for whatever reason, were eager to be seen as standing amidst the avant-garde of the day.

As a result of all these developments, geology rapidly became the most important and fashionable science of the first half of the nineteenth century. Something akin to a geological mania swept the British Isles. For gentlemen the science became a new field-sport wherein the foxy quarry yielded to the fossiliferous quarry, and to judge from Book III of *The Excursion,* Wordsworth's Lake District must have become overrun by the self-styled 'Brethren of the Hammer' as early as 1814. Certainly no gentleman's study was complete without its cabinet of geological specimens. The twelve editions of Charles Lyell's *Principles of Geology,* published between 1830 and 1875, were among the best-sellers of their day. Leading geologists - Lyell being one of their number - received knighthoods or baronetcies, and the Prince Consort attended meetings of the Geological Society of London. He even arranged for the royal children to receive tuition in the science.

In Ireland an interval of more than forty years lies between the public planting ceremony of the tree of applied geology and the equally public planting ceremony of the tree of pure geology. The first ceremony took the form of the appointment of Donald Stewart as the Dublin Society's Itinerant Mineralogist in June 1786. The second ceremony took place in the Provost's House in Trinity College Dublin on 29 November 1831, when nineteen gentlemen gathered to consider the foundation of an Irish geological society to match the Geological Society of London founded in 1807, and the Royal Geological Society of Cornwall founded in 1814. The outcome of their discussions was the establishment of the Geological Society of Dublin in February 1832, under the presidency of Bartholomew Lloyd, the Provost of Trinity College. Within a year the Society had 170 members, including thirteen Fellows of Trinity College, twenty-two members of the medical profession, sixteen military gentlemen, ten noblemen, and five clergymen aside from the Fellows of the College.

The founders of the new Dublin society paid lip-service to the national importance of studies in economic geology, and they expressed the hope that their labours in the science might further the economic development of Ireland. There was even optimistic talk of the Society employing its own geological surveyors much as the Dublin Society had employed Stewart and Griffith. But, once established, the Society settled down to a solid diet of pure geology largely unadulterated by any issues of economic significance. Between the Society's foundation and the close of 1840, its members heard presented 122 communications, but of these only nine would seem to have contained even the slightest of economic components. To suggest that pure, as opposed to applied, geology had no existence in Ireland before 1832 would be absurd. Just a glance at the tables of contents in the first seven volumes of the *Transactions of the Royal Irish Academy*, published between 1787 and 1800, would be entirely sufficient to scout such an obvious a falsehood. It was, nevertheless, within the Geological Society of Dublin that Irish pure geology achieved its first secure institutionalised form, just as Irish economic geology had earlier been institutionalised within the Dublin Society. Among the members of the Geological Society of Dublin their chosen science was not regarded as just a means towards the end of economic expansion; their chosen science was, rather, a highly desirable intellectual end in its own right. If their investigations should perchance prove beneficial to the Irish economy, then so much the better, but what the members of the Society were really concerned with was earth-history and not earth-resources.

These two geological traditions - the earlier tradition of economic geology and the later tradition of pure geology - are nicely encapsulated within the figure of Richard Griffith. As we unravel these two strands from within his life we are led ever more closely towards the political maelstrom wherein the Geological Survey of Ireland was destined to be born in the somewhat inauspicious year of 1845 - the year when the dreaded potato blight arrived in Ireland.

When he returned to Ireland in 1808, Griffith was primarily an economic geologist. On behalf of the Royal Dublin Society, between 1809 and 1828, he surveyed the reserves of all the Irish coalfields, he studied the potential of the Leinster metallic mines, and he examined the economic opportunities presented by many another Irish deposit which came to his notice. This interest in economic geology remained with him throughout his long life (he died in September 1878), but, very soon after the receipt of his 1809 commission to survey the Leinster coal district, he began to be seduced by the sirens of pure geology. As in the cases of so many other geologists who responded to the sirens' sweet song, Griffith's fascination with pure geology took the form of cartographic dreams. He decided - and it most probably happened during the spring of 1811 - that he must complete for Ireland the most detailed geological map that he was capable of achieving. This map became the passion of his life, but its compilation was to prove a gargantuan task. The map was to have a gestation period of almost thirty years.

Griffith recognised that his completed and published map would be of value to many classes of user ranging from the farmer to the engineer. He often alluded to the map's practical utility, but this was really all just window-dressing. It was an effort to impart to Griffith's obsession a gloss of rationality for the benefit of those who did not themselves share his enthusiasm for geology. For Griffith the map was an end in itself. It was an exercise in pure geology. He found intellectual satisfaction in differentiating the 'Tabular Trap' from the 'Trap Porphyry', and the Carboniferous Slate from the Lower Limestone. He enjoyed tramping the countryside tracing out the boundaries of the various geological units and then plotting those boundaries upon his topographical base-maps. He took pleasure in assembling his field-studies like the pieces of a great jigsaw, until, little by little, his geological map of Ireland was brought to completion. He anticipated with eagerness the adulation he must receive as the author of the first comprehensive geological map of Ireland. This last would seem to have been a not unimportant factor. All through his life Griffith felt a deep need to test and prove himself by performing tasks in the public gaze. Perhaps he was the victim of a problem which had its origins in his childhood. His mother had died when Griffith was aged but four. His father had remarried and started a new family which had eventually given Griffith ten step-siblings. It may be that the young Griffith felt a sense of rejection, and perhaps this early wound remained to influence him throughout his life. Perhaps his map was yet another poultice intended to soothe the pain of that childhood injury.

Griffith seems to have put an early version of his geological map of Ireland on display at the Dublin Society during the spring of 1814, but that map can have been nothing more than a crude generalisation. At that date Griffith, in a first flush of youthful enthusiasm, perhaps failed to appreciate the magnitude of the task upon which he was launched. He faced two chief difficulties.

First, Ireland is no small place. It has an area of 83,000 square kilometres. To map the geology of so extensive an island was going to be enormously demanding of time. Indeed, for a lone geologist it was probably an impossible task if the completed map was to attain the high standards now being expected within the fast-developing geological community.

Second, Griffith had no accurate base-map upon which to plot his field-observations. Field-geologists normally record their observations upon pre-existing topographical maps, and they fix the position of their rock-outcrops by relating them to the map's already present detail. But if those details be inaccurate, then the relative positions of the outcrops are false and the geological boundaries become distorted. A boundary which in reality cuts across the country in a straight line may become a series of curves and doglegs when plotted upon a flawed base-map.

These two problems were grievous, but both of them Griffith was able to solve as the years rolled by. The difficulty of the geographical magnitude of Griffith's task was eased after 1830, in which year Griffith assumed duty as the Commissioner of the General Survey and Valuation of Rateable Property in Ireland. In that capacity it was his task to organise the valuation of land and property for the purposes of taxation, and to assist him in the task he was provided with a staff which sometimes consisted of as many as one hundred valuators. It was Griffith's claim that in making their assessments the valuators needed to take into account the nature of the underlying solid rocks. The valuators were therefore given instruction in basic geology and they were told to make geological observation a part of their normal duties. Griffith must have felt very pleased with himself. No longer was he a lone geologist striving single-handed to map the rocks of the whole of Ireland. He now had his hammering henchmen. When officials outside the Valuation Office became suspicious of the amount of geological work being conducted therein, Griffith had resort to the claim that all the work was being done by the valuators on a voluntary basis and in their off-duty hours. This was quite untrue.

Surviving documents make it abundantly clear that between 1837 and 1846 one of the Valuation Office staff - Patrick Ganly by name - was working for Griffith as virtually a full-time field-geologist. Indeed, it is hardly going too far to suggest that from 1830 onwards Griffith was, from behind the doors of the Valuation Office, running a rudimentary but entirely unauthorised geological survey of Ireland. Oddly, the Valuation Office was located within Griffith's Dublin residence at 2 Fitzwilliam Place, and it was thus extremely easy for him to blur the distinction between official duty and private interest. The authorities even had difficulty in trying to determine how far the hall-porter in the house was one of the Griffith family's domestics and how far he was a public servant employed in the Valuation Office! Elsewhere in the house an identical situation prevailed. Griffith was employing a plausible pretext in order to get public servants to make the geological observations necessary for the completion of a purely private geological map of Ireland. Public money was going into a private cartographic pocket.

Griffith's second problem - the base-map problem - was also resolved during the 1830s. In 1824 the Ordnance Survey of Ireland had been established to produce topographical maps for the whole of Ireland at the lavish scale of six inches to one mile (1:10,560). The first sheets of the new coverage - the sheets for County Londonderry - were issued in May 1833, and by November 1846 the entire country had received its six-inch representation. The new sheets proved to be ideal for the purposes of field-geology because they carry a wealth of topographical detail, thus making it easy for the geologist to fix his - or her - position on the ground. The sheets also normally offered ample space for the recording of notes relating to the nature of exposures or the lie of the rocks. Griffith's valuators certainly found the sheets to be invaluable, and the survival in University College Galway of four County Galway six-inch sheets dating from the early 1840s and bearing Ganly's geological field-annotations, would seem to indicate that the modern tradition of Irish six-inch geological field-mapping started among the men of Griffith's Valuation Office. It is a tradition which was later to lie at the very heart of the activities of the Geological Survey of Ireland; it is a tradition which is perpetuated by all modern Irish field-geologists.

The Ordnance Survey might have provided Griffith's men with splendid sheets for use in the field, but there remained the problem of a suitable base-map upon which Griffith's geological interpretations might be laid before the public. For this purpose the six-inch sheets were useless. They were on far too large a scale. A nationwide coverage upon that scale required some two thousand individual sheets. So, despite the Ordnance Survey's magnificent on-going six-inch programme, Griffith by the mid-1830s still saw little prospect of there becoming available an accurate small-scale map suitable for service as the foundation to his projected geological map of Ireland. When he displayed his provisional map before the members of the British Association for the Advancement of Science at their meeting in Dublin during August 1835, he apologised for the fact that his geological lines were plotted upon nothing better than Aaron Arrowsmith's notoriously inaccurate map of Ireland. A solution to this aspect of the base-map problem must then have seemed almost as remote as ever. But in reality a solution lay just around the corner. It was a solution achieved through Griffith's own crafty ability to twist public affairs in the direction of his own private geological ends.

In October 1836 a small commission was established 'to inquire into the manner in which Railway Communications can be most advantageously promoted in Ireland'. Griffith was a member of this new body, and he succeeded in a convincing his three fellow commissioners of the truth of the following two propositions: first, that an understanding of its regional geology was fundamental to the planning of Ireland's future railway system, and second, that before railway routes could be laid out with precision, there must be produced an accurate small-scale map of the country. An approach was made to the Ordnance Survey, and the Survey agreed to compile a new map of Ireland at the scale of one inch to four miles (1:253,440) expressly for use by the Commission. Further, it was decided that this quarter-inch map would be engraved with Griffith's geological boundaries, and that the commissioners would actually publish Griffith's geological map as a component of their own report.

In 1838 the commissioners published a much simplified version (scale approximately 1:633,600) of Griffith's map in the atlas of six maps which accompanied their final report, and the great hand-coloured quarter-inch geological map itself was published in May 1839. Griffith was enormously proud of his achievement, and full well he might be. By any standards the map is a splendid example of

FIGURE 1.3. *Major-General Thomas Colby (1784-1852), the officer in charge of the Ordnance Survey from 1820 until 1846. In 1803 he lost his left hand when a pistol he was holding exploded, and one of the fragments of the weapon 'made a fearful indent in his skull, the mark of which on his forehead was never obliterated'.* (Reproduced from a plate in Charles Close's *The Early Years of the Ordnance Survey*.)

the geological cartographer's art. Over the ensuing sixteen years Griffith lovingly subjected his map to a process of continuous revision so as to incorporate the latest geological discoveries. He personally displayed the map to Queen Victoria and Prince Albert on 31 August 1853 during the course of that year's Great Dublin Industrial Exhibition, and two years later the map was exhibited again, this time at the Paris Exposition Universelle of 1855. The map which went to Paris represents the map in its final form, and to this day that edition of the map remains the finest small-scale geological map of Ireland ever produced. It is a magnificent memorial to a great, if somewhat devious, nineteenth-century Irishman. But it is not here my intention to seek the addition of further lustre to Griffith's encomia. I simply wish it to be noted that since May 1839 there has existed a quarter-inch map depicting the geology of the whole of Ireland.

It is a remarkable fact that during the 1830s two geological surveys of Ireland were being administered from different locations within the city of Dublin. From the Valuation Office, in Fitzwilliam Place, Griffith was conducting his entirely unauthorised geological survey, while from Mountjoy House, up in the Phoenix Park, the Ordnance Survey was organising another geological survey possessed of bona fides slightly superior to those of Griffith's survey. It is now time to turn the spotlight upon that second survey.

The man in charge of the Ordnance Survey was its Superintendent, Lieutenant-Colonel Thomas Frederick Colby, Royal Engineers. When the Survey commenced its mapping in Ireland during 1825, its assigned task was the compilation of a nationwide coverage of maps upon the six-inch scale, but Colby entertained for the Survey far wider ambitions than just surveying and cartography. He hoped that the six-inch sheets would serve merely as some kind of geographical index to a massive compendium of regional information relating to Ireland - a compendium which was to contain data in the realms of science, history, economics, statistics, and society. Exactly how this grandiose scheme was to be achieved was for the moment left somewhat vague, but within the scheme, geology was clearly going to be accorded some prominence. Indeed, from the very beginning of its work in Ireland the Survey set about the task of trying to compile sheets depicting Irish geology.

Colby was himself keenly interested in geology. He had been a Fellow of the Geological Society of London ever since 1814, and, having become an Irish resident after taking to wife a lady from Londonderry, he served in 1836-37 as the President of the Geological Society of Dublin. He had the idea that the Survey would be able to compile some sort of geological map as a by-product of its regular duty of topographical surveying. The scheme was simple in the extreme. While surveying a district the men would collect samples of all the local rocks, record the collection-sites upon maps, and then despatch both the samples and the maps to the Survey's headquarters at Mountjoy House. There a trained geologist would identify the field-specimens and then in some way convert this raw data into some kind of acceptable geological map. To take charge of this geological work Colby appointed Captain John Watson Pringle, a veteran of the Peninsula, of Waterloo, and of the Freiberg School of Mines. Pringle was given the title of Superintendent of the Geological Survey of Ireland, and he assumed his new responsibilities as from 14 November 1826.

Pringle's was as forlorn a hope as any soldier ever faced. There was no way in which this random field-collecting by virtual novices could ever at a distance be transformed into a valid geological map. It was a naive scheme born of men interested in geology but devoid of any real field-experience in the science. Pringle certainly never produced so much as one publishable geological map, but this enterprise, devised by Colby and directed by Pringle, is nonetheless of considerable interest. It was one of the world's earliest attempts at the organisation of an official and nationwide geological survey. As we will see shortly, the Geological Survey of Ireland possesses a close relationship to the geological survey which Colby and Pringle sought to inaugurate in 1826, and it would not have been entirely unreasonable for the modern Irish Survey to have celebrated its sesquicentennial in 1976 rather than in 1995. The Geological Survey of Ireland has some claim to be nine years the senior of the geological survey founded in England in 1835.

The Ordnance Survey had been sent to Ireland to construct six-inch maps, and there was some concern expressed in London when it was discovered that Colby was diverting some of his resources into the compilation of geological sheets. Colby in the 1820s, like Griffith in the 1830s, was conducting a totally unauthorised geological survey of Ireland. Griffith got away with it; Colby did not. In July 1828 the distinguished military engineer Sir James Carmichael Smyth was sent over to Dublin to discover exactly what was going on in Mountjoy House. He acted decisively. On 1 September 1828 he instructed Colby that all the geological investigations were to cease forthwith. Colby's first geological campaign was at an end.

Between the autumn of 1828 and January 1830 the Ordnance Survey attempted no geological surveying, but Colby's enthusiasm for the science remained undiminished. After a decent interval, he somehow obtained permission for the geological work to be revived, and on 13 January 1830 the Survey's field-parties were instructed to re-commence their geological surveying. Pringle was no longer available to take charge of the geological work, and in his stead Colby appointed Captain Joseph Ellison Portlock. This new officer far excelled over Pringle in his understanding of the methodology of modern geology and in his appreciation of the needs of the geological enterprise which was now under his control. Initially, Portlock had to employ the same unsatisfactory methods as had been used by Pringle prior to the Carmichael Smyth edict of September 1828, but after 1832 Portlock was able to convert his geological branch into a full-blown geological survey employing its own civilian staff and conducting its own field-programme. This happened because there had been brought to the fore Colby's ambitious notion that the Ordnance Survey might compile a comprehensive inventory of Irish life both past and present. The man who now

FIGURE 1.4. *Major-General Joseph Ellison Portlock (1794-1864) from a photograph taken late in his life and perhaps shortly after his term as President of the Geological Society of London between 1856 and 1858. In retirement he lived in Blackrock, County Dublin, and he died there, at his residence, Lota in The Cross Avenue, on 14 February 1864. His father had sailed with James Cook on his final voyage of Pacific exploration and Portlock Point near to Diamond Head in Oahu is named in his father's honour.* (Reproduced by courtesy of the British Geological Survey from the original in that Survey's archives.)

placed this project at the centre of the stage was Lieutenant Thomas Aiskew Larcom.

Larcom was based at Mountjoy House, and he was the officer in charge of the Survey's day to day operations. In 1832 he suggested that the Survey should compile and publish descriptive memoirs for every parish in Ireland, each memoir to offer a comprehensive conspectus of its region and to include an account of the parish's geology. This was the Survey's now famed Memoir Project. It was certainly a novel proposal, and at a first glance it perhaps seemed to be a not unreasonable proposal. But closer examination should have revealed that Larcom was suggesting a removal of the lid from off a well-nigh bottomless pit. There are some 2,400 parishes in Ireland! Colby nevertheless accepted the proposal, and in July 1833 the publication of the parish memoirs was formally resolved upon. In that same year - 1833 - the Survey published the forty-nine six-inch topographical sheets for County

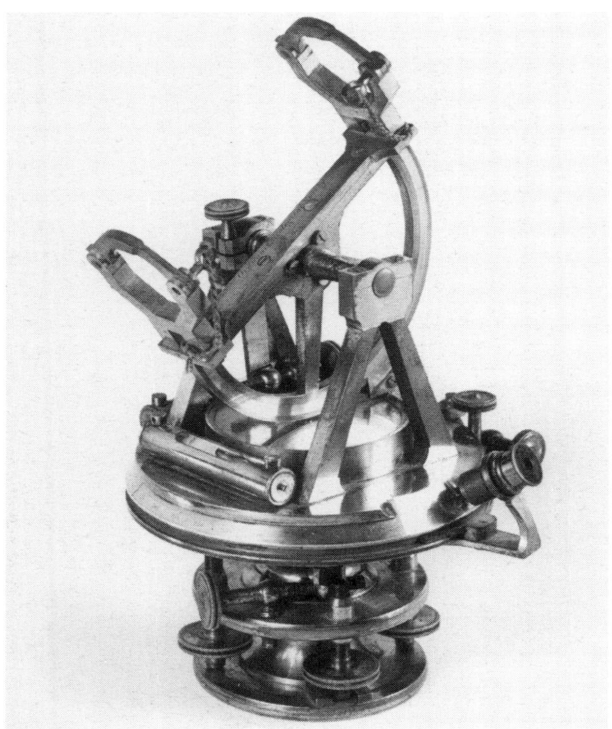

FIGURE 1.5. *An historic instrument: the remains of a theodolite, by Edward Troughton (1753-1835) and William Simms (1793-1860) of London, which once belonged to the Ordnance Geological Survey of Ireland. The instrument presumably dates from around 1830. The inscription 'Ordnance Geological Survey' is engraved upon the telescope bar and is seen in close-up in Figure 1.6. In the 1940s the instrument was being tossed aside during a purge of the Geological Survey's then headquarters at 14 Hume Street, Dublin, when fortunately it was spotted by Mr Murrogh O Brien during one of his visits to the Survey. At the time he was still a mining geologist at Avoca, and for the expenditure of just a few shillings he became the new owner of the instrument. Today it belongs to Dr Aubrey Flegg, one of the Survey's present officers. Dr Flegg has kindly allowed the instrument to be photographed for the present work.*

Londonderry - the first Irish county to receive its six-inch coverage - so it seemed to follow that the County Londonderry parishes would similarly be the first to receive their descriptive memoirs. With this end in mind, Portlock was directed to concentrate all the energies of his department upon the completion of a geological survey of County Londonderry.

In this task, Portlock had among his staff three assistants who were destined eventually to become officers of the Geological Survey of Ireland. First, there was Thomas Oldham, a graduate of Trinity College Dublin, who joined Portlock's department in March 1838. He became Portlock's right-hand man, and Portlock found him to be 'possessed of the highest intelligence and the most unbounded zeal'. Second, there was George Victor Du Noyer, a former art student under George Petrie, and a man whose artistic talents were to prove of inestimable value to Portlock. Third, there was James Flanagan, a fossil and rock collector whom Portlock found to be an 'honest, industrious, and accurate observer'. That these three men served as geologists, first with the Ordnance Survey and then with the Geological Survey, affords us with a clear reminder that, while the Geological Survey of Ireland may not have been founded until 1845, the institution is possessed of strong roots extending down into the earth of Colby's Ordnance Survey.

Of the parish memoirs envisaged by Larcom, only one was ever to be published during the nineteenth century. This lone memoir is for the County Londonderry parish of Templemore, which encompasses most of the city of Derry itself. It can hardly be fortuitous that this was the parish in which Colby had in 1828 found for himself an Irish wife. The memoir was first circulated among selected members of the British Association for the Advancement of Science during their meeting in Dublin in 1835, and the volume was formally published during 1837. Something of the lavishness of the memoir may be gauged from the fact that it occupies more than 350 closely printed quarto pages. Portlock's account of the geology of Templemore occupies only seven of those pages, but the account is accompanied by a small, hand-coloured map of the parish. This is the first official geological map ever published for any part of Ireland. Very appropriately, the scale of the map is one-inch to the mile (1:63,360), the same scale as that later adopted by the Geological Survey of Ireland for its great geological map of Ireland published between 1856 and 1890.

The compilation of memoirs such as that for Templemore was clearly an expensive and time-consuming affair. Were there really to be similar memoirs for every one of some 2,400 Irish parishes? Could such a use of public monies find justification? By January 1840 Portlock had a staff of no less than thirty-five men at work upon various aspects of the Memoir Project, and the authorities were becoming increasingly concerned about the expenditure involved. As in 1828, economy was again the watchword of the day. Portlock had been allowing his men to conduct investigations all over Ulster, but in February 1840 he was instructed to curtail the activities of his department and to focus his remaining resources solely upon the completion of the geological survey of County Londonderry, that being the county where the geological work was furthest advanced. To assist him in bringing this geological task to a speedy conclusion, Portlock was informed that he was being given the services of Lieutenant Henry James, an officer who will shortly be assuming a larger role within my story. In July 1840 there fell a still heavier axe, it was then

FIGURE 1.6. *A close-up of the inscription engraved upon the telescope bar of the theodolite which now belongs to Dr Aubrey Flegg. The instrument was presumably one of the items which the Ordnance Survey handed over to the new Geological Survey of Ireland in 1845, and it serves as a very tangible reminder that the new Survey had strong links with its Ordnance Survey predecessor.*

announced that it had been decided to abandon the Memoir Project altogether.

In Ireland this decision relating to the memoirs aroused some resentment. Sir Denham Norreys and a deputation of the Irish Members of Parliament waited upon the Master-General of the Ordnance, the officer responsible for the Ordnance Survey, to urge a reprieve for at least the geological surveying of Ireland, but they succeeded in securing only two modest concessions. First, Portlock would be allowed to complete his geological survey of County Londonderry and to publish a map and memoir devoted to the region. Second, Lieutenant James would be sent over to England to study the working of the Geological Survey of England and Wales which, in 1835, had been formally established within the British division of the Ordnance Survey.

In 1840 it was understood that Portlock's survey of County Londonderry was virtually complete, and that publication of the map and memoir would follow almost instantly. But Portlock was a geological perfectionist who devotedly worshipped at the new altar of pure geology. He refused to be hurried. He insisted that some of his ground required re-examination. He demanded time for the collection of more fossils. He sought further elucidation far beyond the confines of County Londonderry. His scholarly approach drove the pragmatic Colby to despair. The hitherto warm relationship between the two men became strained, and in January 1843 Portlock was removed from the Ordnance Survey and returned to the regular duties of the corps of Royal Engineers. It was February 1843 before his map and memoir were finally published, and by then Portlock had been posted to the far off Ionian Islands, at that time a part of the British empire. In his Mediterranean solitude (he was living in Corfu) he had the satisfaction of knowing that in geological circles back home his impressive map and bulky memoir were the subject of wide acclaim. They today take their place among the prized classics of Irish geological literature.

When Sir Denham Norreys and the deputation of Irish Members of Parliament waited upon the Master-General during the summer of 1840, they failed to secure any promise that there would be

FIGURE 1.7. *Sir Henry Thomas De La Beche (1796-1855) the founder and first Director of the Geological Survey of the United Kingdom. His spectacle frames were especially made for him in gold by Dollonds of London so that there would be no danger of magnetic interference while he was taking compass readings in the field. In 1818 he married Letitia Whyte of Loughbrickland, County Down, but the marriage proved to be unhappy and the couple separated in 1826.* (Reproduced from a plate in Horace B. Woodward's *History of the Geological Society of London, 1907.)*

established a permanent geological survey of Ireland. Colby nevertheless maintained that such an institution remained essential to Ireland's future prosperity. These are Colby's own words taken from his presidential address delivered to the Geological Society of Dublin on 15 February 1837.

> The situation and the productions of Ireland are favourable to manufactures and to commerce; and a detailed geological survey which shall exhibit its natural resources, cannot fail to give profitable employment to its population.

Colby had tried to establish such a survey under Pringle in 1826, but his infant had been smothered by Carmichael Smyth in 1828. He had tried again under Portlock in 1830, but this time his infant had fallen victim to the 1840 economy axe. Now Colby determined to make a third attempt.

In January 1843 he proposed to his superiors that geological surveying should be revived in Ireland, and for the new survey he suggested the following administrative framework. The geological survey which had existed in England and Wales since 1835 should be enlarged so as to become a geological survey of the United Kingdom, and a new geological survey of Ireland should be developed as a component part of this expanded survey. Captain Henry James (he had attained his captaincy in June 1842) should be appointed as the Local Director of the Irish division within this enlarged survey, his responsibility being to the Director of the new geological survey of the United Kingdom. That Director, Colby suggested, should be Sir Henry Thomas De La Beche, the man who since 1835 had been the very successful Director of the Ordnance Geological Survey of England and Wales. There was one final point to Colby's proposal. In 1843 De La Beche and James were both elements within the population of Colby's Ordnance Survey empire. Colby desired that they should so remain in the future. A new geological survey of the United Kingdom should be firmly under Ordnance Survey control.

Colby's proposals amounted to a vigorous stirring of the Irish geological pot. Within the pot the gruel now began to bubble with individual ambitions, personal jealousies, and behind the scenes intrigue. Initially the government was at a loss to know what should be done, and when eventually decisive action was taken, it was no lesser figure than the Prime Minister himself who took the pot off the boil. As its contents cooled under the Prime Minister's watchful eye, they assumed the form of that institution now familiar to us as the Geological Survey of Ireland. But if we are to understand the Prime Minister's achievement, we must first look into the boiling pot in search of the human tensions which imparted to the gruel its turbulence. Within the pot the agitation was centred upon three poles, each of those poles being associated with an individual who has already featured in the present chapter. They were a distinguished if now embattled trio. They were Colby, De La Beche, and Griffith.

Colby wanted a new geological survey of Ireland to be placed under the wing of the Ordnance Survey because both in Ireland and in England and Wales the Ordnance Survey had for long had a deep commitment to things geological. In Ireland that commitment extended back almost twenty years to Pringle in 1826. The completion of an Ordnance Survey geological map of Ireland had always been one of Colby's ambitions, and perhaps recent developments had served only to heighten his geological aspirations. By 1843 the Ordnance Survey had almost completed its primary mapping of Ireland, and the final set of six-inch sheets - the set for County Kerry - was to be published in 1846. Was the Ordnance Survey now about to retreat from Ireland? Such a retreat was contrary to all Colby's military instincts. Having fought its victorious topographical campaign throughout the length and breadth of Ireland, why should the Ordnance Survey not now launch itself upon a geological campaign destined to defeat the mysteries lurking amidst Ireland's rocks. Having, figuratively, just added to its regimental colours the honour 'Topography of Ireland 1825-46', why, under Colby's command, should they not now seek to emblazon their colours with the new honour 'Geology of Ireland 1844-54'?

Further, Colby was convinced that a geological survey of Ireland under military control would conduct the work with far greater efficiency and expedition than was likely to be achieved with a civilian survey. And let it be quite clear that Colby meant not just a survey directed by Royal Engineer officers but staffed with civilians, as had been the case with Portlock's department. Colby meant a survey staffed at all levels with military personnel. He clearly believed that the geological mapping of Ireland would benefit from the imposition of strict military discipline. He argued, in particular, that newly-trained geological surveyors within a civilian organisation would soon discover that men of their profession were in much demand in the colonies. In consequence there must result an unacceptably high rate of staff-turnover as surveyors left the British Isles to seek their fortunes overseas. Military surveyors would be far less free to desert their posts. Future events in Ireland were to show that here, at least, Colby did have an argument of some validity.

The Geological Survey of England and Wales, which De La Beche had established under the aegis of the Ordnance Survey, was an entirely civilian organisation, although its officers were supposed to wear a dark-blue and brass-buttoned, military-style uniform. But for some reason Colby seems to have felt that Ireland was a different case. Irish rocks were to be mapped by soldiers working for a geological survey which was on parade under the command of the Ordnance Survey. His plan, as outlined in January 1843, involved one of his own officers - Captain James - taking charge of the new survey, and the only civilian involvement was to be that of De La Beche who was to have nominal Irish duties as the Director of the expanded geological survey of the United Kingdom. De La Beche might be a civilian, but he could not in consequence just be disregarded. He was far too good a geologist, far too influential a figure, and far too well-tried an administrator to be left standing on some isolated picket-duty. It should also be remembered that although he counted as one of Colby's Ordnance Survey staff, De La Beche was now Colby's superior in the social hierarchy. In 1842 De La Beche had received the honour of a knighthood, essentially for his role in the completion of some twenty one-inch geological sheets in England and Wales. For his own role in the completion of some two thousand six-inch maps of Ireland Colby never received from his sovereign so much as a single bauble.

Against that setting we turn next to De La Beche's view of the Irish geological situation during the years around 1843. But first a few introductory words about De La Beche's character and background will materially assist our understanding. He was an enthusiastic geologist and he is today numbered among the heroic figures in the history of British geology. But he was also a wheeler-dealer inspired through and through by motives of self-interest. One of his geological contemporaries (Andrew Crombie Ramsay) referred to him as 'an artful dodger', while another (Sir Roderick Impey Murchison) wrote of him in a letter:

> De La B is a dirty dog, there is plain English & there is no mincing the matter. I knew him to be a thorough jobber & great intriguer....

In 1811, aged fifteen, he was expelled from the military college at Great Marlow because of his insubordination, and later, in 1825, his wife sought a legal separation on the ground of cruelty.

During his earlier years his life as a gentleman geologist of leisure was financed by private income derived largely from an estate in Jamaica, but in 1831 a rebellion among the Jamaican slaves, coupled with changes in patterns of trade, left De La Beche in straitened circumstances. He sought escape from his financial predicament through his favourite science. Perhaps there could be found someone who would pay him to wallow in the kind of geological field-work which he so enjoyed. In March 1832 he therefore wrote to the Master-General and Board of Ordnance. He offered to survey geologically the ground covered by eight Ordnance Survey one-inch sheets covering most of southwestern England. He asked for no salary; he merely requested a sum of £300 to cover his field-expenses. The authorities liked the proposal and De La Beche's terms were accepted. By 1835 the eight sheets were complete with all their geological colours. They were assessed by referees and found to be eminently satisfactory. Colby was by no means averse to the further expansion of his cartographic empire, so De La Beche was now appointed to a permanent post at the head of a new Ordnance Geological Survey of England and Wales. In 1835 the civilian De La Beche thus came into occupation of a British post exactly equivalent to the Irish post which the soldier Portlock had been holding ever since 1830.

Unlike Portlock, De La Beche was hungry for status, both within the scientific community and in society at large. Around 1843 his short-term objective was to remain within the Ordnance Survey framework, to secure control of the proposed geological survey of Ireland, to thwart Colby's scheme for running the new survey as a military organisation, and to prevent Colby's puppet, James, from becoming the Local Director in Dublin. De La Beche had his own candidate for the Dublin post standing waiting in the wings. That candidate was John Phillips, a distinguished palaeontologist, one of Britain's best-known geologists, and a member of De La Beche's staff on the Geological Survey of England and Wales. He also happened to be the nephew of William Smith, the pioneer of British geological cartography.

But to say that Phillips was waiting in the wings is hardly true of the situation which developed as 1843 moved on into 1844. De La Beche actually pushed Phillips onto the Irish stage. In 1843 he encouraged Phillips to accept an offer of the newly-founded chair of geology in Trinity College Dublin. Phillips took the advice and he assumed the duties of the chair in March 1844. De La Beche thus got his foot firmly into the Irish geological circle, and he had the satisfaction of knowing that, as the struggle progressed, his own candidate for the Irish local directorship carried a weight of geological metal vastly in excess of that carried by Colby's candidate. James might hold captain's rank, but alongside Phillips he was a geological nonentity. The devious De La Beche gave Phillips to understand that he was virtually certain to be appointed to the Irish local directorship and that there would be no objection whatsoever to his holding of that post concurrently with his Trinity College chair. Poor Phillips - himself frank, open, and guileless - probably never appreciated that he was merely De La Beche's tactical pawn within a grand strategical game.

De La Beche's long-term objective was to place himself at the head of an independent geological survey entirely outside the ambit of the Ordnance Survey and with its sphere of operations extended so as to encompass the entire British Isles. He wanted to escape from the suzerainty of Colby and the Ordnance Survey. He wanted to head his own wide ranging geological enterprise. If he failed to secure control of any new Irish survey, then his geological responsibilities were likely to remain confined to England and Wales for the foreseeable future. If he failed to defeat Colby's plans for running a new Irish survey as a military organisation within the Ordnance Survey, then De La Beche's ambitions for independence in Britain were likely to be stifled by the official observation that geology was an Ordnance Survey responsibility in Ireland and must therefore remain so in Britain. De La Beche had already founded and taken control of one institution lying outside Colby's domain - the Museum of Economic Geology in Craig's Court, London, founded in 1835 - and he now recognised that if he played his cards aright in Ireland, there might be important dividends for him back home in Britain.

During 1843 the geological shadow-boxing within the Irish ring seemed to be a straightforward affair involving two sets of contestants. In one corner there stood Colby, James, and the supporters of the Ordnance Survey, while in the opposite corner there stood De La Beche, Phillips, and the supporters of the Geological Survey. All these principal contenders, let it be noted, were English rather than Irish. Suddenly, in 1844, the situation was changed dramatically. An Irishman leaped into the ring claiming to be a third contender for the prize. He was Richard Griffith.

On 25 March 1844 Griffith wrote to the Chancellor of the Exchequer (Edward Goulburn). He drew attention to his own geological activities over a period of more than thirty years, and he implied that he already possessed so much geological information that any new geological survey of Ireland would only prove to be a totally unnecessary squandering of public money. He offered to make all his geological maps and other records available in the public interest, and he concluded his letter with the following observation which had clearly been crafted so as to warm the cockles of a Chancellor's heart.

> What we require here is a good fossilist, & if such were appointed I think I could undertake the Geological department and complete it at a comparatively trifling cost to the public.

It is not here proposed to detail all the cadenzas and pirouettes performed by Colby, De La Beche, and Griffith as they each sought to draw attention to their respective bids for the control of any new geological survey of Ireland. Nor do I here propose to trace the ebb and flow of their respective fortunes as the struggle progressed. It is, nonetheless, interesting to reflect upon the relative merits of the three contending claims.

Colby's was a bid which can only be dismissed as absurd. He may have been enthusiastic about geology, but he clearly had no understanding either of the nature of geological field investigation or of its demands upon an individual's scientific insight. His notion that ordinary soldiers might be sent out to map the rocks of Ireland was a mental aberration. We must agree with Charles William Hamilton, the President of the Geological Society of Dublin, who in February 1845 observed of Colby's proposal:

> ... it was treating Geology as if it were a work which could be done by the day or by the piece; it was throwing experience, and that tact which experience gives, out of the question, and acting upon the supposition that a clinometer could be put into the hands of a sapper, to be used as mechanically as a theodolite....

FIGURE 1.8. *'The Father of Irish Geology': Sir Richard Griffith close to the end of his long life. This portrait first appeared in the* Dublin University Magazine *for 1874 and it is derived from a photograph taken in Dublin by Thomas Cranfield of 115 Grafton Street. Griffith's pride in his great geological map of Ireland is reflected in the fact that he clearly wished to be posed with one of the versions of the map. The version which he has brought into the studio is the 'pocket version' of the map, which had been completed in August 1853, and which was intended to be of assistance to the officers of the Valuation Survey during the course of their duties. Historically the map is of great interest as being the first colour-printed geological map of the whole of Ireland.*

Here neither we nor Hamilton can fairly be accused of any misunderstanding of Colby's proposed methodology for the geological surveying of Ireland. On 26 November 1844 Colby did actually send James off to County Donegal with six soldiers drawn from the Corps of Royal Sappers and Miners. His orders were that the men were to receive geological instruction and then be set to work upon the task of mapping the geology of the entire county! We may only gasp with astonishment. Ill educated soldiers devoid of geological experience were being turned loose upon the rocks of one of the most geologically complex of all the Irish counties.

De La Beche's bid, in contrast, was thoroughly sound. He was himself an able and experienced geologist; he had founded the Geological Survey of England and Wales; and he had successfully guided the fortunes of that survey since 1835. Further, in Phillips, De La Beche had found for himself a splendid running mate. Phillips was just as experienced a geologist as his chief, and he was a tested and proved administrator because for many years he had been Assistant General Secretary of the British Association for the Advancement of Science. The only weakness in De La Beche's bid was that neither he nor Phillips had much experience of either Ireland or Irish geology.

In retrospect it is clear that Griffith's bid was by far the strongest of the three. He had to his credit more than thirty years' experience of Irish geology. In 1839 he had published a fine quarter-inch geological map of Ireland, and he was keeping the map up to date by a policy of on-going revision. For almost fifteen years he had been running an unofficial geological survey from within the Valuation Office, and in notebooks, maps, sections, and fossil collections that office now contained a wealth of material relating to the geology of Ireland. Finally, Griffith was a man who, in various capacities, had already given ample token of his possession of administrative powers of a high order.

But Griffith faced a serious difficulty in seeking the embellishment of his claim with suitable corroborative detail. The more of that detail he revealed, the clearer it would become that he had been guilty of misapplying Valuation Office funds to geological ends of an essentially private nature. The more he revealed, the more he was likely to raise doubts first about his own probity, and second about his suitability for appointment as the senior officer of a new geological survey of Ireland. Griffith had to navigate as best he could between the Scylla of ill-advised revelation and the Charybdis of undue modesty.

In the event, the struggle for control of the new geological survey of Ireland was decided not so much by the kinds of criteria just mentioned, as by the abilities of each of the contestants to find friends within the London-based power-wielding hierarchy. Here Griffith was at a grave disadvantage. He was resident in Dublin, tied to Dublin by his Valuation Office duties, and largely without friends along London's corridors of power. Even upon his own Irish doorstep his bid for the control of any new geological survey of Ireland for some reason failed to win local support. In Dublin, Griffith seems to have earned respect rather than amity. Perhaps some were even jealous of his achievements. That certainly seems to have been the case with C.W. Hamilton. In 1844-45, for instance, Hamilton was the President of the Geological Society of Dublin, and he boldly advised the authorities that Griffith's bid was not one deserving of official acceptance.

Colby and De La Beche were both resident in London (Colby had removed himself from Dublin to London in 1838), and there they both doubtless had many influential friends. But De La Beche enjoyed an advantage which was now to prove decisive. He was on the best of terms with none other than the Prime Minister himself, Sir Robert Peel. De La Beche had secured the ultimate ally.

Peel was no stranger to the world of science. For several years he had been closely associated with the scientific circle centred upon the Geological Society of London; scientists were regular members of house parties at Drayton Manor, Peel's seat in Staffordshire; geologists such as De La Beche, Richard Owen, Roderick Murchison, and William Buckland were preferred for varied public honours during Peel's ministry of 1841-46; and in 1848 there was even a move to elect Peel to the presidency of the Royal Society. Peel once confessed to some distaste for De La Beche's deviousness, but the two men do nevertheless seem to have become firm friends. That relationship was now about to exert a profound and lasting influence upon the study of Ireland's geology.

De La Beche broached with the Prime Minister the vexed question of the geological survey of Ireland, and he clearly succeeded in presenting his own solution to the problem in a highly favourable light. Indeed, when late in 1844 Peel crystallised his thinking upon the subject into an official memorandum, his arguments were so nicely oriented towards De La Beche's long-term objective of a civilian survey outside Ordnance Survey control, that it is tempting to believe that De La Beche was actually looking over Peel's shoulder as the document was drafted.

In his memorandum Peel observed first that the union of the topographical and the geological surveys had resulted in some inconvenience. He therefore wondered whether it might not be advisable to release the Ordnance Survey from all its geological obligations so that a completely fresh civilian department could be established and charged with responsibility for the investigation of geology throughout the entire United Kingdom. Second, he recollected that there was in Britain one government-financed geological enterprise which was already quite outside the jurisdiction of the Ordnance Survey, namely the Museum of Economic Geology which since 1835 had stood in Craig's Court, London. That museum was under De La Beche's direction, and it housed the collections made by the Ordnance Survey's British geologists, but, by some strange twist of fate, the museum was not under the control of the Master-General and Board of Ordnance, but rather under the aegis of the First Commissioner of Her Majesty's Woods, Forests, Land Revenues, Works and Buildings. Since the First Commissioner already had the museum under his wing, Peel mused, then why should he not also assume responsibility for a refurbished and expanded geological survey of the United Kingdom?

Peel's idea (or was it really De La Beche's idea?) became the burden of a Treasury minute drawn up on 27 December 1844. The Ordnance Survey would lose all its responsibility for geology, a new geological survey of the United Kingdom would be established, and the new survey would be answerable to the First Commissioner. These proposals were submitted to the First Commissioner (Lord Lincoln, later the Duke of Newcastle) on 1 January 1845, and they met with his instant approval. Indeed, Lord Lincoln seems to have been almost enthusiastic about the idea of enlarging his already extensive empire, because on 13 January he completed a comprehensive memoir explaining exactly how the proposed new institution might operate. The salient features of this important memorandum are as follows.

1. Both the existing Geological Survey of England and Wales and the new geological survey in Ireland should be placed under the office of the First Commissioner, where both surveys would henceforth be under the immediate control of De La Beche as General Director.

2. De La Beche should divide his time between the British and the Irish surveys, but, to assist him in the performance of his duties, there should be appointed a Local Director on either side of the Irish Sea. The Local Director in England and Wales should be Andrew Crombie Ramsay (he had joined De La Beche's staff in 1841) and the Local Director in Ireland should be James who would be seconded from the Royal Engineers in order to fill the office.

3. An annual grant of £1,500 should be made available for the purposes of the Irish survey. There was accepted an estimate made by De La Beche that the geological surveying of Ireland would occupy not more than ten years, and the total cost of the Irish survey was therefore accepted as being £15,000.

4. As a counterpart to the Museum of Economic Geology in Craig's Court, London, there should be established a Dublin Museum of Economic Geology with the Irish chemist Robert Kane as its director. The museum should be responsible for conducting all the Irish survey's chemical analyses, and in return it should become the repository for all the Ordnance Survey's specimens presently in store at Mountjoy House and for all future specimens collected by the new survey.

The Treasury intimated its acceptance of all these proposals in a letter to Lord Lincoln dated 31 January 1845, and only one small amendment was later introduced, that being to clarify Kane's status. It was decided that he should be responsible not to De La Beche, as was originally intended, but directly to the First Commissioner himself.

The die was cast. The Geological Survey of Ireland was about to come into existence. Griffith's bid for control of the new survey had failed utterly. Not even a niche was going to be found for him within the new institution. The Geological Survey of Ireland has no roots within Griffith's Valuation Office. Down to 1847 Griffith persisted with his unofficial survey, but he eventually had to admit that the game was lost. In 1848 he withdrew, leaving the field exclusively to De La Beche and his men. Griffith must have been bitterly disappointed. So, too, must Colby. For twenty years he had struggled to found an effective geological survey of Ireland, but now he had to admit defeat. And it was by no means just a local Irish defeat. He had also been routed in England and Wales. His former survey empire was being partitioned, and his onetime geological provinces upon either side of the Irish Sea were being handed over to a civilian in the shape of his own former subordinate, De La Beche. True, Colby did have the satisfaction of seeing his own preferred candidate appointed to the Dublin local directorship, but this was hardly a victory because by accepting the post, James was automatically removed from Colby's control.

The one man who was able to rub his hands in glee was De La Beche. He had obtained virtually everything for which he had been playing. He now stood at the head of his own independent Geological Survey and he ruled a geological empire which spanned the Irish Sea. The only fly in the ointment was James. De La Beche had wanted Phillips in the Dublin local directorship, but he now found that he had to rest content with James. It was presumably a sop to Colby. Phillips, who had been sitting in Trinity College awaiting his call to survey duty, resigned his chair, packed his bags, and returned to England. There is no evidence that De

La Beche felt any remorse for having misled and misused his colleague.

The Act establishing the Geological Survey of Ireland - 8 & 9 Victoriae cap. 63 - did not receive the Royal Assent until 31 July 1845, but the new administrative structures authorised under the Act were all in place by 1 April 1845. That is the date upon which the Geological Survey of Ireland came into existence. Some might consider 1 April as not the most auspicious date in the calendar for the birth of a new institution, but that the Survey has flourished and survived to celebrate its sesquicentennial shows that its inauguration was no act of an April Fool.

CHAPTER TWO

YOUTH
1845-1854

> In Ireland where the maps are on a scale of six inches to the mile, very great precision may be obtained, both as regards the lines of mineral veins and the outcrop of coal beds, and the like detail will be secured in the Great Britain Survey in those districts for which maps of the same scale are to be adopted.
>
> Sir Henry De La Beche in his Instructions for the Local Directors of the Geological Survey of Great Britain and Ireland, 22 May 1845.

I make this assertion fearless of contradiction. No geological survey anywhere in the world has been born into surroundings more splendid than those into which the Geological Survey of Ireland was born in 1845. The infant Survey was accommodated in the magnificent Dublin Custom House with which James Gandon had decorated the northern bank of the River Liffey just a little way downstream of what is today O'Connell Bridge. The Custom House, completed in 1791, has been acclaimed as one of Europe's noblest buildings.

The Survey men were by no means the first geologists to find shelter within the limestone walls of the Custom House. In 1842, three years before the establishment of the Geological Survey of Ireland, the government had granted rent-free accommodation there to the Geological Society of Dublin. In the Custom House the Society held its meetings, there the Society maintained its library, and there the Society organised a museum which was open to the public upon Mondays and Thursdays. Now, in 1845, a second, if embryonic geological museum was arrived in the Custom House. Somewhere down the corridor from the Geological Survey's apartments, Robert Kane was beginning the assembly of the specimens which were eventually intended to form the Dublin Museum of Economic Geology. Thus, in 1845, and for a short time thereafter, the Custom House was the veritable hub of the Irish geological world. But it was a hub lacking in durability. The Survey and Kane's museum were shortly to move out to a fine building especially acquired and reconstructed to meet their joint needs. The Geological Society of Dublin was to suffer a more brutal fate. In September 1847 the Society was rudely evicted from its chambers to make way for the swollen establishment of the Poor Law Commissioners necessitated by the Potato Famine which then held Ireland in its grip.

It was on 5 February 1845 that James wrote to the Inspector-General of Fortifications intimating his willingness to be seconded from the corps of Royal Engineers to become the Local Director of the new Survey. In that post he was, of course, responsible to De La Beche as the Director of the Geological Survey of the United Kingdom. It was nonetheless the First Commissioner of Her Majesty's Woods, Forests, Land Revenues, Works and Buildings who eventually (a year later than might have been expected) drew up the regulations spelling out James's precise duties as the Irish Local Director. These regulations were forwarded to James, through De La Beche, on 29 April 1846.

From the regulations James learned that each year he was expected to spend the eight months between 10 April and 10 December in the field assisting his staff, inspecting their work, and carrying out his own personal mapping programme. The remaining four months of each year he was to spend in the Dublin office digesting the previous season's work, but if he wished he was permitted to pass one of those four months in London either at the Survey's headquarters or keeping in touch with the progress of geology in general. The First Commissioner clearly regarded Dublin as something of a geological backwater! The Local Director's annual salary was £300, to which there was added the sum of £50 to cover travel expenses incurred within a 15-mile radius of any field-station from which the Local Director might be working. All other travel-expenses were to be made the subject of individual claims.

The presence of James in the Local Director's office was a very human reminder of the continuity existing between the former Geological Branch of the Ordnance Survey of Ireland and the new Geological Survey of Ireland. As we will see shortly, there were other human links between the two bodies, and this sense of continuity was reinforced on 28 October 1845 when James assumed

FIGURE 2.1. *The Dublin Custom House viewed from the southeast. Rooms within the building accommodated the Geological Survey of Ireland from April 1845 until October 1846.*

responsibility for all the botanical, geological, and zoological specimens collected by the Ordnance Survey during the years when the Memoir Project had held sway. Other items were handed over too. Presumably it was then that the geologists acquired the theodolite featured in the previous chapter (Fig. 1.5), and then there certainly changed hands the splendid fossil drawings which one George Victor Du Noyer had prepared for Portlock's Londonderry memoir of 1843. Of Du Noyer we will shortly hear further, but for the moment we have to say our farewells to Colby. He deeply resented having to relinquish all this Ordnance Survey material to the Geological Survey. He was a soldier, and the word 'surrender' was no part of his vocabulary. But surrender it was, and to exacerbate matters, he was having to surrender everything to one of his own former subordinates who had become a turncoat and joined the enemy.

James's first major task as Local Director was clearly that of recruiting a staff for the new Survey. Initial appointments for field-surveyors were to be made at the grade of Temporary Assistant Geologists, where the pay was seven shillings per diem for a six-day week. After the completion of a six-month probationary period, such men were eligible for promotion to the grade of Assistant Geologist where the pay was ten shillings per diem, again for a six-day week. The number of such appointments which could be made was controlled by the fact that the total annual budget for the Survey was set at £1,500.

On 21 May 1845 the First Commissioner wrote to De La Beche emphasising that all the appointments made in Ireland must be to the Geological Survey of the United Kingdom and not to the Geological Survey of Ireland. It was to be made clear to all candidates that, if appointed, they were liable for service anywhere within the British Isles. The logic behind the First Commissioner's directive is easy to understand. On De La Beche's own estimation, the geological surveying of Ireland was expected to be completed within ten years. At the conclusion of the survey, the First Commissioner clearly envisaged the transference of the Irish surveyors to Britain, where the geological surveying was clearly going to be a more protracted affair.

Those being recruited to the Survey were bound by two significant prohibitions. First, they were debarred from the making of any unauthorised geological communications to either private individuals or public bodies. All the geological information acquired by the Survey was clearly going to be a strictly guarded public property. Second, members of the staff were forbidden the assembly of private collections of minerals or fossils. This rule was evidently imposed because within the Ordnance Survey, during the 1830s, Portlock had run into difficulty with staff who had been collecting specimens as a part of their official duties, but who had then been selling all their best material to waiting private customers. All such entrepreneurial tendencies were now to be suppressed.

The first field-surveyor appointed to the Survey was Frederick M'Coy. He was the son of Simon M'Coy, a noted Dublin physician who in 1849 was to become the first professor of materia medica in the newly-founded Queen's College Galway. M'Coy junior early developed a passion for natural history, and such was his local reputation, that around 1840, when he can have been little more than twenty years of age (1823, the year commonly quoted as that of his birth, must be an error), he was invited to undertake the examination and arrangement of Richard Griffith's rapidly expanding collection of Irish fossils. Collaboration between the doyen of Irish geology and his young assistant resulted in the publication of a synopsis of the Irish Carboniferous Limestone fossils in 1844, and of the Irish Silurian fossils in 1846. M'Coy also worked upon various other Dublin collections, including those at the Royal Dublin Society and the Geological Society of Dublin, together with the private collection assembled by Henry Charles Sirr, the Dublin Town-Major who long before had played his part in the arrest of both Lord Edward Fitzgerald and Robert Emmet.

Where the collection of the Geological Society of Dublin was concerned, M'Coy was deemed to have given less than satisfaction, and his engagement as the Society's Curator was terminated in February 1842. But whatever may have been his failings in that particular case, there is no doubt but that by 1845 he was one of Ireland's most experienced palaeontologists. Indeed, initially James hoped to employ M'Coy as the Irish Survey's specialist palaeontologist who would be solely responsible for the determination of all fossils collected by the Irish staff. De La Beche thought otherwise. He made it clear that all the Irish organic remains were to be the exclusive responsibility of Edward Forbes (see Fig. 10.4), the Survey's London-based palaeontologist. M'Coy was therefore appointed to the Survey as an ordinary field-surveyor, but in view of his palaeontological expertise - and despite his lack of experience as a true field-geologist - he was appointed as a Temporary Assistant Geologist at the full rate of pay of ten shillings per diem. He was offered his post on 22 May 1845 and he accepted two days later.

M'Coy, with his sturdy frame, reddish hair, florid complexion, and warm heart, possessed many of the characteristics of the stock Irishman. Some might further regard his blunt determination and pepperiness when thwarted as two further characteristics derived from the land of his birth. It is odd that he, the first surveyor appointed to the staff, should eventually have come to enjoy a wider scientific reputation than that vouchsafed to any of the men who followed him into the ranks of the Irish Survey. He and James were the only serving or former officers of the Irish Survey ever to receive the accolade of knighthood, and it is strange that both these future knights should have departed from the Survey under circumstances which, at the time, seemed to augur ill for their future careers. M'Coy, it should be explained, was to earn his scientific eminence not by hammering at Irish rocks, but rather by sitting in an Australian chair.

FIGURE 2.2. *(Sir) Henry James (1803-1877), the first Local Director of the Geological Survey of Ireland. Reproduced from a contemporary photograph in the archives of the Survey. The original bears the manuscript dedication: 'Yours truly, Henry James'.*

The second field-surveyor to be appointed was Walter Lindsay Willson who was offered his post as Temporary Assistant Geologist on 18 June 1845. He had previously worked for five years as a civilian employee with the Ordnance Survey, and he accepted James's offer on 23 June.

The third field-surveyor was Lewis Edwards, who arrived in Ireland on 8 September 1845, having been brought over from Britain to assist with the proposed mapping of the Castlecomer and Slieveardagh coalfields. Although he had no previous experience of Survey work, he came with strong recommendations, and he was supposed to have some familiarity with the geology of coalfields. He failed to live up to expectations. It soon became clear that he was incompetent, and he was dismissed as from 18 October 1845. His remains to this day the briefest career in the entire history of the Irish Survey, and although one turbulent later officer - George Henry Kinahan - was frequently to be threatened with dismissal, Edwards is the sole Irish Survey geologist ever actually to have experienced such a fate.

The last field-surveyor to be appointed during the inaugural year was Andrew Wyley who, before joining the Survey, had taught for two years in the Revd John Scott Porter's Classical, Commercial, and Mathematical School in Belfast's College Square. The Presbyterian Porter, 'a prince among preachers', was also a strong supporter of the Belfast Natural History and Philosophical Society, and there we perhaps have a clue as to the origin of Wyley's own interest in natural history. His name had been highlighted for the Survey because by chance one of his referees - a clergyman from Lisburn, County Antrim - had recently shared a coach with De La Beche on a journey from Waterford to Clonmel.

Wyley's testimonials spoke highly of his personal qualities, although one is left wondering what may have lain behind the enigmatic observation of an acquaintance some years later that Wyley was 'a cultured but very curious man'. In his letter of application, Wyley claimed to be proficient in mechanical philosophy, chemistry, mathematics, mensuration, surveying, and draughtsmanship, but while mathematics had been his livelihood, geology had been his pastime. He explained that he had already assembled a collection of Irish geological specimens, but this was presumably a collection of which he now had to dispose. He was offered his Survey post on 27 September 1845, and he reported for duty at Arklow, County Wicklow, on 7 October. While with the Survey he is said to have perfected the mechanism for a breech-loading rifle some ten years before the Prussians first used such a weapon with devastating effect at the battle of Sadowa in 1866.

In addition to the four field-surveyors, James appointed two Fossil Collectors and one General Assistant. The senior of the Fossil Collectors was James Flanagan (see Fig. 10.2) who was offered his post on 28 March 1845, although it was not until 24 May that he finally intimated his acceptance. He had worked earlier on the Ordnance Survey's triangulation of Ireland and then under Portlock on the geological survey of County Londonderry. Both Portlock and James had high opinions of his abilities. For Portlock he had proved an 'honest, industrious, and accurate observer', while as early as 15 April 1843 James had written to De La Beche noting that Flanagan was 'a very useful fellow, and a capital collector'. In his new post he was paid four shillings and sixpence per diem. The second Fossil Collector was one Thomas Murphy, and the General Assistant was James Penny, whose task it was to preside over the Survey's Dublin office.

During 1845 there were thus appointed to the Survey a total of five geologists (James, M'Coy, Willson, Edwards, and Wyley), two Fossil Collectors, and one General Assistant, but this was far from being the full extent of the forces which were now being deployed ready to begin the geological conquest of Ireland. Geological artillery - some of it artillery as heavy as that available anywhere in the world - was being imported from across the water.

First, on 21 June 1845, Trevor Evans James, a Welshman, was despatched to Ireland as an Assistant Geologist. He had been serving as an officer of the Geological Survey of Great Britain since May 1840, and De La Beche now sent him over as a stiffening for the inexperienced Irish team. But his Irish sojourn was of only brief duration. On 1 October 1845 James the Local Director wrote to James the Assistant Geologist advising him that De La Beche required his services back in England, and that he was to proceed posthaste to Derby. That was the official reason for Trevor James's departure from Ireland. The real reason for his going was that the Local Director had taken a strong personal dislike to his Welsh namesake and had insisted upon his removal, although there had admittedly also arisen certain doubts about the Welshman's geological competence. Certainly De La Beche found it necessary to dismiss him from the British Survey as from 30 September 1846.

That personality-clash occurring between the two men named James, and within just a few months of the Irish Survey's establishment, was to prove a sad portent. Throughout the nineteenth century there were few periods when the atmosphere of the Irish Survey was not being polluted by the fumes of personal antagonism. Within the Survey of the United Kingdom as a whole, the Irish Branch was to become notorious for its long-lasting feuds.

Second, and a piece of artillery of vastly heavier calibre than Trevor James, there was De La Beche himself. He was present in Ireland for much of the summer of 1845, and he returned regularly thereafter, often remaining for several months on end. He took his Irish responsibilities very seriously, and of his successors in the post of Director or Director-General, only Sir Archibald Geikie (Director-General 1882 to 1901) came anywhere near to matching De La Beche's deep personal

FIGURE 2.3. *Edward Forbes was famed for his comical doodles featuring gnomes and other fanciful creatures. This is a pastiche of eight of the drawings which featured in his 1861 biography by George Wilson and Archibald Geikie. There the story of the large creature here placed centrally on the right is told as follows. At a Council meeting of the Geological Society of London, Gideon Mantell (1790-1852) proposed that the remains of the* Dicynodon *in the Society's museum should be cleaned and dressed. Forbes was present and he immediately made this sketch to illustrate the creature in its cleaned and dressed state!*

involvement with Irish geology. His Irish visits were much more than mere tours of inspection. Examine the field-areas being worked by his staff he most certainly did, but he also liked to engage himself in some of the actual field-mapping. He enjoyed being a part of the action. During the Survey's earliest field-seasons, for example, he joined his officers in the running of long geological sections inland from the shores of St George's Channel. One of these sections ran inland for a distance of some 64 kilometres, from the sea near Arklow Rock, to Bilboa, standing close to the boundary of counties Carlow and Laois. The eastern portion of this section was the work of De La Beche alone. It was the Director himself who carried the line from the blown sand at the coast, through the 'greenstone and felspathic porphyry' of Arklow Rock, across the 'blue argillaceous slate' of Slievefoore, and on up to the 'green trappean ash' at the summit of Croghan Kinshela.

Third, there was imported from time to time a piece of artillery designed expressly for the reduction and capture of fossils. He was, of course, the Survey's distinguished Palaeontologist, Edward

FIGURE 2.4. *(Sir) Warington Wilkinson Smyth (1817-1890), Mining Geologist to the Geological Survey of the United Kingdom from 1845 until 1851.* (Reproduced from a plate in Archibald Geikie's *Memoir of Sir Andrew Crombie Ramsay,* 1895.)

Forbes, a man of immense personal charm and magnetism. His premature death, only a few months after leaving the Survey in order to succeed Robert Jameson in the Edinburgh chair of natural history, came as a profound shock to British science at large. In Ireland he was responsible both for the determination of the Survey's fossils and for their arrangement in the museum (see p.257). But he also liked to savour the Irish countryside, and he was frequently to be seen at work in some of the richer of the Irish fossiliferous localities. Some of his habits must have seemed a trifle odd to those of his Irish hosts who were not inclined to scientific pursuits. When he was preparing his work on the British mollusca, for instance, he always carried in his pocket a tin-box containing half a dozen of the slugs he was in process of describing. While staying at the old vicarage in Monkstown, County Cork, he horrified the maid by baiting her damp kitchen with turnip slices and other delectables appropriate to the appetites of his slimy friends, seeking in this way to increase the variety of the species present within his pocket menagerie.

Fourth, the final piece of regularly imported geological artillery was (Sir) Warington Wilkinson Smyth. He was a Cambridge graduate who had displayed such energy behind an oar upon the Cam that he had earned himself both the sobriquet 'the steam engine' and a place in the winning university boat of 1838. After widespread experience of mines upon the continent of Europe, he in June 1845 joined the Geological Survey of the United Kingdom as its Mining Geologist. In Ireland, between 1845 and 1851, he undertook special studies of the mines of County Wicklow, and of the Castlecomer and Slieveardagh coalfields.

The nine geologists and the two Fossil Collectors who have just been paraded represent the human resources - the very substantial human resources - which were available to the Irish Survey during its first field-season. The Survey itself, of course, provided all the material resources necessary for successful work in the field, and some indication of the range of equipment provided for a surveyor comes from a note written by James on 3 November 1845. The note records that Trevor James had drawn from the Survey's stores the following items, and he was now liable for their return as a result of his departure from Ireland: 2 sketching cases; 1 50-foot measuring chain; 1 set of arrows for use with the chain; 1 pair of parallel rulers; 1 clinometer; 2 hand-held magnifiers; 2 protractors; 1 chisel; 2 hammers; 1 3-foot rule; 1 moleskin bag and strap; 1 portfolio; 2 notebooks; 1 acid bottle; and 1 box with key. The box was presumably intended to contain all the equipment during an officer's removal from one field-station to another.

During the days when the Geological Survey of Great Britain was a division of the Ordnance Survey, all De La Beche's officers on duty were expected to wear their blue, brass-buttoned, military-style uniform. The wearing of this uniform ceased at the end of March 1845 with the divorce of the Geological Survey from the Ordnance Survey. The uniform was therefore never the official dress of the Irish Survey. The military link might have gone, but for some decades in Britain, at least, there did persist a tradition which served to remind the officers of their former military connection. It seems that upon joining the Survey each new officer was issued with a set of brass Survey buttons emblazoned with the royal crown and crossed hammers, and these buttons were worn at those dinners when the self-styled 'Royal Hammerers' gathered in London to celebrate the end of each field-season with feasting, songs, and general merriment.

I just cannot say whether sets of Survey buttons were ever issued to geologists joining the Irish Survey. Senior members of the Irish staff certainly did annually travel to London to contribute to the joviality of the Royal Hammerers, so perhaps sets of Survey buttons did then grace Irish waistcoats. The songs composed by the officers, and performed at these dinners, were treated as a particular Survey art form. It was an art form with Gilbertian parallels. This, for example, is the final verse of one of the two songs sung by Ramsay at the dinner held on 16 January 1850 with De La Beche in the chair. It serves to remind us that at least the senior and more successful of the Survey's officers saw themselves as belonging to a close-knit and highly exclusive band of brothers. The song's allusion to 'Carlisle' is a reference to the Earl of Carlisle who was then the First Commissioner of Her Majesty's Woods, Forests, etc.

The Survey needs no strangers,
No scurvy council's brother;
We'll work with Daddy De La Beche,
And stick to one another;
With six-inch sections, maps, reports,
We yet shall see the day
When Carlisle
Shall blandly smile,
And double all our pay,
And every man shall keep his wife
when he doubles all our pay.

The then Local Director of the Irish Survey was present at that London dinner, and he doubtless joined with gusto in the chorus to Ramsay's song. He was himself shortly to take a wife.

Again, I cannot say whether the officers of the Irish Survey ever held their own local dinners to mark the close of a field-season. I certainly know of no surviving reference to any such events. Perhaps the strained (to put it mildly) personal relationships which so often existed within the Irish Survey were not conducive to institutional prandial pleasures. But I must briefly return to the subject of uniforms and the Irish Survey. The Local Director (in April 1867 he became the Director) of the Survey was regularly invited to Dublin Castle to attend levees of the Vice-Regal Court. For such occasions he was expected to appear resplendent in the court dress appropriate to a civil servant of the fourth class. In the heyday of Victoria's reign that dress consisted of a blue, gold-embroidered coat, white kerseymere breeches, and white silk stockings, the *tout ensemble* set off by a black beaver cocked-hat with an ostrich feather and a black-scabbarded sword. I just cannot resist the observation that I would love to have seen some recent Directors of the Survey departing for the Castle thus attired!

I have devoted the last few paragraphs to trivialities. Equipment, uniforms, buttons, dinners, and songs all pale into insignificance when placed alongside the vital problem which has now to be brought under review. It is the problem which James had to face in 1845 - the problem which seemed to gnaw at the very heart of the new Survey. Had he been invited to state the precise nature of the problem James might have responded as follows. 'The Geological Survey of Ireland has been brought into being, and I have been placed at its head with the promise of an annual subvention of £1,500, but what exactly are we supposed now to do?'

We must not allow all the accumulated wisdom of our sesquicentennial hindsight to diminish the magnitude of that problem as it must have appeared in James's 1845 perspective. He and his officers were embarked upon a novel undertaking of deceptive complexity. For reasons which will shortly emerge, the extension of De La Beche's Survey into Ireland involved much more than the simple transposition of techniques, learned amidst the British rocks, across the Irish Sea, and into an Irish context. It was not simply a case of playing the now familiar English game within a new Irish arena. The Irish Survey had to devise its own distinctive Gaelic game, and in so doing its officers were to be forced back upon their own intellectual resources.

FIGURE 2.5. *The 'coat of arms' of the Royal Hammerers, designed by William Hellier Baily (1819-1888) in 1849. From 1857 until his death, Baily was an officer of the Geological Survey of Ireland.* (Reproduced from an illustration in the *Geological Magazine* for June 1901.)

A parallel between the Ordnance Survey and the Geological Survey would seem apposite. The Ordnance Survey had been making maps ever since its inauguration in 1791, but not until its arrival in Ireland in 1825 did it have to face up to the multitude of problems spawned by the task of having to map an entire nation at the large scale of six-inches to one mile (1:10,560). The Irish challenge forced the Ordnance Survey to the development of new skills and new techniques. At the time when De La Beche incorporated Ireland into his geological empire, he already possessed vast experience in the compilation of geological maps. But down to 1845 he had never had to erect his geological sheets on the foundation of the kind of Ordnance Survey maps which were available to him in Ireland. Like the Ordnance surveyors of twenty years earlier, De La Beche and his Irish officers faced a distinctive Irish challenge. They, too, had much to learn.

The act of 1845, establishing the Geological Survey of Ireland, referred at the outset to 'the completion of a geological survey of Great Britain and Ireland'. There is no specific reference to maps, but the implication seems to be clear enough: James and his men were expected to present the results of this geological survey in cartographic form. On this subject the act offers no further enlightenment. In a manner so typical of its age, it is concerned primarily with the issue of private property. How was a landowner's right to forbid trespass to be reconciled with a Survey officer's need of access in order, as the act so quaintly puts it, 'to break up the surface'?

So it seemed that James was responsible for the preparation of a geological map of Ireland. But De La Beche's memorandum of 22 May 1845, addressed to his two Local Directors, gave no indication as to how this end was to be achieved. The document contains that passing reference to the Irish six-inch maps which heads this chapter, and its 22 closely written pages are replete with discussion of general geological principles, but the document singularly failed to inform James of the manner in which his men were to use their field-maps or to work their ground. Were they to walk their ground along selected lines of transect? Were they to locate geological boundaries and then follow them wheresoever they might lead? Or were they to attempt the recording of every outcrop of rock they were able to discover? On these critical matters De La Beche had nothing to say. He merely recorded this nebulous comment.

> The system of observation adopted in the Geological Survey of Great Britain, is well known to the Local Directors, having been found effective and productive of the required results, it will be merely necessary to remark that no alteration is contemplated in that system, further than the more complete organisation of the service and its extention [*sic*] into Ireland may require.

James must have been thoroughly familiar with the system De La Beche had been using in England and Wales. Back in 1842 James had spent four months on secondment from the Ordnance Survey of Ireland to the Geological Survey of Great Britain, and he had then mapped for De La Beche in both the counties of Hereford and Gloucester. But did his English experience really have any relevance to his new Irish situation? Here we arrive at the nub of the problem.

In England and Wales all the British Survey's field-work had been conducted upon small-scale Ordnance Survey sheets. Indeed, most of the field-work had been carried out using sheets drawn to a scale of only one inch to one mile (1:63,360). In southern Britain, where De La Beche's men had been at work, the one-inch sheets had represented the only map coverage available. In Ireland a completely different situation prevailed. There, in 1845, an Ordnance Survey one-inch map was nonexistent. The basic Irish map coverage was at the vastly more generous scale of six inches to one mile (1:10,560), and it was upon these sheets that James and his men were now going to have to plot their field-observations.

There is a world of difference between one-inch field-mapping and six-inch field-mapping. The Survey in Britain had been playing its snooker upon a child's-sized table; the Survey in Ireland was about to cue in upon a table of championship proportions. During the 1830s members of Portlock's team had conducted some six-inch field-mapping in mid-Ulster (see p.9), and while a member of the Valuation Office, Ganly had completed a little field-mapping upon that same scale as a contribution towards Griffith's geological survey of Ireland (see p.7). But the venture upon which the Geological Survey of Ireland was now launched was really a venture without precedent. Nobody anywhere in the world had as yet attempted to field-map the geology of an entire nation upon so lavish a scale as six inches to one mile.

The appointed task of the new Geological Survey of Ireland was thus to compile a geological map of Ireland - a map which the public would clearly expect to represent a substantial improvement upon the quarter-inch geological map of Ireland by Griffith which had been available ever since 1839 (see p.7). As a means to that end James and his men were going to conduct a nationwide field-survey based upon the six-inch sheets of the Ordnance Survey. Slowly, as they developed the necessary skills, there was to dawn a realisation that those six-inch sheets were ideal for the Survey's purposes. The sheets carry such a wealth of topographical detail that the location of almost any rock-outcrop is instantly obvious without recourse to the use of a compass or a chain, and the sheets themselves are so spacious that an abundance of detailed geological observation may be recorded directly upon the sheet itself.

James was left that spring of 1845 with one final question. It was a geographical question. Where in Ireland was his Survey to commence its field-operations? Portlock had mapped a wide area in mid-Ulster, and in 1844 James himself had started work in County Donegal (see p.16), but instead of ordering a revision and extension of these earlier surveys, De La Beche very wisely resolved to make a completely fresh start. On 22 May 1845 he wrote to James directing him to open his campaign in southeastern Ireland in an area comprising counties Dublin, Wicklow, Kilkenny, Carlow, Waterford, and Wexford, and James himself was instructed to proceed to a field-headquarters located in either County Waterford or County Wexford.

De La Beche decided to tackle this corner of Leinster for two reasons. First, his British surveyors were now at work just across the St George's

Channel in Wales, and he hoped that a mapping of the coastal regions on either side of the sea would enable his two Survey teams to elucidate each other's geological problems. Second, southeastern Ireland contains such known mineral resources as the copper lodes at Avoca, and the coal-seams at Castlecomer, and De La Beche was anxious to demonstrate from the outset the economic potential of the Survey's work.

On 5 June 1845 James ordered from the Ordnance Survey four sets of the 141 six-inch sheets covering counties Waterford, Wexford, and Wicklow, and by the end of that month all was ready for that exciting step which in Survey parlance was always known as 'breaking ground'. During that first field-season the main weight of the Survey's effort was thrown against the slates and limestones of southern County Wexford. James and his wife took up residence in Wexford town in a furnished house rented by the week, and from there, on 30 July, he wrote to John Phillips, his former rival for the local directorship, reporting that a period of splendid weather had allowed them to enjoy long days in the field. The two Fossil Collectors were doubtless in more humble accommodation. Flanagan had been set to work upon the (Ordovician) slate exposures along the picturesque eastern shores of Waterford Harbour around Arthurstown and Duncannon, while Murphy had been given the somewhat less attractive task of grubbing around for Pliocene shells in the so-called Wexford 'manure gravels' which are really glacial tills containing an ice-dredged fauna.

Meanwhile Smyth was farther to the north. He was taking a look at the Castlecomer Coalfield. Thirty years earlier Griffith had been sanguine of its potential but Smyth was far from impressed with what he saw. On 30 September 1845 he wrote to Ramsay from Carlow.

> We are going to get in the Kilkenny coal which proves to be a very poor shallow concern, just the leavings of a tearing denudation, the dregs at the bottom of a tay-cup, and yet poor Paddy thinks no small beer of his coalfield!

Towards the end of that summer many of the geologists gathered in the little seaside town of Fethard. There Forbes penned to Ramsay a letter, dated 14 September 1845, which affords us with an all too rare glimpse of Survey life in the field.

> I am here in a little village near Hook Point, in the midst of Mountain Limestone fossils, examining their distribution - all very interesting. The Captain [James], a very nice fellow named Willson, who is of his staff, and that thorough Welshman, little J [T.E. James], peppery uncomfortable, and marvellously stupid and uninformed (as I find on close quarters), are my companions. We make a very merry mess, however, and the Welsh squire's absurdities - for he is in misery in Ireland - make us laugh. Sir Henry [De La Beche] was with us till two days ago, working like a trooper, and when not at work telling funny stories. In a few days I leave this and go with the Captain (who sports a ferocious pair of egg-brown moustaches) to look at the Pleistocene beds in Wexford. Thence I go with Sir Henry to Dublin.

Fethard stands on the southern coast of County Wexford, and at the northern end of the Hook promontory. About the promontory there is a marked insular atmosphere which must have made it attractive to the young Survey. It is a compact area, a finite area, a clearly limited area. It could be mapped without leaving boundaries trailing off into the uncertain space of unmapped adjacent sheets. To map the Hook is to achieve a sense of solid accomplishment. Its rocks are beautifully exposed in continuous coastal sections, and during the summer of 1845 it became the first neatly defined piece of Ireland to have its mapping completed by the Survey. But, as we shall discover shortly, there was soon to vanish that sense of proud accomplishment which filled the Survey men as they left the Hook in the autumn of 1845.

The history of the Survey over the forty years that followed 1845 is the history of the Survey's fan-like extension of its mapping northward from the Hook. At Fethard, in 1845, De La Beche, James, and all the Survey men thought that they were embarked upon a task of just ten years' duration. In reality, their century was to be approaching its close before the Survey's primary geological mapping of Ireland was finally completed. The Survey opened on Ireland's southeastern coast in 1845, and it closed on the northwestern coast in 1887. Of the nine men who contributed to the breaking of ground in County Wexford during the summer of 1845, it seems that M'Coy alone was left alive to see the great task come to completion. Perhaps by 1887 he neither knew nor cared what was happening in Ireland. By then he had lived 'down under' for more than thirty years.

De La Beche was intensely proud of his claim to descent from one of William the Conqueror's knights. There was therefore something singularly appropriate about his now finding himself at Fethard, County Wexford. When he examined the local six-inch sheet (Wexford Sheet 50) he will have noticed at Baginbun Head, just to the south of Fethard, a landscape feature recorded upon the sheet as 'Strongbow's Entrenchment' (see Fig. 2.6). This feature is the fortification supposed to have been erected by the Anglo-Normans in 1169, following their landing at Bannow Bay and at the start of the Anglo-Norman conquest of Ireland. Now another knight of Norman blood had arrived at the Hook bent on a different type of Irish conquest. Strongbow is buried in Dublin's Christ Church Cathedral, and there he has his monument; De La Beche is buried in London's Kensal Green cemetery,

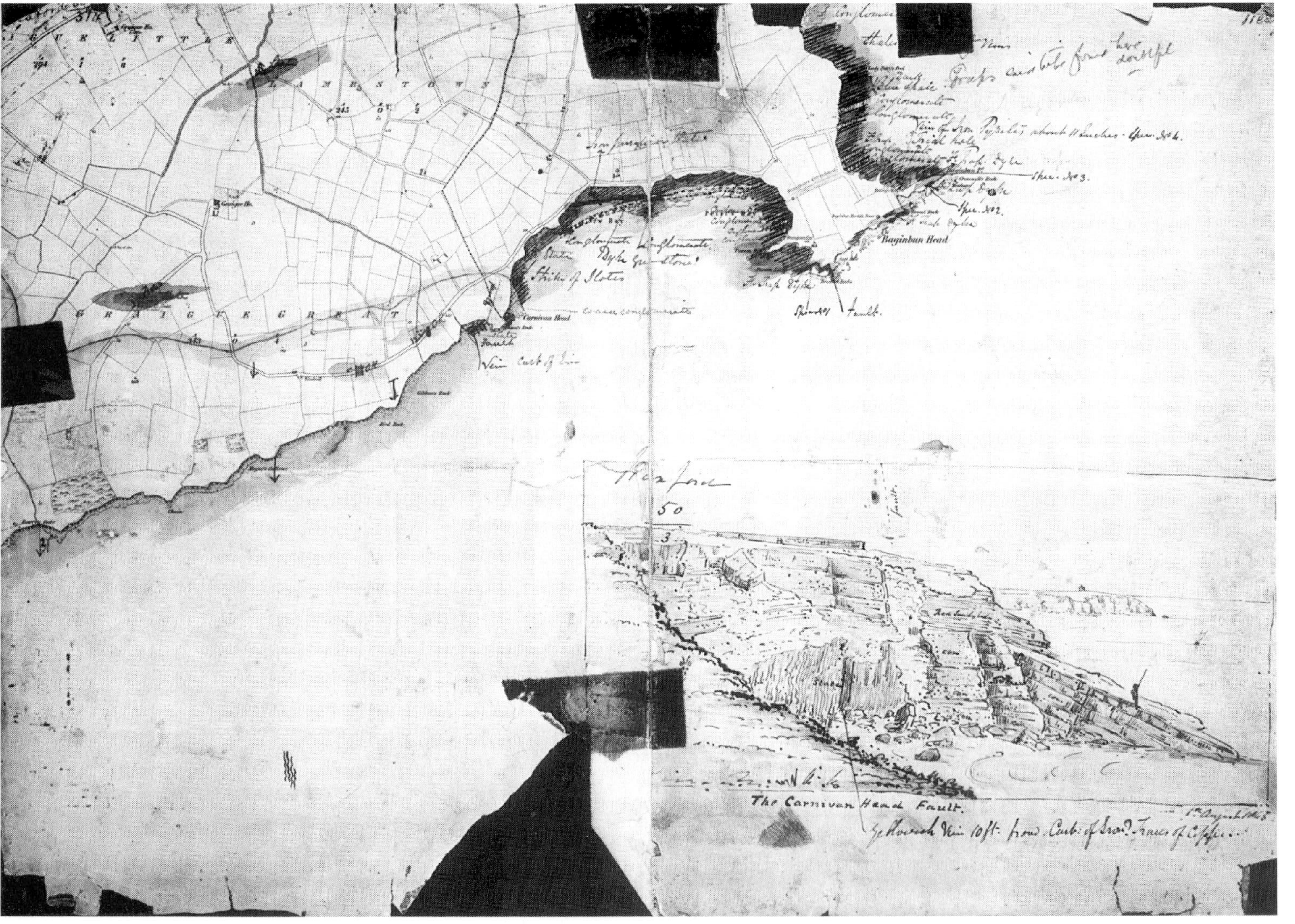

FIGURE 2.6. *A field-sheet dating from the Survey's first field-season. The sheet, here reproduced at a reduced scale, is the southwestern quarter of six-inch Sheet 50 of County Wexford, and it depicts a part of the Hook Head Peninsula. The sketch entitled 'The Carnivan Head Fault' is dated 1 August 1845, and at least some of the field annotations appear to be in the hand of De La Beche himself. At Baginbun Head the Ordnance Survey base-map records 'Strongbow's Entrenchment' and even 'Site of Strongbow's Tent'. Around the Head, the geological notes indicate the sites at which three rock specimens, numbered 1, 2 and 3, have been collected. Were these the very first specimens ever to be collected by the Geological Survey of Ireland? This historic sheet is today in poor condition and the dark forms upon the Figure are places where some well-meaning but misguided individual has sought to repair damage by applying Sellotape.*

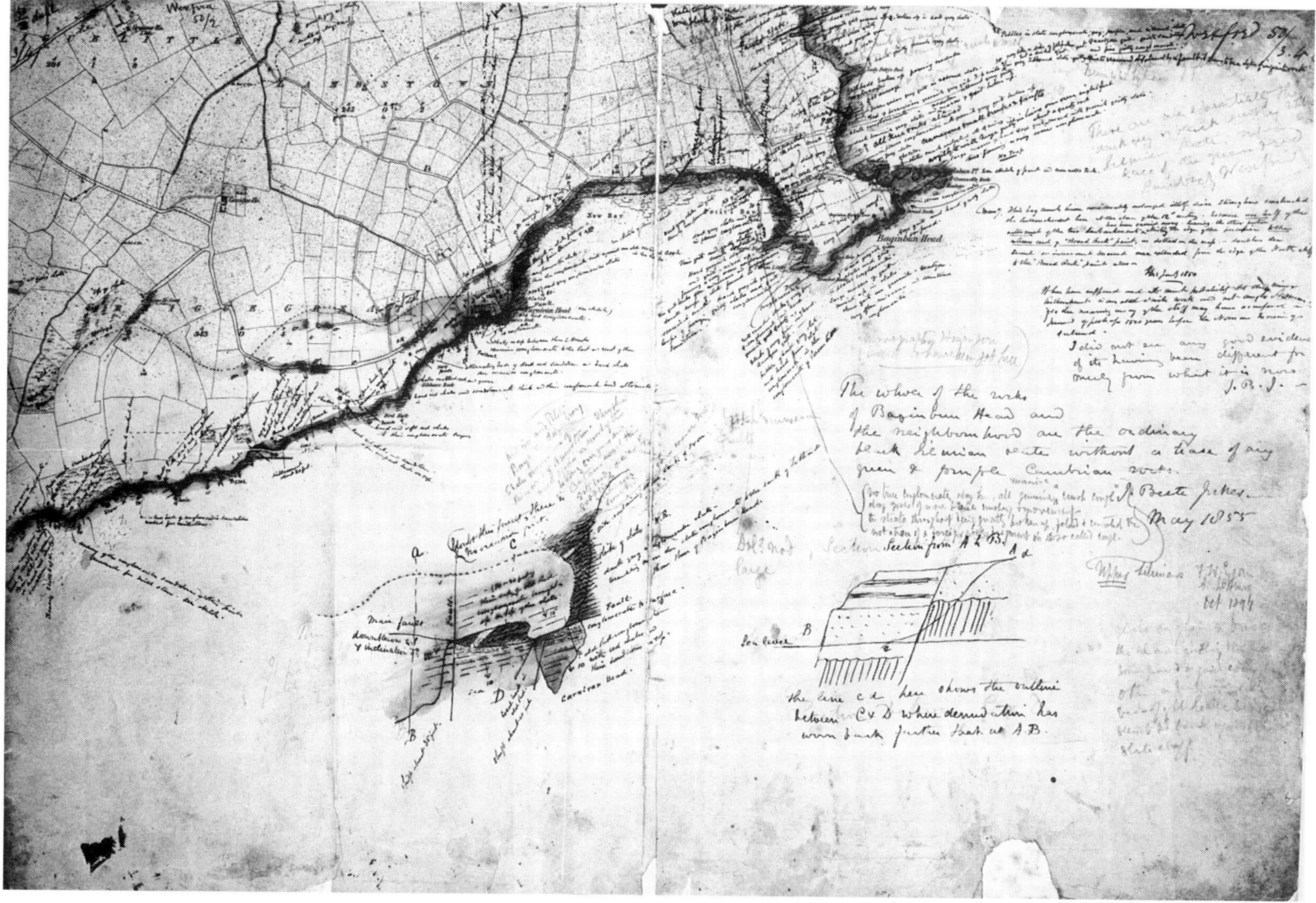

FIGURE 2.7. *The current version of the field-sheet for the County Wexford six-inch Sheet 50 southwest (Sheet 50/3). This is the sheet which will be shown to any enquirer requesting access to the Survey's reference collection of six-inch field-sheets of the Hook Head region. The sheet carries the work of the many officers who have investigated the region since the first field-season in 1845. It carries dated annotations by Du Noyer (January 1850), Jukes (May 1855), and Egan and McHenry (October 1897). This sheet, like many another of the field-sheets, reveals the officers as engaged in dialogue with each other. For example, Du Noyer has added a note claiming to have seen evidence that Baginbun Head has undergone substantial coastal erosion since the time of the Norman invasion of Ireland. But Jukes writes of the Head : 'I did not see any good evidence of its having been different formerly from what it is now'.*

but he has his Dublin monument in the institutional form of the Geological Survey of Ireland.

The news of this fresh 'Norman invasion' of Ireland was clearly far from welcome within the Dublin office of the Commissioner of Valuation. For thirty years Richard Griffith, now the Commissioner, had felt a keen proprietary interest in the geology of Ireland. Now De La Beche and his men were trespassing upon Griffith's preserve. They were threatening the completion of a map which was bound to supersede the great quarter-inch (1:253,440) map which Griffith had laid before the geological world as recently as 1839, and to which he was himself so devoted. Griffith felt that something had to be done . He made a token protest. He sent Patrick Ganly, his trusted geological assistant, down to investigate the country where the Survey was now at work, Thus, during the summer of 1845, De La Beche's official Survey and Griffith's entirely unofficial survey were both mapping in the same ground. James warned M'Coy that he must have nothing to do with Ganly, and on 4 October 1845 James wrote to Phillips observing that Griffith

> ...is so conscious of the inaccuracy of his work that he has actually had one of his men (Ganley[*sic*]) dodging our lads from Dublin & Enniscorthy, New Ross, Waterford, & Bunmahon. We have seen him at work at all these points in our district!

This game of hide-and-seek Griffith very soon abandoned.

The first annual report of the Geological Survey of Ireland was sent to De La Beche on 2 February 1846. In it James informed his chief that the survey of County Wexford was finished, that maps, sections, and other illustrations of the geology of the county were in active preparation, that large portions of counties Carlow, Kilkenny, and Waterford had been mapped, and that there had been gathered a great deal of information relating to the mines of both counties Waterford and Wicklow. This was an impressive achievement for only ten months of work. According to the report five per cent of the country was now mapped, and it really did begin to look as though ten years of work might well be sufficient for the completion of the survey. But De La Beche would have done well to have read that report through spectacles fitted with sceptical lenses. As will shortly emerge, the contents of that first annual report owed far more to James's vivid imagination than to the field activities of his still very inexperienced staff.

In the spring of 1846 James became the first head of the Irish Survey to face a problem which was to become all too familiar to each of his successors - the problem of finance. On 12 May 1846 he wrote to De La Beche expressing the view that it was impossible to maintain the then establishment of the Irish Branch upon an annual budget of only £1,500. As an economy measure he suggested that Wyley, his most recent recruit, should be transferred to England just as soon as he had completed his current Irish assignment. But De La Beche had no wish to receive Wyley. Indeed, he considered that he should be dismissed as 'a very inferior man for our purposes'. In the event, Wyley remained with the Irish Survey until 1855. It was Murphy, the Junior Fossil Collector who became the sacrificial victim. He had given entirely satisfactory service but the winds of economy blew chill and his appointment was terminated in May 1846.

In the same month as Murphy's dismissal, James himself left the Survey on four weeks' leave of absence. The Commissioners of the Board of Works had invited him to survey the sites of a number of harbour works which it was proposed to construct around the Irish coast as a Famine-relief measure. In view of the prevailing national emergency, it was eventually agreed that he might undertake the task, although De La Beche considered that the youthful Survey could ill afford the loss of its Local Director at the opening of a new field-season. Perhaps this journey around the coast was important for James. Perhaps it gave him the opportunity to ponder upon the geological course that his personal career was now taking. Certainly when he returned to Dublin he brought with him a minor bombshell. On 20 June 1846 he wrote to De La Beche asking to be relieved of his duties as Local Director.

For De La Beche this came as a complete surprise. Nothing in their relationship hitherto had suggested that James was in any way dissatisfied with his lot, and even now his resignation was supported by a minimum of explanation. In his letter he merely observed:

> [I am] finding that my position on the Geological Survey of Ireland is not such as I had reason to believe it would be when I undertook the duties of Local Director, and that the powers and means which have been entrusted to me are insufficient to enable me to carry on the duties in a satisfactory manner either to the public or to myself....

In his official correspondence over the next few weeks James was a little more forthcoming about the reasons for his action. He claimed that when he accepted the post, De La Beche had given him to understand that one of his Survey's chief tasks would be the collection of specimens for Kane's Museum of Economic Geology, but now De La Beche had informed him that the assembly of museum material must in no way be allowed to interfere with the Survey's primary function of field-mapping. James protested that he was being allowed no control over the Irish activities of either Forbes or Smyth. He grumbled - here with some justice - that both of the supposedly experienced Assistant Geologists sent over from Britain had proved to be incompetent.

And James complained of what he termed the 'drudgery' of geological field-work.

It is difficult to take most of his stated grievances very seriously. They look like trumped-up excuses being offered in justification of a resignation being made for other, and more fundamental reasons which James did not care to divulge. That complaint about the drudgery of geological field-work probably comes closest to the mark. By June 1846 it must have become clear to him that he was inadequately equipped to be admitted as a true brother of the hammer. He was at heart only a shallow careerist in geology, and during the 1845 field-season his close association with such full-blooded geologists as De La Beche, Forbes and Smyth must surely have convinced him that he was not truly of their ilk. They were inspired with a missionary zeal to shed illumination upon the darkest secrets lurking within the earth's vaults. Their field-mapping was an exciting and almost spiritual exercise. But, as James confessed, for him it was mere drudgery. He must have been disturbed to discover from the regulations promulgated in April 1846 that such dull toil was supposed to be his lot for no less than eight months of each year.

And then there was the question of status. James, possessed of that 'ferocious pair of egg-brown moustaches', was an egocentric and ambitious man. By 1846 he must have recognised that he had taken a wrong turn. The local directorship was not going to yield the independence and social importance which he so desired. He was now a captain of four years' seniority, and he probably felt that a command subordinate to the civilian De La Beche, and consisting of only three Assistant Geologists, one Fossil Collector, and one General Assistant, was hardly fit duty for an officer of his rank and a gentleman of his standing. Colby had never been happy about James's secondment to serve in such a civilian organisation as the Survey, and perhaps by 1846 James himself had come around to a similar point of view.

It may also be that James's action was tinged with pique. On 16 February 1846 the Lord Lieutenant had conferred a knighthood upon James's museum colleague, Kane, and, filled as he was with aspirations, James may well have been resentful. He can hardly have overlooked the fact that in age Kane was no less than six years his junior.

Surprised though he may have been by the turn of events, De La Beche was far from being despondent. James had never been his first choice for the Dublin post, and a closer acquaintanceship had evidently convinced De La Beche of his Local Director's limitations. Certainly De La Beche now felt that he was relieved of an incubus. On 9 July 1846 he wrote from Dublin to Ramsay:

> It had been a lucky thing that the Captain resigned, otherwise I really don't know the amount of mess into which our Irish Survey might have got. His notion seems to have been that he was to do little or nothing personally in the field - and altogether he seems to have considered the affair as mere employment - until he could step into something else - That something else has turned up in the shape of Engineer to the Portsmouth Dock Yard - and right well ought we to be pleased therewith.

James had left his Dublin post just five days before those words were written, but his departure from the Survey was by no means the end of his career in the public service. From 1846 he was superintendent of the constructional works in Portsmouth dockyard, and he achieved sufficient scientific eminence to ensure his election to Fellowship of the Royal Society in 1848. Two years later he returned to the Ordnance Survey as superintendent of the Edinburgh office, and from there he was in 1854 translated to that Survey's Southampton headquarters as Director-General. Thus the man who has to be indicted as a failure in the Dublin local directorship, found himself only eight years later at the head of an organisation far larger than the Geological Survey of Ireland was ever to become. Strange to relate, his regime in Southampton proved to be an outstanding success. He received his knighthood in 1860, and he rose to the rank of Lieutenant-General before ill-health forced his retirement in 1875.

James's successor as Local Director was a Dubliner - Thomas Oldham. He was born on 4 May 1816, the eldest son of Thomas Oldham and his wife, Margaret Boyd, Thomas senior being a broker with the Grand Canal Company. Thomas Oldham junior attended school in the city, and then he entered Trinity College Dublin, where he received his B.A. in the spring of 1836. At that time the College possessed no school of engineering, but it was towards the industrial arts that Oldham now turned his attention. He resolved to become a civil engineer, and he left for Edinburgh, there to obtain experience in the subjects of his newly-chosen profession. While in the Scottish capital he joined the class of Robert Jameson, the professor of natural history in the University of Edinburgh, and it was perhaps at Jameson's feet that the young Irishman found his love for geology.

When he returned to Ireland in March 1838, it was to assume not a post in civil engineering , but an office with the Ordnance Survey as Captain Portlock's chief geological assistant. In that capacity he played a major role in the geological mapping of mid-Ulster. In Portlock's eventual 1843 report upon the geology of the region, he was generous in his praise of Oldham whom he described as 'possessed of the highest intelligence and the most unbounded zeal'. Oldham remained with the Ordnance Survey

FIGURE 2.8. *Thomas Oldham (1816-1878), the second Local Director of the Geological Survey of Ireland (1846-1850) and the first Superintendent of the Geological Survey of India (1851-1876). When he left Ireland he was aged thirty-four, and this is probably a photograph taken later in his life. His son, Richard Dixon Oldham (1858-1936), and his brother, Charles Aemilius Oldham (1831?-1869) were also officers with the Indian Survey. Oldham died at Rugby on 17 July 1878.* (Reproduced from a plate in Archibald Geikie's *Memoir of Sir Andrew Crombie Ramsay,* 1895.)

until the final relics of Portlock's department were disbanded in January 1843. But not for long was he without geological employment. In June of that same year he became Curator of the museum of the Geological Society of Dublin, this being the post from which M'Coy had recently been removed. Oldham filled the post to everybody's satisfaction, and it became his stepping-stone into the academic world. In November 1844 he was appointed assistant to Sir John MacNeill, the first professor of civil engineering in Trinity College Dublin, and then in April 1845 he succeeded Phillips to become the College's second professor of geology.

Although Oldham ceased to be Curator to the Geological Society of Dublin in January 1845, he remained one of the Society's staunchest supporters. Between November 1843 and January 1851 he presented to the Society no less than twenty-six papers, and over the same period, in addition to his curatorship, he varyingly served the Society as president (1848-50), as secretary, as assistant secretary, and as a member of council. His scientific attainments were recognised by his election to Membership of the Royal Irish Academy in 1844 and to Fellowship of the Royal Society (on the very same day as James) in 1848. His most renowned geological discovery was that fossils existed in the ancient Bray Group rocks of County Wicklow, a discovery made in 1840 but not reported to the Geological Society of Dublin until 12 June 1844. Shortly thereafter the fossils were named *Oldhamia* in honour of their discoverer (see p.257).

Oldham was unquestionably in a geological class far superior to that of James, and he was to prove an excellent Local Director. His formal letter to De La Beche accepting the office was written in Oldham's chambers at 5 Trinity College on 27 June 1846, and he became the new Local Director as from 4 July. There was no necessity for him to resign his College appointment; the College had agreed that he might hold his Survey post concurrently with his chair. Oldham thus achieved that duality of appointment to which Phillips had unsuccessfully aspired two years earlier.

James had in large measure been foisted upon a reluctant De La Beche; Oldham was De La Beche's personal choice for the post. On 9 July 1846 De La Beche wrote to Ramsay from Dublin:

> The more I see of Oldham the more I am disposed to consider he will be successful - I like him much - besides he will agree so much better with Sir Robert Kane - the Captain rather roughed up the latter.... I will go with Oldham into the country on Monday for about 3 weeks.

Those three weeks served to strengthen De La Beche's conviction still further, and on 26 July he again wrote to Ramsay, this time from Bunclody in County Wexford:

> Oldham and self continue to get on famously and I am right well contented with him. Our captain was a failure - the more I see of the work supposed to be done the more I see that somehow he seems to have supposed that this said work was to be done as mechanically as that of sappers on a Trigl. Survey and his mind seems to have been engaged in making up the supposed good work of others and not in getting a grasp of it himself. Oldham appears to me to have a philosophical mind - quite ready to go ahead in the school we have been forming - As a colleague you will find him worth 50 of the other.

The Survey's other senior staff were also quick to recognise that in Oldham they had found a true kindred spirit. Soon after Oldham's appointment Forbes wrote to De La Beche:

> I am glad to hear all things go well in Ireland. The opinion you entertain of Oldham's talents is what I expected. I have always been impressed with the notion, that his abilities are of a far higher order than those of any other Irish geologist.

Similarly, on 8 August 1846, Ramsay wrote to his chief from his Welsh field-station at Dolgelley, observing of Oldham:

> I like his notes - They are hearty and cordial .... I feel as if I should like him better and better the more I know

> him. I am certain we are much better adapted for each other than the grandiose Captain, and we shall pull together in your triumphal car like fun.

Amidst all these pleasantries James introduced the sole jarring note. On 2 July, in one of his final acts as Local Director, he wrote the following paragraph to De La Beche.

> I do not know whether or not you are aware of the fact, that there has for some time past existed a sort of feud between Oldham and M'Coy, and that at the very last meeting of the Geological Society here there were read some angry letters between them arising out of observations made by Oldham on M'Coy's work on the Carboniferous fossils at some former meetings. I was in the country at the time, and have not seen the letters, but it is clear that Oldham's appointment as Local Director, makes M'Coy's position peculiarly unfortunate, and I should think it would be advisable to remove him to England.

At this distance in time it is impossible to decide upon the rights and wrongs of this altercation between Oldham and M'Coy, but it clearly generated considerable heat. M'Coy wrote a paper critical of Oldham which the Council of the Geological Society of Dublin rejected at its meeting on 17 June 1846 with the observation 'that Council consider it desirable that all personal allusions should be avoided in controversial papers of scientific character'. De La Beche nevertheless decided not to take the matter very seriously. He failed to act upon James's advice that M'Coy should be removed to England, and thus the scene was set for the little Survey drama which was to be enacted during the summer of 1846.

Within a few days of assuming his new office, Oldham arrived at an unwelcome conclusion: James had left the affairs of the Survey in chaos. Oldham could find no adequate record of the Survey's activities during his predecessor's tenure of the local directorship. He soon realised that in his annual report of February 1846 James had grossly exaggerated the extent of the ground covered during the first field-season. More especially, James's claim to have completed the mapping of County Wexford now proved to be entirely false. On 6 August 1846 Oldham wrote to De La Beche:

> Of the fair plans and sections alluded to by Capt. James in February last I find none in this office, with the exception of three sections, so prepared that I could not recommend them for publication.

There was even a suspicion that James was guilty of misappropriating public property. In July 1845 the Stationery Office had specially bound all the fossil drawings prepared by Du Noyer for Portlock's 1843 Londonderry memoir, but Oldham could now find no trace of the volume in the Custom House. It later transpired that James had taken it with him to Portsmouth, and when taxed with the matter, the culprit meekly explained that he had only been trying to get the volume back into Portlock's hands. But Portlock was in Corfu rather than on the shores of Spithead, and in any case the volume belonged to the Survey in Dublin rather than to a soldier serving overseas. Happily, the volume did eventually return to Dublin where today it is one of the Survey's treasures.

One of Oldham's first tasks as Local Director was to inspect the work of his staff in the field. What he saw did not always meet with his approval. Wyley's mapping was already known to be suspect, and Oldham was far from satisfied with what the former Belfast teacher now had to show him. But under Oldham's guidance there was some improvement, and on 22 October 1846 he wrote to De La Beche from Ashford, County Wicklow, remarking upon Wyley's progress and recommending that his pay should in consequence be advanced to 8/6 per diem. To this proposal De La Beche speedily assented, but Oldham was never entirely happy about Wyley. As late as 3 October 1849 we find him writing to De La Beche from Wexford complaining that Wyley was never going to make a good field-man, that he was 'extraordinarily erratic', and that all of his mapping needed to be very carefully checked.

It was nevertheless for M'Coy that Oldham reserved his most severe strictures. On 29 August 1846 he wrote from Bunclody, County Wexford, to M'Coy at Borris, County Carlow, complaining in vigorous terms about the quality of M'Coy's work in the Bunclody region. Oldham claimed that alluvial deposits had been completely disregarded; that geological locations had been misplaced on the six-inch field-sheets by as much as half a mile; that rock outcrops had been marked where none existed and vice versa; and that many important localities had clearly never been examined at all. He demanded of M'Coy an explanation before reporting the matter to De La Beche. In his reply, dated 1 September, M'Coy protested that Oldham's complaints were insufficiently detailed to allow of adequate rejoinder, but this exchange must have bearing upon the fact that M'Coy decided to resign from the Survey as from 30 September 1846. Only eighteen months had elapsed since the foundation of the Survey, and already, for one reason or another, there had departed five of those - James, Edwards, T.E. James, M'Coy, and Murphy - who had broken ground during the previous year.

We cannot know how far Oldham's critique of M'Coy's mapping arose from a genuine concern for the quality of the Survey's work, and how far there was an element of personal hostility towards M'Coy stemming from their previous clash to which James had drawn attention. But it does seem probable that Oldham's complaint of slipshod work was grounded in fact, and it should be remembered that four years earlier a similar complaint had earned M'Coy a virtual dismissal from his curatorship at the Geological Society of Dublin. Oldham certainly continued to complain bitterly about the quality of M'Coy's work for months after the culprit had departed the Irish scene. On 7 April 1847, for instance, he wrote to De La Beche about the mapping in eastern County Wexford.

> Error after error turning up near Courtown. Limestones marked where not existing - and omitted where they are - and similar mistakes of other kinds - The whole of that area, being a critical one, will have to be gone over carefully - Is not this too bad. Some of M'Coy's work.

On 7 May Oldham at Courtown Harbour wrote again to De La Beche in the same vein

> I have been here for the last ten days - making the most of all the fine weather we had, which was not much - a district so badly examined I never saw - but this is all past now.

For M'Coy this contretemps was but a temporary set back in an otherwise outstanding career. From Ireland he went to Cambridge to a post in the Woodwardian Museum, where Professor Adam Sedgwick was soon enthusing over the young Irishman's talents, and in 1849 M'Coy re-crossed the Irish Sea to assume the chair of mineralogy and geology at Queen's College Belfast. Five years later there came another move, this time to the antipodes where he became professor of natural science in the new University of Melbourne. There he speedily achieved renown because of his scientific attainments, his pugnacious character, and a sartorial perfection that made him one of the dandies of Victoria. He received his knighthood in 1891, and when he died in 1899 he was the grand old man of Australian science. In 1935 the Melbourne students founded a M'Coy Society in his memory.

If, upon his field-sheets, M'Coy really did misplace outcrops by as much as half a mile, then that was an unforgivable offence. It could only indicate egregious carelessness. One must, nevertheless, have some sympathy with M'Coy. Neither he, nor any other of the Survey's officers, would seem to have received any clear instruction from James as to the nature of their duties. Even James himself probably had little insight into the niceties of six-inch field-mapping. It will be remembered that as recently as December 1844 - and long after his personal experience of small-scale geological mapping with the Survey in England - he had naively fallen in with Colby's plans by leading six untutored soldiers off to County Donegal to map the county's geology at the six-inch scale (see p.16).

In his own way, De La Beche had also been naive. Perhaps to satisfy his own devious political ends, he had announced that the geological mapping of Ireland would occupy no more than a period of ten years. But whatever his motives may have been, this estimate must have found its way into the moleskin field-bags of the Irish officers. They carried the estimate around with them as they tramped the Irish countryside. It must have influenced their style of field-work. If Ireland was to be mapped within a period of ten years, then, in crude measure, it meant that rather more than three complete counties had to be surveyed every year. Such an enforced rate of progress was hardly conducive to detailed six-inch mapping. The ten-year estimate and meticulous six-inch mapping were incompatible. The ten-year estimate and British-style small-scale mapping might have been compatible, but during the 1840s Ireland possessed no equivalent to the one-inch map which was so basic to the British Survey's programme.

Sometime during the 1970s, one of the Survey's office staff - John Duffy by name - discovered behind a cupboard in the Survey's then headquarters, an envelope bearing the inscription 'Old field-maps. Destroy'. Fortunately that directive had never been implemented. Inside the envelope there were a number of field-sheets - some of them M'Coy's - dating from the Survey's field-seasons of 1845 and 1846 (see Fig. 2.9). A number of other early field-sheets are also now to be seen in the Survey's archives, and without exception they all convey the same message: the young Survey was just footling around. On the field-sheets (they are mostly quartered Ordnance Survey six-inch sheets) the officers have merely followed the principal roads and a few of the streams, marking crudely and vaguely the general localities where different types of rock had been observed. There is little or no attempt to record dips, to draw geological boundaries, or to depict the character of the terrain. In short, all those early field-sheets represent geological mapping of an extremely inferior and rudimentary character. The arrival of Oldham was timely. He brought experience of the six-inch mapping which had served to underpin Portlock's 1843 report on the geology of mid-Ulster. That experience he was able to call upon as he sought to set his new charge in motion along the right lines.

The poor quality of the early mapping, and the consequent necessity for a re-examination of the ground, resulted in the Survey making only slow progress between 1846 and 1850. Not until the latter year, for instance, was the Survey able to return to the Hook peninsula to complete a more effective mapping than that achieved during 1845. But there were two other factors causing delay. First, there was the disturbance created in 1846 when the Survey had to remove itself from the Custom House to the newly acquired building which was to be the

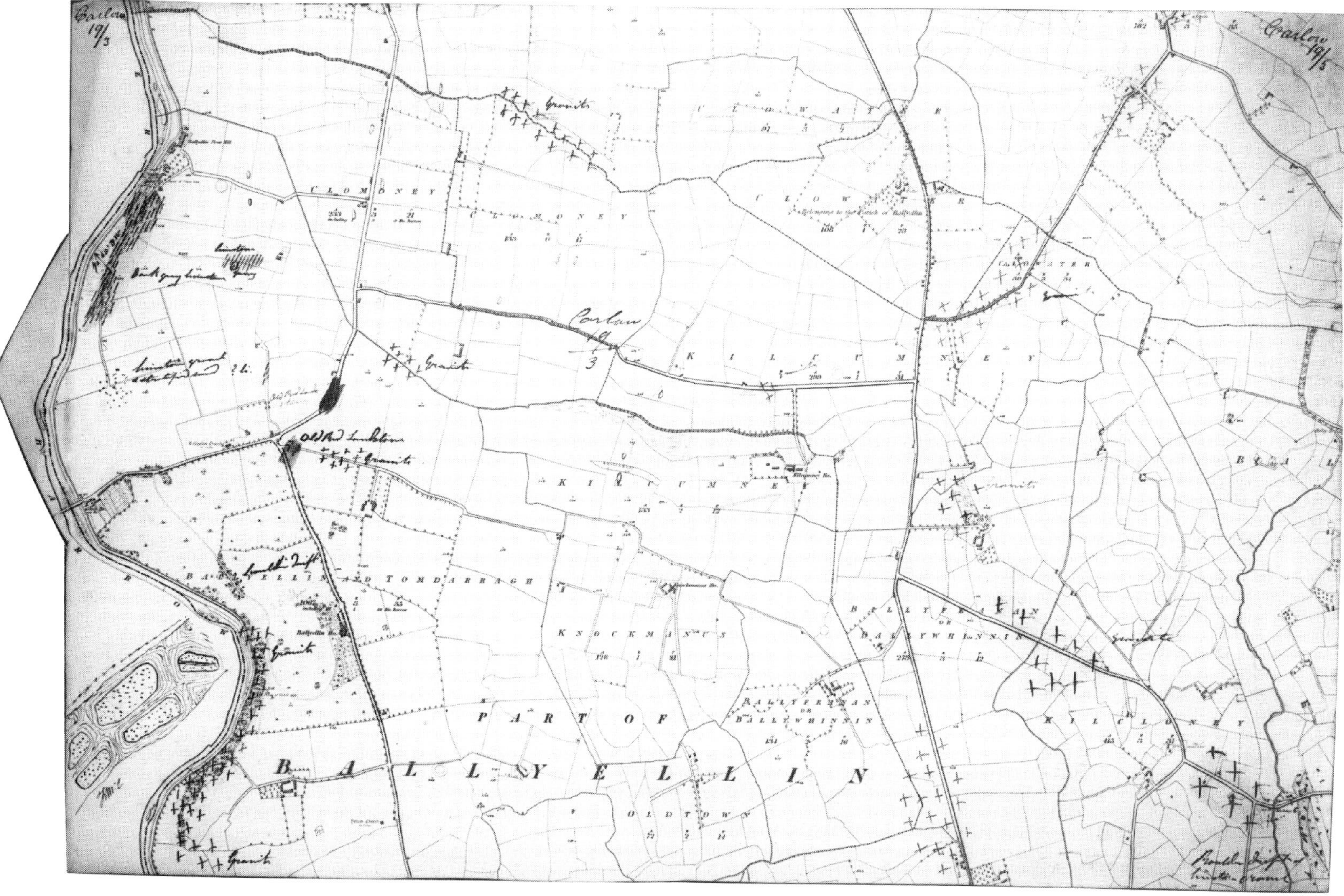

FIGURE 2.9. *One of M'Coy's six-inch field-sheets dating from 1845 or 1846, here much reduced in scale. The sheet is the southwestern quarter-sheet of County Carlow Sheet 19. The River Barrow, forming the county boundary, lies on the west of the sheet and M'Coy has affixed his monogram to the sheet's bottom, left-hand corner. The lack of recorded field-observations, and the lack of precision are both clearly in evidence. M'Coy has obviously done little more than walk along a few of the roads. Crosses and a splash of red represent granite, dashes washed in blue represent limestone, and a '7' symbol washed in red-brown represents Old Red Sandstone. There is no attempt to plot geological boundaries, and we are left to wonder how M'Coy thought that his field-studies might be converted into a geological map of Ireland. Only one measurement of dip is recorded. The field-sketch in the bottom left-hand corner is evidently a representation of spheroidally weathered granite core-stones set within a matrix of rotten granite or growan.*

FIGURE 2.10. *Number 51 St Stephen's Green, the home of the Survey from October 1846 until March 1870. This is the building as it appeared in 1983. The two wings were added between the autumn of 1848 and the spring of 1850, during the building's conversion into the Museum of Irish Industry. The Survey was accommodated on four floors in the south (right-hand) wing. Today the building is the headquarters of the Office of Public Works, but the forty panels of Irish marble erected by Sir Robert Kane in the entrance hall during 1850 are all still in place.* (From a photograph by Terence Dunne of Trinity College Dublin.)

Survey's more permanent home. Second - and much more seriously - there was increasing delay caused as a result of the Survey being burdened with the task of collecting large numbers of geological specimens for use within the museum. This time-consuming work was unpopular with the officers, and it was a responsibility which was to drive both Oldham and his successor to despair.

In his memoir of 13 January 1845 the First Commissioner had suggested that the Survey and the Dublin Museum of Economic Geology should be housed together within their own especially prepared building. During 1845 various options were considered, and the choice eventually fell upon the house standing at 51 St Stephen's Green East. The house was acquired, but some reconstruction and extension of the building was necessary to fit it for its new role as a museum and Survey headquarters. This work was carried out under the direction of the noted architect George Papworth, and it was evidently 1854 before the last of the contractor's men had departed the scene. But long before then the Survey had moved in to take over its new accommodation. It was on 7 October 1846 that Kane informed De La Beche of his readiness to receive the Survey into its new apartments, and by the July of 1847 the Survey was fully established in that fine city square known to Dubliners simply as 'The Green'.

Within the reconstructed number 51 the Survey was housed at the front of the building and chiefly within the newly constructed southward extension. On the hallway-floor the Survey had space within the Museum's library. There the General Assistant worked, and there were kept the Survey's letter and account books. On the floor above was the room where all the Survey's maps were stored, and this room also served as the Local Director's office. On the top floor there lay a large workroom for the use of the Survey's officers whenever they happened to be in Dublin. Finally, in the basement, the Survey had the use of a large cellar for the storage of specimens, and for the unpacking of casks of rocks, minerals, or fossils as they arrived from officers in the field (see Chapter Ten).

Unfortunately the transfer to The Green occasioned some friction between Kane and Oldham over the ownership of the property which hitherto had been located in the Custom House. Kane's demands were certainly comprehensive, and at one stage he was even claiming as Museum property all the Survey's hammers, collecting-bags, and instruments. Were it able to communicate with us, that theodolite featured in Figure 1.5 must tell a tale of its being the victim in a vigorous tug-of-war! Eventually it was agreed that everything should be handed over to Kane except for two categories of article: first, those items necessary for the Survey's day to day activities, and, second, the fossils, plants, and books which had once been the property of Portlock's department in the period of the Ordnance Survey's Memoir Project. The apportionment of the material was declared complete on 9 July 1847, but for long thereafter relations between Kane and the Survey remained far from harmonious. De La Beche deeply regretted that the Dublin museum had in 1845 slipped from his grasp, and he must have been furious in 1847 when it was announced that the Dublin Museum of Economic Geology was being renamed 'the Museum of Irish Industry' (see p.262).

The upheaval occasioned by the removal from the Custom House was soon over, but the delay caused to the mapping programme by the collection of museum samples dragged on from year to year. It had always been understood that the Survey would collect rocks, minerals, and fossils for Kane's museum in Dublin and for that at Craig's Court in London, but in the summer of 1846 Oldham received instruction that henceforth he was in addition to collect on behalf of the museums in the new Queen's colleges in Belfast, Cork, and Galway. This was just about bearable; it merely meant that his men had to find five samples of each type of specimen instead of the two which had sufficed hitherto. The real problem was a request now made by Kane. It was Kane who added the straw which all but broke the camel's back. On 16 April 1846 he wrote to James asking the Survey to collect soil-samples, what he wanted being outlined as follows.

> A collection of specimens, showing every kind of soil and subsoil which is met with in each county - the locality of each being marked and the area over which it extends being defined as well as circumstances allow - some note of the characteristic vegetation of each kind of soil should be attached.

Some of these samples were intended for display in the Museum, while others were to go into Kane's Museum Laboratory for chemical examination. It was a tall order. Kane was really asking the Survey to undertake nothing less than a national soil survey alongside its national geological survey. But Kane had the ear of the authorities, and on 24 September 1846 the First Commissioner formally instructed the Survey to commence the collection of soil-samples. Initially, De La Beche was anxious to co-operate because he hoped that the chemical analysis of the soils would yield some indication of their agricultural potential, thus allowing the Survey to be of some direct assistance to the Irish economy. That was the theory; in practice the soil-samples were for five years the principal irritant affecting the Survey's relationships with the Museum. Their cohabitation of number 51 with Kane was for the Survey never to be an entirely happy experience.

In his first annual report, dated 5 March 1847, Oldham frankly admitted that the Survey had been making but slow progress, and he went on to remind De La Beche of the difficulty he was facing in trying to run the Survey in Famine-stricken Ireland.

> The very distressed state of this county & the consequent demand for all persons at all competent to superintend the execution of numerous works intended for the relief of the poorer classes, has further rendered it extremely difficult to procure such aid as we require, so that our staff of assistants has been smaller than we wished.

As a result, the post left vacant by M'Coy's resignation four months earlier was still unfilled. Willson, the erratic Wyley, and Flanagan now represented Oldham's entire field-force. Nothing had as yet been published, but Oldham reported that 1,500 square miles (3,900 square kilometres) of southeastern Ireland had now been adequately mapped, including 23 of the 47 six-inch sheets of County Wicklow, 22 of the 54 sheets of County Wexford, 9 sheets of County Carlow, 9 of County Kilkenny, and 2 of County Waterford. In addition he recorded that Smyth had completed his examination of the Castlecomer Coalfield, of the mineral district of County Wicklow, and of the copper mines at Knockmahon in County Waterford. Finally, large numbers of specimens had been collected both for the Dublin museum and for the museums of the three Queen's colleges.

Oldham probably felt uneasy at having to admit that his two-year-old Survey still had nothing to show as a publishable earnest of its labours. Then - as now - the authorities expected tangible evidence of the Survey's field-activities. He therefore made a small propitiative offering to the Earl of Bessborough, the recently appointed Lord Lieutenant, and a man who happened to enjoy a warm relationship with Daniel O'Connell. The offering took the form of three sheets of horizontal sections based upon the Survey's work in southeastern Ireland, and covering the mining districts of County Carlow, Queen's County (Laois), and County Wicklow. The three sheets were delivered to Dublin Castle on or just before 7 April 1847, but if Oldham really was seeking to curry favour in high places, then his little ploy was largely negated by the activities of the grim reaper. The

Lord Lieutenant died of hydrothorax in the Castle on 16 May 1847 after less than a year in office. On the previous day his friend O'Connell, bound for Rome, had died in Genoa.

A week after sending the three sheets of sections off to the Castle, Oldham displayed two of the same sheets to the Geological Society of Dublin at a meeting held upon 14 April 1847. But about all of these sheets there has to hang a certain air of mystery. What were they? Their precise character is nowhere made clear. In all probability they were manuscript versions of some sheets of horizontal sections which the Survey was to publish in printed form during the summer of 1848.

During the field-season of 1847 Oldham concentrated his resources - such as they were - on completing the survey of County Wicklow, partly because of its mineral resources, and partly because it afforded a useful base-line study for the geology of the whole of Leinster. In June of that year Willson was stationed at Dunlavin in the slate country on the western side of the Wicklow Mountains, and Wyley was based at Roundwood amidst the slates to the east of the same mountains. For some reason Flanagan was farther south; he was collecting at Camolin down in County Wexford.

The remoteness of certain parts of the Wicklow Mountains somewhat hindered the Survey that year. On 18 June 1847, for example, we find Willson writing from Dunlavin to report that he had failed to find any suitable lodgings from which to map six-inch Sheet 16 and part of Sheet 22, two sheets covering the uplands around the head of the Kings River and Table Mountain. He therefore requested permission to hire a horse and car by the day to facilitate him in reaching the more remote parts of his area. This request Oldham immediately sanctioned. Earlier in that year a very different delay had been occasioned in the Survey's field-programme. It was a trivial delay, but nonetheless a delay filled with great poignance. On 20 March 1847 Oldham circulated the following note to each member of his staff.

> Wednesday next the 24th inst. being appointed by Her Majesty & Council, as a day to be set apart for general humiliation in consequence of the awful distress prevalent in this country, attendance to their duties will not be required from the assistants on that day.

As Forbes observed during the first of his two Irish visits in 1847, the Famine had converted Ireland into 'a land of misery and tears' (see p.258).

Systematic, sheet by sheet mapping, of course had to be the Survey's priority, but in April 1847, Oldham was authorised to undertake an investigation of a somewhat different type. The sections laid bare during the construction of the rapidly expanding railway system of England and Wales had presented geologists with unique opportunities for field-study. At its Glasgow meeting in 1840 the British Association had set up a committee charged with the responsibility of placing upon permanent record as much as possible of the geological information being revealed in cuttings and tunnels. De La Beche was a member of that committee, and certainly by 1841 the Survey in England and Wales was paying close attention to what had come to be known as 'railway geology'.

It was decided to extend this type of work into Ireland, and the new task was assigned to Portlock's former artistic assistant, George Victor Du Noyer (see p.10). Following upon the collapse of the Ordnance Survey's Memoir Project during 1842, Du Noyer had been declared redundant, and he had spent some time as the drawing master in the newly established College of St Columba - the 'Irish Eton' - then located at Stackallan House in County Meath. In May 1847 he was appointed as a temporary Survey officer and instructed to prepare geological sections of the strata exposed along all the lines of railway radiating from Dublin. It was just over sixty years since the Dublin Society had appointed Donald Stewart to perform a similar duty along the banks of the Grand Canal (see p.2). Equally interesting is the fact that with Du Noyer's appointment to the Survey, exactly half of its staff - Oldham, Du Noyer, and Flanagan - were former members of that team which had worked with Portlock in mid-Ulster during the 1830s.

Du Noyer started work by following the line of the Dublin and Drogheda Railway, which had been opened in 1844, and in the November and December of 1847, with De La Beche's permission, he brought the results of his study to the notice of the Geological Society of Dublin. By the March of the following year he had drawn detailed sections not only along the Dublin to Drogheda line, but also along the Midland Great Western Railway, which by then had pushed its head almost as far west as Mullingar. But difficulties arose when he transferred his attention to the line of the Great Southern and Western Railway, because the company refused him access to its property. This was evidently the first time that a Survey officer anywhere in the British Isles had been refused such a facility, and De La Beche was annoyed. He instantly invoked the powers bestowed upon him under the Parliamentary act of 1845. He served the directors of the railway company with legal notice of his intention to send Du Noyer onto their property. Reluctantly they acquiesced. After completing his work on the Great Southern and Western in the later summer of 1848, Du Noyer moved on to examine the line of the Dublin and Belfast Junction Railway northward of the Boyne.

Throughout all this railway work, Du Noyer proved himself to be a most competent Survey officer, and on 30 September 1848 he was transferred to the regular staff of the Survey as a belated replacement for M'Coy. To his chagrin, however, he was informed that his sixteen months of special service on railway geology would not exempt him from the six-month probationary period normal for an Assistant Geologist. It was 14 April 1849 before De La Beche sanctioned Du Noyer's appointment to a permanent post. His railway sections were never published, but they still exist in the Survey's archives drawn upon rolled strips of squared paper, each many metres in length. The sections themselves are beautifully depicted in Du Noyer's artistic hand at a vertical and horizontal scale of one inch to forty feet (1:480), and they afford a valuable record of geological exposures now lost because today the walls of most of the railway cuttings are vegetated.

As the mapping of County Wicklow drew to its completion during the autumn of 1847, there came to the fore what is best termed 'the base-map problem'. It was the problem which had confronted Griffith during the 1830s (see p.6). He had his various field-sheets, but down to 1839 there was available no suitable map of Ireland upon which he might actually publish the results of his field-investigations. Now the same problem was haunting the Survey. De La Beche and Oldham were both anxious to publish the Survey's Irish work upon a one-inch map (1:63,360) comparable to that being used in Britain, but, despite De La Beche's entreaties, the Ordnance Survey had still not resolved upon the compilation of an Irish one-inch series. Under James, the Survey had tried to construct its own one-inch map by reduction from the six-inch (1:10,560) scale, but it had proved an onerous task with which Oldham had not persisted. Yet the Survey had to publish.

De La Beche and Oldham decided that there was only one solution to their problem. They would have to call into service the small-scale county maps of the so-called Townland Index series. These were maps originally intended as index maps depicting the sheet-lines of the six-inch coverage of each of the counties. Portlock had already made the Townland Index maps the basis for his geological map of mid-Ulster published in 1843, but De La Beche and Oldham now took their decision only with the greatest of reluctance. They both recognised the absurdity of field-mapping upon the six-inch scale and of then eliminating a good deal of the carefully plotted detail during the course of reduction to the county index sheets which are mostly drawn to a scale of only half an inch to the mile (1:126,720). In any case the half-inch scale was only twice that of Griffith's existing geological map of Ireland. Surely the Irish public would be expecting from its new Survey something more innovative than just a glorified Griffith map.

The very fact that the Townland Index maps were county maps was itself unfortunate because a county is an arbitrary and quite inappropriate unit for geological study. De La Beche pointed out that an important structural entity such as the Leinster Coalfield extends into three different counties, and its representation upon three county maps must visually destroy its unitary character. But any attempt to fit the county maps together was foredoomed to failure because most of the counties have been plotted upon their own individual graticule. The sole available alternative to the Townland Index maps was the six-inch sheets themselves, but while the publication of a few six-inch geological sheets might be called for in certain complex mining districts, the issuing of a nationwide coverage upon that scale was entirely out of the question. It would have involved the preparation of some two thousand sheets, and many of these sheets would have appeared as monochromes indicating that only one type of rock was present within the region. In October 1847, therefore, De La Beche asked the Ordnance Survey to prepare a slightly modified version of the County Wicklow Townland Index to serve as the basis for the forthcoming geological map of the county.

The geological map of County Wicklow - the Survey's first publication - appeared on 26 July 1848 bearing the title *Index to the Townland Survey of the County of Wicklow geologically coloured* (Plate I). Proudly, Oldham put the map on display at the meeting of the British Association held that year in Swansea between 9 and 16 August. The base-map is derived from the ordinary Townland Index at a scale of half an inch to the mile (1:126,720), and the geological map still displays the lines of the county's 47 six-inch sheets. The Townland Index has nevertheless been modified in three ways. First, engraved lines have been added to represent both the geological boundaries and the course of the various horizontal sections which the Survey now had ready for publication. Second, part of County Dublin has been added to the map so as to represent the northern terminus of the Leinster Granite along the shores of Dublin Bay between Booterstown and Dalkey. Third, in the southeast, part of northern County Wexford has been added in order to avoid an abrupt ending of the Croghan igneous complex at the county boundary.

The geology is represented upon the map by hand-applied colour-washes, and all told it affords an accurate enough representation of the county's geology. The map's greatest weakness arises from the Survey's attempt to be overly ambitious. Oldham has tried to represent upon the map both the county's solid geology and its overlying

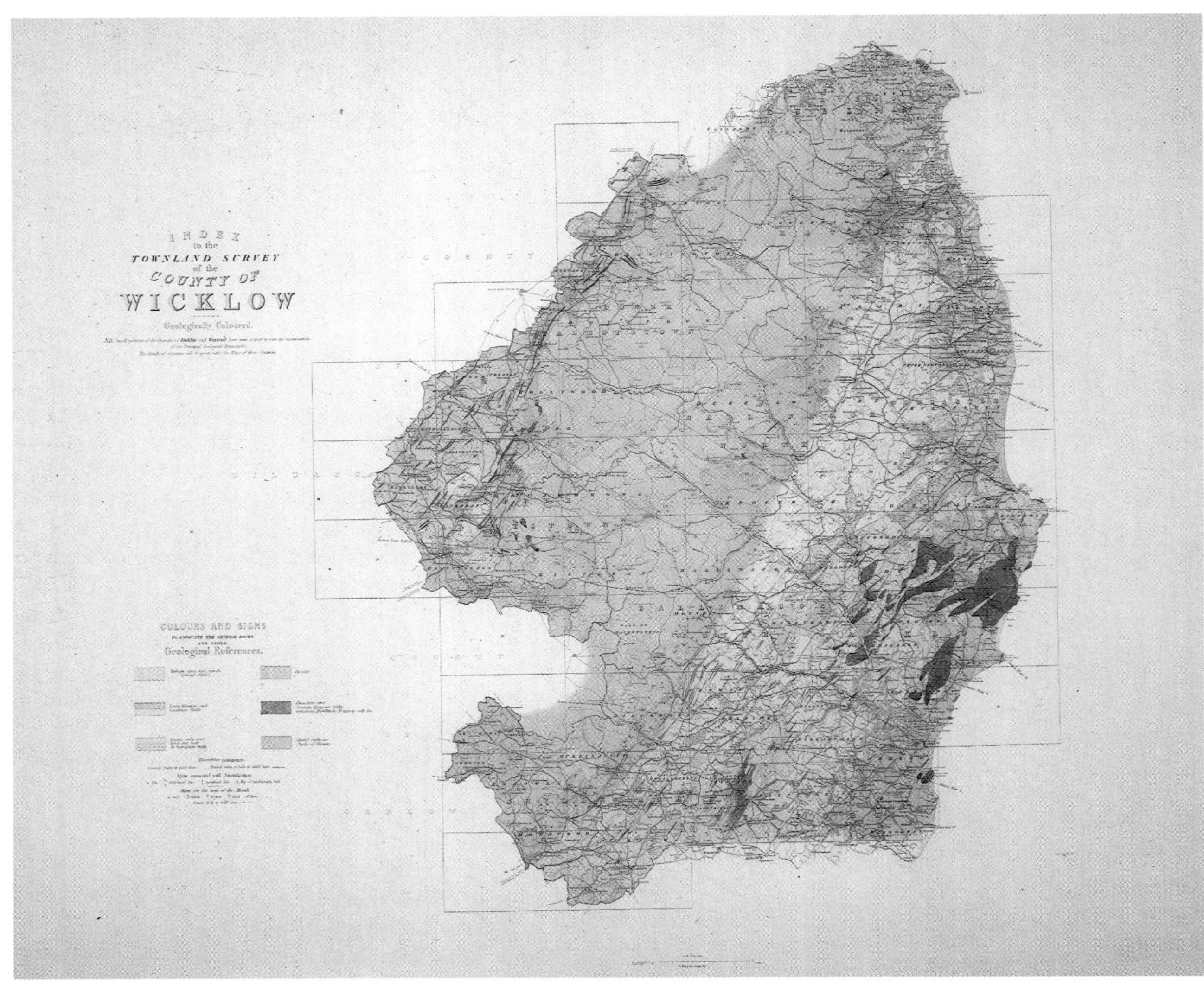

PLATE I. *The geologically coloured Townland Index map of County Wicklow, here reduced from its original half-inch (1 : 126,720) scale. This sheet, tinted by hand and published on 26 July 1848, was the first map to be issued by the Geological Survey of Ireland. Counties are inappropriate units for geological study, and here, for the sake of geological completeness, the sheet in the north encompasses a part of County Dublin, and in the south a part of County Wexford. The effect of the drift stipple is best seen in the eastern portion of the map.* (Reproduced from a map in the archives of the Survey.)

unconsolidated deposits. A very fine stipple has been introduced to show what the map's key terms 'Tertiary clays and gravels ("glacial drifts")', and, while locally the result is legible and even pleasing, there are other areas where the addition of the stipple has brought some confusion into the entire geological picture. The Survey still had much to learn. Overall the map is nonetheless an attractive example of geological cartography, and we may well understand Oldham's pride in the Survey's earliest publication. The map is now rare - perhaps even extremely rare. Only two hundred copies were printed and coloured, these being sold to the public at seven shillings apiece as compared with a price of two shillings and six pence charged by the Ordnance Survey for the standard Townland Index sheet.

The Townland Index maps may have been upon too small a scale to satisfy the Survey, but their use as a geological base-map did seem to offer one slight advantage. Even Oldham himself admitted as much during a meeting of the Royal Irish Academy on 13 November 1848. This advantage stemmed from the fact that Kane was then preparing two series of county maps of Ireland. One series depicted land valuation, and was based largely upon the work of Griffith's Valuation Office. The other series consisted of county soil-maps (Kane termed them 'agrological' or 'agronomic' maps), and was based largely upon the soil-samples being collected by the Survey. It was hoped that a comparison of Kane's maps with the Survey's maps drawn to the same scale would establish the existence of important but hitherto unrecognised relationships between geology and agriculture. In this way the activities of the Survey might be given a direct relevance to Ireland's agricultural improvement.

Sadly, this effort at bridge-building between geology and agriculture never really proceeded beyond the drawing-board. Early in the 1850s Kane abandoned the construction of his two proposed series of maps, and none of them was ever published. Indeed, for many decades there was lost all trace of even the manuscript versions of the maps. But in November 1993 four of the manuscript sheets (land valuation maps of counties Donegal, Tyrone, and Wexford, and a soil map of County Kildare) appeared in an auction room in Blackrock, County Dublin. There the significance of the sheets was fortunately recognised by Dr Arnold Horner of University College Dublin. When the sheets came under the hammer he was able to acquire the three land valuation maps on behalf of his College. The fourth sheet - the soil map - has unfortunately again been lost from the public view.

At the same time as the geological map of County Wicklow made its appearance in 1848, the Survey also published four sheets of longitudinal or horizontal sections across southeastern Ireland (Horizontal Sections 1, 2, 3, and 4, later designated 'Old Series'), drawn to the standard Survey scale of six inches to one mile (1:10,560). The sections cover a total length of well over two hundred kilometres, and they had been surveyed on the ground by De La Beche, Oldham, and Smyth. It was evidently copies of some of these sections which, in the April of the previous year, Oldham had both presented to the Lord Lieutenant and then exhibited before the Geological Society of Dublin. But the publication of the sections had been delayed until 1848 because of their intimate relationship to the geological map of County Wicklow.

It is interesting to note that in their construction of sections the Survey seems to have taken all the altitudes and other topographical detail directly off the six-inch Ordnance map. Here the Irish Survey possessed a decided advantage over its British counterpart. In the absence of a six-inch coverage in Britain, the geologists there were having to survey their section lines with chains and theodolites. This was to prove a formidable undertaking in the mountainous districts of North Wales where De La Beche's men had just started work.

The 1848 tally of publications included one other item: Smyth's plan of the Avoca mines drawn to a scale of one inch to three hundred feet (1:3,600) and entitled.

> *Plan and sections of the Ovoca Mines County Wicklow. Comprising the copper and iron-pyrites mines of Ballymurtagh, Ballygahan, Tigroney, Cronebane, and Connary.*

The plan's exact date of publication remains uncertain but one copy was presented to the Royal Irish Academy on 9 November 1848, and another copy was seemingly presented to the Geological Society of Dublin at its monthly meeting five days later.

On 9 May 1849 the Survey published its second county map, this one being for County Carlow, and four weeks later - on 13 June - there appeared the companion map for County Kildare. These two maps are in exactly the same style as the earlier County Wicklow map, and with them there should have been published a similar map of County Wexford. But in his annual report for 1848 Oldham explained that he was withholding the Wexford map because he remained doubtful about the accuracy of some of the Survey's early mapping. Perhaps he had M'Coy's work chiefly in mind. Oldham certainly had his men back in County Wexford during the field-season of 1848 for an extensive programme of revision and re-mapping.

As was then the practice, many copies of the newly published county maps went on a complimentary basis both to individuals and to institutions, but the public at large evidently took little interest in the three maps. As late as 3 April 1855 Messrs Hodges and Smith of Grafton Street, Dublin, the sole Irish agents for the Survey's maps, had taken only 73 copies of the Wicklow map, 15 of the Carlow map, and 20 of the Kildare map. This was hardly big business. Oldham himself now harboured grave doubts about the maps. In his annual report for 1848 he complained that the Townland Index maps were 'exceedingly ill adapted for the proper exhibition of the features of Geological structure', and in his report for the following year he returned to the subject at some length. He emphasised again that the index maps were on far too small a scale for the Survey's purpose, and he now pointed out that while the index sheets used for the maps of Wicklow, Carlow, and Kildare had all possessed a common scale of half an inch to one mile (1:126,720), there was no such uniformity of scale among the index sheets for the remaining twenty-nine counties. The forthcoming geological map of County Dublin, for example, was based upon an index sheet with a scale of one inch to one and a half miles (1:95,040). He concluded by entering a strong plea that the Ordnance Survey should again be pressed to prepare a one-inch map for the Survey's use.

In the autumn of 1848 the Survey's involvement in the collection of soil-samples for the museum engendered serious friction between Oldham and Kane. The Survey's complaint was that the collection of the soils was seriously hindering the task of mapping the solid geology. Certainly the geologists must have spent an appreciable proportion of their time digging holes and carrying soil-bags. Between 20 February 1847 and 16 November 1848 no less than 330 soil-samples were despatched to Kane from counties Carlow, Dublin, Kildare, Kilkenny, Wexford, and Wicklow, and from Queen's County (Laois), each sample being accompanied by a form upon which the collector had to answer fifteen questions about both the soil and its environment. For his part, Kane complained incessantly that the individual samples he received were too small for sound analysis - he demanded at least two pounds (900 grams) of soil in each sample - that the samples were being inadequately documented, and that they were from sites too widely scattered to afford a satisfactory picture of the areal distribution of soil types.

The whole sorry business seems to have come to a head on 13 November 1848 at a meeting of the Royal Irish Academy when an angry Kane taunted Oldham by reminding him that the Survey was not collecting soils merely of its own volition as a gesture of goodwill towards the Museum. Rather had the Survey received specific orders to undertake the work from no lesser individual than the First Commissioner himself, acting 'upon the application of Sir Robert Kane'. On the following day Kane addressed a long and forceful letter to De La Beche putting the Museum's case, and stressing, in particular, that the Survey had provided him with the woefully inadequate total of only 48 soil-samples from the whole of County Wicklow. On 27 November De La Beche forwarded the letter to the First Commissioner together with a covering statement of his own presenting the Survey's point of view.

In his memorandum De La Beche observed that if the Survey was to become seriously involved in the assessment of agricultural potential, then it should have upon its staff an agricultural geologist qualified in soil chemistry and trained to consider soils within the full complex of their environmental setting. This was a strikingly modern-sounding pedological proposal, and De La Beche suggested that such an officer should be appointed for a trial three-year period at a cost of £250 per annum. De La Beche's efforts at empire building had the happy knack of succeeding, but this particular proposal never came to anything, and the storm over soil-samples gradually passed away. As early as 27 November Oldham wrote to his staff reminding them of their continuing responsibilities in respect of the collection of soil-samples, and this duty they by no means shirked. Between 6 December 1848 and 24 September 1850 there arrived at number 51 a total 451 soil-samples collected in counties Carlow, Dublin, Kilkenny, Waterford, Wexford, and Wicklow.

In 1850 the staff of the Survey consisted of Oldham, three Assistant Geologists (Du Noyer, Willson, and Wyley), one General Assistant (Joseph G. Medlicott who had replaced Penny in October 1846), and Flanagan, the Fossil Collector. Of these six men, only Du Noyer and Flanagan remained in Ireland by 1857. It was the fulfilment of a prophesy. In 1843 Colby had urged the view that a civilian geological survey would prove to have an unacceptably high rate of staff turnover. Officers would resign to seek their fortunes overseas. This is exactly what now began to happen. The first to depart was Oldham himself.

In March 1850 the Board of the East India Company offered Oldham the newly-created post of Superintendent of the Geological Survey of India at a salary of £800 per annum. For Oldham, who was eager to marry a certain Miss Dixon of Liverpool, this offer was a sore temptation, but he nevertheless responded to the Indian overtures with a negative. De La Beche was informed of what had happened, but he did nothing to make it easier for Oldham to remain in Ireland. Soon all Oldham's initial hesitation was overcome when the East India

Company's offer was renewed later in 1850 at a salary now more than three times the £300 which he was earning as Local Director in Dublin. Oldham submitted his resignation to De La Beche on 14 November 1850, the resignation to take effect from the end of that month.

In a letter to the First Commissioner, Oldham explained the reasons for his having felt less than happy about the Dublin post. First, he pointed out that the standing accorded to the Local Director in Dublin left much to be desired. He was regarded as equivalent to the Local Director for England and Wales, but this was unjust because for most of the year the latter officer had his Director close at hand, whereas the Local Director in Ireland was much more isolated and he therefore carried a far greater burden of personal responsibility. Second, the high cost of living in Ireland was making it difficult for him to exist upon his Dublin salary. He pleaded the inadequacy of the £50 paid to him in lieu of travelling expenses incurred within a 15-mile radius of his various field-headquarters, and he claimed that over the previous four years these local travelling expenses had on average amounted to £73 per annum, with the additional £23 coming out of his own pocket. Similarly, he observed that the cost of his accommodation while on tours of inspection was proving to be very high, and again he frequently had to dig into his own resources because hotel charges were commonly well beyond the limit of reimbursement which he could claim from the Survey. All this rings true - certainly far truer than those excuses which James had offered in explanation of his own resignation just four years earlier.

Oldham remained in Dublin until January 1851, when he and the new Mrs Oldham left for the East. There Oldham assumed his fresh geological duties in March 1851. In India he discovered that the establishment of the geological survey consisted of one peon and one writer; there were no European assistants; there was no provision for field-work; and the survey's few records were stored in one box in the Surveyor - General's office. It was a far cry from 51 St Stephen's Green, and one of Oldham's first acts in India was to write home inviting Medlicott to go to his assistance in Calcutta. Medlicott was perhaps relieved to have the opportunity of shaking Irish dust from his feet. As a member of the Church of Ireland, he had recently effected a clandestine marriage to a Roman Catholic girl, and his enraged father, the rector of Loughrea, had for a while banished him from the family home. Medlicott resigned from the Survey in September 1851 and he joined Oldham in the following December.

J.G. Medlicott was the first of five members of the Irish Survey who were enticed to India by Oldham's attractive offers. But this link between the Irish and the Indian surveys was only one part of a much broader link which now developed between Ireland and the Indian Survey. From Oldham, in 1851, down to 1920 almost twenty Irish geologists joined the Geological Survey of India, and during the seventy years between 1851 and 1921, there were only sixteen years when the Indian Survey did not have an Irish geologist at its head. Oddly, at home in Dublin things were very different. There the Irish Survey had at its head a native-born Irishman for rather less than half of that seventy-year period.

When Oldham submitted his resignation, the Irish Survey was still well short of the sixth anniversary of its foundation. Yet here was De La Beche now seeking for his third Local Director for the Dublin office. It was not an easy post for him to fill. There was nobody suitable within the ranks of the Irish Survey itself; Du Noyer, Willson, and Wyley were all far too inexperienced. Nor was there any other obvious candidate lurking anywhere else upon the Irish scene. Oldham had been found waiting in the Dublin wings in 1846; four years later the Dublin wings were empty of an appropriate player. De La Beche therefore turned to the ranks of the British Survey in search of his new Irish Local Director. He sent to Ireland one of the finest geologists ever to have made a career amidst the Irish rocks. The new Irish Local Director was Joseph Beete Jukes. He is deserving of a fanfare; his arrival at number 51 is a crucial moment in the history of the Survey.

Jukes was born at Summerhill, near Birmingham, on 10 October 1811. He was the only son of a local manufacturer, the family evidently having made its money in the button trade. His interest in geology developed while he was still a boy, and it owed much to the influence of Jane Jukes, his aunt and senior by twenty years, who was herself a talented enthusiast in the science. As I write there sits beside me the scrapbook in which Jane proudly recorded the details of her nephew's distinguished career. Being a woman, she had to rest content with Beete as her surrogate within the real world of science. She merits here her little memorial. She was born in Birmingham just before the 'Church and King Riots' of July 1791, and she died at 3 Crescent West, Birmingham, on 10 August 1873.

During the 1820s geology appeared to offer little in the way of career opportunities even to a young man, and Jukes therefore bowed to the wishes of his widowed mother. The family had for long been Dissenters, but his mother dreamed of enhancing her respectability through the possession of a son in Holy Orders within the established church. With this in mind, Jukes in 1830 went up to St John's College Cambridge as an exhibitioner. There, it has to be admitted, he found his pleasure in the open air rather than the library, and one wonders whether on his rambles around Cherry Hinton or Madingley he ever came across a student from Christ's College out hunting for beetles. If he did, then it was surely the first meeting between Jukes and Charles Darwin. As I will suggest in Chapter Nine, Darwin's most famed work was later perhaps to shape Jukes's thinking as he grappled with a major problem in Irish geology.

One Cambridge experience Jukes and Darwin certainly did share. They both met and developed an admiration for Adam Sedgwick, the distinguished professor of geology. Darwin seemingly never joined Sedgwick's class, but Jukes did. He enrolled against the advice of his tutor, who held so dubious a subject as geology to be unsuitable food for the mind of a prospective ordinand. That tutor was evidently right. Sedgwick's discourses held Jukes enthralled. As he sat at the professor's feet, all thought of entering the Church melted out of Jukes's soul. He resolved instead to dedicate his life to Sedgwick's science. It was a moment of rebirth. His real father had died when Jukes was aged only seven, but now Jukes declared Sedgwick to be his new paternal parent. In their lifelong correspondence he normally addressed Sedgwick as 'my dear father'.

Coming down from Cambridge in 1836, Jukes lived for almost three years as an itinerant geologist, walking the English byways, hammer in hand, and covering his modest expenses by means of courses of geological lectures delivered before local societies. A typical programme was that for 1837. In April he began a course at the Literary, Scientific, and Commercial Institution of Liverpool; in October at the Mechanics' Institution in Birmingham; and in December at the Literary and Philosophical Society of Leicester. It was all fine experience as a prelude to the lecturing duties which were to come his way in Ireland during the 1850s (see p.277).

Soon Jukes felt the call of lands and rocks more distant. From April 1839 until November 1840 he held the rigorous office of Geological Surveyor to the colony of Newfoundland, and, having failed to secure the chair of geology in University College London during the summer of 1841, he in April 1842 again sailed away from England. This time he was embarked as Naturalist aboard H.M.S. *Fly* (485 tons, 18 guns) bound for Australia and the East Indies. Interestingly there was on board an Irish connection. The commanding officer of the *Fly* had links with County Down. He was Captain Francis Price Blackwood, son of Sir Henry Blackwood, Nelson's 'Prince of frigate captains'. Jukes spent almost four years in the antipodes, visiting Singapore, Java, New Guinea, and Norfolk Island, in addition to Australia and the Great Barrier Reef.

FIGURE 2.11. *Joseph Beete Jukes (1811-1869), seemingly attired in his smoking jacket. At various times in his life he was much addicted to 'the weed', and as early as 2 April 1850 he informed Ramsay that he had just finally renounced tobacco for the seventh time! Some thought that heavy smoking might have been a cause of his mortal illness, but Augusta Jukes protested that he had shed the habit long before his death.* (Reproduced from a plate in Horace B. Woodward's *History of the Geological Society of London*, 1907.) (See also Figure 3.11.)

His years in the *Fly* may have been scientifically less fruitful than those of Darwin in H.M.S. *Beagle* or Thomas Henry Huxley in H.M.S. *Rattlesnake*, but at a personal level it is clear that Jukes was a vastly experienced geologist by the time the *Fly* dropped anchor in Spithead on 19 June 1846.

His appetite for overseas travel for the moment satiated, Jukes on 14 August 1846 wrote to De La Beche soliciting a post with the British Survey. An interview followed and the weather-beaten traveller clearly made the right sort of impact. On 18 August De La Beche wrote to Ramsay:

> I have had a very satisfactory interview with Jukes, who appears a very fine fellow, and to love knowledge for its own sake.

It was a sound assessment. Jukes was offered a Survey post at nine shillings per diem, and he was told to present himself on 1 October at Bala, in Merioneth, for training under Ramsay and William Talbot Aveline.

Jukes had now entered into his element. As a field-surveyor he was an outstanding success. Meticulous in his attention to detail, and possessed of a superb eye for country, he became perhaps the finest field-geologist of his day. Within less than a year of Jukes's joining the Survey, Ramsay recorded in his diary that Jukes 'produces better work and understands it better than any man on the Survey'. The four years which he now passed mapping in North Wales and the English Midlands were surely the happiest in Jukes's life. By day his bulky form proved to possess quite remarkable powers of endurance in even the roughest of terrain; by night his booming voice and ringing laughter made him the life and soul of the party at those hostelries which served as the Survey's field-headquarters. As one of his colleagues observed: 'A more joyous, generous, kindly spirit lived not among us'. Innocent in the devious ways of the world, Jukes was a man without guile who existed solely for his chosen science. But those few idyllic years rapidly came to an end. If we are to understand what now happened, I must ask my reader to bear in mind one simple fact: on Saturday 22 September 1849, in the parish church at Harborne, near Birmingham, the Hon. and Revd Towry Law pronounced Jukes and Miss Georgina Augusta Meredith to be man and wife. Jukes was a geologist burdened with new financial responsibilities.

Little more than a year after the wedding, De La Beche offered Jukes the Dublin local directorship in succession to Oldham. Initially Jukes was reluctant to accept the offer. He dreaded the thought of severing those close personal ties which now bound him so intimately to his colleagues on the Survey in England and Wales. Two considerations nevertheless eventually caused him to a reassessment of the situation. I now present those two considerations in the order in which I am convinced that Jukes himself would have wished them to appear. The first consideration is scientific, the second is economic.

Jukes was a geological perfectionist. He felt that hitherto all his field-mapping for the Survey had fallen far short of his ideal. It had merely been British-style one-inch mapping. It had imposed upon him severe limitations. It had denied him the opportunity of recording all those minutiae of field-geology which so fascinated him. There was only one place in the world where he might face the challenging but deeply rewarding task of widespread, large-scale field-mapping. That place was Ireland. The Irish Survey's programme of six-inch field-mapping was for Jukes an almost irresistible bait.

And then there was the 'dirty dog' barking about money. By the autumn of 1849 Jukes's salary was £300 per annum, and exactly the same as that of the Local Director in Dublin. (Not until 1854 was the Irish Local Director's salary raised to £400 per annum.) De La Beche nevertheless had the barefaced effrontery to tell Jukes that in real terms he would find the Irish salary to be far higher than his British salary. On £300 in Ireland he and Augusta would find themselves able to enjoy a standard of living substantially improved as compared with the somewhat frugal existence being allowed to them by a British salary of £300.

This was an example of De La Beche's duplicity at its most flagrant. His regular visits to Ireland had given him first-hand experience of the high cost of living which had to be faced by a Survey officer in post-Famine Ireland. He knew from Oldham's letter of resignation that he and his own new wife doubted their ability to live adequately off the Local Director's salary, even when it was supplemented by a second income derived from a tenure of the chair in Trinity College Dublin.

In fairness to De La Beche it has to be recognised that he was the victim of conflicting interests. On the one hand there was the broader Survey interest. He had to fill the Local Director's office in Dublin and he had to entice thither the best man he could find. Jukes was that man. On the other hand there was the narrower personal interest. Jukes was a friend, a devoted disciple, and a loyal Survey officer. De La Beche had decided that the broad Survey interest must be paramount. Perhaps he was right.

The six-inch maps were Sirens luring Jukes to Hibernia's shores. As yet he knew nothing of De La Beche's deceitful ways. His initial hesitation about Dublin evaporated. On 20 September 1850 he wrote to De La Beche from Llangollen accepting the Irish local directorship. Eight weeks later, on the morning of 29 November, his Survey colleagues Ramsay and Alfred Selwyn saw him aboard the Irish packet at Holyhead (see p.277), and that afternoon Jukes ascended the steps of number 51 ready to assume the responsibilities of his new office.

That was a golden day in the history of the Survey, and a red letter day in the history of Irish geology. In Jukes's own life, and, I suspect, in that of Augusta, it was a black day. It ushered in eighteen somewhat miserable years. Jukes had made an error. Almost immediately he began to discover that conditions in Ireland were not to his liking, and it must very soon have dawned that he had been duped by his chief. He arrived in Dublin on a Friday. The following Monday he wrote to Ramsay:

> It's very dark & dreary here & I can't say I admire Dublin. There's devil a decent place to be had for lodgings under £2 a week and there's no intermediate grade between the dirty & the magnificent.

Perhaps as an Englishman he felt himself to be an unwelcome intruder upon the Irish scene. Certainly

FIGURE 2.12. *Kiltorcan Old Quarry, County Kilkenny (S557345), the site of Flanagan's 1851 discovery of richly fossiliferous beds in the upper Old Red Sandstone. The fossils were first brought to the notice of the scientific world by Edward Forbes during the meeting of the British Association for the Advancement of Science held in Belfast in September 1852. Since then many another geologist has visited the site, and in 1976, with the assistance of Roadstone Ltd, the site was reinvestigated under the direction of Professor William Gilbert Chaloner, then of Birkbeck College London.* (Photograph by the author.)

only a week before he crossed to Dublin he had written to Sir Roderick Murchison:

> Oldham tells me that in one of their leading papers there are, appended to a notice of his going to India, some sharp remarks on importing an Englishman to succeed him.

It may be that nationality had something to do with Jukes's first major disappointment in Ireland. In October 1850 he had applied for the soon-to-be-vacant Trinity College chair which Oldham had held concurrently with his local directorship. But the Board of the College decided to pass Jukes over and to appoint the Carlow-born Revd Samuel Haughton (see p.277). Thus Jukes was denied that professorial salary with which Oldham had supplemented his Survey income. This was a serious matter because at every turn Jukes discovered the hollowness of De La Beche's promise that he and Augusta would be able to live very economically in Ireland. Indeed, the high cost of living in Ireland is a constantly recurring theme in Jukes's letters dating from his early Irish years. Here, for example, is Jukes writing to Ramsay from Dublin on 6 March 1852 (see also p.295).

> As to the expense of living in Ireland you must either make up your mind to it, or you must sink down into a state of dirt and discomfort which makes life miserable. There is no middle class here, & accordingly no accommodation for such a class. You can't have middle class lodgings nor middle class inns, there are no country lodgings to be got anywhere. There is no medium, you must either live like a gentleman of fortune, or you must altogether cease to mingle in gentleman's society.

For whatever reason, Jukes seems to have been quite unable to adapt himself to conditions of life in Ireland. From almost the very moment of his arrival, his character underwent a strange transformation. Gone was the carefree geologist of yore, and in his place there stood a man overwhelmed by the responsibilities of his new office. His friends noticed with concern the change that came over him, and when Ramsay enquired as to what had happened, Jukes responded from Dungarvan, County Waterford, on 14 June 1851

> I am sorry I have grown so matter-of-fact. I can hardly tell you why it is, but I feel that it is so. I hardly know whether it is the air of Ireland, or the nature of the work here, or what; but certainly much of the zest of life has departed, and nothing but duty and business remain. Not that we are unhappy, but only in a sort of

FIGURE 2.13. *Buildings in the main street of Ballyhale, County Kilkenny, during 1987. The town has changed little since James Flanagan found the richly fossiliferous beds at nearby Kiltorcan during 1851. Flanagan spent the last few months of his life at Ballyhale, and he died there on 14 April 1859. He lies in an unmarked grave somewhere in a local Roman Catholic burial ground.* (Photograph by the author.)

> negative state. It may partly proceed perhaps from the utter want of society. We have not made a single acquaintance anywhere.

Change there certainly had been, but Jukes remained a field-geologist of outstanding ability. This talent he was now to deploy in the interests of Irish geology, and under his control the Geological Survey of Ireland for the first time became a thoroughly efficient and effective body. Jukes remained at the head of the Survey for less than twenty years, but during that period he impressed upon the Survey a character which it was to retain right down to 1924.

One of Jukes's earliest tasks in Dublin was to oversee the publication of two further geological sheets based upon the Ordnance Survey's Townland Index maps. These two sheets were first, the long-delayed map of County Wexford, and second, the map of County Dublin. Both the maps appear to have been published during May 1851, and the Wexford map is in the same general style as the three earlier sheets depicting counties Carlow, Kildare, and Wicklow. But the Dublin sheet differs from all the others in that, as Oldham had warned (p.42), its scale is one inch to one and a half miles (1:95,040) instead of half an inch to one mile (1:126,720).

On the Dublin sheet there is some evidence of inadequate editorial attention because some manuscript corrections have had to be introduced into the map's key. Perhaps in the spring of 1851 Jukes was still not entirely *au fait* with his new duties. But his lapse, if such it was, can have excited little public comment, because even by the spring of 1855 Messrs Hodges and Smith had managed to sell only a measly 21 copies of the Dublin sheet. By that same date the combined sales of all five of the county maps amounted to only 155 copies. In their own day those county maps were something of a cartographic flop, and paradoxically, it is that fact which today results in their elevation to the status of being prized collectors' items.

At the beginning of his first Irish field-season, Jukes went off to inspect the work of his geologists. He was not entirely happy with what he saw. From Waterford he wrote to Ramsay on 31 May 1851:

> Our fellows here seem all good fellows, as good as on the English survey, but sometimes they do astound me not a little and then that leaves an uncomfortable feeling afterwards.

He was, of course, anxious to press ahead with the mapping as rapidly as the mental and physical limitations of his staff might allow. Very soon after his arrival in Dublin he lighted upon the collection of soil-samples as one area where time could be saved. As early as 10 March 1851 he wrote to De La Beche saying: 'Had we not better try to get rid of the soil affair?' On 18 March De La Beche replied asking Jukes to estimate the amount of time that his officers were spending upon soil-sample collection. He responded three days later. He reported that the collection of the samples was occupying each of his men for an average of eight days in every quarter. This was clearly a substantial proportion of their time, but collection nonetheless continued. During 1851 Kane acknowledged the receipt of 398 samples taken from the soils of counties Cork, Kilkenny, Tipperary, and Waterford. Between 9 March 1852 and 1 July 1852 a further 142 samples were returned, but then the flow of samples suddenly ceased. It was nevertheless not until January 1853 that Jukes and Kane formally agreed that the Survey's involvement in soil-sample collection should be terminated.

During Jukes's early years in Ireland the Survey worked steadily westwards through the south of Ireland from County Kilkenny, across counties Waterford and Cork, and on into County Kerry. Of course there were problems. In 1852 bad weather virtually halted all the Survey's field activities for two months. In 1854 we find Jukes complaining of the delays being caused by the officers encountering extensive spreads of peat and impenetrable thickets of furze. In 1856 there was another bad summer. And always the staff were wasting long hours tramping between their lodgings and their ground because there was never available sufficient money to allow for the regular hire of cars or horses.

But those years also saw scientific excitement, and never more so than during Jukes's very first Irish field-season. Flanagan was then searching for fossils in Wyley's ground on one-inch Sheet 157 (New Ross) when he came upon immensely rich beds of beautifully preserved fossils in the upper Old Red Sandstone at Kiltorcan in County Kilkenny. In September 1851 Jukes and Forbes together went to see what their Fossil Collector had discovered. They went to Flanagan's field-quarters (I presume he was living at Ballyhale) to see his treasures laid out for their inspection; they climbed up the slope eastward of the town to see for themselves the exposures which were to make Kiltorcan one of the classic sites of Irish geology. Among the fossils found there was a large freshwater bivalve shell. Despite Jukes's good natured protests, Forbes announced that he proposed to name this particular fossil *Anodonta jukesii* (now *Archanodon jukesi (Forbes 1853)* (see Plate XII).

Despite their environmental and financial difficulties, and buoyed up by their little episodes of excitement, Jukes's men now began to press ahead at a goodly rate. The notion of completing a geological survey of Ireland within a limited period of only ten years was quietly forgotten as, under Jukes's watchful eye, the officers concentrated upon the challenging but enthralling task of detailed six-inch field-mapping. In that task all the officers now had considerable experience; in that task some of them were now beginning to display considerable skill.

By the summer of 1854 the Survey had pushed its mapping-front westwards through Munster, over the crest of the Shehy Mountains, and down to the salt-water shores of Bantry Bay. The officers were into that magnificent region where Europe's frayed extremities finally yield to the fury of the Atlantic. They were surrounded by peninsulas where rugged Old Red Sandstone mountains look down upon island-flecked inlets. On a summer's day of blue skies and still, clear air, the region presents a succession of visions which by any standards are breathtaking in their splendour.

Thursday 24 August 1854 was perhaps just such a day. Jukes and his wife had their field-headquarters in the town of Bantry. Ramsay was visiting from Britain. That morning, after breakfast, Jukes and Ramsay left Bantry by car, bound for Glengarriff. Augusta, side-saddled upon Dolly, rode out for a mile or two with them. Despite consultations with several physicians, Beete and Augusta never succeeded in producing any children. Instead, they surrounded themselves with animals. Two of those animals now yapped excitedly around Dolly's fetlocks: Carlo, the setter, and Tommy, the Scots terrier. Jukes and Ramsay had important business to discuss. They were on their way to meet with De La Beche around on the other side of Bantry Bay. He was staying at Glengarriff. And what was that important business? Why were the Director of the Geological Survey of the United Kingdom, his Local Director for England and Wales, and his Local Director for Ireland all come together in this beautiful but remote corner of Munster? This is something to be reserved for explanation in the next chapter. For the moment we mentally simply rejoin Jukes and Ramsay beneath the hot morning sun. Augusta turns Dolly's head southwards back towards Bantry, and leads Carlo and Tommy home. The two geologists continue on north over the Coomhola River, past the gates of Ardnagashel House, and on along the shores of Glengarriff Harbour. I suppose that there were seals to be seen in the harbour then just as there are today.

CHAPTER THREE

MATURITY 1854-1890

> ... and that generally the survey had made as much progress in their work as was possible with the very scanty staff, and the very inadequate means that had hitherto been placed at their disposal (hear, hear). On a future occasion he hoped to give the society something more definite, and to announce results of a more gratifying character (hear, hear).
>
> From a press report of J. Beete Jukes's presidential address to the Geological Society of Dublin on 8 February 1854 and preserved in Jane Jukes's scrapbook.

Eccles's Hotel at Glengarriff is today one of the best-known of the many visitor-receiving establishments in the southwest of Ireland. But unlike the majority of its late twentieth-century rivals, Eccles's is a venerable institution. In its brochure I see that it claims to be one of the oldest established hotels in Ireland. It was certainly there in 1854. It then wore a configuration somewhat different from that familiar to the modern tourist, but the site is unchanged. The hotel has always stood alongside the road from Bantry, with the hotel windows looking out over Glengarriff Harbour and towards Garinish and a more distant Whiddy Island. Thackeray stood at one of those windows in 1842 wondering why tourists thought it necessary to go to the Rhine or Saxon Switzerland in search of the picturesque.

It seems that in 1854 there were still only two hotels in Glengarriff. Of the two, Eccles's was slightly the more accessible because the scheduled car from Bantry always paused right outside the hotel's door. Many is the time when Victorian ladies from Leamington, Leeds, or London must have laid aside their petit point and rushed over to a window to wave to a departing friend, or to spy upon new arrivals as portmanteaux were lifted off the car and passed to the hotel's attendant porters. In 1854 the hotel was owned and managed by Thomas Eccles. Under his supervision the establishment had already earned a considerable reputation for its excellence. Thackeray tells us that it even possessed a waiter who prided himself upon his ability to distinguish the 'gintlemin' from the rest by the manner in which they imbibed their whiskey.

Who were the guests resident in the hotel on Thursday 24 August 1854? I do not know. Was De La Beche among their number? I just cannot say. What I may declare with confidence is that De La Beche was certainly present in Glengarriff that day. This granted, there would seem to be a strong likelihood of his having chosen to sample the hospitality of the region's best-known hotel. Indeed, in my imagination, I entertain little doubt upon the matter; Sir Henry was surely that day one of Thomas Eccles's guests.

Late in the morning of 24 August 1854 a lady in the hotel did perhaps put down her petit point and move over to a window intent upon discovering the cause of the disturbance outside. A car up from Bantry had just halted. Two bearded gentlemen in their forties were alighting. The lady of the petit point knew nothing of the identity of the two gentlemen, but the reader of the last few pages will already entertain suspicions. We saw them into their car at the close of the previous chapter. They were, of course, Jukes and Ramsay. De La Beche doubtless came out to greet them. Perhaps together they all went back into the hotel to partake of Mr Eccles's excellent luncheon priced at one shilling and six pence per head. Or perhaps they were content merely to order a noggin, thus giving that waiter a chance to assess whether or not they were real 'gintlemin'.

Should there have been a needle-working lady at one of the hotel's windows observing this latest arrival, what she witnessed must have appeared to be an amiable and fraternal scene enacted within a delightful and tranquil setting. That setting was certainly splendid - it reminded the Glaswegian Ramsay of Loch Lomond - but the human aspects of the encounter were not quite what they appeared. The lady watching was not to know that these three men were come together in an effort to resolve a long-running scientific disagreement. It was a disagreement which held profound significance for the Geological Survey on both sides of the Irish Sea. It was a disagreement over the scale of the field-sheets to be used by the Survey in its field-programme. It was a disagreement which had

FIGURE 3.1. *Glengarriff Harbour, August 1993. Eccles's Hotel is the large complex of buildings standing close to the shore on the extreme right of the photograph.* (Photograph by the author.)

clouded Jukes's earliest years in Ireland. The nature of the disagreement must now engage our attention.

The Survey had published its geologically-coloured Townland Index maps of counties Dublin and Wexford during May 1851. The next county sheet scheduled for publication - the sixth such sheet - was that for County Waterford. On 10 March 1852 Jukes exhibited a draft manuscript version of this map to the Geological Society of Dublin, but the map was destined never to be published. Its fate was sealed by a policy change arising from a dispute which developed between Jukes and De La Beche. The dispute had its origins early in 1851. It was a dispute which may have been aggravated by the transformation which came over Jukes's character following his arrival in Ireland, and by his growing realisation that his chief had been less than honest with him about the nature of the conditions he was likely to encounter in Ireland.

Paradoxically, at the root of the dispute there lay an agreement. Both Jukes and De La Beche shared a dissatisfaction with the small-scale Townland Index maps which had been pressed into service as base-maps for the Survey's published geological sheets. But beyond that basic point the two men parted company.

Jukes held that the best alternative to the publication of the small-scale county maps would be the publication of geological versions of the six-inch (1:10,560) maps themselves. He regarded the detailed six-inch field-mapping being conducted by the Irish Branch as the chief glory of De La Beche's entire Survey. He dreamed of seeing nothing less than a nationwide Irish coverage of published six-inch sheets.

For his part, De La Beche quite rightly regarded a national coverage of published six-inch sheets as entirely out of the question. As we noted earlier (p.39), such a coverage would have involved the production of some two thousand sheets, each 90 x 60 centimetres in size, and over much of Ireland the geology is so uniform that a substantial number of the sheets would have displayed scarcely so much as a single geological line. From this point, De La Beche proceeded to argue that since the six-inch sheets were never themselves going to be published, then it followed that six-inch field-mapping was itself a waste of the Survey's time. Was it not ridiculous to spend months tracing out the minutiae of field-phenomena only to lose so much of the carefully recorded detail during the course of reduction to some smaller scale? De La Beche had evidently changed his mind since he wrote those words which appeared at the head of the previous chapter (see p.19).

There was some logic in De La Beche's case. In Britain the Survey had from the outset been forced to work within the confines of small-scale Ordnance Survey sheets. For most of the time, De La Beche's team in Britain had been both mapping and publishing upon the same scale - upon the one-inch map (1:63,360). So why, De La Beche mused, should the Irish staff not both survey and publish upon the best small-scale sheets available to them - upon the Townland Index maps? Admittedly, the Townland Index maps were not ideal, but geologically-coloured Townland Index maps had now been published for five counties. Had the time not arrived for a review of the situation? Was this not the moment for the time-consuming luxury of six-inch field-mapping to be stopped?

An abandonment of six-inch surveying, it seemed, must accelerate the Irish Survey's rate of progress. De La Beche was painfully aware of the fact that back in 1845 he had agreed that a new geological map of Ireland might be completed within a period of no more than ten years. Now the close of that ten-year period loomed uncomfortably close, and maps remained to be published for twenty-seven of the Irish counties. Those twenty-seven of the Irish counties included all twelve of Ireland's largest counties.

It would appear that in February 1851 Jukes did actually receive from De La Beche a specific instruction to abandon all six-inch field-mapping, and to work henceforth upon what Jukes himself once described as 'those footy little county maps'. His confrontation with De La Beche formed the subject of a letter which Jukes wrote to Ramsay on 3 March 1851. Therein Jukes explained that upon his receipt of De La Beche's directive his initial response had been to consider resigning from the Irish local directorship. But more studied consideration had tempered his anger.

> I perceive that would be a foolish and also a cowardly way of acting. The interests of the survey here being committed to my charge, I am bound to stick by it and fight for it to the last. Sir H., therefore, gets a letter from me this morning, telling him the six-inch map was one of my greatest inducements to come here; that I was disgusted and disappointed when I found they were not published geologically, and that I am resolved not to rest till they are so published .... Taking a strictly 'service' view of the matter, I can show the absurdity of paying £1500 per annum out of the public purse for merely a slightly-amended edition of Griffiths' [*sic*] map. The real question is the amount of *detail* and *accuracy* of work.

In the event Jukes persuaded De La Beche to accept a compromise, but it was a compromise in which the Director yielded more ground than did his man in Ireland. For his part De La Beche accepted that the Irish Survey would persist with its six-inch field-mapping, but Jukes, on the other hand, had to concede that the publication of a nationwide coverage of six-inch geological sheets formed no part of Survey policy. The publication of six-inch sheets would be confined to just a very few areas where mining was of importance.

Thus far the score was about even, but the contest was swung in Jukes's favour by De La Beche's second concession. He agreed to the abandonment of the series of county geological maps based upon the Townland Index sheets. This was a concession which became an option for De La Beche only as a result of a development which was now taking place within the Ordnance Survey. Ever since Colby's arrival in Ireland during the 1820s (see p.8), the Ordnance Survey had been considering the compilation of a one-inch (1:63,360) coverage of the country. But it was 26 April 1851 before the Treasury finally authorised the Ordnance Survey to commence the construction of such a map by reduction from the six-inch (1:10,560) sheets. It was this new one-inch map which De La Beche now agreed should replace 'those footy little county maps' as the base-map for all the Irish Survey's future standard published sheets. The die had been cast. From the 1850s down to the 1880s it remained normal practice for the Survey to field-map upon the six-inch scale and then to publish its work upon the one-inch sheets.

De La Beche thus had the satisfaction of knowing that as soon as the new Irish one-inch topographical sheets began to come from the Ordnance Survey, his own staff would be laying comparable one-inch geological sheets before the public on both sides of the Irish Sea. Where the Irish six-inch field-mapping was concerned, De La Beche nevertheless continued to entertain doubts and reservations. And that, via a somewhat circuitous route, brings us back to Eccles's Hotel at Glengarriff upon that sunny morning of 24 August 1854.

In 1854 De La Beche resolved to extend the Geological Survey's activities into Scotland, and he had deputed Ramsay, the sole Scot upon his staff, to go north to break ground in Scotia. De La Beche expected Ramsay to use one-inch maps in the field in Scotland, as was normal practice in England and Wales, but the Ordnance Survey had just published some six-inch sheets of the country around Edinburgh, and, inspired by Jukes, Ramsay was determined to try his hand at a six-inch survey of the Edinburgh region. De La Beche disapproved, but Ramsay remained resolute. He informed his chief that as a preliminary to his Scottish enterprise he proposed to visit Ireland. He wanted to learn exactly how Jukes's men were using their six-inch sheets. As Ramsay explained to De La Beche:

> It would be a great mistake on my part to omit seeing what they do, and how they do it, in Ireland. It does not follow that the same rules should be applied in Scotland; but whether or no, I want to see how they keep, cut, use, and abuse their maps, what their portfolios are like, how they handle them in the field, and twenty other things that may save us much time and trouble in Scotland, and which only eyesight can instruct upon.

Ramsay arrived in Dublin on 22 August 1854, and he immediately went down to Bantry to see Jukes and his officers in action. That is how, two days later, Jukes and Ramsay came to be seated in a car on their way north to meet with De La Beche at Glengarriff. It was there, beside the waters of Bantry Bay, that De La Beche and Ramsay thrashed out the policy to be adopted by the Survey in Scotland; it was there that Ramsay secured his Director's permission to adopt Irish-style six-inch field-mapping in that portion of the United Kingdom which in those days was so often designated merely as N.B.

Thus the fate of the geological mapping of Scotland came to be decided at Glengarriff and most probably within the establishment belonging to Thomas Eccles. Perhaps the modern hotel should wear a plaque in commemoration of the event. It was certainly an event which we will do well to remember. Here was the Geological Survey's eminent Local Director for England and Wales come to a remote corner of Ireland in order to learn how a six-inch geological survey was to be conducted. The episode is a reminder that the Geological Survey of Ireland was no inexperienced offspring clutching to its parent's coat-tails. Rather was the Geological Survey of Ireland an innovative institution from which the British Survey had much to learn.

The difference between De La Beche and Jukes over six-inch field-mapping was really a difference over means and ends. For De La Beche all such field-mapping was merely a means towards an end, that end being the publication of one or more small-scale geological maps. For Jukes all such field-mapping wore an entirely different complexion. It was a highly desirable end in itself. It was something possessed of its own intrinsic value - something in need of accomplishment quite independently of any relationship which it might possess to the publication of small-scale geological sheets.

Jukes was a man of vision. The Geological Survey of Ireland was, of course, going to publish maps based upon field-observations made by its officers, but he considered that the Survey's prime function must be to serve as a national archive of geological information. In his eyes it was the Survey's task to collect information about the rocks of Ireland, to store that information, and to make that information available to all who might have need of it. In the fulfilment of this task he ascribed a pivotal role to the six-inch field-maps. To employ a concept drawn from a far later age, those maps were to be the Survey's microchip. The Survey was going to transfer all the information resulting from six-inch field-surveying to a constantly up-dated set of six-inch maps. That set was to be maintained in the office, and there it would offer an encapsulation of all the data available relating to the field-geology of Ireland.

During the course of a presidential address to the Geological Society of Dublin, delivered on 14 February 1855 in House 35 of Trinity College, Jukes explained exactly why he regarded six-inch field-mapping as essential for any well-run national geological survey. Preserving his own words as far as possible, the following are the salient and thoroughly cogent elements of his case.

1. 'A national geological survey should be conducted with the most minute accuracy possible to be attained', thus obviating the necessity for repeated re-surveying. Further, we must ensure that 'even in wide and barren districts composed exclusively of one particular kind of rock, such as granite or Old Red Sandstone, every square foot of ground be examined, and every exposure of rock carefully marked upon the map'.

2. The field-geologist can locate himself with precision upon a six-inch sheet, and the map is itself large enough to accommodate all those observations which in one-inch field-mapping have to be recorded in accompanying note-books.

3. When necessary, detailed geological cross-sections may with ease be drawn directly from the six-inch field-sheets.

4. The accuracy of any smaller-scale maps can easily be tested by reference to the six-inch field-sheets, and the explanation for any suspected errors is speedily discerned.

5. A national geological survey should be 'carried on with reference not so much to what may be thought our immediate requirements, as to the wants and requirements of the future'. Six-inch field-sheets can be filed away and kept in perpetuity as 'a great public document of reference'. They will, for example, be available to serve as the basis for the production of such smaller scale geological maps as may be needed, or as the foundation for reports of the mineral potential of properties prepared at the request of individual land-owners.

In the previous chapter (p.47) I observed that Jukes imparted to the Survey a character which it retained right down to 1924. That statement I now reaffirm, but with one proviso. Where the six-inch cartographic data-base is concerned Jukes's influence did not die in 1924. It lives on. The reference collection of annotated six-inch maps which he founded is still in daily use by Survey officers, and by those who come to the Survey seeking guidance over their Irish geological problems.

The discussions at Glengarriff on 24 August 1854 have scientific and cartographic significance, but they also wear a certain melancholy significance. They were a feature of the last of De La Beche's many visits to Ireland. Although still only in his fifties, De La Beche's health had begun to fail - at Glengarriff, Ramsay noted that his chief's mind was 'far, far gone' - and he died on 13 April 1855 following upon a stroke. Ramsay had for long entertained hopes of becoming De La Beche's successor, but it was not to be. The new Director was appointed on 5 May 1855, and he came from without the ranks of the Survey. It was a strange nomination. The new Director was the haughty gentleman-geologist, Sir Roderick Impey Murchison, the man famed for his establishment of the Silurian System within the stratigraphical column.

'The King of Siluria', as he liked to be titled, was no stranger to Ireland. As an ensign in the 36th Foot he had sailed to the Peninsula from Cork in 1808, and towards the close of the Napoleonic War he had been stationed at Armagh. Later, having laid aside the sword in favour of the hammer, he had attended the meetings of the British Association for the Advancement of Science in Dublin (1835), in Cork (1843), and in Belfast (1852), and during the summer of 1851 he had searched for a base to his Silurian System in the wild country southward of Killary Harbour.

In the summer of 1856 Murchison returned to Ireland, this time as the Survey's Director. He arrived in Dublin on 15 August, and spent a few days in the city before going down to Kilkenny to inspect ground being mapped by Willson. From there Murchison proceeded to Limerick, where he stayed at Cruise's Hotel, a noted establishment which Murchison considered really had 'nothing to boast of, save a very civil landlord'. Perhaps the Director was in an ugly mood; the weather had turned nasty and his efforts to purchase a set of waterproof clothing in Limerick had met with no success. From Limerick he went to Tarbert, and thence by steamer to Tralee, there as yet being no rail link into northern County Kerry. In Tralee, on 21 August, he met up with Jukes, Du Noyer, seventy-one-year-old Richard Griffith, and John

FIGURE 3.2. *Sir Roderick Impey Murchison (1792-1871), from* Vanity Fair *for 26 November 1870. He is there described as 'A Faithful Friend, an eminent Savant, and the best possible of Presidents'.*

William Salter, who two years earlier had succeeded Forbes as the Survey's Palaeontologist.

The next six days they all passed together in an examination of the geology of the Dingle Peninsula, which, as we will see shortly (p.63), was presenting the Survey with some perplexing problems. The sportsman in Murchison was doubtless pleased to note the presence of 'immense large trout, white and brown' in a tarn high up on the slopes of Mt Eagle at the western extremity of the peninsula, but the geologist in him must have been even more delighted by an admission now finally wrung from Griffith.

Ever since 1840 Griffith's quarter-inch map (see p.7) had represented the rocks throughout the western half of the Dingle Peninsula as all being of Silurian age. Repeatedly since his visit to the region following upon the Cork meeting of the British Association in 1843, Murchison had urged Griffith to temper his claims as to the extent of the Silurian strata both within the Dingle Peninsula and throughout southwestern Munster generally. Now, in August 1856, Murchison at last secured Griffith's concession that, setting aside the undoubted Silurian strata around Dunquin and Ferriters Cove, it was better to regard the remaining rocks of the western half of the peninsula as being of Old Red Sandstone age rather than as being Silurian. But Griffith's great map had already entered upon its final form, and Griffith's change of mind was never to receive cartographic expression.

Murchison left Dingle on 28 August, and in bad weather he travelled southwards to the Gap of Dunloe and thence to Muckross. There the foul weather continued on 29 and 30 August, but then all was transformed, and on his final two days in County Kerry he had the pleasure of seeing the Lakes of Killarney bathed in sunshine and at their glorious best. Indeed, he was moved to describe Muckross as 'an enchanting place', and it was perhaps with some reluctance that on 2 September he joined the train bound for Dublin. The next day he spent with Jukes inspecting ground in County Wicklow, and on 4 September he left for Holyhead in the paddle-steamer *Cambria* with 'wind southerly; swell heavy; lots of sick people'.

Murchison had not enjoyed his Irish visit. Despite his two glorious days at Muckross, his three weeks in Ireland seem to have left him only with memories of inadequate hotels, unappetising food, uninteresting geology, and day after day of drenching rain. It must also be noted that he shared with De La Beche a deep prejudice against all those manifestations of the Roman Catholic faith which are so widespread in Ireland. Following his return to England, Murchison wrote to Ramsay as follows.

> I really must declare that the geology of Ireland is the dullest ('tell it not in Gath') which I am acquainted with in Europe. If St Patrick excluded venomous animals he ought to have worked a miracle in giving to the holy isle some one good thing under ground. But no! everything has had a curse passed upon it. There are as good Cambrian rocks as need be, they are all like the Longmynd, and won't give good slates. Then there are as good Carboniferous Limestone and Millstone-grits as any in Scotia, but it is pitiable to see the miserable small packets of broken culm at intervals of scores of miles, which are dignified by the name of Coal-measures. Then as to mines it is *nil,* except what used to be called the curse of the miner (pyrites).

When Ramsay met Murchison immediately after his Irish tour, the Director exclaimed: 'catch me going to Ireland again!' He almost kept his word. He did return for the Dublin meeting of the British Association in 1857, but otherwise, although he remained Director and then (after March 1867) Director-General of the Survey until his death in 1871, he seems never again to have set foot upon Irish soil. Murchison's dereliction of his Irish responsibilities threw upon Jukes a heavy onus, and very understandably Jukes resented not receiving from his chief that support and assistance which should have been his due.

Between May 1851 and December 1856 the Irish Survey published nothing. For much of that period Jukes must have suffered from a deep sense of frustration. He was awaiting the appearance of the first of the new Ordnance Survey one-inch sheets. As soon as they arrived at number 51, the Survey would have to begin the laborious task of transferring information from the six-inch field-sheets to the new one-inch base-maps so as to bring into being a geological map of Ireland at the one-inch scale (1:63,360). As he waited it must have been galling for Jukes to see that Griffith's map still held the centre of the Irish geological stage. At the Great Dublin Industrial Exhibition, on 31 August 1853, Griffith personally demonstrated his cartographic masterpiece to the Queen and Prince Albert, and when a geological map of Ireland was required for the 1855 Exposition Universelle in Paris, it was again Griffith's map which was put upon display. According to De La Beche's original estimate, by 1855 the Survey should have virtually completed its mapping of Ireland's geology, but in reality the Survey had placed before the public little more than the five county maps which were now in process of being superseded.

While he impatiently awaited the arrival of the earliest of the one-inch sheets, Jukes, perfectionist that he was, began to be nagged by doubts relating to the Survey's early field-surveying. Was the work executed under James and Oldham really of sufficient quality to withstand public scrutiny when published upon the one-inch scale? Certainly much of the work dating from Oldham's day had been intended for publication only upon the small-scale Townland Index maps. Was it really now suitable for publication upon the more demanding one-inch scale? Jukes's answer to that question lies concealed within the statistics here plotted as Figure 3.3.

During Jukes's first year as Local Director - 1851 - the Survey mapped the impressive total of 3,017 square kilometres of fresh territory, and in 1852 a further 2,573 square kilometres were mapped. But in 1853 and 1854 the totals for new territory mapped fell dramatically. To some extent this decline was a result of the loss of experienced staff, of inclement weather, of the mountainous character of the terrain now being encountered in West Cork and Kerry, and of the difficulty of securing field accommodation near to the ground under examination. But there was another reason. Jukes had finally decided that some of the Survey's early mapping in Leinster was indeed insufficiently precise to withstand publication on the one-inch scale. He therefore determined to have large areas of southeastern Ireland re-examined.

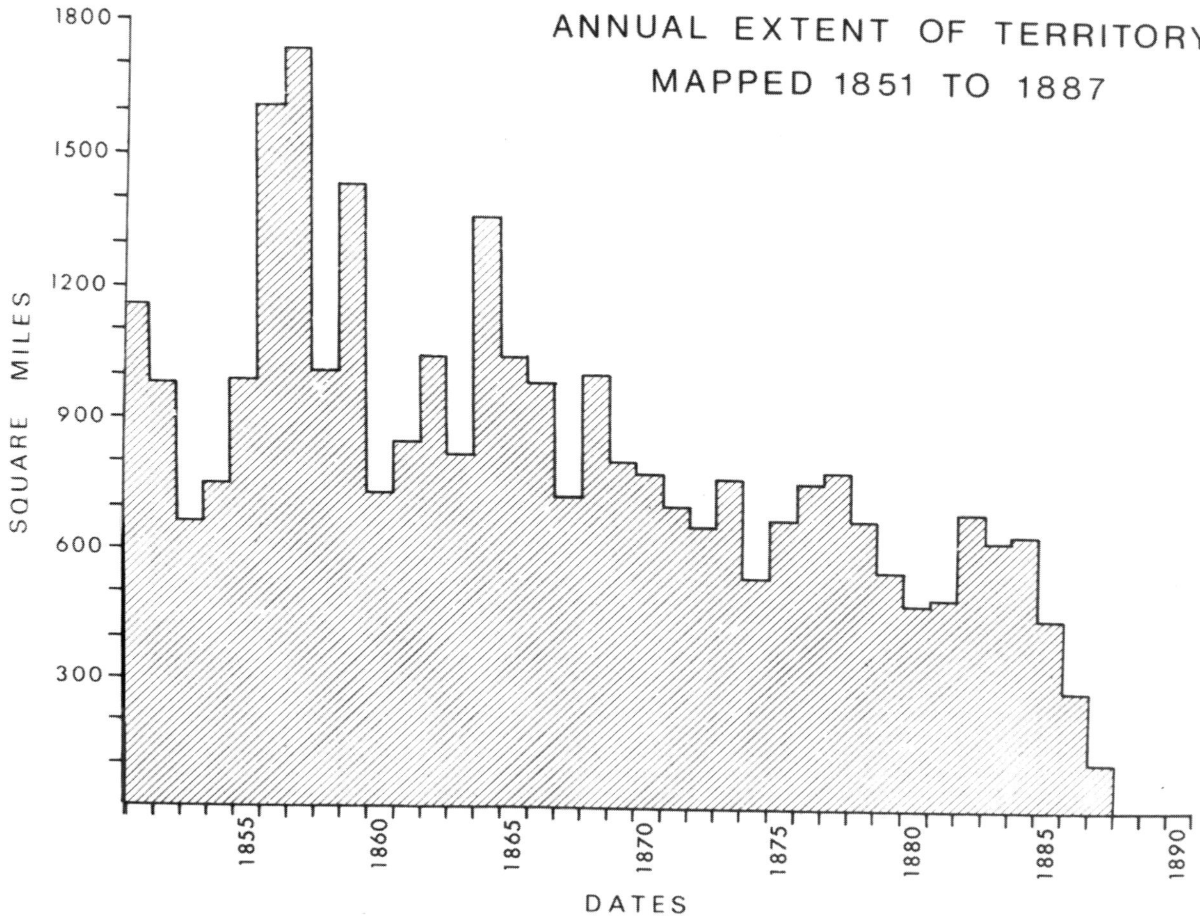

FIGURE 3.3. *The area of ground mapped by the Irish Survey each year from 1851 down to the completion of the primary survey of Ireland in 1887. Based upon the manuscript annual reports of the Local Director, or Director, of the Irish Survey.*

Jukes and Wyley spent the greater part of the summers of 1853 and 1854 re-mapping old ground in counties Wexford and Wicklow, and occasionally the experience brought back to life the joyous Jukes of old. Here, for instance he writes to Ramsay from Rathdrum, County Wicklow, on 15 June 1853. The Sullivan mentioned is William Kirby Sullivan, the chemist to the Museum of Irish Industry. He was responsible for all the Survey's chemical analyses.

> I am going to get Sullivan down here next week, and we mean to work the very entrails out of all the traps hereabouts, and not leave 'em a single atom of mystery to pride themselves on any longer. Worst of it is, when one has made out the chemistry and mineralogy, one can't see the geology in this confounded rolly-polly wood covered country.

This meticulousness on the part of Jukes left the ailing De La Beche feeling exasperated. The southeast of Ireland was territory that James was supposed to have finished in 1846, and that Oldham had revised during his own local directorship, but now here was Jukes insisting upon further revision in the 1850s. De La Beche died just a few days after the Irish Survey's tenth anniversary. If success was to be measured in terms of maps published, then the Irish Branch had given him little cause for decennial celebration.

On Saturday 11 October 1851 the Great Exhibition at the Crystal Palace finally closed its doors to the public. As a legacy, the exhibition left behind a strong British awareness of the national importance of what were termed 'the fine arts and practical science'. As a direct result of this new consciousness there was established, in March 1853, the Department of Science and Art, to which there was assigned the task of developing a nationwide educational programme designed to enlist science and the arts in the cause of industrial improvement and expansion. Among the bodies taken under the wing of the new Department were both the Geological Survey of the United Kingdom and the Museum of Irish Industry.

During the following year - 1854 - its new masters bestowed upon the Museum an expanded educational role through the establishment of a fresh institution styled the Government School of Science Applied to Mining and the Arts attached to the Museum of Irish Industry. Jukes was appointed as the School's first professor of geology (he, of course, remained the Survey's Local Director) and he soon proved himself to be a very effective and popular lecturer. Irish audiences now began to benefit from those lessons which Jukes had learned twenty years earlier as an itinerant lecturer upon the English circuit. Five of those who joined his Irish lectures went on to become officers of the Irish Survey (see Chapter Eleven).

In the aftermath of the Great Exhibition the climate in official circles was entirely favourable to the Geological Survey. It seemed to offer an obvious area in which science might be harnessed to the interests of industry, and the Treasury therefore sanctioned the augmentation of the Survey's staff upon both sides of the Irish Sea. When Jukes took over the Survey in December 1850, its staff consisted of the Local Director himself, one Geologist (Du Noyer), two Assistant Geologists (Willson and Wyley), one General Assistant (J.G. Medlicott), and one Fossil Collector (Flanagan). Of these, Medlicott departed in September 1851 to join Oldham in Calcutta, Wyley resigned in January 1855 to become Government Geologist in Cape Colony, and Willson left in November 1856 to join his four former colleagues who were now in India, Willson explaining in his letter of resignation that it was impossible for him to maintain a family upon his Irish salary in a land where, he claimed, the cost of living had more than doubled in a mere five years.

As replacements for these departing officers, and as augmentations to his staff, Jukes appointed a total of ten men (six Assistant Geologists, two General Assistants, and two Fossil Collectors) between October 1851 and July 1856. He must have been well content with the calibre of the men now being attracted to the Survey. Both the General Assistants - John Studdert Kennedy and Henry Benedict Medlicott - and four of the Assistant Geologists - Frederick James Foot, George Henry Kinahan, Samuel Medlicott, and Joseph O'Kelly - had been students in Trinity College Dublin, and of these six, five held the College's Diploma in Engineering, possession of which indicated attendance at classes in geology.

The most notable of Jukes's appointments was that of Kinahan. He joined the Survey at Bantry just three days before the Glengarriff meeting between De La Beche, Jukes, and Ramsay, and he received his training in that district under Du Noyer and Wyley. Kinahan was the son of a Dublin barrister, and the holder of the Trinity College Diploma in Engineering. He had turned to geology after a year spent as a civil engineer, and he was eventually to earn Jukes's approval as 'a hardworking and indefatigable explorer of wild & difficult districts'. But he also earned another and less enviable a reputation. He was destined to become the most cantankerous and turbulent Survey officer of all time.

The most strange of Jukes's appointments was that of John Kelly. Hailing from Borrisokane in County Tipperary, Kelly, in 1814, had become assistant to Richard Griffith at the Dublin Society (see p.6). For almost forty years he remained in Griffith's employ, but in 1853 ill-health forced his retirement, and he found himself facing old age without any pension entitlement. Jukes evidently took pity on him, and in July 1856 he appointed Kelly as an Assistant Geologist charged expressly with the duty of taking responsibility for the Survey's office. For the remainder of his working life Kelly thus performed in number 51 much the same duties as he had long performed in Griffith's Valuation Office.

By the time of De La Beche's death in 1855, Jukes's men were advancing northwards along a front extending from Berehaven, through Kenmare and Millstreet, to Mallow. The Survey now possessed completed six-inch field-sheets for the greater part of Leinster and Munster. But the Ordnance Survey was proceeding only slowly with the preparation of the one-inch map, and Jukes therefore still lacked any means of laying his officers' work before the public at the scale agreed upon earlier in the decade. It is now time to see how this situation was finally remedied. It is now time to observe the birth of the one-inch geological map of Ireland.

Although the production of a one-inch coverage of Ireland had been authorised in April 1851, it was two and half years before the Ordnance Survey sent the first of the new sheets over to number 51 to have the geological lines added. Originally the Ordnance Survey intended to cover Ireland in fifty-nine one-inch sheets, each sheet having a size of 90 x 60 centimetres, these being the same dimensions as those of the Ordnance Survey's six-inch sheets. This was far too large a size for convenient use in the field (the Geological Survey, of course, normally cut its six-inch sheets into quarters for use in both the field and the office), and in consequence the Ordnance Survey soon changed its plans by deciding to issue the new one-inch map in sheets a quarter the size of those at first intended. Until October 1858, however, the smaller sheets were regarded as quarter sheets of the full sheets envisaged earlier, being numbered, for example, 40 S.E. or 47 N.W.

Jukes believed, probably wrongly, that he himself had been instrumental in bringing about this change in the Ordnance Survey's policy. He once recounted that, late in August 1852, De La Beche had passed through Dublin on his way to the Belfast meeting of the British Association, and that while in Dublin De La Beche had enquired of his Local Director as to the size he thought the new one-inch sheets should be. Jukes, familiar as he was with the quartered six-inch sheets used by the Survey, responded that their size was the largest that could handled with comfort in the field. He therefore recommended this to his chief as the most appropriate format for the new sheets.

It was in November 1853 that the earliest of the new one-inch sheets reached Jukes. They were the four quarter sheets comprising Sheet 36 and covering a large portion of County Wicklow. After plotting the geological boundaries upon the sheets, Jukes had geological colours added, and in this form Sheet 36 was exhibited to the Geological Society of Dublin on 14 December 1853. Jukes despatched the sheet back to the Ordnance Survey in February 1854, and in the following August it returned to his hands, now with all the geological details engraved. This proof map, with colours added, he exhibited to Section C (Geology) of the British Association meeting at Liverpool that September, and publication should have followed soon thereafter. Instead there ensued almost three years of delay.

In his presidential address to the Geological Society of Dublin on 14 February 1855, Jukes blamed the delay first upon a shortage of engravers in the Ordnance Survey, and second upon the military upheaval occasioned by the outbreak of the Crimean War in March 1854. That the delay became prolonged until late in 1856 was nonetheless chiefly the result of a policy change within the Survey itself.

Originally it had been intended to represent no drift deposits upon the one-inch maps, a decision which was doubtless influenced by the earlier want of success in trying to depict both the solid and the drift geology upon one and the same map in the Townland Index county series. It should also be noted that in England and Wales it had long been De La Beche's policy to disregard most of the drift mantle and to publish sheets that were essentially representations of the solid geology alone. Perhaps he had never thought very deeply about the problem of depicting the drifts because he had begun his own mapping in southwestern England well beyond the limits of Pleistocene glaciation. But now the issue of drift mapping was raised urgently in the Irish context.

On the morning of 2 February 1856 a visitor arrived at number 51 to see Jukes. The visitor's name was John Doyle. He was the manager of the map department in the shop of Messrs Hodges and Smith, standing at 104 Grafton Street, just around the corner from The Green. Doyle had come to inspect some of the new one-inch sheets, and upon seeing them he immediately expressed disquiet at the absence from the sheets of any comprehensive representation of the drift overburden. That afternoon he wrote to Jukes formally upon the subject. He observed that the absence of the drifts was bound to affect the sales of the sheets adversely because the purchasers of Irish estates were almost invariably interested in the character of the drift mantle present upon their domains. 'In fact', Doyle continued, *'that* is the chief if not the only geological feature of interest to most buyers of the maps'. Jukes professed to be impressed by this commercial pleading, and he immediately forwarded Doyle's letter to Murchison together with a covering letter of his own indicating his concurrence with Doyle's observations. Jukes further suggested that the drift should be represented by some system of stippling similar to that which had been employed upon the Townland Index sheets.

This little episode involving Doyle has about it a slightly unnatural air. Was it, perhaps, a little ploy engineered by Jukes? Was Jukes eager to represent drifts upon the new Irish sheets, but was he encountering Murchison's opposition? Was Doyle therefore enlisted to add commercial reinforcement to Jukes's argument based upon scientific logic? If stratagem it was, it certainly succeeded. Murchison replied to Jukes on 6 February 1856 agreeing that the drifts should be represented upon the sheets, but, in characteristic fashion, leaving to Jukes the decision as to exactly how the task was to be accomplished.

While all this was happening, there was continuing the production of the 'driftless' one-inch sheets. During February 1856 Jukes received from the Ordnance Survey the sets of sheets comprising sheets 36, 41, 47, and 53, covering the whole of southeastern Ireland, the sheets all carrying their engraved geological lines and merely awaiting the addition of their geological colours. The decision to portray the drifts now meant that all these sheets had to be returned to the Ordnance Survey for modification.

The chief drift deposits needing to be added were, of course, the extensive spreads of gravels and sands which obscure the solid geology over so much of Ireland. These spreads (they are now known to be of glacial origin) Jukes had finally decided to depict by means of a rash of stipple, and in returning the sets of sheets 36, 41, 47, and 53 to the Ordnance Survey, he asked for there to be prepared special stipple plates so that the symbol could be added to the sheets already printed. This makeshift method proved to be a failure. Uneven shrinkage of the paper made it impossible to secure a satisfactory registration of the new stipple plate upon the previously printed sheets. It was therefore decided to scrap all the sheets already printed (a few of them seem to have got as far as having their geological colours added) and to print fresh copies of the sheets using the original copper plates, but with the drift limits and the stippling now engraved thereupon.

On 24 November 1856 fifty copies of each of the new version of sheets 36 and 41 were ready for colouring, and for this they were despatched to London. It was there that all the Geological Survey's maps were then coloured by Charles Bone and his staff, a system of centralised colouring having been introduced to ensure that all of the Survey's maps - both British and Irish - carried the same uniform range of tints. By the end of December 1856 the first of these sheets were back in Dublin and in the hands of Messrs Hodges and Smith ready for sale, and by 8 April 1857 a proud Jukes was in a position to present sets of twenty-one quarter sheets to both the Royal Irish Academy and the Geological Society of Dublin. Those copies of the sheets destined for sale were priced at from one shilling to two shillings and six pence depending upon the extent of the territory represented.

Students of the one-inch map should note that in the bottom left-hand corner of the four quarter sheets comprising Sheet 36 is the erroneous statement that the sheets were all published in June 1855, while in the similar corner of the four quarter sheets of Sheet 41 is the equally erroneous statement that the sheets were published in February 1856. These were evidently the dates upon which it had been hoped to publish the sheets before the various delays intervened. But the false dates are a trivial blemish. What really matters is that almost twelve years after its inception, the Survey had now begun to publish the series of geological maps which for one hundred years were to constitute the basic national coverage of geological sheets available for sale to the public (see Plate II).

The base-map for all these early one-inch geological sheets is the Ordnance Survey's one-inch 'outline edition' issued between 1856 and 1862. It is an edition upon which hills are represented largely just by a scattering of trigonometrical points. Between 1855 and 1895 the Ordnance Survey did compile a 'hill edition' of the one-inch sheets, whereupon topography was graphically represented by the use of hachures. Jukes would doubtless have been happier with these hachured sheets as his base-map, despite the problems that might have arisen in mountainous areas through geological detail becoming obscured by heavy hachuring. Certainly in 1873 Jukes's successor decided to employ the hill edition as the base-map for all the Survey's subsequent one-inch sheets, but in the 1850s such an option was not available to Jukes. He had to publish geological sheets from Leinster, whereas, very inconveniently from his point of view, the Ordnance Survey had decided to make topographical sheets from Ulster the subject for its earliest essays in one-inch hachuring (see Plate III).

On 16 April 1858 Jukes wrote to the Ordnance Survey observing that their regard of the published one-inch sheets as quarter sheets was inconvenient. He therefore suggested that henceforth the quarter sheets should each be accorded full sheet status and be numbered consecutively. The implementation of this proposal in the October of that year meant that eventually Ireland was covered not by fifty-nine large-sized one-inch sheets, but rather by 205 small-sized sheets extending from Sheet 1 (Malin Head, County Donegal), to Sheet 205 (Toe Head, County Cork). Following upon this renumbering, the eight quarter sheets comprising the original sheets 36 and 41 - the Survey's first published one-inch sheets - became sheets 120, 121, 129, 130, 138, 139, 148, and 149.

The story of the Survey between 1856 and 1890 is essentially the story of the one-inch map. The final pre-publication editing of the one-inch sheets was the responsibility of Jukes and then of his successor, but as from 1855 the head of the Irish Survey was burdened with another and closely related task. It was on 1 December 1855 that Murchison wrote to all the Survey's staff explaining that henceforth it was his wish that every British and Irish one-inch geological sheet should be accompanied by an explanatory memoir. For the benefit of his staff Murchison outlined their new responsibilities as follows.

> You will be pleased to note in the first instance, the physical features of the tract you have surveyed which best exhibit the relations of the rocks. You will then record the names and positions of the localities, whether natural escarpments, river banks, quarries, shafts or adits, which have afforded the clearest evidences; and you will also give, as far as possible, the names of the organic remains and minerals, and point out the lithological structure of the strata, together with their dip and directions.

Each memoir was to be written by the geologist who had surveyed the ground in question, his name, as Murchison expressed it, 'being thus publicly associated with our great national undertaking'.

The first of the Irish memoirs was published on 28 July 1858. It was written by Jukes, Du Noyer, and Wynne, and it describes that area of southern County Tipperary and northwestern County Waterford which is depicted upon one-inch Sheet 45 S.E., a sheet which was shortly to be restyled Sheet 166. This memoir, together with its four companions published during 1858, were all entitled *Data and Descriptions,* while the equivalent works published in 1859 and later were simply entitled *Explanations,* but it is as 'the memoirs' that these publications have become familiar to many generations of Irish geologists. Most of the memoirs contain around 40 pages, and many of those published during Jukes's regime are embellished with attractive illustrations derived from artistic works by Du Noyer and Wynne. Today, the dog-eared condition of the russet paper covers of so many of the memoirs located within institutional collections, bears ample testimony to the heavy usage which those memoirs have received over the decades.

In January 1859 Jukes estimated that a geologist could map a one-inch sheet, and then write its accompanying memoir, all within a period of twelve months, and by 29 June 1861 he was able to report as published the very creditable total of twenty-six memoirs. There was some understandable delay in compiling memoirs for certain of the one-inch sheets of southeastern Ireland because that mapping had largely been carried out by Oldham, Willson, and Wyley, none of whom were still with the Survey by the time Murchison's memoir directive arrived at number 51. But eventually every single sheet in the Irish one-inch series received its accompanying memoir or part-memoir. It was a remarkable achievement.

The memoir scheme was never popular with the Survey staff. Most of the officers saw themselves not as desk-bound, pen-pushing authors of academic monographs, but as rock-hammering field-surveyors ever anxious to get to grips with a fresh piece of ground. Jukes and his successor certainly had difficulty in extracting memoir contributions from some of the more recalcitrant of the staff, but their efforts were well worth while, if for no other reason than that the necessity of writing the memoirs made the geologists think more deeply about the phenomena which they were investigating and recording upon their maps. In short, the unwelcome literary task of preparing memoirs probably had the effect of making the Survey men more reflective field-geologists. The classic illustration of this point is provided by Jukes himself, and it is a theme which here provides the substance of Chapter Nine.

The directive requiring them to prepare memoirs may have served to stimulate the minds of the geologists, but the general public took little interest in the new publications. The normal print-order for the early memoirs was 250 copies, but by 29 June 1861 there had been sold in Ireland not more than twenty-three copies of any one of the twenty-six Irish memoirs published by that date. Substantial sales had been expected for the two memoirs covering the Castlecomer Coalfield (sheets 128 and 137), and in these cases the print-order had therefore been doubled to five hundred copies, but only sixteen copies of Sheet 128 had been sold by 29 June 1861, and only twenty-three copies of Sheet 137. In the cases of two memoirs (sheets 131 & 132 and 136) only one copy of each had been sold. Even today, well over a century later, the Survey still possess within its stores substantial numbers of unsold copies of many of the memoirs. Only one of the memoirs has achieved the status of being a bibliographical rarity, that being the memoir to sheets 7 & 8, dealing with the Giant's Causeway and published in 1888.

The Survey's 1860 field-programme was planned upon a modest scale; Jukes, with Murchison's permission, decided to use the year partly for the consolidation of the memoir publication programme, and partly for the preparation of the earliest of a new series of longitudinal sections. The first four of these sections (they were styled 'New Series' to distinguish them from the earlier sections published by Oldham in 1848) were published in April 1860 at the six-inch scale (1:10,560). They are engraved, but hand-coloured, and eventually there were thirty-seven sheets of such sections in the series, the last of them (Sheet 35) appearing in December 1894. The lines followed by the sections were marked upon the published one-inch sheets, and the sections were intended to add a vivid third dimension to the two dimensional cartographic representation of the geology. Of the one-inch sheets, 104 were provided with at least one longitudinal section, and among the sheets of sections, particular interest attaches to Sheet 6, published in October 1860. That sheet depicts the Slievenamuck Fault with a throw of 1,200 metres, and in February 1861 Professor Samuel Haughton, of Trinity College Dublin, hailed this dislocation within the Munster rocks as 'the grandest proved fault in the world'.

During the 1860s the Survey mapped an average of 2,418 square kilometres of fresh territory every year, the annual average for an individual officer being 208 square kilometres of new ground. Throughout the 1860s Jukes's men continued to advance northwards on a broad front extending across the whole of Ireland, from the shores of the Irish Sea to those of the Atlantic. One-inch sheets had already been published for the country around the cities of Cork, Dublin, and Limerick, and Jukes now decided that Ireland's fast-growing second city could no longer be kept waiting. In 1867 he therefore resolved to develop a new mapping enclave in eastern Ulster and well to the north of his main mapping front. Du Noyer was given responsibility for this new work, and it was while he was thus engaged that disaster overtook him and his family. They all passed the Christmas of 1868 at his field-station in Antrim town, but immediately after the festival, scarlet fever arrived in their midst. His eldest daughter died of the fever on 2 January 1869,

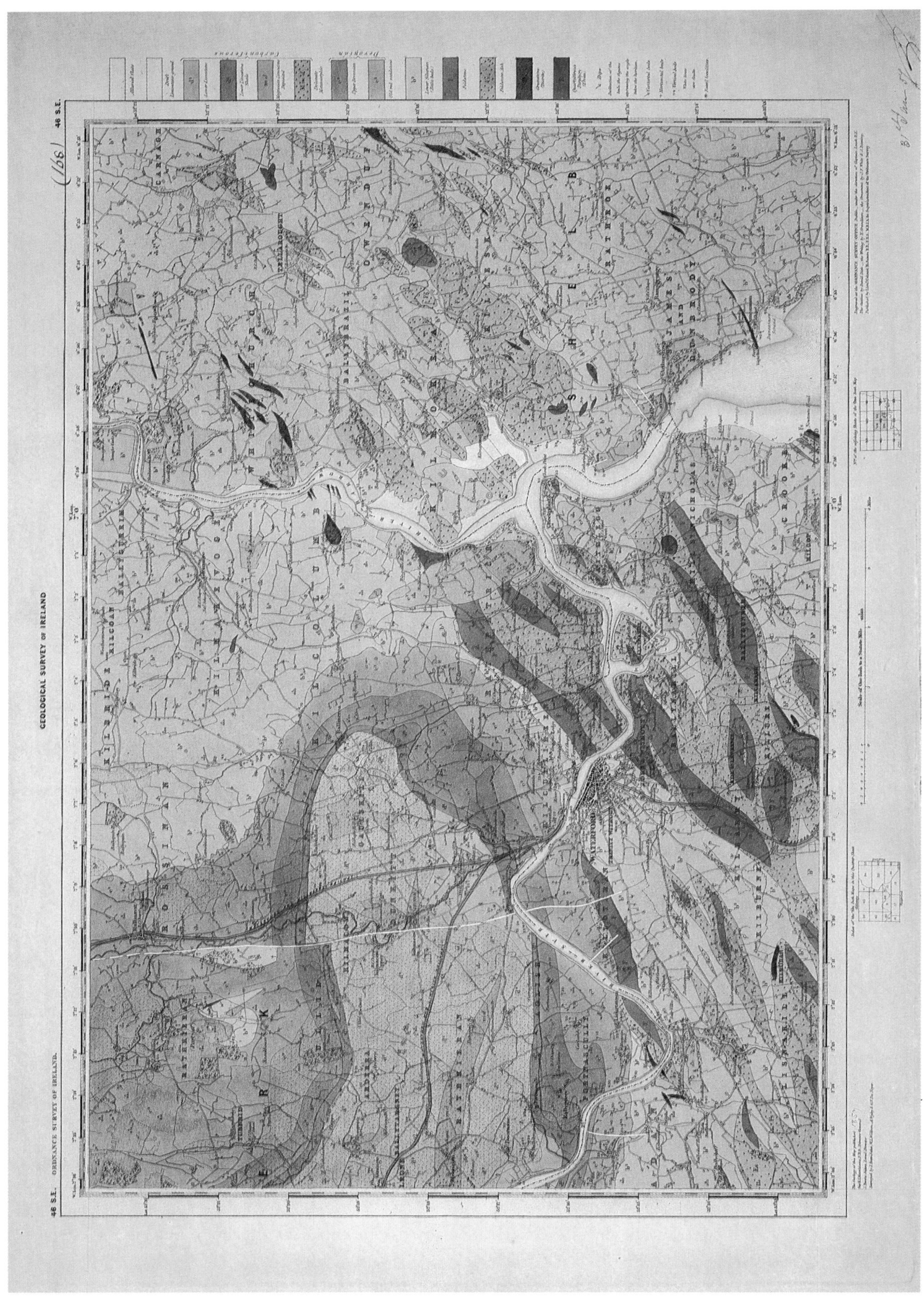
GEOLOGICAL SURVEY OF IRELAND
ORDNANCE SURVEY OF IRELAND
46 S.E.
(168)
WATERFORD

and Du Noyer himself became its victim just a few hours later, following upon an illness of four days' duration. He lies buried in the midst of that very province where thirty years earlier he had learned his geological skills from Portlock and Oldham.

By July 1869 the Survey had published 117 of the 205 one-inch sheets needed to cover the whole of Ireland. Enormous credit is due to Jukes for maintaining such a steady output of high quality work in the form of maps, memoirs, and sections. It is nonetheless interesting to note that he was no longer thinking of the Survey's task as being one of finite duration. When he appeared before a Select Committee on 31 May 1864, he was invited to comment upon the time necessary for the Survey to complete its mapping of Ireland's rocks. Such an estimate he declined to offer

> ... because nobody knows the kind of rocks that may be met with; the rocks in the north-western part of Ireland are of a kind that has never been thoroughly examined anywhere in the world, and nobody knows how long they will take us. Moreover as we go on with the Geological Survey we introduce improvements in the nature of our operations; I must say also that it appears to me that the Geological Survey is indefinitely extensible. The scientific examination of the earth is just as inexhaustible as that of the heavens....

When he published the lecture he had delivered in December 1866 at the Museum of Irish Industry, Jukes returned more forcefully to this theme of the Survey as an enterprise in pure rather than in applied science. He now emphasised that while the Survey possessed immense utilitarian value - its cost, he suggested, would be repaid in economic benefit many times over - it should be recognised that its principal achievement was upon a more lofty and intellectual plane through a deepening of the human understanding of the history and structure of our globe.

> Men of science have of late years pandered too much to the utilitarian quackery of the age, and it is time that some one should stand up to protest against it. Government and the House of Commons should be told that science must be supported and encouraged for her own purely abstract purposes, independently of all utilitarian applications.

This argument he developed by drawing an analogy between the Geological Survey and the government-financed Royal Observatory at Greenwich. Was the Royal Observatory not allowed to probe the secrets of the universe to depths far beyond those necessary for the solution of practical problems in navigation? Then why should the same freedom not be granted to the Geological Survey? Why did the Survey not receive official encouragement to probe the secrets of earth-history to depths far beyond those necessary to permit the answering of mundane enquiries from the coal-miner or the civil engineer. Jukes's argument was cogent enough, but it remains an argument to which governments within these islands have usually turned the deaf ear.

Any field-geologist setting about the compilation of a geological map will encounter problems belonging to one or other of five generic groups.

First, there are the methodological problems. How should the ground be worked? Should cross-country traverses be made, should geological boundaries be walked out, or should the geologist seek to map every single exposure?

Second, there are the environmental problems which hinder the task of the observer. The extent of the drift cover, the presence of forest, the degree of weathering of an exposure, the spread of lichen over an outcrop, the angle of the sun, the dampness of the rock's surface, even the wetness or dryness of the geological observer - all these factors will affect what the geologist sees in the field.

Third, there are the problems which arise from the fact that geologists carry certain intellectual preconceptions with them during the course of their mapping. Throughout the middle years of the nineteenth century, for instance, most British geologists believed that their islands had recently experienced a deep submergence. Such a drowning was then an article of the geological faith. In his *Geological Observer* of 1851, De La Beche offered a map of the British Isles as they must have appeared when inundated by an ocean standing a thousand feet higher than that of today, and in his *Siluria* of

PLATE II . *One of the earliest of the one-inch sheets : Sheet 46 S.E., published in 1857, and later restyled Sheet 168 (Waterford). The sheet is here reproduced at a diminished scale, the inner frame of the original sheet measuring 46 x 31 centimetres. The ground covered by the sheet was mapped by Jukes, Du Noyer, Willson, and Wyley.*

Like all the sheets of the one-inch map issued before 1873, this sheet is based upon the Ordnance Survey's outline edition of the one-inch map whereupon relief is somewhat inadequately represented by little more than a scattering of bench-marks and trigonometrical points.

The manuscript annotation in the bottom right-hand margin indicates that the newly printed copy of the sheet was examined in the Ordnance Survey on 31 January 1857, and the monogram is that of James Duncan who was the Principal Engraver in the Irish Ordnance Survey from 1827 until 1866. Duncan having given his approval, the sheet would then have been sent to Britain to receive its geological colours. Oddly, somebody has omitted to have the year of publication engraved upon the copper plate from which the sheet was printed.

Later editions of this sheet appeared in 1863 and 1901, and there may well be many another minor variant of the sheet. (Reproduced from a copy of the sheet in the archives of the Survey.)

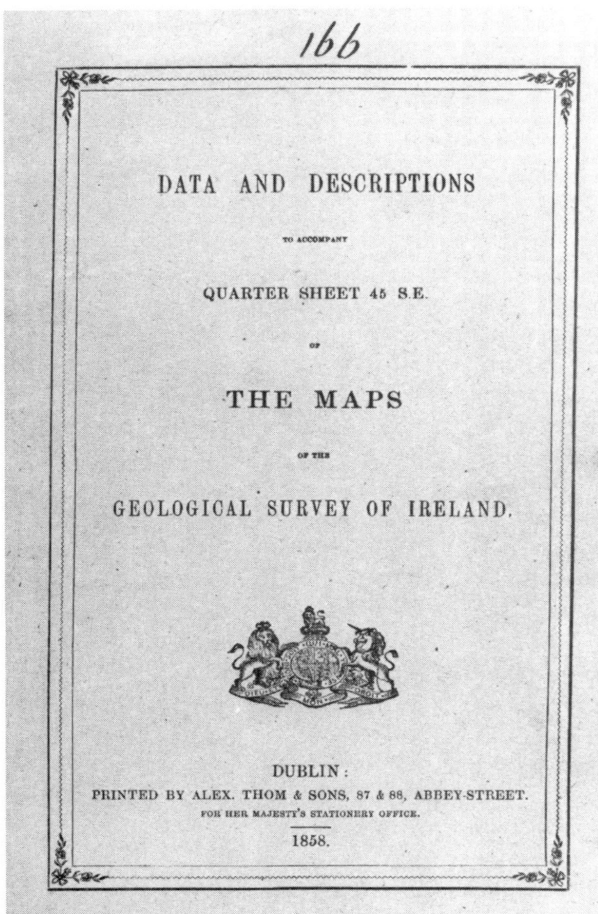
166

DATA AND DESCRIPTIONS

TO ACCOMPANY

QUARTER SHEET 45 S.E.

OF

THE MAPS

OF THE

GEOLOGICAL SURVEY OF IRELAND.

DUBLIN:

PRINTED BY ALEX. THOM & SONS, 87 & 88, ABBEY-STREET.

FOR HER MAJESTY'S STATIONERY OFFICE.

1858.

FIGURE 3.4. *The cover of the first of the one-inch sheet memoirs: the memoir to Sheet 45 S.E. published on 28 July 1858. This sheet was shortly redesignated Sheet 166, hence the manuscript addition at the top of the cover. The size of the memoir is 15.2 x 24.2 centimetres, and it contains 28 pages, including three with illustrations derived from sketches by Du Noyer.*

1854, Murchison wrote of vast areas of northern Europe as having recently lain beneath an Arctic sea. We now know that all this was false dogma, but, with authorities such as these behind them, it is small wonder that Du Noyer thought himself able to discern the effects of deep submergence within the Munster landscapes, or that Kinahan considered the Irish Midlands to be littered with sandbanks left stranded following the inundation.

Fourth, there are the problems arising from the need to interpret the observed phenomena. How many phases of deformation are represented in the strata? In what sort of environment were the rocks deposited? Is the entire sequence perhaps inverted as a result of earthmovements?

Finally, there are problems of classification. Is this rock best described as a rhyolite or as a trachyte? Is this bed of limestone exposed on the floor of a dry valley the same as that present upon a hill-top five kilometres distant? Is this sill Ordovician or Eocene in age?

The Survey's officers encountered all these five groups of problems in varying degree. The methodological problems they first faced in the vicinity of Hook Head as they broke ground during the summer of 1845. Their resolution of the methodological problems will be engaging our attention shortly (see p.77). The environmental problems were, and are, ever present. Some of them will be mentioned in my final chapter (see p.296). To the problem of the preconceptions which geologists carry with them into the field there is no real solution. Scientists can never hope to divorce themselves from the age to which they belong. It is a difficulty which will be illustrated further in Chapter Eight. The problem of interpretation is the very essence of geological field-investigation. Every coastal cliff, every river-bed, every hillside exposure, and every gravel pit - they all pose a multitude of challenges to the geologist's ability to understand the natural world. Each of the Survey's published one-inch geological sheets must represent an infinity of interpretative judgements made by officers in the field.

It was nevertheless the final category of problems - the problems of classification - which most obviously taxed the Survey's staff. The one-inch sheets which they were compiling are essentially stratigraphical documents designed to reveal the age and type of rocks present at any particular locality. It was classificatory problems connected with the age and the type of rocks which constantly demanded answer. Sometimes the problem was so simple that it scarcely needed to be expressed: 'Is this rock granite or is it schist?' On other occasions the issue might be rather more complex: 'Are these slates of Wenlock or Llandovery age?' In yet other cases the classificatory problem could only be answered in a very arbitrary fashion: 'Where in this drift - encumbered landscape do I draw a boundary between the sandstone exposed to the north and the limestone exposed to the south?'

Local classificatory problems such as these were legion, but in Jukes's day three classificatory problems of far wider implication engaged the attention of the Survey. These three problems were first, the subdivision of the Irish limestones, second, the stratigraphy of the Dingle Peninsula, and third, the age of the slates in southern County Cork. We must now glance at each of these problems in turn.

In 1837 Griffith had proposed a tripartite division of the Irish limestones into a Lower Limestone, a Calp Limestone, and an Upper Limestone, and these three categories he gradually introduced into his quarter-inch geological map. The young Survey adopted Griffith's scheme, and in the Survey's early notation the Lower, the Calp, and the Upper limestones became respectively the d^2, d^3, and d^4 limestones. But here we have a good

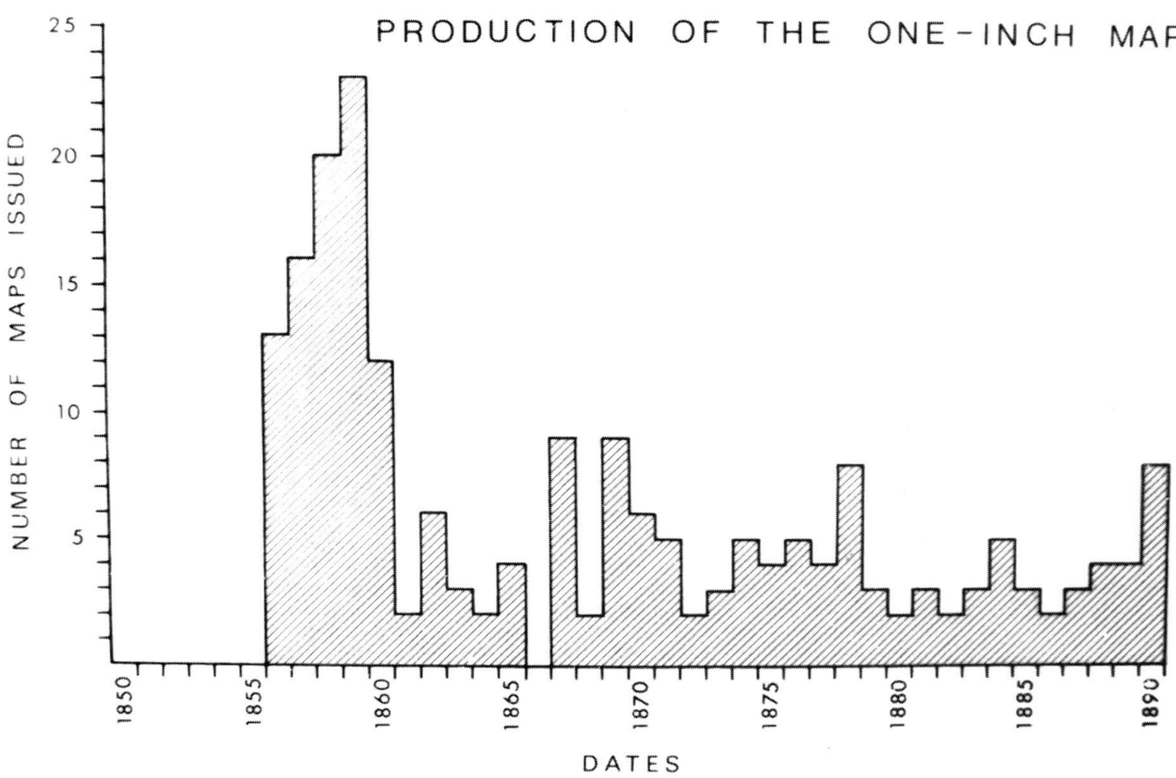

FIGURE 3.5. *The output of the 205 component sheets of the one-inch geological map of Ireland. Based upon the manuscript annual reports of the Local Director, or Director, of the Irish Survey. The dates featured upon the one-inch sheets themselves are not always reliable.*

example of the Survey taking the field equipped with a preconception of dubious validity. Certainly Jukes's officers soon found themselves in trouble because in the field it proved difficult to categorise the limestones according to Griffith's model. On many of the one-inch sheets there appears the comment that it had not proved possible to delimit one or other of the three limestones within the area in question, and on other sheets - on Sheet 164 (Charleville), for instance - the colour representing the d^2 limestone is simply allowed to merge into the colour representing the d^4 limestone.

Jukes had early recognised that there was neither lithological nor palaeontological justification for a nationwide tripartite division of the limestones, and in September 1867 he announced that the Survey would henceforth abandon its attempt at subdivision of the limestones. The three categories of limestone nevertheless continued to feature upon many of the Survey's later one-inch sheets, and even today (1995) the three categories are still depicted in all their deceptive verisimilitude upon the Survey's popular 1:750,000 map of Ireland.

Jukes's second major classificatory problem lay in the remote Dingle Peninsula of County Kerry in the area covered by one-inch sheets 160, 161, 171, and 172. It was during the 1850s that the Survey found itself at grips with the rocks of Dingle. De La Beche, Forbes, and Jukes were there in 1852, and Griffith, Jukes, Murchison, and Salter made their visit to the peninsula in 1856, but most of the mapping was executed by Du Noyer and by the still somewhat inexperienced Arthur Beavor Wynne, who replaced Wyley in April 1855. The fruit of their labours was published upon the four one-inch sheets during 1859.

Within the Dingle Peninsula the local sequence of the rocks, proceeding from the oldest to the youngest, is broadly as follows:

1. At the far northwestern end of the peninsula, in the country around Dunquin, there are steeply dipping mudstones, siltstones, and sandstones, all containing fossils indicating for the rocks an upper Silurian age.
2. Immediately to the east, and conformable upon the Silurian strata, is a thick sequence of mudstones, siltstones, sandstones, and conglomerates, all looking very much like the Old Red Sandstone found elsewhere in southern Ireland. Despite much searching, however, these rocks refused to yield any fossils that could be used to confirm their age.
3. Still farther to the east, and resting with marked unconformity upon the indeterminate beds lying to the west, are the grits, sandstones, and slates of the undoubted Old Red Sandstone.

Nowhere in the south of Ireland has a major unconformity been discovered within the true Old Red Sandstone sequence, and, in view of this, there arose the question of the age that should be ascribed to the rocks which in Dingle come between the fossiliferous Silurian strata and the confirmed Old Red Sandstone. Were they best regarded as belonging to the upper Silurian or to the Old Red Sandstone?

Griffith, despite Murchison's misgivings, had chosen to map the intermediate beds as Silurian, but Jukes decided upon a more cautious approach. The Survey simply categorised the beds in question as 'the Dingle Beds' of uncertain age, and as the Dingle Beds - the Dingle Group in modern terminology - they have ever since appeared upon geological maps of the region. Jukes's caution was well advised because it now seems probable that the rocks of the Dingle Group are partly upper Silurian (upper Ludlow and Downtonian) and partly Devonian (Gedinnian).

Jukes's third major classificatory problem lay in the far south of Ireland, in the area depicted upon the fifteen one-inch sheets numbered 191 to 205. Throughout most of southern Ireland the Old Red Sandstone is succeeded first by the thin beds of the Lower Carboniferous Shales, and then by the thick sequence of the Carboniferous Limestone, but in southern County Cork there is a marked change in the character of the Carboniferous sediments. There the Old Red Sandstone is overlain not by the Lower Carboniferous Shales and the Limestone, but rather by a thick series of arenaceous and argillaceous rocks known to the Survey as 'the Carboniferous Slates' and to more recent geologists as 'the Cork Beds'. A question thus had to be answered. What is the chronological relationship between the Carboniferous Slates in the south and the shales and limestones farther to the north?

Jukes decided that the southern slates and the Carboniferous rocks to the north were really all of the same age, and that they owed their different characters merely to the fact that the two sequences of rocks had formed in different sedimentary environments. Here he drew upon his personal experience in Australian waters during his years in H.M.S. *Fly*. He remembered that off the coast of New Guinea he had seen places where the waters inshore of a barrier reef were clouded with mud, while only a short distance away, seaward of the reef, the waters were crystal clear. Something similar, he suggested, must have happened in County Cork during Carboniferous times, with turbid waters existing in what is today southern Cork, while slightly farther north there were clear waters populated with forests of crinoids.

Jukes was right - a facies change is indeed involved - but his wider extension of the concept brought him into conflict with the geological establishment of that day. In papers read in 1865 and 1866 to the Royal Geological Society of Ireland (prior to 1864 it had been the Geological Society of Dublin) and to the Geological Society of London, he argued that the slaty and supposedly Devonian rocks of north Devon were in reality of the same age as the Carboniferous slates of County Cork. The English rocks were thus really of Lower Carboniferous age rather than being Devonian. He claimed that any real understanding of the true character of the supposed Devonian rocks of Devon must be based upon a study of the rocks of southern Ireland, and he further insisted that such a study would reveal that

> ... the true Devonian rocks are everywhere synchronous with the Carboniferous Limestone, their palaeontological differences depending on *habitat* and *province,* and not upon *time.*

This was tantamount to a denial of the existence of an independent Devonian System, but the controversy that Jukes stimulated was largely concerned with rocks beyond Ireland's shores and it need here concern us no further.

In Britain during the 1860s there was some concern at the slow pace with which the Geological Survey was proceeding with its task in all parts of the British Isles. It was therefore decided to expedite the work by augmenting the Survey's staff. Benjamin Disraeli, the Chancellor of the Exchequer, must have been in magnanimous mood, because on 24 November 1866 Murchison was informed that as from 1 April 1867 his own title would become Director-General instead of Director, while the authorised establishment of the Irish Branch of the Survey would from that date be as follows:

1. Jukes as Director instead of Local Director
2. One officer in the new rank of District Surveyor
3. Four Senior Geologists
4. Up to twelve Assistant Geologists or Temporary Assistant Geologists.

Within the civil service, as elsewhere, there had now dawned what Gladstone had termed 'the age of examinations', and all candidates for these new junior posts in the Survey had to secure a nomination, sit a geological test, and then pass the appropriate examination set by the Civil Service Commissioners. Richard Glascott Symes in 1863 had been the first officer appointed after jumping the examination hurdle (he failed at his first attempt, finding the examination 'more severe than I had anticipated'), and candidates sitting the Commissioners' examination in 1867 had to display their proficiency in handwriting and orthography, in arithmetic (including vulgar and decimal fractions), in English composition, in drawing, in Euclid

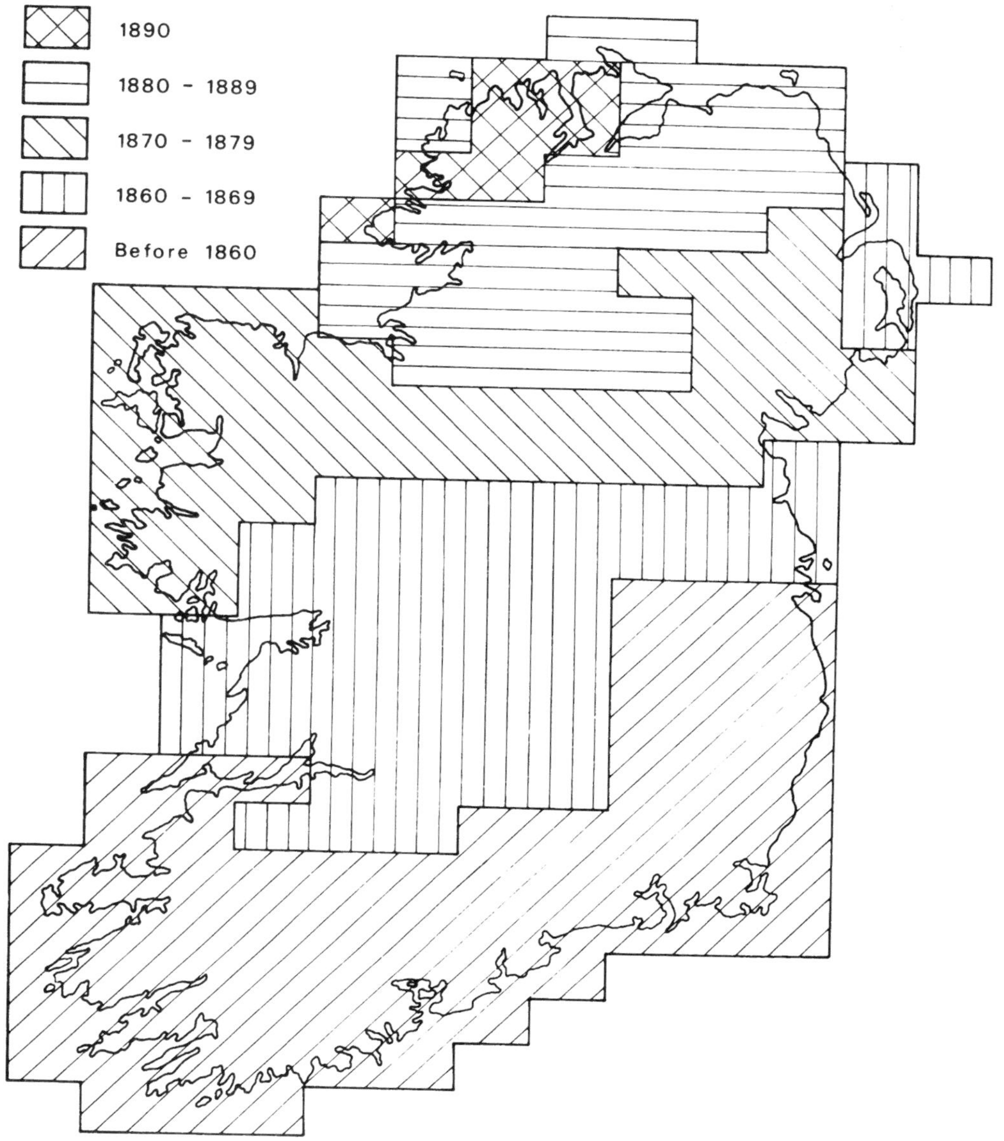

FIGURE 3.6. *The spread of the one-inch geological map over the surface of Ireland. The shading indicates the dates at which the various groups of one-inch sheets were published.*

(Book I), and in the use of common mathematical instruments.

On the eve of this expansion Jukes had a staff of five geologists - Du Noyer, Kinahan, Joseph O'Kelly, William Hellier Baily (see p.260), and Symes - and most men in Jukes's position must surely have been delighted at the proposed threefold increase in their establishment. But not so Jukes. There was something wrong. As will be explained shortly, his mental equilibrium was disturbed. The Survey expansion of 1867 casts him in an unflattering light. It summoned from him a welter of disparaging remarks about his officers, and it released from him a good deal of anti-Irish sentiment. On 5 February 1867 Ramsay wrote to Archibald Geikie:

> Poor Jukes is in a sort of semi-despair about all this business, and considering that he will be adding ten more Irishmen to his already Irish lot, I don't wonder at it. His chief man [Du Noyer?] lately informed him that he had given up taking and recording dips, as he found it to be useless! Jukes simply longs for the day when he will be able to retire, from age, and wear out the fag-end of his days, unworried by Irishmen and Boilermen, and I considerable sympathise with him.

On 15 June following, Ramsay again wrote to Geikie:

FIGURE 3.7. *Number 72 Upper Leeson Street, Dublin. The home of Beete and Augusta Jukes – and of their pet animals – from 1855 until 1869.* (Photograph by the author, 1995.)

> Jukes is exceedingly fidgety. He has not a man in Ireland that he can trust to training others. Also, they are all so unruly, that without rules (printed) every one will be in rebellion.

Ramsay can hardly be accused of having misrepresented Jukes's sentiments because that same summer Jukes himself wrote to Geikie as follows:

> I think I am getting a good batch of new men, worse than some of the old ones I could not have especially my two Seniors Du Noyer & Kinahan who can neither spell nor write English, & whose excessive bumptiousness & conceit are in the nth power of their ignorance. I have been very near reporting Kinahan to the Dr. General & asking his dismissal from the service this spring.

Exactly the same message went to London on 28 April 1868 when Jukes wrote to Trenham Reeks at the Survey's Jermyn Street headquarters.

> But at present I feel decidedly against more ignorant assistants. Had poor Foot lived I might have got through better but at present my two seniors Du Noyer & Kinahan are almost at open war with me & all correspondence is stilted official stuff.

There Jukes was clearly still feeling the death of Foot; he had been drowned on 17 January 1867 while trying to rescue two skaters who had fallen through the ice on Lough Key in County Roscommon. Jukes's sentiments of sad regret were doubtless genuine enough, but it has to be made clear that the Survey's correspondence files, the field-sheets, the one-inch maps, the memoirs, and the wider geological literature contain nothing to justify the calumny which Jukes was now directing against his staff. What we are obtaining here is not a perceptive insight into the professional bankruptcy of the Irish Survey, but rather an insight into the imaginings of Jukes's now sadly afflicted mind.

Despite some misgivings, Jukes decided that Du Noyer, his longest-serving officer, should become the first Irish District Surveyor. Back in 1861 Jukes had told Ramsay that Du Noyer 'was at times insane', that he 'had been brought up to me out of the country mad', and that Du Noyer's mother had also gone mad. Jukes now complained to Murchison that while Du Noyer was an accomplished draughtsman and an accurate observer, he could not be trusted with any independent work because of

FIGURE 3.8. *A group of the Survey staff taken around 1860. Standing, from left to right : Wynne, Mooney (General Assistant), O'Kelly, Jukes, and Baily. Seated : Foot and Du Noyer. Absent are Galvan, Kelly, and Kinahan.* (Reproduced from an illustration in Robert Lloyd Praeger, *Some Irish Naturalists : a Biographical Note-book*, 1949, by kind permission of the Dundalgan Press.)

'his want of all powers of generalisation and logical reasoning'. Du Noyer's tenure of the post was tragically brief because of his death in January 1869 (see p.59), and Jukes, again with some reluctance, agreed that Kinahan should be Du Noyer's successor as District Surveyor as from 1 March 1869.

Eight new members of staff were appointed between 1867 and 1869: Richard Joseph Cruise; Frederick William Egan; Hugh Leonard; William Benjamin Leonard; Joseph Nolan; William Acheson Traill; James Liley Warren; and Sidney Berdoe Neal Wilkinson. Of these eight, only three had university qualifications - Egan, Traill, and Warren were all graduates of the University of Dublin and were either diplomates or licentiates of the Trinity College Engineering School - and it may be that university graduates were reluctant to enter for competitive examinations of the type now being demanded of candidates for Survey appointments. Certainly the Survey posts themselves can hardly have looked very attractive. The pay was only seven shillings per diem, the posts were only as Temporary Assistant Geologists (the government clearly still looked forward to the day when, the mapping completed, the Survey could be disbanded), and there was no entitlement to superannuation.

The eight men appointed attained varying degrees of proficiency as field-geologists - Egan was perhaps the best, W.B. Leonard was probably the worst - but none of them ever gained any high eminence within the geological world. If we look across the water to Scotland we see that during the 1860s the Scottish Survey gained such recruits as James Croll, James Geikie, John Horne, and Benjamin Neeve Peach, all of them men destined to achieve international reputations. The Irish recruits of that period were hardly men of a water to match that of their Scottish brethren.

Perhaps the most notable attribute of the Irish recruits of the years between 1867 and 1869 was their proneness to accident and premature death. Warren died in 1872, seemingly of tuberculosis. W.B. Leonard was drowned at Belmullet, County Mayo, in 1876. Hugh Leonard was injured in a cliff

FIGURE 3.9. *The Lansdowne Arms Hotel, Kenmare, County Kerry. The hotel was perhaps the scene of Jukes's accident on the morning of 27 July 1864. The upper illustration is from the* Irish Tourist's Guide Advertiser *dating from the early 1860s. The lower illustration is the author's photograph of the hotel as it was in August 1993.*

fall at Ballycastle, County Mayo, in 1875, and he had to retire from the Survey six years later as unfit for further duty. Finally, in the summer of 1899, Egan was thrown from a car near to Rathdrum, County Wicklow, and he eventually died as a result of his injuries. But if some of Jukes's new recruits were accident prone, then I now have to point out that their fates were merely a reflection of the sad end which awaited their chief himself. By the time of the 1867 expansion of the Survey, Jukes was in trouble.

Towards the end of July 1864 Jukes was staying at Kenmare, County Kerry, during the course of one of his regular tours of inspection. Perhaps he had based himself at the Lansdowne Arms, an hotel which still flourishes in the town. On the morning of Wednesday 27 July, with his car waiting at the door, Jukes slipped on the hotel staircase and plunged headlong down to the flagstone floor of the hallway. Initially he seemed to have suffered little ill-effect. After a few minutes delay, he continued with the day's field-programme as planned. But complications soon followed.

During August 1864 he began to suffer from severe headaches, and he was forced to take sick-leave as from the beginning of September 1864. A continental excursion was resolved upon as suitable therapy, but while geologising near Coblenz, at the end of September, he suffered a seizure accompanied by partial paralysis. Murchison arranged for him to be granted extended leave until the end of January 1865, but when Jukes returned to his duties in February 1865, he was a shattered man who experienced long fits of deep depression, regular, if temporary, bouts of amnesia, and periodic blackouts. His judgement was seriously impaired, and he found difficulty in reaching administrative decisions. The drowning of Foot and the death of Du Noyer plunged Jukes into the depths of despair, and his increasing want of tact in his dealings with his officers led to serious friction within the Survey. All this has to be remembered as constituting the background to those calumnies noted earlier as uttered by Jukes against his staff.

As best he could, Jukes continued his editing of the one-inch sheets and their accompanying memoirs. Around the Christmas of 1866 he even summoned up the energy to compile an attractive small-scale geological map of Ireland. This map - 'Jukes's Map' as it came to be called - was published on 1 July 1867 by Messrs Hodges and Smith in Dublin and by Edward Stanford in London. Its scale is almost one inch to eight miles (1:506,880), and it has to be admitted that the map is something of a hybrid. The southern half of the sheet is based upon the work of the Survey (presumably he had Murchison's permission to employ Survey material in this manner), while the northern half, depicting country as yet largely unmapped by the Survey, is derived from Griffith's quarter-inch (1:253,440) map in its final, 1855 form.

In the spring of 1868 Jukes collapsed while travelling with Kinahan in a car somewhere in the wild country around Clifden, County Galway, and he was taken back to his inn unconscious. Augusta Jukes was summoned from South Wales, and Jukes's physician was called from Dublin, but by the following morning Jukes had recovered sufficiently to permit his continuing with his programme of inspection. On 5 March 1869 he suffered a similar collapse at Holywood, County Down, but on this occasion it was two days before he was fully restored to consciousness. Again he struggled to recover his former self, and on St Patrick's Day 1869 he wrote to Archibald Geikie:

> I believe I was living too low, and am now taking a glass of claret at lunch & two or three at dinner. They say that for the last two or three days I seem better than I have for the last two years, so I may hope perhaps eventually to get something like what I used to be.

Pleasant though the claret 'cure' may have been, Jukes was really now beyond any assistance that could be rendered by either medical science or the vintners of Bordeaux.

About Jukes's illness there has to linger an air of mystery. Augusta and other members of his family clearly blamed everything upon the accident at Kenmare in July 1864, but some of his contemporaries were not entirely convinced by the family's logic. Instead, they sought their own explanations, these ranging from over-indulgence in tobacco to martyrdom in the cause of a particularly demanding science. There is certainly ample evidence that Jukes's mental problems long pre-dated anything which may have happened at Kenmare during the summer of 1864. The first of his vituperative outbursts seems to have occurred as early as July 1860, when, as a result of some trivial misunderstanding, Jukes over-reacted by accusing Wynne of gross insubordination. In the margin of the Survey's correspondence dealing with the affair Wynne himself later - presumably during the 1880s - wrote the following comment:

> Such attacks of irritation were not characteristic - but premonitory of the subsequent sad calamity which befell one of the best of men.

A mystery there may be, but the sad events of the spring and early summer of 1869 are clear enough. In April, Jukes had just finished the editing of one-inch sheets 82 (Clogher) and 95 (Headford) when renewed illness struck him down. He was granted six months' leave of absence, but this time there was no question of his leaving Ireland in search of health through a continental sojourn. He was too far gone. On 8 May 1869, by the authority of Augusta and two physicians, he was admitted to Hampstead House, a private lunatic asylum standing in the Dublin suburb of Glasnevin. There he died on 29 July 1869. In an act symbolic of their unhappy relationship with Ireland - in an act regretted by their Dublin friends - Augusta removed her husband's body back to his native Warwickshire for burial. He lies in Selly Oak, Birmingham, in the still surprisingly secluded graveyard of St Mary's parish church, where grey squirrels scurry about amidst tottering and deeply weathered memorials cut from the local sandstones. Sadly, of his grave there is now no identifiable trace.

Jukes's successor as Director of the Geological Survey of Ireland was Edward Hull. Born in Antrim town on 21 May 1829, Hull was the son of a Church of Ireland curate. He was educated at schools in Edgesworthstown, County Longford, and Lucan, County Dublin, before entering Trinity College Dublin in 1846 to study for the Diploma in Engineering. Within the diploma course it was Oldham's lectures in geology which both gripped and disturbed the young Hull - disturbed him because until then his sole encounter with earth-history had been through the opening chapters of *Genesis* (see p.276). He received his engineering diploma in 1849 and his B.A. in 1850, but the great period of Irish railway construction was almost at an end, and he failed to secure any engineering appointment in Ireland.

Somewhat at a loose end, he in the autumn of 1849 visited number 51 to take his leave of Oldham, and the professor suggested that Hull should approach De La Beche to inquire about the possibility of a post with the Geological Survey of England and Wales. Armed with Oldham's letter of introduction, and supported by Murchison, whose sister had married Hull's cousin, the young Irishman tackled De La Beche. The outcome was for Hull eminently satisfactory. On 1 April 1850 he became a Temporary Assistant Geologist with the Survey of England and Wales. He received six months' training under Jukes in North Wales, and thereafter he was sent to map in England, where his chief area of activity was the South Lancashire Coalfield.

Initially, Hull seems to have achieved an acceptable standard in his work for the Survey, but after a while his mapping became increasingly slipshod. Following an inspection of some of Hull's ground, Ramsay noted that the Irishman's work was getting 'worse and worse', and De La Beche instructed Ramsay to secure Hull's resignation as an alternative to dismissal. The kindly Ramsay interceded upon Hull's behalf, but there was little improvement in the quality of Hull's work. In 1858 he was passed over for promotion to the rank of Geologist, despite his nuptial relationship with Murchison, who was now become the Survey's Director.

Perhaps this setback persuaded Hull to mend his ways. In 1859 he certainly obtained the promotion denied to him in the previous year, and during the Survey expansion of 1867 he received further advancement when he was appointed to the Geological Survey of Scotland with the rank of District Surveyor and as second in command under Archibald Geikie. In Scotland he was assigned responsibility for the mapping of the Lanarkshire Coalfield - coal and coalfields were now his speciality - and in execution of this duty he took up residence in Glasgow. There his stay was brief.

In Dublin Jukes's health was deteriorating, and in April 1869 he was granted his six months' leave of absence. Clearly somebody had to be appointed to administer the Irish Survey in Jukes's stead. Murchison chose Hull for the task. He was appointed as Jukes's locum-tenens on 28 April 1869, and he sailed over to Ireland on 6 May, just two days before Jukes was committed to Hampstead House. When Jukes died, Hull was clearly well placed to secure for himself the succession. That is what happened. In October 1869 he was named as Jukes's successor both as Director of the Geological Survey of Ireland and as professor of geology in the institution which had once been the Museum of Irish Industry, but which since August 1867 had assumed a new role as the Royal College of Science for Ireland.

Over the next twenty years it was Hull who pressed ahead the Survey's programme of one-inch map and memoir publication. Much credit is due to him for the fact that, despite many a difficulty, the one-inch map of Ireland was brought to completion in 1890. That conceded, it also has to be observed that Hull is not to be numbered among the greatest of the Survey's Directors. As a scientist he was decidedly second rate. He was certainly no Jukes.

In 1910 - admittedly very late in his life - Hull published an autobiography. It is a revealing work. He emerges therefrom as a sycophant of shallow intellect. He displays a naivity of approach to a variety of issues, and, occasionally, a blatant ignorance which others might have preferred to conceal. He admits, for instance, to having lived in Dublin for many years before discovering - and then through the agency of a visitor - that Trinity College - Hull's own alma mater - possessed a world-famed manuscript known as the Book of Kells! I will leave my reader to ponder upon the significance of one other feature of Hull's autobiography. Nowhere therein does parental pride cause him to allude to the fact that his daughter Eleanor was a leading Celtic scholar of the day and one of the founders of the Irish Texts Society, established in 1898 for the publication of texts in the Irish language.

In his politics Hull was a staunch Conservative and Unionist entirely out of sympathy with any Irish aspirations towards Home Rule. He was an equally staunch supporter of the Church of Ireland. During his years in Dublin he took an active part in the affairs of the Island and Coast Society of Ireland, a Church of Ireland body founded in 1833 'for the education of children and promotion of Scriptural truth in remote parts of the coast and adjacent islands'. During his retirement years in London he was equally active in the affairs of the Victoria Institute founded in 1865 for the reconciliation of 'any apparent discrepancies between Christianity and Science'.

When we examine Hull as a geologist, we discover that some of his work can only leave us astounded and aghast. A sense of blank amazement engulfs us as we peruse some of his published papers. He was not one to be over concerned with the painstaking investigation of detailed field-evidence. Rather was he constantly falling victim to the seductive charms of grandiose schemes of speculative synthesis - schemes which a few moments of reflection should have shown to be specious. His expansive approach to the earth sciences is epitomised in the title of a book which he published in 1882. Other geologists were devoting years of study to just a few square kilometres of ground, but Hull chose to write upon *Contributions to the physical history of the British Isles. With a dissertation on the origin of western Europe, and of the Atlantic Ocean.* He possessed a mind that was determined to impose simplistic order upon the natural world. Above all he was dangerously convinced of his own ability to solve problems which had for long perplexed the most distinguished of his predecessors. He was destined, in 1879, to launch the Irish Survey upon the most absurd and disastrous campaign in the whole of its one-hundred-and-fifty-year history.

When Hull departed from Scotland bound for Ireland, there were perhaps sighs of relief within the Scottish Survey. It may be that in Edinburgh the Scottish Director felt himself relieved of an incubus. When Hull arrived in Dublin one, at least, of the Irish officers considered himself to have had an incubus thrust upon him. That officer was Kinahan. As the Irish Survey's District Surveyor, Kinahan believed that he should have been appointed to take charge of the Irish Branch during Jukes's illness. He resented the Scottish District Surveyor being sent over to usurp a position which Kinahan felt to be rightfully his. At his remote field-station in Recess, County Galway, Kinahan fumed at the thought of this interloper seated in the Director's office at number 51. Hull might be Irish by birth, but what did this booby know of Irish geology? He, Kinahan, the most experienced of Ireland's practising geologists, had been cruelly slighted.

Within hours of his learning of Jukes's death on 29 July 1869, Kinahan wrote to Murchison demanding both Hull's removal and a recognition of his own claims to the Irish directorship. Another similar letter followed on 8 August, but Murchison proved to be impervious to all such pleas. Nepotism rather than geological skills might have sent Hull to Dublin, but Murchison was clearly satisfied that Kinahan was no real alternative to Hull. Already, by 1869, it was becoming clear that Kinahan was mentally unstable, and there was growing evidence of his inability to establish a normal rapport with his Survey colleagues.

In Survey folklore relating to the events of 1869, Kinahan was in the past commonly depicted as the innocent victim of bureaucratic partiality and anti-Irish prejudice. Should there be any who may still be tempted to subscribe to such an interpretation, I would say this: take a look at Kinahan's post-1869 record and, more especially, at what happened in 1883-84, when, for a few months, Kinahan did find himself in charge of the Survey (see p.88). Perhaps Hull was not the happiest of choices for the Irish directorship, but Murchison was surely right to have excluded Kinahan from the appointment. Sadly, that exclusion, coupled with Hull's presence in the Director's office, had dire consequences. Kinahan resolved to make his Director's life as difficult as possible, and there developed between the two men a bitter feud of twenty-years' duration. The atmosphere was poisoned for all those working within the Irish Survey, and the Irish Branch achieved notoriety throughout the entire British geological community.

One of Hull's first tasks in Dublin was to find for the Survey a new and more spacious home. Number 51 had served the Survey well enough in the early years, but by the mid-1860s the Survey was in need of expanded accommodation. There were steadily increasing numbers of six-inch field-sheets to be filed. Every year storage-space had to be found for a fresh batch of field-notebooks. Newly published one-inch maps and memoirs were constantly arriving in quantity. And in March 1864 shelf-space had to be provided for General Portlock's substantial collection of geological literature which his widow had decided to present to the Survey. The final straw was the expansion of 1867. Its consequence was that work-rooms had to be found for the several new officers who would, of course, from time to time be leaving their field-stations in order to pursue their labours in Dublin.

Expansion within number 51 was out of the question, especially after 1867, when the former Museum of Irish Industry assumed its new

FIGURE 3.10. *Edward Hull (1829-1917), Director of the Survey between 1869 and 1890.* (Reproduced from the frontispiece to Hull's autobiography, *Reminiscences of a Strenuous Life,* 1910.) See also Figure 3.11.

pedagogical role as the Royal College of Science for Ireland. The young College was making its own spatial demands in satisfaction of the needs of its professors and students. Jukes began the search for a new Survey headquarters as early as August 1865, but it was left for Hull to complete the quest. Initially, in October 1869, Hull was anxious to transfer the Survey to a house in Upper Merrion Street, the street in which the Duke of Wellington is said to have been born, but in the end the Survey went to number 14 in Hume Street, a street of terraced Georgian houses just around the corner from number 51 in The Green. Hume Street may have lacked association with historical figures of the magnitude of the Iron Duke, but, strangely, number 14 stands just across the street from the house in which Sir Richard Griffith was born in 1784.

The Survey's move from The Green to Hume Street took place in the spring of 1870. Hull's first full day in number 14 was 31 March 1870, and on 8 June he wrote to Reeks in London:

> We are now completely settled in our new offices which are the envy & admiration of all beholders.

Hull had every reason for feeling pleased. Number 14 provided the Survey with eleven rooms - several of them of goodly size - in addition to ample storage accommodation in the cellars. The sole drawback was that the house lacked any apartment suitable for the public display of the Survey's collections of rocks and fossils. The greater part of the collections were therefore left behind at number 51 where they presumably continued to be much used by students studying geology at the Royal College of Science (see p.265). There was certainly nothing temporary about the move to Hume Street; number 14 was to remain the Survey's headquarters for well over one hundred years. The house became an intimate part of the Survey's history, and, antiquated though its apartments were by the 1980s, there were many officers who felt pangs of nostalgic regret when the time came to transfer from Hume Street to the fine new premises over at Beggars Bush.

Murchison never set foot inside the new Irish headquarters. He suffered a stroke on 30 November 1870, and he died on 22 October 1871. His successor as Director-General was Andrew Crombie Ramsay, whose name has already featured many times in these pages and who had for long been Jukes's friend and confidant. Sadly, Ramsay was past his peak by the time he received his appointment as Director-General in March 1872, but he nonetheless took his Irish responsibilities far more seriously than had Murchison

Ramsay visited Ireland regularly to make tours of inspection, and during these excursions it was Irish Pleistocene deposits and landforms which especially engaged his attention. Ever since spending his honeymoon in Switzerland in 1852 he had been a devoted student of all aspects of our glacial legacy, and in 1859 he had pioneered the view that glaciers have played a major erosive role in shaping many of the world's present landscapes (see p.244). The ice-gouged Wicklow Glens, the glacially-scoured moutonnée landscapes of Connemara, the ice-dumped moraines of the Midlands, and the wide scattering of drumlins, eskers, and kames all served to make Ireland a land well suited to Ramsay's geological tastes.

His first tour as Director-General occupied almost four weeks in the autumn of 1872. It took him all along the Survey's then mapping front from Carlingford and the Mourne Mountains, through the drumlin swarm of northern Ireland, past Boyle, and on northwards to Sligo. Writing to Archibald Geikie about this tour, Ramsay observed:

> I have seen all the staff but two, and a very nice set of fellows they are.

In view of this favourable impression, based upon his first-hand experience, one wonders what Ramsay now made of all that denigration of his 'Irish lot' which had featured so regularly in the private correspondence of the ailing Jukes.

FIGURE 3.11. *Three successive Local Directors, or Directors, of the Irish Survey as they feature in a photograph album in the archives of the British Geological Survey. Hull is on the left, Oldham in the centre, and Jukes on the right.* (Reproduced by kind permission of the British Survey.)

Sir Andrew Ramsay - he was knighted at Windsor Castle upon the eve of his retirement - left the Survey on 31 December 1881. He was succeeded by the Survey's third successive Scottish Director-General - by Archibald Geikie. Although not always the most popular of men, Geikie was a highly talented individual whose interests ranged from Horace and Ovid, to igneous petrology and the history of science. He was certainly one of the most internationally renowned geologists of his generation.

Sir Archibald - he received the accolade at Osborne in July 1891 - knew Hull well; he had been Hull's Director in the Edinburgh office between 1867 and Hull's departure for Dublin in May 1869. In the light of that experience Geikie perhaps felt it prudent for the Director-General to keep a close eye upon Hull's doings with the Irish Survey. Or perhaps Geikie just enjoyed Irish rocks and Irish society. Whatever the reason, as Director-General he took very seriously his Irish responsibilities (see p.110). He claimed to have visited Ireland at least once every year during his term as Director-General from 1882 until 1901, and he revived a Survey tradition which had been dormant since the days of De La Beche. This was the tradition that the Survey's senior officer should himself become personally involved in the field investigation of actual Irish geological problems. The memoir to Sheet 17, for instance, contains a discussion of the rocks exposed on the shore of Lough Swilly near Manorcunningham, written by Geikie and dated 23 March 1885, while the memoir to sheets 31 (in part) & 32 of 1891 contains a chapter by Geikie devoted to the supposed Archaean rocks of the Lough Derg inlier near Pettigoe in County Donegal.

Hull thus received a full measure of support from the two Directors-General under whom he served following Murchison's death in 1871. But where his own subordinates were concerned the situation was less satisfactory. When he took over the Survey during the summer of 1869, Hull found himself possessed of a somewhat inexperienced staff. Of his twelve geologists, only four had more than two years of service to their credit; all the remainder were men recruited as a result of the 1867 expansion. Even the value of the four experienced men was diminished by problems. Baily was disgruntled and could not always be relied upon to complete his work to schedule. He had been imported from the British Survey in 1857 as a specialist in palaeontology, but he was deeply resentful of the fact that he was denied the title of 'Palaeontologist in Ireland', and instead had to rest content with a geological rank followed by a parenthetical '(Acting Palaeontologist)'. There is also a hint of his having suffered from an alcohol problem (see p.261). O'Kelly had been largely restricted to office work since 1866 as a result of bronchial problems developed in consequence of the rigorous conditions he had experienced while mapping in the Slieveardagh Coalfield during the winter of 1858-59. And then there was Kinahan.

FIGURE 3.12. *Mr and Mrs George Henry Kinahan during the 1860s. They were married in St Thomas's church, Dublin, on 12 November 1855, fifteen months after Kinahan joined the Survey. Mrs Kinahan, the former Harriette Anne Gerrard from County Westmeath, died on 18 May 1892.* (The illustration is reproduced from a photograph in the *Kinahan Papers* in the Library of the Royal Irish Academy, and it is here featured by kind permission of the Academy.)

His temperamental instability, and his feud with Hull, were seriously diminishing the reliability of his field-work. That left Symes as the sole geologist of experience upon whom Hull could place a full reliance.

The men appointed as a result of the 1867 expansion were, of course, rapidly learning their trade, and a good deal of Survey time must have been expended upon the induction of new officers. During Hull's regime, between 1869 and 1890, seven geological recruits arrived in Hume Street, and they constituted a substantial proportion of the *dramatis personae* involved in the final acts of the primary mapping of Ireland. First, in July 1870, there was Edward Townley Hardman, a former Drogheda Grammar School boy and a graduate of the newly-founded Royal College of Science for Ireland. Second, in May 1871, there was William Edmund L'Estrange Duffin, the son of Maghera rectory in County Down, a graduate of Trinity College Dublin and one of the College's licentiates in engineering, but a man who remained with the Survey only until February 1874, when he resigned to become County Surveyor in the Western Division of County Limerick. Third, in June 1874, there was James Robinson Kilroe, another graduate of the Royal College of Science, a former science teacher in Sir Titus Salt's Institute at Saltaire, and a man destined to become the Survey's chief authority upon the soils of Ireland. Fourth, in February 1875, there was William Fancourt Mitchell, yet another graduate of the Royal College of Science, a former apprentice at the Vulcan Foundry at Newton-le-Willows in Lancashire, but a man who proved to be one of the Survey's more unfortunate appointments. In a confidential report of 1889 Geikie described Mitchell as 'a most unsatisfactory member of the staff'.

The fifth appointment was the most interesting. It was the appointment of Alexander McHenry. Born in County Antrim in 1847, the son of a policeman, McHenry attended school in Dublin under the noted educationalist and scholar Patrick Weston Joyce. After leaving school he joined Jukes's geological class at the Museum of Irish Industry, and the young man's enthusiasm and patent ability soon brought him to Jukes's notice. Upon Jukes's recommendation, he in January 1861 was appointed to the Survey as a Fossil Collector in replacement of the deceased Flanagan. In that role his admirable qualities soon became apparent to all his new colleagues. He was given unofficial promotion to the part-time post of Acting Assistant Palaeontologist, and in December 1872, following upon Warren's death, Baily, Kinahan, O'Kelly, and Symes presented to Hull a memorial wherein they urged that McHenry should be given the now vacant geologist's post. Hull concurred, but the

FIGURE 3.13. *Number 14 Hume Street, Dublin, the headquarters of the Survey between March 1870 and May 1984. The photograph was taken in 1982 while the Survey still occupied the building. The three windows on the first floor are those of the room which was used as an office by Grenville Cole (Director from 1905 until 1924) and by all subsequent Directors of the Survey. It seems that Hull may originally have used as his office the two-windowed room to the right of the street-door.* (From a photograph by Terence Dunne of Trinity College Dublin.)

Civil Service Commissioners insisted that McHenry must pass the necessary qualifying examination. He attempted the examination in June 1874, but he failed. The four memorialists again espoused his cause, and the eventual outcome was a waiving of the examination requirement in McHenry's case. He was appointed as a Temporary Assistant Geologist as from 26 March 1877. In his new rank he fully lived up to his colleagues' expectations, and in Geikie's confidential 1889 memorandum he noted that McHenry 'is, on the whole, the most efficient member of the staff'.

Hull's sixth and seventh appointments both arose from the deaths of serving officers. When O'Kelly died in 1883, Hull brought back to the Survey a veteran from earlier years - Arthur Beavor Wynne. Wynne had joined the Survey in 1855 but he had resigned in 1862 in order to join the Geological Survey of India. There he laboured for twenty years, but in 1883 ill-health caused his return home to Ireland, and in that same year he found himself reinstated with the Irish Survey to take charge of the Hume Street office.

FIGURE 3.14. *Richard Glascott Symes (1840-1906). His father, Glascott Richard Symes, was a leading Dublin physician with a large practice in Kingstown. After twenty-seven years of service with the Irish Survey, Symes was in 1890 transferred to the Geological Survey of Scotland. There his health was seriously impaired following a carriage accident in which he was involved near Campbeltown in Kintyre.* (Reproduced from a photograph kindly made available by Mr Glascott J. R. Symes of Dublin.)

The final appointment resulted from Baily's death in 1888. Hull then claimed that the Survey no longer had need of a palaeontologist because:

> Little now remains to be done in Irish Palaeontology except to add to the collections from time to time from new openings.

He therefore recommended that Baily should be succeeded not by another palaeontologist, but by a petrologist. The proposal was accepted, and to this new post there was in 1888 appointed a twenty-two-year-old Liverpudlian named John Shearson Hyland.

The appointment of Hyland reflects the fact that Hull was much interested in the new science of microscope petrology. Ramsay had little sympathy with the new technique; as he expressed it: 'I don't believe in looking at a mountain with a microscope'. But Hull recognised that the preparation of extremely thin slices of rock, and their study beneath a special petrological microscope, could yield important insights into both the character of a rock and its history. This was an innovation within the Irish Survey for which Hull deserves much credit.

As early as 16 May 1871, Hull wrote to Murchison asking him to approve expenditure upon the following items necessary to equip the Survey for microscope work:

Jordan's Lapidary Machine for slitting & polishing specimens	£10. 10. 0
Microscope suitable for examining slit specimens of minerals	£15. 0. 0
Achromatic condenser	£ 1. 0. 0
Polarizing apparatus	£ 1. 12. 6
	£28. 2. 6

Soon notes by Hull upon the microscopic character of the local rocks began to appear in the Irish sheet memoirs, the first such note featuring in the memoir to one-inch Sheet 48 (Banbridge) published in May 1872. Similarly, in periodicals such as the *Geological Magazine* and the *Journal of the Royal Geological Society of Ireland,* we find papers by Hull dealing with the petrology of the Lambay Island porphyry, the County Limerick volcanics, and the Galway and Wicklow granites.

When Hull assumed responsibility for the Survey in 1869, there had been published one-inch geological sheets for the whole of Ireland to the south of a line running from the shores of Galway Bay, northward to Lough Mask, and thence eastwards to the coast of the Irish Sea in County Louth (see Fig 3.6). In the summer of that year the field-staff was distributed as follows: Hugh Leonard was mapping the granite and schist islands of County Galway; Cruise was at Roundstone and Clifden; Warren was in the schist country at Letterfrack; Kinahan was at Recess where he and his family had for some years been living in an old police barracks; Nolan was on the shores of Lough Mask at Toormakeady; Symes was in the drumlin-drift country at Westport; Wilkinson was on the Carboniferous Limestone at Swinford; W.B. Leonard was in the Longford-Down Massif at Kingscourt; Egan was amidst the Silurian rocks at Banbridge; and Traill was observing the Mountains of Mourne sweep down to the sea at Newcastle in County Down.

Slowly, year by year, the mapping-front was pushed northwards, while from Hume Street there flowed a steady stream of new one-inch sheets, new memoirs, and new sheets of longitudinal sections. Hull has to be admired for his success in maintaining an excellent record of publication despite the fact that, initially at least, many of his officers were inexperienced and in need of training. That said, I do have to admit that the Survey's letter-books reveal Hull himself to have received from London

FIGURE 3.15. *Sir Andrew Crombie Ramsay (1814-1891), Director-General of the Geological Survey of the United Kingdom from 1872 until 1881.* (Reproduced from the frontispiece to Archibald Geikie's *Memoir of Sir Andrew Crombie Ramsay*, 1895.)

many a reprimand because of his carelessness in editing some of the Survey's publications.

Hull introduced few innovations where the Survey's field-mapping was concerned; he was well content with the tested methods which he inherited from the Survey of Jukes's day. It is time now to examine those methods in some little detail. They are the methods which gave to us the great one-inch geological map of Ireland.

Each geologist was assigned his ground by the Director, and thither he was despatched equipped with two sets of the six-inch sheets covering his area, and two sets of the one-inch Ordnance Survey sheets of the same district. The six-inch sheets were each cut into four quarters for ease of handling, and one set of these - the 'working sheets' - was employed in the field, while the other set - the 'duplicate sheets' - was accorded fair-copy status.

Upon the working sheets an officer was instructed to record neatly every single exposure of rock. In 'obscure districts' he was particularly enjoined to explore all trenches dug to received the foundations of buildings, and to examine ditches around the margins of fields. But in those areas where the surveyor's problem was a plethora of outcrop rather than a scarcity of rock - in areas such as the bare limestone terrain of the Burren or the glacially-scoured country of Donegal - officers were permitted to base their conclusions upon the running of a number of closely-spaced cross-country traverses. As much detail as possible was to be recorded upon the six-inch sheets, but sketches and additional details might be entered in field-notebooks.

All the field-work was recorded upon the working sheets in pencil, but in the evening an officer was supposed to re-inscribe his day's work in Indian ink so that his annotations would retain their legibility come rain, come storm. Similarly, in the evenings, or upon wet days when out-of-door activity was impossible, he had to transfer all his work from the working sheets to the duplicate sheets, the latter being intended for preservation in perpetuity as the Survey's basic archive of Irish geology. But there was no intention of releasing the often field-worn working sheets for destruction once the transfer of information had been completed; the working sheets, too, were destined for preservation in the Survey's Dublin headquarters.

FIGURE 3.16. *Sir Archibald Geikie (1835-1924), Director-General of the Geological Survey of the United Kingdom from 1882 until 1901.* (Reproduced from a plate in Horace B. Woodward's *History of the Geological Society of London,* 1907.)

From time to time at his field-station, an officer was required to transfer the essentials of his work to the two sets of one-inch sheets with which he was provided, and in this manner he was able to see his detailed six-inch mapping fitted into its broader regional context. One of these sets of one-inch sheets was for the officer's own use; the other set was to be kept up-to-date and available for despatch to Dublin when requested, so that either the Director or the Director-General could periodically review the progress and significance of the work.

When the mapping of any one-inch sheet was complete, it was the officer's task to send the sheet to Dublin for the Director's approval, and, approval granted, the geological sheet was returned to the officer together with another clean copy of the same Ordnance Survey one-inch sheet. To that sheet the officer now had to add all the details, symbols, and lines (geological boundaries were marked in carmine and faults in blue) which he wished to see upon the eventual published geological sheet. Next, the annotated sheet went to the Ordnance Survey for the geological information to be engraved, and shortly thereafter the officer received his first proof of the new geological sheet. Upon this proof he was required to mark any desired changes in red, and then to tint in sepia those portions of the sheet which were to receive the drift stipple. When these final details had all been engraved by the Ordnance Survey, the officer received his second proof, and to this he had to affix the standard geological colours. This proof was then designated the 'pattern copy'. It was the prototype from which the published sheet was prepared by the Geological Survey's colourists in England.

Where the published one-inch sheets were concerned, Hull introduced only one innovation worthy of particular mention. Jukes, of necessity, had employed as a base-map the Ordnance Survey's one-inch outline edition upon which little attempt is made to depict relief (see p.58). But as the Survey pushed into northern Ireland, the geologists found themselves in a region for which there were available the Ordnance Survey's excellent hachured sheets of the one-inch hill edition. Hull, doubtless anxious to illustrate the relationship of geology to topography, in 1873 decided to change the Survey's one-inch base-map from the outline edition to the hill edition for all the sheets lying to the north of a line drawn roughly from Dundalk to Clew Bay.

The first geological one-inch sheet upon a hachured base - Sheet 28 (Antrim) - was published in October 1874. Three adjacent geological sheets - sheets 21 (Larne), 29 (Carrickfergus), and 36 (Belfast) - had already been published on the outline edition base-map, and, in order to preserve a uniformity of style for the map in northern Ireland, the original versions of these three sheets were withdrawn. New versions of the three sheets, based upon the hachured base-map, were published between 1876 and 1883. In some cases the new hachured geological sheets have a somewhat mirky and overburdened appearance (sheets 26 (Draperstown) and 43 (Manorhamilton) for instance), but most of the hachured maps are extremely handsome specimens of geological cartography. Especially fine examples are sheets such as numbers 10 (Kilmacrenan), 15 (Dunglow), 34 (Ballygawley), and 58 (Monaghan).

By the close of 1879 forty-nine one-inch sheets had been published under Hull's direction, and of these it is sheets 59 (Castleblayney), 60 (Newry), 70 (Dundalk), and 71 (Carlingford) which hold the greatest scientific interest. These four sheets, published between August 1875 and December 1876, depict the Tertiary Slieve Gullion ring-complex. The complex is a great circular intrusive mass of igneous rock located in County Armagh at the western end of the Caledonian Newry Granite (a granite body which, incidentally, the Survey believed to have resulted from the ultra-metamorphism of the local Silurian strata). The complex is some 10 kilometres in diameter, and its tough rocks form a striking circle of rugged hills centred upon Slieve Gullion itself. The rail-traveller speeding between Dublin and Belfast obtains an excellent view of this remarkable topography as the train penetrates the southeastern quadrant of the ring around Jonesborough.

The ground occupied by the ring-complex was mapped by Egan, Nolan, and Traill, and they executed their task well. They nonetheless failed to differentiate adequately between the various types of igneous rock present. As a result they remained largely oblivious to that spectacular annular pattern of geological outcrop which later geologists were to bring to light. Thus, while the Survey trio were aware that they had lighted upon something unusual, they failed to appreciate that here was a type of structure which was altogether unknown to geological science. Not until ring-structures had been fully described later in the west of Scotland, did William Bourke Wright, himself a former officer of the Irish Survey, point out in 1924 that the Irish officers had partially mapped an identical structure almost half a century earlier.

In addition to the one-inch sheets, the Survey under Hull maintained a steady output of the accompanying sheet memoirs. Some of these memoirs had now become substantial monographs. The 1878 memoir describing most of northern County Galway (sheets 93 & 94), for instance, contains 177 pages (it sold for nine shillings), and the 1891 memoir on northwestern County Donegal (Sheets 3, 4, 5, 9, 10, 11, 15, & 16) was of equal size. Hull was himself a regular contributor to the memoirs, and when Traill resigned from the Survey (Traill resigned in August 1880 because his wife of one year was ill and Hull refused to grant him further leave to care for her) after mapping the Mourne Mountains but before completing the memoir (sheets 60, 61 & 71), it was Hull who personally undertook to remedy the deficiency.

Hull also continued the new series of six-inch (1:10,560) longitudinal sections inaugurated by Jukes in 1860 (see p.59), and publication of the series of thirty-seven sections was finally completed in December 1894. Where these sections were concerned, Hull did feel compelled to modify the Survey's field-technique in one respect. In Britain, under both De La Beche and Murchison, the absence of any six-inch Ordnance Survey coverage had commonly forced the geologists to undertake the laborious task of mapping the topography along the line of their sections by means of chain and theodolite. It was largely this type of work which had engaged Hull in North Wales during his six months of apprenticeship under Jukes in 1850. But in Ireland, James, Oldham, and Jukes had never found it necessary to survey their sections in the British manner. Possession of the admirable six-inch maps had allowed the Irish officers to derive their topographical detail directly from the Ordnance Survey sheets.

Now things were changed. In the mountainous districts of the west of Ireland, Hull concluded that the six-inch sheets carried insufficient altitudinal detail to permit the construction of accurate topographical sections. We therefore find him writing to Murchison on 11 April 1871 asking him to sanction the purchase of two 5-inch theodolites and some steel chains. Presumably the Irish Survey thereafter adopted the British Survey's methods of section running.

One other innovation of Hull's regime must be mentioned. Jukes had once hoped that it would be possible to publish geological sheets at the six-inch scale, but De La Beche had declared such cartographic lavishness to be entirely beyond the realms of financial possibility (see p.39). Now under Hull, between 1874 and 1877, there were published ten six-inch geological sheets covering the Connaught and Tyrone coalfields, and the iron-ore

ORDNANCE SURVEY OF IRELAND.
GEOLOGICAL SURVEY of IRELAND
SHEET 32.
Cancelled June 1891
EXPLANATION of Geological Signs and Colours
Carboniferous Rocks
Metamorphic Rocks
Igneous Rocks
LOUGH DERG
LOUGH ERNE

mining district located near Larne in County Antrim.

Early in 1878 Hull felt the moment to be opportune for the issue of a new geological map of the whole of Ireland in the tradition of Jukes's map of 1867 (see p.69). Like Jukes's map, Hull's map was a private venture rather than a Survey publication, and both Hull and his publisher - Edward Stanford - can hardly have been unmindful of the fact that the British Association was scheduled to meet in Dublin during August 1878. There were going to be many visiting geologists seeking for guidance in their exploration of Ireland's rocks.

Hull's map was published on 30 March 1878. Hand-coloured, its scale is one inch to about eight miles (1:506,880), and it sold for thirty shillings, dissected, mounted upon linen, and in a slip-case. Upon the map Hull admitted that in plotting the geology of those areas not yet mapped by the Survey - County Donegal was the principal region in this category - he had sought guidance from Griffith's map of 1855, and this was to be the last occasion upon which the author of a geological map of Ireland was forced to seek inspiration in Griffith's masterpiece. Griffith's splendid quarter-inch map was about to be superseded by the Survey's magnificent one-inch map. It was an appropriate moment for Griffith to make his exit. He died on 22 September 1878, only two days after entering his ninety-fifth year.

Hull's map incorporates many refinements of detail not present upon Jukes's map of 1867, but a comparison of the two maps reveals between them a pair of striking differences.

First, Jukes had depicted all the Carboniferous beds above the limestone simply as Coal Measures, but, in the light of his considerable experience of coalfields throughout the British Isles, Hull now claimed to be able to divide the Irish Upper Carboniferous strata into the Yoredale Shales at the base, then the Millstone Grit, and finally the Coal Measures at the top. The extent of the Coal Measure strata was thus far smaller upon Hull's map than upon that of Jukes. As a stalwart Unionist, Hull perhaps took pleasure in thus reminding the Nationalists that Ireland was not a land richly endowed with black diamonds. Some of those Nationalists, perhaps misled by the extent of the Coal Measure strata depicted upon Jukes's map, had been arguing that Munster contained one of the largest coalfields within the British Empire. But, so the argument continued, British entrepreneurs had refused to exploit Munster's riches for fear of endangering the prosperity of the English coalfields. By showing the true and very limited extent of Munster's Coal Measure strata, Hull was demonstrating that it was the harsh realities of Irish geology, rather than Albion's perfidy, which explained the absence of Irish counterparts to Bradford, Gateshead, or Wigan.

Second, most of the copies of Hull's map incorporate what purported to be a major improvement in the representation of the geology of the south of Ireland (but see the caption to Fig. 3.17). The story of that supposed improvement, and of its sequel, must for the next few pages hold our attention. I am about to remove the lid from off a can of worms. The events now to be unfolded represent the most disreputable episode in the entire 150-year history of the Survey. Collective responsibility for what happened clearly has to be laid at the door of Hume Street, but within the building there is really only one officer who is culpable. That officer is the Director himself - Edward Hull.

During the 1870s Hull was clearly exercised by the unresolved problem of the Dingle Beds lying far to the south of the Survey's then mapping-front. He saw the problem as one in need of being mopped up. The age of those enigmatic rocks must be

---

PLATE III. *One-inch Sheet 32 (Pettigoe) issued in November 1885 and here reproduced at a diminished scale. The inner frame of the original sheet measures 46 x 31 centimetres.*

After 1873, all the one-inch sheets being published for the northern portion of Ireland were based, as here, upon the Ordnance Survey's one-inch hill edition, whereupon relief is represented by means of hachures.

This sheet was originally mapped by Mitchell, Symes, and Wilkinson. The latter officer found for himself a wife at Cliff House, on the Lower Limestone in the sheet's southwestern corner. In the haste to complete the primary mapping of Ireland during the 1880s, much of the country here depicted was mapped on the ground on the one-inch scale rather than upon the six-inch. A later Survey officer – W.B. Wright – spent the field-season of 1910 re-mapping the Pettigoe region upon the six-inch scale (see p.227).

Around 1885 the official colourist for all the Survey's sheets was Mrs E. Williams of 4 Stratford Villas, Camden Square, Camden Town, London. This is almost certainly an example of her work.

The manuscript inscription in the upper margin of the sheet should be noted. Although first published in the state here shown, during November 1885, a revised version of the sheet was issued as early as June 1891 and all copies of the original version remaining in store were declared to be cancelled, This serves as a reminder that many of the one-inch sheets exist in varied states.

The revision of June 1891 related chiefly to the rocks here represented as quartzite, quartz schist, mica schist, and gneiss. During 1889 Geikie and McHenry re-examined the ground occupied by these ancient rocks, concluded that they were identical to the Archaean rocks of the Scottish highlands, and resolved upon the issue of a revised sheet depicting the rocks as Archaean. (Reproduced from one of the several 'Cancelled' copies of the sheet in the archives of the Survey.)

established once and for all. Further, he was convinced that, since the year of Jukes's demise, important light had been shed upon the age of the Dingle Beds as a result of the Survey's mapping of the rocks in the vicinity of Killary Harbour, located on the boundary between County Galway and County Mayo.

In the Dingle Peninsula, as we have seen (see p.63), the stratigraphical sequence consists of fossiliferous upper Silurian rocks overlain unconformably by the unfossiliferous Dingle Beds which, in their turn, are overlain with marked unconformity by the undoubted Old Red Sandstone. Hull believed that around Killary Harbour the Survey had located rocks - the 'Mweelrea Beds' and the 'Salrock Slate Series' - which, on the basis of lithology, were to be correlated with the Dingle Beds, but which, unlike the Dingle Beds, contain a modest peppering of fossils. Those fossils were regarded as being of upper Silurian age, and that, he reasoned, must be the true age of the perplexing rocks of the southwest. (He was evidently unaware that Griffith had already advanced much the same argument back in January 1845.)

After due reflection upon the entire problem represented by the succession in the southwest, Hull arrived at the following three conclusions.

1. Because of their conformable relationship to the upper Silurian rocks, and because of the evidence from Killary Harbour, the so-called Dingle Beds must themselves be of upper Silurian age.
2. Jukes and other geologists had pointed out that the rocks of the Iveragh Peninsula lying to the south of Dingle Bay - rocks known as the 'Glengarriff Grits' - were lithologically identical to the Dingle Beds, but because of the absence of any unconformity between the Glengarriff Grits and the Old Red Sandstone reposing upon the Dingle Beds, the Grits had been mapped as Old Red Sandstone rather than as Dingle Beds. This, Hull decided, was an error. On the basis of their lithological similarity, he concluded that the Glengarriff Grits and the Dingle Beds must be grouped together and that both the sets of strata must be assigned to the upper Silurian.
3. Since there is no unconformity to be found in the sandstones and grits to the east of the Iveragh Peninsula, then it follows that an extensive tract of country in Kerry and West Cork - a tract which the Survey had mapped as Old Red Sandstone - must now instead be assigned to the upper Silurian.

Hull first gave cartogaphic expression to these conclusions in his map of Ireland published in March 1878, but at that time he evidently had very little field experience of the rocks in question. His 'solution' to the problem of the Dingle Beds was merely a piece of arm-chair geology. Clearly the proposed new classification had to be considered in the light of the field evidence, so, in September 1878, after the close of that year's Dublin meeting of the British Association, Hull set off for the southwest, taking with him O'Kelly and McHenry. His choice of companions is interesting. O'Kelly, with his bronchial problems, can hardly have been the most vigorous of field-assistants, while McHenry, who had been promoted from Fossil Collector to Assistant Geologist only the previous year, was in no position to restrain his Director should he suspect him of trying to view the field-evidence through the distorted lens of a preconceived theory.

Guided by the field-sheets prepared in Jukes's day, Hull and his companions visited sites around Dingle, Killarney, Kenmare, Sneem, and Glengarriff. A mere few days of investigation sufficed to convince Hull that his new interpretation of the local stratigraphy was indeed valid. He tells us that O'Kelly and McHenry were likewise convinced that the truth was at last discovered, but we may only wonder at a mentality which allowed Hull to imagine that within a few brief days he could achieve that understanding which had eluded Ganly, Griffith, and Jukes despite their painstaking studies extended over many years.

Hull boldly announced his new interpretation to the Geological Society of London on 9 April 1879, and he secured Ramsay's permission to send McHenry back to Munster to map out the detail of the new classification. That revision occupied McHenry for the years 1879, 1880, and 1881, and it was a revision which raised even nonscientific eyebrows in Westminster. For reasons of economy, the government wanted the one-inch maps of the British Isles to be completed as speedily as possible, and questions were now asked in the Commons as to why revision mapping was being undertaken in Ireland in advance of the completion of the primary mapping. Such questions were fully justified. McHenry's efforts were just a waste of Survey time.

At a first glance, Hull's re-interpretation of the Munster stratigraphy looks plausible enough. But a more thoughtful reflection should have been sufficient to convince any geologist that here lies a baited trap. If the geologist swallows the attractive idea that the Dingle Beds are equivalent to the Glengarriff Grits, and that both are of upper Silurian age, then there must follow a series of concomitant problems, the resolution of which will lead the geologist into deeper and deeper trouble. The perceptive Jukes doubtless saw the nature of the trap and avoided it; the less discerning Hull fell into the trap, and soon found himself in serious difficulty.

The character of the trap is extremely simple. Throughout Munster the rocks which the Survey had mapped as Old Red Sandstone are succeeded with evident conformability by rocks of Carboniferous age. But if the strata beneath the Carboniferous beds are regarded as upper Silurian

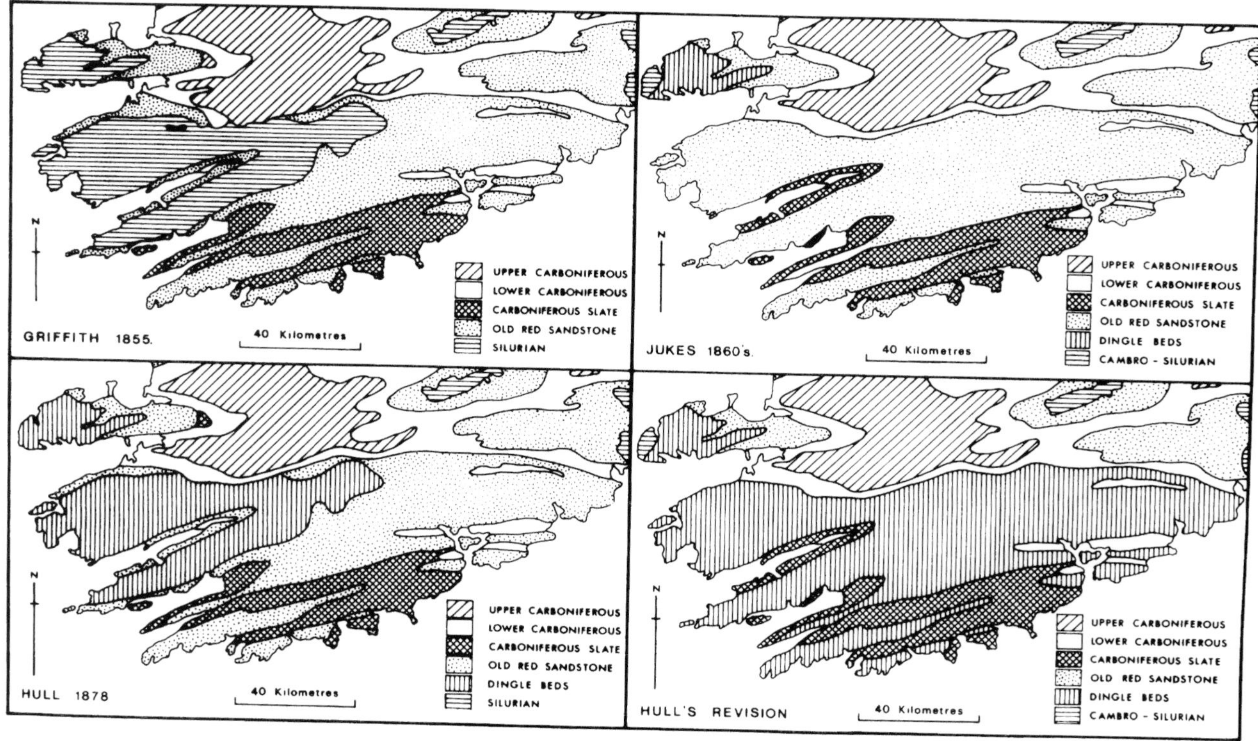

FIGURE 3.17. *Changing stratigraphical interpretations of the geology of southwestern Ireland from Richard Griffith in 1855 to Edward Hull around 1880. This figure was originally prepared for publication in 1983, and at that time all the copies of Hull's 1878 map to have come to my notice carried the lines as depicted in the lower left diagram. As explained in the text (see below), some of those lines are not engraved, but are late stage manuscript additions. I now know that at least one copy of Hull's map of 1878 exists without any manuscript lines, and its representation of the geology of the southwest is identical to that featured upon Jukes's map of 1867. This copy of Hull's map without the manuscript additions is now in my own collection. Perhaps some significance is to be read into the fact that this particular specimen of the map was in July 1882 presented by Kinahan's friend, the geologist Maxwell Henry Close, to Kinahan's son, Gerrard A. Kinahan. Had Close perhaps asked the publishers to colour a copy of the map without introducing the manuscript additions? Was Close perhaps acting upon the assumption that evidence of Hull's absurd revision could only prove anathema within the Kinahan household?*

rather than as Old Red Sandstone, then how is the observed conformable relationship to be explained? Surely it is absurd to believe that most of Munster could have remained unaffected by diastrophism throughout those aeons during which thousands of metres of Old Red Sandstone were being deposited elsewhere within these islands. In fact it was patently obvious that in some parts of Munster major earthmovements had indeed occurred during the interval between the Silurian and the Carboniferous. Even Hull had to allow that in the Dingle Peninsula undoubted Old Red Sandstone rested upon the Dingle Beds with marked unconformity. As he struggled to extricate himself from this dilemma, Hull had resort to various contrivances which do nothing to enhance his geological status in the eyes of posterity.

On his map of March 1878, Hull groups the Dingle Beds and the Glengarriff Grits together without specifically claiming the rocks as being of upper Silurian age. The problem of the conformable relationship between these strata and the overlying Carboniferous rocks he handled in two ways.

First, he introduced narrow outcrops of Old Red Sandstone between the Dingle Beds and the synclinal Carboniferous strata around the Kenmare River and Bantry Bay, thus implying that there had been a continuity of sedimentation from the Silurian into the Carboniferous (Fig. 3.17).

Second, he introduced a line running through northwestern County Cork delimiting the Dingle Beds to the northwest from the Old Red Sandstone to the southeast, and he thus confined the problem of a continuity of sedimentation from the Silurian into the Carboniferous to that area lying northwestwards of the line. This line in northwestern County Cork, together with the lines separating the Dingle Beds from the Old Red Sandstone around the Kenmare River and Bantry Bay, were clearly added to the map at a late stage because they are all manuscript lines and not a part of the map's engraved format. Indeed, the map bears trace of Hull's slapdash editorial methods because he has allowed the index number '4', indicating Old Red Sandstone, to survive in two localities within the area which was now coloured as Dingle Beds. Many users of the map must have been puzzled as to what was intended.

Hull derived all the manuscript lines delimiting his Dingle Beds directly from Griffith's quarter-inch map, and none of them has any reality in nature. They are all lines which Ganly had 'invented' for Griffith so that the grits and conglomerates of West Cork and Kerry could be represented as Transition Clay Slate (1839-40) and then as Silurian (1840 onwards), and separated from the similar rocks farther to the east which were represented as Old Red Sandstone. In short, Griffith's map had carried these lines because they were necessary to extricate Griffith from much the same stratigraphical difficulty as that in which Hull had now enmeshed himself. That boundary which Hull revived in order to separate a Dingle Bed region in the west from an Old Red Sandstone region in the east was just about the worst line upon Griffith's map. It was essentially a topographical boundary which Ganly had plotted in some haste during bad weather in January 1839. It was a line in which even Ganly himself had soon lost all faith. Yet this was the line upon which Hull in 1878 chose to bestow a fresh lease of life.

Perhaps Hull felt uneasy about his delimitation of the Dingle Beds upon the 1878 map, because when he visited the southwest in September 1878 he seems to have been approaching his stratigraphical problem in a slightly different manner. If it could be demonstrated that there was an hitherto unrecognised unconformity at the base of the Carboniferous, then he was free to regard all the pre-Carboniferous rocks of the southwest as being of upper Silurian age, and he could dispose of those dubious-looking outcrops of Old Red Sandstone around Bantry Bay and the Kenmare River.

Discovery of this postulated unconformity became the prime objective of Hull, O'Kelly, and McHenry as they toured the southwest in the autumn of 1878. Hull claimed to have found that for which he sought. Initially, he admitted the somewhat elusive character of the unconformity, but he claimed to have satisfied himself that on the northern side of the Kenmare River, in the district around Sneem, there was indeed an unconformity to be discerned at the base of the Carboniferous. Slightly later he was less guarded about his achievements during the tour of 1878.

> The general result was that, both along the shores of Kenmare and Glengariff [*sic*] Bays, we found the clearest evidence of a great hiatus between the Glengariff beds and those which immediately overlie them in those districts; resulting in the entire absence of the Old Red Sandstone at the base of the Carboniferous beds.

In the light of his supposed discovery, Hull believed that the way was now open for him to eliminate the Old Red Sandstone from the whole of western Munster lying to the south of Dingle Bay. He now read the stratigraphical sequence as consisting simply of the upper Silurian Dingle Beds, or Glengarriff Grits, overlain directly by the lowest beds of the Carboniferous sequence, with the Old Red Sandstone intervening between the upper Silurian rocks and the Carboniferous strata only within the Dingle Peninsula.

Henceforth Hull intended that the Survey should represent the rocks of most of western Munster as upper Silurian rather than as Old Red Sandstone. He saw himself as bringing the Survey around to a view very similar to that which had been enshrined in Griffith's quarter-inch map ever since 1840. Hull thought that Griffith should be one of the first to learn of the Survey's conversion. Towards the close of his southwestern tour in September 1878, Hull wrote a letter from Eccles's Hotel at Glengarriff, to Griffith in Dublin, announcing the discovery of a major post-Silurian hiatus in the stratigraphy of the southwest, but it was a letter that Griffith was never to receive. He died on 22 September, shortly before the letter was delivered to his Dublin residence at 2 Fitzwilliam Place. Perhaps Hull was in any case mistaken in believing that Griffith would have welcomed the news out of Eccles's Hotel. During his visit to Dingle with Murchison in 1856 Griffith had come around to the view that the Dingle Beds were perhaps, after all, better included with the Old Red Sandstone rather than with the upper Silurian strata exposed at Dunquin (see p.54).

Having satisfied himself of the existence of a basal Carboniferous unconformity in the southwest, Hull saw himself as facing only one further problem in connection with his stratigraphical re-interpretation. How far eastward in Munster did the upper Silurian strata extend into the ground which had formerly been mapped as underlain by the Old Red Sandstone? What Hull now wanted to find - needed to find - was a major unconformity which had somehow been overlooked by all previous investigators of Munster's geology. He had to discover an unconformity separating the upper Silurian rocks to the west from the overlying Old Red Sandstone to the east. If the unconformity could be located in the vicinity of that boundary which Ganly had drawn for Griffith in 1839, and which Hull had used upon his map of 1878, then so much the better. But in 1879 Hull was already admitting that the upper Silurian rocks extended 'father east than the meridian of Cork, and may possibly be found entering the sea about Youghal Bay'.

The location of the unconformity, and its tracing out upon the ground, were clearly tasks that would occupy a great deal of time - far more time than Hull personally could devote to the project. It was for this reason that he secured Ramsay's permission to send McHenry down to Munster to revise the mapping during 1879, 1880, and 1881, and during 1882 Cruise was also sent south to undertake revision in County Cork.

Presumably McHenry was under orders to find the elusive unconformity, and a soul-destroying task it must have proved. He and his colleagues would seem to have had little sympathy with the re-interpretation that Hull was requiring them to enforce. In 1880 Kinahan reported that during conversation after their visit to the southwest with Hull in September 1878, O'Kelly had expressed serious doubts as to whether his Director had read the field-evidence aright, while McHenry had preferred to draw a diplomatic veil of silence over the entire episode. It was not until 1905 - fourteen years after Hull's departure from Ireland - that McHenry summoned up the courage to confess in print that he had no faith in the re-interpretation which he had been required to impose. The Survey's archives reveal that in June 1879, just two months *after* Hull presented his re-interpretation to the Geological Society of London, Baily, McHenry and Richard Clark (he in 1877 had succeeded McHenry as Fossil Collector) were despatched to the southwest to search for fossils that would confirm the upper Silurian age of the Glengarriff Grits. But the trio brought no comfort to Hull. In his report dated 18 June - did Hull notice that it was Waterloo Day? - Baily affirmed that on palaeontological grounds the Glengarriff Grits could not possibly be of Silurian age. They could only be Old Red Sandstone.

As ever, Hull's most vigorous critic was the turbulent Kinahan. He attacked his Director's scheme through the pages of a variety of geological periodicals, and in a forthright paper presented to the British Association at Swansea on 26 August 1880. That particular eruption was perhaps the cause of Hull's precipitate departure from the Swansea meeting to undertake a spontaneous excursion to the less actively volcanic environment represented by the Auvergne. To both Ramsay and Geikie, Kinahan protested that his own early mapping in the southwest was being mutilated to make it conform to Hull's new model, and in a letter to Ramsay on 8 June 1879 he objected to McHenry being:

> ...engaged drawing fanciful boundaries which may make nice looking maps, but are an outrage on geology.

In his regular confrontations with Hull, Kinahan was by no means always in the right, but in opposing Hull's re-interpretation of the Munster stratigraphy Kinahan was entirely justified. Hull had launched the Survey upon a wild-goose chase. Modern geologists would agree with Kinahan that in the far southwest there is no great hiatus between the Glengarriff Grits and the overlying Carboniferous rocks, and even at Sneem, Hull's type locality for the unconformity, Hull's successors have been entirely unable to discern that unconformity which Hull claimed was present (see p.227).

The same is true farther to the east. The major unconformity between the supposed upper Silurian strata of the west and the Old Red Sandstone of the east - the unconformity for which McHenry had to search - was just a chimaera. Nowhere between the Iveragh Peninsula in the west and the Lismore-Youghal region in the east is there any regionally significant stratigraphical discontinuity. The rocks throughout this tract of country either all had to be upper Silurian or else they all had to be Old Red Sandstone, and since Hull had already advocated an upper Silurian age for the rocks in the west, he had no alternative but to re-classify as upper Silurian all those rocks of eastern County Cork which previously had been mapped as Old Red Sandstone. It was there, in eastern County Cork, that the full absurdity of Hull's re-interpretation became painfully apparent; it was there that the trap was fully sprung.

The town of Fermoy (Sheet 176) stands upon the Carboniferous rocks flooring the North Cork Syncline. A few kilometres to the southwest of Fermoy, anticlinal sandstones and conglomerates rise above the syncline to form the Nagles Mountains; a few kilometres to the northeast of Fermoy, seemingly identical sandstones and conglomerates rise above the syncline to form the Kilworth and Knockmealdown mountains (see Plate XI). The rocks rising on either side of the syncline, let it again be emphasised, are lithologically identical, but, according to Hull's re-interpretation, the rocks to the south of Fermoy were Dingle Beds or Glengarriff Grits of upper Silurian age, while the rocks to the north of Fermoy were Old Red Sandstone of Devonian age. The rocks to the south were to be designated as b^6 and tinted with a muddy grey-brown; the rocks to the north were to be designated c^2 and tinted with a rich red-brown. It was ridiculous but Hull had no alternative.

Hull did allow the Dingle Beds to extend as far east as the shores of the St George's Channel on Sheet 188 (Youghal). But farther to the north, in the Fermoy region, he this time could find no *modus vivendi* for himself by invoking yet another eastward extension of his upper Silurian rocks. He was at the end of a road. To the east the beds forming the Kilworth and Knockmealdown mountains rest upon true Silurian strata with marked unconformity. The

Kilworth and Knockmealdown rocks thus had to be of Old Red Sandstone age.

Hull was asking the geological world to extend its credulity to the acceptance of three suppositions.

> 1. That while the pre-Carboniferous rocks on either side of the North Cork Syncline might appear to be identical, this was an illusion. The rocks to the north of the syncline were of Old Red Sandstone age while those in the south were of upper Silurian age.
>
> 2. That within the width of the North Cork Syncline - a distance of a mere 5 kilometres - the entire Old Red Sandstone sequence of southern Ireland - a sequence containing thousands of metres of strata - simply died out.
>
> 3. That while it was admittedly difficult to discern in the field, there was really a major discontinuity intervening near Fermoy between the supposed upper Silurian rocks to the south of the North Cork Syncline and the overlying younger strata on the northern side of the syncline.

McHenry had failed to find any real unconformity to support Hull's conception of the Munster stratigraphy, so the Survey had to invent an unconformity just as Ganly had invented an unconformity for Griffith in 1839. Adjudication as between the relative merits of two fictitious unconformities perhaps absurd, but it can at least be said that Ganly's unconformity followed a topographical boundary. Hull, on the other hand, was inviting his geological contemporaries to indulge in an act of blind faith which was entirely unsupported by field-evidence of any type.

All the published one-inch sheets depicting those parts of Munster revised by Cruise and McHenry between 1879 and 1882 now carry an inscription such as 'Revised in 1880 by Alex. McHenry M.R.I.A.', and a reader might be misled into believing that the sheets had been published soon after the date of the revision. The truth is more complex. A new edition for the Killarney region (Sheet 173), incorporating revisions by Cruise and McHenry, was published in 1883, and in the same year revised versions of sheets 171, 174, 175, and 176 were engraved by the Ordnance Survey. Publication of those four sheets was deferred, however, because Geikie wished to examine the revision in the light of the field-evidence. In the spring of 1884 he therefore toured the southwest in company with McHenry himself, and Geikie's verdict was that publication of the revised maps, whether engraved or not, should for the moment be delayed.

It would be satisfactory to be able to record that a few brief days in the field had been sufficient to convince an astute Geikie of the speciousness of Hull's re-interpretation, but in reality such was not the case. In 1884 Geikie delayed the publication of the revised one-inch sheets not for scientific reasons, but simply upon the grounds of political expediency. At the time, he was under severe governmental pressure to bring the entire geological survey of Britain and Ireland to a speedy conclusion. He knew that his political masters would object strongly if they saw the Irish Survey diverting some of its energies into the preparation of revised maps in advance of the completion of the outstanding one-inch sheets of northern Ireland.

Once the national coverage of one-inch sheets was complete - the final sheet was published in November 1890 - then the situation was changed, and, with Geikie's approval, the geologists in Hume Street - Hull himself had now gone into retirement - began to prepare the revised Munster sheets for publication. There were thirty sheets involved (sheets 171, 172, 174-177, and 182-205), and on 12 November 1890 a first batch of fifteen of the revised sheets was despatched from Hume Street to the Ordnance Survey for engraving. On many of the sheets only small changes had to be introduced, but the Ordnance Survey moved slowly, and not until 5 November 1892 did revised versions of the last of the thirty sheets arrive back in Hume Street. Next, the geologists prepared coloured pattern copies of the revised sheets, and on 18 November 1892 twenty-two of the pattern copies were sent over to London for Geikie's approval. It was at this juncture that skeletons began to be found in cupboards.

On 29 November 1892 Geikie wrote to Dublin expressing his disquiet with certain features of the geology being depicted upon the pattern copies, and he soon fastened upon the Fermoy sheet - Sheet 176 - as the most dubious sheet in the set. On 28 January 1893 he wrote to Hume Street as follows:

> Would you ask McHenry to draw me a rough section of what he supposes to be the structure of the ground along the eastern margin of Sheet 176....I specially want to know the evidence for the sudden disappearance of the Old Red Sandstone southwards when it is so copiously developed north of the Fermoy-Lismore syncline.

McHenry replied on 31 January 1893; the truth came out at last. First, he confessed that during his revision he had never seen even so much as a hint of an unconformity intervening between Hull's upper Silurian Dingle Beds and the overlying Carboniferous strata.

> In the very many sections that I examined the two sets of rocks were perfectly conformable. In no instance did I notice what could be looked upon for a moment as otherwise.

Second, he admitted that ever since 1880 he had been convinced that the pre-Carboniferous rocks on either side of the North Cork Syncline were really identical. But, he explained, Hull had told him that the geology lying northward of the syncline was none of his concern, and McHenry, the policeman's son and former Fossil Collector, now protested to the Director-General that 'my duty was to simply obey my instructions'. So much for the geological map as an exercise in objective observational science.

Faced with such admissions, Geikie had before him only one possible course of action. As in 1884, he decided to withhold the revised sheets, but this time his motive was not political expediency. It was, rather, a desire for scientific rationality. The annual report of the Irish Survey for 1893 contains the following note:

> The publication of revised editions of a large number of maps in the South of Ireland has been postponed - further consideration being deemed necessary by the Director-General.

The revised version of Sheet 173 had been published in 1883, and some copies of at least two of the other four sheets engraved that year - sheets 174 and 175 - also seem to have reached the public sometime between 1883 and 1892, although the publication of these sheets was never officially announced.

And what was the fate of the other sheets revised by McHenry between 1879 and 1881? Many of them were never published. On 27 October 1894 the geologists in Hume Street received from Geikie a directive informing them that henceforth all the rocks which Hull had reclassified as Dingle Beds were to revert to being coloured as Old Red Sandstone. Jukes's interpretation was to be restored. Early in the twentieth century the problem of the Munster stratigraphy was again brought prominently before the Survey, first, during an investigation of the drifts of the Cork region in 1903 (see p.118), and second, during a revision of the geology of the Killarney and Kenmare district between 1911 and 1913 (see pp.138 and 227). These two surveys highlighted surviving inconsistencies upon the Munster sheets, and as a result, Grenville Cole, the then Director of the Irish Survey, prepared new versions of all the thirty sheets affected by Hull's 1879-82 revision. All the sheets revised by Cole were issued on the eve of World War I bearing the inscription 'Re-edited 1913'.

Since the Survey had perpetrated the ill-advised Munster revision, it was only just that, in the fullness of time, the Survey should have made recompense by itself publishing a damning critique of Hull's conception of the region's stratigraphy. This happened when Wright prepared the new memoir for the Killarney and Kenmare district - a memoir which, after some delay, was eventually published in 1927 (see p.158).

One question about Hull's revision of the Munster stratigraphy remains to be asked. Why did he devise and cause the Survey to carry through so doubtful a geological project? The answer may be that around 1878 he had strong personal reasons for wishing to capture the geological limelight. Throughout the 1870s it must have been clear that Ramsay was unlikely to remain Director-General for very long. Now if the next Director-General was to come from within the ranks of the Survey, then it follows that Hull must have perceived himself as being one of the three most likely contenders for the office. The other two obvious candidates were Archibald Geikie, then the Director of the Scottish Survey, and Henry William Bristow, the Survey's Senior Director for England and Wales. Hull was senior to Geikie in the service, and he was more in the public eye than was Bristow. Perhaps he believed that by publishing a few seminal papers - by doing something startling in the south of Ireland - he would be able to strengthen his claims upon the Survey's senior post and go some way towards countering the very considerable reputation that Geikie had already achieved through the wielding of his own facile pen.

Is it entirely fortuitous that between April 1877 and January 1882 Hull read to the Geological Society of London five rather grandiose papers? In one of those papers he made a clear bid for geological immortality. He attempted to establish the concept of a Devono-Silurian stratigraphical episode, and he thus sought to join that elite band consisting of those few geologists who have been founders of geological systems. The last two of these five papers were read to the Society on 11 January 1882, just four weeks and three days after Geikie in Edinburgh had received a letter from the Earl Spencer inviting him to accept the directorship-general. The succession decided - the prize lost - never again during his tenure of the Irish directorship did Hull publish a paper in the *Quarterly Journal* of the Geological Society of London.

If it really was personal ambition which clouded Hull's geological judgement during the 1870s, then as a scientist he must of course stand condemned. But there was an extenuating circumstance. We must have a sneaking sympathy for Hull as a man. If he really was trying to escape from Dublin to London, then his desire so to do is readily understandable. In Hume Street he was having serious problems of a personal nature. Kinahan was proving intractable and was evidently resolved to make his Director's life as intolerable as possible.

During the nineteenth century the Irish Survey was not infrequently the scene of personality clashes between some of its officers. Henry James had taken exception to T.E. James in 1845; Oldham had fought with M'Coy; and Jukes had crossed swords with Baily, Du Noyer, and Kinahan. But all such affairs pale into insignificance as compared with the feud between Hull and Kinahan which shattered the peace of Hume Street, burst into the chambers of several learned institutions, and even infiltrated into the geological literature. The pouring of oil upon the troubled Irish waters became one of the principal tasks of both Ramsay and Geikie during their respective terms as Director-General. No history of the Survey can afford to overlook this lamentable episode.

Kinahan was a large, tough, shaggy individual. From October 1876 until October 1882, he and his family lived at Avoca, in the mineral district of County Wicklow, and there he was known to the locals as 'the big miner'. Geikie once described him as being 'not the kind of antagonist one would care to encounter in a personal scuffle'. Of his devotion to geology there can be no doubt. Almost forty years of continuous activity in the field gave him an unrivalled knowledge of Ireland's rocks, and throughout his life there flowed from his pen a steady stream of papers, pamphlets, and books.

Some of Kinahan's work for the Survey was admirable. On 24 March 1868, for instance, Jukes wrote to him as follows:

> On examining the six-inch maps of the Galway district which you have sent me I have only to give every praise to he neatness of the execution of the work and the care with which the observations seem to have been made.

On the other hand, much of his work - especially his later work - was idiosyncratic, confused, and deficient in scientific logic. Many of his six-inch field-sheets are crude and untidy. Some of his mapping the Survey even refused to accept. In June and November 1884 Geikie and Hull inspected Kinahan's revision mapping of sheets 148 and 149 around Gorey in County Wexford, and they found the work so unsatisfactory that they ordered the destruction of the type for the memoir that Kinahan had written to accompany the two sheets - a memoir which was already at page-proof stage. On 21 December 1885 Geikie wrote to Hull about Kinahan's work upon Sheet 17 in County Donegal:

> With regard to the Map, I do not think the alterations are yet satisfactory. Mr Kinahan's conception of the structure of the district is so entirely different from those of his colleagues, and I must add from my own, which I formed after examination of his ground with him, that I do not think any further progress can be made with the Map until you take an opportunity of going over the disputed ground with him, and with one or more of the officers who have worked the adjacent tracts.

In less serious vein, but indicative of his slapdash approach, there is this story of Kinahan which circulated widely within the British Survey. One day, in a work-room in Hume Street, Kinahan encountered two of his colleagues comparing their maps of adjacent ground and trying to relate their respective lines. 'Joinin'-up, eh?', observed Kinahan, 'If I see throuble brewin', I just dhraw a hell of a fault along the whole confounded frontier, and cut off every blessed line'.

In temperament Kinahan was highly variable. Sometimes he was placid, pliable, and filled with child-like innocence. This was the mood in which Geikie discovered him when he went down to Avoca on 30 June 1882, and that evening Geikie found himself returning to Dublin by train with an armful of flowers as a gift from the Kinahans to the Hulls. But for much of the time Kinahan was a victim of black moods during which he was clearly intolerable and perhaps even physically dangerous. Jukes had trouble with him from about 1866 onwards, and few of Kinahan's colleagues were immune from his vituperations.

In 1872 Kinahan and Cruise spent three months together running sections in Connemara where, as regulations allowed, they hired two assistants and shared the cost involved. Later, in his capacity of District Surveyor, Kinahan applied to the Survey for a refund of the money which the two officers had laid out, but when the reimbursement was made, he pocketed the entire sum and refused to concede Cruise's entitlement to a share. In 1877 Hugh Leonard was sent down to County Wexford to assist Kinahan in his revision of Sheet 158 around Enniscorthy. Kinahan demanded his colleague's immediate withdrawal as being 'perfectly useless', yet Leonard was his own brother-in-law. When McHenry was despatched to Cork and Kerry in 1879 to begin the Munster revision, Kinahan protested that his own early mapping was 'being put into the hands of ignorant officers'. In 1883-84, when, as the second-in-command, Kinahan took charge of the Survey during Hull's absence in the Middle East (see p.97), he fell out with Wynne in the Survey's office. The cause of the altercation was Wynne's efforts to re-organise the storage of the six-inch field-sheets, and when Hull and Geikie read the resultant correspondence they were appalled. Geikie always tried to be sympathetic towards Kinahan, but on 25 February 1884 even he wrote to Hull observing that Kinahan had written to Wynne:

> ...in a tone that seems purposely meant to be insolent and irritating, and is as far removed as possible from the language which should be used by a superior officer to those under his charge. The perusal of this correspondence has painfully convinced me that in future it will be impossible for me to allow Mr Kinahan to occupy any position of authority over his colleagues.

Henceforth Kinahan insultingly addressed Wynne only as 'the Office Keeper' instead of employing his proper title of 'the Resident Geologist'.

But it was Hull himself who was cast in the role of Kinahan's principal *bête noir*. Hull seated in the Director's office was a thorn buried deeply in Kinahan's flesh; the pain made him angry and sometimes resulted in his becoming mentally unhinged. Hull himself sometimes lacked tact and forbearance in his dealing with Kinahan, and occasionally he, too, descended into fits of ill-advised fury. On 9 January 1882, for instance, he wrote a letter to the *Geological Magazine* criticising some of Kinahan's views, and couched in such terms that one can only express surprise that the editor - Henry Woodward - should have accepted the letter for publication. Kinahan must have found wry satisfaction in the fact that two months later Hull had to publish a retraction of the letter, expressing 'regret for having allowed myself to pen it'.

Hull was thus by no means an entirely blameless element within this turbulent relationship, yet there can be no doubt but that the guilt lay overwhelmingly upon Kinahan's side. In view of the relentless and severe provocation that Hull experienced, the wonder is not that he occasionally lost his equilibrium, but rather that for most of the time he managed to keep the work of the Survey moving forward so smoothly and so effectively. We must sympathise with the request that Hull made to Geikie on 25 August 1882. He had himself just lost the opportunity of escape from Ireland through promotion to the office of Director-General, and in despair he now wrote to Geikie inviting him to remove Kinahan from Ireland to the Survey of Scotland or to that of England and Wales. But Geikie chose to take no such action.

Trouble between Kinahan and Hull erupted within only weeks of Hull's arrival in Dublin, and on 9 August 1869 Kinahan's truculence earned him a reprimand from Murchison. Thereafter the next twenty years saw a series of continual skirmishes which resulted in Kinahan receiving repeated warnings from the Director-General, many of those warnings involving threats of dismissal if he failed to mend his ways. Indeed, on a number of occasions he was informed that he would have been dismissed had the Director-General not been aware of the hardship that must befall his wife and family were he to be deprived of both his post and his pension. Any blow by blow discussion of the encounters between Hull and Kinahan would require a full book; all that can be offered here are samples illustrative of the four types of tactic employed by Kinahan during his conduct of the war.

First, he used obstructionist tactics. In September 1869 he delayed the proofs for the memoir to Sheet 95 (Headford) by insisting that he had to revise the punctuation. In January 1871 he explained that the pressure of his other work was making it impossible for him to complete indexes for certain of the memoirs for which he was responsible. In the summer of 1876 he tried to hold up publication of Sheet 93 (Clifden) by protesting that certain important faults had been omitted. In December 1881 he explained to Hull, with mock sincerity, that indoor work upon his maps was impossible at Avoca during the winter because the configuration of the Vale of Avoca resulted in the winter sun affording him with insufficient illumination. In September 1886 he protested that he was unable to prepare a certain sheet memoir because he had been sent too few sheets of foolscap, while in January 1888 he complained that he was unable to colour his maps because he had been sent only inferior brushes and he needed sable-haired brushes!

And then there was the case of the memoir to sheets 138 and 139 covering southern County Wicklow. These two sheets had been published in 1856, but there was no accompanying memoir, so while he was stationed at Avoca around 1880 Kinahan was under instruction to remedy this lacuna. His revision of a part of the two sheets was inspected by Geikie and Hull in the Avoca-Aughrim-Woodenbridge-Arklow district on 27 and 28 March 1884, and they refused to accept Kinahan's interpretation of the local structure. In a report dated 3 April 1884 Geikie wrote:

> The revision of the maps by Mr Kinahan appeared to me altogether reckless and not warranted by any evidence to be obtained on the ground itself....If the work were everywhere as worthless as where I have personally tested it, the gravest consequences would follow.

Hull therefore took upon himself the task of completing the missing memoir, making use of some of Kinahan's material with appropriate acknowledgement. Kinahan was furious. He fought a delaying action over the memoir, and during Hull's absence from Dublin in March 1888 he sent to the Director's room for various maps and documents relating to the memoir, modified the proofs of the memoir to his liking, and then sent them off to London to be printed. When Hull returned to Hume Street there took place in the Director's room, on 28 March, a particularly ugly scene at which Cruise, McHenry, and Wynne were the witnesses, it having been Hull's policy since April 1876 never to interview Kinahan without a third party being present. That particular Wednesday morning, however, Hull may have regarded his three colleagues not so much in the role of passive observers, as in the role of a potential bodyguard should physical violence occur, because we are told that Kinahan struck a defiant pose before storming from the room uttering threats.

In fairness to Kinahan it should be noted that he may have felt a rather poignant relationship with the memoir to sheets 138 and 139. His son Gerrard had turned to geology, and some of his observations had found a place within the memoir, but Gerrard himself had been killed by a poisoned arrow on 27 May 1886 while participating in a mineral survey in the Niger basin of West Africa.

Second, Kinahan employed the tactic of studied insolence. On 3 March 1871 he began a letter to Hull: 'I am in the receipt of your letter dated in hieroglyphics'. In his official report upon his activities during 1872 he claimed to have spent his time in mapping, in the running of sections, and in trying to defend his character 'from the calumny of Mr Hull'. On 8 November 1881 he wrote to Hull observing that he was an incompetent Director and that he ought to resign. Should he decline to accept this advice, then Kinahan wanted to know how much of his salary Hull was prepared to make over to him for the performance of those duties which were beyond Hull's ability. When he submitted his quarterly financial return for the second quarter of 1887, Edward Best at the Survey's London headquarters noted that Kinahan had 'had the brainless folly to write the remark which you will see'.

Ramsay was the shocked witness of one of Kinahan's episodes of monstrous insolence. In August 1877 Ramsay and Hull were touring County Wicklow, and they arranged to meet Kinahan at the beautifully situated Woodenbridge Hotel on 17 August, Kinahan having been instructed to come down from Avoca bringing his field-sheets together with any correspondence that might have arrived for either Ramsay or Hull. He appeared bearing Ramsay's mail but he had deliberately left his field-sheets behind, and upon Hull enquiring about his own letters, Kinahan retorted angrily: 'Am I to be Mr Hull's postman!' Ramsay noted in his diary that Kinahan was 'outrageously savage in his conduct to Hull', and he continued:

> Altogether he was so insulting to Hull & so sulky with me, that after a 1/2 hours thought, I told him I had decided not to go further in that direction & he might return to his quarters.

Third, Kinahan employed the tactic of regular disobedience. Repeatedly he refused to obey Hull's orders, raising against them a multitude of what Geikie once termed 'frivolous objections'. He refused to conform to the Survey's rules for the nomenclature of rock types. He refused to sign for maps that he borrowed from Hume Street. He flouted the Survey's rules by publishing papers without first obtaining permission. He objected when he was required to move from one field-station to another, and his removal from Avoca to Letterkenny, County Donegal, in October 1882 was the cause of particular acrimony. In County Donegal, in 1884, he wanted to map the Fanad Peninsula, but it was a part of the ground which Hull had already assigned to Cruise. Kinahan nevertheless went off with the six-inch sheets of Fanad, and he proceeded to map the region. In October 1888 he had to be severely reprimanded for wasting time in the unauthorised mapping of a part of the Inishowen Peninsula which had already been surveyed by Cruise.

Finally - and here the Irish Survey's dirty linen was displayed for all to see - Kinahan sought publicly to subvert Hull's reputation as a geologist. Whenever Hull entered into print on some aspect of Irish geology, there commonly followed a reply from Kinahan expressing his vigorous disagreement with Hull's conclusions. Often, it seems, the burden of Kinahan's geological writings owed just as much to personal malice as to the principles of scientific reasoning.

When Hull spoke to the Royal Geological Society of Ireland on 11 January 1871 on the subject of the Ballycastle Coalfield, Kinahan replied in the December issue of the *Geological Magazine*. When Hull wrote about the drifts so magnificently displayed in the coastal cliffs southward of Killiney in County Dublin, Kinahan wrote claiming that Hull had misunderstood what he had seen. When Hull proposed his re-interpretation of the stratigraphy of Munster, Kinahan mounted a major counter-attack through the pages of a number of journals including those of the *Transactions of the Manchester Geological Society*. At first sight the involvement of that particular journal in an Irish dispute might seem incongruous, but the wily Kinahan had doubtless discovered that Hull had been an honorary member of the Manchester society since 1874. When Hull turned to microscope petrology, Kinahan followed suit, and so the confrontation continued until that day in 1891 when Hull finally shifted his residence from Dublin to London.

Today Kinahan is one of the best remembered figures of the nineteenth-century Irish Survey, and there is a widespread belief that he played a major role in the Survey's mapping programme. Such a view stands in need of revision. In Jukes's day Kinahan certainly was one of the Survey's stalwarts. His name features upon twenty-seven one-inch sheets issued between his joining of the Survey in August 1854, and Jukes's death in July 1869. But with the advent of Hull, Kinahan's role was changed. From July 1869 down to the autumn of 1890 Kinahan's name appeared upon only eleven new one-inch sheets, and of these, no less than seven had been surveyed either in whole or in part during Jukes's tenure of the directorship. For comparison, Symes's name appears upon twenty-nine new sheets issued during Hull's regime.

Throughout the greater part of Hull's directorship, Kinahan was stationed far to the south of the Survey's northward advancing mapping-front. As the Survey's sole officer in the rank of District Surveyor, Kinahan should have been at that front co-ordinating, supervising the younger men, and bringing to bear upon their field-problems his long geological experience. But that is not what happened. Rather did Hull station him far to the south of the mapping-front, first at Wexford (1872 to 1876) and then at Avoca (1876 to 1882). From these stations his assigned duty was merely revision mapping. Not until Kinahan was transferred from Avoca to Letterkenny in October 1882 did he again find himself working alongside his colleagues in the mapping of virgin territory.

Until the October 1882, it seems to have been Hull's policy (and perhaps that of the Director-General himself) to keep Kinahan at work as far away as was possible from the ground being investigated by his brother officers. Perhaps there was a real fear that his explosive temperament might damage the progress of the enterprise. When Hull went to the Middle East in the winter of 1883, leaving Kinahan in charge of the Survey (see p.97), Geikie was at pains to emphasise that there was no need for Kinahan to transfer himself to Dublin, and in particular it was stressed that it was entirely unnecessary for him to visit his colleagues to inspect their work. For his part, from 1869 onwards, Kinahan was perhaps resolved to do for the Survey nothing which might in any way redound to Hull's credit. The Survey's suppression of Kinahan's revision of one-inch sheets 138. 139, 148, and 149, and of the accompanying memoirs that he had written, meant that during his six years of residence at Avoca he contributed virtually nothing to the Survey's published progress.

Kinahan undoubtedly possessed geological talents, but there is no escaping the conclusion that from 1869 onwards he was to the Survey more of an incumbrance that an asset. Geikie appears to have held Hull in low esteem, and he always seems to have felt some sympathy for Kinahan, but on 5 March 1889, when Geikie wrote his confidential report on the future of the Geological Survey of Ireland, even he could offer nothing more than the following curt verdict:

> Mr Kinahan is no longer either bodily or mentally capable of doing useful work for the Survey, and ought to be retired.

It may be that Kinahan's problems were related to the kind of existence which a Survey officer was required to lead. Day after day an officer was alone in the field with his maps. Week after week he spent in the solitary tracing of abstruse boundaries across wind-swept and rain-sodden landscapes. Month after month he had to live surrounded by a peasant people with whom he shared little in common. It must have been easy to become introverted. Within an officer's mind it must have been common for problems - both human and scientific - to expand out of all reasonable proportion.

What wives and children may have thought of the demanding Survey life-style has passed without record. What did Harriette Kinahan think of her five years at Recess in County Galway? What did Frances Du Noyer think of being taken off to 'the Black North'? What did Mrs W.B. Leonard think of living at Glenamoy, County Mayo, in a 'miserable hovel with a clay floor' (see p.298)? I just do not know. What I do know is that as early as 22 September 1852, Jukes wrote to Ramsay about Augusta:

> I am almost beginning to fear she will not be able to stand our wandering life much longer.

But I have no wish to imply that Survey officers perceived their duties to be compulsively obsessive. Many officers found that their geological responsibilities afforded them with the opportunity to develop a wide variety of other interests. The rocks of Ireland may have been their bread and their butter, but Survey duties gave them excuse for their indulgence in a number of other passions.

Jukes was an acute observer of the Irish scene, and the author (under the pseudonym 'Cosmopolite') in 1858 of three articles published in *The Times* on 'The State of Ireland'.

Foot, Kinahan, Symes, and Wynne were all keen natural historians, and Kinahan and Wynne were in 1857 elected Corresponding Members of the Natural History Society of Dublin. Kinahan wrote about the bats, birds, ferns, and fish which he had observed during his Survey work in Connaught. Symes was a leading ichthyologist and ornithologist of the day, and while investigating the rocks of the Burren, Foot also studied the region's botany, meteorology, and zoology. He even sought to transpose his geological techniques into the world of plant geography. This he did by paralleling his map depicting the distribution of the region's strata types with a second and pioneering map illustrative of the distribution of certain Burren plant types.

Archaeology is another subject which very naturally attracted the attention of nineteenth-century Survey officers. They belonged to an age when the movement for Celtic Revival was seeking to retrieve Ireland's past from within the enveloping mists of time, and here Survey officers were peculiarly well placed to make significant contribution. Indeed, the Irish landscape is so replete with archaeological sites that there must have been many occasions when officers bent upon their duties almost literally tripped over the remains of ages far more recent than those normally of concern to the geologist. Kinahan wrote about the crannoges of Lough Rea in County Galway. Nolan wrote a little book about the history and antiquities of Glendalough in County Wicklow. Hardman published a number of archaeological papers in the *Proceedings of the Royal Irish Academy.* Du Noyer was deeply involved in the affairs of the body which in 1890 became the Royal Society of Antiquaries of Ireland.

That reference to Du Noyer opens the window upon another field activity which engaged the attention of Survey officers. Several of them were very competent artists, and their professional itineraries afforded inspiration for their pencils, their pens, and their paints. Indeed, even a cursory examination of the six-inch field-sheets reveals that many officers could not resist the urge to add to their sheets decorative sketches devoid of all relevance to the geological work in hand. Sometimes it was a vignette of the pandemonium within an Irish town upon fair-day. Sometimes it was an impression of a tumble-down cabin, its former inhabitants gone to seek their fortune in some foreign land. Sometimes it was a sketch of a favourite canine field-companion 'hot after chasing a hare'. Among these Survey artists there are two deserving of especial mention: Wynne and Du Noyer.

Wynne was an accomplished water-colourist whose work featured regularly in Dublin exhibitions during the later nineteenth century. On 10 November 1891 Nolan wrote to Wynne:

> Congratulations on the favourable notices of your sketching club work in the papers. I didn't see the show yet.

The walls of my own drawing-room are decorated with three examples of his water-colours. One is an early painting of St Mary's Abbey at Howth, in County Dublin. Another is a painting of redwood trees in California, presumably painted as he journeyed home from India in 1883. The third, entitled 'Solitude' and exhibited at the Dublin Sketching Club exhibition of 1889, is of Lough Dan in County Wicklow. Into that picture, Wynne has introduced a dash of artistic licence. Having recently returned from the East, he clearly felt the rounded, granite skyline of the Wicklow Mountains to be lacking in dramatic appeal. He has therefore introduced snow-capped Himalayan-style peaks as a backcloth to the Wicklow lake!

Du Noyer was the most talented of the Survey artists. Trained under George Petrie, he has left for us a substantial artistic oeuvre of remarkable diversity. His work ranges from botanical and zoological subjects, to paintings of archaeological remains, and landscape panoramas. He even provided some large wall-pieces intended as illustrations to accompany Jukes's geological lectures at the Museum of Irish Industry (see p.277). The large number of archaeological paintings which he presented to the Royal Irish Academy resulted in the grateful Members electing him an Honorary Life Member on 23 February 1863. It is singularly appropriate that he should have received his ultimate seal of artistic approval during the Survey's sesquicentennial year of 1995. The National Gallery of Ireland then paid its own particular tribute to both Du Noyer and the Survey by mounting an exhibition devoted to Du Noyer's artistic achievements. The exhibition, sponsored by Bord Gáis Éireann and entitled *Hidden Landscapes*, was opened before a large invited audience on 20 June 1995, and it remained on view until 31 August following (see frontispiece).

To pass from this artistry on the part of Du Noyer and his colleagues to my next topic is surely to descend from the sublime to the gross. I allude to the indulgence of many an officer in the so-called gentlemanly field-sports. Some officers combined their geology, their natural history, their archaeology, or their artistic talents, with the handling of gun or rod. Kinahan, for example, was a shooting man. His non-geological field activities sometimes brought him into serious conflict with agents and gamekeepers. Once Jukes had to be introduced in the role of mediator. Symes was another officer who was just as handy with a gun as with a hammer. But he was also an enthusiastic fisherman. When he was mapping in County Mayo during the late 1860s he always tried to conclude a day in the field with an hour spent beside some river, rod in hand.

The Survey's field-sportsman *par excellence* was Wilkinson. His autobiography, aptly entitled *Reminiscences of Sport in Ireland*, is a remarkable volume. It is a saga of bags and catches, laced, of course, with tales of those giant fish which escaped to fight another day. Of geology, the science which gave to him his livelihood for almost half a century, there is not a mention. Wilkinson merely informs us that he was a professional surveyor. He evidently considered geology to be *infra dignitatem*. When a fresh edition of his autobiography was published in 1987, as a contribution, let it be noted, to the literature of the field-sports, the author of a new introduction to the volume very naturally made the mistake of jumping to the conclusion that Wilkinson, like his father, had been employed upon the Ordnance Survey of Ireland.

Wilkinson informs us that on his most memorable day with the gun he brought down 125 head of game and wildfowl on the bogs near Swinford in County Mayo (Sheet 65). The outstanding year in his fisherman's log was 1881,

FIGURE 3.18. *Du Noyer was a prolific artist whose work reflects a deep interest in all facets of the Irish landscape. These four vignettes are typical of the scenes to be found in his sketchbooks or added to his field-sheets. The four have kindly been found and assembled for me as here by Dr Jean Archer from items within the Survey's archives.*

Du Noyer seems particularly to have relished the sketching of boats, ships, and the sea. The upper scene of a sloop and a brigantine in a choppy sea is to be found upon his County Dublin six-inch field-sheet, Sheet 12/1. The little watercolour occupies the offshore area of the sheet to the east of Donabate.

Lower left a sea-dragon, with another sloop, adds a humorous touch to an enlargement which Du Noyer had felt it necessary to make of Crossfarnoge Point, lying upon the County Wexford six-inch sheets 51 and 52. The enlargement is dated April 1850, and has been produced from the six-inch sheets by means of the 'squares method'.

Lower right is an ink drawing dated October 1852 and entitled 'Joint surface, Black Slates. Bullens Bay. Old Head of Kinsale. Cleavage resembling Bedding'. To provide scale, Du Noyer has added what is presumably a self-portrait. This drawing is in Geological Sketches of G.V. Du Noyer, *volume II, p.18, in the Survey's archives.*

Attached to the central illustration there would seem to be a sad little tale. Mr Buff, a spaniel, was for many years Du Noyer's field companion. He features in numerous of his master's sketches. This particular drawing, inscribed 'Alass poor Buff', features upon Du Noyer's County Kerry six-inch field-sheet 66/3 in the waters of Lough Leane near to Killarney. The implication is perhaps that Mr Buff met a tragic end in the lake while engaged upon some watery escapade.

when he landed 102 salmon and grilse, mostly on Lough Melvin (sheets 43 and 44) and on the River Erne. But to his lifetime's regret, he never caught a salmon weighing more than 25 lbs (11 kilos).

His wife Alice (she came from Belleek and was herself adept with a rod) tied his flies, and he boasted that he never fished on Sundays. Despite this wifely assistance, and in view of this self-imposed temporal limitation, the reader of Wilkinson's autobiography can only express amazement that he should ever have found time enough to look out his maps and to take himself off to examine a rock. But the Director's annual reports reveal that in reality Wilkinson mapped just as much ground as did any of his colleagues. Indeed, in 1884 his personal total of 99 square miles (260 square kilometres) mapped was larger than the total achieved that year by any of his colleagues.

Director's reports and areas of territory mapped bring us back to the Survey's true sphere of activity - back to geology. In January 1880 the Survey still had to complete and publish thirty-nine of the 205 one-inch sheets necessary to finish the new geological map of Ireland. The rocks remaining to be mapped ranged from the grey limestones of County Sligo to the black basalts of County Antrim. But at the heart of the surviving *terra incognita* there lay the geological fortress of County Donegal, an ancient complex of contorted schists, knotted gneisses, and gnarled granites. No Irish county presents the geologists with a greater challenge. No Irish county displays a more intricate structure. No Irish county imposes upon the geologist a more stringent test of both intellectual capacity and physical stamina. Hull and his officers would clearly have liked to make a slow, cautious, and reflective approach to this, their final major problem. Time was essential, but time, alas, was not on their side.

When it suits them, government departments can have remarkably long memories. Ramsay, Geikie, and Hull all now found that De La Beche's words spoken to Peel during the 1840s were by no means forgotten in official circles. A geological survey of Ireland, he had said, should occupy no more than ten years. By 1880 the Survey had been at work for thirty-five years, and a substantial tract of ground still awaited examination. The authorities waxed impatient. Whitehall demanded that the Irish Survey should bring its work to a speedy conclusion.

On 6 September 1880 his superiors addressed to Ramsay a letter complaining of what they perceived to be a want of energy in the prosecution of the Geological Survey's operations throughout the United Kingdom. They protested that despite the augmentation of the staff since 1867, the annual extent of territory mapped had for ten years been declining. On 26 March 1881 Ramsay was informed that the Survey was to undertake no further revision without first receiving permission from higher authority. On 11 July 1881 Ramsay was told that his superiors had found entirely unacceptable his estimate that the Irish Survey needed a further ten years in which to complete its task. The pressure was on. This was a very different world from that in which James, Oldham, and Jukes had spent ten years upon the production of nothing more than five of 'those footy little county maps'.

In order to expedite affairs, Hull introduced three changes into the Irish Survey's programme. First, he abandoned his plans for publishing fifty-four further six-inch sheets covering mining districts in Queen's County, and in counties Antrim, Carlow, Kilkenny, and Tipperary. Second, he stopped the preparation of duplicate sets of the six-inch sheets; henceforth the working copies of the six-inch sheets were for some years the only ones available. Third, all the revision work in progress was halted, apart from some minor revision carried out by Cruise in Munster during the summer of 1882. McHenry was sent up to County Antrim, and Kinahan - under protest - was removed from Avoca, first to Letterkenny, and then to Rathmelton on the shores of Lough Swilly. Thus by the autumn of 1882 Hull had his entire force deployed at grips with the rocks of Ulster.

One further modification of the Irish Survey's well-tested methods was not of Hull's making; it was the result of a directive from on high. In their search for means of stimulating the geologists to greater efforts, the officials within the Department of Science and Art had lighted upon the six-inch field-mapping which was now the Survey's normal practice throughout the British Isles. Might the Survey's progress not be accelerated if the six-inch mapping was abandoned and a reversion made to the old-style one-inch mapping? The point was put to Ramsay. He clearly doubted the wisdom of such a change, but he was a tired man upon the verge of his retirement. He had no heart for battle with his departmental mandarins. He gave ground.

As a result we find Hull sending a circular dated 9 August 1881 to all his officers. He explained that he had received orders requiring future field-work to be conducted upon one-inch sheets, instead of upon the familiar six-inch sheets. The principle for which Jukes had fought so strenuously during the early 1850s was thus lost largely by default thirty years later. Henceforth six-inch field-mapping would be permitted only in areas of unusual geological complexity or in regions possessing important mineral resources.

For the Department of Science and Art it was something of a Pyrrhic victory. Hull's men claimed, with much justice, that far from accelerating their work, the use of one-inch field-sheets would

PLATE IV. *The work of a compulsive artist. About 1855 Du Noyer was mapping the geology of the country represented upon the County Tipperary six-inch Sheet 90, which includes the Old Red Sandstone of the northern slopes of the Knockmealdown Mountains. There Bay Lough caught his eye and inspired his artistic instincts. He produced his brushes and paints, turned over his field-sheet (Co. Tipperary 90/2 & 4), and left us with this delightful vignette upon the sheet's reverse. The modern geologist instantly recognises that what Du Noyer here depicts is a beautiful example of a cirque, dating from Ireland's recent glacial period, and containing a moraine-dammed tarn. To all this, in the 1850s, Du Noyer and his colleagues were still oblivious. In the distance, to the north, are the Galty Mountains.*

actually retard their progress. In particular, they protested that they would be wasting a great deal of time trying to fix the location of exposures upon the one-inch sheets, a task which was so simple upon the six-inch scale. As a result there arrived in Hume Street a steady stream of requests from the field-staff seeking permission to be allowed to continue with six-inch mapping. The first four such applications arrived in August and September 1881 from Egan in Coleraine, Hardman in Sligo, Kinahan in Avoca, and Symes in Ballymena. All these requests were granted, and by June 1882 more than half of the staff had received Hull's permission to continue working upon six-inch sheets in the traditional manner.

As the officers moved into County Donegal their thoughts very naturally turned to the lessons learned by geologists who elsewhere had grappled with areas of similar complexity. In a paper read to the Geological Society of London on 20 February 1861, Robert Harkness, of Queen's College Cork, had observed that the Donegal rocks display certain similarities to the rocks of the Northwest Highlands of Scotland, and this point was not lost upon Hull. On 7 May 1880 he wrote to Ramsay seeking permission to make an official visit to the Northwest Highlands to see whether the lessons of Highland stratigraphy might have any relevance to an understanding of the geology of Donegal.

Approval granted, the Scottish visit took place later that same month. Hull took Symes with him, and in Scotland they travelled under the guidance of Geikie who was then still the Director of the Scottish Survey. A train of the Highland Railway deposited the visitors at the little station of Garve, near Dingwall, whence they travelled north-westwards, over the Moine Schists and the Durness Limestone, to reach the Torridonian Sandstone in the vicinity of Ullapool. From there they moved northwards to Inchnadamff, and then on to Scourie and Rhiconich to inspect the Lewisian Gneiss. Finally, they turned southeastwards to cross the Moine Schists via Loch Shin in order to regain the Highland Railway at Lairg. They thus made two parallel traverses of the Northwest Highlands some 50 kilometres apart, and they also saw a good deal of the fascinating geology exposed along the western seaboard. But it was hardly time well spent; it was a case of the blind leading the blind.

The stratigraphical interpretation which Geikie presented to his Irish visitors was the interpretation which he and Murchison had offered as far back as 1861 - an interpretation which involved belief in an eastward younging succession, from a Fundamental (Lewisian) Gneiss at the base, up through a Cambrian (Torridonian) Sandstone, to a Lower Silurian series containing the Durness Limestone near the base and the Crystalline (Moine) Schists at the top. The concept of a stratigraphical sequence in which sedimentary strata, such as the Torridonian Sandstone and the Durness Limestone, were overlain by schists, had long troubled certain geologists. But it was not until Charles Lapworth began his now classical studies in Sutherland in 1882 - studies based, be it noted, upon six-inch mapping - that it became clear to all that the apparent stratigraphical succession in the Northwest Highlands was really an illusion. The respected Law of Superposition was there inapplicable. The Crystalline Schists were actually ancient rocks imported into the region from the east along low-angle thrust-faults.

When Hull described his Scottish journey before the Royal Geological Society of Ireland on 20 December 1880, he certainly entertained no thoughts of massive overthrusting. Instead, he had returned from Scotland nagged by one question above all others. Were there to be found in Ireland ancient rocks equivalent to the Fundamental Gneiss which he had seen so splendidly displayed in the heavily glaciated country around Scourie and Rhiconich? For some years there had raged a debate as to whether other outcrops of such ancient rocks - they were then usually termed Laurentian rocks - might exist elsewhere within the British Isles. Now, on 20 December 1880, Hull informed his Dublin audience that during the ensuing summer he would be going to County Donegal in an effort to resolve the question. Did northwestern Ireland contain a counterpart to the Fundamental Gneiss of the Scottish Highlands? Were Hibernia's very foundations to be found exposed somewhere north of the Erne and west of the Foyle?

Upon his map of 1855 Griffith had already indicated the high antiquity of certain rocks in the north and west of Ireland by designating them as 'Azoic (Primary System)', but the absence of obvious Cambrian strata from the greater part of Ireland rendered difficult the positive identification of any still older Pre-Cambrian rocks. Hull was nevertheless full of his usual self-confidence when, in May 1881, he set off for County Donegal accompanied by Symes and Wilkinson.

At that time, Hull subscribed to the view - a view then widely current among Irish geologists - that the Irish granite bodies were largely a result of high-grade metamorphism rather than being a product of the intrusive emplacement of magma. Indeed, at around this period, Hull commonly referred to areas such as Iar-Connaught or the Gweebarra River basin of Donegal as being underlain by gneiss rather than by granite. Influenced by this theory, and guided by Griffith's map (although over twenty-five years old, it was still the only detailed geological map of Donegal), Hull, Symes, and Wilkinson spent almost two weeks examining the southeastern margins of the Donegal

Granite from Fintown to Glen, and the northwestern margins of the Granite from Creeslough to Dunlewy. Hull's conclusion was that what Griffith had represented as granite was really a body of Laurentian gneiss identical to the Fundamental Gneiss of the Scottish Highlands, while the adjacent schists Hull categorised as being of Lower Silurian age, and thus equivalent to the Crystalline Schists of Scotland.

Hull announced his 'discovery' of the existence of Laurentian rocks in Donegal in *Nature* on 26 May 1881, and he went on to argue that the 'gneisses' of the Ox Mountains, Belmullet, and Iar-Connaught were also probably all of Laurentian age. So far as Belmullet and Iar-Connaught were concerned, Hull's decision came too late - the one-inch sheets covering those regions were already published - but Laurentian rocks did feature upon five one-inch sheets published after 1881. They appeared first upon Sheet 26 (Draperstown) published in 1882, the strata designated as Laurentian being the rocks of the Tyrone Igneous Group, and in 1884, Sheet 55 (Sligo, Dromahair, Drumkeeran) represented a portion of the Ox Mountains inlier as 'Metamorphic beds of uncertain age (probably Laurentian)'. The other three sheets showing Archaean or Laurentian rocks are numbers 24 (Donegal, Stranorlar), 31 (Ballyshannon), and 32 (Pettigoe) covering the Lough Derg inlier. The rocks of the inlier had been depicted as quartz schist when the three sheets were first published between 1885 and 1888, but they were redesignated as Archaean gneiss when new versions of the sheets were issued in 1891-92 (see Plate III).

Strangely, when the six sheets covering northwestern Donegal - sheets 3, 4, 9, 10, 15, and 16 - were published in 1889 and 1890, the Donegal Granite was not depicted as a gneiss of Laurentian age. This was because a tour of Donegal with Geikie during October 1887 had caused Hull to abandon his earlier belief that the Donegal Granite was essentially of metamorphic origin. He now accepted that the Granite was an intrusive rock consolidated from an igneous melt, and as such it could only be younger than its enclosing rocks. If, as he still believed, the schists encircling the Donegal Granite were rocks of Lower Silurian age, then there was no way in which the Granite itself could be regarded as being of Laurentian vintage.

Hull's 'discovery' of Laurentian rocks in northwestern Donegal may speedily have proved to be a delusion, but the Survey did make two significant and unexpected finds during the survey of Donegal. First, while mapping the Fanad Peninsula in 1885 the officers came upon a downfaulted outlier of Old Red Sandstone which had featured upon no earlier geological map of the region. Second, in 1887 Kilroe found two tiny outliers of Lower Carboniferous sandstone atop the quartzites of Slieve League at an altitude of 600 metres. Geikie was taken to see the outliers on 24 October 1887, and they made upon him a profound impression as indicating the scale of the denudation experienced by Ireland's Carboniferous strata. From the outliers he drew the inference:

> ... that the Irish coal-fields, now so restricted in extent, once spread far and wide over the hills of Donegal, from which they have since been gradually denuded. Truly the woes of Ireland may be traced back to a very early time, when not even the most ardent patriot can lay blame on the invading Saxon.

Important though it was, the programme of field-mapping underpinning the one-inch sheets was by no means the be-all and end-all of the Survey's nineteenth-century existence. By Hull's day the Survey was widely recognised as possessed of a significant public role, and there now flowed into Hume Street a steady stream of public and private enquiries. Just two examples will serve to illustrate the point. On 14 August 1871 a County Wicklow landlord arrived to ask about the mineral potential of his estate. Hull thought him 'a perfect gentleman'. It was Charles Stewart Parnell up from Avondale and then thinking about home economics rather than Home Rule. In the autumn of 1888 Hull received another visitor. On this occasion it was somebody who, far from wishing to sever Ireland from Britain, proposed instead to bind the two together with a bond of steel. He was an engineer representing a group of speculators who were hoping to raise the finance necessary for the construction of a submarine railway tunnel between Larne and Stranraer. He wanted to know whether their plan was likely to encounter any geological problems.

Hull was also involved in some consultancy work far beyond Ireland's shores. In 1873 he went down the Danube to report upon the mineral potential of an estate somewhere near to the Iron Gate. It was a commission for which he never received the promised fee. In 1890 (not 1886, as he claims in his autobiography) he crossed to the United States, accompanied by Hyland, in order to explore a large Tennessee mineral property on behalf of a London syndicate. The two geologists crossed from Queenstown to New York in the brand-new, Belfast-built liner *Majestic*, and this time Hull received what he termed 'a substantial bonus'.

The oddest of Hull's overseas commissions was that to the Middle East in 1883-84. Prior to this episode Hull lacked experience of desert travel, he was ignorant of Arabic, and his knowledge of the Middle East was derived largely from his assiduous studies in the Old Testament. But for some reason the London-based Palestine Exploration Fund asked him to lead an expedition which was to map the

FIGURE 3.19. *Boulders of Wicklow Granite forming the memorial which marks the grave of George Henry Kinahan in the Church of Ireland graveyard at Avoca in County Wicklow. His wife Harriette is also buried here, but the granite has not held well its carved inscription and the wording is now scarcely legible.* (Photograph by the author.)

topography and geology of the Wadi Araba lying between the Dead Sea and the Gulf of Aqaba. A young major of the Royal Engineers - an Irishman from County Kerry - had agreed to spend his leave with the expedition assisting in the topographical surveying. The geologist and the soldier introduced themselves to each other at Shepheard's Hotel, Cairo, in November 1883. According to Hull the two of them got along famously, but we now know that the soldier developed a strong personal dislike of Hull. He was contemptuous both of Hull's ignorance of the Arab and of Hull's persistent fear that the expedition was on the point of being annihilated in an Arab ambush. Of the soldier's own bravery there could be no question. He was Horatio Herbert Kitchener, the future Earl Kitchener of Khartoum. While Hull and Kitchener were exploring the Biblical Wilderness of Zin, Kinahan in Ireland was creating a personal wilderness of sin. He had been left in charge of the Survey, and, as we have seen (p.88), the few months of Hull's absence from Hume Street amply demonstrated Kinahan's unfitness for executive responsibility.

One other officer was involved in an overseas assignment. In February 1883 Hardman was seconded 'on special colonial service' to Western Australia. There his investigations proved to be of enormous value, and he played the major part in the discovery of the Kimberley Goldfield. The Western Australian government was anxious to appoint him to the post of State Geologist, but the local Legislative Council raised financial objection. With some reluctance, Hardman had to return to Ireland in 1885 when the London authorities refused to grant him any extension of his leave of absence. That return was disastrous for Hardman and his family. Only eighteen months after arriving back in Ireland, he was struck down by typhoid, his constitution having been undermined by a chest infection recently developed as a result of working in bad weather around Woodenbridge in County Wicklow. He had been sent there to prepare a memoir to sheets 138 and 139, Kinahan's proposed memoir having been declared unacceptable. Ironically, in Western Australia there had just been removed the financial objections to his appointment as State Geologist, but it was now his widow who received £500 as a gratuity from the Western Australian government in recognition of Hardman's auriferous discovery at Kimberley.

In April 1887, as Hardman fought for his life in Dublin's Adelaide Hospital, two of his colleagues were up in County Donegal putting into place the final pieces of that immense jigsaw puzzle which is the one-inch geological map of Ireland. By the previous summer - the summer of 1886 - the

Survey had completed its mapping of every county save for Donegal. During that summer almost the entire weight of the Survey had been thrown against the rocks of the far northwest. Then Cruise, Egan, Kilroe, McHenry, Mitchell, Nolan, and Symes had all completed the mapping of their assigned Donegal ground. When 1887 dawned, only 94 square kilometres of Donegal remained to be surveyed, 78 square kilometres being in Kinahan's ground around Rathmelton and Church Hill, and 16 square kilometres being in Wilkinson's ground out upon the Rosguil Peninsula.

During the summer of 1887 it was Wilkinson who completed his ground first. Kinahan decided that he would have to defer the examination of some of his ground until access became easier after the harvest. The harvest was early that year - it had been an unusually hot, dry summer - and Kinahan remained at his field-station in Rathmelton until the end of October. It must have been one evening towards the close of that month when Kinahan plied his hammer upon the very last rock exposure to receive examination during the Survey's primary geological mapping of Ireland. The campaign which had opened at Hook Head in the summer of 1845, was now come to a close forty-two years later by the shores of Lough Swilly.

Although the primary mapping of Ireland was now complete, the Survey still had before it three further years of work connected with the mapping. That work was of five types.

First, pattern copies of the final one-inch sheets had to be prepared, and the publication of the sheets themselves had to be arranged. Three new one-inch sheets were published in 1887, four in 1888, five in 1889, and seven in 1890. The final sheet to appear was Sheet 10 (Kilmacrenan). It was published on 21 November 1890, and it is a most attractive and striking sheet, depicting a region of high geological complexity around Creeslough and Letterkenny.

Second, the accompanying sheet memoirs had to be completed, and the last of them - the memoir to sheets 22, 23, 30, and part of 31 - was published in April 1892.

Third, the regular preparation of duplicate copies of the six-inch field-sheets had ceased in 1881 in order to expedite the progress of the survey, and this deficiency now had to be remedied. In October 1888 Hull reported that some two hundred six-inch field-sheets remained to be copied.

Fourth, eleven sheets of longitudinal sections had to be prepared for northern Ireland, and the last of these (Sheet 35) was not published until December 1894.

Finally, as a result of the Science and Art Department's opposition to six-inch field-mapping, several areas of County Donegal had been mapped only upon the one-inch scale. One such an area was the Slieve League Peninsula, and it was now decided to re-map the peninsula on the six-inch scale. The task was assigned to Kilroe, and he completed his re-investigation during the summer of 1889.

While the final Irish one-inch maps and memoirs were being prepared for publication, Geikie decided that it was desirable for some of the Irish staff to visit Scotland in order to see something of the exciting discoveries which the Scottish Survey had been making in the Northwest Highlands. Following upon Lapworth's seminal work in Sutherland in 1882, Geikie had immediately set some of his most experienced staff to work in the region, and their revelation of the presence of a series of folds and over-thrusts of awe-inspiring complexity had begun to excite the attention of the entire geological world.

Geikie had badly burned his fingers in the Northwest Highlands. For far too long he had clung to his own and Murchison's false interpretation of the stratigraphy of the region as a normal sedimentary succession. Now he had made ample acknowledgement both of his own error and of the brilliance of Lapworth's tectonic interpretation, but he was determined that he and the Survey would not be caught out for a second time. If the rocks of the Northwest Highlands enshrined some lesson that the Irish Survey should learn, then that lesson must be administered before the Irish officers finally committed themselves through the publication of the remaining Donegal one-inch sheets and memoirs. The rocks of northwestern Ireland were patently similar to those of western Scotland. Was it not likely that they had shared a common history?

The party selected for the Scottish excursion consisted of Kilroe, Kinahan, McHenry, Nolan, and Wilkinson, and they crossed from Belfast to Greenock on the night of 4-5 July 1888. In the Northwest Highlands they visited much of the same ground around Inchnadamff as Hull had seen in 1880, and their guide was the leader of Geikie's team in the area, the redoubtable and much loved Benjamin Neeve Peach. The Irish party was back in Dublin by 24 June, and each member of the group was then required to write for Geikie a report relating what they had seen in Scotland to their experience of Irish geology. Those reports were not very enlightening; the Irishmen understandably found it difficult to relate the geology of Donegal to that of the Northwest Highlands. This, for instance, is an extract from Nolan's equivocal report dated 10 July 1888:

> I do not think we shall find evidence for anything like the extensive displacements that have occurred in Sutherlandshire, yet it seems not improbable that some such movements have played an important part in shaping the geology of Donegal and may serve to explain much that is now obscure.

Geikie himself remained persistent. If the ancient rocks of Ireland contained secrets comparable to those which the Scottish rocks had so long concealed from him, then Geikie was determined to unmask those secrets. In the spring of 1889 he therefore brought Peach over to Ireland, and he and Peach scoured counties Mayo and Galway in the company of McHenry and Hyland. From Benwee Head, County Mayo, they travelled to Belmullet, to Achill Island, and thence via Westport and the southern shores of Clew Bay, to Killary Harbour. From there they moved on to Clifden, along the margin of the quartzites forming the Twelve Pins, past the old constabulary barracks at Recess which for many years had been a home for the Kinahan family, and so on to Galway city. But Geikie had to admit that the excursion had been disappointing. Even the discerning eye of Peach had seen little more in the rocks than had the eyes of the men of the Irish Survey some twenty years before.

As Geikie travelled through Ireland in that spring of 1889 he must have carried with him one problem which was administrative rather than geological. What should happen to the Geological Survey of Ireland now that it had accomplished its appointed task of mapping the country's geology? Back in London there were politicians and civil servants who had always regarded the Geological Survey of Great Britain and Ireland as engaged upon a task of finite duration. Once the geological map of the British Isles was completed, then surely the Survey could be disbanded. The Irish section of that map had been finished first, so clearly the Irish Survey must now pay the penalty of becoming the first part of the Geological Survey of the United Kingdom to be extirpated by Whitehall's scalpel of economy. Geikie was well aware of the danger. He saw no hope of trying to maintain the Irish Survey at anything like its 1889 levels of staffing and finance. Even Hull was pessimistic. He could see little future role for the Survey. On 24 October 1888 he wrote to Geikie saying:

> ... unless for a few isolated districts, I regard the field work of the Survey as so accurate and complete in all its details that I cannot regard a general revision of the Geological Survey of Ireland as either necessary or desirable.

On the other hand Geikie was convinced - and rightly so - that Ireland had a continuing need for a Geological Survey presence. Some compromise was clearly called for. Early in March 1889 Geikie recommended to his superiors that the Geological Survey of Ireland should be spared, but that its establishment should be reduced. Just a small staff should be left in Dublin and charged with the task of handling routine geological enquiries from the public, with the responsibility of keeping the one-inch sheets available and up-to-date, and with the duty of undertaking occasional field-revision as the need arose.

Negotiations around this proposal evidently took place throughout much of the remainder of 1889, and not until 2 December was Geikie in a position to communicate to Hull the official news of the final verdict. Hull himself, together with Kinahan, were both to retire on pension, each having served with the Survey for close upon forty years. Symes and Wilkinson were to be transferred to the Geological Survey of Scotland. Cruise, Mitchell, and Wynne were all to be pensioned off, Cruise and Mitchell because Geikie regarded them as being geologists of inferior quality (Mitchell had developed a drink problem while mapping in Donegal) and Wynne because he was now aged fifty-four. The Irish Survey was to be left in the charge of Nolan, who was given the new title of Senior Geologist, and his staff was to consist of Egan, Hyland, Kilroe, and McHenry, together with Clark, the Fossil Collector.

Over the next few months 14 Hume Street must have been the scene of many a farewell as Hull's men began to go their several ways. Symes and Wilkinson became members of the Geological Survey of Scotland as from 1 April 1890. Cruise, Mitchell, and Wynne retired on 31 August, and on that same day there ended Kinahan's long and turbulent association with the Survey. One can but wonder whether, on his final day in Hume Street, Kinahan chose to come down the creaking stairway from the room on the top floor which had been his since the close of mapping programme - he had complained of his banishment to what he termed a garret - down to the first floor, past the entrance to the office inhabited by the despised Wynne, and to the door of the Director's room, there to knock as a preparatory to talking of Hull a polite adieu.

Hull's own final day as Director of the Survey came just one month later. He passed into retirement on 30 September 1890. The Director-General came over to Dublin to mark the occasion, and it was, indeed, an occasion fully worthy of formal recognition. Even down to the present day, Hull remains the longest-serving Local Director or Director in the history of the Irish Survey. Nobody in their right senses would seek to place him within the geological pantheon, but, despite many a difficulty, he had brought to completion the great one-inch geological map of Ireland. His was no mean achievement. According to the Survey folklore of yesteryear, Hull expected his cartographic accomplishment to bring him the honour of a knighthood. That never happened. In 1891 he left Dublin for London, hoping there to continue his geological career as a consultant. He was, presumably, a very disappointed man.

CHAPTER FOUR

SURGERY
1890-1905

... the popular notions as to the vast mineral wealth of Ireland, or her hidden coal-fields, waiting only for development, are myths unworthy of a serious and reflective age.

Grenville Cole in an essay published in 1902 under the auspices of the Department of Agriculture and Technical Instruction for Ireland.

An Irishman who had a bit of a set-to with a Corsican gentleman at a Belgian cross-roads one day in June 1815 observed of their encounter that it was 'the nearest run thing you ever saw in your life'. As he sat in his office reflecting upon the events of 1890, Joseph Nolan might well have recollected Wellington's words. The Geological Survey of Ireland had survived, but that survival had only been by the thickness of a petrologist's microscope-slide. For us, however, the margin whereby survival had been achieved is now of little moment. All that does matter is that there was still firmly affixed to the door of 14 Hume Street a handsome brass plate inscribed 'Geological Survey of Ireland Office'.

Just as the allied victory at Waterloo left Europe to face a multitude of complex problems, so did the post-1890 persistence of the Geological Survey of Ireland carry in its wake a series of troublesome concomitant issues. Like a tangled skein of yarn, these issues were all intimately intertwined, but if we seek to unravel them, we find that in essence there are to be discovered just three strands. These are the strands which constitute a major part of the fabric of the present chapter. It is a chapter which sees the Survey being buffeted by some of the same storms as those which swept through the Irish nation at large as the nineteenth century gave way to the twentieth.

The first strand is that which involves the reasons underlying the existence of the Survey. The Survey had been established in 1845 expressly to complete a new geological map of Ireland. That task was accomplished with the publication of the final one-inch sheet in November 1890. What comes next for a scientist who has just been to Stockholm to collect a Nobel Prize? What comes next for the mountaineer who has just returned to Kathmandu after standing atop Mount Everest? What comes next for a Survey which, after forty-five years of toil, has just completed its assigned task?

The second strand is that of colonialism. Ever since the year of its foundation the Geological Survey of Ireland had merely been a part of a wider geological survey of the entire British Isles. The Irish Survey was under the immediate control of a Director-General who sat in Jermyn Street, just off London's Piccadilly Circus. The Survey was ultimately administered from the Board of Education office in Whitehall. The purse strings of the Survey were held by the Chancellor of the Exchequer in Downing Street. During the first forty-five years of its existence there had been only four years when the local head of the Irish Survey had been an Irishman promoted from within Ireland. Even the one-inch sheets, issued from Hume Street and sold by Hodges, Figgis & Co. in Grafton Street, were all coloured in London by brushes held between English fingers.

But as 1900 approached Ireland began to awaken. Ireland was asserting itself. Ireland was increasingly determined to assume responsibility for its own affairs. Ireland desired the freedom to shape its own destiny. Geology was hardly foremost in the minds of those who were now so vociferously demanding Home Rule for Ireland, but the Survey was clearly one element within the game now being played. The men of Hume Street were at grips with the very rocks from which Ireland was built. Among those rocks there were deposits essential both for the nourishment of Irish agriculture and for the stimulation of Irish industry. The Survey thus had within its purview some of the most fundamental of the resources essential to the wellbeing of the Irish nation. The study of Irish geology therefore seemed to be far too important a field to be left to the vagaries of some London-based organisation. Ireland's rocks are the foundation upon which the Irish people must build their prosperity. Those rocks must be explored under Irish direction and in the interest of the entire Irish community.

The third strand is that of a widespread public perception of the Survey as an institution which had failed the Irish nation. The Survey itself, together with the wider international world of the science of geology, might both regard the completion of the one-inch map of Ireland as a splendid achievement. There were nonetheless those in Ireland who adopted a very different view. What was so commendable about this map which the Survey had presented to the Irish nation? Was it not a sterile and academic document? Did it not simply display rocks largely according to their age? Was it not just a map by geologists and for geologists? What did it matter to a smallholder on the shores of Killala Bay that his cottage stood upon a mass of porphyritic dolerite? Did even a quarryman in Killaloe really need to know that upstream of him the rocks upon either side of Lough Derg had been mapped as Upper Silurians of Llandovery age?

Surely what did matter was that the Survey should locate the geological resources which the Irish people needed to lift them out of the slough of poverty and into a new age of prosperity. The Survey should be locating clay for Irish potteries. It should be finding sand for Irish glassworks. It should be discovering iron-ore for Irish foundries. Above all, it should be ascertaining the whereabouts of the coal necessary for the furnaces of Ireland's envisaged industrial powerhouses. Every year the firemen of the Midland Great Western Railway of Ireland were feeding some 60,000 tons of coal into the fireboxes of their locomotives. Why was this coal being dug from Taffy's Welsh pits rather than from Paddy's own Irish mines? That Ireland must somewhere contain all the geological prerequisites for industrial prosperity passed without question among those who looked forward to the thriving Ireland of a new age. Were the Irish not among God's chosen people? Was it not unthinkable that the Creator could have been so unmindful of His Irish flock as to have left their island deficient in the mineral resources necessary for the generation of national wealth? Did the gold and silver of the eighth-century Ardagh Chalice and the Tara Brooch not bear magnificent testimony to the fact that in Ireland there must be the geological resources necessary to sustain a second Irish Golden Age?

Admittedly, we now know that Ireland did indeed contain mineral riches which nineteenth-century methods of prospecting had failed to bring to light. But the religio-philosophical style of reasoning then implicitly, if not overtly, adopted must in geological circles today evoke at best the smiles of incomprehension and at worst the howling laughter of derision. There is nevertheless no escaping the fact that outside the geological community there was for long in Ireland a tendency to don the spectacles of pure faith before speaking of the nation's geological resources. The wearing of such spectacles served nicely to simplify thinking about the true objectives of a geological survey of Ireland.

As in some great game of hide-and-seek, such a survey should be concerned with a search for the divinely bestowed but concealed mineral wealth. Such a survey should dedicate itself to the exploration of the local world of Irish economic geology rather than to the advancement of the broad international field of the geological science. Such a survey should consist of Irish geologists devotedly deploying their skills in the practical interest of their compatriots.

In the eyes of those entertaining views such as these, the achievement of the existing, British - administered Survey seemed to be woefully inadequate. Ever since its foundation in 1845 it had been given freedom, finance, and facilities, but its only tangible attainments appeared to be a one-inch map of Ireland, constructed largely upon historical principles, the slim sheet memoirs, so many of which remained unsold, and a few cases of geological specimens now displayed within the galleries of the new Dublin Museum of Science and Art located in Kildare Street (see Chapter Ten). The Survey was seen as having short-changed the Irish people. Not only had the Survey failed to locate Ireland's God-given treasure-chest of geological riches, but the Survey seemed never seriously even to have embarked upon the hunt for the treasure-chest.

There here has to be mentioned a somewhat different but rather more extreme interpretation of what the Survey had been doing. There were those of a strongly nationalistic bent who chose to believe that the British-controlled Irish Survey had never actually been neglectful of its primary economic duty, but that it had most certainly indulged in a gross and malevolent deceit. The argument went as follows. Ireland must be replete with great mineral wealth. As a result of its field-operations the Survey now knows exactly where that wealth is located. But British mining and industrial interests across the water are fearful of Irish competition and the Irish Survey is therefore under instruction to throw a cloak of secrecy over all its discoveries relating to Ireland's subterranean riches.

Anyone familiar with the Survey and its activities has difficulty in understanding how an argument such as this could ever seriously have been entertained. It is nonetheless an argument which has repeatedly cropped out at various levels within Irish society. There seems little reason for believing that even today the argument has finally been laid to its rest. When Grenville Cole wrote the words reproduced at the head of this chapter he perhaps had in mind an interpretation of the Survey's work such as might have been adopted by an extreme nationalist convinced of Albion's perfidy in everything. Thirty years later the *Irish Press,* on 25 April 1933, reported the following passage from a speech delivered by the then Minister for Industry and Commerce.

> As regards raw material, we have large coal areas, but the quality of the deposits has yet to be established. We are arranging for exhaustive examinations as a

> preliminary to the development of iron, copper and zinc deposits.
> We have found the geological reports prepared by the British Government to be most unreliable, and I think it fair to assume they were deliberately made so in order to prevent development in those directions.

The Minister involved was the thirty-three-year-old Sean Francis Lemass who in 1959 was to become a notable Taoiseach in succession to Eamon de Valera.

Soon after the Survey's 1984 removal into its new premises at Beggars Bush, there was mounted in the new building an exhibition illustrative of the geology of Ireland and the work of the Survey. One afternoon a gentleman in his sixties entered the exhibition where he fell into conversation with a Survey officer who happened to be present. The visitor explained to the officer that the Survey had once possessed an abundance of information about Ireland's mineral wealth but that on instructions from London the information was treated as highly confidential. It was kept locked in a safe to which only the Survey's Director had access. Before the British left Ireland in 1922, the visitor recounted, the safe and its contents were secretly removed to England where they doubtless still lie in some archive reserved for the most sensitive of documents. The gentleman explained that he had become privy to these facts while attending the undergraduate lectures of that Irish university of which he was a proud alumnus.

Chill winds associated with each of the three strands now introduced were soon to rattle the windows and threaten the roof of 14 Hume Street, but only gradually did the storm attain its full intensity. Indeed, the 1890s were a decade of relative tranquillity as compared with the five years which followed 1900. During that last decade of the nineteenth century the Survey faced only two problems of any magnitude. The first of those problems the Survey shared with many another Irish family: the threat of eviction. The second of those problems arose from the first of the three strands just introduced above: what was to be the Survey's function in the aftermath of the completion of the one-inch map?

On 3 December 1891 the Office of Public Works informed Nolan that his request for a room in 14 Hume Street to be fitted out as a geochemical laboratory had been rejected because the Survey would shortly be moved into smaller premises. A house which had once been home to fifteen geologists was deemed to be far too large for an emaciated Survey of only one third that size. On 16 May 1892 Geikie instructed Nolan to go to inspect 2 Kildare Place to see if it would make a suitable new headquarters for the Survey, but in the event the Office of Public Works implemented neither this particular threatened eviction nor any of its several later successors. The Survey remained in 14 Hume Street until the removal to spacious new premises at Beggars Bush during May 1984.

Where the post-1890 function of the Survey was concerned the situation initially seemed clear enough. Soon after his appointment as Senior Geologist in Charge, Nolan was informed by Geikie that henceforth the duties of the Survey were to be threefold. First, the Survey was to deal with geological enquiries as they arrived from government departments, from other public officials, from industry, and from the ordinary people of Ireland. Second, the Survey was to have curatorial responsibility for all its own specimens now housed in the Dublin Museum of Science and Art. Third, the Survey was to engage in on-going revision of the one-inch map so that its sheets could always be relied upon as embodying the most up-to-date interpretation of Irish regional geology.

In March 1889, when he wrote his confidential report on the members of the Irish Survey, Geikie evidently envisaged that the staff of the reduced Irish Survey would be undertaking one further responsibility. In Britain he had been encouraging certain of his staff in the preparation of synoptic stratigraphical memoirs devoted to the deposits of some given epoch or period. Clement Reid's monograph *The Pliocene Deposits of Britain*, published in 1890, was the first of this new genre of British Survey publication, and Geikie seemingly hoped to inaugurate a similar series of publications within the Irish Survey. It must have been for this reason that in his confidential evaluation of each Irish Survey officer he was at pains to assess their literary ability. He noted, for example, that Cruise was 'but an indifferent writer' and that Symes 'has no literary power', whereas Nolan 'is a good Surveyor, and can write'. But all such assessment was effort wasted; no Irish stratigraphical memoirs were ever undertaken although it may be that Kilroe's *Soil-Geology of Ireland*, published in 1907, should be thought of as approximating to the stratigraphical memoir concept. Geikie certainly gave his blessing to Kilroe's project when it commenced in 1897, and just four years later one of his final acts as Director-General must have been to give his approval to Kilroe's completed manuscript. There is no record of what Geikie may have said when he opened *Nature* for 7 November 1907 to find therein a somewhat damning review of Kilroe's work.

During the 1890s the Survey doubtless handled with efficiency the many and varied geological enquiries which must have arrived in Hume Street. In 1894, for instance, the enquiries dealt with related to coal and peat resources, pottery clays, bauxite, barytes, oil shales, alum shales, water supply, building stones, ornamental stones, and the

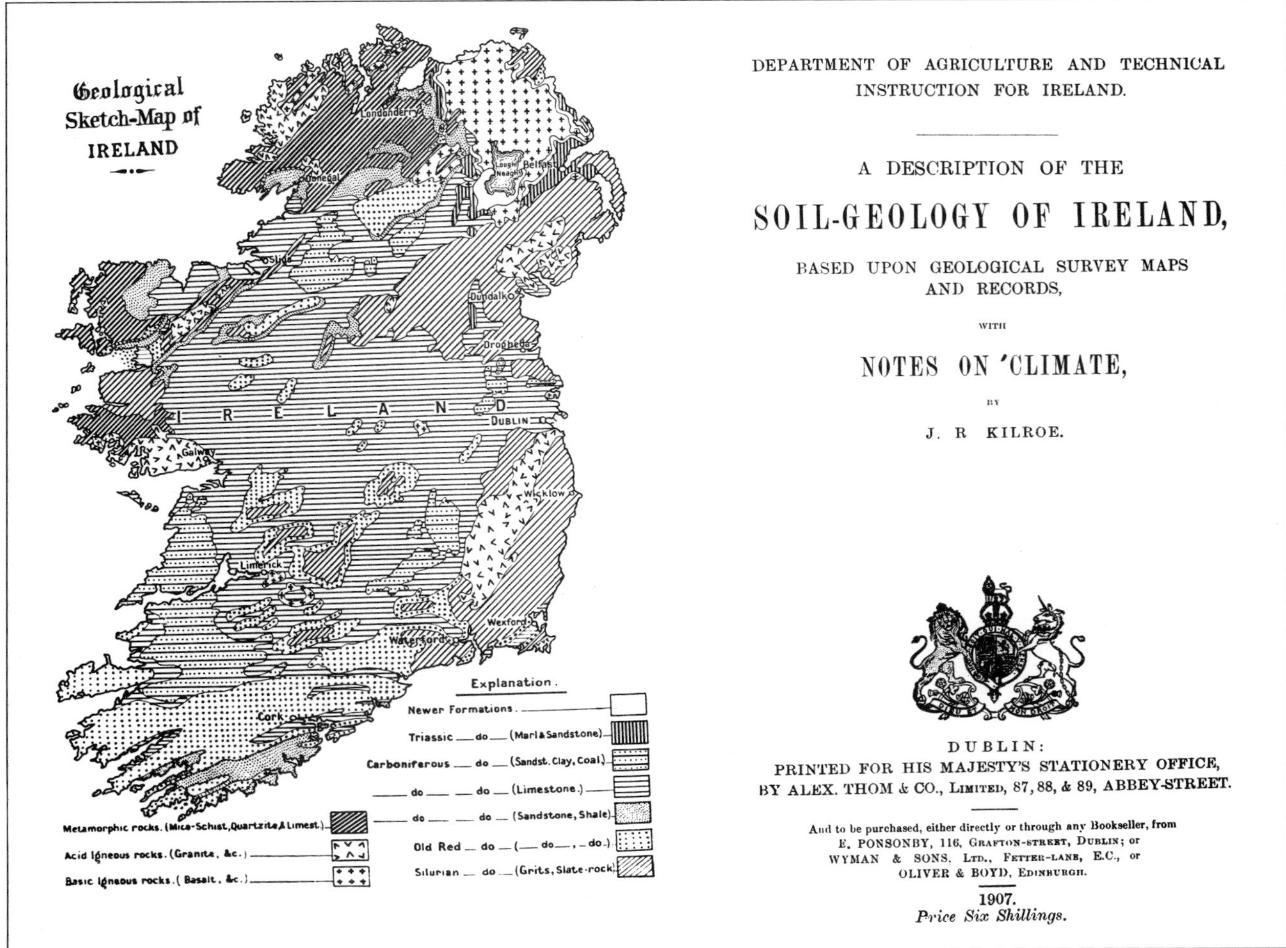

DEPARTMENT OF AGRICULTURE AND TECHNICAL INSTRUCTION FOR IRELAND.

A DESCRIPTION OF THE

SOIL-GEOLOGY OF IRELAND,

BASED UPON GEOLOGICAL SURVEY MAPS AND RECORDS,

WITH

NOTES ON 'CLIMATE,

BY

J. R KILROE.

DUBLIN:
PRINTED FOR HIS MAJESTY'S STATIONERY OFFICE,
BY ALEX. THOM & CO., LIMITED, 87, 88, & 89, ABBEY-STREET.

And to be purchased, either directly or through any Bookseller, from
E. PONSONBY, 116, GRAFTON-STREET, DUBLIN; or
WYMAN & SONS, LTD., FETTER-LANE, E.C., or
OLIVER & BOYD, EDINBURGH.

1907.
Price Six Shillings.

FIGURE 4.1. *The frontispiece and title page of Kilroe's* Soil-Geology *reduced to about three-quarters of their original size. On 7 November 1907 the book's reviewer in* Nature *observed: 'To produce such a book is a noble ambition, but we fear that the materials for it hardly exist as yet in the case of Ireland, for throughout Mr. Kilroe's book we are struck by the paucity of data really bearing on the point at issue'.*

mineral deposits of Achill Island. That last enquiry arose from a visit to Achill by Lady Aberdeen on behalf of the Irish Industries Association and in the shocked aftermath of the disaster off Westport Quay in which 33 of the islanders - mostly women and girls - had been drowned. Similarly, all the officers clearly bestowed much time upon the arrangement and then re-arrangement of the Survey's collections in the Dublin Museum of Science and Art (see Chapter Ten). But for the historian the most visible of the three kinds of task undertaken by the Survey was that of map revision.

A hundred years ago an anonymous British Survey author wisely declared that 'it is the necessary fate of all geological maps to become antiquated'. By the 1890s advances within the geological science certainly demanded that the one-inch map should be re-examined in the light of the latest knowledge. Here there were three topics of particular concern. First, was there sufficient evidence to justify some of Ireland's most ancient rocks being re-classified as Archaean or Pre-Cambrian? Second, igneous petrology had been revolutionised by the microscopic study of rocks in thin-section, and in view of this development there was need to refine the nomenclature of the igneous rocks as they had been depicted upon the one-inch map. Third, Lower Palaeozoic palaeontology had developed apace during the second half of the nineteenth century and it was imperative that Ireland's Lower Palaeozoic strata should be re-investigated in the light of the palaeontological evidence now available.

During his visit to Ireland in 1889 Geikie had been impressed by the similarity of some of the County Galway rocks to the Lewisian Gneiss of northwestern Scotland, that being a rock of undoubted Archaean age. Indeed, he later observed of his Galway experience, 'had I been brought blindfolded to this region I would at once have supposed myself to be in Sutherland, or among the Outer Hebrides'. At Hull's instigation, Archaean or Laurentian rocks had already appeared upon two of the one-inch sheets published during the 1880s -

upon Sheet 26 (Draperstown) and Sheet 55 (Sligo) - and Geikie was now very anxious to know whether there could be discovered stratigraphical evidence which would allow of other Irish rocks being accorded Archaean status. Much of the necessary re-investigation fell to McHenry during the field-season of 1892. He spent the June of that year among the ancient rocks of southern County Wexford. During early July he joined Egan, Kilroe, and Watts in the search for an Archaean legacy in the Erris district of County Mayo. Later the same month he ran a section from Lough Conn, across the Ox Mountains, and on to Manorhamilton through a region where Archaean rocks were already represented upon one-inch Sheet 55. During August he searched for Archaean rocks in counties Antrim, Cavan, and Donegal before joining Geikie on a tour of inspection through the north and west of Ireland. That summer McHenry traced 45.8 kilometres of geological boundary, examined 20 kilometres of coastal section, and collected 575 rock-specimens. It is sobering to reflect that some of the problems which perplexed McHenry during that distant summer of 1892 are still perplexing us even today. It has proved remarkably difficult to establish the true age of some of the most ancient of Ireland's geological foundations.

The microscopic study of rocks in thin-section had been introduced into the Survey by Hull as early as 1871 (see p.76), and when Baily died in 1888 it was resolved to convert his former palaeontological post into a new petrological appointment. The first to hold that new office was the Liverpudlian, John Shearson Hyland. He had studied in Leipzig under the famed Ferdinand Zirkel, and he was the first Survey officer to arrive decorated with a Ph. D. That degree he had earned with a dissertation devoted to some rocks sent to Germany from Kilimanjaro by Hans Meyer who in 1889 made the first (?European) ascent of the mountain. Hyland held the petrological appointment in Dublin for a mere three years, and his resignation in 1891 was received in Hume Street with some satisfaction because he had proved to be a troublesome colleague. Oddly, while he was in Dublin he became an undergraduate on the books of Trinity College. The next Temporary Assistant Geologist (Petrologist) was William Whitehead Watts, and when he was translated to London in 1893 to assume responsibility for petrological work in Jermyn Street, the Dublin post went to William Johnson Sollas who combined his Survey duties with those of the chair of geology and mineralogy which he had held in Trinity College Dublin since 1883. Sollas was appointed to the chair of geology at Oxford in 1897, and the Survey's next petrologist was Henry Joseph Seymour, a young graduate of the Royal University of Ireland (1898). In addition to his petrological duties with the Irish Survey, Seymour was soon examining thin-sections of Scottish rocks sent over to Hume Street by officers of the Scottish survey. In 1900, for instance, Seymour examined 193 microscope-slides of Irish rocks and 115 slides of Scottish rocks sent to him from the Edinburgh office.

An insight into a typical year's work for the petrologist is provided by the instructions which Sollas received for his guidance at the beginning of 1895. He was told to describe the slides taken from the igneous rocks at Carlingford. (He actually described 298 slides that year but many of them were derived from County Galway rocks collected by McHenry.) He was to go into the field to revise the igneous rocks on one-inch Sheet 71 (Carlingford) and then proceed to Newcastle, County Down, to see if there was need for a revision of the igneous rocks on Sheet 60 (Mourne Mountains). He spent six weeks in the field, modernised the nomenclature of the local igneous and metamorphic rocks, but reported that on the whole he had found the earlier mapping to be 'extremely faithful and accurate'. His final assignment was slightly unusual. It evokes memories of Du Noyer back in 1847. Sollas was instructed to spend one week photographing the significant sections revealed during the construction of the newly-completed railway line from Galway, through Oughterard and Recess, to Clifden. (There was a photographic dark-room in Hume Street at least as early as 1899 and Sollas was evidently an enthusiastic photographer.)

By far the largest of the three tasks of revision undertaken by the Survey during the 1890s was that of re-classifying the Lower Palaeozoic strata. It was unfortunate that the primary mapping of Ireland should have taken place at a time when palaeontological knowledge had been insufficiently far advanced to allow of an adequate differentiation of the rocks below the Old Red Sandstone. The deficiency now had to be remedied and this revision was pressed ahead field-season by field-season until it was completed during 1900.

Normally, Clark, the Fossil Collector, was the first to move into a district selected for re - examination, his task being to search for the fossils which later would guide his geologist colleagues in their drawing of boundaries. Clark must have been particularly pleased with himself in 1896. He was collecting from the rocks of the Longford-Down Zone in the area covered by sheets 58,59,68,69,79,80, and 90, and he knew that previously the Survey had failed to find fossils in the Lower Palaeozoic rocks depicted upon Sheet 58 (Monaghan). But now he succeeded in finding there four fossiliferous localities which indicated that

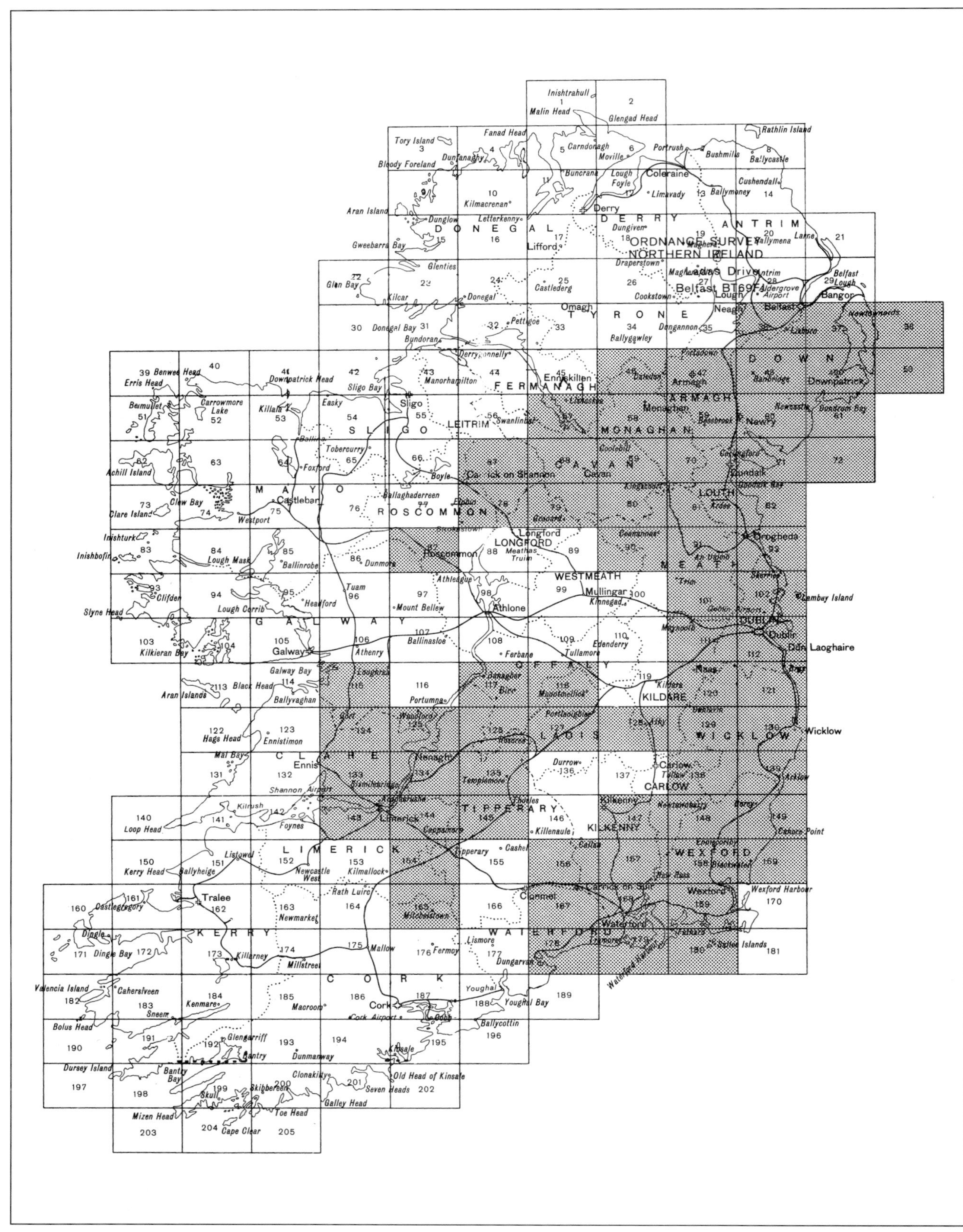

FIGURE 4.2. *The distribution of the sixty-seven new one-inch sheets published between 1900 and 1902 and showing the revised classification of the Irish Lower Palaeozoic rocks. Most of the revision mapping was the work of Kilroe. He had re-examined the rocks in parts of Ireland other than those covered by the sixty-seven sheets, but in those other areas his work was regarded either as insufficiently detailed or as insufficiently extensive to justify the preparation of new editions of the existing one-inch sheets.*

some of the rocks belonged to the Llandeilo while others belonged to the Llandovery. Since the Survey possessed no specialist palaeontologist after Baily's demise in 1888, all Clark's problem fossils were determined by Edwin Tulley Newton of Jermyn Street, by Benjamin Neeve Peach of the Scottish Survey, or by Charles Lapworth of Mason College, Birmingham.

As Clark completed his investigations, the geologists moved in, and year by year they re-examined the rocks from the Waterford coast north into County Down, and from Wicklow Head west into Clare Island. In terms of the area re-investigated, the lion's share of this work fell to Kilroe who re-explored the Lower Palaeozoic rocks of at least ten of the Irish counties. He seems particularly to have enjoyed the time he spent re-mapping in the country around Maum Bridge in County Galway. On 8 June 1894 he signed the visitors' book in the local hotel and expressed his gratitude to Miss Wallace, the new proprietrix, for 'the attention and anxiety to please' which she had evinced during his stay of five weeks' duration.

Most of this revision of the Lower Palaeozoic strata was laid before the public in a series of sixty-seven revised one-inch sheets published in 1900, 1901, and 1902 (Fig. 4.2). Mention of the appearance of these sheets affords a convenient moment at which to introduce a caveat for the benefit of the geological community. Geologists commonly suppose that each of the Survey's one-inch sheets exists in only a single state. They assume that any one-inch sheet which may come to hand represents the ultimate Survey verdict upon the geology of any given region. This is both naive and unjust to the Survey. The one-inch sheet consulted as authoritative by the modern geologist may well be a sheet which in reality was superseded by one or more later issues. From its earliest days onwards the map was a living document subject to constant modification. Not until the 1920s was the map allowed to die. Only then did rigor mortis set in as the map became a fossil. But the would-be student of the evolutionary history of that fossil faces substantial problems. On the one hand there is extant no written record of the sequence of states through which each sheet of the map has passed, while on the other hand there is at present no complete collection of the 205 one-inch sheets illustrative of their successive conditions. The one-inch geological map of Ireland has yet to find its cartobibliographer.

Nolan himself seems to have taken little part in any of the Survey's revision mapping carried out during the 1890s. In his annual reports to the Director-General he repeatedly explained that he had been preoccupied by his administrative duties in Hume Street. Those duties he clearly performed with efficiency and success. He emerges from the Survey's letter-books as an amiable individual devoid of scientific pretensions but possessed of a warm personal relationship with all his staff save for the querulous but ephemeral Hyland. Hume Street was a far happier place under Nolan than it had ever been during those twenty years of confrontation between Hull and Kinahan.

Although by birth a Queen's County (Laois) man, Nolan became passionately devoted to the beautiful landscapes of County Wicklow, and it was there that he conducted such personal field-work as he undertook during the 1890s. He took it upon himself to map the glacial deposits and the peat of the Wicklow Mountains region, and this programme he continued year by year until rheumatism ended his field career during the summer of 1900. None of his Wicklow field-sheets seem to survive within the Survey and virtually no publications of any kind ever resulted from his Wicklow peregrinations. I suspect that for Nolan field-work eventually became just an excuse for a satisfying day passed amidst his beloved mountains. If a summer's morn dawned fair he would forget about Hume Street and get out his six-inch sheets. A short stroll from his Sandymount home brought him to the railway and he was soon rattling over the metals bound for the scenic glories of Glenealy, Avoca, or Woodenbridge. But here there was nothing unique about Nolan; many another geologist has found that a professed devotion to field-study may be used in justification of temporary withdrawal from the cares of the world. What the soul-searcher finds in the house of retreat, the geologist finds in the bed of a stream or the face of a quarry.

Geikie followed all the Irish revision work with the closest attention possible, both at a distance, by correspondence from Jermyn Street, and on the ground itself by regular and prolonged tours of inspection. The ensuing passage comes from a letter which he wrote to McHenry on 9 May 1894, and it serves to exemplify Geikie's ebullience.

> I am writing to Mr. Kilroe and you with the request that you will keep me informed of the progress of your respective areas. I may not be able to join you as early as I had hoped, but I am intensely interested in the problems you are attacking, and I feel very hopeful that your results, if cautious and careful work have led up to them, may be of signal service to the whole Survey. So every now and then report to me what is doing and how the problems are beginning to look. Never mind any previous theories either your own or other peoples'. But try to get securely at the actual facts.

Geikie was a somewhat self-centred individual not overly given to the praise of others, but he patently held McHenry in high esteem. In his confidential report upon the Irish Survey in March 1889 he evaluated Mac (for so he was familiarly known to his

FIGURE 4.3. *Nolan's men in 1895, the year of the Geological Survey of Ireland's Golden Jubilee. From left to right: Egan, Kilroe (seated), Nolan, Clark, and McHenry (seated). The empty chair was perhaps intended as a reminder that Sollas was absent. Between them, the five geologists present had by 1895 given to the Survey a total of 128 years of service.* (Reproduced from an original in the archives of the Survey).

colleagues) as 'on the whole, the most efficient member of the staff', and in his autobiography, published in 1924, Geikie remembered Mac as 'one of the most helpful and efficient travelling companions I ever had the good fortune to meet with'. It was in Mac's company that Geikie had a brush with death during a tour of inspection in July 1899. He was in County Wicklow examining some of the Lower Palaeozoic revision mapping, and about the 17th of the month he was near Rathdrum travelling in an open car with Mac and Egan. Their horse took fright and the car was overturned. Mac escaped with nothing more serious than cuts and bruises. Geikie suffered from shock and he went off to the Hebrides to recuperate, advised by his physician to do nothing more strenuous than 'lie in the bottom of a boat'. But poor Egan suffered severely. His shoulder was injured and his liver was damaged. The shoulder was examined by X-ray (Egan was surely the first Survey officer to benefit from Röntgen's 1895 discovery) and it slowly mended. Bravely, Egan returned to his duties but the damaged liver proved serious. Jaundice set in and after much sickness he died on 6 January 1901. He was the ninth officer of the Survey to die, as it were, 'on active service'.

It was, of course, in his capacity as Director-General that Geikie made his regular Irish tours of inspection. But it does seem that when he was in Ireland Geikie had some entitlement to wear a second hat. Although nowhere specifically spelled out, there does seem to have been a tacit understanding that after Hull's retirement in 1890, Geikie had subsumed the office of Irish Director. This perhaps explains how we came to possess a geological map of Ireland which has always been known as 'Geikie's map' just as we have 'Jukes's map' of 1867, and 'Hull's map' of 1878.

Geikie's map - a most ambitious, attractive, and useful map - is at a scale of ten miles to the inch (1:633,600) and it bears the title 'Map showing the surface geology of Ireland'. Upon the map Ireland's superficial deposits are represented in the categories of blown sand, peat, alluvium, or glacial drift, and in the absence of any such deposits the map indicates the character of the solid rocks which rise through the drift overburden. The map was compiled in Hume Street under Geikie's direction, he being notoriously adept at employing Geological Survey officers upon tasks which were essentially private ventures of his own.

The various stages in the production of the map may still be traced in the surviving manuscript sheets within the Survey's archives. Work started in 1894, and all the relevant information was first abstracted from the one-inch sheets and then plotted upon a quarter-inch (1:253,440) map. This manuscript quarter-inch map was exhibited at the International Geological Congress held in Paris in 1900. The quarter-inch map was next reduced to the eventual scale of 1:633,600, with Kilroe doing the northwestern portion of the map, Egan the northeastern, McHenry the southwestern, and Nolan the southeastern. On 24 November 1899 uncoloured 'boundary' versions of the map were in Hume Street for correction but it was 1906 before the map was finally published, 'with government authority', by the renowned firm of John Bartholomew at the Edinburgh Geographical Institute. Geikie's name is featured prominently upon the map but over in Dublin both Kilroe and McHenry must surely have felt aggrieved that all their work had been allowed to pass without acknowledgement. Nolan and Egan, the two other officers who had worked upon the map, were past caring about such a slight. By 1906 they had both for some years been entombed within the deposit which the map represented in blue and designated simply as 'drift'.

Geikie's map became one of the best-known of all the geological maps of Ireland. It obtained a wide currency because copies were folded into a pocket at the rear of Kilroe's 1907 *Soil-Geology of Ireland*. In that form the map was still to be obtained through the Government Publications Office in Dublin as recently as the early 1970s when the book, with map, was still selling at the 1907 price of six shillings or 30 pence! Through the agency of the Department of Agriculture and Technical Instruction for Ireland, copies of the map were evidently also circulated to Irish colleges and schools, accompanied by a brief descriptive memoir from the pen of Professor Grenville Cole of the Royal College of Science for Ireland.

Cole we shall be encountering again shortly. For the moment it is the just-mentioned government department which must engage our attention. We have arrived at a turning point in the history of the Geological Survey of Ireland, and the Department of Agriculture and Technical Instruction played a vital role in the machinations which surrounded the Survey during the period between 1900 and 1905. Those were without question the most fateful five years in the entire 150-year history of the Survey.

The Department of Agriculture and Technical Instruction for Ireland originated in the recommendations of the so-called Recess Committee convened during the summer of 1896. The new Department was brought into being by the passage through the Westminster Parliament of the Agriculture and Technical Instruction (Ireland) Act of 1899, and the Department began its operations on 1 April 1900. The entire enterprise was very much the brainchild of (Sir) Horace Curzon Plunkett who had already made a profound impact upon Irish life through his involvement in the movement towards agricultural co-operation. As the Vice-President of the new Department he was its *de facto* Director, it having been agreed that the Chief Secretary should be nothing more than a 'sleeping' President.

It was Plunkett's hope that during the new century just dawning the activities of the Department would make real that national prosperity which hitherto had been only a dream. This golden age was to be achieved as a result of two broad developments. First, the new Department was to bring together all the offices having a bearing upon the national economic wellbeing. Previously these offices had been widely scattered among various departments of state; now, in the interest of increased efficiency, they were all to be consolidated under Plunkett's control within the Department's headquarters in Dublin's Upper Merrion Street. Second, through the activities of the Department and its officers, modern science was to be enlisted in the cause of Irish prosperity. Science teaching was to be developed in Irish schools, the agricultural colleges were to be revivified, relevant statistics were to be collected and analysed, advisory schemes were to be developed for the benefit of Irish farmers, fisheries research was to be undertaken (the 375 - ton steamship *Helga* was purchased for the purpose), and expert advice was to be made available to Ireland's existing and potential industrialists.

Among the varied bodies for which the new Department now became responsible were the Dublin Museum of Science and Art, the National Library of Ireland, the Royal Botanic Gardens at Glasnevin, the Dublin Metropolitan School of Art, and the Royal College of Science for Ireland. Formerly these five institutions had all been administered from London under the aegis of the Department of Science and Art. Ever since 1853 the Department of Science and Art had also been responsible for the administration of the Geological Survey of the United Kingdom, but in 1900 the Geological Survey of Ireland formed no part of the package which was handed over to Plunkett. Why? Hume Street was literally just around the corner from Plunkett's office at 4 Upper Merrion Street and his Department certainly understood the importance of geological knowledge to Ireland's future prosperity. In 1902 the Department even published a geological map of the country between Clew Bay and Galway Bay in illustration of an essay on the ponies of Connemara! The Geological Survey of Ireland was nonetheless for the moment allowed to remain as a colonial outpost of the British Geological Survey. In explaining this fact two different perspectives have to be adopted. One is the perspective as seen from London and the other is the perspective as seen from Dublin.

Seen from London there was a desire to preserve the integrity of the Geological Survey as an entity concerned with the geology of the United Kingdom as a whole. The rocks on the two sides of the Irish Sea stand in the closest mutual relationship and scientifically it seemed absurd to allow the Irish Sea to become a boundary separating the territories of two teams of entirely independent geological surveyors. In 1845 De La Beche had instructed James to open his Irish campaign in Leinster because the rocks of Wexford and Wicklow might elucidate problems in Welsh geology; Jukes had always believed that the key to the geology of Devonshire was buried in Munster; and only recently Geikie had been trying to install some kind of common circuit which would illuminate the ancient rocks of Scotland and northwestern Ireland.

At the human level, officers had traditionally been appointed to the Geological Survey of the United Kingdom rather than to one of its regional components. This had allowed a fruitful exchange of officers from one part of the United Kingdom to another. Jukes, Baily, and Hull had all been transferred from Britain to Ireland, while H.B. Medlicott, Symes, Wilkinson, and Watts had all gone from Hume Street to the British Survey. Similarly, the Geological Survey of the United Kingdom was actually functioning as a unitary whole. Since 1888, for instance, the Irish branch had possessed no palaeontologist and most of its fossils were determined in Britain. The British Survey, on the other hand, was weak in petrology and Seymour had therefore been studying thin-sections sent over to Dublin by the Geological Survey of Scotland.

One final point relating to the London perspective has to be made. With the exception of Murchison, every Director or Director-General of the Geological Survey of the United Kingdom had found pleasure in having Ireland as a part of his administrative empire. Regular expenses-paid excursions across the Irish Sea to encounter Irish rocks and Irish friends were stimulating and gratifying experiences. Nobody from Jermyn Street had enjoyed these visits more than did Geikie. In his autobiography he observed of Ireland:

> The geology, the scenery, the antiquities and the people all interested me; and I can say with truth that in no part of my duties did I find more pleasure than in those which took me to Erin.

It is easy to understand why Geikie in particular would have viewed askance any proposal for the amputation of the Geological Survey's Irish limb.

I turn now to the perspective upon the issue as it appeared in Dublin eyes and, more especially, as it appeared in Horace Plunkett's eyes. At this juncture Plunkett saw no reason to urge a severance of the Irish Survey from the British. But while his conclusion might coincide with that of Geikie, the two men must have arrived at their common standpoint after following entirely different logical paths. Geology might be fundamental to Plunkett's envisaged Irish golden age but did the Irish Survey's files contain the type of information which was needed? What Plunkett wanted was applied geology, economic geology, practical geology. What the Survey had on offer seemed to be academic geology, theoretical geology, speculative geology. The Survey had just spent ten years in re-classifying the Irish Lower Palaeozoic strata and in refining the nomenclature of the Irish igneous rocks. In Plunkett's vision the nation had been hungry for nourishing information about coal, cobalt, copper, and clays. What the Survey had fed to the nation was an indigestible diet of the Llandeilo and the Llandovery accompanied by tooth-breaking masses of epidiorite and elvanite. Plunkett's view of the Survey was perhaps identical to the view of the Survey which Kane had entertained fifty years earlier (see p.262). Even officers of the Survey itself had qualms of conscience upon this point. Here is Kilroe writing to his Director-General on 8 March 1901.

> I have frequently been asked by land agents and others interested in the Country's wellbeing in what respect the Survey is of any benefit to the taxpayer, and have found it extremely difficult, with such a dearth of Irish minerals, to supply a satisfactory and convincing answer.

Did the Department of Agriculture and Technical Instruction really wish to take such a Geological Survey under its wing? Was the *international* scientific idealism of the Survey ever likely to be reconciled with the severely practical *national* idealism of Plunkett and his Department? Surely it was prudent to leave the Irish Survey with its British parent. In this way the scientific expertise of the Survey would be available to Plunkett if and when it was needed, while his own Department would be at liberty to develop within itself that variety of applied geology which Ireland's future prosperity seemed to demand.

In opting for such a course, the Department was favoured by one singularly happy occurrence. From the very instant of its inauguration the Department had found itself in possession of a seed which might be encouraged to develop into a new geological bureau of precisely the type necessary to meet the Department's needs. By assuming responsibility for the Royal College of Science for Ireland, the Department had already acquired its own eminent geologist in the diminutive form of Professor Grenville Arthur James Cole, who since 1890 had been the college's professor of geology. Henceforth the Department was to use Cole as its geological consultant. His professorial duties within the College of Science were light, and as from 1900 he was increasingly referred to as 'geologist to the Department of Agriculture and Technical Instruction'. And that, in the eyes of the Department, was merely a beginning.

Its failure to insist upon a lopping of the Irish Survey from its British trunk was thus no act of generous magnanimity upon the part of Plunkett and his Department. Rather was the Irish Survey being marginalised as largely irrelevant to the needs of Ireland in the twentieth century. At the same time a path was being left clear for the development of a new bureau of applied geology within the Department itself.

Geikie was a shrewd man. He can hardly have been oblivious to the reality of what was afoot in Upper Merrion Street. On the morning of 26 July 1900 he attended an informal meeting to discuss the future relationship between the Irish Survey and the Department of Agriculture and Technical Instruction. The meeting seems to have been most amicable, but there are about it three features suggesting that Geikie perceived himself to be negotiating from a position of some weakness. First, the meeting took place not in Hume Street, but in Upper Merrion Street. Second, Sir Archibald Geikie, F.R.S., Director-General of the Geological Survey of the United Kingdom, and arguably the world's most renowned geologist, met that morning not with Plunkett himself but only with Thomas Patrick Gill, the Secretary of the Department. Third, Geikie made the following series of breathtaking concessions.

He accepted that in future 'the economic side of geology' in Ireland would be the responsibility of the Department rather than of the Survey. More specifically, it was agreed that henceforth the Department rather than the Survey would handle all matters relating to the mapping of Ireland's soils, all enquiries concerning mineral resources and building materials, and all geological investigations associated with construction sites, sewerage schemes, cemetery development, and the like. This concession alone was sufficient to shake Hume Street to its very foundations, but Geikie was prepared to surrender even more of the Survey's traditional territory. He agreed that the Survey would now renounce its interest in the solid rocks of Ireland and would instead devote its resources to the mapping of Ireland's unconsolidated superficial deposits. Even here Geikie was prepared to see the Survey reduced to being little more than an adjunct to the Department. The Survey's proposed programme of drift mapping was merely intended to provide an underpinning to the soil maps which the Department had decided to construct as one of its contributions towards the improvement of Irish agriculture. The Department was therefore to be allowed some control over the manner in which the Survey developed its drift-mapping programme.

On the afternoon of 26 July 1900 Geikie wrote for Gill a memorandum recording the various points upon which they had agreed during their discussion that morning. On the subject of the Survey's proposed drift mapping Geikie wrote as follows:

> But as the Drifts in Ireland are much more uniform and simple than they are in the centre and south of England, I have great hope that the requisite revision will not prove to be either a long or laborious undertaking, though until we have tried some bits of it in different parts of the Country, it may not be possible to speak very definitely.

This was a remarkably sanguine appraisal to come from a geologist who was widely experienced in the details of the Irish landscape. He should have known better. The full significance of Geikie's words will become apparent shortly.

What lay behind Geikie's far-reaching concessions made that July morning in 1900? Geikie was then in his sixty-fifth year but there was nothing effete about him. His County Wicklow car accident now lay a year behind him and before him he had twenty-four remarkably active years including five when he was President of the Royal Society (1908-1913). A charitable interpretation of what transpired in Gill's Upper Merrion Street office would be that Geikie chose to set aside the narrow interests of the Irish Survey in favour of the wider interests of Ireland as a whole. As we have seen, he seems to have had a real affection for the country, and he may have believed that what he had agreed in his discussions with Gill was all in the best interest of Ireland and its people. There is also available a less charitable interpretation. Geikie's character contained some odd quirks. By July 1900 he knew that he would shortly be retiring from his post as Director-General. Now it could be that out of spite he wished to leave his successor with an empire somewhat diminished as compared with that over which he himself had presided with such personal satisfaction.

The agreement between Geikie and Gill had no official standing. It was a gentleman's agreement only. Certain of its provisions nevertheless received almost instant official blessing. On 14 April 1900 there was established a committee charged with the task of enquiring into the organisation, staffing, and future responsibilities of the entire Geological Survey of the United Kingdom. The chairman of the committee was John Lloyd Wharton, an Old Etonian, a Yorkshire Member of Parliament in the Conservative interest, and a director of the North-Eastern Railway Company. The committee met thirteen times and it submitted its confidential report on 24 September 1900. Many of the committee's discussions were actually held in Geikie's Jermyn Street office, and where Ireland was concerned the committee would seem to have lent an attentive ear to what Geikie had to say. The committee noted that there already existed a complete one-inch map depicting Ireland's solid geology. Since the country was largely dependent upon agriculture, the committee was satisfied that what was now required was an equivalent large-scale map representing Ireland's superficial deposits. The preparation of such a map, the committee considered, should now become the Irish Survey's primary task. This was exactly what Geikie and Gill had agreed upon just two months earlier, and, doubtless so advised by Geikie, the committee clearly imagined the mapping of the Irish drifts to be an undertaking of no great magnitude.

The committee went on to offer a proposal far more radical than any to have emerged from Geikie's discussions in Upper Merrion Street.

> ... the collections of the Irish Survey are now housed in the Dublin Museum, which is in the charge of the Department of Agriculture and Technical Instruction for Ireland. We are disposed to think that the survey in Ireland should be continued as a separate branch for a period only sufficient for the completion of the re-survey of the drifts; after which the remaining staff might be removed to Great Britain and the responsibility for keeping the maps up to date transferred to the Irish Department above mentioned, with the help of its Professor of Geology.

It began to look as though 14 Hume Street would soon be falling vacant. The saving to the Exchequer accruing from the closure of the Irish Survey would, incidentally, have been minimal. Throughout the 1890s the annual cost of the Irish Branch had been around £2,000 which was some 12 per cent of the total annual cost of the Geological Survey of the entire United Kingdom.

The Wharton Committee made one other recommendation of note within the present context. It was suggested that a permanent Consultative Committee should be established to serve the Geological Survey of the United Kingdom in an advisory role. This new body came into being in November 1901 under the chairmanship of Professor John Wesley Judd, a former Geological Survey man and Grenville Cole's erstwhile mentor and colleague at the Royal School of Mines. Of the nine other members of the new committee, four, including Wharton himself, had served upon the Wharton Committee and were presumably in agreement with its views upon the future of the Irish Survey. Sollas's appointment to the Consultative Committee afforded it with some direct insight into the affairs of Hume Street and the nature of Irish geology, but it was another appointment which carried the greatest significance so far as the Irish Survey was concerned. Plunkett was nominated to the committee as the representative of the Department of Agriculture and Technical Instruction for Ireland. Upper Merrion Street fingers were now firmly lodged in the Hume Street pie.

Queen Victoria's death on 22 January 1901 was widely regarded as marking the close of an era. Within three months of the queen's final journey to Windsor there took place two retirements which similarly mark the close of an era for the Geological Survey of Ireland. The first retirement was that of Geikie from the directorship-general on 1 March 1901. On 1 May following, a dinner was held in London in Geikie's honour. Lord Avebury presided and among the eighty-eight distinguished gentlemen present were Cole, Hull, Seymour (representing the Irish Survey), Sollas, and Watts. Geikie's successor was (Sir) Jethro Justinian Harris Teall. It was the first time since De La Beche's death in 1855 that the head of the Geological Survey had not been a Scotsman by birth. Teall was an Englishman from Gloucestershire, and perhaps the absence of Celtic blood from his veins influenced his attitude towards Ireland. He certainly displayed none of Geikie's interest either in the problems of Irish geology or in the affairs of Hume Street.

The second retirement was that of Nolan, Senior Geologist in Charge in Hume Street. Having attained the age of sixty, he retired on 30 April 1901. Perhaps his colleagues gave him a dinner at Maple's, Morrison's, or some other well-known Dublin restaurant of the day. If they did, then the event has passed without record. Nolan had for some time been suffering from rheumatism and cardiac problems. He was dead within the twelvemonth.

Nolan's retirement meant that a new man had to be found to assume local responsibility for the Irish Survey. Geikie had agreed with Gill that the Irish Survey would in future concern itself chiefly with drift mapping. The Wharton Committee had recommended the adoption of the very same policy. It therefore followed that the new officer in charge of Hume Street should be a geologist familiar with the particular problems involved in the mapping of superficial deposits. Kilroe had recently been taking a deep interest in such matters but he would be eligible to retire in 1908 at the age of sixty and it seemed desirable that the post should be given to a younger officer. Over in England there was an officer with all the right qualifications. He was aged forty-two, he was a first-class field-man with an international reputation in Pleistocene geology, and he was willing to be transferred to Ireland. His name was George William Lamplugh.

Lamplugh was born in 1859 at Great Driffield, which stands just to the south of the Yorkshire Wolds. After his father's death, his mother removed the family down to the coast at Bridlington, and it was there that the young man embarked upon a commercial career in the office of a local merchant. But the sight of the white Cretaceous Chalk of Flamborough Head, the outcrops of the Speeton and Kimmeridge clays on the shores of Filey Bay, and the widespread smear of boulder clay all had their formative influence upon young Lamplugh's mind. They helped to make of him an enthusiastic and entirely self-taught amateur geologist. He started to attend scientific meetings and he began to publish scientific papers based upon his increasingly astute field-observations. His achievements brought him to the notice of Archibald Geikie who in 1892 offered him a post with the Geological Survey as a Temporary Assistant Geologist. Any man other than Lamplugh would surely have spurned Geikie's offer. Temporary Assistant Geologists faced an uncertain future and their salary was substantially less than that which Lamplugh was already earning in the commercial world. This financial aspect was a very material consideration since he now had a wife and family to support. But he hesitated not a moment. A professional geologist he just had to be. As such he enjoyed a career of considerable distinction. He was elected a Fellow of the Royal Society in 1905; he became the Assistant to the Director of the Geological Survey in 1914; and between 1918 and 1920 he was the President of the Geological Society of London. It was the kind of career which would have delighted Samuel Smiles.

Lamplugh took charge of the Irish Survey on 1 May 1901 in the rank of District Geologist. As if to emphasise the new relationship existing between the Survey and the Department of Agriculture and Technical Instruction, he that very day went over to leave his card in the office at Upper Merrion Street. Shortly thereafter Lamplugh and his men broke ground for what initially was intended to be a drift survey of the whole of Ireland. In launching the new survey Lamplugh obviously faced problems involving scientific methodology: how should the Irish drifts be classified and exactly what characteristics of the drifts were to be recorded upon the field-sheets? On all such matters Lamplugh clearly had his own strong views, formulated and tested during his Geological Survey

FIGURE 4.4. *George William Lamplugh (1859-1926). The illustration is reproduced from a plate in* The Geological Magazine *for August 1918.*

work in Britain and during his more distant excursions, some of which had taken him as far afield as British Columbia and Alaska. But in addition Lamplugh faced two major logistical problems, one of them human and the other geographical.

The human problem was that except for Kilroe, Lamplugh's five members of staff had little experience of the kind of geological task which now was theirs. McHenry, then approaching sixty years of age, had spent the last forty years almost exclusively in the investigation of problems in Irish solid geology. Clark was essentially a palaeontologist and museum curator. Seymour had been the Survey's petrologist since 1898 but now he had to return his microscope and his slides to their respective cabinets as he took to the field to be retrained as a drift man. Lamplugh's fifth officer was a novice who had joined the Survey as recently as 12 April 1901 in replacement of the deceased Egan. The novice's name was William Bourke Wright and under Lamplugh's tutelage the young man soon began to display the talents which were destined to make him one of the world's best-known Pleistocene geologists. It was those talents which have earned him a prominent place within Chapter Eight of the present volume. At the outset,

Lamplugh's Hume Street team hardly seemed well suited to the task now in hand and much credit is due to their captain for the fact that by example and inspiration he speedily converted his officers into an effective group of Quaternary geologists.

Lamplugh's geographical problem related to the spatial priorities of the new survey. Where should the drift mapping begin? During his discussion with Gill, in July of the previous year, Geikie had agreed that the Department of Agriculture and Technical Instruction should have some control over the manner in which the Survey developed its drift-mapping programme. Whether, in the event, the Department's officers really did exert such influence is unclear. What is clear is that Lamplugh undertook first to map the drifts of the Dublin region and then to map the drifts lying in and around each of the other major Irish population centres.

For the moment gone were the days when Survey officers spent their time grappling with abstruse geological problems set in thinly populated regions where the landscape was dotted with little more than scrawny sheep and concealed poteen-stills. A mapping of the drifts around Belfast, Cork, Dublin, Limerick, and Londonderry was literally going to place the officers onto the doorsteps and into the backyards of one quarter of the Irish population. The programme of drift mapping was designed to show how immediately relevant a geological survey was for the Irish people whenever they took up a spade to build a new bridge, to lay out a new sewer, or to dig a new grave. In 1900 Geikie might have agreed that the Department should henceforth assume responsibility for Irish economic geology, but in 1901, and through its drift mapping, the Survey was laying firm claim to a responsibility for Irish applied geology.

The drift survey of the Dublin region involved the mapping of some 400 square kilometres of country spread across thirteen six-inch sheets. This task was completed during the six months between May and November 1901. In character the mapping was concerned with a simple delimitation of the basic drift elements within the landscape and there was little attempt to present those elements as chronological ciphers within some geohistorical story. The officers were required to map such drift units as the blown sand of the North Bull, the recent intake at Booterstown, the alluvium of the Liffey valley, the raised beach around Sutton, the 'river-gravel terraces' on the Dodder upstream of Rathfarnham, and, of course, the boulder clay, which was divided into the clay 'mainly of non-calcareous material' around the flanks of the Dublin Mountains, and the clay 'containing much limestone' which mantles most of the remainder of the landscape.

Even within Ireland itself there can be few modern geologists possessed of any familiarity with the detail of the events surrounding Lamplugh's drift survey of the Dublin region. Every geologist in the world is nonetheless familiar with three terms which were introduced into the vocabulary of geology during the course of the survey. Lamplugh found that locally certain of the Dublin boulder clays had become cemented into a solid mass through the action of percolating waters charged with calcium carbonate. Such cemented deposits, he suggested, should be termed 'calcretes'. Similarly, deposits cemented by silica precipitation might be termed 'silcretes', and deposits cemented by iron precipitation might be termed 'ferricretes'. Those three terms were coined as the men from Hume Street looked down upon Dublin from the adjacent hills, the terms were introduced into the literature by Lamplugh in December 1902, and today the terms are in universal usage.

With the Dublin drift survey completed, in 1902 Lamplugh and his little team went north to map the drifts of the Belfast region. Further identical surveys followed in the Cork region during 1903 and in the Limerick region during 1904. As we will discover shortly, Lamplugh ceased to be an officer of the Irish Survey during 1904, but after his departure one final drift survey was undertaken, that being of the Londonderry region and carried out during 1905 and 1906.

One-inch drift maps from these five surveys were all published with commendable rapidity as follows:

Dublin	1903 (falsely dated 1902)
Belfast	1904
Cork	1905
Limerick	1906
Londonderry	1908

John Andrews has explained that early in the 1850s, when the Ordnance Survey was arranging the sheet-lines for its one-inch map of Ireland, it was Dublin which in every sense called the tune. The sheet-lines were arranged so that the Irish capital lay plumb in the middle of what was to become one-inch Sheet 112, while all the other Irish cities had to take their chance with the sheet-lines no matter how inconveniently they might fall. At the heart of Belfast, for instance, the *Titanic* came close to sliding across the corners of four one-inch sheets when she was launched from slip number 3 in Harland and Wolff's yard on 31 May 1911. The Dublin drift map has sheet-lines corresponding to the Ordnance Survey's one-inch Sheet 112 and to the Geological Survey's own one-inch solid geology sheet first published in 1859. To this day one-inch Sheet 112 remains the sole one-inch Geological Survey sheet of the original series to have been published in both a solid and a drift version. In the cases of Belfast, Cork, Limerick, and Londonderry the existing one-

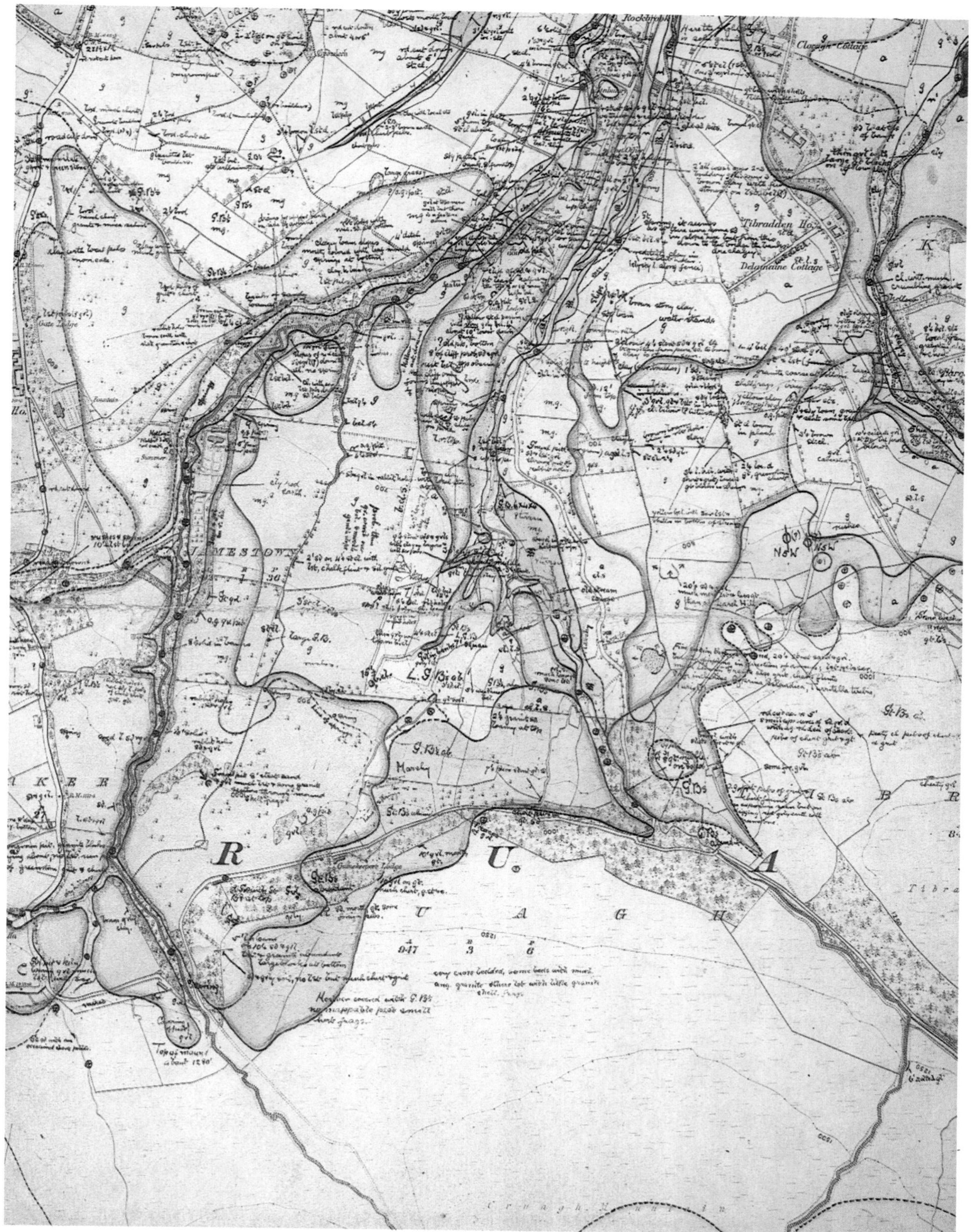

PLATE V. *The work of a novice, but one who was heir in a great tradition. One of Wright's six-inch field-sheets dating from the drift survey of the Dublin region in 1901. The sheet is a portion of County Dublin Sheet 25/2 depicting part of the foothills of the Dublin Mountains northward of Cruagh Mountain. In addition to mapping the drift geology, Wright and his colleagues were also recording land-use. Letters inscribed upon the individual fields of the sheet represent land-use according to the following notation: g Grass Land; mg Meadow Land; ng New or Rotation Pasture; a Tillage Land.*

inch sheet-lines proved too inconvenient and the Ordnance Survey therefore prepared new one-inch base-sheets for the use of the geologists. Each of these four drift sheets overlaps either two or four of the earlier one-inch solid sheets.

Perhaps in an effort to overcome the Survey's colonial image, it was originally hoped that all the drift maps would be printed at the Ordnance Survey's office in Phoenix Park, Dublin. But the Ordnance Survey itself was lukewarm about this proposal. On 29 October 1901 the Ordnance Survey warned the Geological Survey that the colour-printing facilities available in Phoenix Park were inferior to those available at the Ordnance Survey's headquarters in Southampton. A Dublin colour-printed map was not going to be as good as a Southampton colour-printed map. The experiment was nonetheless tried. The Dublin drift sheet was printed in Phoenix Park with the colours added in a series of lines and stipples. It was the Geological Survey of Ireland's first colour-printed map but, sadly, it would appear to have been pronounced a cartographic failure. The remaining four drift sheets were all printed in Southampton with flat sheets of colour replacing the lines and stipples of the Dublin map (see Plate VI).

Each of the five drift sheets was accompanied by a substantial new descriptive memoir, the memoirs all being published between 1903 and 1908. Within the memoirs the account of the local solid rocks is taken largely from the earlier sheet memoirs edited by Jukes or by Hull, but the discussion of the local drifts is in each case both entirely new and remarkably comprehensive. The Survey's desire to be seen as doing something of material value to the Irish people is reflected in the inclusion within each memoir of a section devoted to economic geology. The Belfast memoir, for instance, devotes seventeen of its 174 pages to economic geology, the contents of the section being arranged under the heads of metalliferous ores, gypsum, rock salt, peat, building materials, house sites, water-supply, agricultural geology, and soils. Another innovation reflecting changed times was the inclusion of some fine photographic plates within the memoirs. Those in the Limerick and Londonderry memoirs are plates from a camera belonging to Seymour, but the plates in the other three memoirs are all the work of the noted Belfast photographer Robert John Welch.

The six-inch field-sheets compiled by Lamplugh and his officers during the drift survey all survive within the archives of the Geological Survey at Beggars Bush. To examine those sheets is to experience a surprise. We discover that the Survey was not only mapping the drifts. The officers were performing two other tasks — tasks which receive no mention upon the published maps, within the pages of the memoirs, or, indeed, among the Survey's surviving correspondence files. The officers were not concerned solely with the mapping of the drift phenomena; they were also making a field-by-field map of rural land-use and, as the opportunity arose, they were recording observations of soil character (see Plate V).

Land-use they mapped according to the categories of grass-land, meadow-land, new or rotation pasture, or tillage-land, and their observations, now a century old, must surely possess interest for historians of Irish agriculture. The notes upon soils are of a very rudimentary character. Clearly officers were never expected to dig deep soil-pits or even to use a soil-auger. All that was attempted was a recording of any revealed soil character according to the simple scale of clayey, loamy, stony, gravelly, sandy, or peaty (but see p.130).

In these fascinating field-sheets, through the land-use mapping and the notes upon soils, we again see reflected the Survey's determination to render its activities as relevant as possible to the everyday issues of Irish life. The Survey's new-found interest in soils perhaps holds a special significance. As we have seen already, the Department of Agriculture and Technical Instruction was thinking of undertaking some kind of soil survey of the whole of Ireland. By making its own observations upon Irish soils the Survey was perhaps attempting to stifle the opposition and to pre-empt for itself the entire field of Irish soil science.

When Lamplugh died in 1926 his obituarist in the *Geological Magazine* observed, without any explanation, that the deceased's few years in Dublin 'were not the happiest of his life'. Initially such an assessment must evoke puzzlement. Lamplugh did a fine job in Hume Street. Within a mere four years he supervised drift surveys of the regions around Dublin, Belfast, Cork, and Limerick, and he saw into print the resultant drift maps and memoirs for Dublin, Belfast, and Cork. His relations with his staff seem to have been entirely harmonious and following his departure from Hume Street his former Irish colleagues presented him with what is described as 'a set of pictures'. Was this, perhaps, a set of James Malton's prints of Dublin? What we do know is that, to Lamplugh's delight, the gift reached him in England on his forty-sixth birthday, 8 April 1905. If we wish to learn of Lamplugh in the wider Irish context we may turn to the *Irish Naturalist* for October 1904. There we find a note entitled 'Denudation in the Geological Survey' regretting Lamplugh's departure from Hume Street with the following words.

> He had endeared himself to every one with whom he came in contact in Ireland, and was already a guide, philosopher, and friend to young geologists throughout the country.

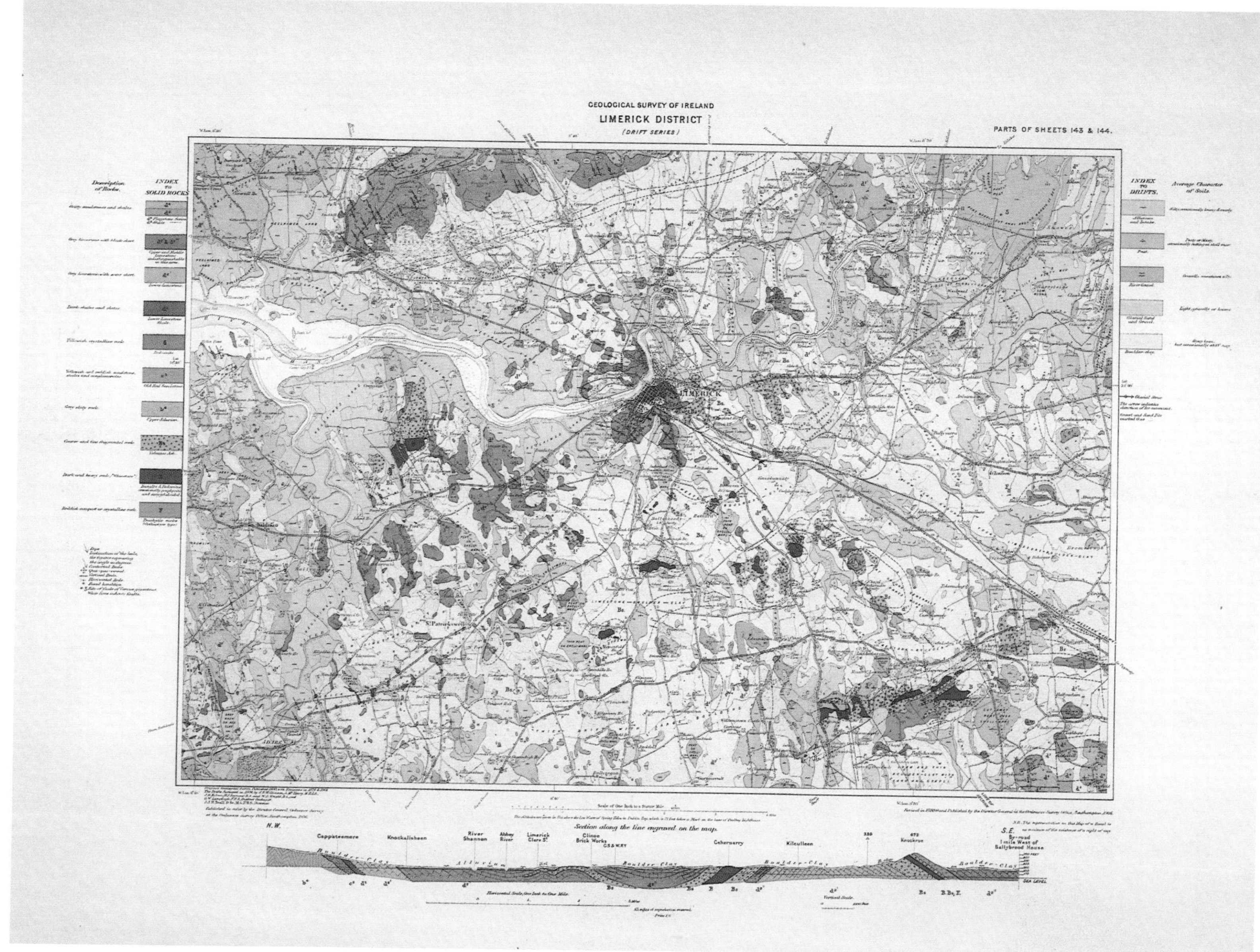

PLATE VI. *The 1906 colour-printed drift map of the Limerick district, here reduced in size. The inner frame of the original measures 46.5 x 30.5 centimetres.*
(Reproduced from a copy in the collection of the Geological Survey of Ireland.)

Why, then, was so successful and esteemed a geologist unhappy in his Irish billet?

At the root of Lamplugh's Irish problems there lay one simple fact: he was a geological perfectionist ever striving to attain the unattainable. Everywhere about him in Ireland he found that he had to rest content with less than that perfection for which he craved. In Hume Street it aggrieved him to discover that the Irish Survey had no real set of Standard Copies for the one-inch map. The Irish officers, unlike their British counterparts, were content to treat as Standards the one-inch manuscript sheets compiled directly from the six-inch field-sheets. In many cases these compilation sheets carried evidence of changing interpretations introduced during the reduction of the six-inch field-observations to the published one-inch scale. In other cases these compilation sheets were deficient in detail which was actually present upon the published one-inch sheets. For Lamplugh such working documents were unworthy of Standard Copy status. Again, in November 1901, when Lamplugh recalled all the one-inch Colourist's Pattern Copies from the colourist in England (the colourist was now Mr F. Dyer but he worked at the same address in Camden Square, London, as the aforementioned Mrs E. Williams) he found them to be faded, soiled, and worn and quite unfit to serve their intended purpose. On 2 January 1902 he therefore set about the gargantuan task of having prepared a new set of Colourist's Pattern Copies.

Problems of a very different nature confronted Lamplugh in 1903 when he went south to conduct the drift survey of the Cork region. The solid rocks of that portion of Munster had been mapped originally by Jukes and his men during the 1850s, but after 1878 Hull had introduced his unwise revisions affecting the region's Old Red Sandstone, and after 1890 Geikie had insisted upon some dubious modifications among the Carboniferous strata. So far as Hull's revision of the Old Red Sandstone is concerned, that term 'unwise' is really far too generous an adjective to employ. As we have seen, the revision reflected both a wilful misreading of the field-evidence and crass stupidity upon the part of the perpetrator of the revision (see p.82). Lamplugh was aware of all this, but the then current one-inch sheets carried some of the suspect revisions, so what was he to do? He had to have a map of the solid geology of the Cork region as a base-map to his drift survey. Was he to employ the Survey's latest one-inch sheets, incorporating revisions which he knew to be erroneous? Or was he to revert to the interpretation published upon the one-inch sheets of Jukes's day and thus cast public aspersion upon the competence of more recent Survey officers? Good scientist that he was, Lamplugh decided that scientific truth must be placed before institutional loyalty. He opted for a reversion to the interpretation of the region's solid geology as it had been depicted upon the one-inch maps published by Jukes in 1858.

For Lamplugh this little episode in County Cork had far wider implications than those just outlined. The problems in Cork represented the lifting of the lid off another potential can of Survey worms.

First, the two officers who had carried out the revisions at the behest of Hull and Geikie were McHenry and Kilroe. Both these officers had always protested that from the outset they had entertained grave doubts about the validity of the revisions which they were required to introduce. They both pleaded that in their revision mapping they were only doing what their superiors had instructed them to do. They had been acting under orders. But the Cork affair left a nasty smell in Lamplugh's nostrils. He clearly felt that McHenry and Kilroe had debased their science by allowing themselves to be inveigled into becoming the instruments whereby grievous error was introduced into the fabric of Irish geology. They were both charming field-companions but their scientific escutcheons were tarnished. And now these two men were Lamplugh's chief lieutenants. He had to rely upon them to produce work of the high standard which he expected, but in the light of the past were they really capable of meeting his demands? Had Teall placed into his hands a sadly flawed weapon?

Second, if such atrocities had been inflicted upon the geology of County Cork, then what crimes against geological truth might have been committed by the Survey elsewhere in Ireland? Was the Survey's geological edifice riddled throughout with the woodworm of error? Would the fabric crumble into dust wherever Lamplugh chose to test its soundness with his hammer? During the summer of 1903 Teall's Assistant, Horace Bolingbroke Woodward, visited Cork to inspect the progress of the drift survey. There Lamplugh introduced Woodward to some of the problems arising from the revisions ordered by Hull and Geikie. Woodward was clearly shocked. If what he had seen in County Cork was typical of the Irish Survey's mapping of solid rocks, then that Survey's standards were far inferior to those of the British Survey. Woodward left Ireland convinced that the country needed much more than a survey of its drift deposits; there was need, he considered, for a complete nationwide revision of the mapping of Ireland's solid geology.

(In fairness to the officers of the Victorian Irish Survey it has to be said that Lamplugh's fears were largely groundless and that Woodward was over-reacting. In the Cork region they were seeing displayed the most glaring of the Survey's misdemeanours. Had Woodward tested the quality of the Survey's mapping elsewhere in Ireland, then he must surely have moderated his claim for a resurvey of the entire island. It was Wright who perceptively observed that such a nationwide revision of the solid rock mapping would be '(between ourselves) more to the interest of The Staff than to that of the General Public.')

Lamplugh's unhappiness was further compounded by the fact that for much of his period in Dublin he must have felt somewhat like a bone in contention between a pair of dogs. One of the dogs lived in a kennel in London's Jermyn Street and the other had his kennel in Dublin's Upper Merrion Street. During 1901 Teall and Lamplugh were both involved in discussions with Gill on the subject of relations between the Survey and the Department of Agriculture and Technical Instruction. At a lower level Lamplugh and Cole met on several occasions to try to resolve the problem of responsibility for economic geology. It was that problem — the vexed question of economic geology — which gave to Lamplugh his first serious Irish headache.

In his discussions with Gill in July 1900 Geikie had agreed that in future all issues connected with Irish economic geology would be handled not by the Survey but by the Department of Agriculture and Technical Instruction. This decision clearly denied the Survey the opportunity of demonstrating the relevance of its work to the immediate needs of the Irish people. It was a decision which in practice was difficult of application. It was a decision which left Lamplugh discomfited. On 8 October 1901, for instance, Mr Wandesforde of Castlecomer arrived at Hume Street soliciting the Survey's advice over the sinking of some trial boreholes in the Coal Measures near to Banteer in County Cork. Was this to be regarded as an economic matter? What was Lamplugh to do? The problem was discussed with Gill at the Department, and on this occasion a compromise solution was achieved. It was decided that McHenry from the Survey and Cole from the Department should both go down to Banteer and there act jointly like Marco and Giuseppe Palmieri in Barataria.

Perhaps this little episode brought the issue to a head. Certainly on 22 January 1902 Teall formally instructed Lamplugh that henceforth all matters involving economic geology were to be left entirely to the Department. That very evening Lamplugh met with Cole in the Conversation Room of the Royal Dublin Society in Leinster House to explore further the common problem of economic geology, and on 11 February 1902 Cole wrote to Lamplugh explaining that it was now Gill's wish that the Survey should forward all economic enquiries directly to Cole at the Royal College of Science. The Survey, nevertheless, fought a brave rearguard action through the inclusion within its new drift memoirs of those essays upon economic geology to which reference has already been made.

Cole was far from happy with his fresh responsibilities in the area of economic geology. He was an academic geologist. He was a petrologist. He had teaching responsibilities. He suffered the physical disability of dwarfishness which rendered extended programmes of field-work difficult for him. He had no wish to be at the beck and call of every misguided soul who had mistaken 'fool's gold' for the genuine article or quartz crystals for diamonds. He saw himself as the hapless victim of what he believed to be the Survey's dereliction of its economic responsibilities. It was his own bad luck that the Department of Agriculture and Technical Instruction should have taken over those responsibilities in the immediate aftermath of an administrative reshuffle which had placed the Royal College of Science under the Department's wing, thus leaving Cole in the exposed position of being the Department's sole geologist.

Cole had been a professor with abundant time for research and for writing. Now he was expected to assume the mantle of an itinerant economic geologist. It is impossible not to sympathise with him in his predicament. It is certainly easy to understand why, as they sat in the Conversation Room at Leinster House on 22 January 1902, Cole explained to Lamplugh that the Department would have to provide him with an assistant whose prime task would be the undertaking of field-investigation. That assistant was soon forthcoming although his appointment was achieved in a somewhat circuitous manner.

The Department had mounted a widely praised display at the Glasgow International Exhibition of 1901 and there was a desire to emulate this success at the Cork International Exhibition of 1902. More especially, the Department desired to display in Cork a collection of the Irish rocks and minerals which were possessed of economic significance. Richard Clark from the Survey was a member of the Cork exhibition's committee in the department of raw materials and minerals, but Plunkett, Gill, and their minions in Upper Merrion Street had no intention of involving the Survey in the development of the Department's Cork exhibit. The Department had other plans involving one Edward St John Lyburn.

Lyburn had studied mining at the Royal College of Science for Ireland where he had become an Associate in 1893. He was thus one of Cole's former students. After graduation he worked as an assayer and mining engineer in southern Africa, but in 1898 he was back in Ireland holding a Department of Science and Art scholarship which enabled him to spend six months examining the auriferous deposits of the Gold Mines region of County

Wicklow. In June 1898 he read before the Royal Dublin Society a paper on mining in Swaziland and the Transvaal, and in December 1900 he presented before the same society a paper on the Wicklow gold deposits. These public appearances had their effect; somebody in the Department of Agriculture and Technical Instruction noticed both Lyburn and his credentials. On 23 December 1901 he was invited to assume responsibility for the collection of the geological materials which were to be included in the Department's Cork exhibit.

Lyburn spent the first three months of 1902 travelling throughout Ireland collecting specimens for the Cork display. He sought the assistance of a wide range of officials from county surveyors and quarry owners, to town-clerks and the members of the Irish Land Agents' Committee, but he makes no mention of his ever having rung the bell at 14 Hume Street. His Irish activities resulted in his writing of an account of the nation's rock and mineral resources, and this account he published in the Department's annual report for 1901-2. In the account he drew attention to many a geological resource which he claimed to be worthy of exploitation. There was lead at Glendalough and in County Monaghan. There was coal in counties Kilkenny, Tipperary, and Tyrone. There was slate at Killaloe. There was limestone to be quarried at Foynes. And there were minerals and slates to be worked in West Cork. All this information he managed to present in a manner which seemed to imply that he was reporting a series of startlingly original discoveries. The geological image of Ireland which he sought to present is epitomised in the following passage from his essay.

> It is unnecessary for me to add that Ireland, from a prospector's point of view, remains "unscratched", or, in other words, very little prospecting has been done in the country.

This was fair neither to the Geological Survey nor to those who had spent mints of money in their efforts to develop Irish mines. Lyburn's words were nevertheless sweet music in the ears of the denizens of Upper Merrion Street. Lyburn had his reward. As soon as funds could be made available he was appointed as Economic Geologist to the Department of Agriculture and Technical Instruction.

In this manner did Cole obtain a geological assistant, while the Department could now claim to possess its own geological bureau. In this manner, too, did the Survey acquire a local rival. It was a rival which might well have been prepared to boast that it was excelling over the Survey. Were Cole and Lyburn not under Irish control and doing work of direct, day-to-day relevance to the Irish populace? For half a century had London not deliberately directed its own colonial-style Survey into the making of esoteric studies of a type which fascinated your English professors but which were quite incomprehensible to Manus up in Donegal or to Donnchadh over in Clare? Nemesis was on her way from upper Merrion Street, down Ely Place, and into Hume Street.

While Lyburn was collecting his exhibits for the Cork exhibition of 1902, the report of the Wharton Committee was brought back to the centre of the stage. The report had been confidential and even today copies of the report are far from easy to find. Plunkett nonetheless somehow obtained access to the document. He did not like what he read therein. The report had, of course, recommended the appointment of a Geological Survey Consultative Committee and Plunkett had himself just been appointed to that new body. On 1 February 1902 he wrote to the secretary of that committee a letter which had two objectives. First, there came a trivial point. Plunkett presented his apologies for his inability to be present at the inaugural meeting of the Consultative Committee on 3 February 1902. Second, and of vastly more importance, he sought to make it clear that he found entirely unacceptable the Wharton Committee's decision relating to the Geological Survey of Ireland.

The Wharton Committee, it will be remembered, had recommended that the Survey should be instructed to complete a drift survey of Ireland, it being understood, as Geikie must have advised, that such a survey would occupy no more than just a few years. Further, the committee had recommended that at the conclusion of this task the Geological Survey of Ireland should be abolished. Its remaining officers should be transferred to Britain and thereafter the Department of Agriculture and Technical Instruction should shoulder the public responsibility for all aspects of Irish geology. Plunkett now protested that the Irish national interest demanded the continued existence of an effective Irish geological survey. But his own Department, he claimed, lacked the resources necessary to allow it to assume full responsibility for a geological survey of Ireland. He therefore demanded that the Geological Survey of Ireland should not be evacuated to Britain upon the completion of the drift survey. Rather should the Geological Survey of Ireland in its entirety be handed over to the Department of Agriculture and Technical Instruction. Upper Merrion Street was proposing to swallow Hume Street.

For the moment London chose to take no action upon the matter. Plunkett's discovery that the Wharton Committee had proposed the abolition of the Geological Survey of Ireland must nevertheless have been a significant factor prompting Plunkett in the appointment of Lyburn as the Department's

Economic Geologist and thus in the addition of a geological bureau to Plunkett's already expansive empire.

This chapter approaches its denouement. There are now in place all the elements of the final scene save one. Just as Ireland was creating problems within the Palace of Westminster, so, too, was Ireland creating problems within Jermyn Street. Teall lacked Geikie's enthusiasm for Ireland. Woodward had returned from Cork in 1903 convinced that the Survey's work in Ireland fell far short of British Survey standards. Lamplugh was unhappy in his colonial billet and wanted to return to England. He had reservations about the competence of his senior staff; the able Wright, his most junior officer, was in 1904 a candidate for transfer to the British Survey; and even Lamplugh himself seems to have harboured doubts about the public utility of the drift survey. Thanks to Geikie, the Survey had already lost from the Irish geological bone the juicy morsel of Irish economic geology, and ever since February 1902 Plunkett had been pulling vigorously at the remainder of the bone. The old Jermyn Street dog was losing interest in the contest with its young Upper Merrion Street rival. It was Lamplugh who gave to the story its final element. It was he who threw into the arena the bombshell which finally caused the Jermyn Street dog to retreat into its London kennel.

Exactly when Lamplugh discovered his bombshell is not clear. He perhaps discussed it with Teall late in 1902 or early in 1903, but it made its earliest formal appearance in a confidential memorandum which Lamplugh addressed to the Board of Education on 21 April 1903. His explosive information was that Geikie and the Wharton Committee had both subscribed to a mistaken belief. They had both been egregiously wrong about the time necessary for the completion of a drift survey of Ireland based upon six-inch field-mapping. Such a survey was really a most complex task. In the light of his experience with the drift surveys of the regions around Dublin and Belfast, Lamplugh was now in a position to offer a forecast. Assuming the Survey's present resources, a complete and detailed drift survey of Ireland would occupy not less than one hundred and forty years! It could be expected to take more than three times as long as the Survey's solid survey carried out between 1845 and 1890. The drift survey was unlikely to be completed before the year 2042.

This was the height of absurdity. Nobody - certainly not Teall and Lamplugh - considered that a drift survey of Ireland was worthy of such an expenditure of money and time. The moment had arrived for Hume Street and Jermyn Street to decorate themselves with white flags.

The Department of Agriculture and Technical Instruction had throughout these months been maintaining its insistence that it be given control of the Survey. This, for example, is Gill writing to the Board of Education on 21 May 1904.

> The Department consider that if they had under their charge the staff of the Geological Survey in Ireland they could greatly increase the value of the economic side of Geology to the country without in any degree impairing the progress of the survey work on its scientific side.

The Board of Education now agreed. On 1 July 1904 the Board wrote to the Treasury saying that the moment had arrived for the Geological Survey of Ireland to be transferred to the control of the Department of Agriculture and Technical Instruction for Ireland. On 15 March 1905 an Order in Council effecting the transfer was sealed by the Lord Lieutenant (the Earl of Dudley) and Privy Council in Ireland in the Council Chamber at Dublin Castle.

But Plunkett and Gill were not going to be allowed to capture Lamplugh. Like Douglas MacArthur at Corregidor, Lamplugh slipped away from Ireland to fight further Pleistocene battles elsewhere. As early as 29 February 1904 he was told that he was being reappointed to the Geological Survey of England and Wales in replacement for Charles Edward Fox-Strangways who was on the point of retirement. The new head of the Geological Survey of Ireland was nominated on 27 February 1905. It will surely come as no surprise to readers to learn that he was the Department's senior geologist, Professor Grenville Cole. He was accorded the title 'Director' and it was the first time that the Survey had truly been headed by such a figure since Hull's retirement fifteen years earlier. But the office did have about it a slightly hollow ring. Nolan and then Lamplugh had both been full-time Survey men; Cole was to be merely a part-timer. He was expected to continue the execution of his professorial responsibilities in the Royal College of Science, and as Director he received an addition of only £100 to his salary. This sum, it was made clear, was not regarded as pensionable, and again one is left with a feeling that Cole had received a somewhat raw deal. There was, nevertheless, ample precedent for what Cole was now being asked to do. Oldham, Jukes, and Hull had all combined the direction of the Survey with the performance of professorial duties.

Teall made his final official crossing of the Irish Sea late in March 1905. At a ceremony in Hume Street on 1 April 1905 he formally handed the Geological Survey of Ireland over to Gill as the representative of the Department of Agriculture and Technical Instruction for Ireland. The ceremony must have taken place in the large, first-floor, front room which was now to become Cole's office. When, forty years ago, I first knew that room, its walls were hung with Du Noyer paintings, while between the windows there stood the cases especially made to contain those of Major-General Portlock's books which his wife had presented to the Survey back in 1864. The room was probably in very much the same state on 1 April 1905. Lamplugh had officially been an officer of the Geological Survey of England and Wales since 17 October 1904, but he had lingered in Ireland and was present in Hume Street for the handing-over ceremony as we must presume Cole similarly to have been. Perhaps for the occasion Clark, as Superintendent of Maps, had put on display a few of the Survey's more interesting sheets: the recently-published drift sheets of Belfast and Dublin, some colourful one-inch sheets, and maybe one of Oldham's county maps dating from the 1840s. Of one thing we may surely be confident: those attending the ceremony will hardly have overlooked the fact that to the very day it was the Survey's Diamond Jubilee.

An Irish institution had now assumed responsibility for a Survey which had hitherto been a colonial venture administered out of London. Irish geology was now to benefit from Home Rule. But it must not be assumed that Hume Street was the scene of great rejoicings on 1 April 1905. It is difficult to believe that the departure of Teall and Gill was followed by any popping of champagne bottles. In advance of the take-over nobody would seem to have asked the officers of the Geological Survey of Ireland what their own views in the matter might have been. Lamplugh and Wright had both voted with their feet by leaving for England once they saw the direction in which the wind was blowing. The remaining Survey officers were deeply concerned by what had happened. Even Cole had his reservations. Their combined disquiet will crop out early in the chapter which follows.

CHAPTER FIVE

RECUPERATION
1905-1924

The present staff of the Survey, in addition to the economic geologist attached to the Department, may be regarded as forming, under the chief officials of the Department, a bureau for the supply of geological information respecting Ireland, and for the investigation of her natural features and resources.

Grenville Cole in an essay published in the *Journal* of the Department of Agriculture and Technical Instruction during 1905.

The Dublin and South Eastern Railway was always more familiarly known as the Dublin Slow and Easy Railway. As such it features in the writings of Samuel Beckett. He knew the line well. His parents lived in Foxrock and he was a frequent Dublin-bound passenger out of Foxrock station. On early journeys his destination was his school in Earlsfort Place; on later journeys he was bound for the cobbled squares of Trinity or for some secluded corner in Davy Byrne's. At all times he was a close observer of his fellow passengers. He probably often noticed the dapper but diminutive gentleman with the sparkling eyes and a head which must have excited the fingers of any Victorian phrenologist. That gentleman lived in Carrickmines and he boarded the city-bound train at the last station before Foxrock. The gentleman was Professor Grenville Cole.

By birth Cole was English; by adoption he was Irish. He had arrived in Ireland in 1890 to assume the chair of geology in the Royal College of Science and he rapidly became an Hibernophile. In his concern for Ireland's wellbeing he would have yielded nothing to Horace Plunkett. His anger was aroused whenever he considered England to be giving Ireland less than a fair deal. A small illustration comes from the year 1915. It is a case a little like that of Sir Hugh Lane's pictures (once under the exclusive control of the National Gallery in London) or that of the great Birr telescope's speculum (still in the Science Museum in London). Cole discovered that certain Irish fossils collected by Captain Joseph Portlock around 1840 were in the Museum of Practical Geology in London. Cole decided that they should be in Dublin. He therefore wrote a memorandum requesting their repatriation and this he persuaded Thomas Gill to forward to London on behalf of the Department of Agriculture and Technical Instruction. The tone of Cole's communication was somewhat petulant. It certainly annoyed London. The authorities there considered it to be ridiculous that they should have been troubled with so trivial a matter in the midst of a global war. Cole they likened to some German plenipotentiary presenting a demand on behalf of *das Vaterland*. Not unreasonably, London refused to take any action.

All this is not to suggest that Cole was ever a green nationalist. Far from it. He was a red, white, and blue Unionist. There can have been no more loyal a professor present when King Edward laid the foundation stone of the new Royal College of Science for Ireland on 28 April 1904 or when King George declared open the magnificent completed college on 8 July 1911. In 1914 Cole did his bit for king and country by becoming a khaki-clad and bicycle-mounted (he was ever a cycling enthusiast) despatch-rider around Dublin for the Loyal Volunteers. He was clearly proud that at the outbreak of the war three members of the Survey staff should have joined the colours in response to Kitchener's call. By 1917 he was able to take satisfaction from the fact that his only son was in uniform and swinging along the French pavé to the strains of *Tipperary*. As we shall see shortly, Cole's political views may well have been one factor bearing upon the manner in which the Survey was regarded by Ireland's new masters in the aftermath of the nation's gaining of independence.

Cole may have been small in stature, but he was no intellectual lightweight. By the time he became Director of the Irish Survey his active and fluent pen had brought to him an extensive reputation. As early as 1889 he had received from the Geological Society of London the balance of the proceeds of the Murchison Geological Fund, and by 1905 he had to his credit two geological books, both in several editions, together with over a hundred geological research papers. He had also been responsible for sundry other publications of a more general nature, these including two delightful volumes (one co-authored with his wife, Blanche, a former student of Cole's) descriptive of cycling tours in Europe during those halcyon days before Gavrilo

FIGURE 5.1. *Grenville Arthur James Cole.* (From an original portrait in the archives of the Geological Survey of Ireland.)

FIGURE 5.2. *Grenville Cole addressing a party in the field at some unknown location. The plate is of somewhat poor quality but it has been included as a reminder that Cole was a man of small stature. Was this perhaps an excursion of the Dublin Naturalists' Field Club? Cole was certainly a vigorous supporter of the Club. He was the Club's President in 1896-97, and its Vice-President in 1894-95 and 1916-17.* (From an original in the archives of the Geological Survey of Ireland.)

Princip pulled the trigger in Sarajevo. In retrospect it seems strange that Cole should have had to wait until 1917 before being elected to Fellowship of the Royal Society of London. He was the third (and perhaps the last?) geologist to be accorded that distinction while serving as an officer of the Irish Survey.

When he arrived in Hume Street, Cole found awaiting him a staff consisting of four men. Those four had between them given to the Survey a total service of 110 years. Only Seymour was under the age of fifty. The transfer of Wright to England in 1904 had left an Irish vacancy and that vacancy was now filled by the appointment of yet another quinquagenarian. Cole had told the Department that because of his responsibilities in the Royal College of Science (and perhaps because of his increasing problem with rheumatoid arthritis) he could not be expected to undertake close oversight of his officers in the field. It was therefore decided to appoint a geologist who could be given the task of supervising all the Survey's day-by-day field activities. His rank was to be that of Senior Geologist. The man selected for the post was none other than one of the Irish Survey's former officers; Sidney Berdoe Neal Wilkinson.

Wilkinson had originally reported for duty with the Survey on 1 August 1867, way back in Jukes's day, and in 1890, following the completion of the one-inch map, he had been transferred to the Geological Survey of Scotland. He had never been a particularly talented or enthusiastic geologist and he had only joined the Survey in the first place because he was at a loose end after several times over failing to pass the examination necessary for entrance to the army. The fact that his father was then a Captain in the Royal Engineers had lacked nepotic significance in the eyes of the authorities at the Horse Guards; the fact that his father was then in charge of the Irish Ordnance Survey's establishment at Mountjoy Barracks, in the Phoenix Park, may perhaps have greased Wilkinson's entry through the backdoor of the Geological Survey of Ireland. Be that as it may, we must suspect that his 1905 decision to return to Ireland was inspired by no particular love for Irish geological problems. It was simply that Wilkinson was a zealous field-sportsman and he probably felt that his ambitions with gun and rod were more likely to be achieved in Ireland than in Britain.

If Wilkinson's return to Hume Street represented an unexpected event in the area of personnel, there

FIGURE 5.3. *The 'Gentleman Geologist'. Sidney Berdoe Neal Wilkinson about to take to the field. It is not clear whether on this particular occasion he proposed to carry his hammer, his rods, or his gun.* (Reproduced from the 1987 edition of Wilkinson's *Reminiscences of Sport in Ireland*.)

was one other event in the same area which might have been expected to occur but which in reality failed to take place. The Department might reasonably have been expected to transfer Edward Lyburn from Upper Merrion Street and into Hume Street. This the Department failed to do. Lyburn remained where he was as Economic Geologist to the Department, and although Cole on several occasions suggested that Lyburn might like to move himself into one of the vacant rooms in Hume Street, no such a consolidation of the Department's geological expertise occurred during Cole's years as Director.

It may be that Lyburn's absence from Hume Street was no bad thing. His presence might well have resulted in dissonance. His views on the state of Irish geology were hardly likely to win him friends within the Survey. For almost sixty years its officers had been exploring the rocks of Ireland, yet in 1902 Lyburn had temerously claimed that, from the point of view of a prospector, Ireland was still in the condition of being 'unscratched'. Around the time of Cole's assumption of the directorship, the Survey's officers would surely have rounded upon such a critic in their midst. They were in a fractious mood. Morale was at a low ebb. They were disturbed by what had happened to the Survey - their Survey - on 1 April 1905.

Two respected Survey officers - Lamplugh and Wright - were gone to Britain. The new man in charge of field operations was Wilkinson, a returned emigrant. Clark, Kilroe, and McHenry could all remember him from days of old as a somewhat odd and withdrawn individual. The new Director was a quite unknown quantity in the Survey context. He was lacking Survey experience; he was merely a part-time Director; and he had been foisted upon Hume Street by the bureaucrats of Upper Merrion Street.

Formerly the Irish Survey had only been one component within the very much larger Geological Survey of the United Kingdom - a Survey which, to use some words of Seymour's, enjoyed 'a prestige second to that of no other Survey in the world'. Now the Irish Survey had been torn from her revered British parent. She had been forced into bed with a controversial Irish upstart of a department which was already cohabiting with its own Economic Geologist. The Survey's new master knew nothing of the life to which she had been accustomed. She had lived in a world of science. Her social circle had been replete with Fellows of the Royal Society and of the Geological Society of London. Her visual pleasures had been sought in the galleries of the Museum of Practical Geology and those of the British Museum's department of natural history. Her reading had been found within the *Geological Magazine* and the monographs of the Palaeontographical Society. Her playthings had been clinometers and petrological microscopes. Now she had to adjust to living with a master who shared none of these interests. His prime concerns were the weight of fleece produced by Roscommon hoggets, the mode of slaughtering Limerick pigs, the shape of Galway lobster pots, and the marketing of Carrickmacross lace. She was told to employ herself usefully in the interests of her new master and those of the Irish people, but at the same time she was forbidden all conversation with the Irish people on the subject of economic geology. Economic geology was reserved for Lyburn.

The transfer of the Survey to the Department brought in its wake an immediate and very practical problem. The Department had made inadequate financial provision for the Survey's field-programme during the summer of 1905. As the money ran out Cole had to recall McHenry and Seymour from their field-stations during August, and Kilroe and Wilkinson had to abandon their field-work prematurely at the close of September. As that summer he sat in Hume Street, compelled to restrict himself to office work when he should have been tramping the countryside, Seymour perhaps mused over the predicament in which the Survey had been placed. He certainly now became the spokesman for his disgruntled colleagues, and on 26 April 1906 he addressed to Cole a substantial memorandum outlining the grievances of the staff. Some of the points which he made are points already adumbrated within the present chapter, but he also offered four other observations of interest and importance.

First, the staff were of the opinion that in appointing Cole as Director there had been established an ominous precedent. The Department was clearly regarding the directorship as an ancillary duty for their professor of geology in the Royal College of Science. Since there seemed every probability that this chair would always be filled from Britain, it followed that the Survey was now threatened with a succession of part-time Directors fished from within the British academic pond. (Here the fears of the officers were to prove groundless. They knew nothing of the academic developments which were to be triggered by future political change. Cole was the last individual to hold the directorship concurrently with an academic appointment and the Royal College of Science itself ceased to exist as a separate entity in 1926.)

Second, the events of 1905 had left the Irish Survey in an atrophied state. Before April 1905 the Irish Survey had been free to call upon the expertise of British Survey officers as the need might arise. Now this opportunity had been removed. Since Baily's death in 1888, for instance, the Irish Survey had possessed no specialist in palaeontology and

Irish fossils had regularly been sent to Britain for identification. Who was now going to serve as the Survey's palaeontologist? Similarly, the regular visits to Ireland by the Director-General had always served to assist the Irish officers in their setting of Irish geological problems within the broader context of the British Isles as a whole. Now such visits were at an end. The events of 1905 had indeed left the Survey in a state of scientific impoverishment.

Third, in days gone by there had been some interchange of officers across the Irish Sea. Only recently Lamplugh and Wright had gone off to join the British Survey while Muff had come to Ireland to work upon the Belfast and Cork drift surveys. The new situation seemed to preclude all such staff mobility. Henceforth, the Irish Survey would have to be content with a narrower and self-contained existence. This clearly had repercussions for the officers themselves and, again, for the progress of Irish field-geology.

Finally, the officers claimed that the 1905 amputation had seriously diminished their career prospects. Before the surgery they had been part of a large organisation in which they could consider themselves as eligible for promotion through various grades up to the rank of the directorship-general and the knighthood which had invariably been coupled to that office. Now they were part of a very much smaller organisation wherein the new relationship of the Irish directorship to the chair of geology in the Royal College of Science seemed to debar them from aspiring even to the directorship of their own Survey. It now appeared that officers of the Survey were trapped in what was virtually a dead-end-job. This, Seymour observed, must have serious implications.

> I feel strongly that under present conditions of promotion the right type of scientific man will not join the staff in Ireland, and as a necessary consequence the standard of work accomplished is likely to fall below the level of that done in adjoining countries. We should then occupy the unique and to my mind humiliating position for a Geological Survey of having our geological problems worked out for us by experts from across the channel, instead of having competent men on our own staff to deal with our own problems.

Perhaps here Seymour was writing with the pen of a prophet. Certainly readers might like to return to Seymour's words after a reading of the next chapter in the present volume. Cole himself accepted the thrust of Seymour's argument and he carried the point forward to the Department in a memorandum of his own dated 12 July 1905.

Seymour remained disillusioned. At heart he seems to have been a devoted Survey man. He was certainly an officer of promise. But he resigned from the Survey as from 1 November 1909 upon his appointment to the chair of geology in University College Dublin. That chair he held for almost forty years, but during those years he published very little geological research. The events of 1905 seem to have blighted the development of his research career. The man who as a fresh-faced graduate had once undertaken petrological studies on behalf of both the Irish and the Scottish surveys now allowed his geological instincts to wither. What happened to Seymour was a microcosm of what was shortly to happen to the Survey as a whole.

The Survey now had to fend for itself, but although the umbilical cord spanning the Irish Sea had been severed, there did persist a few tenuous links between the Irish and the British surveys. Seymour had complained that transfers across the Irish Sea would not be possible in the aftermath of 1905, but during the spring of 1907 he was himself allowed to spend eight weeks gaining experience with the British Survey by mapping around Matlock, in Derbyshire, under the supervision of Charles Bertie Wedd. (Perhaps Seymour hoped that the experience might lead to his being offered a permanent post with the British Survey.) In 1910, as we will discover shortly, Wright was allowed to transfer back to Ireland from the Geological Survey of Scotland, and very occasionally British Survey officers crossed to Ireland to assist in the solution of Irish problems. In November 1911, for example, two officers of the British Survey - Robert George Carruthers and Gabriel Wharton Lee - visited Bundoran to help with the identification of a base to the Carboniferous succession.

Down certainly to the 1920s the Irish Survey's maps, sections, and memoirs continued to feature in the catalogues being issued to the public from Jermyn Street, but gradually the two surveys drifted apart. It was like two terrestrial plates diverging after an episode of rifting. By 1935 the two surveys were separated by a metaphorical gulf far wider than the Irish Sea itself. In the July of that year the British Survey celebrated its centenary with a series of festivities. Delegates were in attendance from many parts of the empire and from thirty-three foreign countries including Afghanistan, Costa Rica, Haiti, and Salvador. But the Geological Survey of Ireland sent no delegate. Trinity College Dublin was represented by its Vice-Chancellor (Sir Thomas Francis Molony) and Seymour was present as the representative of the Royal Dublin Society, the Royal Irish Academy, and University College Dublin. But nobody had asked Seymour to add Hume Street to his representational brief. Perhaps it was all just an unfortunate oversight. Or was it? By 1935 the Irish Survey was a part of the Department of Industry and Commerce and its Minister was Sean Lemass. It was just two years earlier that he had been reported as having blamed the British

Government for duping the Irish people through the issue of misleading information about the true scale of Ireland's mineral wealth (see p.102).

The failure of the Department of Agriculture and Technical Instruction to provide an adequate grant for the Survey's field-programme during 1905 was regrettable. On a more positive note the Department did then take one imaginative and praiseworthy step. The Department conceded that the severance of the Irish Survey from its British counterpart had indeed resulted in Hume Street losing its former access to the expertise enshrined within the British Survey. To meet this difficulty the Department from 1905 onwards annually made available a subvention for the appointment of what were termed Temporary Professional Assistants. The idea was that, through the temporary engagement of selected specialists, the Survey would be able to buy in whatever geological expertise might become appropriate as the Survey's work developed. During the year 1905-6 the Department made £120 available for this type of appointment, and the contributions made by various of the Temporary Professional Assistants will be mentioned as our story unfolds.

When Cole assumed responsibility for the Survey he faced no easy task. What was now the Survey's *raison d'être?* He had to lead the Hume Street brigade but in what direction were they to proceed? As he sat in his new saddle surrounded by his staff no Captain Nolan came galloping over from Upper Merrion Street brandishing his sword and shouting 'There, my lord, is your enemy'. One thing alone was clear: the Survey was expected to undertake duties which both possessed practical significance for Ireland and held promise of economic enrichment for the Irish people. Anything was likely to be taboo if it merely excited the hammer-wielding greybeards into that kind of excited chatter which was incomprehensible to everybody outside the geological fraternity.

A re-orientation of the Survey towards applied geology might at first sight have appeared to be a solution to Cole's problem. But in reality that path was effectively barred by the presence of Lyburn over in Upper Merrion Street. Throughout his directorship Cole was to receive repeated official reminders that all public enquiries arriving in Hume Street and relating to economic geology were instantly to be referred to Lyburn. Cole himself included this very directive in the printed regulations which he completed for the Survey on 1 January 1914. (New Year's Day was a holiday only for those who had joined the Survey before 21 March 1890.) Economic geology was strictly Lyburn's bailiwick and there were those in the Department who would seemingly have wished to interpret the term 'economic geology' in its very broadest sense. Indeed, in his discussions with the Department in July 1900 (see p.111) had Sir Archibald Geikie not conceded that 'the economic side of geology' might be taken to encompass phenomena as varied as mineral resources, building materials, construction sites, sewerage schemes, and cemetery development?

Geikie's own efforts to find some utilitarian role for the Irish Survey had resulted in the launching of a nationwide drift survey. That project had become the victim of infanticide. Lamplugh was the unquestioned authority upon all matters relating to the drift and there was nobody prepared to quarrel with his conclusion that a complete drift mapping of Ireland would occupy the Survey for at least one hundred and forty years. Equally, there was nobody prepared to justify the proposal that over the next one hundred and forty years the Survey should devote itself to the completion of some two hundred one-inch drift sheets which in the event might prove to be of limited economic value.

Cole sought to give justification to the existence of the Survey by following three different avenues. Nowhere is he explicit upon the subject of his policy - the Survey's archives offer no confidential insights based upon documents marked 'for internal information only' - but an overview of the Survey's work during the first five years of Cole's regime renders clear his strategy. It was a nicely balanced strategy which had been carefully conceived and which was eminently successful. By 1910 Cole had steered the Survey-ship into far calmer waters than those in which she had been buffeted during the first five years of the century.

Cole's first avenue involved relating the Survey's work to Irish agriculture through the investigation of Irish soils. In this way the Survey would be able to assist Ireland's chief industry. As Cole explained in 1908:

> The study and description of soils, which represent the actual surface-material on which we live, seem appropriate to a Geological Survey acting under a Department of Agriculture and Technical Instruction.

Cole's second avenue led him upon a search for economic problems which the Survey might legitimately tackle using its own scientific expertise but without treading upon the tender toes of Lyburn or the Department. The Survey might be debarred from itself responding to enquiries of an economic nature addressed to Hume Street, but surely nobody within the Department would have the effrontery to complain if the Survey were to make significant economic discoveries during the course of its field programme.

Cole's third avenue was that of unashamed pure geology. Cole was a geologist of culture and perception. He recognised that in the past, both in its own right and through its association with the British Survey, the Geological Survey of Ireland had enjoyed a not inconsiderable international reputation. For the sake of both Ireland and the Survey itself, Cole wished the newly independent Survey to suffer no diminution in its global prestige. But how was the continuance of such prestige to be ensured? It was certainly not going to be ensured by shunting economic enquiries over to Lyburn, by assisting Mr Wandesforde with his boreholes at Banteer, or by reporting to the Department on the character of the soils to be found in its new Avondale Forestry Station. Full prestige would be achieved only if officers of the Survey were known to the world at large through their making of regular contributions to the internationally recognised corpus of geological knowledge. Cole was not only the Director of the Survey; he was also an academic holding a chair in a major institute of higher learning. By 1905 he already possessed his own distinguished record of research publication and he was clearly determined that Survey officers should be accorded the opportunity of making fundamental contributions to the international literature of their science. In any case, history demonstrated that the pure geology of one day might tomorrow be valued as possessed of the highest practical significance.

There was nothing idiosyncratic about Cole's decision to involve the Survey in the study of Irish soils. His decision merely mirrored events in Britain. There, around 1905, the British Survey was seriously contemplating the compilation of what it was proposed to term 'agronomic maps' for the use of agriculturalists, while in 1906 the same Survey published a second edition of H.B. Woodward's very successful memoir on *Soils and Subsoils from a Sanitary Point of View*.

Cole gave effect to his own policy on soils in a variety of ways. He acquired the pedological expertise which the Survey needed by appointing Timothy Hallissy as a Temporary Professional Assistant for a period of forty weeks during the year 1905-6. Hallissy was a graduate of the Royal University of Ireland in chemistry and physiology (1893) and an Associate of the Royal College of Science for Ireland in agriculture (1904). He had been teaching agricultural science in the college run by the Franciscan Brothers at Mount Bellew in County Galway, and while a Temporary Professional Assistant he taught soil-physics in the Royal College of Science. With the Survey, Hallissy's task was the mechanical analysis of soils. He was re-appointed as a Temporary Professional Assistant for a part of each year until October 1908, when he was appointed to the Survey's permanent staff as a Geologist just two days after the creation of a vacancy through McHenry's retirement. Cole and Hallissy together visited the Rothamsted Agricultural Experimental Station at Harpenden in Hertfordshire (Kilroe had been a slightly earlier visitor) and the lessons learned there were put to some purpose when a top-floor back-room in Hume Street was converted into a soils laboratory. In his annual report for 1908-9 Cole observed of this new facility:

> The Survey laboratory promises to be of increasing utility in the determination of substances in soils that may be beneficial or harmful to particular kinds of crops or trees.

Hallissy was a native of Blarney in County Cork and on the top-floor in Hume Street he was soon joined in succession by twin brothers who shared his natal place: Thomas Haigh and William D. Haigh. The twins graduated in the Royal College of Science for Ireland in 1908. William in August 1909 became a Temporary Professional Assistant with the Survey, his specialism being the chemical analysis of soils, while his brother went home to Munster to become a science-master in Cork Grammar School. William was regularly re-appointed in his Survey post down to the close of 1912, and in January 1913 he was succeeded by his ex-schoolmaster brother. Thomas remained with the Survey as a Temporary Professional Assistant until September 1914 when he obtained leave of absence to enlist in the Royal Dublin Fusiliers. With that regiment he served throughout the war, including the Gallipoli campaign, and he rose to the rank of sergeant-major before receiving a commission in January 1918. Of the three Survey officers who marched off to war in 1914 he alone survived.

The Survey was involved in soil investigations in many parts of Ireland. When Cole assumed the directorship, plans were already afoot for a drift survey to be made of the Londonderry district during the 1905 field-season and he allowed these plans to stand. Wilkinson took charge of the project and Cole made it clear that the soils of the region were to be given particular attention. The failure of the Department to provide sufficient funds for field-work during 1905 caused the Londonderry survey to spill over into the 1906 field-season and it was 1908 before there were published the one-inch Londonderry district drift map and its accompanying memoir.

Within the Londonderry region, soil-samples were collected at 28 sites and each collection-site is recorded upon the published drift map together with a notation indicating the character of the soil and subsoil at each site. The soil samples were all removed to Hume Street for examination by Kilroe and Hallissy who studied each sample from such angles as geological origin, chemical composition, physical texture, and capillarity (Figs 5.4 and 5.5). In his preface to the memoir even Cole was moved to comment upon the immense amount of work

FIGURE 5.4. *Soil sampling using the 2-litre collecting box during the drift survey of the Londonderry region in 1906. The figures are perhaps Kilroe on the left, McHenry on the right, and Hallissy, actually filling the box, in the centre. The steel box, 20x10x10 centimetres, had two removable sides, and it was filled with soil by hammering the box into a block of earth spade-dug from a soil-pit. Hallissy (?) is here hammering the box and the spade lies behind him.* (From a photograph in the archives of the Geological Survey of Ireland.)

involved in the analysis of each of the specimens. Whether the results so obtained were of sufficient agrarian or scientific interest to justify such an expenditure of effort I very much doubt.

The Survey was now taking its self-imposed pedological duties very seriously. Analyses of typical Irish soils were made for county agricultural instructors; during the year 1908-9 advice was given to the Department on the soils of its agricultural station at Clonakilty in West Cork; and in 1911-12 a number of soil samples were collected and reported upon in connection with the Department's schemes for afforestation. It should also be remembered that after being delayed for six years within the Department, Kilroe's *Soil-Geology of Ireland* was finally published during 1907. The Department hoped that through its explanation of the principles of soil genesis the book would demonstrate that it was but a short step 'from the victualler's block, and the meal and flour store, to the solid rock of mountain and plain'. But by the time of its appearance even Kilroe probably felt the volume to be a somewhat dated work.

The most ambitious of all the Survey's pedological projects was that carried out upon the former Ballyhaise estate located where the Annalee River wanders through the drumlins of County Cavan. The estate covered some 800 acres (324 hectares) and had for long been held by the Humphry family. Now the estate was the property of the Department. In January 1906 the former Humphry mansion (it is one of Richard Cassels's houses dating from 1730) was re-opened as an agricultural college and the estate itself became an instructional farm. Soon after the opening Kilroe, Seymour, and Hallissy moved in to survey the drifts underlying the farm and to make a map of its soils.

In the early days of geological cartography surveyors had commonly been content merely to plot point information upon their maps. They made little attempt to give any spatial expression to their mapping through the extrapolation of their point-observations into the adjacent ground where exposures were absent. Two Irish examples of such early maps are Robert Fraser's map of County Wicklow of 1801 and George Vaughan Sampson's map of County Londonderry of 1802 (see p.2). It took some time before geological surveyors achieved the confidence necessary to allow them to produce comprehensive maps depicting the

FIGURE 5.5. *The apparatus used by the Survey for observing the comparative capillarity of fine-earth soils, circa 1905 to 1912. The ten glass tubes were each 1 metre long and about 1.5 centimetres in diameter. The lower ends of the tubes stood in a zinc trough containing water kept at a constant level by means of the feed apparatus on the right. The lower ends of the tubes were first blocked with calico and then the tubes were filled with the fine-earths to be tested. The tubes were filled using the zinc scoop which leans against the apparatus on the right. The heights to which the water rose in the tubes were read off for seven days at intervals of 24 hours. To facilitate the readings a mirror was fitted behind the tubes and metre scales are attached to either side of the apparatus. The actual readings were taken by holding between these two scales that most essential of all items of scientific equipment, a piece of string. On the extreme right is the corkscrew used for removing earth from the tubes at the conclusion of an experiment.* (Reproduced from a photograph in the archives of the Geological Survey of Ireland.)

presumed nature of the geology in areas devoid of any outcrop. Much the same sort of development occurred within the Survey where soils were concerned. During the Londonderry drift survey of 1905-6 the officers had been content with point information relating to soils. Upon the published map they merely recorded the sites at which they had collected their 28 soil samples and alongside each site-marker they added their notation indicating the character of the soil and subsoil as determined at that point. Now, at Ballyhaise in 1906, they essayed something far more sophisticated. They set about the task of constructing a true soil map showing the actual spatial distribution of soil-types. They classified the local sites into seven soil-types; they mapped out the distribution of each of the soil-types on the ground using a soil-auger; and they traced out firm boundaries delimiting the field occurrence of each soil-type.

The various office stages in the compilation of the Ballyhaise map are to be traced in a series of maps surviving within the Survey's archives. The draughtsman involved was Martin William Gavin who had joined the Survey in 1903 after thirty-seven years of service with the Ordnance Survey. He must have been pleased in 1908 when Cole selected his manuscript version of the Ballyhaise map at a scale of twelve inches to one mile (1:5,280) for inclusion in the Survey's display at that year's Franco-British Exhibition at Shepherd's Bush in London. He must have been doubly pleased when the Survey's display was awarded a Grand Prix Diploma. The map was finally published in 1910 (it was printed by the Ordnance Survey in Southampton during 1909) at a scale of eight inches to one mile (1:7,920) and with an accompanying 50 page memoir (Plate VII).

In 1910 pedological cartography was still in its infancy and, small though it is, the Ballyhaise map was in the Irish context an innovative scientific achievement. But it proved to be just a flash in the Hume Street pan. The Survey never built upon the foundations laid at Ballyhaise and to this day the map of the former Humphry's estate remains the sole soil map to have been published by the Survey. Something of that map's innovative status is to be gauged from the fact that the second half of the twentieth century was well advanced before there appeared other Irish maps comparable to the Survey's Ballyhaise map. Those new maps were the county soil maps published by the National Soil Survey of Ireland which had been established in 1959 with its headquarters at Johnstown Castle in County Wexford. After an interval of fifty years the men at Johnstown Castle took up the challenge which the men of Hume Street had laid aside after completing their Ballyhaise survey. Cole's advance down the avenue of pedology virtually ceased at Ballyhaise as the Survey turned to more orthodox lines of geological investigation.

Under Cole's able direction the Survey's self-confidence had by 1910 been largely restored. No longer was it felt quite so necessary to pander to the Department's agrarian interests through the study of Irish soils. Pedology had lost its political appeal. Perhaps Hallissy read the runes correctly. He was the Survey's specialist in soils but around the time the Ballyhaise map was published he purchased for himself the sixth edition (June 1910) of Frederick Henry Hatch's *Text Book of Petrology*. I acquired Hallissy's copy of the work from a Dublin dealer only yesterday (20 October 1993) and its existence suggests that the Survey's pedologist felt the necessity for a modest programme of intellectual re-tooling.

The second avenue down which Cole led the Survey was the avenue of economic geology. There he avoided Lyburn by initially focusing upon a single topic demanding a high level of expertise of precisely the type which the Survey was able to command. It was a topic which turned the Survey's attention back to the volcanic northeast.

Northeastern Ireland was an area of extensive Tertiary vulcanism. Time after time glowing lava welled out of great crustal fissures; time and again the telluric blood oozed over the landscape before congealing to form an immense basaltic scab. Today that scab underlies almost 4,000 square kilometres in Ireland's northeastern corner. But the evidence to be read from the scab makes it clear that the bleeding was far from being a continuous process. There was a long period of quiescence during which the terrestrial wounds healed and the flow of blood was assuaged. We now know that the quiescence was of around a million years' duration, but it ended when the region's wounds were again ruptured and when new issues of blood poured out over the old scab.

This sequence of geohistorical events gives to the scab a threefold structure. At the base there are the Lower Basalts. In the middle is the Interbasaltic Horizon, a spectacular red band marking the depth to which the Lower Basalts were weathered during the period of quiescence. Finally, above the Interbasaltic Horizon, there are the various younger basalts produced as a result of the renewed vulcanism. It was upon the Interbasaltic Horizon that the Survey now riveted its attention.

During the formation of the Interbasaltic Horizon Ireland was experiencing climatic conditions of a warm and humid sub-tropical type. Under those conditions the weathering of the Lower Basalts resulted in the formation of pockets both of pisolitic iron-ore and of aluminium hydrate or bauxite. In Cole's day the iron-ore deposits were

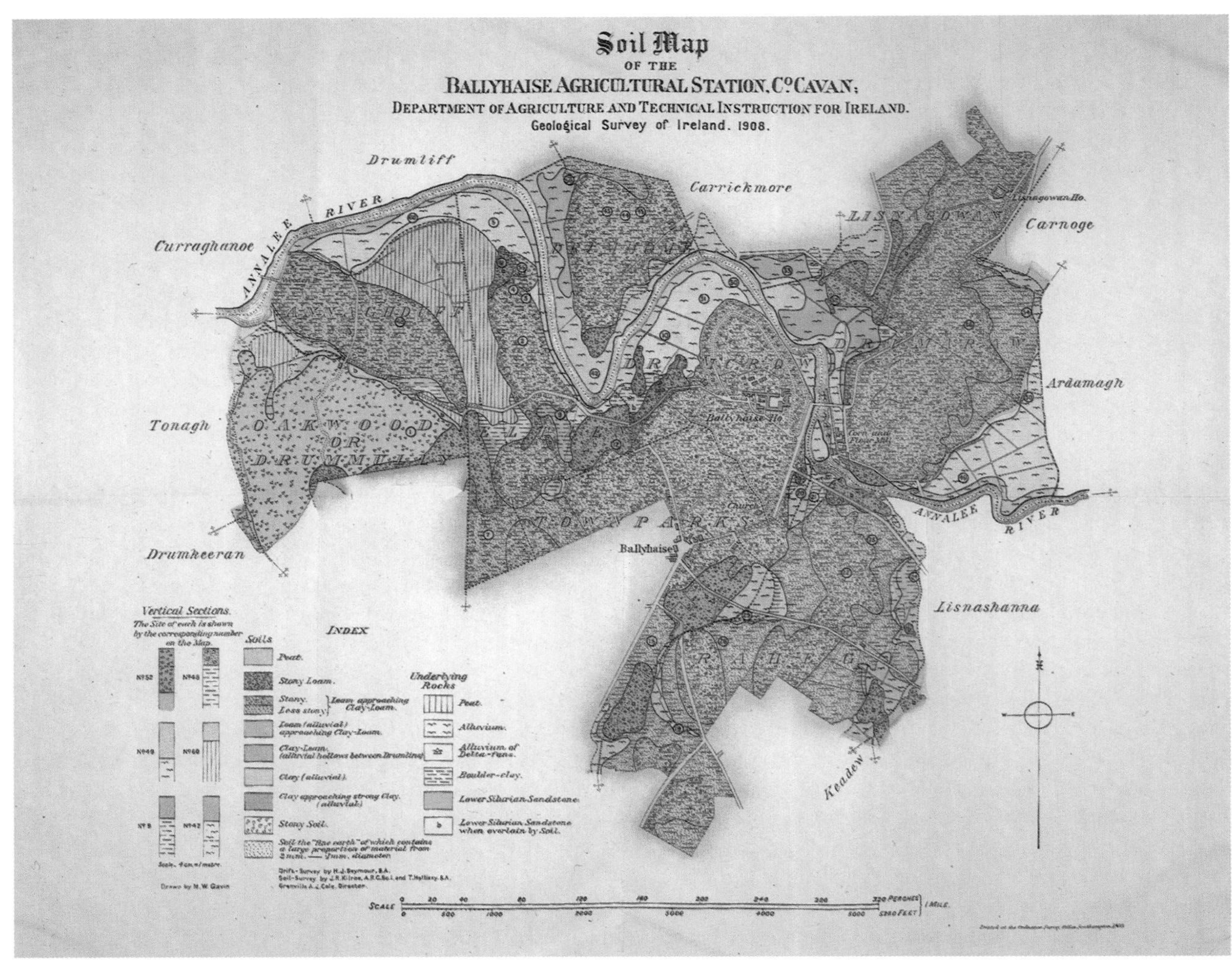

PLATE VII. *The Ballyhaise soil map, colour-printed by the Ordnance Survey at Southampton in 1909. This reproduction is somewhat reduced in size, the original sheet measuring 52 x 44.5 centimetres. The drift survey was by Seymour, the soil survey by Hallissy and Kilroe, and the map was drawn by Gavin, the Survey's draughtsman. The numbered sites are those at which one-litre soil-samples had been taken, and the nature of the samples is discussed in the memoir which accompanied the map. The map was folded and included in an envelope at the conclusion of the Ballyhaise memoir published in 1910. This reproduction of the map is from an unfolded specimen in the collections of the Geological Survey of Ireland.*

being exploited as Ireland's only worked source of that mineral, while there seemed a likelihood that the fast-growing European aluminium industry might well in future find the Ulster bauxites to be a valuable asset.

During the field seasons of 1907, 1908, and 1909 the Survey explored the Interbasaltic Horizon in far greater detail than had been attempted during the original survey in the days of Jukes and Hull. One of the first tasks given to W.D. Haigh when he became a Temporary Professional Assistant in August 1909 was the assembly of published and unpublished chemical analyses of samples from the Interbasaltic Horizon; Charles Edward Moss of the Sedgwick Museum in Cambridge was employed as a Temporary Professional Assistant during 1908-9 to study the fossil plants from the Interbasaltic Horizon; Kilroe made a private visit to inspect the comparable German deposits in the Vogelsberg near Giessen; and Cole entered into correspondence with several geologists overseas who possessed first-hand experience of the current development, under tropical conditions, of analogues to the Interbasaltic Horizon. Among those correspondents were Sir Thomas Henry Holland, the Director of the Geological Survey of India, who had visited County Antrim in 1906 to inspect the Interbasaltic Horizon for himself, and H.B. Muff who had worked on the Belfast and Cork drift surveys and who had spent the year 1905-6 in British East Africa on Colonial Office duties before being appointed as Director of the Geological Survey of Southern Rhodesia in 1910.

From all these investigations there in 1912 resulted an elaborate memoir devoted to the Interbasaltic Horizon and containing a series of colour-printed one-inch maps depicting the outcrop of the Horizon. So far as the Horizon was concerned, these new maps were intended to supersede the representation of the Horizon as it had featured upon the hand-coloured sheets of the original one-inch series. The price of the memoir was three shillings and I notice that on its back cover there is a list of the agents from whom copies might be purchased. In Athlone the agent was a Miss M. Tighe. I wonder how many copies she actually sold.

Lyburn, of course, was no part of the Survey but it is nonetheless interesting to note the kind of activities in which he engaged. While the Survey was up exploring the Tertiary deposits of the Interbasaltic Horizon, Lyburn was down among Ireland's Carboniferous rocks. In 1908-9 and for several years thereafter the Department employed expert lime-burners to give local demonstrations under Lyburn's supervision, and he claimed that as a result a number of defunct lime-kilns had returned to regular use, much to the benefit of the local farmers. But the Survey and Lyburn were soon set upon potential collision courses as they sailed the seas of economic geology. With the investigation of the Interbasaltic Horizon behind them, and in the enjoyment of their renewed sense of self-confidence, the Survey began to turn a blind eye to the signal flying from the halliards of Upper Merrion Street and relating to the subject of economic geology. Cole decided that the Survey would re-examine the stratigraphy of some of the Irish coalfields.

In 1911 Edward Alexander Newell Arber of the Sedgwick Museum was engaged as a Temporary Professional Assistant to examine fossil plants from the Ballycastle Coalfield of County Antrim. During 1913-14 a Staffordshire physician and amateur palaeontologist named Wheelton Hind together with William Thomas Gordon, of King's College London, were both similarly engaged to work upon the Castlecomer Coalfield, Hind to study the fossil mollusca and Gordon to study the fossil plants. Meanwhile Lyburn was just down the road from Castlecomer making a comparable study of the Slieveardagh Coalfield and his resultant report was submitted to the Department during 1913. Perhaps it was only the outbreak of a larger conflict which in 1914 prevented the development of a territorial squabble between Hume Street and Upper Merrion Street with economic geology cast in the role of Belgium.

There was, of course, an element of pure geology in both the Survey's investigations of the Interbasaltic Horizon and in its stratigraphical studies of the Irish coalfields. Those undertakings were nonetheless broadly economic in character. But there were other Survey projects where the pure element far outweighed the applied. Those projects constitute the third avenue down which Cole led the Survey. Down that avenue - the avenue of pure geology - there lie three especially noteworthy projects.

First, during the drift survey of the Londonderry district in 1905 and 1906, Cole became aware of the fact that there was a substantial gap in the Survey's national coverage of six-inch field-sheets. As a result of the directive received from London during the summer of 1881, six-inch field-mapping had largely been abandoned in the northwest in an effort to expedite the completion of the one-inch map (see p.94). The rocks lying in a broad swathe of country extending from the vicinity of Lough Erne northward to the Inishowen Peninsula had never been mapped at a scale larger than that of the published one-inch sheets. This was unfortunate and Cole decided that the deficiency had to be remedied. Various officers assisted in the re-mapping of the neglected districts at the six-inch scale, but the task fell chiefly upon Wilkinson. He began six-inch re-mapping in the northwest during

FIGURE 5.6. *The fisheries protection cruiser and research-ship* Helga *belonging to the Department of Agriculture and Technical Instruction for Ireland. Built at Ayr in 1891 as a steam yacht, she was purchased by the Department and re-equipped for her new role. She had two triple-expansion engines driving twin screws. Her dimensions were : length (overall) 150 feet ; beam 23 feet ; tonnage (yacht measure) 345 tons. It was her deep-sea dredging which yielded the geological specimens described by Cole and Crook in 1910.*

the field-season of 1909, and he continued the work, season by season, until April 1914 when his retirement broke the Survey's final human link with the Survey of Jukes's day. Wilkinson doubtless performed his duties in the northwest conscientiously, but any reader of his autobiography must suspect that what Wilkinson really enjoyed in the northwest was not so much the granites as the grouse - not so much the schists as the salmon.

Second, Cole led the Survey into the investigation of Ireland's offshore geology. Soon after its foundation the Department of Agriculture and Technical Instruction for Ireland had acquired the twin-screw vessel the *Helga* to fill the combined role of fishery-protection cruiser and marine research ship (Fig. 5.6). She had been built at Ayr in 1891 and is not to be confused with the Department's second *Helga* which was launched in Dublin in 1908 and which earned Irish notoriety through her shelling of Dublin's Boland's Mill and Liberty Hall during the 1916 Rising. Between June 1901 and September 1907 the original *Helga* carried out a series of dredgings from the seabed to the north and west of Ireland. Twenty-two sites were investigated, the deepest at a depth of 660 fathoms, and the resultant rock-samples were studied by Cole in collaboration with Thomas Crook, a graduate of the Royal College of Science for Ireland and Cole's assistant there between 1901 and 1905. Their findings were issued as a Survey memoir published in 1910 and in that memoir they announced a remarkable discovery. On the seabed to the west of Ireland there were rocks of an age far younger than might have been anticipated. Onshore most of the rocks are of Carboniferous or greater age, whereas offshore the *Helga's* dredge had brought up rocks dating from no further back than the Cretaceous and the Eocene.

This was by no means the first attempt to understand the nature of the seabed off Ireland's shores. As early as October 1823 Alexander Nimmo, an officer of the Irish Fisheries Board, had presented to the Royal Irish Academy a map of the submarine geology of the waters to the south of Ireland. It is nevertheless Cole and Crook's memoir of 1910 which marks the Survey's entry into the now vitally important realm of offshore geology. As Cole perceptively and presciently observed, the memoir

> ... is an attempt to carry the work of the Geological Survey over part of the continental plateau now covered by the Atlantic.

When he wrote those words did Cole have some vague presentiment of the immense significance which submarine geology was to have for the Survey in a future age of offshore drilling-rigs and seabed pipelines?

Third, Cole involved the Survey in the most renowned collaborative venture ever undertaken by

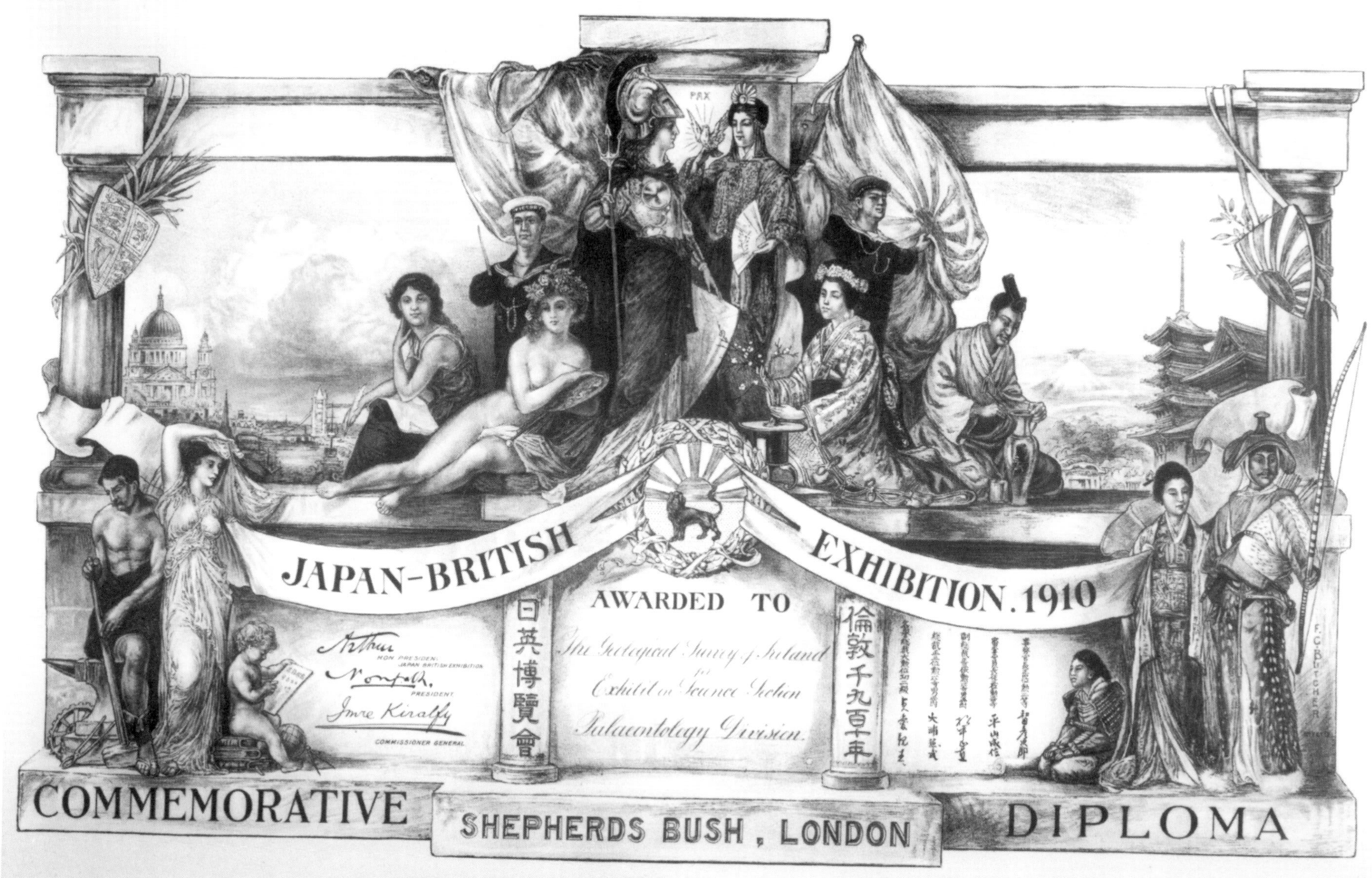

FIGURE 5.7. *An exhibition diploma awarded to the Geological Survey of Ireland in 1910 for its palaeontological exhibit at that year's Anglo-Japanese Exhibition in London. The Japanese might have been forgiven for concluding that clothes were in somewhat short supply within the British Isles.*

natural historians within Ireland. This particular story began on the afternoon of 23 April 1908 when Cole attended a meeting held in the office of Robert Francis Scharff, the Keeper of Natural History in the Dublin Museum of Science and Art. After much discussion it was there decided to undertake a detailed study of all facets of the natural history of Clare Island in County Mayo. The survey was carried out between 1909 and 1911 with financial support from the Royal Dublin Society, the Royal Irish Academy, the Royal Society of London, and the British Association for the Advancement of Science. The survey eventually involved around one hundred Irish, British, and continental naturalists, and their research findings were published as volume 31 of the *Proceedings of the Royal Irish Academy*. Throughout the project Cole was one of the six members of the Clare Island Survey Committee, and he obtained his Department's approval for the Survey's assumption of responsibility for a new investigation of the geology of Clare Island.

The island had originally been mapped for the Survey by Symes during the 1870s and it featured upon the one-inch Sheet 73 published in 1879. For the Clare Island Survey Cole and Kilroe revised Symes's mapping while Hallissy reported in detail upon the island's drifts and soils. Three Temporary Professional Assistants were also involved in the work: E.A.N. Arber studied the Carboniferous rocks; Wheelton Hind examined the Carboniferous mollusca; and W.D. Haigh conducted mineralogical research and soil analyses. The Survey's contribution to the Clare Island Survey was published as an essay by Hallissy in volume 31 of the *Proceedings of the Royal Irish Academy* and as a special Survey memoir published in 1914 and devoted exclusively to Clare Island. With the memoir there came a folded drift map of the island at the unusual scale of three inches to one mile (1:21,120) but with a solid map of the island featured as an inset at its original scale of one inch to one mile (1:63,360). This Clare Island map, like the Ballyhaise soil map, came off Gavin's drawing-board, and it again reflects much credit both upon his draughting skills and upon the training he had received at the Ordnance Survey almost half a century before.

On 20 May 1910 the Survey's Hume Street headquarters was closed for the day. In common with the heads of all public departments, Cole was in receipt of a directive.

> Care should be taken that the window blinds at the various buildings are kept drawn down throughout the day.

The occasion was the day of the funeral of King Edward VII across the water in London. Perhaps as a loyalist Cole really did feel some personal sense of bereavement, but any such sentiments must surely have been abated by the anticipation of a happy event which was scheduled to happen just six weeks later. W.B. Wright was returning to Hume Street to become again an officer of the Irish Survey. Since leaving Ireland in the late summer of 1904, Wright had worked briefly with the Geological Survey of England and Wales before joining the renowned Geological Survey of Scotland. Now, on 1 July 1910, he returned to Hume Street as the replacement for Seymour. With him he brought the warmest of testimonials from John Horne, the senior geologist of the Survey of Scotland.

Many factors doubtless contributed to Wright's decision that he should return to Ireland. He was Irish, Dublin was his birthplace, and his daughter, now Lady Dainton, tells me that there may even have been a sense of filial duty involved. His mother still lived in Dublin and she had recently been struck by a neurological disease which was eventually to leave her bedridden in partial paralysis. She needed care and Wright's elder brother was proving unequal to the task. But surely Wright would never have contemplated such a move had he not been satisfied that Cole had succeeded in imbuing the Irish Survey with a sense of thrusting geological achievement. Wright was to the very core a scientist, a geologist, and a Survey man; by returning to Hume Street in 1910 he was paying his own silent tribute to Cole's achievement.

Cole and Wright formed a close and effective relationship. Wilkinson, the Senior Geologist, was, as ever, busy with his guns and rods, and it was Wright who, from the moment of his return, served as Cole's right-hand-man. For ten years after 1910 Wright was the Hume Street dynamo sending pulses of energy into the Survey and generating waves of inspiration. When Wilkinson retired in April 1914, Wright was immediately appointed as his successor in the post of Senior Geologist. Cole, of course, was merely a part-time Director and responsibility for the affairs of the Survey increasingly devolved upon Wright's willing shoulders. This became particularly true after Cole's health began to deteriorate from around 1917.

During the year following his return to Ireland, Wright broke ground at the start of an important new Survey field-project. This was the drift survey of the Killarney and Kenmare region of County Kerry and it occupied Wright for the three field-seasons from 1911 to 1913. But an account of that survey must be reserved until a later chapter (see p.227) and here I propose to mention just two of the innovations for which Wright was responsible during the years between his return to Dublin in 1910 and the outbreak of the war in 1914.

The first innovation was the inauguration of a completely new geological map of Ireland. Wright felt that the general public, and especially teachers,

INDEX

to the

GEOLOGICAL MAP of IRELAND

On the Scale of Four Miles to One Inch

FIGURE 5.8. *The map that never was. The sheet-lines for the intended quarter-inch geological map of Ireland. Only sheets 2, 5, 11, and 16 were ever published.*

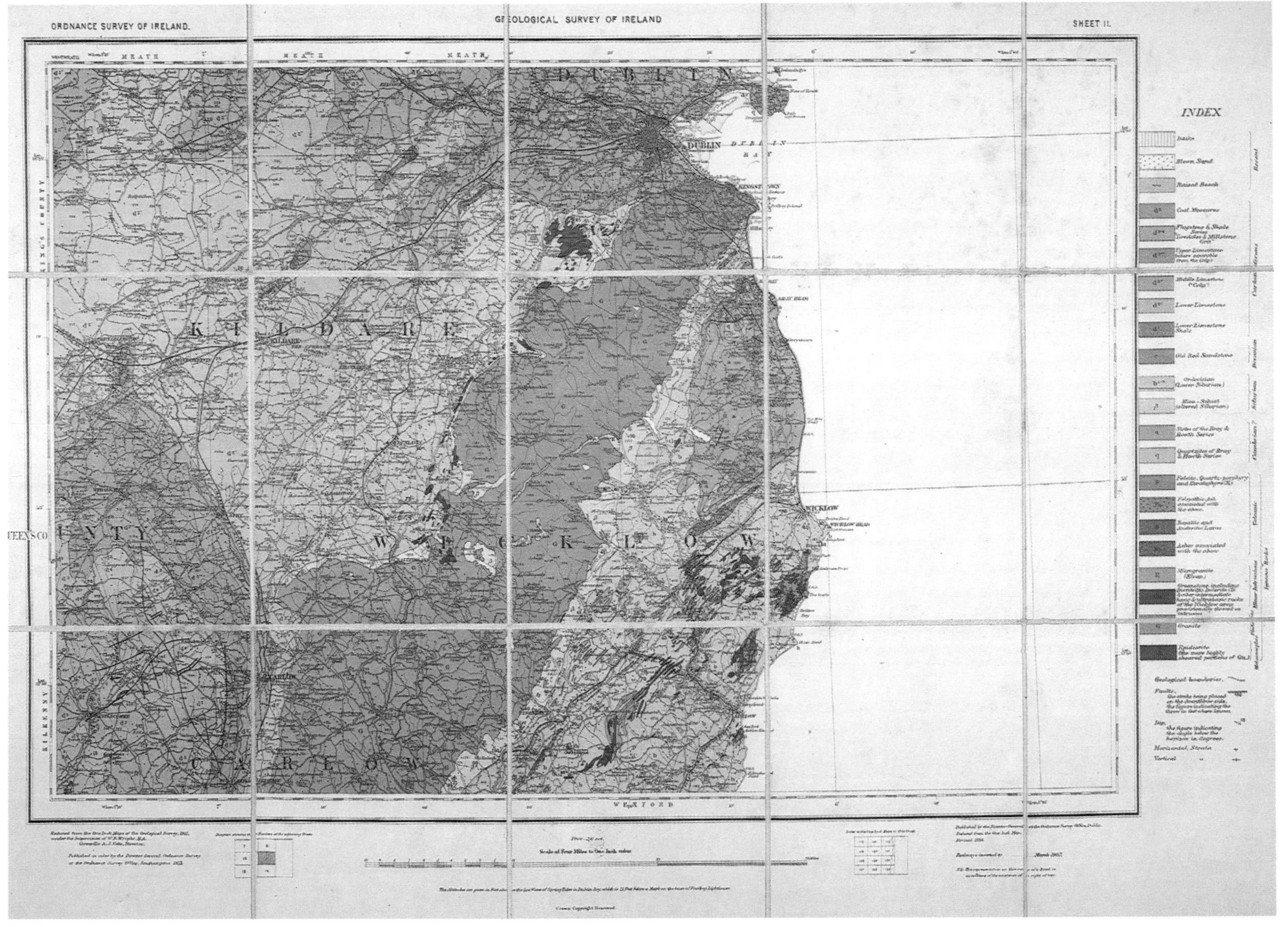

PLATE VIII. *The earliest sheet of the intended quarter-inch (1:253,440) geological map of Ireland in sixteen sheets: Sheet 11. Despite its bearing of the date 1913, the sheet was evidently not published until March 1914. It was compiled by Wilkinson under the overall supervision of Wright as the co-ordinator for the new map. The sheet is here reproduced at a reduced size, the inner frame of the original measuring 47 x 31 centimetres.* Reproduced from an example of the sheet in the author's collection.)

would find useful a geological map of Ireland which preserved most of the detail of the one-inch sheets but which was itself drawn to a rather smaller scale. Such a map would readily afford that conspectus of Irish geology which was only with difficulty to be obtained from the 205 sheets of the one-inch map. England and Wales had since 1896 enjoyed a complete coverage of quarter-inch (1:253,440) geological sheets and in 1907 Wright had in Scotland witnessed the publication of the earliest sheets for a similar Scottish map. Why should Ireland not follow suit with its own quarter-inch geological map? The Ordnance Survey already had on sale a quarter-inch topographical map of Ireland in sixteen sheets so the compilation of a base-map for a quarter-inch geological map of Ireland should present no problems.

In reality the Treasury had given its approval for the compilation of a quarter-inch geological map of Ireland as far back as September 1902, but the exigencies of Lamplugh's drift surveys had then prevented the taking of much action upon the matter. Now, with Cole and Wright backing the project, things began to happen. On 26 April 1912 the Treasury gave renewed sanction to the enterprise and authorised the Ordnance Survey to spend up to £713 on the proposed map. For the map Hume Street adopted the sheet-lines of the Ordnance Survey's existing quarter-inch topographical map of Ireland which meant that a full quarter-inch sheet covered the same area as a block of sixteen one-inch sheets (Fig. 5.8). Wright assumed overall responsibility for the new map and each Survey officer was given the task of compiling one or more of the new sheets.

The construction of the new map was not just a simple exercise in cartographic reduction. The ugly form of the mischievous demon of geological uncertainty would periodically sit grinning upon parts of a sheet as its compiler sought to complete his appointed task. For example, Cole found that there was need for a field re-examination of the igneous rocks falling upon sheets 5 and 8, while on one of Wright's sheets - Sheet 4 - there were problems over the definition of the base of the Carboniferous. That was why Carruthers and Lee of the British Survey explored the Bundoran region in Wright's company during the autumn of 1911.

The first quarter-inch sheet to be completed and published was Sheet 11 which depicts the country southward of the city of Dublin. This sheet had been Wilkinson's responsibility and, despite the marginal claim that the sheet was published in 1913, it really appears to have been published during March 1914 and just a few days before Wilkinson's retirement. Apart from the representation of the superficial deposits around the shores of Dublin Bay, the sheet is exclusively concerned with depiction of solid geology, and it is a most handsome example of the geological cartographer's art. At a price of two shillings and six pence it evidently proved very popular with the map-buying public, although copies of the sheet are now extremely difficult to find. Even the Survey itself can today muster only three or four specimens of the sheet, all of them somewhat soiled. In 1991, and through the kind offices of my erstwhile colleague Frank Mitchell, I acquired a box of maps, most of which had formerly belonged to Augustine Henry, the arborist. It was with great delight that I discovered among the maps the dissected copy of Sheet 11 which is here reproduced as Plate VIII.

Wright's second innovation was one entirely without precedent. In a memorandum dated 6 February 1914 he proposed that the Survey should assume a pedagogical role. His idea was that every field-season the Survey should take under its wing a limited number of carefully selected students drawn from the universities. Each student would be assigned to a Survey officer for training in Survey-style field-mapping and as soon as they had mastered the necessary skills the students would each be given the task of actually mapping a piece of ground on behalf of the Survey. Upon the satisfactory completion of that duty each student would receive a certificate of competence certifying that they had completed the Geological Survey of Ireland course in field-mapping.

All the subsistence and travel expenses incurred by those attending the course were to be borne either by the students themselves or by their universities. The Survey would thus obtain maps of significant pieces of ground at minimal cost to itself. For their part the students would have acquired the experience of working alongside the professional staff of a noted national Survey. That experience would be of direct benefit to the young geologists at the outset of their careers and of eventual indirect benefit to their native land or to the empire at large.

Cole liked Wright's proposal and the Department gave its approval with the proviso that the scheme should be regarded as merely experimental for a period of three years. For the 1914 field-season just one student was accepted. He was A. H. Hutchinson, an Associate of the Royal College of Science for Ireland and therefore one of Cole's former students. Hutchinson worked at Castlecomer under Wright's supervision, and in due course he received his certificate on parchment and headed 'Department of Agriculture and Technical Instruction for Ireland'. I would dearly like to have been able to offer an illustration of that certificate; it was the only such certificate ever awarded.

While Hutchinson was down in Castlecomer developing his skills as a field-geologist, Hume Street itself was the scene of a rather different sort of geological activity. There was being prepared an exhibition display. Several groups concerned for the wellbeing of the city of Dublin had come together in the organisation of a major exposition to be mounted in the former Linen Hall Barracks in Linenhall Street, located in one of Dublin's less salubrious districts northward of the Liffey. The title adopted for the exposition was 'the Dublin Civic Exhibition'. The venture heavily involved the influential Patrick Geddes and his team from Edinburgh, and the project was vigorously supported by the Department of Agriculture and Technical Instruction.

In selecting its own contribution to the exposition, the Survey went back to Lamplugh's drift survey of the Dublin district dating from 1901. Six-inch Sheet 18 of the County Dublin set depicts the entire central portion of the city of Dublin, and the Survey prepared a manuscript drift version of this sheet to form a central feature within the exposition. The drift mapping upon the sheet was entirely the work of McHenry, and at the exposition it attracted such interested attention that Cole decided to publish the six-inch drift sheet in a colour-printed version. This published version is optimistically dated 1915 but it was 1917 before the map actually appeared. Since then it has proved to be an invaluable document for architects, engineers, planners, and all those whose duties bring them into contact with geological problems in central Dublin. To this day the sheet remains the only six-inch drift sheet ever published by the Irish Survey.

Dublin was then notorious for the foul conditions under which so many of its inhabitants had to live and the city had been troubled by social unrest throughout 1913. Many were the hopes which therefore surrounded the Dublin Civic Exhibition. It was opened with due pageantry by the Lord Lieutenant on 15 July 1914 and for a few days it seemed to be making the public impact for which its organisers had hoped. But suddenly perspectives changed. The exposition seemed to assume a parochial and trivial air when set against the background of momentous events which now began to unfold upon the international scene. In the excitement surrounding the outbreak of war there were few who noticed when the exposition closed its doors for the last time on 31 August 1914. It may be that the exposition's chief legacy to Ireland was the published version of the six-inch drift sheet made by McHenry as he tramped the streets of central Dublin during the first summer of a new century.

The Survey's final publication before the outbreak of World War I was something of an oddity. It was a new memoir to accompany one-inch Sheet 58 (Monaghan). The geology of that sheet had originally been mapped by Cruise during 1879 but it now transpired that he had been guilty of a serious error of omission. Admittedly the local landscape is heavily encumbered with drift, but this is hardly excuse sufficient to explain the fact that Cruise had failed to record the presence of a large mass of dark green gabbro lying southward of Monaghan town. Cole was embarrassed, not least because by the early years of the twentieth century the gabbro was being extensively quarried for road metal. Such an error had to be rectified, so Hallissy was assigned the task of revising the sheet and of preparing a fresh memoir. When the memoir was published during the summer of 1914 it contained a new colour-printed version of Sheet 58 at the reduced scale of about 1:168,960. As if in an act of contrition, the revised, 30-page memoir, with its map, was priced at a mere threepence half-penny. Cruise's inferior 16-page memoir, published in 1885, had cost sixpence, and Hallissy was slightly aggrieved that so low a monetary value had been attached to his work of revision.

In August 1914 the Survey possessed a staff of seven men. There were Cole, Wright, and Hallissy, there was Clark the Superintendent of Maps, there was Gavin the Draughtsman, there was Thomas Haigh the 'permanent' Temporary Professional Assistant, and there was a young Geologist named Horas Tristram Kennedy. Kilroe had retired in June 1913 after thirty-nine years of service and Kennedy had been appointed in his stead following the usual competitive examination. Kennedy's parents hailed from County Donegal but he himself had been born in London and was a former Scholar of Trinity College Cambridge. There was also one staff vacancy for a Geologist arising through Wright's promotion to the rank of Senior Geologist following upon Wilkinson's retirement in April 1914. That vacancy was filled as from 11 November 1914 by the appointment of Robert Lepper Valentine, the youngest son of the classics master at Portora Royal School, Enniskillen, and since 1912 an Associate of the Royal College of Science for Ireland. He was obviously an enthusiastic geologist. He had spent the year 1913-14 down at Hook Head trying to apply to the local limestones the principles of zonation devised by Arthur Vaughan among the Carboniferous strata of the Clifton Gorge at Bristol. When Valentine presented himself for the Survey entrance examination he was already wearing the uniform of the Royal Dublin Fusiliers, and by the time of his actual appointment to the Survey he was a newly-commissioned subaltern awaiting his turn to depart for France. But everybody was convinced that the war would be over within just a few months so Valentine's post was left open in anticipation of his joining the Hume Street staff at the conclusion of the hostilities.

FIGURE 5.9. *The dining-room of the Deanery, St Patrick's Cathedral, Dublin, 29 November 1916; the wedding of Lieutenant Horas Tristram Kennedy and Florence Irene Harriet Ovenden. Standing, from left to right: the Bishop of Ossory (J.A.F. Gregg); the Dean of St Patrick's (the bride's father); the bride; G.R. Webb; the bridegroom; I.G.A. Webb; R. Bryce (best man); G. Kennedy; M. Ovenden; A. Boyd. Seated: Mrs Kennedy; D.A. Webb (page); M. Webb (bridesmaid); Mrs Ovenden; Miss Kennedy. Lieutenant Kennedy was killed by shellfire in the Ypres salient on 6 June 1917.* (From a photograph in the collection belonging to the late Dr David Webb of Trinity College Dublin.)

At the outbreak of war Cole, Wright, Hallissy, Clark and Gavin were all too old for military service but Haigh and Kennedy were both in their twenties. These two men immediately volunteered and both were in khaki by September 1914. As was mentioned earlier (p.130), of the three Survey men who were in the army - Haigh, Kennedy, and Valentine - only Haigh survived the war. Valentine died as a Lieutenant on 30 April 1916 as a result of wounds received near Loos, and Kennedy was in the same rank when he was killed by shellfire in the Ypres salient on 6 June 1917 during the battle of Messines. While in France he had met Florence Ovenden from Dublin who was serving with a Voluntary Aid Detachment. She was the younger daughter of the then Dean of St Patrick's and the couple were married in the cathedral during a brief spell of home leave in November 1916 (Fig. 5.9). By his will Kennedy left all his geological books to the Survey's library, and his executors clearly lost no time in complying with his wish. One of his books sits upon my desk as I write and I see that it was added to the Survey's library, on 4 September 1917, less than three months after its former owner was killed somewhere near Armentières. Just a few hours after his death a more renowned Irishman died a short distance up the line in an attack upon Wytschaete: Major Willie Redmond.

Here I have to allude to a piece of folklore which has for long been current within the Survey. The story is told that in 1914 certain officers of the Survey - presumably Haigh and Kennedy - were eager to volunteer for military service but were refused permission to do so. The authorities outside the Survey are said to have regarded geologists as the members of a reserved occupation who were ineligible for military service because their skills were essential to the war-effort upon the home-front. Cole, so the story goes, sympathised with his would-be soldiers and he therefore wrote to the authorities explaining that the geological map of Ireland had been complete since 1890 and that Hume Street would be able to function quite adequately without its younger officers. The authorities, faced with such an admission, removed their prohibition and the officers in question were released to join the queue at the recruiting office. The final twist to the story is that over the next fifty years Cole's letter of 1914, in best civil service style, is said to have been quoted back to successive Directors of the Survey whenever they sought augmentation of their human or physical resources. Cole in 1914 had said that the work of the Survey had really been completed in 1890 and everybody knew that Cole was an honourable man.

This is an entertaining and very convenient story. It explains the Survey's subsequent woes in terms of Cole's patriotic instincts and his desire to alleviate the predicament in which certain of his staff found themselves. But I doubt the story's veracity. Within the Survey's archives I know of no such letter written by Cole at the outbreak of World War I nor have I found any evidence of the civil service subsequently using such a letter as a bludgeon with which to beat the Survey into submission. The 1914 letter seems to have been merely a figment of somebody's overly vivid imagination.

There is nothing imaginary about another strange Survey episode dating from the early months of World War I. Three of its officers having departed to fight the Germans, Hume Street came within a hair's-breadth of obtaining by way of replacement the services of an officer of the Geological Survey of Prussia. Very early in the war Dr W. Henke of the Prussian Survey was captured while serving with the German army, and by January 1915 he was a prisoner-of-war housed in the barracks at Templemore in County Tipperary. At the suggestion of his Director, who happened to be a friend of Cole's, Henke wrote to Hume Street asking whether the Survey would lend him some Coal Measure fossils to work upon during the period of his detention. Cole explored the protocol of such a situation with the authorities. He himself clearly welcomed the proposal and he explained to his superiors that Henke's expertise would be of great value to the Survey in its coalfield studies.

Eventually all was agreed and Wright was scheduled to take the first instalment of fossils down to Templemore. But the episode came to naught. Henke was suddenly transferred to a prisoner-of-war camp located at Holyport near Maidenhead in Berkshire. The incident nonetheless holds symbolic significance. Cole was a loyalist doing his bit for king and country. Belgium had been raped and the British press was full of harrowing stories of the atrocities supposed to have been perpetrated by the advancing hordes of the twentieth century Huns. But for Cole science was above nationality; as a geologist he shared with Henke the membership of an international fraternity. German soldiery might represent the detested enemy, but Henke was a palaeontologist in distress.

The war did bring new faces into Hume Street as vacant offices were allocated to officials involved in the allied war effort. Members of the Department's forestry branch moved into the house, as later did the local Air Ministry auditors. A rather more appropriate arrival was Herbert J. Daly of the Ministry of Munitions of War who had an office in Hume Street during 1917 and 1918. It was Daly's task to inspect all the derelict Irish metallic mines to ascertain whether the reopening of any of them might be of benefit to the allied cause. But the most interesting new face to appear in Hume Street was that of a woman: Miss Mary Josephine Connaughten.

Mary Connaughten was born in Athlone and she was a graduate of the Royal University of Ireland, but Cole first met her in Oxford while he was teaching there at a summer school during 1916. She had completed a course in geology with Professor Sollas and she also held the Oxford Diploma in Geography. Cole offered her a post as Temporary Professional Assistant for part of the summer of 1917 at a salary of two guineas per week. She accepted the offer and in Hume Street she worked upon a card-catalogue of Irish mineral occurrences based upon both the Survey's six-inch field-sheets and its inventory of Irish mines. This was a programme which Cole had launched in 1915 as a part of the Survey's war-effort. Before 1917 Cole may occasionally have employed a lady typist in Hume Street and paid her from the fund for Temporary Professional Assistants, but Mary Connaughten was the first woman to be employed by the Survey in a geological capacity.

It is interesting to note that Miss Connaughten, like all the people in Hume Street, had to work by gaslight whenever artificial illumination was necessary. In October 1916 Wright pressed for the introduction of electricity into the house because such power was needed both for the operation of a rock-cutting machine and for an electro-magnet to be employed in mineral determination. His request was refused. The Board of Works explained that the cost of bringing electricity into 14 Hume Street would be £15 and no such sum was available. It seems that even as late as 1940 work on gloomy days was carried out in Hume Street beneath incandescent gas-mantles.

Short-staffed though the Survey was, a remarkable amount of work was completed during the war years of 1914 to 1918. Hallissy took over Haigh's laboratory investigations, studied soils in County Wexford for the Department, and explored phosphate deposits on the shores of Donegal Bay. Together Hallissy and Wright worked on the Leinster Coalfield and Wright carried out a major revision of the Ballycastle Coalfield. A search was conducted for magnesite in Connemara and for such other minerals as asbestos, molybdenite, and steatite, while Cole began a study of both the Pre-Cambrian rocks of Ireland and the granites of counties Galway, Mayo, Sligo, and Donegal. But there are three other wartime studies which are of especial interest: potash experiments; Wicklow geophysics; and the exploration of a concealed coalfield.

By 1915 potash for fertilizers was becoming scarce and Hallissy suggested that the Survey should undertake a series of experiments to see whether the powdering of igneous rocks rich in potassium could be made to yield a useful fertilizer. The experiments commenced in June 1916 using rocks quarried near Forkill in the Slieve Gullion ring-complex. The rock was crushed and ground by the Dublin firm of W. & H.M. Goulding Ltd, and by 15 February 1917 the Survey had 230 bags of powdered Forkill rock. These bags were distributed to the Royal Botanic Gardens and the Department's Albert Agricultural Institute, both in Glasnevin, and to six Ulster farms located near to Armagh, Castlewellan, Coleraine, Garvagh, Loughgilly, and Newcastle. The powder was applied to experimental plots where either flax or potatoes were being grown, but by 1919 the Survey had to concede that all the results of the experiments were 'absolutely negative'.

About the Wicklow geophysical investigations I am able to write far less than I would wish. The work was carried out during the summer of 1918 and it involved an effort to enlist a modern geophysical technique in the exploration of the long-known deposit of iron-ore located near Ballard and lying some 8 kilometres to the southwest of Wicklow town. But what exactly was done that summer? The Survey's files contain various references to the investigation but, despite the kind assistance of several present Survey officers, I have failed to unearth any scientific account of the real nature of the investigations. Such an account must have existed until at least the 1930s because the Ballard geophysical survey was featured as exhibit G.18 among the forty-nine geological exhibits in the exhibition staged as a part of the bi-centenary celebrations of the Royal Dublin Society in 1931. By way of explanation of the nature of the project I am able to do little more than quote the entire entry relating to exhibit G.18 as it appeared in the Royal Dublin Society's exhibition catalogue.

MAGNETIC SURVEY OF THE IRON ORE DEPOSIT, BALLARD, CO. WICKLOW.

> Made in 1918 by the Geological Survey. On the plan are represented the horizontal components of the magnetic forces due to the lodes alone, the horizontal component of the earth's magnetic force being eliminated. The direction of the lode force is given by the arrows, and its intensity is indicated in blue by shading. The curves separating the blue tints are isodynamic lines, or lines of equal horizontal intensity.

This entry merely whets the appetite of the historian of science. We are clearly here being offered a tantalising glimpse of a pioneering exercise in the application of geophysics to the solution of an Irish geological problem. Professor Tom Murphy of the Dublin Institute for Advanced Studies tells me that he remembers the apparatus used in the survey being on display in the University College Dublin science buildings (formerly the Royal College of Science for Ireland) during the late 1930s but the present whereabouts of the equipment is unknown. The Survey officer responsible for this startling geophysical innovation in 1918 was the talented

Wright. There is one other point about the survey which might enhance its interest in the perception of Irish readers. Ballard had once been a part of the estate owned by Charles Stewart Parnell.

The story of the concealed coalfield again has Wright as its central figure. In February 1917 he gave before the Royal Dublin Society a lecture in which he suggested that the northeast of Ireland might possess hidden resources of coal. There might be present several basins containing coal-rich Upper Carboniferous rocks which are today completely obscured from view by a veneer of post-Carboniferous strata. Borings through the veneer at carefully selected sites, Wright observed, might reveal the existence of workable coal-seams in places where the presence of such resources had never before been suspected. In some way the lecture came to the notice of Edward Hubert Cunningham -Craig, a petroleum geologist working for the Admiralty and the Ministry of Munitions, and through him Wright's ideas were brought to the attention of that Ministry. As a result the Survey was asked to prepare a memorandum explaining Wright's thesis in greater detail. The memorandum was submitted to the Department for the Development of Mineral Resources, one of the components of the Ministry of Munitions, during September 1917, and keen interest was soon being taken in the Survey's document. It was decided to sink a borehole in search of a concealed portion of the Tyrone Coalfield. The site chosen for the boring was close to the southwestern shores of Lough Neagh at Washing Bay and not far from the town of Coalisland. The beds exposed at the surface are the Lough Neagh Clays, and beneath them the bore was expected to pass through a relatively shallow thickness of Tertiary basalt, Cretaceous Chalk, and Triassic sandstone, before entering the Carboniferous strata where, it was hoped, the coal awaited discovery.

Drilling commenced on 17 December 1918 and it speedily became apparent that the Survey had been deceived by the outcrop geology in the vicinity of Washing Bay and Coalisland. In the borehole, both the Lough Neagh Clays and the basalts proved to be enormously thicker than had ever been dreamed possible. The Lough Neagh Clays proved to be 350 metres thick and the borehole did not leave the Interbasaltic Horizon and enter the Lower Basalts until a depth of 527 metres had been attained. The drilling was stopped at a depth of 599 metres without the bore even having penetrated into the Carboniferous beds. If boring had been continued, any coal discovered at such depths would have been quite unworkable.

As an exercise in exploratory economic geology the Washing Bay bore was a fiasco; as an exercise in pure geology it was of immense interest. Indeed, it is probably the most revealing hole ever sunk through Ireland's onshore rocks. Hitherto the age of the Lough Neagh Clays had been uncertain but the boring revealed them to have been caught up in the early Tertiary earth-movements which had affected the region. The clays therefore had to date from the earlier part of the Tertiary and they were thus much older than many geologists had supposed. The boring brought to light many important fossil remains of plants and it of course demonstrated the great thickness possessed by the basalts before they were attacked by Tertiary and later denudation.

Cole clearly had no doubt about the scientific importance of the borehole. It seemed unlikely that such a drilling would ever be replicated and the core resulting from the work at Washing Bay must therefore be preserved for study by future generations. In October 1919 he persuaded the Board of Works to erect wooden racks in the basement of Hume Street, the core was transported from Washing Bay to Dublin, and in the basement of Hume Street the core was stored for more than twenty years. It was an act of gross geological vandalism when, during the 1940s, an uncomprehending Director of the Survey tossed the entire core out into Hume Street and had it carted away. Today the Washing Bay core lies in some Dublin Corporation refuse dump or maybe it was just used as fill upon some Dublin construction site. Wherever it is it must be the most substantial fragment of the Six Counties within the Twenty Six.

On 11 November 1918 Dublin went wild. As the day wore on a vast cheering, dancing, flag-waving crowd thronged the city centre from Sackville Street to St Stephen's Green. Trams were commandeered, men and women in uniform were enthusiastically mobbed, and the singing and counter-singing of patriotic songs reduced that evening's theatrical performances to good-natured chaos. The cause of the jubilation was, of course, the signing of an armistice in a railway siding within the forest of Compiègne. Now, it seemed, all would be returning to something like the normality which had existed prior to August 1914. Certainly that is what initially appeared to be happening in the Survey. Herbert Daly, the foresters, and the Air Ministry auditors all departed from Hume Street. For Kennedy and Valentine there was, of course, to be no joyful homecoming, but as from December 1921 their places were taken by two new Temporary Geologists. The first of these was Thomas John Duffy, an Associate of the Royal College of Science for Ireland who had served in the forces between 1915 and 1919. The second new arrival was Anthony Farrington, a son of the Cork city analyst and a former student in University College Cork and at the Camborne School of Metalliferous Mining. It is interesting to note that, in the 'opportunities for returned heroes' ambience of the day, Farrington in his application to the Survey felt it necessary to account for his lack of war-service. He explained that he had been refused enlistment because of a strained back and a kidney disorder, but here he was perhaps being slightly economical with the truth. In reality he had been in Portugal from 1915 until 1919, and certainly in his later life I recall him as having been a confirmed pacifist.

Thomas Haigh, now out of uniform, decided not to return to Hume Street, but he had merely been a Temporary Professional Assistant and Cole can have foreseen no difficulty about filling that vacancy with other specialists as the need might arise. He did, however, face certain new financial problems. The war had brought about a sharp rise in the cost of living and there had been little commensurate increase in the Survey's annual grant. Indeed, its annual subvention (£2,403 in 1922-23) was very little more than the Survey had been receiving twenty years earlier. A sign of the increased cost of living was that in 1918 officers in the field were entitled to a daily accommodation allowance of six shillings as compared with an allowance of four shillings and six pence in 1914. In the post-war world Cole therefore had to be less lavish in his employment of Temporary Professional Assistants, while Wright's scheme for a Survey post-graduate diploma in field-mapping was never revived.

In Hume Street work now began upon the completion and publication of various projects which had been in abeyance during the war or which had then been undertaken as a Survey contribution to the war-effort.

During 1915 Cole had commenced work upon the card-catalogue of Irish mineral occurrences which two years later had engaged the attention of Mary Connaughten. Not until 1923 was the catalogue finally completed, but in the meantime it in 1922 served as the basis for a substantial memoir devoted to the economic minerals and metalliferous mines of Ireland, the contents being arranged alphabetically from antimony to zinc. The price of the memoir was seven shillings and six pence, a portrait of Sir Richard Griffith formed its frontispiece, Lyburn contributed towards the memoir's compilation, and folded within its covers was a map at a scale of one-inch to ten miles (1:633,600) representing the Irish coalfields in black, the peat-bogs in brown, and the mineral localities in red. This was the Survey's 'mineral map' and it had originally been published during June 1920, although there were certain differences between the two issues of the map, the most obvious of these being that in 1920 the mineral localities were marked in a scarcely legible green rather than in red. In June 1920 there had also been published a version of the map from which the mineral localities had been omitted and this map was known as the Survey's 'fuel map' because it depicted just the coalfields and the peat-bogs. It will emerge shortly that local political developments made it singularly appropriate that the Survey should have published two such maps during the summer of 1920.

Another pair of maps was published in October 1922. These are the colour-printed maps of the Killarney and Kenmare region which arose from the revision and drift mapping carried out by Wright between 1911 and 1913. One map represents the solid geology and aesthetically this sheet is somewhat unpleasing. The Killarney and Kenmare district is predominantly one of Old Red Sandstone and this results in the solid sheet becoming essentially a study in Devonian brown. Far more attractive is the second sheet - the drift sheet. There Devonian drabness is relieved by the representation of its mantling tills and sands in shades of what the cosmetician might describe as arctic blue or luscious pink.

Hallissy had for some years been studying the Irish barytes deposits and during the war he pressed his studies ahead energetically because Britain had no longer been able to obtain barytes from the important German sources. The results of Hallissy's investigations appeared in 1923 as a comprehensive Survey memoir in which are discussed the barytes deposits located in twenty-three of the Irish counties. He also offered some original observations upon the physiographical evolution of the south of Ireland, and his memoir became influential among the geomorphologists who later sought to grapple with that extensive but puzzling Munster landform, the so-called South Ireland Peneplane.

Wright completed his work on the Ballycastle Coalfield soon after the armistice, and in 1921 Louis Bouvier Smyth of Trinity College Dublin became one of the Survey's few post-war Temporary Professional Assistants when he undertook to finish the palaeontological studies which Arber had been conducting in the coalfield before 1914. In 1924 the Survey's new map of the Ballycastle Coalfield was published at a scale of six inches to the mile (1:10,560) and to accompany the map there was simultaneously published a new memoir descriptive of the district. By the time the map and the memoir appeared, Hume Street and the Ballycastle Coalfield lay upon opposite sides of that new Irish phenomenon known as 'The Border'.

The major project resumed after the war was that for the compilation of a quarter-inch (1:253,440) geological map of Ireland. This task remained in Wright's capable hands. By August 1914 there had been published only one of the sixteen sheets necessary - Sheet 11 - but now the work was urged forward with some vigour and three more sheets - sheets 2, 5, and 16 - were published between March

1921 and May 1923. In the margin of Sheet 16 is printed the following note.

> Reduced from the One Inch Maps of the Geological Survey, 1914, under the Supervision of H.T. Kennedy, B.A.

Monuments to the fallen were then being erected throughout these islands. Among his Survey colleagues Sheet 16 must surely have been recognised as Kennedy's geological memorial.

The principal new work undertaken during the post-war years was in the basin of the Upper Liffey in northwestern County Wicklow. It was proposed to construct a hydro-electric generating station on the Liffey at the Falls of Pollaphuca, and in connection with this proposal the Survey undertook both to revise its mapping of the local solid geology and to map the drifts of the entire Upper Liffey basin. The work was carried out chiefly during 1923 and 1924 by Hallissy, Duffy, and Farrington who presumably sometimes set off for the field aboard that notoriously unreliable transportation system, the Dublin and Blessington Tramway. Farrington once told me that it was his experience of mapping the drifts around Blessington which gave to his scientific life its strong Pleistocene orientation. It was therefore a surprise for me to discover that all the surviving six-inch field-sheets of the region are signed not by Farrington, but by either Duffy or Hallissy.

The review just presented of the Survey's achievements during the six years after 1918 might seem to indicate that the Survey was then in a healthy state. Such an interpretation is false. Things were beginning to go wrong. Down to 1920 the Survey had continued to make splendid recovery following the surgery of 1905, but after 1920 the patient took a marked turn for the worse. The Survey began to slide into that state of incapacitating paralysis which was to grip it for almost fifty years. Strangely, Cole's own health mirrors the health of the Survey which for fifteen years he had headed with such notable success. Or was it really so strange? Was Cole's own constitution being undermined by the welter of blows which the Survey now began to receive?

Cole was seriously ill during the closing months of 1919. When he returned to duty early in the following year he was aged only sixty but he had left to him a mere four years of life. It is difficult to believe that those four years were for him anything but desperately unhappy. They saw the disintegration of the establishment world of which he had been a part since his 1890 arrival in Ireland. They saw the Survey take some grievous knocks. They saw the coming to power of men who were hostile to the Survey. They saw the development of a social environment which was inimical to the wellbeing of the Survey. Ireland was winning its independence, but the new state utterly failed to create an atmosphere in which the Survey could flourish as the throbbing geological heart of the young nation.

As we have already noted (p.102), there was in nationalistic circles a deeply entrenched belief that Ireland must possess an immense mineral wealth. But with equal conviction it was held that the British government, determined to keep Ireland impoverished and subservient, had refused to sanction the opening of Ireland's vaults of treasure. As the local arm of that foreign administration, the Survey, both before and after 1905, was seen as having denied the Irish people access to their rightful geological inheritance. Clearly, in the view of eyes of green, the Survey was not to be trusted. As a result fervent nationalists began to look elsewhere for geological enlightenment. In 1920 Dr Guillaume Simoens was brought over from Belgium. In Dublin he was toasted as 'the world's most eminent geologist' and he was invited to report upon the potential of the Slieveardagh Coalfield and to investigate the prospects for successful gold-mining in County Wicklow. Simoens also found himself heavily involved in another Irish geological enterprise - an enterprise which represented a far more serious attempt to marginalise the Survey.

At the General Election held in December 1918 Sinn Féin, the nationalist party, won a resounding victory. The newly-elected representatives turned their backs upon the Westminster Parliament, convened in Dublin as Dáil Éireann, declared Ireland to be independent, and established an Irish government. On 18 June 1919 that government appointed a Coimisiún Fiafruigte Maoin is Tionnscal Éireann (Commission of Inquiry into the Resources and Industries of Ireland) and one of the Commission's first acts was to nominate a Power Committee which undertook to assess and report upon the potential of the Irish coalfields.

Over the greater part of Ireland, and often at gunpoint, Sinn Féin was subverting the existing administration and replacing it by its own new administrative order. No Mauser bullets had smashed the windows of Hume Street, but by setting up a resources committee upon which the Survey was unrepresented, Sinn Féin was merely doing to a branch of Irish geology exactly what it was accomplishing with such outstanding success in so many other fields of Irish life. The Irish Coal Measures were no longer the responsibility of such elements of the British administration as the Survey, Lyburn, or the Department; they were now the responsibility of Sinn Féin and Dáil Éireann. Those two maps which the Survey published during June 1920 - the fuel map and the mineral map - may now be seen in their fuller political context. They were the Survey's answer to the establishment of the Dáil's Commission. They represent the Survey staking its own claim to an institutional responsibility for Ireland's subterranean and surface wealth.

The secretary of the Dáil's Commission of Inquiry was the author, journalist, and Howth gun-runner, Darrell Figgis. He was later to boast that during the struggle for national independence he had seen the inside of ten gaols or other places of detention, but such a record was hardly likely to win for him the approbation of a Unionist such as Cole. There was certainly consternation when a letter from Figgis arrived in Hume Street early in January 1920. The Commission's Power Committee had been relying upon Simoens, 'the world's most eminent geologist', but, whether it liked it or not, the committee now discovered that it would not be able to complete its appointed task without the assistance of the Survey. Figgis had therefore written to Cole inviting him to allow Wright to appear before the committee. Cole was still convalescing after his illness and on 10 January 1920 he wrote to Wright from Orahova, the Coles' home in Carrickmines.

> Dear Wright,
>
> Thank you for your wise letter as to Mr Darrell Figgis's Commission. I confess that, even in a Development cause, I do not like dealing with the avowed enemies of the Commonwealth, and certainly I object to our officers being examined by a body that reports to a foreign (i.e. non-Commonwealth) "government". However, as you prudently suggest, let us keep the peace as far as possible.

A few days later Cole despatched to Figgis a very diplomatic reply and that letter is worthy of quotation *in extenso* as being indicative of the problems now being faced by Cole and other loyalist Irish civil servants.

> Sir,
>
> The Senior Geologist has handed me your letter of 8 January, as to evidence that you suggest might be given by him before a Commission of enquiry into the Resources and Industries of Ireland. Will you kindly inform me as to the terms of appointment of this Commission and the body to which it will ultimately report, and I will then lay the matter before our Department? You mention certain evidences as "challenging the results" of our Survey work; in such cases this Office is always open to enquiry from members of the public in regard to points where published results may seem obscure or perhaps to be modified by more recent discoveries.
>
> I am
> Yours faithfully,
>
> Grenville A.J. Cole
> Director.

In the event both Wright and Hallissy did assist Figgis's Commission and the 'unfailing courtesy and assistance' of the two officers was freely acknowledged when the Commission published its remarkable, fact-filled coalfield report during July 1921. The text of the report was accompanied by a case containing seven lavish geological maps and one geological section. That section must have evoked a wry smile in Hume Street. The Commission had thought fit to reproduce (Sir) Richard Griffith's section of the Leinster Coal District, first published in 1814. In its day it had been a remarkable piece of work; by 1921 it was an anachronism. The seven maps cover all the Irish coalfields in detail, but among the maps the most interesting is map VI which depicts the Ballycastle Coalfield at a scale of six inches to one mile (1:10,560). It is the very map which Wright had prepared for the Survey but which the Survey itself did not publish until 1924. Clearly, whatever moral scruples Wright may have felt, they were insufficient to deter him from displaying before the Commission a manuscript or proof version of his forthcoming map.

The Survey's encounter with Figgis and his Commission was really a most decorous affair. Far more frightening was the atmosphere which developed around the Survey as Ireland became embroiled first in the War of Independence (1919-1921) and then in the Civil War (1922-1923). When the Irish Republican Army set fire to the Dublin Custom House on 25 May 1921 there were lost in the conflagration the manuscript of Cole's forthcoming memoir on Ireland's minerals and metalliferous mines together with all the illustrations for Wright's forthcoming memoir on the geology of the Killarney and Kenmare district (see p.158). There was fear that as a government office 14 Hume Street might itself become somebody's 'legitimate target'. Twice over all the duplicates of the six-inch field-sheets were therefore loaded into the Department's handcart and trundled over to Upper Merrion Street for safe-keeping in the Department's strong-room. There the duplicate set lay from June 1921 until January 1922 and again from January to December 1923.

In many parts of the country the War of Independence saw parties of troops being ambushed, members of the Royal Irish Constabulary being murdered, and so-called 'informers' being executed. In such a jungle what were the survival chances of a map-carrying Survey officer who was reported to the local republicans as having been observed behaving in a suspicious manner? Down in West Cork or up in County Tipperary his survival chances were perhaps little greater than those faced by subalterns such as Kennedy or Valentine on the Somme or in the

Salient. That was certainly the opinion of Mrs Matley. Her husband, the geologist Charles Alfred Matley, had just retired from the British civil service, and in 1921 he proposed to come over to Ireland to work with the Survey as a Temporary Professional Assistant examining the Lower Palaeozoic rocks of counties Dublin and Wicklow. Cole was anxious that he should come, but Mrs Matley refused to sanction her husband's offering of himself as a living target for either the republicans or the crown forces. With reluctance, Cole accepted the decision and on 10 February 1921 be observed in a letter to Matley:

> Dublin is not a pleasant place to settle in just now - no part of Ireland is at present.

It comes as no surprise to find Cole writing as follows in his annual Survey report for 1921-22.

> Owing to the unsettled condition of the country little field-work was attempted, the activities of the staff being confined mainly to work within the office.

Wright decided that he had seen sufficient; the new Ireland was not for him. He evidently let it be known in Jermyn Street that he would welcome the opportunity of a return to the British Survey. That was arranged. He was offered the post of District Geologist in charge of the British Survey's new Manchester office and with special responsibility for the South Lancashire Coalfield. He resigned from the Irish Survey as from 31 March 1921 and he, his wife, their infant daughter, and his bedridden mother all shook themselves clear of the dust of a troubled Ireland. (Sir) John Smith Flett, the Director of the British Survey, wrote to Cole apologising for this poaching of Cole's most talented officer, but nobody understood better than Cole the magnitude of the disaster represented by Wright's departure. Cole had lost a friend, Hume Street had lost its human dynamo, and Irish geology had lost one of its most able and enthusiastic students (Plate X).

On 6 December 1921 there were signed the articles of agreement for a treaty between Britain and Ireland. The Survey now had to adjust itself to living in an Ireland very different in character from that Ireland which had been familiar to Oldham, to Jukes, to Hull, or to Lamplugh. A few trivial events occurring during 1922 serve nicely to exemplify this point. Back in 1910 Cole had been instructed to keep closed the blinds of 14 Hume Street throughout the day of King Edward VII's funeral. Now he received two similar directions but relating to funereal occasions of a nature very different from that of 1910. The blinds of Hume Street were to be closed on 16 August 1922 out of respect for the deceased Arthur Griffith and on 28 August 1922 out of respect for the assassinated Michael Collins. What Cole may have thought of Griffith I have no means of knowing, but in the case of Collins, I very much doubt whether Cole now sought out some portrait of 'the Big Fellow' with which to decorate the wall of his Hume Street office. The outbreak of the Civil War brought to Cole a duty which had never befallen any of his predecessors. Again in August 1922, in common with all heads of department, he was required to secure from each of his staff a declaration that they had not and would not lend support to those who had taken up arms against the Irish Provisional Government. At a more personal level, one would dearly like to know what sentiments were present in Cole's mind as he placed a request before the Department on 21 September 1922. It was a request for a rubber-stamp to allow the overprinting of all the Survey's stationery with the Survey's newly-invented Irish title.

OIFIG AN TOMHAIS CHÉ-EOLAIGH

A very minor administrative request, perhaps, but it was an event which betokened so much.

In September 1922 the military authorities advised that the Royal College of Science for Ireland should be closed because of its proximity to Leinster House where the Dáil was now meeting. For the remainder of his life Cole had to conduct many of his college classes in Hume Street, and the Royal College of Science was itself abolished in 1926. A similar fate was shared by the Survey's geological collections lying in what was now termed the National Museum of Science and Art. The entire museum was closed in 1922, again because its occupation by forces opposed to the Anglo-Irish Treaty would have posed a serious threat to the security of Leinster House. The Survey's collections were then displayed in the so-called Curved Gallery which actually formed a link between Leinster House and the Natural History Museum. During 1924 the government requisitioned the gallery and divided it into offices for clerical assistants attached to the Dáil. The geological displays upon which Cole, Clark, Hallissy, McHenry, Seymour, and Watts had over the years lavished much care, were at short notice swept from their cases and packed into storage crates. More than fifty years were to elapse before most of those specimens were again to see the light of day (see Chapter Ten).

Ireland was partitioned under the terms of the Government of Ireland Act of December 1920. Cole had always rightly urged that Irish geology had to be treated as a unitary whole, but now the six northeastern counties had slipped from his geological domain. On 20 March 1922 he was informed that as a concomitant of partition the Survey's annual grant would have to be diminished. The detached six counties represent 16.5 per cent of Ireland's surface area but the crafty and penny-pinching officials in the Department proposed to disregard this fact in deciding the amount to be axed from the Survey's subvention. They preferred to take account of population. Since the six counties then contained 28.5 per cent of Ireland's population, Cole was told that he must expect to see the Survey's annual grant shrink by considerably more than one quarter. But the authorities over in Upper Merrion Street did allow that Cole might perhaps like to negotiate with them further upon the matter.

The harsh reality of partition became starkly apparent on 18 July 1923. On that day an Ulster hand reached out to grasp the big brass knocker on the front-door of 14 Hume Street. It was Mr Crowe of the Northern Ireland Ministry of Agriculture. He was come to collect all the geological materials relating to the Six Counties. When he left again for Belfast he took with him all the manuscript six-inch sheets for the counties of Antrim, Armagh, Down, Fermanagh, Londonderry, and Tyrone, the six-inch field-sheets relating to the drift surveys of the Belfast and Londonderry districts, twenty-six one-inch Standard Copies covering ground located exclusively within Northern Ireland, all the surviving zinc-plates and wood-blocks for the illustrations in the Northern one-inch sheet memoirs, and last, but by no means least, sixty copies of Portlock's great Londonderry memoir of 1843. Down in the Hume Street basement the core from Washing Bay was left as the most tangible reminder of the Survey's former responsibility for the whole of Ireland.

I suppose that Cole was in attendance to hand all this material over to Mr Crowe and it must have been with some sadness that he watched the various items being carried out through the door of Hume Street. The Portlock volumes had been with the Survey ever since its days in the Custom House under James. A few of the six-inch field-sheets had been with Jukes at 51 St Stephen's Green. And over the years all the maps had been treated with that care and reverence such as in a monastery would be bestowed upon a genuine fragment of the original Cross. Now everything was being handed over to men untrained in geology who would perhaps neither appreciate nor understand the documents which a political decision had brought into their hands. Up in the North there were certainly no geological arms eagerly outstretched awaiting the arrival of the precious Hume Street material. Nobody had thought fit to give Northern Ireland a geological survey of its own and it was not until April 1947 that a branch office of the Geological Survey of Great Britain was opened in the province. But during that long interval the former Hume Street maps must have been well cared for; today those maps are in the safe hands of the Geological Survey of Northern Ireland. I am not sure that I may say the same of the Portlock memoirs. In the 1960s a certain Belfast second-hand bookshop had what seemed to be an unending supply of copies of Portlock's masterpiece. Some of them were rodent-nibbled, and upon enquiry I was told that the volumes had been found in a Belfast warehouse which had been used for government purposes. Were these volumes perhaps the remains of the sixty copies collected by Mr Crowe on 18 July 1923? I like to think so because my own copy of Portlock's memoir came off the shelves of that Belfast bookshop one hot summer's afternoon in 1967. Oddly, it was 18 July, and perhaps I should add that at the time of purchase it was in mint condition with not a trace of rodent dentition.

In mid-March 1924 Cole suffered a minor stroke. He remained undaunted despite this, the latest of his physical tribulations. From his sickbed in Orahova he wrote to Hume Street giving instructions that his office was to be transferred from the large room on the first-floor to the small room on the ground-floor just inside the front door. That room had formerly been Wright's office, but it had been lying unused ever since Wright's departure for Manchester. In all probability Cole never went to Hume Street to occupy his new office. His days on the Dublin Slow and Easy were at an end. He died at Orahova of a second stroke on 20 April 1924. We are told that he had never possessed so much as a single enemy anywhere in the length and breadth of Ireland.

As they stood around his open grave in Deansgrange cemetery his colleagues must have recognised that the Survey had lost a fine Director. Appointed to the office largely to satisfy administrative convenience within the Department of Agriculture and Technical Instruction, Cole had amply demonstrated himself to be a Director in the mould of the great Jukes. Perhaps I should also offer a final reminder: all that Cole had accomplished for the Survey he had accomplished merely on the basis of a part-time occupation of the Director's chair. With Cole laid to rest there was now nobody left capable of preventing the Survey's incipient paralysis from becoming general.

CHAPTER SIX

PARALYSIS
1924-1952

The nature of the services rendered by the Geological Survey is by no means generally understood.

Timothy Hallissy writing in the *Irish Trade Journal* for August 1928

Lying amidst the archives of the Survey there is a set of plans of number 14 Hume Street. The plans seem to date from around 1940, and they were perhaps drawn at the time when electricity was first introduced into the building. They present us with a great deal of detailed information about the internal arrangement of the house as it was some fifteen years after Cole's death. We discover, for instance, that his card-catalogue of Irish mineral occurrences was in the ground-floor room just inside the doorway, while the Survey's set of the journal *Nature* was in the same room on the shelves to the left of the fireplace. But it is the plan for the top floor of the house which presently interests me and, more especially, I wish there to focus upon the smaller of the two rear rooms.

In the days when the house was a private residence, I suppose that smaller room accommodated a nanny responsible for the care of a quiverful of children in an adjacent nursery. On the plan the room bears the title 'Soil Analysis Laboratory'. This is the laboratory which was fitted out for Hallissy about 1908. It is the laboratory where the Haigh twins worked successively upon soil samples from Ballyhaise, Clonakilty, and Clare Island. It is the laboratory where Thomas Haigh must have sat during the hot summer of 1914 wondering whether he should enlist in the Dublins or the Munsters. The plan of the laboratory informs us that the shelves in the room carried apparatus, chemicals, fossils, soil-samples, and blocks for illustrations used in Survey memoirs. Over in the corner, near to the sink, there is marked the presence of a centrifuge, but following the word 'centrifuge' there is added the parenthetical comment 'broken'. The state of that piece of equipment seems nicely to exemplify the state of the Survey during its long years of paralysis.

Down to 1924 the Survey had to its credit a proud record of scientific and cartographic achievement. For eighty years the Survey had ranked among the world's leading national geological surveys. Through important publications, emanating first from 51 St Stephen's Green and then from 14 Hume Street, the names of many of the Survey's officers had become familiar to geological readers the world over. At home the Survey had little by little assembled an invaluable archive of knowledge relating to the rocks of Ireland. In particular, there had been amply fulfilled Jukes's hope that the Survey's six-inch field-sheets would one day be recognised as 'a great public document of reference'. By plunging so boldly into Ireland's offshore waters from the decks of the *Helga*, the Survey had even begun to bring the proximal Atlantic continental shelf within Hume Street's purview. The Survey born in the Dublin Custom House on 1 April 1845 had indeed grown to become a remarkable Irish geological enterprise.

But during the 1920s the entire atmosphere changed. It was almost as though the stroke which Cole experienced at Carrickmines during March 1924 had induced a condition of apoplexy more than ten kilometres away within the nervous system of Hume Street. True, a second stroke sent Cole off to his grave, whereas the Survey survived, but for thirty years after 1924 the Survey was a paralytic and scarcely to be recognised shadow of its former self. At the time of Cole's death the exciting Washing Bay core lying in the Hume Street basement might in both senses have been regarded as the tangible symbol of the Survey's deep commitment to the investigation of Ireland's geology. For the thirty years covered by this chapter I prefer to find my symbolism up in that top-floor rear-room of Hume Street. I offer to you as an emblem the broken centrifuge.

Before describing the clinical detail of the Survey's torpid condition during the decades following 1924, there is one point which must immediately be advanced. I shall eventually endeavour to account for the Survey's lengthy paralysis, but I must without delay emphasise that for what happened there is no simple and ready explanation. Certainly the Survey officers themselves are not to be regarded as convenient scapegoats for the lethargy which now replaced the Survey's former dynamism. Those officers were largely the victims of circumstance. Such efforts as they may have made to maintain the traditions of Hume Street were stifled by forces which were entirely beyond the Survey's control. Similarly, we cannot heap blame upon the officials of the Department of Agriculture and Technical Instruction because on 2 June 1924 the Survey was transferred from that Department to the Department of Education. This transfer, taking place at what for the Survey was a highly inauspicious moment, can only have compounded the Survey's developing problems, but again we must resist the temptation to clutch at facile explanation in terms of departmental maladministration. Really, the Survey's paralysis was complex in its origins. It had causative factors which were deeply embedded within the society whence there came the figures who were now dominant within the newly-independent Irish nation. That point made, it for the moment is the outward manifestations of the Survey's sickness which must receive our attention.

It was during 1924 that it first became clear that the Survey had sailed into waters so troubled that there was a danger of its receiving structural damage. And that takes us back into the National Museum of Science and Art and back to the Curved Gallery where the Survey had its exhibit illustrative of the geology of Ireland. That gallery was a part of the Dublin complex of cultural institutions which centred upon the headquarters of the Royal Dublin Society at Leinster House. In plan the complex took the form of the letter H, with the National Library and the National Gallery paired on one side and the Science and Art Museum and the Natural History Museum paired on the other, with Leinster House itself forming the cross-member (Fig. 10.6). In 1922 a political wave had burst into the heart of this complex when the lecture-theatre attached to Leinster House was adopted as a meeting place for the Dáil. Two years later that same wave surged from Leinster House towards the Natural History Museum sweeping the Survey's exhibits from their display-cases in the Curved Gallery.

Ever since its earliest days in St Stephen's Green, the Survey had provided the Irish people with a display illustrating the geology of their native land. The museum had afforded the Survey both with its chief educative opportunity and with an important means of advertising its own accomplishments. For the Survey its museum gallery had been both schoolroom and shop-window. Now the Survey was peremptorily dismissed from the Curved Gallery. There was no discussion, no offer of immediate alternative accommodation, and no acceptable period of notice to quit. The Survey was simply told to pack its boxes and go (see p.150 and Chapter Ten).

For the moment, just suppose that such an eviction notice had been served upon the Survey by the British administration in the days before Ireland achieved its independence. Imagine the howls of protest which must have arisen from nationalists in every corner of the island as they reacted to an action which deprived the Irish people of access to an understanding of their geological birthright. And in their outcry such nationalists would have received vigorous support from the scientific community on the opposite side of the Irish Sea. Arrangements would have been made for questions to be asked at Westminster. Letters of protest would have arrived from the Royal Society, the Geological Society of London, the British Association for the Advancement of Science, and, of course, from Jermyn Street. But by 1924 the Survey stood alone and vulnerable in a strange new Ireland.

What chance did the Survey have of clinging on to its museum gallery at a moment when even the once powerful Royal Dublin Society was being severely buffeted by the identical political storm? It was in June 1922 that Michael Collins asked to be shown over the society's Leinster House headquarters; the Society's lecture-theatre was shortly requisitioned as a chamber for the Dáil; and by the close of 1924 the Society had been forced to relinquish its final toehold within the building which had been its home ever since 1815. If the well-found company aboard the stately three-decker of Leinster House were incapable of repelling Collins and his Sinn Féin boarders, then is it surprising that the tiny crew of the Survey's museum gallery was so easily overwhelmed? At that time and in that place those in power regarded Dáil secretaries and their typewriters as vastly more important than Dingle slates and their trilobites. And in the new Ireland who was there courageous enough to gainsay such a verdict? The Survey's museum gallery and its specimens were treated much as the monasteries and their sacred relics were being treated in Lenin's Russia.

This episode of the Survey's banishment from its museum gallery affords a nice illustration of the point made earlier. In newly-independent Ireland the Survey wallowed and yawed not because the vessel was crank or poorly handled, but simply because it was being pounded by powerful forces unleashed during the national struggle for freedom.

Next, the Survey found itself the victim both of departmental indecision and of financial stringency arising from the shaky economic situation within the new nation. From 1845 down to 1924 the Survey had never been for one moment without an officially appointed head. In 1846, 1850, 1890, 1901, and 1905 the control of the Survey had passed smoothly from one permanent head to his successor without the intrusion of so much as a single day of interregnum. Only in 1869 was there a slight hiatus in the ordering of the succession. Then, after Jukes's death in July 1869, Hull, who was already in St Stephen's Green as Acting Director, had to wait for almost three months before being confirmed in the directorship. But since Ireland obtained its independence the Survey has repeatedly been plagued by hesitation over the appointment of successive Directors. The departure of each of the five post-1921 Directors has been followed by an interregnum varying in length from one year to almost five years. Indeed, since 1921 the Survey has been without a permanent head for a total of more than fifteen years. Between 1845 and 1921 the Survey ran around as a headless chicken for only 0.32 per cent of the time; since 1921 the Survey has been left to operate in that sad condition for no less than 20.5 per cent of the time.

The interregnum following Cole's death in 1924 is the most striking example of this singularly unfortunate phenomenon. Just six weeks after Cole's fatal stroke there took place the transfer of the Survey from the Department of Agriculture and Technical Instruction to the Department of Education and, where the directorship was concerned, that new Department gave a masterly display of inactivity. It simply did nothing about the vacancy, and it continued to do nothing for well-nigh four years. As the Survey's Senior Geologist (he had succeeded Wright in April 1921), Hallissy very naturally stepped into the breach to perform the day-by-day duties which normally fell to the Director. But from his Department he never received any instruction requesting him to keep the Survey's wheels oiled and turning, and he certainly never received a penny's recompense for the additional duties he was undertaking. He and the Survey were simply abandoned to manage as best they could. Hallissy wrote to the Department on 20 April 1925 and again on 27 November 1927 reminding his superiors of the vacant directorship and of his own anomalous position, but to his letters he received nothing more helpful than curt official acknowledgement. By 1928 Hallissy and his colleagues must have been in a state of some despair.

On 1 April 1928 responsibility for the Survey was again transferred, this time from the Department of Education to the Department of Industry and Commerce. Hallissy resolved to try yet again. On 12 July 1928 he wrote to the Survey's new masters pleading for something to be done. The Department of Industry and Commerce proved to be far more responsive than had the Department of Education. There was immediate action. Hallissy's devotion to duty was recognised and his own position regularised through his nomination as Director as from 9 August 1928. His own former post as Senior Geologist was left vacant, and that rank remained in abeyance until Duffy was promoted to the grade of Senior Geologist in May 1941. Hallissy was the first officer to be promoted to the directorship after rising through the ranks of the Irish Survey. It is a distinction which Hallissy shares only with the present Director of the Survey: Dr Peadar McArdle joined the Survey in 1975, became a Senior Geologist in 1982, and was appointed Director in 1992.

Hallissy was by no means the only Survey officer to suffer as a result of official indecision and penny-pinching. Even more grievous than his problems were those faced by Duffy and Farrington. They had both joined the Survey in December 1921 as Temporary Geologists and at that time it was understood that their salary-scale would be one of £150 per annum increasing by £15 each year to a maximum of £475, but with an efficiency-bar at £400. This was the scale which it was understood they would be joining as soon as they had completed an appropriate probationary period. They both gave the Survey every satisfaction but, despite repeated requests from Hallissy, nothing was done about their appointment to the permanent rank of Geologist. By 1928 the two men were both well past the age of thirty, but they possessed no security in their posts, they received no regular salary increments, and they had no pension entitlements. Worse still in the short-term was the fact that their allowance for field-expenses was entirely inadequate. An officer's field-allowance was then, as now, related to the level of his salary, and even after a once off *ex gratia* salary increment of £50 in 1926, Duffy and Farrington were still being paid only £200 per annum. As a result they found themselves seriously out of pocket whenever their duties took them away from Dublin.

By 1928 Farrington decided that he had endured sufficient of both dubiety and penury. Early that year he resigned from the Survey to become Resident Secretary at the Royal Irish Academy. His departure was a serious loss to the Survey - a loss which became increasingly more apparent as the years rolled by. Farrington was a man who from his undergraduate days in University College Cork had been inspired by a deep interest in the history of our earth. His six Survey years - and especially his drift mapping in west Wicklow - had served to quicken that interest, and although he had published only one paper before he turned his back upon Hume Street, that paper was a presage of important works to come. After 1928 he was never again a professional geologist but throughout his life he devoted such leisure hours as he could find to the exploration of Ireland's more recent geohistory. He proved himself to be a man from the same mould as Lamplugh and Wright, but in his case the authorities controlling the Survey had failed to recognise his true worth. From his pen there eventually came more than fifty papers devoted to the events of the Irish Tertiary and Quaternary, the last of those papers being published in the autumn of 1973, some six months after Farrington's death.

Appropriately that paper, written in association with his friend Frank Mitchell, was concerned with glacial relics in that very region of west Wicklow where fifty years earlier he had commenced his Survey career under Cole's tutelage.

Duffy was either more patient than Farrington or else he was denied the opportunity of easy escape from Hume Street. In his letter to the Department of Industry and Commerce on 12 July 1928 Hallissy again pleaded Duffy's case, but it was March 1929 before Duffy was at long last allowed to join the permanent staff of the Survey.

The Department of Education's failure to fill the vacant directorship or to appoint Duffy and Farrington to permanent posts (between 1924 and 1928 the two men represented half the Survey's geological manpower) must surely have caused Hume Street morale to plummet. But officers had other reasons for feeling profoundly dissatisfied with the treatment being accorded to the Survey within the newly independent Ireland. In particular, the Survey's lines of communication with that wider world beyond Hume Street were being allowed to collapse. Communication is the lifeblood of science and Hume Street was fast turning anaemic as its lifeblood ebbed away. The Survey was being forced to turn in upon itself. Like the nation of which it was a part, the Survey was becoming introspective. Men of the calibre of Ramsay, Geikie, and Teall no longer climbed the stairs up to the Director's office to discuss Irish geological problems and to bring news of London, Edinburgh, or places further afield. Over in the Curved Gallery of the National Museum the Survey had once been able to excite the interest and expand the vision of the general public as visitors studied the Survey's carefully ordered specimens and their accompanying maps. Now the collections were boxed and their former gallery was filled with noisome clatter as busy secretarial fingers typed constituency letters at the behest of T.Ds who in all probability cared little for the distinction between a Wexford goniatite and a Wicklow garnet.

In the days of Cole and Wright the completion of the quarter-inch geological map of Ireland had been eagerly anticipated as an event which would lay before the Irish people a convenient conspectus of the subterranean structure of their native land. Now Hallissy saw the map abandoned in a sadly incomplete state. It features upon the Irish cartographic scene like those gaunt and ruinous homes of the former Anglo-Irish ascendancy which today speck the Irish landscape. The 205 sheets of the one-inch map were the Survey's most significant channel of communication with the Irish people, but in newly-independent Ireland some of the sheets were no longer available for purchase. Even Survey officers themselves found difficulty in securing copies of certain sheets for official use. The Survey's published memoirs had once carried the Survey's name around the world. Now it had to be explained to enquiring foreign librarians that their failure to receive further Hume Street memoirs was not to be attributed to some vagary within the postal service. Rather was it the result of Ireland having virtually ceased to assist its Geological Survey into print.

Here I must return to that point emphasised earlier. The failure of the Survey to maintain its lines of communication with the wider world beyond Hume Street was not a result of any insidious decay acting within Hume Street itself. It was something forced upon the Survey by events operating well beyond the walls of the Survey's headquarters. The Survey did not choose to become introspective; it was forced to become introspective as a result of constraints imposed from outside. This point has already been made in connection with the Survey's banishment from the National Museum. I now wish to establish the same point in connection with the non-publication of the maps and memoirs just mentioned.

As early as the spring of 1922 Cole discovered that the system of colouring one-inch geological sheets had broken down in the aftermath of Ireland's securing of independence. On 22 April that year he was informed that the Ordnance Survey, which was now under the control of the Irish Provisional Government, had available no coloured copies of one-inch Sheet 70 (Dundalk). Six days later, he was angry to discover that coloured versions of Sheet 78 (Strokestown) were also out of stock and, needing the sheet urgently for some official purpose, he had to go off in search of a remaining copy on the premises of Messrs Hodges, Figgis & Co., the Ordnance Survey's Dublin agents. Presumably members of the public now began to discover that even Hodges Figgis were unable to supply needed one-inch sheets. The story behind this evaporation of the former stream of hand-coloured one-inch sheets is one of stark simplicity.

Until around 1906 all British and Irish Geological Survey sheets in need of hand colouring had been dealt with in London by officially appointed colourists working on a contract system. Two of these colourists who worked in Camden Town have already been mentioned by name: Mrs E. Williams and Mr F. Dyer. After about 1906 the colouring of all the geological sheets was carried out by the Ordnance Survey's own colourists at that Survey's Southampton office. But once Ireland became an independent nation all Southampton's responsibility for the colouring of Irish maps was at an end. The task now devolved upon the Irish Ordnance Survey at its office in Phoenix Park, Dublin. And there lay the nub of the problem. The

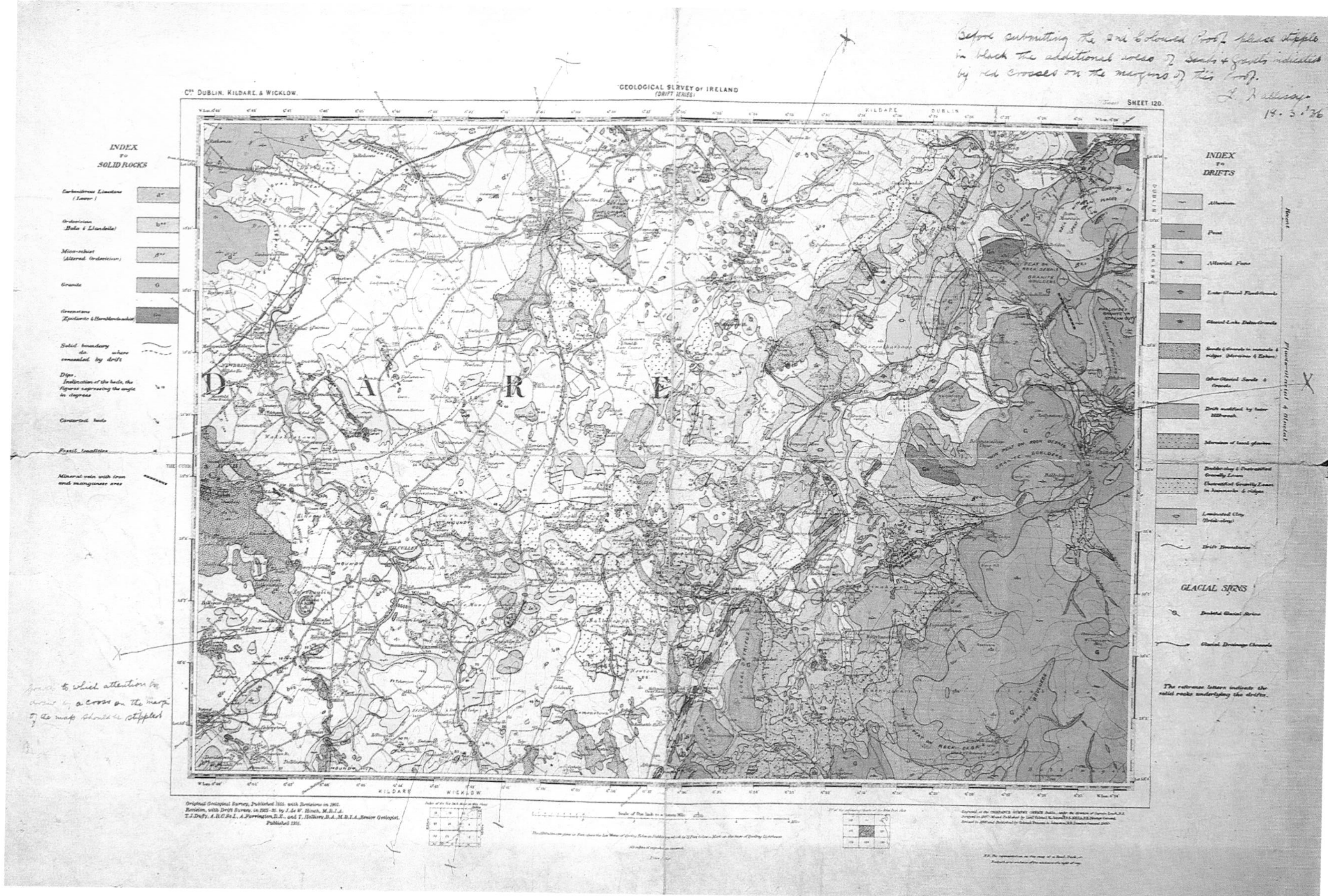

PLATE IX. *The colour-printed proof version of the one-inch drift-edition of Sheet 120 (Naas). This is the sheet which received what Hallissy presumably intended to be his final corrections on 18 March 1936. Over a period of fifteen years this sheet had absorbed a great deal of Survey effort, but the sheet was destined never to be published. Now, sixty years later, and in the above form, the map is for the first time brought into the public gaze. To allow this reproduction the map has, of course, been much reduced in scale. The size of the inner frame of the original is 45.6 x 30.2 centimetres. The base-map is neither the Ordnance Survey's outline edition nor its hachured edition, but rather the more modern contoured sheet.*

Irish Ordnance Survey possessed no colourists and had no experience in the skilled art of affixing tints to geological maps. Steps were soon taken to rectify the situation. Colourists were recruited, trained, and set to work at their task, but in the interim there must have been many members of the public who shared Cole's anger when they discovered that a desired one-inch sheet was unobtainable.

The story of the quarter-inch (1:253,440) map of Ireland had no such happy an outcome. By the time of Cole's death there had been published four of the sixteen sheets necessary to complete the map. The Survey's work upon the remainder of the map was soon far advanced because in the Survey's map archives there are manuscript or printed proof copies of every sheet in the set save for Sheet 9 (see Fig. 5.8). But not one of these sheets was ever actually published. To this day the quarter-inch map remains in its 1923 state of four down with twelve to go. The officers of the Survey were clearly anxious to see the map completed and were striving vigorously towards that end. Equally clearly, officials outside Hume Street did not share the Survey's enthusiasm for the map. I have seen no evidence suggesting that the map was formally put to death after a fair trial involving a review of likely costs *vis-à-vis* potential sales. All the evidence points to the map simply having been allowed to die as a result of official negligence. Those who controlled the valves in the circulatory system linking Hume Street to the outside world had not the wit to perceive that they were conniving in the extermination of what arguably was the most generally valuable map ever engendered within the Irish Survey.

A similar sad story is associated with the drift version of one-inch Sheet 120 (Naas). Between 1922 and 1927 the Survey devoted much time to the study and delimitation of the superficial deposits of this region. Originally the investigation was confined to the valley of the Liffey between Blessington and Ballymore Eustace, and, as we noted earlier (p.148), the work was undertaken because of the proposal to construct a hydro-electric power-station on the Liffey at the Falls of Pollaphuca. In 1923 the Survey's study was extended to encompass the entire area represented upon Sheet 120 and sometime thereafter a manuscript drift map of the region was sent from Hume Street to the Ordnance Survey to be prepared for publication. I see from the Survey diary kept by Mark Cunningham (he joined the Survey in 1930) that he spent the day of my own nativity - 18 January 1932 - affixing tints to a fair copy of the sheet. Between September 1932 and February 1933 Miss Eileen Barnes of 45 Kenilworth Square, Rathgar, spent a total of 376 hours draughting the final version of the sheet for submission to the Ordnance Survey. A late stage, colour-printed proof copy of the resultant sheet exists within the Geological Survey. It bears the printed inscription 'published 1935', and it represents alluvium, peat, alluvial fans, late-glacial flood gravels, glacial-lake delta gravels, drift modified by later hill-wash, and the moraines of local glaciers. Despite the optimistic date of publication carried by the map, Hallissy was still adding his manuscript comments to the sheet as late as 18 March 1936, and, truth to tell, the map was never published at all. Again the Survey had been thwarted in its efforts to lay its work before the public. Today that proof copy of the drift version of Sheet 120 is to be found in the fireproof-store down in the basement of the Survey's headquarters at Beggars Bush. There it lies in one of the steel cabinets which are the coffins of the Survey's stillborn infants dating from the 1920s and the 1930s (Plate IX).

The drift edition of one-inch Sheet 120 was to have been accompanied by a new sheet-memoir. The typescript of the memoir is also lying in the basement at Beggars Bush. Its authors were Hallissy, Hinch, Duffy, and Farrington; it is dated 1936; and its title is *The Geology of the Country around Naas, Blessington and Ballymore-Eustace (Explanation of the Colour-Printed Drift Sheet 120)*. The memoir is complete in every respect save one: on the cover there still has to be added its retail price. But the memoir was never given a price. Nobody has ever purchased a copy. It was evidently never printed. It was certainly never published. In 1931 Hallissy reported that a memoir devoted to the Clare phosphates, illustrated with maps and sections, was almost ready for publication, but this memoir shared the fate of the memoir to drift Sheet 120: it never arrived in the bookshops.

Between 1924 and 1943 the Survey was able to present to the Irish people only two live children. One of these was a memoir published in 1927 and the other was a map published in 1928. These two items must hold for us especial interest as being the only publications to emanate from the Survey during a period of almost twenty years. But as we turn the pages of the memoir, or run our eyes over the map, there soon dawns a realisation that both publications display characteristics which must deny to them our unreserved acclaim. In neither case - and this reverts to my now familiar theme - is blame for the flaws to be laid at the door of 14 Hume Street. The culprits were not the officers of the Survey.

The memoir published in 1927 is the memoir by Wright, Cole, and Hallissy on the Killarney and Kenmare district. It was intended as an explanatory accompaniment to the two one-inch maps of the region - one a solid map and the other a drift - which the Survey had issued in October 1922 (see pp.147 and 228). From a geological standpoint the memoir is a fine and valuable achievement. Its regrettable characteristic is that its publication had been so long delayed. Wright had completed his investigation of the Killarney and Kenmare district in 1913, and Cole had dated his preface to the memoir on 25 July 1916. But publication had been delayed, first because of the Great War, then because of the Irish 'Troubles', and finally because of lethargy within either the Department of Education or the Stationery Office. Such was that lethargy that no official pen was raised to place the ascription 'the late' before Cole's name in recognition of the fact that by 1927 he had been dead for three years.

The map published in 1928 is a representation of the solid geology of Ireland at a scale of one to a million. The Survey had commenced work upon the map in 1924 and it was the first small-scale geological map of Ireland ever to be published by the Survey. In 1924 there had just occurred the transference of the Survey to the Department of Education, and there we would seem to have the key to an understanding of the map's rationale. It was devised primarily for educational use. Indeed, the map was issued as part of a folder, priced five shillings, with the geological map facing a hill-shaded topographical map of Ireland at the same one to a million scale. This juxtaposition of the two maps was intended to illustrate the intimate relationship which exists in Ireland between geology and topography. If physically Ireland is likened to a saucer, then geology explains why the saucer exists.

And in what respect was the 1928 map flawed? Sadly, it is a thoroughly unsatisfactory piece of cartography. The map is far too crowded with detail, the geological tints are uneven in their spread, colour registration is poor, and a general 'smudged effect' renders much of the printing difficult of comprehension. It may be that some of the map's defects result from an attempt to support Irish industry by using locally manufactured paper which was really unsuited for such cartographic purposes. To compare the 1928 geological map with Geikie's splendid drift map of Ireland published by John Bartholomew in 1906 (see p.109) is certainly a chastening experience. Up in Phoenix Park the Irish Ordnance Survey might be proud to be under new management, but the 1928 map of Ireland fails even to attain the lowly cartographic standard of the one-inch Dublin drift sheet of 1903. The poor quality of that 1903 sheet had resulted in all the later drift sheets being printed in Southampton (see p.116); by 1928 the Survey had no Southampton to fall back upon.

The Survey's publication record during those twenty years following Cole's death may have left much to be desired but that is not to imply that the officers in Hume Street were then sitting idly upon their hands or vacantly ogling the nurses in the hospital on the opposite side of the street. The officers - and from 1925 until 1941 they never numbered more than four - continued, as best they could, to provide Ireland and its people with the geological advisory service which was needed. They dealt with the steady stream of official and public enquiries which flowed into Hume Street and which related to topics as varied as water supply, road metal, or the availability of specified types of terrestrial raw materials. One advantage accruing to the Survey from its 1924 transference from the Department of Agriculture and Technical Instruction to that of Education was that Lyburn was no longer hovering upon the scene. The old prohibition upon the Survey's involvement with economic issues was at last at an end. Lyburn and his pre-1914 activities must nonetheless have been in Hallissy's mind during the year 1924-25 as the Survey completed for the Department of Lands and Agriculture a manuscript map indicating the Irish limestones which were suitable for burning in lime-kilns. Similarly, Hallissy must have recalled his own early pedological years when the Survey made the Irish portion of a soil map of Europe for presentation at the first International Congress of Soil Science, held in Washington during June 1927.

In the field the Survey continued to operate as active a programme as limited manpower and financial resources would permit. In 1927, for example, the solid revision and drift mapping of one-inch Sheet 120 was completed; the newly-discovered County Clare phosphate beds were investigated; and the drifts of the Shannon basin between Banagher and Limerick were studied as a part of the Survey's contribution to the success of the Shannon Power Scheme. The excavations for the scheme's Ardnacrusha power station had commenced in March 1926, and thereafter the Survey undertook an examination of all the major geological sections laid bare during the development of the project. And then, of course, there were the coalfields. Virtually every year officers went down to Castlecomer or up to Arigna to examine fresh evidence arising from new boreholes and extended workings, or to offer advice based upon the latest stratigraphical knowledge.

The officers of the Survey were clearly performing their duties to the best of their ability, but there is no escaping the fact that the young Irish Free State took little interest in their doings. Evidence of that scant interest is provided by the proceedings of the Oireachtas. The first eighty volumes chronicling the debates of the Dáil carry their record down to 7 August 1940 but during that period there are only two direct references to the Survey. Both references relate to questions asked about the Survey's coalfield studies and clearly in each case the question was raised by a T.D. who

Visit the Shannon Works!

See this Mighty Project in the making

Arrangements have been made with the Great Southern Railway to issue Return Tickets at Single Fares from all stations on its system to Limerick on week-days, available for return within three days including day of issue, from now on until the 29th of September inclusive.

Conducted Tours daily from the I. O. C. premises
Sarsfield Street, Limerick:—
1st Tour leaves at 10.30 a.m., returning 1.30 p.m.
2nd „ „ 2.30 p.m., „ 6.30 p.m.
BUS FARE 4/- **(Children Half-price)**
Guide's services free.

Those not wishing to avail of these Conducted Tours should apply direct for a permit, giving date of proposed visit.
Conducted Tours on SUNDAYS for large excursion parties ONLY—

Apply to The ELECTRICITY SUPPLY BOARD
GUIDE BUREAU, STRAND BARRACKS, LIMERICK

O'LOUGHLIN
PRINTER
FLEET STREET
DUBLIN

FIGURE 6.1. *The Shannon Power Development Scheme was under construction from 1925 until 1930. At the time it was the largest civil engineering project ever undertaken in Ireland, and it involved the blasting of more than a million cubic metres of rock and the excavation of ten million cubic metres of earth. The completion of the scheme was commemorated on 15 October 1930 by the issue of the first ever Irish pictorial postage stamp (denomination 2 pence). The Geological Survey was responsible for the initial site investigation for the project. The illustration is reproduced from a handbill preserved in the archives of the Electricity Supply Board. It was very kindly brought to my attention by Mr Proinsias Brinkley.*

merely wished to go on record as having been active in the interest of his constituents. In the Seanad the Survey attracted even less attention. The indexes to the first thirty-four volumes of Seanad debates (1922-1948) contain not a single reference to the Survey or its work.

One of the very few occasions upon which governmental attention did focus upon the Survey occurred in 1932. It was the year of the great Dublin Eucharistic Congress. Hallissy was asked whether he wished 14 Hume Street to share with other government buildings the privilege of being illuminated. He declined the offer. The building had still not been wired for electricity and Hallissy considered that illumination by gas-jet posed too serious a fire risk. As a minor aside, there is one other aspect of the 1932 Congress deserving of mention. In common with other heads of department, Hallissy was instructed to facilitate any member of the Survey's staff wishing to take leave during the week of the Congress. It may be that the Survey then closed altogether. Between April 1930 and December 1940 the officers of the Survey were drawn exclusively from Ireland's Roman Catholic community. It was the first time in the history of the Survey that such a situation had existed.

In 1919 the first Dáil had evinced an urgent interest in Ireland's geological resources. To this fact ample testimony is borne by the establishment of the Commission of Inquiry into the Resources and Industries of Ireland, and by that Commission's publication of the remarkably comprehensive 1921 report on the Irish coalfields (see p.148). Why did the youthful state not persist in this early interest? Why did the Survey itself not seize upon so favourable a moment to urge the cause of its national importance? Why was a nurturing of the Survey not a feature of early government policy? To all such questions there would seem to be an abundance of interlocking answers.

The mid-1920s found the Survey severely disadvantaged in seeking to win for itself any kind of public support. The resignation of Wright in 1921, and the death of Cole in 1924, had removed the Survey's two most dynamic, respected, and influential figures. Hallissy was no man to lead a fighting crusade for incisive action, and in any case from 1924 until 1928 he was trapped in that limbo of uncertainty. Was he or was he not supposed to be the Survey's acting Director? Until April 1930 Hallissy's senior officer was the somewhat colourless John de Witt Hinch who had joined the Survey as recently as 1919 in the relatively lowly rank of Superintendent of Maps and Collections. Before coming to the Survey he had worked for twenty-nine years as an attendant in the National Library, and in 1921 he became the last non-graduate to be appointed as a Geologist in the Survey. During the mid-1920s Hallissy's only other officers were the two disgruntled Temporary Geologists, Duffy and Farrington. Hume Street could hardly be expected to become a hot-bed of ambitious, self-seeking intrigue.

The 1924 transfer of the Survey to the Department of Education was disastrous for Hume Street. That Department had no understanding of the nature of the fish which it had just been handed. There was no reason why it should have possessed any such understanding. The Department was concerned with classrooms for children, with the running of the nation's reformatories, with the training of teachers, and with the publication of the numerous Irish-language texts rendered necessary by the attempt to revive the Irish language. The Survey was transferred to the Department of Education only because ever since 1905 the Survey had administratively been pigeonholed with the National Library, the National Museum, and the Royal College of Science. In 1924 those three institutions were all, very appropriately, being handed over to the Department of Education, and when their new departmental masters opened the package they discovered that they had also received the Survey as an unexpected bonus. Perhaps they viewed the Survey with some puzzlement. Even in modern Ireland many of us have encountered well educated people who have laboured under the delusion that geology and archaeology are more or less synonymous. I am fully prepared to believe that in the Dublin of 1924 there may have been civil servants who had little appreciation of the true nature of the Survey's activities.

If such misunderstanding really did exist, then perhaps it was a matter of little moment. In the full national context the Survey shrank into insignificance. It was just one Georgian house, four geologists, one typist, one messenger, and dozens of drawers full of thousands of maps. It was just a speck of civil service dust which was unlikely to detain for long the attention of men who were grappling with the problems of creating the administrative structures of a new nation. In any case, expansion of the Survey was hardly likely because the national economy was weak and public funds were in short supply.

But, just supposing such finances had been available, would they necessarily have gone to the Survey? Was the Survey perhaps still viewed as being in part a lingering vestige of the old British colonial administration? Had it been tainted by the Unionist politics of its recent Director? Perhaps there was in circulation that story of the Survey having colluded in the post-Treaty removal to England of all the vital secrets relating to Ireland's true mineral wealth (see p.103). In consequence, no matter how well-intentioned the Survey's officers might now be, was their surviving file of data not seriously flawed? By 1933 Sean Lemass was the Minister responsible for the Survey and it was in the April of that year that he spoke specifically of the deliberate mischievousness and obscurantism of the geological documentation left by the British administration (see p.102). In some quarters, the Survey's image was perhaps still badly tarnished.

There also persisted that fundamental question which had been hovering around for over thirty years. The one-inch geological map of Ireland had been completed in 1890 so what was the Survey now supposed to be doing? Did the new Ireland really need the services of a geological survey? In the 1920s the country was predominantly an agrarian nation, and it was by no means clear how the Survey's expertise was to be enlisted in the service of Irish agriculture. It was easy to see how a geological survey might assist men who were digging coal or quarrying slates, but how was such a survey to benefit the man who was planting out his potatoes or harnessing his donkey for the morning excursion to the creamery?

In the years before 1922 Irish nationalists had often berated the Survey for its failure to identify Ireland's supposed subterranean riches. Now, in independent Ireland, even the Dáil's own commission of inquiry into Ireland's resources had been unable to locate the mythical mineral wealth. There was both surprise and disappointment. Many - like Sean Lemass in 1933 - clung tenaciously to their cherished belief that one day Ireland's treasury of minerals would be found and, in the long-term, their faith was to be richly rewarded. But others reflecting upon the question began to shift their ground. Are the ways of the Lord not strange? Paradoxically, might it be that the Deity's beneficence towards Ireland was displayed not in the gift of mineral deposits, but rather in their removal? The point was nicely made by Eibhlín de Buitléir (Elenor Butler) in a textbook first published in 1924 and then used by several generations of Irish schoolchildren. She noted that post-Carboniferous denudation had largely removed Ireland's former mantle of Coal Measures, and then she continued:

> For this too, perhaps, we have to be thankful. It is pleasanter to live in health in a land of green fields and of rich harvests than to droop and grow pale in a land besmirched with factory chimneys: and between employment in the open fields and employment in a coal mine or factory there is much to choose.

This was to place a novel gloss upon the seeming relative emptiness of Ireland's mineral vaults. It was a barrenness to be welcomed rather than deplored.

Here Eibhlín de Buitléir was revealing her sympathy for that image of Ireland which was so passionately embraced within the newly-independent Irish Free State. It was to be a Celtic homeland - a nation where the religion of Rome held sway, where Irish was the everyday language, and where supposedly traditional Gaelic values were revived and cherished. So far as possible it was to be a self-contained community where foreign goods were excluded by tariff-walls and where insidious alien concepts were excluded by a strict censorship. This was the Irish idyll of which Eamon de Valera spoke in his famed broadcast to the Irish people on St Patrick's Day in 1943.

> That Ireland which we dreamed of would be the home of a people who valued material wealth only as a basis of right living, of a people who were satisfied with frugal comfort and devoted their leisure to the things of the spirit; a land whose countryside would be bright with cosy homesteads, whose fields and villages would be joyous with sounds of industry, the romping of sturdy children, the contests of athletic youths, the laughter of comely maidens; whose firesides would be the forums of the wisdom of serene old age.

And what could the Geological Survey possibly have to contribute to this new Ireland? The one-inch geological map was complete so what more did the nation need? In any case, did geology's disagreement with the Scriptures not make it a danger to the faith? Was its subscribing to Darwin's notion of 'survival of the fittest' not a threat to public morality? Was its conception of geohistory as an interminable sequence of cycles not subversive of human dignity? The nation desired a knowledge of its folklore rather than its fossils. Ceilidhs and crack were in fashion; conglomerates and copper were not. If the Survey were to be raised from its paralysis might it not prove to be an ogre? If it actually located Irish mineral wealth would the prevailing Irish image not be dented? Who wanted the Irish landscapes of Paul Henry to be converted into something akin to the English townscapes of L.S. Lowry with their boxlike factories, their regimented dwellings, and their matchstick people?

All the factors just mentioned doubtless contributed to the paralysis which overtook the Survey during the 1920s, but that paralysis has to be viewed as just one aspect of a far more general phenomenon. It was just one manifestation of a malaise which began to spread through Irish science as a whole during the 1870s.

In the middle decades of the nineteenth century Irish science had flourished. From biology and mathematics in Trinity College Dublin, to physics in St Patrick's College Maynooth, and astronomy at the castles of Birr and Markree, Irish science then enjoyed a high international reputation. The healthy state of the Survey under Jukes between 1850 and 1869 had merely reflected the robust condition of Irish science as a whole. But after 1870 things began to go wrong. The whole of Irish science began to slide into decay. The reasons for this decay are

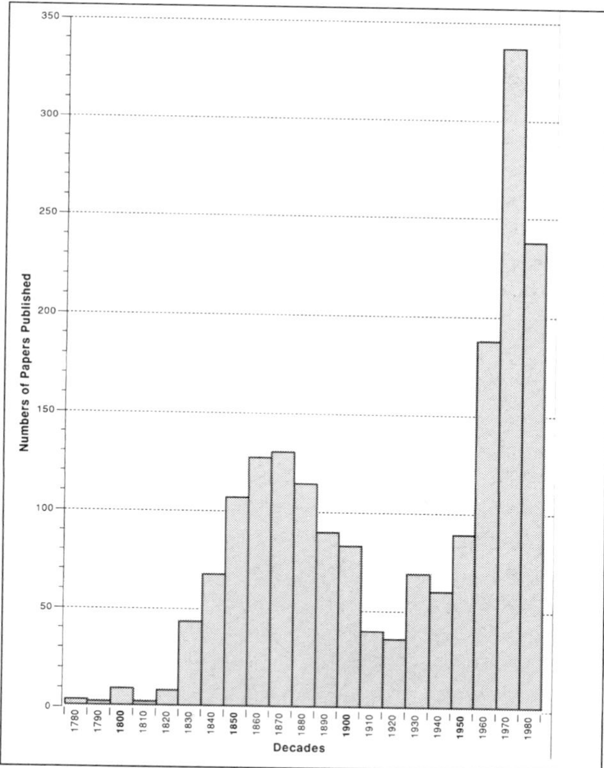

FIGURE 6.2. *The total number of earth-science papers published in Irish scientific periodicals each decade since the 1780s. An earlier version of the diagram appeared, with an explanation, in the* Journal of Earth Sciences Royal Dublin Society, *volume 1, number 1, 1978.*

complex and as yet but little explored. There is, nevertheless, one observation which deserves to be made. Irish science of the mid-nineteenth century was overwhelmingly a creation of the Anglo-Irish ascendancy. It cannot be without significance for our understanding of the history of Irish science that after 1870 the Anglo-Irish ascendancy was itself in progressive decline.

Any further excursion into the factors underlying this decline of Irish science must cause us to stray far beyond the legitimate bounds of this present volume. It is nonetheless appropriate that we should note in outline the story of the sad fate which overtook Irish geology during the decades after 1870. Such an outline both affords us with a microcosm of the fate of Irish science as a whole and enables us to set the paralysis of the Survey in its full disciplinal perspective.

The story of Irish geology after 1870 may be likened to the descent of a staircase with movement from one tread to the next lowest being marked by clearly dated events. Some of these events involved the Survey itself, and in the rehearsal which follows, the reader will encounter several events which are already garbed in familiarity.

Between 1876 and 1882 the former chairs of geology and mineralogy in the Queen's colleges of Cork and Galway were subsumed into more general chairs of natural history. (Queen's College Belfast had taken a similar step in 1860 and in the case of the erstwhile Queen's College Cork it was to be 1979 before geology was restored to the status of being a full chair.) In 1883 the world-famed collection of fossil fish assembled at Florence Court, County Fermanagh, by the third Earl of Enniskillen, was removed from Ireland following the collection's sale to the British Museum (Natural History). In 1890 the Geological Survey of Ireland was reduced to little more than a care and maintenance basis following the completion of the one-inch map, and in the same year there was held the last meeting of the once vigorous Royal Geological Society of Ireland. Four years later the remaining funds of the Society were handed over to the Royal Irish Academy. In 1897 Sollas left Dublin for Oxford and in his stead Trinity College appointed as its new professor not a conventional geologist, but a remarkable hybrid inventor-physicist in the form of the great John Joly.

As a result of the surgery of 1905 the Survey was severed from its renowned British parent and left to fend for itself in a strange new Ireland. During the Great War two out of five of the Survey's officers were killed on active service, and in 1921 Wright decided that his future lay in England rather than in Ireland. In 1922 the Irish people lost their access to the geological galleries of the National Museum, and two years later the Survey's collections disappeared into the storage-crates which were to be their home for fifty years. In 1924 Cole's death removed Ireland's last mainstream geologist possessed of an international reputation, and his chair in the Royal College of Science - a chair which had been held with distinction by Jukes, by Hull, and by Cole himself - was left unoccupied. In 1926 the chair was abolished.

In the human body the pulse rate affords a vital indication as to the condition of a patient. Within the body of science the state of any particular discipline may be assessed by its pulse of publication. The heartbeats of a healthy science send a steady stream of publications pulsing into those channels of literary communication which constitute the arteries of the scientific community. The pulse of Irish geology as revealed by the numbers of geological papers published in Irish scientific periodicals is represented in Figure 6.2. That Figure strikingly demonstrates both the increasingly healthy state of the science between the 1820s and the 1870s and then its marked decline into sickness thereafter. Not until the 1960s did the science regain the vigorous pulse rate which it had displayed a century earlier.

Any geological survey is likely to be a peculiar organism. Such a survey may possess only a single heart, but in all probability that heart will produce not just one measurable pulse rhythm, but two. These two rhythms may respectively be designated 'the official pulse rate' and the 'the private pulse rate'. The official pulse rate is the pulse revealed by the issue of such government-financed publications as maps, sections, and memoirs. This is the pulse rate as measured by the flow of survey publications through the arteries of the state. The private pulse rate is the pulse revealed by the privately produced works which the officers of a survey themselves pass into the arteries of the international community of the earth sciences. This is the pulse rate as measured by the flow of books and papers from a survey and into the normal channels of scientific publication. The official pulse rate measures the success of a survey's officers in laying their work before a local public in the form of official publications. The private pulse rate measures the enthusiasm of a survey's officers in the making of contributions to the international literature of their science.

The official pulse rate of any survey will be affected by factors entirely beyond the control of that survey itself. For example, the level of state funding will clearly have bearing upon a survey's ability to issue official publications. The official pulse rate of the Geological Survey of Ireland was extremely feeble during the years following 1924 because, as we have seen, Hume Street was then feeling the effects of constraints imposed from well beyond its own red-brick walls. Little blame can be attached to the Survey for the weakness of its official pulse rate. But what of the Survey's private pulse rate? That pulse rate was entirely under the control of the Survey officers themselves. Here it has to be admitted that for thirty years after 1924 the Survey's private pulse rate was so feeble as to be almost beyond identification. The Survey's officers were content to register a private pulse rate which was no stronger than their official pulse rate. This state of affairs represented a dramatic change.

From the time of its foundation in 1845 down to 1924 the Survey had always displayed a vigorous private pulse rate. Oldham, Jukes, Hull, Lamplugh, Cole, Du Noyer, Kinahan, and Wright had all fed a steady stream of significant publications into the international literature of their science. But after 1924 this stream dried up almost completely. Between 1905 and 1924 there emanated from Hume Street the remarkable total of thirteen geological books of an unofficial character, eleven of them being exclusively from Cole's fluent pen. Since 1924 not one such an unofficial geological book has ever been written within the Survey. Between 1905 and 1924 thirteen papers by serving Survey officers were published in the two leading Irish scientific periodicals of the day, the *Proceedings of the Royal Irish Academy* and the *Scientific Proceedings of the Royal Dublin Society*. Between 1925 and 1949 only one paper by a Survey officer - Farrington - was published in either periodical. It is largely in vain that we search the international geological literature of the post-1924 era for contributions made by such Survey officers as Hallissy, Hinch, Duffy, McCluskey (appointed 1930), Cunningham, or O'Meara (appointed 1935). The contrast between the behaviour of these professional geologists and that of Farrington is both interesting and telling. After resigning from the Survey in 1928 Farrington had no further professional involvement with geology, yet between 1929 and 1950 he was the sole author of eight geological papers published in the *Proceedings of the Royal Irish Academy* and the *Scientific Proceedings of the Royal Dublin Society* and the part author of two further papers published in the same two journals.

The points just made expose to view a dilemma. On the one hand, is an officer of a geological survey a member of the global community of geology, and as such is that officer expected to make regular contributions to the international advancement of the earth sciences? On the other hand is a survey officer merely a parochial civil servant who is expected to do nothing more than tender geological information and advice within the local community? In short, to what extent should a survey officer aspire to join the leading theoreticians within the science, and to what extent should such an officer rest content with being a local purveyor of expertise in the field of applied geology?

In any geological survey the officers will individually resolve this dilemma by, in varying degrees, blending the international and academic with the local and applied. In the case of the Geological Survey of Ireland the two extremes in this blending process are exemplified on the one hand by Jukes and on the other hand by Hallissy's men.

Jukes never perceived himself to be a civil-service hack. He saw himself first and foremost as a scientist who was grappling with problems at the internationally recognised research frontiers of geology, and who just happened to be paid from the public purse. He was satisfied that his conclusions would eventually be seen to possess practical significance, but that was not their prime purpose. This view he expressed forcefully in 1867.

> Men of science have of late years pandered too much to the utilitarian quackery of the age, and it is time that some one should stand up to protest against it. Government and the House of Commons should be told that science must be supported and encouraged for her own purely abstract purposes, independently of all utilitarian applications.

In newly-independent Ireland, Hallissy and his men took their stand at the opposite extremity of the intellectual spectrum. If we judge them from their failure to maintain within the Survey anything but the faintest suggestion of a private pulse rate, then we must conclude that they saw themselves as geologists possessed of local responsibilities alone. They worked for the Geological Survey just as other employees of the state worked for the Department of Posts and Telegraphs or the Garda Siochana. Nobody really expected a Garda Superintendent to publish learned papers in international journals on the policing of County Mayo or on crowd control at Croke Park. Why, then, should equivalent publications be expected to flow from the pens of the officers in Hume Street?

Things might have been different had Wright not resigned, had Cole not died, or had the new Irish state not denied the Survey's officers the stimulation which would have arisen from the need to maintain a steady output of official publications. A healthy official pulse rate is undoubtedly an encouragement towards the development of a vigorous private pulse rate. As it was, the officers would seem to have lost their geological edge. There had evaporated that lively spirit of geological enquiry which seems to have pervaded the Survey during the years immediately before 1914. Gone were the days when officers from Hume Street had been players upon the international stage. Now the Survey was emulating the Irish Free State by turning in upon itself. In 1939 Ireland opted out of participation in World War II; well before 1939 the Survey had opted out of participation in international geology. Hume Street, let it be remembered, was unrepresented among the many national surveys and other scientific institutions which sent delegates to the centenary celebrations of the British Geological Survey in London during 1935 (see p.128).

In the years following 1924 Survey officers felt it to be far more important to advise Leitrim County Council over its water-supply problems than it was to explore the relationship of the geology of County Donegal to that of Scotland and Labrador. The contentment of ministers and T.Ds now had to be ensured by sending Survey officers on regular missions to the Slieveardagh Coalfield or to Arigna, but there was clearly no need to trouble oneself with thoughts of writing tomes on Irish Carboniferous stratigraphy or the coastal configuration of Armorican Europe.

It was in the aftermath of 1924 that Seymour's 1906 prophecy achieved its fulfilment (see p.128). By losing sight of the broader vistas of their science, the Survey's officers were leaving a major vacuum within Irish geology. Their science was also languishing within the Irish universities and the upshot of all this was that from the 1920s onwards academic geologists overseas began to look upon Ireland as a geologically underdeveloped nation. No longer were the Irish exploiting the geological research potential of their own rocks. The time was ripe for foreign academic geologists to move in, and this influx resulted in the dawn of a colonialist phase in the history of Irish geology. Overseas geologists - they mostly came from British universities - arrived to stake out their claims to pieces of Irish research territory, and by the 1950s a claims map of, say, Galway or Mayo must have looked very like a claims map of the pioneer frontier of the United States one hundred years earlier.

This episode in Irish scientific history deserves to be termed 'the Great Irish Geological Plantation' and it is a movement which was most clearly in evidence during the twenty-five years between 1945 and 1970. It was then that the departments of geology in Imperial College London, King's College London, and the University of Liverpool between them laid claim to virtually the whole of County Donegal. 'Students write theses about the hills of Donegal', exclaimed an *Irish Press* headline on 9 September 1952. Even as late as 1985 there were still more than seventy overseas geologists laying claim to proprietorial research rights over pieces of territory scattered across the length and breadth of Ireland.

The Caucasian colonisation of the American West took place because the Red Indians were weaker than the intruders; the Caucasian colonisation of the 'White Highlands' of Kenya took place because the Kikuyu and the Masai had recently been decimated by smallpox. The Great Irish Geological Plantation occurred because in the newly independent Ireland geology had been allowed to become sick and enfeebled. The colonists arrived because they saw good research problems lying vacant in attractive settings where the local geological community was so small and emaciated as to constitute no intellectual threat to the intruder. It is paradoxical that after winning its political independence, Ireland should have so neglected its native geology that there was ushered in an episode of geological colonialism.

Before going off to occupy their chosen ground, the colonists would almost invariably visit Hume Street and there ask to be shown the six-inch field-sheets encompassing their claim. Then, through the annotations upon the sheets, they would commune with the Survey officers of yesteryear - with Du Noyer, Jukes, Kinahan, McHenry, or Symes - but the modern Survey officer who brought the sheets from their cabinet might well have lacked the confidence and expertise necessary to allow him to become a third element within the geological dialogue.

The occurrence of the Great Irish Geological Plantation may afford striking evidence of the diseased condition of native Irish geology during the decades following the winning of national independence, but in the longer term the episode did bring benefit both to the Survey and to Ireland. Many of the overseas geologists who came to Ireland as intellectual planters developed a deep affection for the country, for its people, and for its rocks. As the opportunity arose some of those planters chose to abandon the 'booleying life-style' of the itinerant summer field-geologist visitor in favour of a permanent Irish domicile. When the Survey finally began to emerge from its paralytic state it was able, after 1967, to recruit to its permanent staff some ten non-Irish geologists who had originally arrived in Ireland as colonists during the Great Irish Geological Plantation. To the Survey those geologists brought a wealth of ready-made expertise of a type which was then hardly available within the still convalescent native geological community.

Hallissy and his officers were at best dormant members of the international geological community. They had allowed their private pulse rate to fade away. They had been forced to acquiesce in a drastic reduction of their official pulse rate. But I must reaffirm the point made earlier. Hallissy and his colleagues were deeply conscientious in the performance of the duties which they saw as theirs. By every means within their power they sought to allow the nation to benefit from the existence of the Survey both through a tapping of its vast storehouse of geological information and through calls made upon the expertise of its officers.

After the 1928 transfer of the Survey from the Department of Education to the Department of Industry and Commerce, the Survey devoted itself almost exclusively to matters of economic geology. Coal, base metals, and industrial raw materials now filled the Survey's agenda to the exclusion of almost everything else. Oddly, the 1928 transfer again brought the Survey into contact with Edward St John Lyburn. He was then serving as Economic Geologist to the Department of Industry and Commerce, but the demarcation disputes between Lyburn and the Survey which had characterised Cole's regime were now a thing of the past. The Survey and Lyburn were held to be playing complementary roles within the field of Irish economic geology. Indeed, for some years McCluskey formed a human bridge between the Survey in Hume Street and Lyburn's office over in the Department's Trade and Industries Branch in Lord Edward Street.

McCluskey graduated from University College Dublin in 1924. Between June 1925 and December 1927 he worked as a geologist with the Phoenix Oil and Transport Co. Ltd in the oil-fields of southern Roumania and then he returned home to work for eighteen months as engineering inspector on the Shannon Power Development Scheme. On 29 September 1928 he wrote to the Survey enquiring whether there might be a post in the offing for a geologist possessed of his qualifications, and he was finally appointed to the Survey as from 30 January 1930 in the rank of Geologist and as a somewhat overdue replacement for Farrington. That a former petroleum geologist should be succeeding a Pleistocene drifts man was surely an indication of the way the wind was now blowing. McCluskey, incidentally, enjoyed a high reputation as a conversationalist. He was one of the social circle which contained Brian O'Nolan (alias Flann O'Brien and Myles na Gopaleen) and he is said to have featured occasionally in the latter's celebrated and witty 'Cruiskeen Lawn' column in the *Irish Times*.

It was in the wake of the Fianna Fáil General Election victory of February 1932 that Sean Lemass became Minister for Industry and Commerce. The new government resolved to develop Irish resources to their fullest extent, and soon it was decided to augment the staff of the Trade and Industries Branch of the Department of Industry and Commerce through the creation of the post of Assistant to the Economic Geologist. It is perhaps significant that this development took place not in Hume Street, with its British and colonial background, but in Lord Edward Street, in a department which was a purely Irish creation. Be that as it may, the man appointed to the new post as from 28 April 1934 was McCluskey. A Survey geologist thus became Lyburn's deputy, but McCluskey's links with Hume Street would throughout appear to have remained close. Lyburn retired during 1938 and on 29 January 1941 McCluskey was transferred back to the Survey where until 1945 he continued to carry the somewhat anomalous title of Assistant Economic Geologist.

Under the aegis of the Department of Industry and Commerce the Survey embarked upon a series of renewed coalfield investigations. The Connaught Coalfield was re-examined between 1929 and 1931; a re-survey of the Leinster Coalfield was completed in 1933; the Slieveardagh Coalfield was re-investigated during 1933 and 1934; and a revision of the Munster Coalfield was completed in 1940. When the Fianna Fáil government came to power in 1932, money was made available for some investigative drilling to be carried out in the coalfields. This work was performed by private contractors with the Survey assuming an overall advisory role. The drilling took place in the Connaught Coalfield during 1934 and 1935, in the Slieveardagh Coalfield between 1935 and 1937, and in the Leinster Coalfield in 1939 and 1940. Outside the coalfields the Survey was also involved in supervising the state-financed exploratory drilling of the gypsum deposits around Kingscourt on the borders of counties Cavan and Meath. This task was Cunningham's responsibility throughout the greater part of 1938 and 1939.

One letter dated 26 May 1937 and written by Hallissy in Hume Street to Cunningham in the Munster Coalfield is worthy of quotation *in extenso* as conveying something of the atmosphere of the Survey during the 1930s. The only words of explanation necessary are that Duffy had just undergone a nasal operation and tonsillectomy, that Miss M. Murray was for some years the Survey's typist, and that a handbook of official phrases in Irish and English was about to be issued for use within the civil service.

> I note what you say about Carrigkerry. If you make a good job of the mapping, the time spent on the survey of the area will not prove excessive. The thickest of the seams, that which appears to have been worked to some extent, will probably be equivalent to the No. II of the Glin-Foynes basin. If you work on this hypothesis, it may help you in the unravelling of the structure.
>
> I have been awfully busy in the office. This sudden interest in mineral development may be due to the imminence of the Election, but there are also big boring programmes contemplated for the immediate future, and of course Water Reports, like the poor, are always with us. I have half a doz. of these lying in front of me at the moment.
>
> Mr. Duffy, who is now quite recovered, is away at Slieveardagh, and it looks as if he will be unable to spend much time this year on the Munster Coalfield.
>
> I will let Miss Murray know that you require a copy of the Irish Phrase book. I understand it is not yet quite ready for general distribution.

The Survey's portrait gallery of former Directors lacks any representation of Hallissy. Perhaps he was shy of the camera and for that there may have been a reason. Those who remember him recollect his suffering from some slight facial deformity. There was, perhaps, something misshapen about one of his eyes. Hallissy was the Survey's sixth Director, but he was the first of the six to retain that office down to the normal civil-service retirement age of sixty-five. Indeed, Hallissy went further. He remained Director down to the age of seventy. On 6 November 1939 his colleagues entertained him to a presentation dinner at the Dolphin Hotel in Dublin's Essex Street, and Cunningham's diary for the following day displays the entry 'Mr. H's Last day in G.S.O.'. It was the close of another era in the history of the Survey.

Hallissy was the last officer with experience extending back to those years before 1914 when Hume Street had possessed a modest international reputation. The officers who sat at table with Hallissy that evening in the Dolphin Hotel were figures who may have been familiar to county engineers, to quarry managers, and to the drilling companies, but to the geological world at large Cunningham, Duffy, McCluskey (he was evidently present that evening although not strictly then an officer of the Survey), and O'Meara were each *homo nullius coloris*. In 1931, when the Royal Dublin Society staged its comprehensive bi-century museum illustrative of the progress of science, art, and industry in Ireland over the previous two hundred years, Hallissy had devoted much time to the preparation of the Survey's contribution. And right well did he perform his task. The items which he put on display reveal him to have possessed a sound grasp of the Survey tradition to which he was heir, among those items being one of Foot's six-inch field-sheets from the Burren, landscape watercolours by Oldham and Du Noyer, fossil drawings by Du Noyer, the Ballyhaise soil map, Cole and Crook's *Helga* specimens, and the map derived from the 1918 geophysical survey at Ballard in County Wicklow.

Now I may be guilty of the perpetration of a grave injustice when I express such a view, but I do suspect that for almost thirty years after Hallissy's retirement there would have been no Survey officer possessed of the historical knowledge necessary for the assembly of so comprehensive a display illustrative of the Survey's achievements. Indeed, I suspect that during those thirty years no Survey officer would have had much interest in even attempting such a display of Survey artifacts. The men who remained in Hume Street after Hallissy's departure were conscientious and capable public servants, but they were essentially practical men who were far more at home in the mud surrounding a Castlecomer drilling-rig than they would have been in Hume Street leafing through the letter-books in search of an understanding of Jukes's mental decline during the 1860s. Hallissy's retirement marked the final severance of that thread of Survey tradition which, despite vicissitudes, had persisted from 1845 down to the 1930s. It was to be the 1970s before the officers of a revivified Survey began to trawl the historical depths in search of the broken end of that cable of Survey tradition which would allow them to re-establish communication with the giants from the past - the giants who had made the Irish Survey the great institution it once had been.

Following Hallissy's retirement Duffy, the senior officer, took over the administration of the Survey pending the appointment of a new Director after the now customary but regrettable delay. That new Director assumed his duties in Hume Street on 24 December 1940. Duffy, Cunningham, and O'Meara must have been surprised by their Christmas present. Their new Director was an Englishman

FIGURE 6.3. *Thomas John Duffy. A graduate of the Royal College of Science for Ireland, Duffy served in the forces from 1915 until 1919. He was an officer of the Survey between 1919 and 1955. The illustration is reproduced from a newspaper photograph featured in the* Irish Press *on 14 April 1944.*

FIGURE 6.4. *Douglas Wallace Bishopp (1900-1977), Director of the Survey from 1940 to 1950. Although English by birth, the influence of South Africa upon him was strong, and many in Ireland thought of him as an archetypal Boer. The illustration is reproduced from a newspaper photograph featured in the* Irish Times *on 27 January 1943.*

seemingly devoid of any previous experience of Irish geology. He was Douglas Wallace Bishopp.

Bishopp had been born in 1900 and he was therefore a few years younger than Duffy, his senior officer. He was educated at Tonbridge School, lying amidst the Wealden hop-gardens, and then at the Royal School of Mines, where he graduated in 1923 in mining and mining geology. Thereafter the world was his oyster. He worked for mining companies in Mexico, the Gold Coast, Tanganyika, and Northern Rhodesia. In the early 1930s he did two spells of duty as a member of staff in the National Museum of Rhodesia at Bulawayo, and it was there that he perhaps first heard tales of the Irish Survey because the Director of the Geological Survey of Southern Rhodesia was then H.B. Maufe who thirty years earlier had worked alongside Lamplugh on the drift surveys of the Belfast and Cork districts (see p.114). Between 1933 and 1936 Bishopp was employed on the Rand goldfields in South Africa, and in 1936 he re-crossed the Atlantic to become an officer of the Geological Survey of British Guiana. It was from South America, via England, that he came to Ireland. Not since Jukes's arrival ninety years earlier had the Irish Survey welcomed so widely experienced a Director. Whether Bishopp preferred Guinness to rum I cannot say, but he can hardly have found easy the transposition from a colonial Georgetown to a post-colonial Dublin which was enduring the scarcities of what in neutral Ireland come to be known as the 1939-45 Emergency. Perhaps the only similarity between British Guiana and the Irish Republic was that they were then both issuing map-bearing postage stamps depicting rather more territory than that over which they actually held effective sway.

The archives of the Irish Survey contain nothing bearing upon the background to Bishopp's appointment. It is nonetheless easy to see what must have happened. Finance was calling the tune. In 1938 Lyburn retired from his post as Economic Geologist in the Trade and Industries Branch of the Department of Industry and Commerce, and in 1939 Hallissy retired from the directorship of the Survey, which, of course, was located within the same Department. Somebody - perhaps even the Minister (Sean Lemass until September 1939 and then Séan MacEntee) - decided to effect an economy by merging the post formerly held by Lyburn with that formerly held by Hallissy. A general geologist in the Jukes - Hull - Cole - Hallissy tradition was no longer felt to be necessary. What was necessary was a severely practical economic geologist in the Lyburn tradition. The post of Economic Geologist in the Trade and Industries Branch was therefore left vacant while an experienced economic geologist was appointed as Director of the Survey. Bishopp was thus at once successor to both Lyburn and Hallissy, and this explains why McCluskey, Lyburn's former assistant, was transferred back from the Trade and Industries Branch to the Survey just one month after Bishopp's arrival in Hume Street.

Bishopp was a colourful character. He was a man large in stature and the very epitome of the drinks-on-the-verandah-at-sundown sort of colonial Englishman. His years under Capricorn had made South Africa his own beloved country, but his paeans of praise for that land were commonly seamed with ugly veins of deep racial prejudice. He wrote - and published - poetry. He was a fine scientist. Like many geologists with experience in southern Africa, he became a convert to the theory of continental drift at time when most geologists in the northern hemisphere were still dismissing the concept as a foolish aberration. In the field he commonly appeared in a kilt, and since a Bishopp tartan was unknown to Caledonian weavers, he chose to appear in the tartan of Clan Douglas. His car was a mighty Lagonda, and to this day those who were his passengers remember the impressive array of cylinders revealed upon the car's bonnet being opened. When the petrol crisis of the Emergency period put that fuel-hungry beast off the road, he took to making his tours of inspection aboard a large and highly audible motor-cycle.

A man of strong opinions, Bishopp was not the easiest of colleagues. In Ireland it was believed that his frequent changes of employment prior to his fetching up in Hume Street had all resulted from his quarrelsome, if not explosive, character. His Irish superiors certainly found him to be demanding, impatient, and stubborn. Two examples will serve to illustrate the point. First, the term 'Northern Ireland' was forbidden in official publications emanating from Dublin. The territory which was so designated by Belfast, was by Dublin simply referred to as 'the Six Counties'. Bishopp regarded this as a petty absurdity. Despite reprimands, he persisted in his use of the prohibited term and he compounded his offence by writing letters of justification to his superiors upon pre-1922 Survey notepaper emblazoned with the royal coat of arms. Second, as some might have thought appropriate for a figure who wore the garb of a Scotsman, Bishopp was a man who counted every penny. (Within the Survey it was believed that he assumed his directorship on Christmas Eve expressly so he would receive a salary over the Christmas holiday!). When the cost of rented accommodation rose in Dublin during the early years of the Emergency, he removed himself and his family to a house at Castlecomer. His public justification for the move was that, as the centre of Ireland's largest coalfield, Castlecomer was the scene of some of the Survey's chief responsibilities. But problems - and acrimony - developed when he began to claim travelling expenses for his regular journeys to Hume Street and to submit frequent hotel bills for his overnight accommodation in Dublin.

Within the Survey the staff developed a grudging respect for Bishopp's ability and expertise, but they found him to be a difficult chief. He was a geologist from a world completely different to their own. He had little patience with them as Irishmen and little sympathy with their Irish way of doing things. Indeed, he made no secret of the fact that he held his officers in low esteem. His particular *bête noire* was O'Meara, the most junior of the officers. The cosmopolitan, English, ex-public-schoolboy back from the colonies could neither understand nor tolerate the shy, slow-talking, stay-at-home farmer's son with a Tipperary accent.

Among modern Survey officers Bishopp's reputation stands low. If he is remembered at all, his ten-year directorship is recollected as one of the Survey's less fortunate episodes. He is ranked with James rather than with Jukes, with Hull rather than with Cole. I here wish to present a somewhat different interpretation. I wish to offer Bishopp as a figure who has been unfairly maligned in the Ireland which he sought to serve. He was a man before his time; Ireland was simply not ready to avail of that kind of expertise which Bishopp brought with him.

When he arrived in Dublin, Bishopp clearly perceived himself to be charged with two sequential responsibilities. First he had to lift the Survey out of its paralytic condition, and second he had to lead a reinvigorated Survey in a search for the native minerals and raw materials which were to be the basis for Ireland's future prosperity. If the Irish government had been content to settle for something less than these twin objectives - if the Irish government had been content with the *status quo* - then surely either Duffy or McCluskey must have been appointed to the vacant directorship. That the Irish authorities had gone to the trouble of looking overseas for their new Director, and that, despite his English background, they had appointed a confirmed economic geologist, seemed to make it as clear as crystal that dynamic and expert action was being envisaged. But Bishopp did not as yet understand the Irish. He arrived expecting to be supported and encouraged in the task which he had been given, but he was soon to be disillusioned. He speedily discovered that the Irish are sometimes high on talk but low on achievement. Promises eloquently delivered are sometimes instantly forgotten. I can see abundant reason why Bishopp should have become angry and frustrated. Ireland was wasting his talents.

Repeatedly Bishopp sought to secure the expansion of the Survey's staff to what he regarded as the minimum acceptable level. In October 1941 he asked the Department to establish a Geophysical Branch within the Survey and to appoint to the Survey a cartographer and officers specialising in petrochemistry, petrography, and hydrogeology. Little happened. In January 1943 he wrote to the British Geological Survey enquiring about their salary scales because he was anxious that any new Irish posts should be advertised with salaries broadly equivalent to those current in Britain. No new appointments were made. In March 1943 he thought he was about to be granted a petrochemist. That officer proved to be a mirage. In April 1943 he informed the Department that he had in view a programme of some twenty years' work for a staff of around ten geologists. In government circles such plans were evidently treated as an Englishman's castles in the air.

It does seem that three new Survey posts - for a geophysicist, a palaeontologist, and a petrologist - were actually approved and twice advertised during 1948 and 1949, but the response was poor because the salaries were meagre as compared with those on offer elsewhere. In June 1949 Bishopp observed sourly that even within the Department of Industry and Commerce the salary-scale for a Meteorological Officer was from £405 to £915 whereas the scale for a Geologist was a mere £350 to £760. Even when good candidates anxious to work in Ireland persisted with their applications, there followed such long delays within the civil service appointments procedure that would be Hume-Street officers had transferred their allegiance elsewhere long before any Survey offers came their way. In this manner did the Survey lose two young scientists who were destined for careers of high distinction: Thomas Murphy, the geophysicist, and Edward Mervyn Patterson, the petrologist. At the close of his first month in Hume Street, Bishopp's officers were Duffy, Cunningham, McCluskey, and O'Meara. Ten years later, when he slammed the door of Hume Street behind him for the last time, his only officers were still Duffy, Cunningham, McCluskey, and O'Meara. So much for the expectations and promises of the intervening years.

Perhaps there were other broken promises. Bishopp would certainly seem to have understood that the Survey was about to be provided either with a completely refurbished home in Hume Street or with a new custom-built headquarters in some other location. Number 14 Hume Street was certainly in need of modernisation. For example, during October 1916 Wright had asked for electricity to be brought into the house but more than thirty years elapsed before the wiring was completed throughout. 'Electrical installation proceeding', wrote Bishopp in his Survey logbook against 26 February 1947. Around that time there was serious talk of the Survey moving to new accommodation over the premises of the Civil Service Dining Club which were then under construction in Earlsfort Terrace, between St Stephen's Green and University College. This accommodation would have contained a small Survey museum, but in total the premises would have been somewhat cramped. In the long-term it was perhaps fortunate that nothing came of the proposal.

While Bishopp was giving instructions about the circuitry within Hume Street and contemplating the ascent of culinary aromas into his proposed Earlsfort Terrace office, he had to face a still more urgent issue relating to accommodation. Ever since the 1890s the Office of Public Works had regarded the Hume Street building as far too large for the Survey's needs. In 1946 it was pointed out to Bishopp that in the public service as a whole the space allocation per person was 70 square feet. In Hume Street each officer was occupying 400 square feet. Bishopp was told that the Survey would have to move. Throughout the mid-1940s the Office of Public Works made strenuous efforts to remove the Survey to Glasnevin. But Bishopp's stubborn character was here to the Survey's advantage. He simply sat tight. He was told that a refusal to comply with the Office of Public Works's request would result in the upper floor of Hume Street being requisitioned for the accommodation of some of the state's legal officers. With an English public-school education behind him, Bishopp must have known that one dictum of the legal profession is *festina lente.* So he stayed put. Again, nothing happened.

The Emergency itself created a multitude of problems for the Survey during the first five years of Bishopp's directorship. The petrol shortage then made field-work difficult. 'Petrol position v awkward. Phone to Supplies', wrote Bishopp in the Survey's log on 3 May 1943. That month the Survey was allocated sixty gallons of petrol to be shared between Bishopp's Lagonda and Cunningham's jalopy of less distinguished marque. It must have been around that time that Bishopp parked his car in favour of a motor-cycle, but even so, throughout much of the Emergency, County Donegal was regarded as lying beyond the Survey's effective range of activity. A good deal of Survey travel during the Emergency was by bicycle (how pleased Cole, that cycling enthusiast, would have been) but even as cyclists the officers faced Emergency - related problems. Again in the spring of 1943, for instance, we find Bishopp trying to obtain four bicycle tyres and inner-tubes to see the Survey through the coming field-season. He was also looking for three pairs of Wellington boots to keep dry the feet of his officers. The discrepancy here is unexplained; the Survey, of course, possessed eight geological feet.

Bishopp was a man of action; he expected to see things happen. In his Hume Street office he must have felt a deep sense of frustration. Nothing was happening over the expansion of the Survey's staff. The question of the Survey's future headquarters was unresolved. And his life was being plagued by trivia such as petrol coupons, bicycle-tyres, and Wellington boots. Angered by his inability to control events outside the Survey, he rounded upon the Survey itself. He began to throw his weight around in Hume Street. He began to purge the Survey of the surviving fragments of a past which he neither cared for nor understood. It is this purge for which Bishopp's directorship today seems to be best remembered.

Bishopp told Duffy to dispose of various odds and ends which had been found lying around the house. Among the ejecta was the greater part of the Troughton and Simms theodolite which was referred to in Chapter One (p.10). In the basement of Hume Street, Bishopp found Wright's Washing Bay core (see p.146) and he resolved that this, too, must go. Bishopp had men working down in the basement during May 1942, so it was perhaps then that the core was unceremoniously tipped from its racks, taken upstairs, and carted off to be dumped who knows where?

The loss of the core was a serious matter for Irish geology, but for the historian of science it is another piece of Bishopp's vandalism which evokes our principal ire. Ever since the beginning of the Survey in 1845 officers in the field had carried notebooks in which they recorded a multitude of varied observations. They wrote notes about outcrops, stream sections, and fossil localities. They sketched geological features, their human field companions, and their canine friends. They recorded some of their daily doings, their hotel charges, and the times of Bianconi cars. By the time of Bishopp's arrival in Dublin there must have been hundreds of such notebooks stored in Hume Street. They clearly offered a unique insight into the life of the Survey and its officers over a period of one hundred years. But for Bishopp the notebooks held no interest. He ordered their destruction. The few Survey notebooks which have survived in archives other than those of the Survey bear silent witness to the historical injury which Bishopp has inflicted upon us.

By way of justification for his spoilage Bishopp would surely have argued that the maintenance of an historical archive was no part of the Survey's responsibility. He was running a geological survey not a museum. His tasks were to seek for useful materials beneath Ireland's surface and to assist the Irish people towards an understanding of the geology of their island. In the actual performance of these twin tasks he and his officers are above our reproach. They did a fine job. To review the Survey's activities over the period of the Emergency is actually to experience an uncanny sense of *déjà vu*. The work in which Bishopp and Hume Street were involved between 1939 and 1945 is so like the work in which Cole and Hume Street had been involved between 1914 and 1918. For a second time the Survey was searching throughout Ireland for materials which, because of renewed international conflict, were again in short supply.

In May 1941 the Battle of the Atlantic claimed 437,000 tons of allied and neutral merchant shipping, and the activities of the Survey's officers during that month nicely illustrate the manner in which the Survey was deployed in seeking to remedy some of the resultant scarcities. Duffy was at Carrickmacross exploring for phosphorite (rock-phosphate). McCluskey was at Castlebar likewise searching for phosphorite, at Arigna hunting for coal, and in County Galway seeking for lead and molybdenite. Cunningham was in counties Dublin and Meath prospecting for phosphorite, and at Kellystown, County Meath, looking for strontium. O'Meara was assisting in the quest for phosphorite in counties Dublin and Meath, while Bishopp himself was holding the fort in Hume Street ('ARP notes etc.' on the 1st of the month; 'To Minister, per J. McC.' on the 13th), investigating the potential of old mines in County Wicklow, and scurrying hither and thither inspecting the work of each of his officers.

Annually down to 1939 Ireland had been importing up to 90,000 tons of rock-phosphate for the manufacture of fertilizers. Such imports were essential to Irish agriculture, but during the Emergency the trade was severely hampered by the shipping shortage. This is why the search for native phosphorite featured so prominently in the Survey's agenda throughout the period of hostilities. But, despite Hume Street's best efforts, no new workable Irish sources of phosphorite were discovered.

The country's sole viable source of phosphorite remained the beds located around Lisdoonvarna in County Clare. That deposit had been discovered in 1924 and it was later developed in a somewhat desultory fashion. In view of the site's national importance it in 1942 was made the subject of a compulsory acquisition order and throughout the remainder of the Emergency the Survey was responsible for all the geological advice offered in connection with the workings. Officers selected the sites for the twenty-two boreholes which were put down in exploration of the extent of the phosphorite, and Cyril James Stubblefield of the British Geological Survey was brought in as a palaeontological consultant. In 1951 McCluskey completed the writing of a proposed Survey memoir devoted to the Clare phosphorites but at that point history began to repeat itself. Back in April 1931 Hallissy had announced that a Clare phosphorite memoir would soon be ready for publication but in the event it never appeared. Twenty years later the same fate overtook McCluskey's memoir. Mining of the Clare phosphorite had ceased in 1947 and somebody in the civil service either forgot about the memoir or else they decided that its publication would now be a waste of public money.

The Survey's Emergency investigations in economic geology did, nevertheless, result in the publication of three Survey memoirs issued between 1943 and 1948 and known as the Emergency period pamphlets. They were the first official publications to have originated within the Survey since 1928, and their appearance restored to the Survey a faint official pulse rate. But, as McCluskey was to discover early in the 1950s, this was just a murmur of brief duration. A further twenty years were to elapse before the Survey was able to shake off its enforced paralysis.

The first of the three Emergency period pamphlets has a slightly unusual history. On 26 January 1943 Bishopp delivered to the Geographical

Society of Ireland a lecture entitled 'Irish Mineral Resources'. Bishopp clearly made a deep impression upon his audience and, during the ensuing discussion, Frank Mitchell suggested that the lecture was of such significance that the national interest demanded its publication. At that time the nine-year-old Geographical Society had never published anything, but Frank Mitchell's proposal was enthusiastically received. The society would itself publish Bishopp's paper. Perhaps Bishopp was able to use this offer as a lever with which to extract a little money out of the safe belonging to the Department of Industry and Commerce. Certainly when the essay was published late in 1943, it carried the imprint not of the Geographical Society but of the Dublin Stationery Office. Frank Mitchell and the Geographical Society would nonetheless seem to be entitled to some of the credit for the fact that 1943 saw the inauguration of the short series of Emergency period pamphlets.

The second and third pamphlets in the series may be dismissed more briefly. Bishopp was the author of the second. It was published in 1947 and is devoted to Irish sources of lime and magnesia of high purity for the manufacture of glass, carbide, and a variety of other chemical substances. Bishopp and McCluskey were the joint authors of the third and final pamphlet. It appeared in 1948 and is concerned with Irish sources of industrial silica.

From the moment of his arrival in Ireland, Bishopp was eager to bring the latest scientific methods to bear upon the exploration of Ireland's subterranean structure. Experienced economic geologist that he was, he fully understood that the search for Ireland's concealed mineral wealth must involve geophysicists equipped with modern geophysical instrumentation. Bishopp probably knew little, if anything, of Wright's pioneering geophysical investigations at Ballard in County Wicklow during the summer of 1918 (see p.145), but he certainly shared with Wright a conviction that the geophysicist might possess the techniques necessary to locate Ireland's buried treasures. As we have seen (p.169), in 1941, Bishopp sought to secure the establishment of a Geophysical Branch within the Survey. That wish was not granted, but he was not left entirely without geophysical support. Indeed, the geophysical research which was based upon Hume Street after 1941 constitutes the most permanently significant aspect of Bishopp's directorship. The story of that geophysical work must now briefly be told.

On 20 February 1941 the Taoiseach, Eamon de Valera, brought into being a body entitled the Emergency Scientific Research Bureau. Its chairman was Professor John Joseph Dowling, the professor of technical physics in University College Dublin, and the task of the Bureau was to advise the government on problems arising from the Emergency and related to the supply of materials for industrial processes. Bishopp's request for the establishment of a Geophysical Branch within the Survey was brought to Dowling's attention. The two men evidently met on 4 March 1941 and the upshot was that Dowling invited one of his graduate-students to undertake geophysical research on behalf of the Bureau but on secondment to the Geological Survey. The graduate student involved was Thomas Murphy who today is a distinguished professor emeritus of the Dublin Institute for Advanced Studies. From 1941 until 1945 Professor Murphy was one half of a two-man team based upon Hume Street. He did the geophysics while Cunningham provided an input of the necessary geological expertise.

Murphy appears to have reported for duty at the Survey on 7 November 1941, and a field-programme using a newly purchased Watts vertical magnetic-field variometer was launched just a few days later. Over the ensuing four years Murphy and Cunningham employed a variety of geophysical techniques to explore the extent of several Irish mineral occurrences. Most of their time was spent in County Wicklow studying the mineralised belt of country which extends northeastwards from Croghan Mountain, through the Vale of Avoca, to the area around Ballard, where Wright had conducted his own geophysical work a quarter of a century earlier. Some of the old mines around Avoca were reopened in 1942 and were being worked by Comhlucht Lorgtha agus Forbartha Mianraí, Teoranta (Minerals Exploration and Development Co., Ltd.) of which company Hallissy was one of the original directors. The object of this mining was the extraction of pyrites as an Emergency source of sulphur to be used in the manufacture of sulphuric acid. The geophysical investigations conducted by Murphy and Cunningham were of immediate assistance to those concerned with the mining, but at the same time their studies possessed a longer term significance because of the fresh light they shed upon the overall structure of the mineralised belt.

Outside County Wicklow, Murphy and Cunningham investigated the pyrrhotite occurrence at Glan, near Oughterard in County Galway, a suspected occurrence of nickel at Slishwood, lying southward of Lough Gill in County Sligo, and the extent of the Tertiary igneous intrusive rocks set amidst the gypsum beds around Kingscourt on the borders of counties Cavan and Meath. Between 1944 and 1946 they also made a nationwide study of geomagnetism involving observations at 892 stations, with an average density of one station for every 8 kilometre square within the national territory.

The Emergency Scientific Research Bureau ceased its operations on 31 March 1945, the changed international situation having rendered the Bureau's continuation unnecessary. Soon thereafter Murphy left Ireland to continue his geophysical studies in the United States, but for some years Cunningham persisted with geophysical investigations in so far as his other Survey duties might permit. It was Cunningham who saw into print the only results of the Emergency geophysical programme ever to have been laid before the public through a Survey publication. That publication appeared in 1949 and it takes the form of a large sheet of paper carrying a pair of stark, black-printed one-to-one-million maps of Ireland placed side by side. In the pair, the left-hand map - Map A - is entitled Lines of Equal Vertical Magnetic Intensity, while the right-hand map - Map B - is entitled Lines of Equal Anomaly of Vertical Magnetic Intensity.

These two maps were the first cartographic offerings to have come from the Survey since the appearance of the somewhat unsatisfactory one-to-one-million geological map of Ireland twenty-one years earlier. But no rapturous welcome awaited the two austere 1949 maps. Perhaps maps of geophysical phenomena were a trifle too esoteric for the Irish geological taste of the day. Copies of the two maps are now difficult to locate and few modern geologists even seem to be aware of the existence of the maps. This is to be regretted because, quite apart from their local Irish significance, the two maps must be regarded as possessed of some modest international significance within the history of both modern geophysics and plate tectonic theory. That significance derives from a note in the margin of Map A and reading as follows.

> ... the anomalies, produced by tertiary basaltic intrusives which appear to be polarised in a direction opposite to that of the present earth's field, are not included.

The phenomenon of reversed polarity in certain of the world's igneous rocks had been recognised long before 1949, but it was Murphy and Cunningham who were the first to identify the phenomenon amidst the rocks of Ireland. When he arrived in the United States soon after the end of World War II, Murphy found that American geophysicists were keenly interested in the discovery which he and Cunningham had made while studying the intrusive rocks at Kingscourt. Within a few years the attention of geologists from around the world had come to focus upon the problem represented by reversed polarity. More especially, the patterns of reversed polarity displayed by certain rocks located upon the world's ocean floors assumed enormous significance during the 1960s as the new plate tectonic theory swept through the international geological community.

Around 4pm on Tuesday 12 September 1950 Bishopp and O'Meara were the only two officers in 14 Hume Street. 'I'm going now', said Bishopp. 'OK', replied O'Meara, 'I'll be here till five'. Bishopp went down the hallway, past the Milners' Patent Fire-Resisting safes containing the six-inch field-sheets, through the front-door, and out into the street. O'Meara thought he was witnessing the routine departure of the Director at the conclusion of yet another day's office work. He was mistaken. Bishopp never returned. He had resigned. His letter of resignation had been written before 15 August but in the interval since then evidently not one member of the Survey's staff had been made privy to his resignation secret. Ireland had clearly exhausted Bishopp's somewhat limited patience. The final straw, he claimed, grew out of the Twigspark lead and zinc property located near Manorhamilton in County Leitrim. That story seems to be a complex one of shady intrigue, fiery Hume Street outbursts, curt solicitor's letters, and even a salted mine. But the essence of the affair is that Bishopp had recommended the rejection of an application for a mining-lease on the property and then his recommendation had been overturned by some superior official. He claimed that high-level political pressure had been exerted behind his back and that his professional standing had been both compromised and impugned. He walked away from Hume Street to become Senior-Geologist-in-Charge with the Geological Survey of Cyprus.

For the Irish Survey the weeks before the Christmas of 1950 were much the same as the weeks before the Christmas of 1940. The Survey was still housed in Hume Street. Duffy was again temporarily in charge, and the other three officers were still Cunningham, McCluskey, and O'Meara. True, the windows now glowed with electric lights, the Washing Bay core was gone from the basement, and the remains of many hundreds of historic Survey notebooks lay rotting in some Dublin refuse-dump. Perhaps, too, that broken centrifuge from the old soils laboratory up on the top floor of the building had shared the fate of sundry other items which had fallen victim to Bishopp's emulation of Hercules in the Augean stables. But the symbolism of that broken centrifuge was still valid. The Survey remained in its paralytic state.

Bishopp had tried - and failed - to lift the Survey into the modern age of geochemistry, geophysics, and hydrogeology. During the year and a half which elapsed before a new Director was appointed, Duffy tried to take the Survey back into the past - back to the days of Archibald Geikie and Lamplugh. On 23 July 1951 he submitted to his superiors a proposal that the Survey should undertake a detailed investigation of Ireland's superficial deposits, the results of the investigation to be published as a national coverage of one-inch drift sheets. It was fifty-one years, almost to the very day, since Geikie had met with Gill in Upper Merrion Street and agreed that the Survey should undertake just such a drift survey as that which Duffy now proposed to resurrect (see p.111). To facilitate the Survey in this new undertaking Duffy requested the appointment of four new officers, all of them to be specialists in drift mapping. Of Lamplugh's estimate that such a survey was likely to take 140 years Duffy said nothing. Perhaps he was insufficiently versed in Survey history to be aware of the events which had led up to the surgery of 1905. Duffy's proposal was despatched to the Department of Industry and Commerce; there it was received; there it was acknowledged; there it was presumably read. Then it would seem to have disappeared into the same Black Hole as had engulfed so many Survey missives over the previous thirty years. But on this occasion official inaction was surely the most appropriate response.

This chapter must end upon a happier note. During Duffy's second period in charge of the Survey there took place a novel development. For the first time a woman was appointed as a full-time officer of the Survey. She was a graduate in geology from the University of Manchester, and she took up her new duties on 1 September 1951. She was Miss Dilys Penelope Lindsey Jones. Duffy wanted her to work in ground adjacent to that being investigated by O'Meara around Carrickmacross and Ardee. Duffy considered it necessary to enquire of Mrs O'Meara whether she might have any objection to his proposal.

CHAPTER SEVEN

REVIVAL
1952-1984

No good purpose would be served by an attempt to assess and apportion blame for the present lamentable state of the Geological Survey. It is sufficient to note that the inability of the Office to carry out its proper functions, has certainly delayed Irish development in a number of fields.

Dr Cyril E. Williams in a memorandum addressed to the Secretary, the Department of Industry and Commerce, and dated 5 September 1967.

Geologists are slightly demented souls, but quite harmless. Such must have been the verdict of many an uninitiated observer who has lingered in order to watch some of the self-styled 'brethren of the hammer' at work in the field. The geologists flit from rock-outcrop to rock-outcrop just as the butterfly of summer flits from flower to flower. At each outcrop they indulge in the same little ritual. First there is a moment of silent and almost prayerful contemplation. Then the mood suddenly erupts into violence as the rock-exposure is attacked with well-aimed hammer-blows. Next, peace is restored as the resultant slivers of rock receive close scrutiny. Then some measurements are made, some hieroglyphics are added to a map, the slivers are labelled and tucked away in pocket or knapsack, and our geologists move on to recommence the ritual at some other site.

Early in the summer of 1956 a stranger appeared in the County Galway village of Tynagh. If anybody paused to watch him, as he wandered in the vicinity of what once had been Spring Garden House, they will have seen him indulging in a strange variant of the little ritual just described. Most geologists pause to examine outcrops of the earth's rocky skeleton; this stranger was behaving in an oddly different manner. He seemed to have interest in nothing but the boulders built into the region's dry-stone walls. He there appeared to be searching for something. His hammer he scarcely used. In some places he knelt upon the succulent sward in order to examine the base of a wall even more closely; in other places he clambered over a wall in order to examine its opposite face; and from time to time he rested his map - case atop a wall in order to consult the documents therein or to leave his hands free for the inscribing of some observation into his notebook. It must have seemed that here was a geologist who was even more demented than most of his kin. But sound reason lay behind this man's apparent madness. What he was doing in County Galway was destined to lead to a transformation within the Geological Survey of Ireland. His investigation of those dry-stone walls was to play its part in a reinvigoration of the entire Irish geological scene. The notes which he then made were shortly to have their dramatic effect upon the very economy of the Republic of Ireland itself.

The geologist who was examining those dry-stone walls around Tynagh was the Survey's Mark Cunningham. His diary for 1956 reveals that, after completing a day's work in the office, he left Hume Street at 5p.m. on Tuesday 19 June to drive to Ballinasloe. For the remainder of that week he explored the countryside around Tynagh, and, after spending the Saturday and Sunday in Dublin (he was a bachelor and he lived at Barry's Hotel in Great Denmark Street), he returned to County Galway on Monday 25 June to spend two further days in the completion of his field-study. When he drove back to Dublin his car was laden with the numerous geological samples which were to engage his attention in Hume Street over the next few weeks, and which were to generate in his diary daily entries such as 'Tyn samps'.

In the Tynagh region, Cunningham was not far distant from his birthplace at Rushestown in the same county. But why was this conscientious and able Survey officer now reduced to the level of examining nothing more substantial than the dry-stone walls created by human hands? An answer to that question involves two other Survey officers. One of them is a nineteenth-century character who has already left his firm footprint upon my story. The other is a new player upon the scene. He is the man who in June 1952 became the Survey's eighth Director and who then took over the Hume Street reins which for more than twenty months had rested in the hands of Tom Duffy.

Tynagh lies on one-inch Sheet 116 (Portumna), published by the Survey during 1865. The field-mapping for the sheet had been carried out by

FIGURE 7.1. *An ex-Director in full vocal flight. Murrogh Vere O Brien, Director of the Survey from June 1952 until February 1964. He is here speaking at a luncheon held for the directors of Northgate Exploration, Ltd, and others, in the Gresham Hotel, Dublin, during the autumn of 1964. He is flanked, on his left, by Patrick Hughes, the President of Northgate, and, on his right, by Dr Duncan Ramsay Derry, a Canadian mining geologist and a director of Northgate.* (From a photograph kindly made available by Ennex International, P.L.C.)

Kinahan, and on his six-inch field-sheet for the Tynagh region (County Galway Sheet 117/1) there appears in the southwestern corner the inscription, in Kinahan's hand, 'Specks of gelina [*sic*] in wall of new grove'. Galena is the principal ore of lead, and upon his field-sheets Kinahan records other nearby sites where there is evidence for the presence of the mineral or where there are sandstone boulders displaying copper staining. In his combined memoir to accompany one-inch sheets 115 (Loughrea) and 116 Kinahan alludes to the evidence of ancient mining having occurred at Carhoon, to the northeast of Tynagh, and to the discovery, amidst the local drifts, of 'boulders of galena'. He also offers this further interesting observation.

> In the vicinity of the old workings various pieces of *galena* and *iron pyrites* were picked up, and the inhabitants of the hamlet there situated informed us "that when the ground thereabouts is tilled in the spring, all their fowl die, being poisoned by something they pick up."

Within the Survey it has always been official policy to keep the six-inch field-sheets and the old memoirs under regular review in the hope of bringing to light deposits which might have come to assume a fresh significance in the context of changing technology and expanding market demand. Thus in Hume Street there did not pass unnoticed Kinahan's reference to 'boulders of galena' or his report of a mysterious vernal murrain among domestic fowl. In his mineral localities memoir of 1922 Cole referred to the evidence of ancient mining at Tynagh, and thirty years later the Survey's new Director resolved that Kinahan's observation merited a further examination of the Tynagh district. That new Director was the bearer of a name familiar in Irish history: Mr Murrogh O Brien.

Murrogh Vere O Brien came to the Survey possessed of a strong background in mining geology. Like two of his predecessors in the Director's chair - like Thomas Oldham and Edward Hull - he was a product of the Engineering School of Trinity College Dublin. During the 1930s, geology was a subject in the Junior, Middle, and Senior years for all engineering students, and it was the geological prelections of Professor L.B. Smyth and Frank Mitchell which whetted O Brien's appetite for the earth sciences. He received his professional degree - Baccalaureus in Arte Ingeniaria - in 1941, and he then joined the firm of Delap and Waller, consulting engineers of Molesworth Street, Dublin. But soon a fresh avenue opened before him. Early in 1942 Mianraí, Teoranta (Minerals, Limited), acting under the influence of the Emergency Scientific Research Bureau, had reopened mines at Avoca, County Wicklow, in order to produce pyrites as a source of much needed sulphur for the manufacture of the sulphuric acid required by the beleaguered Irish fertilizer industry (see p.172). O Brien was appointed to the mines, initially as a surveyor and engineer, and later as a geologist, and he remained at Avoca throughout the Emergency.

In 1945 he resolved to widen his experience. He was given leave of absence from Avoca and he went to London to read the course in mining geology in the Royal School of Mines at the Imperial College of Science and Technology. The course was one of four years' duration, but O Brien was excused from the first two years of course-work, and he completed the programme in half the normal time. The required further practical experience he obtained during a summer vacation spent visiting and working in mines in Sweden and northern Norway, and he proceeded to his degree examination during the June of that memorably hot summer of 1947. His examiners were an impressive bunch: Herbert Leader Hawkins, William Richard Jones, Herbert Harold Read, Alfred Kingsley Wells, and David Williams. These examiners deemed themselves to be well satisfied with the work of their Irish student, and bedecked with his new academic honours, O Brien set sail for North America in order to spend three months visiting Canadian mines and meeting Canadian economic geologists.

From North America O Brien returned both to Ireland and to Avoca. In the aftermath of the Emergency, Mianraí, Teoranta, was committed to an exploration of the Avoca district from the point of view of its copper producing potential, and for the next five years O Brien was the sole staff geologist involved in this investigation. From Imperial College he brought in Professor W.R. Jones as a consultant, but it was another academic who was now to play his part in shaping O Brien's career. As the geologist chiefly responsible for the Avoca explorations, O Brien came into close contact with Michael Anthony Hogan, who was both the chairman of Mianraí, Teoranta and the professor of mechanical engineering in University College Dublin. It was Hogan who had been instrumental in securing for O Brien the leave necessary to allow him to pursue his studies abroad. Now Hogan was again of assistance. When the vacant directorship of the Geological Survey of Ireland was at length advertised, it was he who suggested that O Brien should become a candidate. That advice O Brien accepted. He applied for the post and was appointed Director as from 16 June 1952. (Sir) William Pugh, the Director of the Geological Survey of Great Britain, was a member of the board responsible for the appointment. O Brien recollects one other aspect of his being vetted for the directorship. Following his interview with the board, he was conducted into another room where there sat the celticist David William Greene. Oddly, it was Greene's task to adjudicate upon the candidates' knowledge of foreign languages, while two other gentlemen assessed the candidates' competence in Irish.

O Brien's years in County Wicklow had served to convince him that at Avoca there lay a substantial and workable body of copper ore. In that belief he was shortly to be proved correct as a result of a drilling and tunnelling programme carried through by Mianraí, Teoranta, during the early 1950s, and an Irish subsidiary of the Mogul Mining Corporation of Toronto worked the Avoca deposit between 1955 and 1962. But, O Brien reasoned, if Ireland possessed a major long neglected unworked copper deposit at Avoca, might not other Irish ore bodies lie undetected elsewhere? If nineteenth-century clues were re-examined with twentieth-century techniques and insights might there not be discovered an hitherto undreamed of wealth of Irish minerals? The Irish economy was crying out for stimulation. Unemployment was rife and the nation needed to create jobs in order to assuage a population haemorrhage which during the 1950s was bleeding off as many as 50,000 emigrants each year. Perhaps a partial solution to Ireland's problems lay concealed somewhere within her rocks.

It was not only O Brien who now began to look at Ireland's rocks with hopeful eyes. Ireland itself was changing. At the Department of Finance the vigorous Thomas Kenneth Whitaker was appointed Secretary in May 1956, and he was soon at work upon the notable document issued in November 1958 as the *Programme for Economic Expansion*. Sean Lemass succeeded Eamon de Valera as Taoiseach in June 1959, and immediately began, in J. J. Lee's words, 'to slaughter sacred cows'. And, as I remember so well because of its incongruity, in County Wicklow men wearing miner's helmets now began to emerge from thatched cottages, to mount bicycles which had been resting against turf-stacks, and to pedal off down leafy lanes bound for Avoca and their new job at the St Patrick's Copper

FIGURE 7.2. *The Tánaiste in the Avoca mine, County Wicklow, on 9 September 1953. From left to right: Professor M. A. Hogan, Chairman of Mianraí, Teoranta; the Tánaiste and Minister for Industry and Commerce, Sean Lemass; and Mr T. R. H. Nelson, the mine manager. Murrogh O Brien was also a member of the visiting party that day.* (From a photograph in the Survey's archives.)

Mine. A decidedly threadbare texture became apparent in that old ideal of Ireland as a nation of Irish-speaking farmers who rejoiced in the fact that their green and holy land had been spared such industrial horrors as effluent secreting orifices, raucous factory klaxons, and those space-hungry marshalling-yards where, day and night, shunters assembled trains of coal and ore bound for the insatiable furnaces of boilers and smelters.

The five-year *Programme for Economic Expansion* laid before the Oireachtas in November 1958 (it eventually came to be known as the *First Programme for Economic Expansion)* gave public expression to this changed attitude towards Ireland's mineral-wealth potential. The programme promised that 'additional funds' would be made available to the Geological Survey to allow its undertaking of 'intensive surveys' for mineral deposits 'using the most modern techniques'. There was a still further sign of changing times and a glimpse of broadening vistas for the Survey. The *Programme* promised that new legislation would be introduced to deal with the special problems presented by any future exploration for oil or natural gas within the national territory. This was all in 1958. Not since the early years of the century, and the days of the Department of Agriculture and Technical Instruction for Ireland, had the Survey featured so prominently in a statement of public policy.

It is impossible to know how far O Brien may have been instrumental in this reshaping of the official attitude towards Ireland's mineral resources. On 9 September 1953 he accompanied Sean Lemass, then Tánaiste and Minister for Industry and Commerce, upon a tour of the Avoca mine. Presumably O Brien seized the opportunity to convey the message that a general exploration of Ireland's vaults might well prove to be highly rewarding. In retrospect he nevertheless recollects that such occasions for direct ministerial contact were rare. So far as Whitaker is concerned, O Brien has no recollection of any personal meetings between himself and the author of the 1958 programme, but he suspects that memoranda did pass from Hume Street to Whitaker's office in Upper Merrion Street. So, in one way or another, those in positions of power can hardly have remained entirely unaware of O Brien's conviction that an Irish game of hunt the mineral would be no idle pastime. Certainly, from the moment of his arrival in the Director's chair, O Brien placed economic geology at the very heart of the Survey's agenda.

As Director, O Brien embarked upon a three-pronged campaign to arouse interest in the search for Irish minerals. First, there was the prong of local action within the tiny community represented by the Survey itself. Second, there was the prong of national action within the broader community of the Irish nation at large. Third, there was the prong of international action within that global community consisting of the companies involved in mineral exploration and mining. O Brien's gingering activities along each of these three prongs must recieve our closer attentions.

When O Brien arrived in Hume Street, the Survey was just over one hundred years old, and during its life it had amassed an immense wealth of information about Ireland's mineral resources. Some of that information was on the six-inch field-sheets, some was in the published memoirs, some was on mine-plans, and some was in the card-catalogue of Irish mineral localities made under Cole's direction between 1915 and 1923 (see p.145). The Survey was clearly at liberty itself to bring all this information under review as the exigencies of its other responsibilities might permit. Indeed, as I noted earlier, such regular review had long been Survey practice, and under O Brien the policy was urged with renewed vigour. Perchance something noted upon a field-sheet dating from Jukes's day had hitherto been overlooked. Maybe a comment within a memoir dating from Hull's regime had acquired a fresh significance in the light of mid-twentieth-century market demand. Perhaps some pregnant patterns might be discerned through the application of modern concepts of mineralisation to the contents of Cole's 1922 memoir on minerals of economic importance.

In many cases this review of the documents housed in Hume Street resulted in officers going out into the field to check actual localities as the need and opportunity arose. That, as we have seen, is why Cunningham was busy examining dry-stone walls around Tynagh during the June of 1956, and to his activities in that region we will be reverting shortly. For the moment there is another internal, Survey-generated mineral investigation which is deserving of mention. Again it involved the hard-working Cunningham. Ever since his collaboration with Murphy during the Emergency (see p.172), Cunningham had been regarded as the Survey's acting geophysicist. Towards the close of Bishopp's directorship, Cunningham had been equipped with a Geiger counter and instructed to explore old mine-tailings, and other likely sites, in search of radio-active minerals. In 1947 there had been talk of the development of nuclear power in Ireland using native uranium and employing the local expertise of Erwin Schrödinger, of the Dublin Institute for Advanced Studies, and Ernest Thomas Sinton Walton, of Trinity College Dublin. Cunningham's investigation continued spasmodically during the early years of O Brien's regime, and in consequence readers of the *Irish Times* were one day in 1954 greeted by the headline 'Atom bomb mineral in Ireland?' But Cunningham's little box of tricks was never to be stimulated into paroxysms of excitement at any Irish site. For good or for ill, there were never located any materials possessing radio-activity of economic significance.

FIGURE 7.3. *Mark Cunningham (1908-1980). The illustration is reproduced from a photograph kindly presented to the Survey by Cunningham's relatives. Members of his family have also founded in his memory the annual 'Cunningham Awards' which are administered by the Director of the Survey. One award is made to a member of the Survey's staff for outstanding service, and two other prizes go to two outstanding students within the Irish universities.*

Outside of Hume Street, but remaining within the national context, O Brien lost no opportunity of seeking to arouse Irish interest in the search for local minerals. Here much of the Survey's energy initially was channelled through the activities of Mianraí, Teoranta. Under the 1947 Minerals Company Act, Mianraí, Teoranta, was empowered to undertake a seven-year programme for the exploration and development of Irish mineral resources. The programme allowed for the engagement of economic geologists as consultants, for the prospecting of ground using geological and geophysical methods, and for diamond-drilling at sites deemed to be significant. Various projects - Technical Assistance Projects as they were termed - were undertaken under the provisions of the Act, but two of the projects are here noteworthy because they involved a heavy Survey input.

First, in January 1953, the aforementioned Professor W.R. Jones, formerly of Imperial College London, was engaged as a consultant to the Survey and to the Department of Industry and Commerce. He was set an appallingly difficult task. He was asked to examine all the known Irish mineral districts and then to select three of them for recommendation to the Minister for Industry and Commerce as the ones offering the best prospects for detailed exploratory drilling. For the programme, the Department had already purchased a Craelius diamond drill and a percussion drill, and now the Minister sat back in Kildare Street and awaited the results of the professor's deliberations. Lemass's patience was taxed but little. On 28 April 1953 Professor Jones recommended his first site: the Abbeytown lead and zinc prospect near to Ballysadare in County Sligo. On 17 June 1953 he made his second recommendation: the Murvey molybdenite prospect to the west of Roundstone in County Galway. Professor Jones found the selection of his third site to be rather more difficult. Initially, he favoured the old copper-mining district at Bunmahon in County Waterford, but in July 1954 he finally resolved to offer as his third site the mineralised region at Glendalough in County Wicklow.

O Brien himself was deeply involved in all the investigations which preceded these three recommendations, and once the proposals had received ministerial blessing, a new and heavy burden fell upon the Survey as Cunningham and McCluskey assumed responsibility for the actual drilling programme. Cunningham took charge at Abbeytown, where drilling took place between August and December 1953. Nine holes were drilled with a combined depth of 660 metres, and the drilling revealed the mineralisation to be more extensive than had hitherto been suspected. It seems that Cunningham was under instruction to cease the drilling once a certain horizon was reached, but, noticing extensive dolomitisation in one hole, he gave instruction for drilling to be continued below the specified limiting horizon. The result was the discovery of a lower ore zone. New underground workings were constructed, and the existing mine was given a fresh lease of life of seven years' duration. For forty-one years Cunningham was a stalwart member of the Howth Golf Club in County Dublin; he must have been particularly well pleased with his round of nine holes played at Abbeytown in County Sligo.

McCluskey was in charge at Murvey. There a length of new road had to be constructed to give access to the site, and drilling commenced in December 1953. Thirty holes were eventually put down, with a combined depth of 1265 metres, and the drilling proceeded over a period of some twelve months. During June 1954 O Brien visited Norway both to obtain first-hand experience of molybdenite mining and to discover something about the cost of processing the mineral. Then in March 1955 Professor Jones reported that the Murvey investigation had revealed the presence of 250,000 tons of rock containing 0.13 per cent molybdenite. This, he admitted, was too low a grade to be worked economically, and the site was therefore abandoned to seabirds seeking refuge from Atlantic storms and to the occasional angler come to try his luck upon the waters of nearby Lough Namanawaun.

About Professor Jones's third selected site - Glendalough - little needs to be said. The investigation there was left to a mining company, and the Survey's involvement was minimal. But there were two slightly later projects conducted under the auspices of the Department of Industry and Commerce and with which the Survey was in both senses deeply implicated. One involved the Castlecomer Coalfield and the other involved the Connaught Coalfield.

Coal output from the Castlecomer Coalfield had long been in progressive decline as the collieries faced increasingly serious geological problems. In 1958 the Department therefore resolved to launch a drilling project designed to discover the true nature of the coalfield's reserves. Diamond-drilling commenced in March 1959 and continued until January 1963, the drilling contractors being two English companies. Eventually 117 bore-holes were sunk, and the total depth of rock penetrated was 16,230 metres. O'Meara took charge of the work on behalf of the Survey, but he can hardly have found the assignment entirely to his taste. Geologically the results were disappointing, and the drilling revealed the coalfield's reserves to be far smaller than had hitherto been supposed. Personally O'Meara's own health is said to have suffered grievously under the strain of supervising continuous drilling operations in weather conditions which frequently left much to be desired. Eventually he was forced to hand his responsibilities over to Miss Jones.

The project in the Connaught Coalfield also involved exploratory diamond-drilling. Between July 1960 and September 1962 twenty-four holes were sunk, and in this case McCluskey took charge of the drilling, with a new officer, Dermod

Timothy Downing, supervising some of the work in the mountains. But here, too, a certain sadness surrounds the operations. The Survey's typescript embodying McCluskey's report outlining the results of the work is dated July 1964, but on 8 February in the previous year McCluskey himself had died of a heart attack just after leaving Hume Street bound for some lunch-time engagement.

The third and international prong of O Brien's campaign to arouse interest in Ireland's mineral potential involved his preaching his message of optimism to any members of the global mining fraternity who could be induced to listen. Sometimes he recited his party-piece from behind the Director's desk in Hume Street and to an audience of English prospectors, American financiers, or Canadian magnates. On other occasions he carried his soap-box overseas to serve as a platform from which he could sing his favourite anthem at some international gathering. In September 1958, for instance, he delivered at the Institution of Mining and Metallurgy in London, a comprehensive review of the future of non-ferrous mining in Ireland. His exposition ranged from a description of known mineral localities, and an assessment of Irish taxation policy, to a consideration of the availability of labour and some advice upon the character of the Irish winter.

Six years earlier - in September 1952 - the 19th International Geological Congress had been held in Algiers. O Brien had been there. Where once the Barbary pirates had roistered, O Brien had read to the congress a paper on the Clare phosphates, the paper being based upon McCluskey's unpublished memoir upon the subject (see p.171). The theme of the 20th International Geological Congress, held in Mexico in 1956, was oil, and in response to the call for papers, O Brien prepared an essay on the subject of Ireland's potential as a region suited for oil and gas exploration. This was a topic which in Ireland had been talked about ever since the close of World War II, but the conversations had been over pints of Guinness rather than alongside drilling-rigs. No actual exploration for Irish oil or gas had as yet occurred. O Brien was therefore surprised - perhaps even slightly embarrassed - when he learned that his paper was among those which had been selected for verbal presentation. The delegates in Mexico City were to be illuminated by means of oil and natural gas piped in from a still undiscovered Irish Shangri-la! Nonetheless, O Brien's paper was well received. Among the assembled oil-men his account of Ireland's geological structure aroused particular interest, and in the ensuing discussion one leading American petroleum geologist of vast experience voiced his verdict: Ireland looked a very legitimate oil and gas prospect.

One feature of O Brien's national and international campaign on behalf of Irish minerals was his arranging for the reprinting of Cole's long-out-of-print 1922 memoir devoted to Irish localities for minerals of economic significance. Thus anybody thinking of prospecting for Irish minerals now again had to hand an invaluable vade mecum. Presumably the reprinted version of Cole's memoir was among the varied Survey publications which, during the summer of 1957, were taken from Dublin back home to Wichita, Kansas, by George B. Collins, a lawyer specialising in petroleum affairs. Collins (his grandparents had come from Cavan and Monaghan) had developed a strong interest in Ireland's mineral potential. He had visited Hume Street for talks with O Brien, and he was shortly to play his part in the activities leading to the discovery of the offshore Kinsale Head Gas Field.

O Brien's activities on behalf of Irish economic geology served to regain for the Survey a small place within the global geological community. Not since the distant days of Cole's directorship, and the years before 1914, had the Survey's banner been displayed so prominently at overseas gatherings. The Survey's pulse-rate as measured by its generation of scientific publications might still only be feeble, but at least in O Brien the Survey now possessed a Director who had made himself, the Survey, and Ireland, familiar to economic geologists from all corners of our globe. In 1959 I was a member of staff in Trinity College Dublin, and I recollect that one day my then colleague William Edward Nevill was invited over to the Department of Industry and Commerce for some discussions. I forget exactly what was on the agenda, but since Ted Nevill is a Carboniferous stratigrapher, I suspect that the Department was seeking advice over its drilling programme in either the Castlecomer or the Connaught coalfields. What I do remember is Nevill reporting to me that while with the civil servants he had taken the opportunity to emphasise the outstanding nature of the work which O Brien was doing to stimulate international interest in the search for Irish minerals. That work, Nevill had ventured to suggest, was of vital national significance, and in financial terms it was worth vastly more than the meagre pittance which Nevill believed O Brien then to be receiving by way of salary as the Survey's Director. I doubt whether Nevill did either the Survey or its Director much good, but he certainly spoke the truth.

The Department, nevertheless, was not entirely without appreciation of the work being directed from Hume Street. There was permitted, for example, a modest expansion of the Survey's staff. When O Brien arrived in Hume Street in 1952, the staff consisted of two Senior Geologists (Duffy and McCluskey) and three Geologists (Cunningham, Jones, and O'Meara). By the summer of 1959 the

Survey still had two Senior Geologists (now Cunningham and McCluskey), but the total of Geologists had been augmented to five Downing, Jones, O'Meara, Francis Millington Synge, and Jean Margaret Wilkinson). In addition to these regular officers, financial provision was also being made for the employment of Temporary Field Officers, much as had been the practice during Cole's regime (see p129). The Temporary Field Officers were university geologists or graduate students, and they joined the Survey for a limited period in order to carry out a particular piece of field-mapping. The scheme was introduced in 1953, and that year there were eleven applicants for the two posts available. The two men appointed were John Semple Jackson of University College Dublin, who mapped at Kingscourt in County Cavan, and Desmond Henry Oswald of Trinity College Dublin, who mapped in County Sligo. The following year six Temporary Field Officers worked for a total of twenty-six man-weeks, and by 1960 the Survey's roster of past or present Temporary Field Officers included such familiar British geological names as those of John Frederick Dewey, John Childs Harper, Bernard Elgey Leake, William Stuart McKerrow, Wallace Spencer Pitcher, and Robert Millner Shackleton. These were noble additions to the Survey's fauna even if they were merely birds of passage.

O Brien himself might dream of that day when international mineral exploration companies would be active in Ireland, but in the meantime the more humdrum, day-to-day work of the Survey had to continue. And remarkably varied work it was. Members of the general public came to Hume Street with specimens for identification. Queries from mine-owners and quarry-managers had to be answered. Firing tests were carried out on samples of brick-clay in association with the Institute for Industrial Research and Standards. Reports were prepared for companies seeking silica-sand and other industrial minerals. Advice was given to the Minister for Industry and Commerce over the issue of prospecting licences under the Minerals Development Act of 1940. Work was started - it was never finished - upon a new memoir to Sheet 112 (Dublin). Jones and O'Meara spent several field-seasons mapping the drifts of County Monaghan. A ferruginous water-seepage at Leopardstown Racecourse was examined. McCluskey prepared a report on the geology of the site of a proposed tidal-barrage on the River Fergus at Clarecastle in County Clare. During the summer of 1952, 136 limestone samples were collected, crushed, and then passed on to the State Laboratory for tests to be made as to the suitability of each of the rock types for agricultural purposes. Then officers were of course from time to time called out into the field to examine new exposures or to offer expert advice towards the solution of geological problems. On such missions officers were sometimes able to take with them a valuable new aid in the form of aerial photographs. During the 1950s the Air Corps began to make available such photographs at a scale of six inches to one mile (1:10,560), and in order to familiarise themselves with this new medium O Brien and Cunningham together attended a course in photogrammetry held in the Geology Department of Trinity College Dublin during the spring of 1955.

All these varied activities were clearly enormously demanding of Survey time, but the single most demanding Survey responsibility during the 1950s has yet to be mentioned. Hume Street then contained a young cuckoo which threatened to squeeze equally deserving fledglings from the Survey nest. The cuckoo's name was water-supply. In April 1950 the Department of Agriculture introduced a scheme of grants for the installation of piped domestic water-supply into farm-dwellings. Immediately the trickle of water-supply enquiries flowing into Hume Street became a scarcely-to-be-managed torrent. Duffy cried out for help in a memorandum dated 16 July 1951, but his plea for the appointment of a hydrogeologist met with little response. The Department left him to swim as best he could, and for the final four years of his service (he retired in March 1955) he devoted himself full-time to the preparation of water-supply reports. In 1953 he wrote 534 such reports at an average of well over two reports for each of his working-days.

Like every other Director of the Survey, O Brien soon discovered that his responsibilities were by no means exclusively geological. In Hume Street he had to undertake what might broadly be termed 'housekeeping duties'. For example, soon after his arrival he had to arrange for the removal of an oil-dripping motorcycle which was parked in the hallway of number 14. It was Bishopp's machine which had carried him around the country during the Emergency but which he had abandoned upon his departure from the Survey. Then colour-schemes had to be agreed upon following the Office of Public Works's agreement to a long-overdue redecoration of the house. When the decorators arrived the geologists took some interest in the fact that the man wielding the paint-brush atop a ladder was none other than Mr Behan, father of the borstal boy.

O Brien also had to deal with the following sad little episode. In February 1955 there arrived upon his desk a letter from Miss Bertha Hardman, who claimed to be the last surviving child of the Survey's former officer Edward Townley Hardman. She was then aged seventy-seven, and she explained that she had fallen upon hard times after working as a typist in Glasgow. She reminded the Director that her father had discovered an Australian goldfield, but she confessed that she was now reduced to the writing of begging letters. 'How great are the mighty fallen', she observed. Could the Survey please help? From the British Embassy O Brien obtained the address of the National Assistance Board in Glasgow, and he wrote to Miss Hardman offering advice as to how she should proceed. She was eventually assisted by the members of her late father's Irish masonic lodge. Another tragic episode in which the Survey became marginally involved - an episode which profoundly shocked the Dublin of that day - was the occasion in April 1958 when a woman's body was discovered in the basement area of 15 Hume Street. The Gardai were naturally anxious to know of anything suspicious which Survey officers might have seen or heard.

I now wish to introduce a caveat. I must erect a clear sign warning of danger. Those who have read the present chapter to this point might easily form a false impression. I have written of a Survey where the Director discoursed from Algiers to Mexico City upon the subject of Irish mineral potential, where Cunningham was discovering new mineralised horizons at Abbeytown, where Jones and O'Meara were mapping season by season in County Monaghan, where able overseas geologists were being recruited as Temporary Field Officers, and where Duffy was churning out water-supply reports by the hundred. It would be understandable were a reader to form an image of the Survey under O Brien as an institution which at last had emerged from its decades of languor. Sadly, such an image would be nothing more than a delusion. The recovery of the Survey was to prove a protracted business. In 1962, when O Brien completed his tenth year as Director, the Survey, through no fault of its own, was still in a parlous condition. Without exception, individual Survey officers were performing their duties with ability, energy, and devotion, but the Survey itself was in no condition to meet Ireland's needs as the world moved into the second half of the twentieth century.

The Survey was under-financed and under-staffed. Scientific facilities in Hume Street were either primitive or nonexistent. Any national programme of systematic map and memoir revision was entirely beyond the Survey's resources. Even those relatively unsophisticated water-supply reports were severely taxing the Survey's ability to provide the kind of geological information now being sought by the people of rural Ireland. In 1964 Ireland agreed to participate in the International Hydrological Decade (1965 - 1975) being sponsored by the United Nations Educational, Scientific, and Cultural Organisation. I well remember the shocked dismay with which our National Committee for the Decade heard the Survey's representative (Christopher Robin Aldwell) explain forcefully that the Survey really possessed little understanding of the nation's groundwater resources. All those hundreds of water-supply reports were just makeshift documents based upon little more than surmise and guesswork. Despite those promises enshrined within the 1958 *Programme for Economic Expansion*, little had as yet been done to assist the Survey from its sick-bed. Men in high places had yet to recognise that a modernised Ireland required a modernised Geological Survey.

The impoverished state of the Survey was highlighted when a new edition of the list of Survey publications was issued bearing the date February 1962. To the discerning reader the list made abundantly clear how little the Survey had succeeded in publishing since the acquisition of national independence forty years earlier. But to turn the pages of that little grey-jacketed booklet is to be made aware of a situation far more wretched than that represented by a mere failure to win for the Survey new intellectual ground by means of publication. The catalogue reveals that many a piece of intellectual ground formerly won by the Survey was now become overgrown and lost in the sense that the relevant publications were no longer available for sale to the public. Of the 118 nineteenth-century one-inch sheet memoirs, 39 were recorded as being out of print, the 39 including the memoirs for almost the whole of County Dublin, northeastern County Wicklow, and the greater part of Munster. Lamplugh's drift memoirs for the regions around Cork and Dublin were also out of print, as was Wright's classic 1927 memoir on the Killarney and Kenmare region.

But it was surely geological maps which the Irish public had every right to expect from the Survey, and where maps were concerned the 1962 catalogue presents a dismal picture. Thirty-four of the 205 one-inch sheets are declared to be out of print. Admittedly most of these thirty-four sheets depicted territory located exclusively within Northern Ireland, so their out-of-print status could perhaps be justified, although it should be noted that the drawing of the Border had never deterred the Dublin-based Ordnance Survey from continuing to publish many a topographical sheet of Northern Ireland. Seven of the out-of-print geological sheets were nevertheless in a very different category. They actually straddled the Border and included substantial portions of territory located within the Republic. For once Dublin seemed to be laying claim to rather less territory than that over which it held *de facto* jurisdiction! For the first time since the early months of 1890 parts of the national territory were bereft of a purchasable coverage of one-inch geological sheets.

A still more ominous development is revealed through the pages of the 1962 catalogue. All the prices of the hand-coloured one-inch geological sheets have been deleted. In place of the prices there is merely printed the following note.

> Arrangements have been made for the sale of the sheets of Irish Geological Survey Maps uncoloured.
> The sheets so issued will not necessarily be printed from copper plates.
> Each map will be stamped "uncoloured edition" inside the margin and in red colour.

The tradition of the hand-colouring of Irish geological maps intended for publication extended back to the county statistical surveys issued by the Dublin Society in the earliest years of the nineteenth century (see p.2). Now, in 1962, the tradition was revealed to have died.

We noted earlier (p.156) that down to 1921 the Irish one-inch geological sheets had all been hand-coloured in England, and that following the acquisition of national independence, the Irish Ordnance Survey had of necessity been forced to develop the artistic skills appropriate to their new responsibilities. At the Ordnance Survey's headquarters in Dublin's Phoenix Park those skills were handed down through at least two generations of colourists, the two final colourists - Thomas Barrett and Felix Flood - being recruited by the Ordnance Survey either during or shortly after the Emergency of 1939 to 1945. By the 1950s the Ordnance Survey was finding the colouring of the Geological Survey's one-inch sheets to be an increasingly expensive chore. It may even be that a slowly growing demand for the one-inch geological maps served only to exacerbate the problem. The Ordnance Survey evidently decided that it could no longer continue to shoulder the burden, and both Barrett and Flood were removed to other duties.

A decision taken up in Phoenix Park left O Brien to face a problem down in Hume Street. Yet again the Survey was becoming the victim of circumstances lying entirely beyond its own control. Ever since the appearance of the first sheets of the one-inch geological map late in 1856, that map had been the Survey's single most important published achievement. It is true that since Cole's death in 1924, little, if anything, had been done to keep the map revised and up-to-date. By the 1950s, as I remarked earlier (p.107), the map had become a fossil. But even a fossil may prove invaluable. A substitute for the one-inch map did not exist even as a speck upon the horizon, and an old map was surely better than no map. In view of the Ordnance Survey's withdrawal of its colourists, how was the Survey to ensure the future availability of its greatest published map? Initially, O Brien in 1952 toyed with the idea of reproducing the sheets of the map by means of colour photography, but for some reason the experiment was not proceeded with. During the following year the Survey's own draughtswoman, Maureen Giblin, was given the task of colouring some one-inch sheets as the exigencies of her other duties might allow, but this scheme, too, proved to be unworkable.

The Survey now had to face the unpalatable truth: the story of the hand-coloured one-inch geological map of Ireland was at an end. This was the message implicit in the 1962 catalogue. In future no coloured one-inch geological sheets would be available, aside from the remaining copies of the colour-printed drift-sheets of Belfast, Cork, Dublin, Limerick, and Londonderry, and the paired solid and drift sheets of the Killarney and Kenmare district. Henceforth anybody desiring coloured one-inch geological sheets belonging to the national map would have to purchase one of the 'uncoloured edition' now being offered, and then engage in a do-it-yourself exercise in colouring by numbers. In theory such private colouring was possible because upon the one-inch sheets the different geological units had always been identified by a printed system of notation as well as by their hand-applied colour. But in practice, without access to the Survey's Standard Copies, any private colourist was unlikely to achieve anything like the standard attained over the decades by the professional colourists trained within either the Geological Survey or the Ordnance Survey.

Once the message of the 1962 catalogue had been absorbed by the geological community, a few of its members began to wend their way out to Phoenix Park. They were bound for the Ordnance Survey, there to purchase copies of whatever coloured one-inch sheets might remain in that institution's store-rooms. A magnificent map was in its death-throes, and there were those who craved for a relic. Soon the last of the coloured one-inch sheets had been handed across the Ordnance Survey's sales' counter. Time has now made collector's items of those sheets coloured by Tommy Barrett, by Felix Flood, and by their many brush-wielding predecessors. At our book-fairs - in our auction-rooms - the coloured sheets of the one-inch series today change hands at prices vastly higher than the ten shillings which in 1930 was the price being charged for each of the nine most expensive sheets in the set.

The 1962 catalogue may have pronounced the obsequies of one venerable map of Ireland, but at the same time the catalogue did announce the birth of an Irish cartographic infant. Perhaps thus to juxtapose the two maps makes me guilty of solecism. The old map was a work of art, constructed in 205 sheets, and drawn to the grand scale of 1:63,360. The new map, published in 1962, was a colour-printed, single-sheet representation of

Ireland on the small scale of 1:750,000. It is just about one twelfth the size of its great predecessor. It bears to the one-inch map the same relationship as that existing between a postcard of the *Mona Lisa* and Leonardo's masterpiece itself.

For some reason the Survey chose to regard the new map as a third edition of the one to a million map of Ireland first issued under Hallissy in 1928 (see p.159), and then in a second edition in 1952. To have ascribed such a lineage to the new map seems unfortunate. Not only is the new map drawn to a fresh scale, but it is a vastly more satisfactory example of geological cartography than were either of its so-called first or second editions. Gone is all the typographic clutter, and more modern methods of colour-printing gave to the new map a bright and crisp appearance. It makes a thoroughly attractive wall-piece, and in my teaching-days I always encouraged my students to buy copies of the map with the adjuration that the map was more decorative than a poster, cheaper than a poster, and far more educative than a poster.

Honesty nevertheless compels the admission that upon its first appearance the map evoked some academic guffaws. Early printings of the map carried a number of unfortunate misprints ('Gretaceous' for 'Cretaceous'; 'Quarternary' for 'Quaternary'), but what really stimulated criticism was the map's representation of the Carboniferous Limestone. The map perpetuated Richard Griffith's 1837 division of the Irish limestones into a Lower Limestone, a Middle or Calp Limestone, and an Upper Limestone. In its early days the Survey had sought to apply this tripartite classification in its own mapping, but by the early 1860s Jukes was beginning to suspect that the Survey was following nothing more than a Lower Carboniferous will-o'-the-wisp (see p.62). After a little more experience in the Irish Midlands that suspicion turned to certainty. In September 1867, in the memoir to accompany four one-inch sheets of north-eastern County Galway - sheets 96 (Tuam), 97 (Mount Bellew), 106 (Athenry), and 107 (Ballinasloe) - Jukes announced his conclusion that any nationwide, threefold subdivision of the Irish Lower Carboniferous was entirely specious. Yet almost a hundred years later, in the map of 1962, here was the Survey again pretending that the Lower, Middle, and Upper limestones were indeed Irish stratigraphical realities. The reason for the survival of this geological anachronism into our own age is plain enough: the Survey had never been given the resources necessary to allow of its undertaking a thorough re-investigation of the Irish limestones. Those limestones are by far the most extensive of all Ireland's formations. They underlie almost half of Ireland's area, and their re-investigation would have been an undertaking of major proportions.

Of the 1962 map I have written sufficient. Despite its weaknesses, the map remains in print down to the present day (1995), and its sales-figures since 1962 must surely make of it the most successful Survey publication of all time. On the desks of county engineers, on the walls of mining-company offices, in school-classrooms, and alongside posters of the Rolling Stones in student bed-sits, the map has most effectively brought the Survey's name into the public eye.

We must now step six years backwards from 1962. It is time for us to return to 1956 in order to rejoin Cunningham in those field-investigations which were engaging his attention in the opening paragraphs of the present chapter. It so happens that he is at work in the country lying immediately to the south of that which in 1867 served to convince Jukes of the speciousness of Griffith's tripartite division of the Irish Carboniferous Limestone. Cunningham is, of course, mapping near Tynagh in County Galway.

At Tynagh, as we noted earlier, Cunningham was treading in the footsteps of Kinahan. Now Kinahan was not always the most meticulous of the Survey's officers. In 1890 he even made a frightful pig's ear of the completion of his form applying for superannuation. But here around Tynagh, Cunningham finds little to complain of in the quality of Kinahan's mapping. Guided by Kinahan's field-sheets, Cunningham's emulation of a butterfly soon brings to light many a wall-stone and field-stone flecked with galena or stained with copper. It is all just as Kinahan described the setting ninety years ago.

Individually, each of these stones located by Cunningham sings its own little pianissimo song telling of the presence of some degree of local mineralisation, but only when these individual voices are harmonised into a swelling chorus does the true nature of the Tynagh anthem become clear. Once the individual finds are plotted upon a map, there emerges a clear, meaningful, and exciting pattern. Cunningham is onto something big. This is a classic example of inspired geological field-investigation. It has to be acclaimed as one of the Survey's proudest achievements.

It would be interesting to know the exact moment at which Cunningham became aware that his field-observations were building into a portentous pattern. Was it perhaps as he tramped the ground around the remains of Spring Garden House? Was it as he sat in the commercial room of his Ballinasloe hotel looking at his maps and digesting the fry which in those days was the standard fare emerging from the kitchens of Irish country hotels? Was it back in Dublin, a few weeks later, as he mused over those same maps in the

FIGURE 7.4. *The mill building at Tynagh under construction during 1964. The mine open-pit is located in the middle distance, on beyond the mill building.* (From a photograph kindly made available by Ennex International, P.L.C.)

relative comfort of his Hume Street office? Sadly - foolishly - I never asked him.

And what was this pattern which Cunningham's field-investigation had brought to light? It was simple in the extreme. Cunningham had discovered that when plotted upon a map, the metalliferous boulders in the walls and the fields took the form of a dispersal fan. They had been spread around by the glaciers of the Pleistocene Ice Age. The pattern was exactly like that of smoke drifting downwind from a bonfire. Observe the wind-direction and the form of the smoke-cloud and you have no difficulty about locating the bonfire. From the existing metalliferous boulders around Tynagh, look back up the ancient glacial stream, locate the apex of the fan, and there - perhaps - would be found a veritable crock-of-gold. Cunningham entertained no doubt as to the location of the fan's apex. It was to be found within the townland of Derryfrench, lying in the southeastern corner of Sheet 106 of the six-inch map of County Galway.

The Survey itself was in no position to conduct the necessary detailed investigations at Derryfrench. Cunningham nevertheless did his best. Turn to the reverse of the County Galway six-inch field-sheet 116/2 - the sheet lying immediately to the west of the village of Tynagh - and we find that in 1960 Cunningham has added a table showing the results of his geochemical analysis of nineteen Tynagh specimens using Holman Tests. But thanks to Cunningham and O Brien - and thanks to Kinahan too - the Survey did now have on offer a red-hot tip for the Galway mineral stakes. Was there to be found a punter willing to back the Survey's hunch? O Brien tried. O Brien tried hard. Full of eloquence and enthusiasm he sought to arouse interest in Tynagh among those who controlled the kind of resources necessary for a fuller exploration of the site. Initially there was little response. Tynagh was dismissed as a rank outsider. It lacked pedigree. In its life of more than one hundred years the Survey had never discovered any economic deposits of international significance. Why should the situation now be supposed to have changed? In any case, from The Hague to Toronto - from London to Lusaka - almost the entire global mining fraternity shared a

FIGURE 7.5. *A moment of apprehension; will it work? On 22 October 1965, the Taoiseach officially opened Tynagh mine by moving this lever which detonated an explosive charge in the open-pit of the mine. From left to right: Mrs Loreto Hughes; the Taoiseach, Sean Lemass; David H.B. Fitzgerald, the mine manager; and Patrick Hughes, the President of Northgate Exploration, Ltd.* (From a photograph kindly made available by Ennex International, P.L.C.)

belief that to go looking for minerals in Ireland was scarcely less futile than joining the Galway Blazers in an Irish snake hunt. But O Brien persisted and persistence was to have its reward.

As early as 1957 prospectors did visit the Derryfrench site. They came from Irish Base Metals, Ltd, a subsidiary of the Canadian company Northgate Exploration, Ltd, but they found nothing to set them a-dancing off down the road to Ballinasloe. Three years later, in September 1960, the company did nevertheless undertake an investigation of the soil-chemistry of the locality. It was this study which must have inspired a jig of joy in the headquarters of Irish Base Metals. The initial report arising from the investigations, together with a series of back-up projects, all revealed an impressive zinc and lead anomaly.

Events now began to unfold rapidly. On 29 September 1961 Irish Base Metals lodged an initial application for a prospecting licence covering 57 townlands around Tynagh. Patrick Hughes, the President of Irish Base Metals, was in Hume Street for discussions on 3 October. The next day O Brien went over the ground with representatives of the company. Exploratory diamond drilling commenced on 14 November, although, oddly, John Pyne of the Exploration and Mineral Division within the Department of Transport, Energy and Communications, tells me that the actual prospecting licence for Tynagh (Licence X48) was not approved by the departmental Secretary (J.C.B. MacCarthy) until 28 November 1961, nor was it issued until 21 December. Be that as it may, by March 1963 the sinking of 160 holes, with a total depth of 21,300 metres, had confirmed the existence of a primary ore body beneath a secondary residual zone of mineral accumulation. Finally, after an opening by the Taoiseach (Sean Lemass), the Tynagh mine entered production on 22 October 1965 yielding zinc, lead, copper, and silver.

Tynagh's greatest riches were in zinc and lead, and the discovery of the site instantly placed Ireland among the world's nations best endowed with these two minerals. International financiers and prospectors sat up and took note. Ireland, after all, was not barren. Ireland was a mineral prospect to be

FIGURE 7.6. *Silver from the treatment of the first shipment of lead-zinc-silver concentrates from Tynagh was used to make a gavel and stand designed and crafted by the Irish sculptor Edward Delaney, and commissioned by Irish Base Metals, Ltd. Here, at a dinner in the Shelbourne Hotel, Dublin, on 13 January 1968, the silver piece has just been presented to the Irish Mining and Quarrying Society (founded 1958). Seated, left to right, are Murrogh O Brien (a former President of the Society), David Fitzgerald (President of the Society and mine manager at Tynagh), and D.R. Warfield (Secretary, the Northern Ireland branch of the Institute of Quarrying). Standing, on the left is James Tonner (Inspector of Mines and Quarries), and on the right is Ciaran Blair (a former President of the Society).* (From a photograph kindly made available by Ennex International, P.L.C.)

taken seriously. Through the application of modern methods of geochemical and geophysical exploration, Ireland's vaults might yet be found to contain hitherto undreamed of riches. It was time to fly in to Dublin or Shannon to take a look. In the aftermath of Tynagh, the Irish mining scene was transformed. The desultory mineral prospecting of the 1950s gave way to serious, targeted, and well-funded investigation programmes during the 1960s and the early 1970s. Between 1949 and 1961 only 49 mineral prospecting licences were issued, 26 of them in 1960 and 1961. During the next year alone - 1962 - 113 such licences were issued. By 1968 some six hundred current licences were held, and the total attained its peak in 1974, when 924 licences were current.

This intensive prospecting speedily demonstrated that Tynagh was no flash in the Irish pan. Indeed, during the period from 1961 down to 1974, Ireland proved to be the most profitable exploration area in Western Europe.

In 1962 Magcobar Ireland, Ltd, discovered a multi-million-ton body of barite close to the old mine-workings at Silvermines in County Tipperary. (Wynne had made reference to the existence of 'a mass of gray baryta' at the site in the 1861 memoir to Sheet 134.) The next year, and upon almost the same site, Mogul of Ireland, Ltd, confirmed the presence of a large zinc and lead body. Also in 1963, an exploration group called the Lower Limestone Syndicate located a substantial wealth of copper, mercury, and silver at Gortdrum, again in County Tipperary. In 1970 Tara Exploration & Development Co., Ltd, found a massive lead and zinc body at Navan in County Meath. Finally, in 1974, the Marathon Petroleum Ireland Co. Ltd, announced its discovery of the Kinsale Head Gas

Field in the Celtic Sea some 50 kilometres south of Kinsale.

This widespread search for Irish mineral wealth had a profound effect upon the science of geology within Ireland. Rocks, minerals, fossils, and landforms were suddenly brought into the public gaze as never before. Children in Irish classrooms now learned about the genesis of ore-bodies, that Tynagh was the largest zinc/lead mine in Europe, or that their homeland was become the world's fifth largest producer of barite. Parents in their semis were soon seated before TV screens displaying programmes explaining the essentials of plate tectonic theory or telling of the latest rumoured find out in the mountains over Westport way. By 1973 exploration and mining were in Ireland engaging the attention of so many geologists and prospectors that the time seemed ripe for the foundation among them of a professional body. Preliminary discussions were held in Athlone, Mullingar, and Port Laoise, and the outcome was the inauguration of the Irish Association for Economic Geology. By 1985 the Association had 232 members.

At the focus of all this 1960s geological activity in Ireland there lay the Geological Survey. It was largely the work of the Survey which had inspired the torrent of Irish interest in geology, but the Survey now found itself in no position to exert much influence upon the course of events. If Irish geology of the 1960s be likened to a river in spate, then the Survey has to be seen as a baulk of venerable timber tossed hither and thither by the force of the current. Sometimes the Survey was forced against one bank, at other times it was lodged momentarily against the opposite bank, and for the remainder of the time it was spun helplessly in midstream.

The Survey was neither staffed nor equipped to cope with the situation which had now developed within Ireland. In November 1963 the Minister for Industry and Commerce (Jack Lynch), acting in association with the Organization for Economic Cooperation and Development, established a Research and Technology Survey Team. During the course of its investigations, the team examined the Survey and there resulted the following assessment.

> ... the Team formed the impression that it is now almost entirely an administrative and advisory adjunct to the Department of Industry and Commerce - mainly for advising on prospecting licence applications.

The team recommended that the Survey should be considerably expanded, that it should sponsor aeromagnetic and geophysical surveys, that it should transfer all its data and maps onto magnetic tape, and that it should itself contribute to the offshore exploration for oil and gas through the collection of information relating to promising sections of the continental shelf. There must have been some wry smiles in Hume Street when the team's report arrived there during 1966. But, unlikely though it must have seemed, all that the team had recommended was very shortly to come pass.

In February 1964 the Survey had a staff of only five geologists (O Brien, Aldwell, Cunningham, Downing, and O'Meara). Both as scientists and as human beings their working conditions in Hume Street were decidedly primitive. Apart from the arrival of the electricity, and the installation of a telephone or two, the house and its fittings had changed little since that day in 1870 when Hull and his men had moved over from number 51. North American mining geologists, coming through the doorway to consult six-inch field-sheets or to inspect maps of licensed prospecting areas, must have felt themselves to be entering a time - capsule. But within that capsule the officers clearly performed their duties nobly and to the very best of their ability.

Up on the first floor of the house the Director's room was the scene of innumerable conferences between O Brien and representatives of the mining companies. He tells me that many a morning he found visitors standing unshaven upon the steps of number 14 awaiting his arrival. They would prove to be geological VIPs who had just flown in from Boston or New York aboard flights with breakfast-time touch-downs. In the Director's room examples of Du Noyer's geological artistry looked down upon the discussions, but the three bookcases inscribed 'Portlock Library' which Jukes had ordered to be made in 1864, now stood empty of their volumes. It was a sign of the times. O Brien had given to the Royal Dublin Society all the books from her late husband's library which Mrs Portlock had presented to the Survey in Jukes's day. O Brien preferred his visitors to see the bookcases filled with mineral specimens rather than with musty tomes.

Through the letter-box of number 14 there continued to pour that deluge of enquiries about water-supply which had all but drowned Duffy before his retirement in March 1955. Now the enquiries were chiefly the concern of Bob Aldwell at work in the General Office, next door to the Director's room. And most enthusiastically did he plunge into his task. He was a highly effective representative for the Survey upon the Irish National Committee for the UNESCO International Hydrological Decade (1965-75), and his stimulating May 1973 address to the Galway and Mayo Regional Development Group, on the subject of groundwater, caused the members of the Group to give serious consideration to the appointment of an hydrogeologist on contract.

Down on the ground-floor of number 14, in the untidy room at the rear of the house, there sat Mike

FIGURE 7.7. *In characteristic pose. Mike O'Meara in his office, the rear ground-floor room in 14 Hume Street. It was here that Mike dealt with much of the post-Tynagh deluge of applications for prospecting licences. To judge from the state of the ash-tray, this would seem to be an early-morning photograph.* (From a photograph in the archives of the Survey.)

O'Meara. On the wall behind him, over the black marble fireplace, there hung a framed copy of Du Noyer's geological version of James Fraser's *Travelling map of Ireland* of 1852. Upon the large bench at which he worked - a bench which Hull originally intended for the quartering of six-inch sheets and the dissection and mounting of one-inch sheets - there stood a large ashtray heaped with the residue of Mike's daily intake of nicotine. His was the immense burden of dealing with the Survey's waxing responsibilities in the area of the issuing of prospecting and mining licences. As an excessively shy man, Mike hated having to meet strangers face to face. Within the Survey it was generally believed that he would go into hiding in some Hume Street cubbyhole whenever he detected the threat of intrusion upon his privacy.

In the room next door to Mike - the room which Cole had resolved to make his office in the aftermath of his first stroke - Cunningham grappled with a multitude of queries arriving from government departments, from companies in Ireland and overseas, and from the general public. On behalf of an American corporation, the Industrial Development Authority enquired whether asbestos was mined anywhere in Ireland. Companies wrote asking about the availability of substances such as calcite, dolomite, iron pyrites, kaolin, shale for the manufacture of drainage pipes, the mineral spodumene, or stone for monumental purposes. People clutching geological specimens rang the Hume Street doorbell seeking identification of their finds. Would-be geologists arrived to ask about careers in the science. The curate at Cloonfad, in northern County Galway, reported a mysterious oil-seepage located upon church land. That curate was Father James Horan. For good, or for ill, his name was later to become associated with a Connaught airport rather than with a Connaught oilfield.

And then there were the schoolchildren - dozens of them - who wrote to the Survey soliciting assistance with their classroom projects. I suspect this aspect of the Survey's work to have increased enormously after January 1965 when there was staged the first of the now annual Aer Lingus Young

Scientists' Exhibitions. I wonder where Gay Cassidy and Maev Brennan are now. In the days when Young Scientists' Exhibitions were a novelty rather than an institution, Gay and Maev were pupils in the Holy Child Convent at Ballybrack in County Dublin. From there they addressed the Survey thus.

> My friend and myself are doing a project on Killiney cliff, and request information about how it was formed, what type of rocks and layers make it up, and what makes it fall down every so often. We would be very grateful for any information please.

In reply they received a two-paged typed letter in single-line spacing. They certainly had no cause for complaint.

But all this was desk-bound, paper-pushing, office work. Did the Survey of O Brien's later years have no field-programme? Had the occupants of Hume Street lost their hammers and their map-cases? Of course not. It nevertheless does have to be admitted that during the last forty years the pressure of other duties has allowed Survey officers to spend a far lesser proportion of their time in the field than was formerly the case. Certainly far gone are those Victorian days when an officer - and his family - would disappear off into the field, perhaps for years on end. Many a modern officer must have regretted this development. O'Meara certainly did.

O'Meara was at heart a field-man, and it is highly appropriate that one of the Survey's principal field-programmes during the 1960s should have involved O'Meara, working in close collaboration with his friend and colleague, Francis Synge. In 1958 there had been established a National Soil Survey, and in their mapping of soils, the pedologists very naturally turned to the Survey for information about the Irish drifts as the parent material from which most of our soils have been derived. It is interesting to recollect that had the drift survey inaugurated by Lamplugh in 1901 been persisted with, and had his estimates proved to be valid, then by 1960 the Survey would have mapped the drifts of approaching one half of Ireland. But Lamplugh's survey had been aborted, so now O'Meara and Synge, assisted by various of their colleagues, took to the field to make reconnaissance drift surveys of a type which it was hoped would materially assist the soil Survey in its task. In this programme the geologists mapped the drifts of counties Carlow, Kildare, and Limerick, and a map showing the drifts of the latter county - the map was the work of O'Meara and Synge, assisted by Aldwell and Jean Margaret Wilkinson - was published at a scale of 1:126,720 in 1966 as a part of the memoir devoted to the soils of Limerick.

Issues of ethics and morality have scarcely ever surfaced within the story which I have to tell. But around the Christmastide of 1963 such issues did arise behind the door of 14 Hume Street. At the centre of the problem there stood the Director himself. O Brien had served in that post for more than eleven years. When he arrived in Hume Street in 1952, his ambition had been to deploy the Survey's expertise and information resources in an effort to bring into being an Irish mining industry of international significance. In the light of the recent discoveries at Gortdrum, Silvermines, and Tynagh, that ambition was in late 1963 on the point of realisation. Indeed, it may be that O Brien had succeeded beyond the most sanguine of his earlier expectations.

O Brien had come to the Survey from the antiquated and moribund Irish mining industry of the 1940s. It was perhaps now time for him to step back into the modernised and exciting world of the Irish mining industry of the 1960s. There were certainly those within that industry who recognised the Director of the Survey to be a man possessed of unusual and valuable talents. So, the inevitable happened. A tempting offer was made. O Brien was invited to join the Tara Exploration & Development Co., Ltd, as the General Manager. He accepted. He resigned from the Survey as from 13.00 hours on Saturday 29 February 1964. It was the Survey's loss. On the other hand, for his new company, for Ireland, and, presumably, for O Brien himself, it was an auspicious leap-year leap to have made. He now began to assist his company towards its 1970 discovery of the huge zinc and lead body at Navan.

But where within this event do there lurk ethical and moral considerations? The answer is simple. As the Director of the Survey O Brien had been privy to a good deal of confidential information communicated by the mining companies. It was material freely imparted to him as the head of the national geological survey, but, at the same time, it was material to which other and competing mining companies might dearly have liked to secure access. O Brien was now about to join one of the mining companies. Was he at liberty to divulge to his new company the sensitive information which he had received as the Director of the Survey? The issue troubled O Brien. He was determined to be punctilious in the matter. Once it became clear that he really was leaving the Survey to join Tara Exploration, he arranged that all negotiations with the mining companies involving business of a confidential nature should be handled by one of his officers rather than by the Director himself.

On Monday 2 March 1964 Cunningham, the senior officer, took over the administration of the Survey. It was to be yet another of those protracted interregna, this one being destined to last for just over three years. Eventually, in 1966, the vacant directorship was advertised, and, seemingly, advertised widely. Reference to the vacancy certainly featured in a publication emanating from the Institution of Mining and Metallurgy in London. Perhaps its presence there had something to do with the fact that O Brien had been nominated to the committee now charged with the responsibility for filling the vacant directorship. O Brien was a member of the Institution and, indeed, on 16 June 1966 he was the guest-speaker at an Institution dinner held at Martinez Spanish Restaurant in London's Swallow Street. Be that as it may, the Institution's notice relating to the Hume Street vacancy certainly came to the attention of one far-distant geologist working beneath an equatorial sun and seated virtually on the shores of Lake Victoria. That geologist was the Commissioner, the Geological Survey and Mines in the newly independent state of Uganda. He was in Entebbe. It was said that he was the only Director of a geological survey anywhere in the world who was able to take a shot at a crocodile while standing beside his office desk. Not, of course, that he actually ever did avail of the opportunity of displaying his marksmanship in such a manner! The name of that geologist was Cyril Edward Williams.

Bishopp had been an Englishman who was widely believed to be a South African; Williams was a genuine South African, born in Durban, Natal, in 1922. From school he proceeded to the University of Capetown, but his studies there were interrupted by the call to arms of World War II. He joined the South African Air Force, and he eventually flew Martin B-26 Marauder bombers in the Mediterranean sphere of operations. An unusually heavy aircraft for its twin-engined size, the Marauder had the reputation of being a difficult plane to fly. Truth to tell, it was widely known as 'the widow maker'. But Williams successfully completed sixty operational missions, and with the conclusion of hostilities (he was about to leave for southeastern Asia when Japan capitulated) he returned to the less hazardous life of being a student in the shadow of Devil's Peak on Table Mountain.

From the campus of the University of Capetown he must often have gazed out eastwards towards the suburb of Athlone; on sultry December afternoons he must have driven down the western side of the Cape Peninsula, along the shores of Bantry Bay, and down to the Cape of Good Hope itself. Little can he have realised how closely his later years were to become enmeshed with the real Athlone and the real Bantry Bay. It was nevertheless upon that campus, nestling beneath Devil's Peak, that he began the journey which was to take him to both Westmeath and West Cork. His graduation in geology opened the door upon a varied career as a geological surveyor in South Africa, in East Africa, and in such other locations as Mauritius and the New Hebrides. In 1962 he became Deputy Director of the Geological Survey of Uganda, and during the following year he was appointed Commissioner, the Geological Survey and Mines of Uganda.

In the Uganda of 1966 the episode of Idi Amin was still more than four years distant, but Williams perhaps began to sense that the time had arrived for the Ugandans to assume responsibility for their own affairs. He certainly began to feel that his own future lay elsewhere. He had been given to understand that he had only to ask and there would be found for him a senior post with the Geological Survey of South Africa. Such a return to his own homeland must have seemed a very natural course for events to take. But then his eye was captured by the notice relating to the vacancy in far-off Hume Street.

Williams had never set foot upon the Emerald Isle. He nevertheless possessed a tenuous link with Ireland. In common with countless millions of others around the world, his family tree contained an Irish branch. His maternal grandmother had hailed from Limerick, and his mother had been born in Dublin. He thought it might be interesting to see something of Ireland. Why not apply for the vacant Irish directorship? He did. He recollects in due course being informed by the Civil Service Commission that for the post they already had their eye upon a particular and strongly favoured candidate, but that if Williams wished to come to Dublin, then the selection committee would be happy to see him. But on the subject of expenses the Civil Service Commission was adamant. There was for Williams to be no expenses-paid trip from Entebbe to Dublin. If he came, there was no question of the Irish taxpayer footing the bill.

Williams was undeterred. His meeting with the selection committee was arranged to take place during the autumn of 1966, and Williams remembers how cold Dublin felt after the heat of Uganda. To explore what happened behind the door of the interview room would involve a breach of confidence. All that I will mention is one simple point, but a point nonetheless indicative of changing attitudes within Ireland. Unlike Murrogh O Brien in 1952, Williams was never asked about his knowledge of Ireland's first language. That was a good thing. A little Afrikaans or Swahili he might

FIGURE 7.8. *Dr Cyril Williams (front left) on the steps of 2 Fitzwilliam Place, Dublin, on the afternoon of 14 June 1979. From 1828, until his death in 1878, this house was the the residence of Sir Richard Griffith. Dr Williams has just unveiled a plaque commemorating the association between the house and the man who has been hailed as 'the Father of Irish Geology'.* (From a photograph by Terence Dunne of Trinity College Dublin.)

have managed, but of Irish he then knew not a word. It was not held against him. Neither at the interview, nor during the course of his subsequent Irish career, did Williams ever feel that his overseas origins were disadvantageous either to himself or to the office which was placed in his care.

Within geology, Williams was a specialist in igneous petrology and vulcanology. These were hardly fields which can have ranked at the top of any listing of Hume Street's most urgent needs. In the eyes of the Civil Service Commission's panel, Williams nevertheless possessed two important credentials making him eminently suited to the Irish directorship. First, throughout his career, he had taken a keen interest in all aspects of economic geology, and he had himself been notably successful in the discovery of hitherto unknown mineral deposits. Second, he had already demonstrated his ability to fill competently the kind of post for which he was now under consideration. He had founded a geological survey in the New Hebrides, and for three years he had been directing the work of the Geological Survey of Uganda. The panel was impressed. Williams was offered the Irish directorship. He accepted.

While in Dublin for the interview, Williams, very naturally, paid a visit to Hume Street. There he talked with Cunningham. It would be interesting to have a transcript of whatever that veteran campaigner in Irish geology may have had to say to his visitor on the subject of the future of the Irish Survey. It would have been still more interesting to have been a fly upon the wall at another discussion which shortly took place thousands of kilometres from Hume Street and in another hemisphere. Upon his return to Uganda from Ireland, Williams discovered that Douglas Bishopp was in Pretoria working for the Geological Survey of South Africa. Early in 1967 he visited the Transvaal expressly to meet the man who more than sixteen years earlier had slammed the door of Hume Street behind him for the last time. He found Bishopp still to be very bitter about his Irish experience. Bishopp wished Williams well in his new post, but he emphasised that Williams would find enormous problems awaiting him in Dublin. He clearly deeply resented the 1940s failure of the Irish administration to support him in his efforts to expand and modernise the Survey. To this day (1995) Bishopp's words still ring loudly in Williams's ears. 'You're going to be wasting your time in Dublin'.

A few weeks later, in March 1967, Williams arrived in Ireland to assume his new duties. Bishopp's words spoken in Pretoria had hardly been encouraging, and now here was Williams seated in what once had been the office of a deeply frustrated Bishopp. Bishopp had tried to bring the Survey into the twentieth century. He had failed. O Brien had sought little more than the employment of the Survey as a mineral prospecting tool. Tynagh was Ireland's reward and O Brien's personal ticket of leave back into the mining industry. In March 1967 it became the turn of Williams. What was he to do with the tiny four-man (Aldwell, Cunningham, Piers Gardiner, and O'Meara) institution now placed in his hands? He really had little choice. The challenge which faced Williams in 1967 was much the same as the challenge which had faced Bishopp in 1940. He had to modernise the Survey. He had to re-create the Survey. He had to give to Ireland the Survey which it needed to face the demands of the second half of the twentieth century. And all that meant a massive expansion in terms of personnel, accommodation, equipment, and capital expenditure.

Initially, prospects looked bleak. One of his earliest tasks was to call in the army to remove a collection of dangerously unstable chemicals. When he made his first tour of number 14 he must have been shocked. The top floor of the house had virtually been abandoned. I and my then Trinity College colleague, John Andrews, had been up there a couple of years earlier and we found that in one of the back rooms - in Hallissy's old soil analysis laboratory - some shelves had collapsed jettisoning onto the floor most of the Survey's Victorian letter-books, together with a wealth of other historic literature. I also have a vague recollection that there was in one room ample evidence of Dublin pigeons having secured access to the building through a broken casement window.

For the first sixteen months following the arrival of Williams, this Hume street *status quo* remained largely undisturbed. There might be a new Director seated behind the three first-floor windows of number 14, but not overnight was there to be accomplished a raising of the Survey from the sick-bed where it had lain ever since Cole's death in 1924. Williams proceeded slowly but methodically. He set about familiarising himself with Irish geology in the field. He had discussions with Professor Jimmy Brindley of University College Dublin (he offered to lend the Survey a petrological microscope), with Professor Charles Holland of Trinity College Dublin (he had been in Ireland only a few months longer than Williams), and with Professor Tom Murphy of the Dublin Institute for Advanced Studies (he had been the Survey's geophysicist during the Emergency). He had long sessions with Cunningham, whom he found to be entirely pessimistic about the Survey's chances of being granted a programme of modernisation. And Williams himself began to prepare a memorandum for submission to his superiors outlining his proposals for the future of the Survey.

The memorandum which Williams prepared is entitled *Reorganisation of the Irish Geological Survey*, and it occupies twenty foolscap pages. In the document he explains that because of its many decades of neglect, the Survey now needs to be reconstructed *ab initio*. But, he suggests, this is no bad thing. Ireland has the opportunity to create the most modern geological survey unit to be found anywhere in the world. He asks for a new and properly equipped building adequate to the needs of a dynamic scientific institution. He explains the need for new salary scales so that the Irish Survey will be able to compete for the best international talent available. He requests a dramatic expansion in the staffing of the Survey. The new institution will need 34 geologists (geochemists, hydrogeologists, marine geologists, palaeontologists, petrologists, etc.), 23 technicians (field, laboratory, and library assistants, museum curators, motor mechanics, etc.), and 14 office staff (ranging from office superintendents to office cleaners). He explains that financial provision must be made to allow geological staff to have periodic study leave, to give them regular opportunity for attendance at international conferences, and to permit their engagement in bilateral exchange programmes. All this, it is suggested, might be funded from the royalties paid by the Irish mining industry. Finally, Williams offers a timetable for the implementation of his proposals between December 1967 and December 1969.

Williams signed his memorandum on 5 September 1967, and on that day, or very soon thereafter, the document was sent over to Kildare Street to J.C.B. MacCarthy, the Secretary of the Department of Industry and Commerce. Williams thereby fulfilled a charge laid upon him at the time of his appointment. When the directorship had been advertised during the previous year it had been explicitly stated that the new Director would be expected to plan and then to implement a modernisation of the Survey. Further, it was made clear that the new Director could expect to receive full official support at all stages of the work. Much the same had been said to Williams during the course of his interview in the autumn of 1966. He had now produced his plan for the Survey. He had asked for the first steps towards modernisation to be taken in December 1967. He sat back in Hume Street and awaited news of the assistance and support which he understood himself to have been offered. Nothing happened. As he waited, Williams must have imagined a smug Bishopp down in Pretoria saying 'There, I told you so'.

Several times in previous chapters I have sought to emphasise that during the decades following the acquisition of national independence, the Survey found itself a victim of circumstance. The paralysis which for so long afflicted the Survey was not caused by internal failings within Hume Street so much as by weaknesses within that larger administrative machine wherein the Survey was but a tiny cog. The initial fate of Williams's 1967 memorandum serves nicely to illustrate the point. He has told me what happened.

Somebody outside Hume Street had agreed that the reinvigoration of the Survey must be made a priority. Williams had been selected and commissioned to carry the task through. He had produced his plan and submitted it to his Department. Now he waited for the response. He waited through the winter of 1967-68. He waited through the spring of 1968. He waited through the summer of 1968. He waited into the autumn of 1968. And still nothing happened. Late in 1968 he made an appointment to see MacCarthy, the Secretary of the Department. He found MacCarthy to be most amiable, but when Williams broached the subject of the memorandum, MacCarthy's response left Williams dumbfounded. 'What memorandum?', said MacCarthy. The memorandum was moving through the Department with such excessive slowness that even after the passage of more than a year it had still not reached the desk of the departmental Secretary, the man for whom the document was intended.

I fully understand that my reader, experienced in the ways of officials the world over, may be tempted to offer another, alternative, explanation of MacCarthy's words. His plea of ignorance, my reader may protest, was just a ploy. He really knew all about the memorandum. He was merely stalling. He was playing for time. At a first glance such an explanation might look attractive. When we discover what happened next such an explanation collapses. Again I rely upon the memory of Williams himself.

There and then, in MacCarthy's office, Williams produced a copy of the memorandum. MacCarthy looked the document over. He was a very experienced civil servant. He had been the Secretary in Industry and Commerce for more than twelve years. He speedily grasped the thrust of Williams's case. He turned to Williams. He asked searching questions. They discussed. MacCarthy picked up his phone. Within seconds he was in conversation with a senior official in the Department of Finance. Arrangements were made for a meeting to be held in Finance just two days later. Things were now moving fast. Williams tells me that he entered the meeting in Finance hoping to secure sanction for the appointment of twelve geologists to the Survey's staff. He came away from the meeting having been granted sanction for the appointment of thirteen geologists!

The Survey's long years of emaciation were at an end. Oddly, it was just one hundred years since the ailing Jukes had seen the Survey through its expansion of 1867-68. And why - eventually - had Williams found the Department of Industry and Commerce, and then the Department of Finance, to be so sympathetic to his cause? There were doubtless several reasons, but one must surely be paramount. In post-Tynagh times it was increasingly recognised that to the Irish nation, geologists might be worth vastly more than their own weight in gold. Between 1965 and 1968 the value of the gross output of Ireland's mines had increased by a staggering 1230 per cent. Between 1965 and 1973 the value of the gross output of Ireland's mines increased from £800,000 to £27,000,000.

Australians speak of the convicts who arrived with Captain Arthur Phillip 'in the First Fleet'. The Survey contains no convicts, but officers do speak of those who joined Dr Williams 'in the First Intake'. Between November 1968 and the close of 1971, there arrived in the Survey eighteen new geologists, geochemists, geophysicists, and the like. Now it was Cunningham's turn to be dumbfounded. The eighteen form an interesting group. Among them there was only one woman - Loreto Farrell. Of the eighteen, five were Irish by birth and coming to the Survey direct from an Irish university. Five were Irishmen who were returning home to assume a Survey post after holding overseas appointments or after studying in overseas graduate schools. Most of the remaining eight had been participants in what earlier I termed 'the Great Irish Geological Plantation' (see p.165). They were non-Irish geologists who had originally come to Ireland to stake out for themselves a claim to a piece of Irish research territory. But they had taken a liking to the country, to its rocks, and to its people. Through their acceptance of one of the new Survey posts they were able to become permanent residents within the land of their choice.

Deepak Inamdar is not to be numbered among the former geological planters, but his appointment was certainly one of the more interesting among the arrivals belonging to the First Intake. A graduate of the Maharaja Sayajirao University of Baroda, he in 1969 was a graduate student in geophysics in the University of Glasgow. Seeing that the Survey proposed to appoint a geophysicist, Inamdar applied and was offered the post. During the nineteenth century, Oldham and five other Survey officers had left Ireland bound for the Indian Survey; now in the twentieth century an Indian geologist had joined the Irish Survey in part repayment of the old debt.

Between September 1972 and May 1975 no new geological appointments were made to the Survey. The First Intake was being digested. But during 1975 there began the selection of the Second Intake, and between May 1975 and November 1980 a further nineteen geologists were recruited. Of course, not all the geologists who joined the Survey in either of the two intakes chose to remain permanently with the Survey. The buoyant international demand for geologists ensured that the Survey was bound to suffer some leakage. Nonetheless, in 1986 the Survey had a geological staff numbering twenty-eight officers. That was around twice the size attained by the Survey in its Victorian heyday, and it was a far cry from the four officers who in March 1967 had gathered to greet Williams upon his first morning in Hume Street.

This expansion in the number of the geological staff was matched by a similar increase in the size of what eventually came to be known as the Support Services Division. A Drilling Unit was established under Kevin Crilly, by 1987 the Cartography Unit had a staff of fourteen, while the office staff numbered twenty. Only in the area of technical assistance did the Survey fail to achieve the style of growth which might have been expected. In 1987 the Survey possessed three Senior Technicians (Christopher Daniel McDonnell, Thomas McIntyre, and John Clive Murray), but these three chiefs were left without any tribe to lead into battle. Thereby hangs a little tale - one of several little tales which it is best to leave for exploration by some future historian of the Survey.

By 1970 the rapidly expanding size of the Survey far exceeded the capacity of 14 Hume Street. The provision of a modern, custom-built headquarters for the Survey was a matter of some urgency. Discussions upon that subject commenced around 1968, but in the interim the Survey clearly had to be found temporary accommodation. Number 14 for the moment remained the nerve-centre for the

FIGURE 7.9. *John Duffy at work in the Survey's building at 4 Kildare Street around 1980. As Paperkeeper he was responsible for the printing of many of the Survey's publications. On 18 December 1987 he became the first recipient of the Survey Cunningham Award 'in recognition of his outstanding contribution to the work of the Survey over eighteen years in the areas of map curation, printing of publications and service to the public'.* (From a photograph in the Survey's archives.)

Survey, but the inscription 'Suirbhéireacht Gheolaíochta Éireann. Geological Survey of Ireland', now began to appear on doorways in other parts of Dublin southward of the Liffey.

For a while another house in Hume Street - number 19 - was used by the Survey. By an odd coincidence the expansion took the Survey back into St Stephen's Green, to a house - number 46 - very close to the Survey's old home at number 51. A little distance away, in Kildare Street, the former Motor Registration Office at number 4 was handed over to the Survey. And a very seedy building it proved to be. Upstairs there was an area which staff were not supposed to enter because the floor was rotten, and in the basement, behind a door which was jammed ajar, a chamber was literally knee deep in ancient legal documents. They presumably dated back to the nineteenth century when the building had contained the offices of Rooke and Rooke, solicitors.

Another building which was pressed into Survey use was a portion of the former biscuit factory belonging to Messrs W. & R. Jacob, and Co. Ltd, in Bishop Street. There several of the Survey's staff were located throughout most of the 1970s. There, too, was housed the Survey's library. That was most inconvenient. A Hume Street officer wishing to keep an eye on the incoming periodical literature had to walk down Hume Street, across The Green, up York Street, along Aungier Street, and into Bishop Street. The entire Bishop Street set up was bizarre. Messrs W.& R. Jacob were in process of relocation at a new factory in Tallaght, but at the time of the Survey's arrival some types of biscuits were still being manufactured in Bishop Street. Survey officers had permission to avail of the facilities of the factory's canteen, but if they did so, they had to run the gauntlet of the rich Dublin ribaldry of the women on the work-floors. I gather that forthright comments as to the sexual proclivities and prowess of certain officers led to a sharp reduction of their intake of caffeine.

There were some consolations. I am told that on Thursday afternoons there was opened a little hatch on the ground floor of the building. There Jacob's pensioners and Survey officers were entitled to buy bags of broken or misshapen biscuits for just a few pence. That little tradition must have terminated around 1976. By then biscuit manufacturing had ceased in Bishop Street. Demolition of the old factory commenced, and the Survey staff located in their corner of the building continued their work to the alarming sounds and vibrations of tumbling girders and crashing masonry. Several of us recollect within the Survey's part of the building an unlocked second-floor door which opened only upon a vista of the spire of St Patrick's Cathedral. The time had arrived for the Survey to leave Bishop Street.

From Bishop Street the Survey staff and the library were in September 1979 moved to Baggot Bridge House, a brand-new office building standing close to the Grand Canal. It was a different world from the biscuit factory, even if the partition-walls between offices were now so thin that neighbours could not avoid listening in to telephone debates as to whose turn it might be today to collect the children from school.

During the 1970s Williams's Survey empire thus became widely scattered around the city of Dublin. But his empire also extended into nearby County Wicklow. Cole had once found storage space for the Washing Bay core in the basement of Hume Street; Williams required far more spacious premises for the hundreds of metres of core which the Survey now began to acquire. A large core-store was therefore developed within the walls of the former Glencree

FIGURE 7.10. *The Survey's drilling-rig at work during the spring of 1985. The site is amidst the Namurian rocks at Coolbaun, to the northeast of Castlecomer and in the Leinster Coalfield.* (Reproduced from a photograph in the archives of the Survey.)

Reformatory, located at the head of Glencree and some twenty kilometres distant from Dublin city-centre. It was out at Glencree that the Drilling Unit stored all its equipment.

The Survey of the 1970s possessed one other outpost. To service its needs in the field, the Survey had now been equipped with a small fleet of Landrovers and with two caravans fitted as mobile laboratories. When not in use, these vehicles were all kept at the Royal Hospital in Kilmainham. The officer in charge of the vehicle-fleet was Michael Max, and it seems that at the time of their purchase it was agreed that in the event of some national emergency, all the Landrovers would be handed over to the army for military use.

Both to its contemporary observers, and to its historian, the expansion of the Survey between 1968 and 1978 appears as quite breathtaking in its magnitude. When Williams arrived upon the scene, the Survey consisted of five men rattling around in the empty recesses of Hume Street. Ten years later the Survey was become a well-staffed institution possessed of offices scattered through the southern portion of the city of Dublin, with its own transport-fleet, and with a storage facility in County Wicklow. As we will discover shortly, there was also under construction in Dublin a magnificent new home for the Survey. What the aggressive and blunt Bishopp had failed to accomplish during the 1940s, had been achieved by the affable and gracious Williams during 1968 and the years following.

And why the difference? The answer is surely simple. Bishopp had lived in an Ireland where the idea of a revitalised Geological Survey was dismissed as involving an absurd squandering of public monies. Williams had arrived into an Ireland which was still rejoicing at events in Tynagh, and where other even richer discoveries were being eagerly anticipated. This post-Tynagh post-Navan transformation of the Irish attitude towards the Survey is strikingly illustrated by the Survey's subventions recorded within the pages of the annual *Estimates for Public Services.* Ralph Horne has very kindly looked out for me the following figures. They speak eloquently for themselves.

	1965	1967	1969	1971	1973	1975
Staff numbers	10	10	24	32	43	73
Salaries (£s)	11,484	14,561	37,114	58,372	91,490	245,983
Equipment, stores, etc. (£s)	-	-	6.300	17,000	60,000	300,000

Should there be required any further evidence of the changed environment within which the Survey now existed, then that evidence is afforded by a summons which Williams received one day during 1969. He was called to a meeting with George Colley, the Minister for Industry and Commerce, so that the Minister might learn at first hand of the developments taking place within the Survey. Williams remembers his Minister's parting words: 'If you should need any assistance, don't hesitate; come straight to me'. Those were sentiments entirely without precedent in the whole history of the Survey.

By the close of 1975 the Survey had a staff of twenty-eight geologists, but of that number only three (Aldwell, Gardiner, and O'Meara) had a length of continuous Survey service exceeding that of Williams himself. I introduced that adjective 'continuous' deliberately because there was one other officer in 1975 - Synge - whose total service did exceed that of Williams, but it was service divided into two terms. Having originally joined the Survey in 1957, Synge had resigned in 1963, disillusioned by the Survey's failure to develop any publications policy. He went into the world of academic research in Northern Ireland and in Britain, but in 1969, sensing that a new era was dawning within the Survey, he returned to Dublin to assume responsibility for the Survey's Quaternary Division.

Williams may have commanded an army of new recruits wherein O'Meara was really the sole seasoned veteran, but Williams speedily established within the Survey a strong *esprit de corps.* He made himself freely accessible to all his staff. Without any sense of patronage, he referred to them as 'my boys and girls'. He was popular. From O'Meara to John Duffy, the Paperkeeper, there was a strong sense of purpose. Exciting things were happening. Tasks of national importance were being undertaken. Survey morale soared. The return of Synge in 1969 was a sign of the times. In 1976, when Dave Naylor left the world of petroleum geology to take charge of the Survey's mapping programme, he accepted a massive reduction in his salary merely for the pleasure of living in Ireland and for the satisfaction of joining the Survey in its great new enterprise. Williams's success in inspiring the Survey with a new sense of community and purpose is by no means the least of his many achievements.

When he first arrived in Hume Street, Williams can have known little or nothing of the history of the institution now placed in his care. This lacuna he speedily remedied. I suggested above (p.167) that during the decades after the 1920s the Survey had lost contact with its distinguished past. Williams sought to effect a cure for this amnesia. He wished to inspire his boys and girls with a memory of the great tradition to which they were heir. The Survey's Victorian and Edwardian letter-books were now properly cared for, and two of the volumes received a full conservation treatment. Many of the Survey's Du Noyer paintings were remounted. The volumes constituting the Portlock Library were brought back from the Royal Dublin Society and rehoused in their original bookcases. In 1970 Williams asked me to give a lecture to the Irish Geological Association (founded 1959) on the history of the Survey, his hope being that his officers would attend such a meeting in force.

That the Survey has in 1995 chosen to celebrate its sesquicentennial in such style clearly indicates that the Survey has now fully re-established contact with its past. This is the message which has this year been carried around the world upon Irish envelopes and packages. At the Survey's suggestion, the sesquicentennial was celebrated by the issue, on 27 July 1995 (not on 6 July 1995 as stated in the philatelic magazine of the Irish post office) of a 52 pence (the denomination necessary for an airmail letter) Irish postage stamp bearing a geological map of Ireland. That miniature map must be the most widely circulated Irish geological map of all time because half a million of the stamps were printed. The tiny map is derived from a sheet compiled by the Survey in 1975 for inclusion within the *Atlas of Ireland* published by the Royal Irish Academy in 1979. Perhaps, too, that my reader now holds the present volume, bearing the Survey's imprint, is just one further sign of Williams's success in awakening the Survey to a remembrance of its past.

We noted earlier (p.156) that following the attainment of national independence in 1922, both Ireland and the Survey became profoundly introspective. Before Cole's death in that - for the Survey - calamitous year of 1924, the majority of the Survey's geologists had seen themselves as possessed of dual allegiance. On the one hand they were local Irish Survey men; on the other hand they were members of the great international community of geology. After 1924 the situation changed. Most of the Irish Survey officers opted out of the international geological community. Men such as Cunningham, T.J. Duffy, McCluskey, and O'Meara were content to be nothing more than competent and conscientious civil servants. But around 1970 both Ireland and the Survey were transformed. In 1965, Sean Lemass as Taoiseach, had his memorable talks with Terence O'Neill, the Premier of Northern Ireland, and in 1973 Ireland joined the European Economic Community. Within the Survey it was Williams, arriving from another continent, who threw open the Survey's windows to admit a gust of international air. He wanted his officers back into the international community of geology.

As I observed earlier in this chapter (p.195), in his memorandum of September 1967 on the reorganisation of the Survey, Williams had specifically indicated his wish that Survey officers should rejoin the international geological community through attendance at overseas conferences and through bilateral staff exchange programmes. But he also recognised that membership dues would have to be paid to the international community in the form of publications submitted to international periodicals. He wanted his officers to publish. He wanted to be able to feel the Survey's pulse rates coming back to life. He wanted to sense that throb as Survey officers pumped their work into the international circulatory system of their science.

In order to stimulate Survey authors, Williams founded within the Survey an in-house journal entitled *Geological Survey of Ireland Bulletin*. The first issue is dated November 1970, and fifteen parts were published before the journal was suspended following the publication of volume 4, number 3, during 1991. The *Bulletin* was intended to provide an organ for the publication of refereed papers arising from the Survey's investigations, so that matters, in Williams's words, 'are fully aired and discussed before being finalised in maps and memoirs'. Eventually, exactly one hundred papers appeared between the covers of the *Bulletin* - covers which all featured drawings by either Oldham or Du Noyer - and of that total of papers, eighty-eight involved Survey officers as authors. Writing for the *Bulletin* was no part of the official duties of a Survey officer. That so many officers did so write is a clear indication that the Survey was again ticking with a private pulse rate. The Survey was once more an intellectually stimulating pond in which to swim.

What had happened to the Survey's private pulse rate was soon paralleled by the development within the Survey of a similarly reinvigorated official pulse rate. In the forty-three years between Cole's death and Williams's arrival in Hume Street, there had trickled from the Survey as new publications nothing more than two small-scale maps of Ireland (1928 and 1962), two outline geophysical maps of Ireland (1949), Wright's Killarney and Kenmare

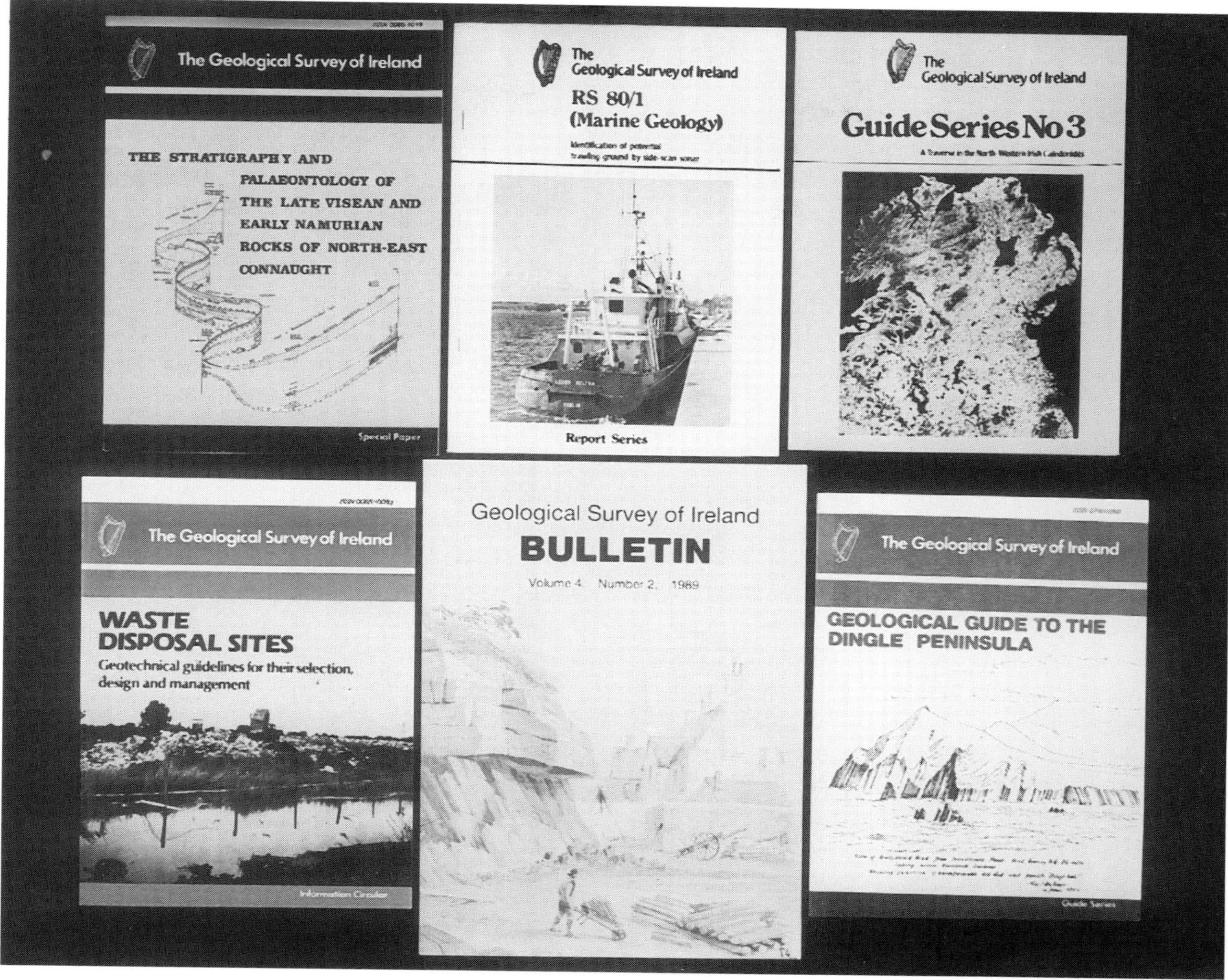

FIGURE 7.11. *An example of each of the series of Survey publications inaugurated soon after Cyril Williams assumed the directorship of the Survey.*

memoir (1927), and the three Emergency period pamphlets (1943, 1947, and 1948). Now that feeble trickle was replaced by an avalanche. Neither Ireland nor the international geological community could any longer entertain doubts as to whether the Survey might be alive or dead. The Survey was, as Williams expressed it in 1970, 'once again in business'.

Aside from the *Bulletin,* Williams's avalanche of Survey publications consisted of works belonging to one or other of four main series.

First, inaugurated in 1970, there is the series of *Information Circulars* designed for the publication of general descriptive articles, excursion guides, bibliographies, and the like. Two examples drawn from the series are the introduction to the Geological Survey by Ralph Horne and Piers Gardiner (1970, IC/2) (Horne and Gardiner constituted a Publications Unit responsible for all the Survey's early publications), and the pamphlet on the selection, design, and management of waste disposal sites by Donal Daly and Geoff Wright (1982, IC 82/1).

Second, inaugurated in 1973, there is the *Report Series,* which is intended for works which are unsuited for publication through one of the standard geological channels, but which are nonetheless deserving of wide circulation. This series is especially intended for research findings in geochemistry, geophysics, and hydrogeology, and some instances are Pat O'Connor's reconnaissance radiometric survey of the Irish Republic (1981, RS 81/1), or the memoir to the compilation magnetic map of Ireland by Michael Max and Deepak Inamdar (1983, RS 83/1).

Third, inaugurated in 1976, there is the *Guide Series,* which comprises field-guides to selected regions of outstanding geological interest. The guides are intended for the interested amateur, just as much as for the professional geologist, and by

1984 the series contained four guides. The first of these was Ralph Horne's widely-used, several times reprinted guide to the rocks of the Dingle Peninsula (perhaps there should be an Irish-language version for sale at An Daingean), and the most recent is a multi-authored guide to the Caledonides of the west of Ireland (1983, GS4).

Fourth, inaugurated in 1971, there are the *Special Papers*, these being monographs by non-Survey authors dealing with important topics, but at a length which makes it impossible for them to secure a publication outlet in one of the scientific periodicals. The first of the *Special Papers* was by Henk Visscher of Utrecht, and was devoted to the Permian and Triassic beds of the Kingscourt Outlier (1971, *Special Paper* No. 1). The most recent addition to the series is by a former Survey officer - Ken Higgs - and his two collaborators reporting upon their studies in the palynology of Ireland's Tournaisian rocks (1988, *Special Paper* No.7).

From the *Bulletin* to the *Special Papers,* this was a remarkable outpouring of geological literature. The Survey, like a desert after rain, had suddenly burst into flower. Librarians around the world opened new catalogue files entitled 'Ireland, Geological Survey of'. To Hume Street there began to be delivered letters from geological surveys in almost every continent requesting the establishment of publication exchange agreements. With remarkable speed, and with outstanding success, Williams had taken the Survey back into that international league where once it had played in the days of Jukes, Hull, and Cole.

But there is another side to the coin. To set against this success in the field of literature publication, there has to be recorded the existence of a major failure. It was a failure possessed of serious repercussions. The effects of the failure are undoubtedly still with us. Indeed, it may be that some future historian of the Survey, decades hence, will conclude that the effects of a Survey failure during the 1970s and 1980s still lingered on to influence official attitudes towards the Survey during the early years of the twentyfirst century. And what was the nature of the Survey's failure? It was both simple and rudimentary. The Survey found itself incapable of satisfying the growing local and overseas demand for modern medium and large-scale maps depicting Ireland's geology.

The one-inch geological map of Ireland had been allowed to die during the 1920s, when the policy of on-going revision was abandoned. Sheets from the map - even the last few hand-coloured sheets - were still on sale around the time of the Tynagh discovery, and these remaining sheets were eagerly snatched up by the incoming prospecting and mining companies. But the old map, splendid though it had been in its own day, was now just a cartographic anachronism. For the newly-arrived companies to be forced to resort to such a map was rather like asking a team of engineers to lay out a projected underground railway system for the city of Dublin on the basis of nothing more substantial than John Rocque's map of the city published in 1756.

By the 1960s everybody with an interest in the geology of Ireland recognised that the rocks of the country would have to be resurveyed. New knowledge needed to be brought to bear. New techniques needed to be employed. New maps needed to be published. These must surely have been among the salient arguments underpinning the official decisions of 1966 and 1968 both to overhaul and to expand the Survey. From the outset, Williams himself certainly attached a high priority to the completion of a new geological map coverage of Ireland. In his seminal memorandum of 5 September 1967 he had listed twenty-three objectives for a revitalised Survey, but the first of them was:

> To undertake complete revision and geological mapping of all areas of the Republic....

Under James the Survey had in 1845 launched itself upon an ultimately successful nationwide mapping of Ireland's solid rocks. Under Lamplugh the Survey had in 1901 embarked upon an abortive nationwide mapping of Ireland's drift deposits. Now, under Williams in 1968, the Survey was about to begin a comprehensive resurveying of both Ireland's solid and drift deposits.

As new officers joined the Survey during the years following 1968, they were assigned to individual pieces of field-ground just as officers joining a warship are assigned to their action stations. Williams's commendable idea was that areas of known mineral potential should be investigated first, so it was to counties such as Tipperary, Waterford, and Wicklow that officers now found themselves despatched. The annual summer exodus of officers to their allotted ground once again became a feature of Survey life. In 1976 Dave Naylor was appointed to the Survey, becoming Assistant Director two years later, and he assumed overall responsibility for the entire mapping programme. He regularly inspected each officer's ground, and perhaps not since the days of Archibald Geikie, Edward Hull, and G.W. Lamplugh had officers benefitted from so close a supervision of their mapping. All that mapping, of course, was still being carried out upon the Ordnance Survey's six-inch (1:10,560) sheets, just as it had been ever since those pioneering days around Hook Head during the summer of 1845.

Six-inch sheets might be ideal for geological field-mapping, but during the 1970s Williams and Naylor had to face precisely the same problem as had confronted James, Oldham, and Jukes during the first seven years of the Survey's life. It was the old base-map problem. The six-inch scale is far too large a scale for a national coverage of published geological sheets. So, that granted, upon what scale should the Survey seek to lay its maps before the public? De La Beche and Jukes had in 1851 opted to employ the new one-inch map for this purpose, but for Williams and Naylor there was to hand no such simple a solution. The Ordnance Survey was in the process of going metric. After a life of more than one hundred years, the one-inch topographical map of Ireland was now at the Ordnance Survey declared to be defunct. But no similarly scaled metric replacement map had as yet appeared.

Williams and Naylor had several rounds of talks with the Ordnance Survey. The outcome was a decision to await the completion of the first sheets of a new Ordnance Survey 1:50,000 topographical map of Ireland. The Ordnance Survey gave to the geologists a verbal assurance that such sheets would become available late in the 1970s or early in the 1980s. The delay was clearly to be regretted, but the Geological Survey had the satisfaction of knowing that the promised sheets would form the basis for a geological map of Ireland slightly larger in scale than the Survey's old one-inch map (1:63,360). A remarkable Victorian achievement was seemingly about to be surpassed in every respect. Jukes in the 1850s had waited for more than two years for the arrival of the first one-inch topographical sheets from the Ordnance Survey. It was not unreasonable for Williams now to have to wait a similar length of time for the arrival of the first of the Ordnance Survey's new 1:50,000 topographical sheets. But Williams was soon looking back over the decades with envious eyes. The cartographic fates who had smiled upon the Survey of Jukes's day with such benevolence, were now in a very different and meaner mood.

Jukes was in charge of the Survey for nineteen years. During that period he saw published 117 one-inch geological sheets covering well over one half of Ireland. Williams was in charge of the Survey for twenty years. During that period he saw published not so much as a single sheet of the 1:50,000 geological map of Ireland. Further than that, aside from the maps included in the *Bulletin,* the *Information Circulars,* or other of the Survey's new serial publications, the Survey between 1967 and 1987 published not one geological map of any description. The Williams era was for the Survey one of stark cartographic famine. But, to avoid misunderstanding, I must instantly add my rider. Williams was not culpable. Naylor was not culpable. There was nobody within the Survey at whom an accusing finger might justly be pointed. It was all another example of that sad phenomenon which we have encountered so often in previous pages. The Survey found itself manacled as a result of decisions taken elsewhere and quite beyond the Survey's sphere of operational influence.

The story of the Survey's failure to issue any sheets of a new national geological map of Ireland during the years of Williams's regime must be one of some complexity. It would be inappropriate for me to pry too deeply into so recent an event. Perhaps the story will one day be told following the opening to scholars of the appropriate files of government departments, the Survey, the Ordnance Survey, and the trade unions. For the present it is sufficient to note that the 1:50,000 base-map promised by the Ordnance Survey failed to materialise. During 1988 the Survey therefore abandoned the notion of a 1:50,000 geological map of Ireland. Instead, the Survey proposed to solve its base-map problem in a fresh manner. It was decided that the Survey would itself photographically enlarge the existing Ordnance Survey half-inch (1:126,720) map of Ireland to a scale of 1:100,000, and then employ this new map as the basis for the modern national coverage of geological sheets. It was an odd marriage to arrange. It was a little like the marriage of a nonagenarian groom to his teenaged bride! The geological interpretation is new, but its base-map dates back to the eve of World War I.

The new coverage of geological sheets is known as the Survey's Bedrock Map Series, and it will depict the geology of the whole of the Republic of Ireland in twenty-one sheets. Each sheet is to be accompanied by an informative, colour-illustrated memoir, the sheet and its memoir nestling in cosy cohabitation within a plastic folder. The Survey has moved a long way since the days of the hand-coloured one-inch sheets and their austere, brown-jacketed memoirs. The first of the Bedrock Map Series - Sheet 6 (North Mayo) - was published in September 1992, and it is hoped to have all the twenty-one sheets of the map published by early in

1997. I will not try to explain why, in a series of twenty-one sheets, one of the four sheets published during 1994 was Sheet 25 (South Cork)! As with so many things in Irish life, it is all to do with 1922 and Partition!

Williams's years as Director may have been years of cartographic famine, but he did inaugurate, and see carried through, two important surveys, using modern methodologies which would have left the likes of Oldham, Jukes, or Hull agape in puzzled bewilderment. These two surveys were pieces of contract work commissioned by the Department of Industry and Commerce or, later, by the Department of Industry, Commerce and Energy on behalf of the Survey, and making use of special funding.

The first survey was a nationwide vertical aerial photographic survey carried out between 1973 and 1977. The £100,000 contract was awarded to the French Institut Géographique National, and its cameras were flown at an altitude of 15,000 feet to yield a photographic coverage with a nominal scale of 1:30,000. All the resultant negatives are today held by the Ordnance Survey on behalf of the Geological Survey.

The second survey was an airborne magnetometer survey, and here the contract went to the English firm of Hunting Geology and Geophysics Ltd. This survey was not nationwide. It covered just 49,000 square kilometres in the eastern, central, and western portions of the country, and the objective was the location of areas of potential mineralisation. The survey was completed in three phases between August 1979 and September 1981, and all the resultant electromagnetic tapes are stored in the Survey.

While these two exotically modern surveys were being conducted far above Ireland's surface, there continued at ground-level all the Survey's more traditional and multifarious activities. The post-Tynagh mining-boom brought to the Survey an enormously increased work-load. In 1987, for instance, the Survey evaluated 377 applications for mineral prospecting licences, and assessed 213 applications for licence renewal. The modernisation of the Irish nation made fresh demands upon the Survey. In 1973 the Survey was invited to contribute a geological perspective to the planning of what was eventually to become the Dublin Area Rapid Transit system, and a few years later the Survey became involved in studying the route of the gas-pipeline which was to carry Dublinwards the product of the Kinsale Head Gas Field. Increasing concern for the environment brought the Survey's expertise into fresh focus, and today the Survey is responsible for the assessment of the environmental impact studies required before many a development can receive its go-ahead. And all the time the Survey was conducting its activities against the backdrop of increasing public interest in the earth sciences. Each year the Survey now handles around one thousand enquiries from the general public.

In any review of the work of the Survey during Williams's directorship, there is one other sphere of activity which just has to receive mention. It was novel and it was important. Further than that, several of the officers who were involved, today remember the episode as one of the most rewarding and enjoyable aspects of their entire career within the public service. I refer to the Survey's involvement with the great international debate upon the subject of the Law of the Sea.

During the decades following the end of World War II, many nations became increasingly concerned about their legal rights within and under the waters off their coasts. Not the least of the questions at issue was that of the national title to any offshore mineral resources. The debate - a sometimes acrimonious debate - culminated in the establishment of a United Nations Seabed Committee in the late 1960s, and then in the holding of the Third United Nations Conference on the Law of the Sea between 1974 and 1982. The Conference met first in Caracas in 1974, and there followed eleven other sessions, involving more than 150 nations in ninety-three weeks of negotiations.

Ireland took a keen interest first in the work of the Seabed Committee, and then in the deliberations of the Conference. The Irish delegation normally contained two or three Survey officers, the six officers involved in the work being Cyril Williams himself, Gardiner, Keary, Naylor, Riddihough, and Robinson.

The Survey officers were widely regarded as having made a notable contribution to the various debates, and Gardiner tells me that upon several occasions he found himself negotiating on behalf not just of Ireland, but also on behalf of a whole group of other nations which are also possessed of wide continental margins. Amongst those that he was acting for were Argentina, Australia, Canada, New Zealand, and the United Kingdom! Indeed, Gardiner even earned for himself an eponymous place within the legal history-books. At one point in the discussions there was need for a clearer legal definition of the outer limits of the so-called continental rise, marking the edges of our continents in regions of wide continental margins.

FIGURE 7.12. *An artist's impression, dated 1976, of the Survey's new headquarters at Beggars Bush. The buildings around the new structure are all parts of the old barracks complex.* (Reproduced from a copy of the drawing in the archives of the Survey.)

At the group's New York meeting in 1976 he offered a suggestion. It found widespread acceptance and was soon enshrined in international thinking as the 'Gardiner Formula' or the 'Irish Formula'.

While the day-by-day work of the Survey was being conducted from offices in Hume Street, Kildare Street, the former biscuit factory, or Baggot Bridge House, important - dramatic - developments were taking place elsewhere. Bulldozers were digging. Concretes were hardening. Cranes were lifting. Bricks were piling. Pipes were arriving. A new headquarters for the Survey was under construction. Planning for a new headquarters had commenced very soon after Williams's arrival in Ireland. Number 14 Hume Street was totally unsuited to the Survey's needs, and by 1970 the dispersion of the Survey's facilities around the city of Dublin was proving highly inefficient and entirely unacceptable. Something just had to be done.

The first question to be solved was the geographical one. Where should the new headquarters be located? A number of possible sites was considered. One of the proposals reviewed involved the Survey being provided with a new building to stand alongside the Ordnance Survey's headquarters in Phoenix Park, Dublin. This would have been a neat solution. Since the two Surveys had been born as Siamese twins in 1825, and then separated in 1845, such a reunification up in the Park would have had sentimental appeal. But that was not to be. By 1972 it had been decided to rehouse the Survey in a new building located within the early nineteenth-century (1827) infantry barracks at Beggars Bush, in Dublin's Haddington Road, and little more than one kilometre distant from Hume Street.

The military had long since marched out through the gates of Beggars Bush Barracks for the last time, and by the 1960s its ranges of buildings were in use as a government stationery store. At the former barracks, construction work commenced on behalf of the Survey during 1974, but soon problems of several types arose. For lengthy periods the building-site lay forlorn and silent, while over in Hume Street, Williams must have felt that his patience was being severely taxed. If, while he waited, he had found the time to leaf through some of the Survey's archives, he might have come across some documentation about an odd little episode relating to Beggars Bush. It might, perhaps, have suggested to him that the choice of the barracks site was not an entirely happy one for the Survey to have made. Many decades earlier the Survey had itself reported upon the Beggars Bush site as one of ill-omen. The story is as follows.

During the 1870s the military authorities became concerned at the unexpectedly high death-rate among troops garrisoned at Beggars Bush. The Survey was asked to investigate the site to discover whether there might be any geological explanation for the fact that the undertaker's hearse was so frequently being summoned to the barracks

FIGURE 7.13. *The Survey's final days in Hume Street. On the left is a view of the cluttered hallway looking towards the street-door. The 'Milners' patent fire-resisting' safes on the right of the hall were purchased in May 1891, during Nolan's regime, expressly to house the six-inch field-sheets. For that purpose they are still used during the 1990s. Atop the safes there normally stood plaster busts of Jukes and Portlock, but these had evidently been removed to a safer place by the time the photograph was taken. On the right, in the spring of 1984, one of the safes is lifted away from number 14* en route *to Beggars Bush.* (From photographs in the archives of the Survey, the exterior photograph having been taken by Dr Jean Archer.)

mortuary. McHenry was sent over to see what he could discover. He offered an hypothesis.

McHenry noted that the barracks stands upon the very edge of a great spread of boulder clay and immediately inland from a former coastline. All the land eastward of the barracks is reclaimed slobland. (The Survey's six-inch drift map of the city of Dublin, 1917, actually represents the old coastline as running along Shelbourne Road, just below the eastern wall of the barracks, and where the old cliff-line actually forms a part of the perimeter defences of the barracks.) McHenry suggested that the reclamation of the slobland had been assisted by the dumping there of large quantities of foul waste from the city of Dublin over a long period of time. That gave him the explanation he needed to account for the high military mortality rates. The decaying refuse of centuries was releasing noxious vapours which were escaping to the surface along the former coastline and where the boulder clay met the onetime slobland. The air of the barracks was being foully polluted by miasmas arising from a geological boundary located at the foot of the eastern wall of the barracks.

Modern sanitary engineers would doubtless dismiss McHenry's reasoning as absurd, but the Victorians favoured miasmic explanations for much of the ill-health which surrounded them. Certainly Kinahan was entirely convinced by the logic of his colleague's argument. The *Freeman's Journal* for 29 January 1889 contains a letter by Kinahan reminding the authorities of the existence of this 'death line' at Beggars Bush Barracks, but McHenry's postulated miasmas would long since seem to have dissipated themselves. So far as I am able to judge, the health of Survey staff would seem today to be far better at Beggars Bush than it ever was in Hume Street half a century ago! I have certainly never heard of any part of the new building having to be fumigated, as happened to one office in Hume Street during 1942 (see p.301)! Nor has the presence of the 'death line' done anything to deter the recent conversion of other portions of the old barracks into highly - desirable, up-market town-houses.

The Survey's new building was eventually completed early in 1984, and the removal from Hume Street, Kildare Street, and Baggot Bridge House was completed in May 1984. And a splendid new building it was. Hull had been immensely proud of his new premises in Hume Street during the spring of 1870; now Williams and his staff could with justice take an even deeper pride in their new Beggars Bush home. Perhaps no Survey in the world was better accommodated. Certainly visitors from other surveys began to express envy as they were conducted around the new Beggars Bush facilities.

In the early stages of the planning for the new building, the Survey had enjoyed the enthusiastic support of John Allen, the then Chairman of the Office of Public Works. Williams had first met Allen at a party somewhere in Dublin. He soon discovered

FIGURE 7.14. *The staff of the Survey at Beggars Bush during 1984 and very soon after the transfer to the new building. A few members of the staff were not present for the taking of the photograph, and among those absent was the present Director of the Survey, Dr Peadar McArdle. The original of the photograph is in the archives of the Survey.*

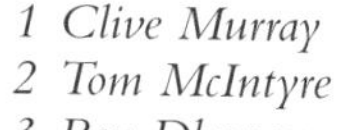

1 Clive Murray
2 Tom McIntyre
3 Ben Dhonau
4 Gerry Stanley
5 Dan Tietzsch Tyler
6 Bob Aldwell
7 Willie Warren
8 Chris McDonnell
9 David Ivers
10 Conor MacDermot
11 Mary Gormley
12 John Dooley
13 Eddie McMonagle
14 Dave Barry
15 Donal Daly
16 Tony Callaghan
17 John Duffy
18 Noel Keogh
19 Piers Gardiner
20 Bill Morrissey
21 Bernie Glendon
22 Christina Bolger
23 Shane O'Brien
24 Andy Sleeman
25 Margaret Rooney
26 Maureen Donnelly
27 Linda McDermott
28 Loreto Farrell
29 Mel Howes
30 Maeve Boland
31 Rachael Harper
32 Teresa Donnellan
33 Michael Kinsella
34 Archie Donovan
35 John Morris
36 Barry Long
37 Geoff Wright
38 Valerie O'Neill
39 Aubrey Flegg
40 Ronnie Creighton
41 Tony Johnson
42 Eugene Daly
43 Ray Weafer
44 John Pyne
45 Anne Murphy
46 Jean Archer
47 Amos Walsh
48 Tom Reilly
49 Andrew Flood
50 Peter Fitzpatrick
51 Pat O'Connor
52 Cyril Williams
53 Ralph Horne
54 Janet Ball
55 Siobhan Murphy

FIGURE 7.15. *The Research Vessel* Lough Beltra. *Originally operated by the National Board for Science and Technology, the vessel is presently under the control of the Department of the Marine. She has frequently been used for Geological Survey research projects carried out as a part of the Survey's marine geology programme. She was formerly a fishing vessel and she has an overall length of 21.1 metres.*

that around midday Allen commonly strolled over from the Office of Public Works, at 51 St Stephen's Green (the building, of course, was the former Museum of Irish Industry), to take lunch in the Shelbourne Hotel. There Williams joined him upon many an occasion. In her history of the hotel, Elizabeth Bowen reminds us that the hotel's coffee room 'rings, and has rung, with grand racy talk'. Perhaps it was some of that grand racy talk which resulted in the Survey being presented with so splendid a new abode.

The architects for the Beggars Bush building were the Dublin firm of Tyndall, Hogan, and Hurley, and, most appropriately, their plans incorporated within the structure a nice functional stratification. The upper of the six floors - Floor Four in the system of numbering now in use - was devoted to laboratories for electronics, geochemistry, micropalaeontology, radiometrics, x-ray diffraction, and the like. Floor Three was given over to bedrock mapping, and to cartography - and, I must add, to the Survey Tea Room. Floor Two was allocated to geophysics, to Quaternary geology, to hydrogeology, and to marine geology. Floor One was reserved for the Survey's mineral resources division, for the Director, and for the Survey's other senior members of staff. The Ground Floor supported the Public Office, a good-sized library, and a large exhibition area. Finally, down in the capacious basement, there was a lecture - theatre, additional exhibition space, a rock-store, and further laboratory accommodation with facilities for the crushing and milling of rocks.

That was the magnificent and cohesive plan. But even before the Survey had arrived in Beggars Bush to take up residence, things had begun to go awry. By the summer of 1983 the entire eastern end of the unfinished building (four out of its eleven bays) had been taken from the Survey and allocated to another branch of the public service. Since the arrival of the Survey in May 1984, a good deal of space within the remainder of the building has been taken over by the Survey's parent Department, and used for purposes which are not all entirely germane to the

FIGURE 7.16. *In the exhibition area at Beggars Bush on 30 October 1987. On behalf of the Survey, Ralph Horne makes a presentation to Cyril Williams on the occasion of his retirement from the directorship.* (Reproduced from a photograph in the archives of the Survey.)

activities of the Survey itself. Equipment intended for installation in those top-floor laboratories was never fitted, and even the laboratories themselves have been decommissioned and turned to other uses. But a full description of all the most recent events at Beggars Bush is no part of my brief. The terminal event for this history of the Survey has to be the Survey's removal to Beggars Bush in the spring of 1984. I do, nevertheless, propose to take one small step on beyond that terminal date and down a little way towards the present. That step brings me to 30 October 1987. More precisely, that step brings me to 4.30 on that Friday afternoon.

On that day and at that time the staff of the Survey, and their invited friends, gathered in the exhibition area of the Survey's new headquarters. Oddly, it may well have been to the very day the centenary of Kinahan's completion in County Donegal of the Survey's primary geological mapping of Ireland. But in Beggars Bush that afternoon, neither Kinahan nor Donegal were foremost in our thoughts. We were assembled for another purpose. Cyril Williams was retiring. We were there to sip wine, to pay our tributes, and to say our farewells. The ninth Local Director or Director of the Survey was departing. Of the nine, only one other - Hallissy - had remained in office until the normal age for retirement. Of the nine, only one - Hull - had held the directorship for longer than Williams, and Hull's tenure of the office surpassed that of Williams by a mere five months. But no directorship of the Survey had ever witnessed within the Survey anything like the remarkable transformation of the Williams era. An antiquated period-piece of a Survey had almost miraculously been converted into a modern and dynamic Survey.

That evening, as Cyril Williams descended the steps outside the Survey's new home - as he walked away across the former parade ground where once there had barked red-jacketed sergeant-majors - his mind perhaps reverted to his first visit to Dublin and to the pessimistic views which Cunningham had then voiced about the Survey's future prospects. Perhaps Williams paused to look back at the new building, its windows now illuminated and giving the whole edifice the appearance of some great liner lying at her berth. Perhaps he remembered another conversation - a conversation in far distant Pretoria. 'You're going to be wasting your time in Dublin'. It

FIGURE 7.17. *Three Directors of the Survey: Murrogh O Brien (1952-64) left, Cyril Williams (1967-87) right, and the present Director, Peadar McArdle, standing. The illustration makes an interesting comparison with the three Directors featured in Figure 3.11 on page 73. In September 1995 the Forum of European Geological Surveys convened in Ireland in commemoration of the Irish Survey's sesquicentennial. An excursion followed the meeting, and Frances McArdle caught this picture at the Hodson Bay Hotel, County Roscommon, on the evening of 6 September 1995.*

must have been with a deep sense of satisfaction that he turned on his way towards the old barracks-gate and then out into the busy world of Haddington Road.

On the following Monday morning the Survey entered upon the fifth of its protracted post-1922 interregna. This time Ralph Horne was left as the Survey's temporary helmsman. Not until February 1992 was Peadar McArdle appointed to be the new Director. Those two geologists - the Survey's two helmsmen over the last eight years - have sometimes found themselves to be handling the Survey in the midst of decidedly choppy waters. But all that is something best left for some future historian of the Survey. I propose to conclude this chapter back in the company of Cyril Williams.

He came to Ireland from an office overlooking the crocodile-infested waters of Lake Victoria. In his retirement he lives in County Clare in a house overlooking the yacht-studded waters of Lough Derg. One afternoon during the glorious summer of 1995 I sat with him on the patio of his residence. He had cooked for us a bowl of potjie - a recipe from his native South Africa. We ate and we talked of his Survey years. 'You know', he said, 'perhaps we were just *too* successful in our expansion of the Survey'. That observation I leave behind to be pondered by the Survey's future chroniclers.

CHAPTER EIGHT

DELVING THE DRIFT

I may, perhaps, here be allowed to remark, that there is in Ireland a vast field for any geologist who would take up the subject of the drift with a determination to work it thoroughly out.

J. Beete Jukes in his presidential address to the Geological Society of Dublin on 8 February 1854.

Ireland and a chesterfield sofa share one characteristic in common: they are both very well upholstered. Almost everywhere the solid rocks of Ireland's frame are hidden from view beneath varying thicknesses of those unconsolidated deposits which the geologist designates under the omnibus term 'drift'. The drift is of many types. The peat-bogs, which have been so widely exploited by Bord na Móna, represent one type of drift. A second type is the alluvium which borders so many an Irish river from the Bann to the Bandon. A third type is the wind-blown sand of those dunes, from Brittas to Belmullet, where lotioned sunbathers laze on hot July days. The peat, the alluvium, and the wind-blown sand are all depicted upon maps compiled by the Geological Survey of Ireland, but none of these three types of drift has ever become the focus for a major geological controversy. Their nature and origin is patently obvious; they offer little meat for the kind of debate so relished by scientists. But there is within Ireland a fourth major category of drift deposit. The fourth category contains the materials which are by far the most extensive of all Ireland's drifts, and for two hundred years the drifts of this fourth category have stimulated incessant interest and discussion. In that discussion the officers of the Geological Survey of Ireland have ever been to the fore.

The fourth category of drift comprises three classes of deposit. First, there are immense spreads of rubble consisting of boulders of various sizes set within a matrix of sand or clay. Such deposits may

FIGURE 8.1. *Till and bedded gravels exposed on the banks of the Dinin River below Castlecomer and near to Jenkinstown House (S480646). The sketch was made by Hardman and it originally featured in the second edition (1881) of the memoir to one-inch sheets 127 etc. (Kilkenny and Tipperary coalfields). In the original caption* a. *is described as Upper Boulder Clay and* b. *as Middle Gravels.*

FIGURE 8.2. *Bedded glacial sands and gravels in the valley of the Doonane River at the southwestern foot of Keeper Hill in County Tipperary (R774651). The deposits were laid down close to the front of the so-called 'Midlandian Ice Sheet', the most recent of the great glaciers to have swept Ireland's surface.* (Photograph by the author.)

be tens of metres thick and they might convey the impression that Ireland must have been traversed by some gigantic, load-shedding dump-truck, its tailgate wide open. Geologists know such deposits as 'boulder clay' or 'till' (Figs 8.1 & 8.7). Second, there are sheets of sands or gravels, the materials arranged in a layered sequence and with all their components nicely sorted according to size. This is the kind of deposit in which our sand martins might like to excavate their tunnelled homes. Geologists distinguish this type of deposit as 'stratified drift' (Fig 8.2). Third, there are boulders - sometimes huge boulders - which lie prominently in the landscape like stranded whales upon some ocean beach. Often they are boulders of a rock entirely different in character from that of the rocks upon which they rest. As striking features of the terrain, they have often received their own individual names, and many of them have taken a place in the folklore of their locality. The geologist simply terms them 'erratics' (Fig 8.3). The boulder clays, the stratified drifts, and the erratics had all attracted the attention of Irish geologists long before the Geological Survey of Ireland became an item in any Chancellor's budget. Such drift deposits were so striking a landscape feature that they simply commanded attention. But the attention they received was not quite the same sort of attention as that which was being bestowed upon other of Ireland's rocks.

Where the solid rocks were concerned - the granites, the slates and the limestones - it then seemed entirely sufficient to describe their character and their extent. It appeared that geologists here had only two questions to answer. First, what kind of rock was present at any given locality? Was it a granite, a greywacke, the Old Red Sandstone, the Carboniferous Limestone, or perhaps the Cretaceous Chalk? Second, over what geographical area did that particular kind of rock persist? Was it a small intrusive feature underlying no more than a few square metres, or was it a vast sedimentary sheet to be traced across the greater portion of an entire county? Even the youngest of these solid rocks possessed a high antiquity and there seemed little need for speculation as to the nature of the environmental conditions which might have prevailed at the remote period of any given rock's genesis. Plain geo-description was what was called for rather than analytical geohistory. What mattered was the simple anatomy of the earth; studies in the earth's environmental psychology were something left for the future.

FIGURE 8.3. *The Cloughlowrish Stone, an erratic of Old Red Sandstone conglomerate lying to the northwest of Stradbally in County Waterford (X335995). The sketch was made by Du Noyer about 1850 and it originally featured in the memoir to one-inch sheets 167 (Carrick-on-Suir) etc. Du Noyer considered this to be perhaps the largest erratic in Ireland. The Stone is still there (1994) although now somewhat obscured by tree-growth.*

But the boulder clays, the stratified drift, and the erratics were entirely another matter. They were clearly very recent additions to the Irish scene and yet they seemed to betoken environmental conditions utterly different from those prevailing today. Under what circumstances had the rubbly boulder clay originated? The stratified drifts had apparently formed in water, but what water? Above all, what force of Nature had placed the erratics in their present positions? The drifts seemed to be the key to an understanding of some remarkable episodes in recent earth-history. The drifts seemed to be trying to tell us something. In Ireland, as elsewhere, it was students of the drifts who pioneered the study of palaeo-environments. The question 'In what sort of environment did the boulder clay form?' was soon followed by similar environmental questions relating to far older deposits such as the Ulster Interbasaltic Horizon, the Munster Sandstones, or the Leinster granites.

The officers of the Geological Survey came face to face with the problem of the Irish boulder clays in County Wexford during the Survey's very first field-season. They were soon speculating as to the nature of the environmental conditions under which such deposits had been formed. But if we are to understand the conclusions to which they were then led, we must first take a retrospective glance at the events which occurred during the twenty years before the Survey's 1845 inauguration. There was general agreement among almost all of the geologists who before 1845 had looked at the Irish boulder clays, stratified drifts and erratics. A simple palaeo-environmental explanation seemed to be to hand. Clearly, Ireland had recently been submerged beneath the waters of a transgressive sea. The deposits were all possessed of a marine origin. The boulder clay must have been formed in exposed locations where storm-waves had kept the sea-bed in a state of constant agitation. The stratified drifts had seemingly accumulated in the more tranquil waters of bays and lagoons. The erratics had evidently been transported by icebergs which floated upon the transgressive waters and gradually melted, thus releasing their bouldery cargoes to be scattered at random over the one-time sea-bed. In this manner, three important elements within Ireland's drift mantle seemed adequately to be explained in terms of the former presence of a marine environment. This was the then generally accepted Marine Submergence Theory of drift formation.

Once in place, the Marine Submergence Theory was found to be capable of explaining many another feature of the Irish landscape aside from the boulder clays, the stratified drifts, and the erratics. For example, did the scratches or striations to be seen upon many an Irish rock-surface not mark the places where debris-laden icebergs had run aground like ill-conned ships? And then there were the eskers. All over the Irish Midlands the stratified drifts form not expansive sheets of debris, but, rather, long, narrow, serpentine ridges. Where they rise out of damp bog-lands these ridges used to serve as useful routeways and that earned them their Irish designation as 'eiscir' meaning a ridge or elevation (Figs 8.4 and 8.5). Ireland is the internationally recognised type-area for such

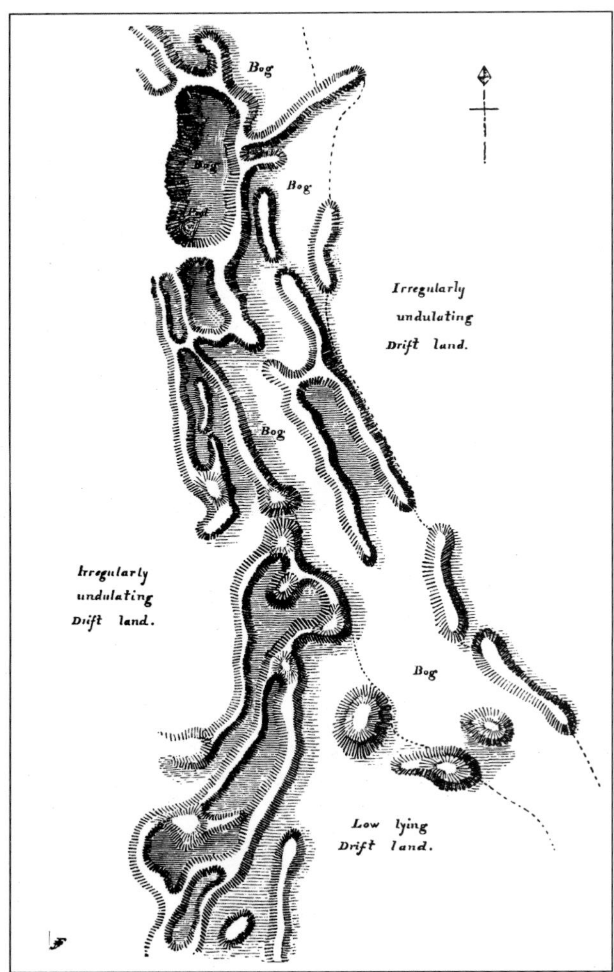

FIGURE 8.4. *A plan of eskers lying to the west of Streamstown, County Westmeath, as mapped by Foot on one-inch Sheet 99 (Mullingar). This plan was originally published in the memoir to one-inch sheets 98 (Ballymahon) etc. in 1865.*

phenomena, and today all such features are known as eskers whether they snake across the landscapes of Westmeath or those of Wisconsin. Now if Ireland had recently been largely submerged in water, then might the eskers not be sandbanks formed as tides and currents rearranged the sediments lying upon the bed of the transgressive sea? That was certainly the explanation which Bartholomew Lloyd, the Provost of Trinity College Dublin, expounded before the Geological Society of Dublin on 8 February 1832 when he delivered to the Society its first anniversary address.

For Lloyd and his contemporaries the Submergence Theory scarcely required further corroborative evidence, but such evidence was nevertheless soon to hand. In 1835, just in time for that year's Dublin meeting of the British Association for the Advancement of Science, John Scouler, of the Royal Dublin Society, announced that he had found fragments of marine shells in the boulder clays at both Bray, in County Wicklow, and Howth, in County Dublin. Every geologist knows that the fossils contained within a deposit indicate the kind of environment in which the deposit was formed. The submarine origin of the boulder clay was therefore evidently now proven. The last of the pieces in a great geohistorical jigsaw-puzzle seemed to have fallen into place. And a very nice picture the completed puzzle seemed to present. As British geologists attending the 1835 British Association meeting looked at the completed Irish picture they must have felt a sense of satisfaction. Quite independently, on the basis of evidence within their own island, they had arrived at geohistorical conclusions identical to those of their Irish colleagues. The geological choirs on either side of the Irish Sea were singing the same anthem. The great submergence was not just an Irish phenomenon; it had affected the British Isles in their entirety.

(Here a caveat whispered into my reader's ear might prove helpful. Early in Act II of Gilbert and Sullivan's opera *H.M.S. Pinafore* there is a song that opens with these lines.

> Things are seldom what they seem,
> Skim milk masquerades as cream.

As we proceed with this chapter those words must reverberate within our heads. The tale of the deciphering of the most recent stages in Ireland's geological history has really been a form of detective story. As in all good whodunnits there has to be an eventual twist in the plot. For the moment, however, the plot merely thickens.)

Now the spotlight swings to focus upon a single individual. Among those attending the 1835 British Association meeting in Dublin there was the great Swiss naturalist Louis Agassiz. Indeed, during the meeting he was one of the five distinguished scientists upon whom the University of Dublin chose to confer its degree of LL.D. *honoris causa.* But Agassiz was about to raise to Cain. He was about to administer to the newly-completed jigsaw-puzzle such a shaking that its pieces were eventually to fly asunder.

Less than a year after his attendance at the 1835 British Association meeting, Agassiz commenced a study of the Swiss glaciers. He speedily arrived at an important conclusion. The modern Swiss glaciers, he postulated, are merely the shrunken relics of former glacial giants which once thrust their snouts to points far beyond the limits of their present shrivelled descendants. But if this was true of the Swiss glaciers, then was it not also likely to be true of all the world's glaciers? Had every one of the world's modern glaciers not once been bloated to far beyond their present dimensions? That, however, was by no means the limit of his speculations. He

FIGURE 8.5. *A sketch of an esker by Du Noyer. The drawing was made from Rahugh Moat (N383320), County Westmeath, and it was originally published in 1865 in the memoir to one-inch sheets 98 (Ballymahon) etc.*

had given birth to a still more remarkable brainchild. He now believed that our entire globe had recently experienced an episode of refrigeration and that a mere geological yesterday there had existed vast glaciers in regions of the world where today such icy phenomena are entirely unknown. One evening in July 1837 Agassiz and his friend Karl Schimper invented a dramatic and emotive title for this postulated episode of refrigeration. It should be termed, they suggested, *die Eiszeit* - the Ice Age.

Agassiz wanted to test his novel hypothesis. It was comparatively simple to demonstrate that the Swiss glaciers must indeed once have extended far downstream of their present snouts, but were such glacial relics as striated pavements, roches moutonnées, and moraines to be found in regions where today there exist no glaciers? The British Isles seemed to offer ideal ground for such a testing of the validity of *die Eiszeit* . In 1840, therefore, Agassiz arrived in these islands expressly to search for phenomena which might be explained as the handiwork of former British and Irish glaciers. If such ice-fashioned relics could be found, then he proposed to use them in an attempt to convince the influential British geological community that *die Eiszeit* was no aberration of a brilliant scientific mind now gone berserk. Rather was *die Eiszeit* to be received as a cold fact of the natural order.

Agassiz opened his British campaign with a tour of Scotland and there he was brilliantly successful. He discovered his glacial relics in abundance and with those relics he sought to prise the scales from the eyes of his accompanying British geologists. Next, it was Ireland's turn and his Hibernian campaign was no less successful than had been that in Scotia. He was able to point out that some of the boulder clay along the flanks of the Dublin Mountains was really the moraine of former glaciers, and he found many another glacial relic in counties Cavan, Down, and Fermanagh. When he cleared Ireland's shores after a whirlwind tour of little more than a week's duration, he left behind him an Irish geological community which was dazed - perhaps even shocked - but it was a community where a few perceptive souls did now concede that in future it might perhaps be necessary to view the Irish landscape through a novel lens of Swiss manufacture.

With all the wisdom of hindsight, we are able to appreciate that Agassiz was entirely correct. Ireland has most certainly experienced recent glaciation. But for his contemporaries the issue was by no means so easy of resolution. Agassiz had sailed into Irish waters to loose off a remarkable broadside, but it did not follow that Irish geologists would instantly strike their colours and surrender their swords. That sort of drama might be appropriate to the quarterdeck of a seventy-four in Nelson's day, but controversy in science is a very different type of engagement.

In 1840 it seemed to many that acceptance of *die Eiszeit* was tantamount to a betrayal of the hard-won uniformitarian principle which is ensconced at the very heart of modern geology. That principle finds expression in the renowned aphorism 'the present is the key to the past'. There are no glaciers in Ireland today and to evoke former glaciers in explanation of present Irish phenomena looked dangerously like a return to those dark days when so many events in earth-history had been explained in terms of violent catastrophes. To suppose that ribbons of ice had once streamed out of the Dublin Mountains towards Rathfarnham or Tallaght was just too spicy a notion for the palate of most Irish geologists. Surely all the features which Agassiz proposed to explain in terms of his glaciers were at least as well explained in terms of the Submergence Theory. Why should Irish geological heads be drained of their accustomed salt-water only to be refilled with chill glacier ice?

FIGURE 8.6. *Thomas Oldham's 'marine bar' sweeping across the floor of Glenmalur at Baravore, County Wicklow (T066943).* (Photograph by the author.)

Every Irish geologist is familiar with the sea. Neptune is everywhere Patrick's neighbour. A marine transgression is easy to envisage. It requires nothing more than a slight readjustment in the relative levels of land and sea. On the other hand, few Irish geologists of the 1840s had ever encountered a glacier. The nearest glacier is a thousand kilometres distant. To conjure up Irish glaciers would require a major transformation of the cosmic order. Maybe Agassiz never shaved with Ockham's razor but Irish geologists most certainly did.

The arguments just presented constituted philosophical and psychological objections to the Glacial Theory but all the time there lurked in the background one other objection which was fundamental and in both senses thoroughly down to earth. That objection arose from the existence of those shelly boulder clays. In 1835 Scouler had announced their presence at Bray and Howth; by 1838 he had traced the same deposits inland across the Dublin lowland up to an altitude of 65 metres in the Dodder valley; and by the 1840s it was clear that identical shelly boulder clays were to be found plastered over the landscapes on both sides of the Irish Sea. The presence of those fragmented seashells in the boulder clays around the Irish Sea seemed to convey a clear message. The boulder clays were of marine origin. They had never possessed a glacial parent. Agassiz *was* deluded.

Now there came a shock. On 9 March 1842 Charles William Hamilton reported to the Geological Society of Dublin that he had indeed discovered what he considered to be the footprints of former Irish glaciers around the shores of Bantry Bay, in the Dingle Peninsula, and on Keeper Mountain in County Tipperary. This was startling. Here was a well known Irish geologist (he was soon to be elected President of the Geological Society of Dublin) conceding that there really was some truth in the message which Agassiz had delivered. But how much truth? What was the real nature of *die Eiszeit?* Had that episode merely witnessed the development of a few scrappy glaciers in some of the

FIGURE 8.7. *A section exposed in Oldham's 'marine bar' at Baravore, County Wicklow. The material revealed is really till forming part of one of the late-stage moraines left by the retreating onetime Glenmalur glacier.* (Photograph by the author.)

Irish uplands, or had it, as Agassiz himself claimed, been a period when powerful glaciers marched from their mountain redoubts to engulf the adjacent lowlands completely? Had the glaciers been contemporary with the marine transgression which deposited the shelly boulder clays, or were the glaciation and the submergence events of slightly differing age? For fifty years after 1840 it was questions such as these which gripped the attention of geologists not only in Ireland, but throughout the world. What was being sought was some kind of composite theory which would amalgamate the old Submergence Theory with the new Glacial Theory.

During the nineteenth-century the Geological Survey was essentially concerned with the classification, mapping, and description of Ireland's solid rocks. Various types of drift were, of course, both depicted upon the published one-inch sheets and alluded to in the memoirs, but at the official level the nineteenth-century Survey took little interest in deposits younger than those of Tertiary age. The boulder clays, the stratified drifts, the erratics, the blown sand, the alluvium and the peat were all merely so much dust atop the stratigraphical column. The Survey existed to explore Ireland's solid rocks, and if there were found seams of fuel or veins of ore, then so much the better, but a search for lodes of geohistory amidst the drifts was no part of the Survey's main agenda.

At the level of the individual Survey officer a very different situation prevailed. The debate surrounding the Glacial Theory was one of the major geological issues of the day and as they worked their way through the Irish countryside, Survey officers took the keenest interest in all the field-evidence pertinent to the icy problems under international review. Ireland proved to be wonderfully rich in such evidence, and their duties afforded Survey officers with unrivalled opportunities for the exploration of that evidence. As a result there flowed from Survey pens, and into the scientific periodicals, a multitude of papers descriptive of drift phenomena and interpretive of their geohistorical significance.

In one paper, published just a few weeks after he became the Survey's Local Director, Oldham was very sceptical about the former existence of Irish glaciers. Somebody (I wish I knew who) had been up Glenmalur in County Wicklow and close to the Baravore ford they had identified what they claimed to be the moraine of an ancient glacier (Figs 8.6 & 8.7). Oldham was suspicious of the conclusion.

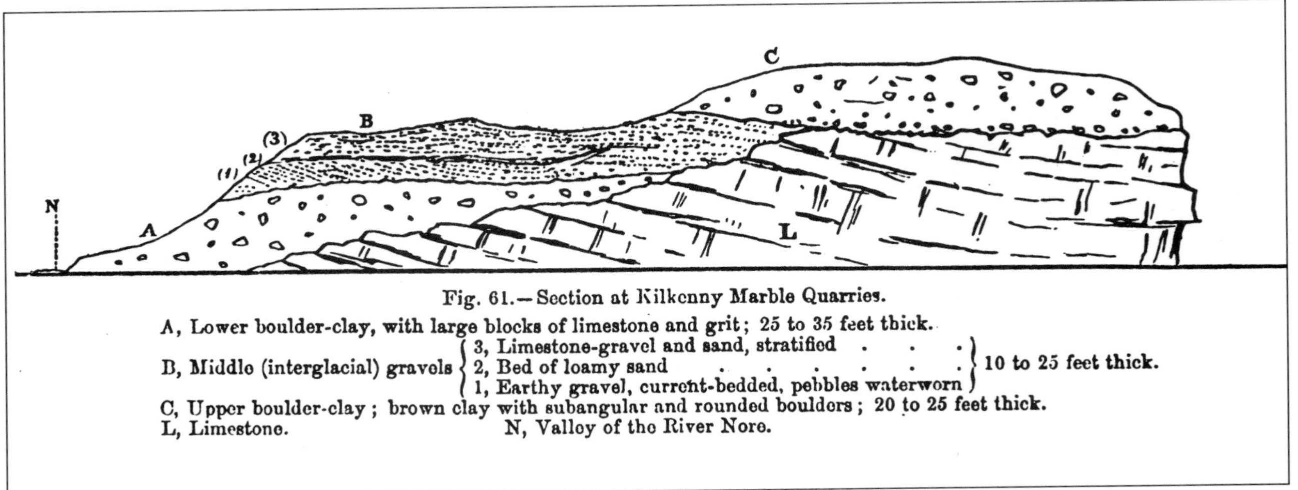

FIGURE 8.8. *Edward Hull's 'type section' for the Irish Pleistocene deposits: the section at Kilkenny Marble Quarries. Reproduced from Figure 61 in the second edition (1877) of James Geikie's* The Great Ice Age. *Hull featured the section again in the first (1878) edition of his own book* The Physical Geology & Geography of Ireland.

During 1844 and 1845 he had made a careful study of the shelly boulder clay over a wide area on the east coast of Ireland from Drogheda southward to Bray Head. He was satisfied that the shelly beds were all a result of recent submergence, so what was this about a former glacier in Glenmalur? He went down to Baravore to examine the evidence for himself and on 10 June 1846 he reported back to the Geological Society of Dublin. He was entirely satisfied that the supposed moraine was nothing more than a marine bar formed when the recent transgression converted the glen into being a long arm of the sea. Today any undergraduate student of geology would be expected instantly to recognise both the morainic character of the feature at Baravore and the presence locally of many another landform testifying to the former presence of a Glenmalur glacier. But, experienced field-geologist though he was, Oldham in 1846 could see no evidence of glacial action anywhere in the vicinity. His eyes were not yet adjusted to the illumination which Agassiz had made available.

As the years passed, other Survey officers did become adjusted to the new illumination. They began to recognise that the Irish landscape abounds with the relics of former glaciers. In one sense, however, Oldham's little paper of 1846 might be regarded as an exemplar which was followed by all other nineteenth-century officers of the Irish Survey. When they wrote on the subject of the Irish drifts they all emphasised the significance of a postulated marine transgression. Indeed, during the second half of the reign of Queen Victoria the entire United Kingdom contained no more fervent an exponent of the Submergence Theory than the gentleman who was the Director of the Irish Survey between 1869 and 1890.

Edward Hull was no genius. As we have seen, he was addicted to the devising of naively simplistic solutions to the most complex of geological problems. Perhaps he had some good points, but I do confess that he will ever recall to my mind that line of Pope's:

> For fools rush in where angels fear to tread.

During the 1860s, while he was an officer of the Geological Survey of England and Wales, Hull had studied the drifts in south Lancashire. There he claimed to see evidence of three consecutive Pleistocene events: first, a massive ice-sheet glaciation; second, a glacial or interglacial submergence; and third, a smaller-scale local glaciation. This supposed discovery shaped all his future thinking on the subject of the drifts. When he returned to Ireland in 1869 he began to search for a similar tripartite sequence within the Irish drifts. His was the kind of mind which finds that which it believes must exist; he might have found his motto in St Matthew's gospel, chapter 7, verse 7:

> Seek and ye shall find.

Certainly his search amidst the Irish drifts was soon rewarded. What he saw convinced him that his lesson learned beneath the emblem of the red rose was fully applicable beneath the emblem of the shamrock.

At the base of the Irish drift succession, resting upon glacially polished and striated rock-surfaces, Hull claimed to find a Lower Boulder Clay of stiff texture and dark, perhaps bluish hue. This deposit, he asserted, dated from the ice-sheet phase in Ireland's Pleistocene history. Next, in the middle of the succession, there came the laminated Middle Sands and Gravels containing marine shells and formed during the deep Glacial or Interglacial submergence which had left only Ireland's highest mountain peaks emergent. Finally, the youngest member of the succession was a reddish Upper Boulder Clay brought into being during a district glaciation taking place in upland regions as Ireland rose slowly from the glacial sea. Some of this boulder clay was of subaerial origin, but the greater part was a submarine deposit formed as debris was released from melting icebergs. By the same mechanism, all the Irish erratics were ice-rafted to their present stations. The Upper Boulder Clay was supposed to be very patchy in its modern extent. This was because the clay had still been plastic as it emerged from the sea and it fell a ready prey to marine erosion as it passed through the zone of wave action. Most of the resultant debris was moved over the seabed by currents which there shaped the debris into the shoals now familiar to us as the Irish eskers.

This was Hull's conception of the Irish Pleistocene, and his type-section revealing of the tripartite succession was evidently located in a marble quarry close to the River Nore in County Kilkenny. That, at least, was the section which he sketched for inclusion in the second edition of James Geikie's classic *The Great Ice Age* published in 1877 (Fig 8.8). Through the pages of that influential work, through his own writings, and through the Survey's memoirs, Hull's views obtained wide currency. The notion that Ireland had experienced a deep glacial submergence eventually enjoyed a life-span in excess of sixty years. In 1910 Hull included within his autobiography, a somewhat incongruous chapter defending the Submergence Theory, and even as late as 1920, through a paper published within the august *Philosophical Transactions* of the Royal Society of London, Professor John Walter Gregory of Glasgow was still advocating a marine origin for the Irish eskers. Perhaps water loomed large in that professor's subconscious; he was destined to be drowned in the Urubamba River of Peru during 1932.

Kilroe tried to apply Hull's tripartite division of the Irish drifts to the area around Killiney during the 1901 drift survey of the Dublin region. He speedily abandoned the attempt. Today we recognise that both the Submergence Theory, and Hull's entire image of the Irish Pleistocene, amounted to nothing more than a chimera. But this needs evoke little surprise. History repeatedly shows us that even widely experienced and deeply conscientious geologists may be led to conclusions which eventually are discovered to have been fallacious. The task of the geohistorian is fraught with difficulty. To attempt a reading of the record of the rocks is to attempt the breaking of a complex cypher. As John Ruskin once observed in the light of his own geological studies:

> For the more I endeavour to read Nature patiently, the more I find she is always trying to deceive us....

We may only wonder which of the tenets of our modern geological creed will, in the fullness of time, prove to have been no more securely grounded than was Hull's chronology of the Irish Pleistocene. But now I have to impart to my plot its promised twist. The shelly boulder clays are a perfect illustration of the point which Ruskin sought to make. They had most cruelly deceived us. Ever since their discovery during the 1830s the shelly boulder clays had seemed to be crucial evidence germane to any reconstruction of Ireland's Pleistocene story. Now it was discovered that they were not quite what they appeared to be.

Here we must momentarily quit Ireland and its Geological Survey and transfer ourselves to Scotland where we meet James Croll, an officer of the Geological Survey of Scotland. In Scotland, geologists had been discovering that shelly boulder clays, identical to those in Ireland, were widespread in Caithness and elsewhere along the shores of the North Sea. In the *Geological Magazine* for May and June 1870 Croll offered a novel explanation for these shelly deposits. They were not to be read as evidence of submergence; they were a result of a former glacier having dredged a pre-existing seabed. Like some gigantic bulldozer, the glacier had gouged the shelly material off the floor of the North Sea, incorporated the debris into its own ground moraine, and then pushed the entire agglomeration out of the North Sea basin and onto the Caithness landscape. Such a bulldozing glacier could only have been a gross and brutal agent, and Croll's hypothesis thus explained the fact that in Caithness, as throughout the British Isles, the shells within the fossiliferous boulder clays were normally found in a highly fragmented state.

Gradually this ice-dredging hypothesis came to be accepted as the true explanation for all the shelly boulder clays of the British Isles. During 1894 and 1895, Sollas actually did some experiments with model glaciers - he termed them 'poissiers' - made of pitch and designed to test the ability of real glaciers to move material from a lower to a higher level. Since he wore two different hats during his Dublin years it is unclear whether these experiments were conducted in Hume Street or in Trinity College. Be that as it may, as the new ice-dredging hypothesis assumed its place within the geological creed, the old Submergence Theory gradually drained out of the geological literature.

One vigorous exponent of the ice-dredging hypothesis was the American geologist Henry Carvill Lewis, who toured Ireland in both 1885 and 1886. On the latter occasion he inspected the shelly drifts of the Dublin region in the company of Hull and the Revd Maxwell Henry Close, a most acute

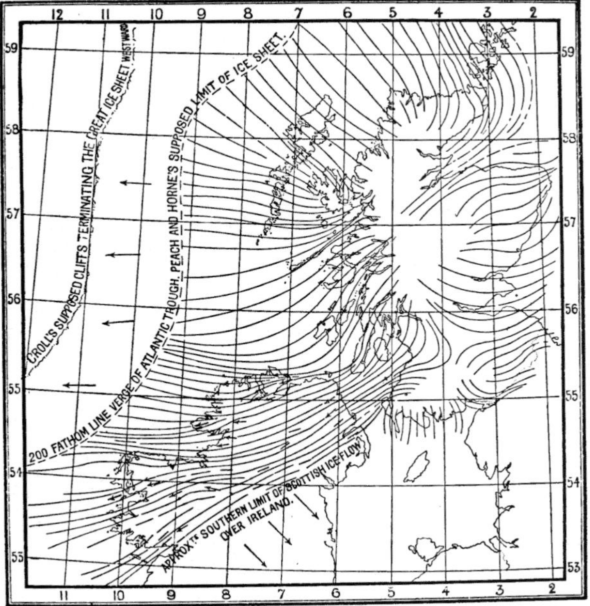

FIGURE 8.9. *The Scottish invasion. Kilroe's map of the Scottish ice flowing across northern Ireland. The directions of flow of the ice in Scotland were taken from the second edition (1887) of Archibald Geikie's* The Scenery of Scotland. *Originally published in the* Quarterly Journal of the Geological Society of London, *44(4), 1888.*

amateur observer of Irish glacial phenomena. They must have had together a most lively discussion. Lewis and Close were both satisfied that the shelly deposits expansed before them were indeed a result of ice-dredging; Hull stuck resolutely to the Submergence Theory. (Oddly, if we are to believe a report in the *Irish Naturalist* for March 1896, Close later abandoned the ice-dredging hypothesis.) It was around this time that Lewis wrote in his notebook:

> I believe this doctrine of a post-pleiocene [*sic*] great marine submergence in Britain to be the most pernicious one ever propounded in geology. For the last fifty years it has retarded the investigation of post-pleiocene phenomena all over Europe and America.

The recognition that the shelly drifts might not be what they at first seemed was a salutary reminder that any deciphering of Ireland's Pleistocene story was going to be a protracted business. Another reminder came in 1888. With the six-inch field-mapping of Ireland completed, it was decided in Hume Street to abstract all the glacial striations recorded upon the published one-inch sheets for the north of Ireland and then to re-plot the striations upon a map of Ireland at a scale of one inch to ten miles (1:633,600). The construction of this synoptic map was chiefly Kilroe's responsibility, and the pattern displayed by the completed map evoked some surprise. Without realising the fact, the Survey, over the years, had been recording in northern Ireland two sets of striations. There was one set with a broadly northward orientation and another set with a broadly westward orientation.

The striations with the northward orientation were clearly the work of an Irish ice-sheet flowing from an ice-centre in the Irish Midlands, but the striations with a westward orientation proved that at some time northern Ireland must also have been invaded by a great body of ice flowing out from Scotland and towards the Atlantic Ocean (Fig 8.9). But which ice had arrived first? Had Irish ice been forced to yield to the Scottish invader or had the Scottish invader been repelled from Ulster's shores by a sturdy development of local glaciers? Acceptance of the reality of *die Eiszeit* was beginning to reveal in its train that multitude of chronological problems which to this day continues to fascinate all students of the Irish Pleistocene.

When, in 1891, Hull published the second edition of his *Physical Geology & Geography of Ireland* he referred to Kilroe's study of the two sets of striations in northern Ireland, but otherwise his account of the Ice Age in Ireland remained much as it had been in the first edition of 1878. His conception of Irish glacial stratigraphy still involved belief in the existence of a Lower Boulder Clay, a set of Middle Sands and Gravels, and an overlying Upper Boulder Clay, and this conception he evidently carried with him into his London grave in October 1917.

About Hull's obstinate adherence to an outmoded interpretation of the field-evidence there is perhaps nothing unusual. Thomas Kuhn has observed that scientists rarely abandon an old paradigm in favour of a new. Within the scientific community paradigm shifts commonly occur only as younger scientists, equipped with a new paradigm, step into the shoes of their departing seniors. So it was in the case of Pleistocene studies within the Geological Survey of Ireland. As the older men sodden with the Submergence Theory left Hume Street - men such as Hull, Kilroe and Kinahan - their places were taken by younger men who were possessed of a deeper awareness of the remarkably complex story enshrined with Ireland's glacial drifts. Sometimes even those younger men had difficulty in locating the path towards a seeming truth. During the summer of 1893, for instance, that will-o'-the-wisp, the Marine Submergence Theory, led Sollas and Robert Lloyd Praeger into the Irish Midlands to spend a fruitless day searching for seashells amidst the gravels of an esker lying close to Port Laoise.

If some date has to be selected to mark the dawn of the modern era in the Survey's investigation of Ireland's Pleistocene legacy, then that date has to be 1 May 1901. It was then that Lamplugh arrived in Hume Street to assume control of the Irish Branch

FIGURE 8.10. *W. B. Wright (seated on the left) and some of his College contemporaries posed upon the steps of the Museum Building in Trinity College Dublin. The photograph was perhaps taken on the day of Wright's Commencements in 1900. The four men may well be that year's four Senior Moderators in Mathematics, Experimental Science, and Natural Science.* (Photograph reproduced through the kindness of Barbara, Lady Dainton.)

and to inaugurate a drift survey which initially was intended to be nationwide in its extent. In Lamplugh, Ireland had acquired a fine Pleistocene geologist. He was well seasoned in the study of drift phenomena, he had first-hand experience of present-day glaciers, and he enjoyed a good command of the international Pleistocene literature. All this is reflected in the admirable drift mapping carried out under his direction in the environs of Dublin, Belfast, Cork, and Limerick between 1901 and 1904. Each of the maps and memoirs arising from the surveys is thoroughly modern in tone. Gone is the old Marine Submergence Theory; the so-called Land-Ice Theory now reigned supreme. Lamplugh explains all the Irish shelly gravels in terms of seabed-dredging by an immense 'West British Glacier' which was once in occupation of the Irish Sea basin.

> In the Dublin district it is evident, from the direction of the striae and the character of the transported material, that the 'Ivernian' ice, flowing from W.N.W. around the northern shoulder of the Dublin Mountains, was barred from its direct course into the basin of the Irish Sea by the 'West British' ice which filled that basin; and the complex drifts of the area are the result of the overlapping of the two sheets upon the same tract at different stages of the glaciation.

Lamplugh had set Irish Pleistocene geology squarely upon the right lines.

Lamplugh was present in Ireland for only four field-seasons, but the drift surveys of Dublin, Belfast, Cork, and Limerick, important though they are, by no means constitute the sum of his contribution to Irish Pleistocene studies. He made another and more human contribution. While in Ireland his enthusiasm for all matters glacial, and his tutelage amongst the Irish drifts, inspired the Irish Survey's youngest officer with a determination to

FIGURE 8.11. *One of the many 'dry gaps' which attracted Wright's attention during the drift survey of the Dublin region in 1901: the Dingle, which cuts across a granite ridge near to Carrickmines (0215224). The plate featured in the new, 1903 memoir to one-inch Sheet 112, and is derived from a photograph taken by Robert John Welch (1859-1936), the noted photographer from Belfast.*

follow in his chief's scientific footsteps. That young officer's Pleistocene investigations were destined eventually to win for him a place among that select band of Geological Survey of Ireland officers whose names have become familiar the geological world over. That young officer was William Bourke Wright.

Wright was born in Dublin in 1876, the son of one of the city's watch and clockmakers. His father died when William was only a child, and his mother worked at home as a seamstress in order to eke out the family's meagre financial resources. He was educated at the Masonic Orphan Boys' School, his father having been a Mason, and upon leaving school William would seem to have taken some kind of employment in an effort to earn the money necessary to allow him to enter Trinity College Dublin. He was thus rather older than the average Junior Freshman when he came on the College books on 17 June 1895. Throughout his undergraduate years finance remained a problem and he went off the College books during the academic year of 1897-98, presumably in order to replenish his savings through a return to paid employment. His academic career was nonetheless one of distinction. He was elected to Scholarship in 1899, and during the following year he took first class Moderatorships with gold medals in both mathematics and natural science. In the university he studied geology under the great John Joly, who had succeeded Sollas in 1897, but, paradoxically, it seems to have been the Junior Sophister classes in astronomy which first aroused Wright's interest in terrestrial glaciers. In those classes he encountered the then highly esteemed work entitled *Climate and Time* written by the same James Croll who had advocated an ice-dredged origin for the shelly drifts of Caithness. In that book Croll sought to explain the Ice Age in terms of variations in the eccentricity of the earth's orbit and his elegant hypothesis aroused within his youthful reader a deep interest in the stately gavotte of the terrestrial ice masses.

Wright joined the Geological Survey on 12 April 1901 and that day Nolan wrote of him:

> He seems to be a nice young fellow and likely to make a good officer.

As has happened to many novice Survey officers, Wright spent his first days in Hume Street making duplicate six-inch sheets for the reference collection, but more exciting duties awaited him. The Survey had just resolved to embark upon its ambitious programme for the mapping of the Irish drifts, and within a few days of Wright's reporting to Hume Street, Lamplugh arrived to take charge of the Survey in its new enterprise. When the drift survey of the Dublin region commenced during May 1901, Wright and his colleague Seymour were

FIGURE 8.12. *The Courtmacsherry Platform at Howe's Strand, County Cork (W559429). Reproduced from the paper by Wright and Muff in the* Scientific Proceedings of the Royal Dublin Society, *10(2), 1904. The figure in the photograph is perhaps H. B. Muff. The 'stack' upon the platform by which the figure stands has now (1994) all but disappeared.*

taken out to the Howth peninsula, lying to the north of Dublin Bay, there to receive their field-training under Lamplugh himself. It was a true master class and the two young officers learned quickly. They were soon assigned their own personal ground. First, Wright mapped the drifts on Howth and around Raheny and Finglas, before moving to the south of Dublin to map the deposits in the foothills of the Dublin Mountains between Glenasmole and Stepaside (Plate V). It was in those foothills that he paid particular attention to some of the remarkable 'dry gaps' which feature upon the one-inch Dublin drift map of 1903 and which became the subject of two papers which he published arising from his first field-season as a professional geologist. Within the papers he correctly interpreted the gaps as being parts of channels excavated by glacial meltwaters which had once flowed around the mountain flanks.

Those two papers by Wright serve again to remind us of the nature of paradigm shifts within science. Back in 1878 the senior member of Hull's staff, the veteran Kinahan, had erroneously interpreted such County Wicklow features as The Scalp and the Glen of the Downs as being a result of marine erosion during the Great Submergence. Then in 1901 along comes Wright, a novice fresh from college - an impudent whipper snapper as I am sure he would have appeared in Kinahan's eyes - and he offered what today we would hold to be the true explanation for all such features. These channels are, indeed, late glacial features ripped out by meltwaters draining from an ice-sheet occupying the Irish Midlands. And why the difference between the two men? Even scientists are largely children of their age. Kinahan and Wright were born almost 50 years apart. Kinahan's nativity had placed him into the world of Daniel O'Connell; Wright belonged to the age of Eamon de Valera. Science, like politics, changes with time. Incidentally, de Valera's mathematical interests earned him election to the Royal Society of London in 1968 whereas Wright's devotion to Pleistocene geology never secured for him that coveted distinction.

Wright spent the field-season of 1902 mapping drifts with the Survey in the Belfast region, and in 1903 he went south to assist with the extension of the drift survey into the Cork region. It was there that he and his Survey colleague Herbert Brantwood Muff made a discovery which ever since

FIGURE. 8.13. *Wright and Muff's section in Courtmacsherry Bay.*
1. Raised-Beach Gravel and Blocks.
2. Blown Sand.
3. Lower Head.
4. Boulder Clay.
5. Upper Head.

has fascinated every student of the Irish Pleistocene. While examining the shores of Cork Harbour the two geologists became aware of the presence of a shelf cut across the local Devonian and Carboniferous rocks and standing a couple of metres above the level of the highest of modern tides. They found the shelf to be backed by a cliff, and resting upon the shelf they were able to identify several deposits, including boulder clay. That boulder clay was of vital significance. Its presence proved that the shelf beneath must pre-date the glaciation responsible for the deposition of the boulder clay (Fig 8.12).

This was exciting. Over almost the whole of southern Ireland there is an immense geological hiatus. There are scarcely any rocks dating from the aeon between the close of the Carboniferous and the advance of the Pleistocene glaciers. But the platform around Cork Harbour fitted somewhere into this interval. To stand upon the platform, it seemed, was to stand upon a fragment of Ireland as it had existed upon the eve of the glaciation. To stand upon the platform was to enter a geological time-machine. In their jubilation - and in their off-duty hours - Wright and Muff speedily extended their study out from Cork Harbour and along the entire south coast of Ireland from Baltimore in the west to Carnsore Point in the east. This was a distance of 240 kilometres and almost everywhere they looked they found a rock-platform and overlying deposits identical to those with which they were now so familiar inside Cork Harbour. But the following extract from a letter sent by Lamplugh to Wright on 15 April 1903 suggests that in his enthusiasm Wright had trodden upon the toes of at least one of his Survey colleagues.

> There is an unwritten etiquette on the Survey that one man shall not traverse another's ground without previous arrangement between them & much ill feeling & jealousy has sometimes arisen from breaches of this custom.

Wright and Muff announced their discovery to the British Association meeting at Southport in 1903, in the pages of both the *Geological Magazine* and the *Irish Naturalist*, in a comprehensive and beautifully illustrated paper read to the Royal Dublin Society on 16 February 1904, and, of course, in the appropriate section of the Cork drift memoir of 1905. Their drawing of a typical section across the platform is reproduced in Figure 8.13. The interpretation which they and other geologists place upon the section affords a nice example of the manner in which earth-scientists are able to build a fascinating geohistorical story out of terrestrial phenomena which the uninitiated would scarcely even notice. The geologist is somewhat like Sherlock Holmes. The geologist uses scraps of field-evidence to reconstruct geohistory just as Holmes at the Abbey Grange was able to reconstruct the events of the previous evening using nothing more than a torn bell-rope, a twisted poker, a single blood-stain, and three wine-glasses, one of them containing beeswing. The story derived from the deductions of our two Survey 'detectives' goes as follows.

The rock-platform and the cliff behind it were both cut by wave action at a time when the level of the sea was slightly higher than it is today. Since the platform has a constant height, we must assume that its present elevation is a result of the sea-level having fallen rather than the land having risen. Such a rising of land must surely have resulted in the platform becoming warped.

The blocks and pebbles resting directly upon the platform are part of a shingle-beach contemporary with the platform itself. About the shingle there is one point of particular interest. It contains a few far-travelled elements such as pebbles of Cretaceous Chalk and pieces of granite from the Mourne Mountains. Such material was probably rafted to the beach frozen within icebergs, and this proves that the shingle dates from a time when conditions in Ireland were already becoming arctic.

The sand at the rear of the beach-shingle is wind-blown but it must have become lodged in its present position after the stranding of the icebergs and after sea-level had begun to fall. Otherwise, had the sea still bathed the entire platform, then the sand must have been eroded and washed away.

The rubble overlying both the blown-sand and the raised-beach gravels consists of angular debris of local origin. It is a scree or 'head' deposit produced by the frost shattering of the old sea-cliff. The presence of such material indicates that at the time of its formation the climate was becoming increasingly rigorous.

Above the lower head is a deposit containing material which is partly of local origin and partly imported from elsewhere. The stones within the deposit are less angular than those in the head and many of them bear striations. This mass of rubble is a boulder clay proving that after the formation of the lower head the region became engulfed by glacier ice.

The final deposit is the upper head. In character it is very similar to the lower head and it indicates a second episode of frost-shattering under periglacial conditions prevailing after the glacier had departed but before the climate had ameliorated to anything like its present condition.

In Wright and Muff's day this remarkable feature of the coast of southern Ireland was known as 'the pre-glacial raised beach', but today the wave-cut bench is termed 'the Courtmacsherry Platform' after the location in County Cork where the two Survey officers found the feature to be particularly well displayed.

During the field-season of 1904 Wright joined with his colleagues in the survey of the drifts around Limerick, his own ground lying north of the Shannon in County Clare. But half way through the season he went around to say his farewells. At his own request he had been transferred to the Geological Survey of Great Britain. The reasons underlying his request are not known. Perhaps he simply wished to expand his geological horizons. Maybe he was unsettled by the knowledge that Lamplugh, his mentor, was clearly proposing to wipe Erin's mud from his boots at the earliest opportunity. Possibly, like other members of the Irish staff, Wright deplored the impending severance of the membrane linking the geological twins on either side of the Irish Sea. But whatever the reason, the move brought to Wright inestimable geological benefit.

The field-season of 1905 he spent mapping drifts in the English Midlands alongside Lamplugh who was now returned home. Then, in 1906, Wright went north to join the Geological Survey of Scotland, and for the next four field-seasons he was a member of that survey's famed West Highland Unit. On the mainland he mapped the complex geological structures of Glencoe and Glen Nevis; in the Hebrides he grappled with the cone-sheets and dyke-swarms of the Isle of Mull where his personal ground was in the vicinity of Loch Bà. Among his field-colleagues were Muff (he changed his name to Maufe in 1909), his erstwhile Cork companion, and such legendary figures as Charles Thomas Clough and Edward Battersby Bailey. Back in Edinburgh the man in charge of the Scottish survey was the famed John Horne, one of the heroic figures from the great Highland Controversy of twenty years earlier. Wright was delighted to find himself again working alongside Muff because they had become firm friends during their days together on the Belfast and Cork drift surveys. Indeed, his desire to renew their companionship may well have been one of the factors which drew him to Scotland. It was nonetheless Bailey who was Wright's geological idol. Although Bailey was Wright's junior by five years, it was to Bailey that Wright always felt a particular debt of gratitude for his example and for his unspoken lessons in the craft of the field-geologist. They worked together during the summer of 1907 as they mapped the geology of the Inner Hebridean islands of Colonsay and Oronsay.

In the West Highlands, Wright was in the presence of some of the actual features which in 1840 had convinced Agassiz that the British Isles really had been held in the grip of *die Eiszeit*. Wright's chief Survey engagement might be with the ancient Torridonian beds of some of the Inner Isles and with the Tertiary intrusives of Mull, but his Pleistocene interests remained fully alive. Around Glasgow he studied examples of those low, boulder-clay hills which are known to the geological world by their Irish title of 'drumlins'. Beyond the Highland Boundary Fault he examined glacial

FIGURE 8.14. *In noble company. Wright with the Geological Survey of Scotland. A photograph taken at that Survey's headquarters, 33 George Square, Edinburgh, by A. MacPherson during the winter of 1909-10. The personnel present, reading from left to right. Back Row: H. McVey; H. B. Maufe; D. Tait; R. G. Carruthers; E. B. Bailey; A. Macconochie. Seated Row: R. Lunn; C. T. Clough; J. Horne; L. W. Hinxman; G. W. Lee; E. M. Anderson. Front Row: M. Macgregor; W. B. Wright; B. Lightfoot.* (From an original photograph in the archives of the Geological Survey of Scotland and reproduced with that Survey's kind permission.)

landforms ranging from cirques and rock-basins to moraines and erratics. While in Colonsay he identified what he regarded as a pre-glacial platform of marine erosion now standing some 40 metres above sea-level. Facilitated by the award of a grant through the Royal Society - and by the employment of an Abney level - he was able to trace the same platform in the adjacent islands of Islay, Mull, Iona and the Treshnish group. He allowed that any correlation of this platform with other elevated wave-cut platforms elsewhere in the British Isles would be premature, but when he published on the subject in 1911 he clearly leaned towards the view that this platform in the Western Isles was contemporary with the much lower platform which he and Muff had identified in the south of Ireland. The difference in elevation between the pre-glacial platform in the south of Ireland and that in the Western Isles might, he suggested, be a result of block-faulting. It was a correlation and explanation which he later abandoned.

On a very clear day, as St Columba is reputed to have noticed, the far distant coast of County Donegal is to be seen from Oronsay. As he gazed southward from the raised beach at Eilean nan Uan did Wright dream of home? In 1907, as he and Bailey walked back from Oronsay to Colonsay across the sands exposed at low-water, did he think of his former Hume Street colleagues beginning their survey of the Interbasaltic Horizon just across the North Channel from the Oa of Islay? As he sketched the pre-glacial platform at Uragaig in Colonsay (the sketch is reproduced in his 1911 paper) did he feel a nostalgia for the similar platforms at Howe's Strand and Clonakilty? As he sat in Mull by the shores of Loch Bà musing upon the intrusive heat of Tertiary cauldron subsidence did he relish the thought of a cooling encounter with an Irish Pleistocene glacier? Perhaps. But, as we noted earlier (p.138), his daughter offers a far more prosaic explanation of the little event now about to unfold. Wright's mother was still resident in Dublin, she was ill, she was in need of care, and

Wright's elder brother, Charles Edmund Wright, was proving incapable of shouldering the burden. In 1910 arrangements were therefore made to permit Wright to leave Scotland and to return to the Geological Survey of Ireland without any loss of either seniority or pension entitlements.

Wright arrived back in Hume Street on 1 July 1910, and when Wilkinson retired in April 1914, Wright was promoted to the rank of Senior Geologist. As such he was the Irish Survey's senior full-time officer. We saw in Chapter Five that for ten years after 1910 Wright was both Cole's first lieutenant and the Survey's great dynamo. Innovative ideas flowed from him as he threw himself enthusiastically into a multitude of Survey tasks. He took charge of the project for the quarter-inch map. He devised the scheme for the development within the Survey of a diploma course for post-graduate students. He was responsible, during 1918, for the geophysical survey of the iron-ore deposit at Ballard in County Wicklow. And throughout World War I he spearheaded the Survey's involvement in the search for new coal resources at Castlecomer, in eastern County Tyrone, and at Ballycastle, County Antrim. But whatever the nature of the Survey task immediately to hand, Wright's mind continued to be fascinated by the problems encompassed within the Irish Quaternary.

He spent most of his first field-season back in Ireland - the season of 1910 - in the Pettigoe region up-grading the old one-inch field-mapping to the six-inch scale. He nonetheless found the time for a study of the drumlins lying around the head of Donegal Bay (he demonstrated them to a party from the Geologists' Association on 9 August 1912) and for some musings upon the problem presented by the presence of submerged forests in certain of the County Donegal lakes. But almost immediately a far larger assignment came his way. The memoir to one-inch Sheet 184, covering the mountainous country between the Kenmare River and the Lower Lake of Killarney, had been published in 1859 and by 1910 the stock of copies was almost exhausted. This was obviously far too important a tourist area for the memoir to be allowed to pass out of print, but some revision and expansion of the earlier work was clearly desirable. It was therefore decided that the Killarney and Kenmare region should be liberated from the established one-inch matrix and treated as a special region to be accorded its own new one-inch solid and drift sheets drawn to revised sheet-lines devised with the tourist interest in mind. The lines of the two new geological sheets were arranged so that they were almost coincident with the lines of the northern portion of the highly acclaimed one-inch topographical map of the Killarney district which the Ordnance Survey was to publish in 1913. Further, it was decided that the two new sheets would be accompanied by a fresh memoir focusing upon the region's magnificent array of Quaternary drifts and landforms. When such drift surveys had been undertaken between 1901 and 1906, the Survey had, season by season, expedited the work by throwing all its officers into the task. Now it was decided to leave the surveying of the Killarney and Kenmare region entirely to Wright alone.

The inauguration of this project meant that the Survey was according to the Killarney and Kenmare region the same style of treatment as that already accorded to the regions around Dublin, Belfast, Cork, Limerick, and Londonderry. Cole had scarcely been involved in so much as one of these earlier drift surveys, whereas Wright had been involved in all the drift campaigns save that around Londonderry. It therefore seems highly likely that the impetus for the new drift survey came from Wright rather than from Cole. Perhaps the moment was peculiarly opportune for Wright to have broached such a proposal with his Director. In 1910, following the International Geological Congress at Stockholm, Cole had joined Lamplugh and a number of other geologists on an excursion to Spitzbergen under the leadership of the eminent geochronologer Baron Gerard de Geer. The paper on the glacial features of Spitzbergen which Cole read before the Royal Irish Academy on 8 May 1911 makes it abundantly clear that matters glacial were then very much to Cole's taste. Wright, incidentally, had also been at the Stockholm conference. He had been given permission to attend in Survey time but at his own expense. He, too, had joined one of the conference excursions. He had been to Lappland.

Wright must have been a happy man when, at the opening of the 1911 field-season, he headed for the southwest to break ground for his exciting new project. He had even secured for himself a special allowance in compensation for having to use as his field-station so notoriously expensive a resort as Killarney. That allowance must have come in handy; he spent at least a part of his first Kerry field-season based upon one or other of two Killarney hotels: the New Hotel and the International Hotel. But his first field-station in the southwest seems to have been at Kenmare, where he based himself at the Lansdowne Arms which was perhaps the very hotel where Jukes had met with his accident in July 1864 (see p.67). On 6 May 1911 Wright took a day off from glacial geology in order to go to Sneem to inspect the unconformity which Hull claimed to have discovered in the Tahilla river during the autumn of 1878 (see p.84). Wright was shocked by his own discoveries. He found that on the six-inch field-sheet Hull had misplaced the critical site by a quarter of a mile, that the drawing of the site accompanying Hull's published paper bore no relationship to reality, and that Hull's unconformity was merely the delusion of a warped mind. When, that evening, Wright penned a note to Cole (he apologised to his Director for the scrawl, explaining that he was tired and lying upon a sofa) he castigated Hull, observing that he would never have got himself into such a geological mess had he possessed even 'the brains of a cat'. Wright was never a man to mince his words.

Within three months of his arrival in County Kerry, Wright received a visit from a distinguished man of science - William Morris Davis, the most renowned geomorphologist of that day. Davis had organised a pilgrimage of two months' duration around some of the most notable of the European geomorphic sites, and the first of his pilgrims forgathered in Killarney upon 1 August 1911 under the local leadership of Cole and Wright. It was Wright who introduced the party to the Gap of Dunloe - a fine example, noted Davis, of a glacial distributary pass in Sölch's classification - and it was Wright who introduced the party to many another relic of the region's glacial past. He also took them off his immediate ground, down, we may presume, the spectacular metals of the Cahersiveen railway, and over to Valencia Island so that the visitors might inspect the impressive evidence of marine erosion in Europe's frayed end around Bray Head.

Wright continued his studies in the southwest during the field-season of 1912 and he returned to Kerry to complete his work during the summer of 1913. Perhaps, during that summer, he made an excursion southward from Kenmare, across the Caha Mountains, and down to Glengarriff. Perhaps he went to look at the drumlins lying around the head of Bantry Bay, the most southerly of all Ireland's drumlins. There he may well have encountered Rear Admiral David Beatty's squadron of lean, grey battlecruisers. He may have seen them lying to anchor off Widdy Island; he may have heard the distant thunder as they exercised their main armament out beyond Bear Island. Retrospectively the image of those three-funnelled steel monsters within so idyllic a natural setting must surely have assumed the significance of an omen. War was close. In their own small way Wright's investigations in the Killarney and Kenmare region were destined to become entangled in the events which followed the climacteric of 1914.

Wright must have completed the writing of his memoir on the Killarney and Kenmare region around that day in May 1916 when three of Beatty's battlecruisers revealed their unsuspected fragility by blowing up off the Jutland Bank. Ships which had lain so impressively off Bantry were now become the coffins of three thousand sailors. Cole added his preface to the memoir at a time when even Londoners could hear the barrage on the Somme. In the news-sheets there were accounts of mountains of dead Tommies lying under the guns of the Schwaben Redoubt; accounts of the besieging of Tomies Mountain by ice streaming from its redoubt over the Kenmare River had to await the restoration of peace. And while they waited, Wright's memoir was itself caught up in violence. All the illustrations intended for the memoir were destroyed when the IRA set fire to the Dublin Custom House on 25 May 1921.

The new one-inch solid and drift maps of the Killarney and Kenmare region were both published in October 1922, when eight hundred copies of each were printed. On 12 January 1920 Wright read to the Royal Irish Academy (he had been elected a Member in 1912) a paper in which he discussed some of his conclusions about the deglaciation of the Killarney and Kenmare district, but the publication of his Survey memoir on the region was delayed until July 1927. By that date Wright was no longer resident in Ireland and, as we noted earlier (p.159), nobody in Dublin even troubled to amend the memoir to indicate that Cole, the author of the preface, had lain in his grave for the last three years. That aside, the memoir, containing 120 pages, is an admirable piece of work. It offers a superb illustration of the geologist acting in the guise of a Sherlock Holmes. Through a minute and painstaking examination of a region the skilled geologist is able to reconstruct the story of events which occurred long before there existed human eyes to see or human minds to reason. Wright measured some striations on Knocknagullion, he located an erratic close to the railway near Cleady, he mapped a series of moraines below Lough Caragh, he studied the strand-lines of a former lake in the Slaheny valley, and he examined an esker in the mud flat to the south of the Great Southern Hotel at Kenmare. From these pieces of evidence, and from innumerable other specimens of field-phenomena, he was able to offer for the first time a detailed account of the glacial and post-glacial events which have occurred in that most famed of all Ireland's scenic districts. Ever since its appearance his memoir has been the valued vade mecum of all those eager for understanding of the anatomy of the magnificent Reeks-spined country betwixt the two arteries of Roughty and Laune. Sadly, the memoir has been long out of print. Its original price was one shilling and sixpence; today a geologist anxious to acquire a copy on the second-hand market will require rather more than just a couple of coins.

Wright was associated with one other project which, in the phraseology of the day, was kiboshed by the events of the summer of 1914. In the spring of that year he and Cole hatched a plan for an international conference devoted to Irish

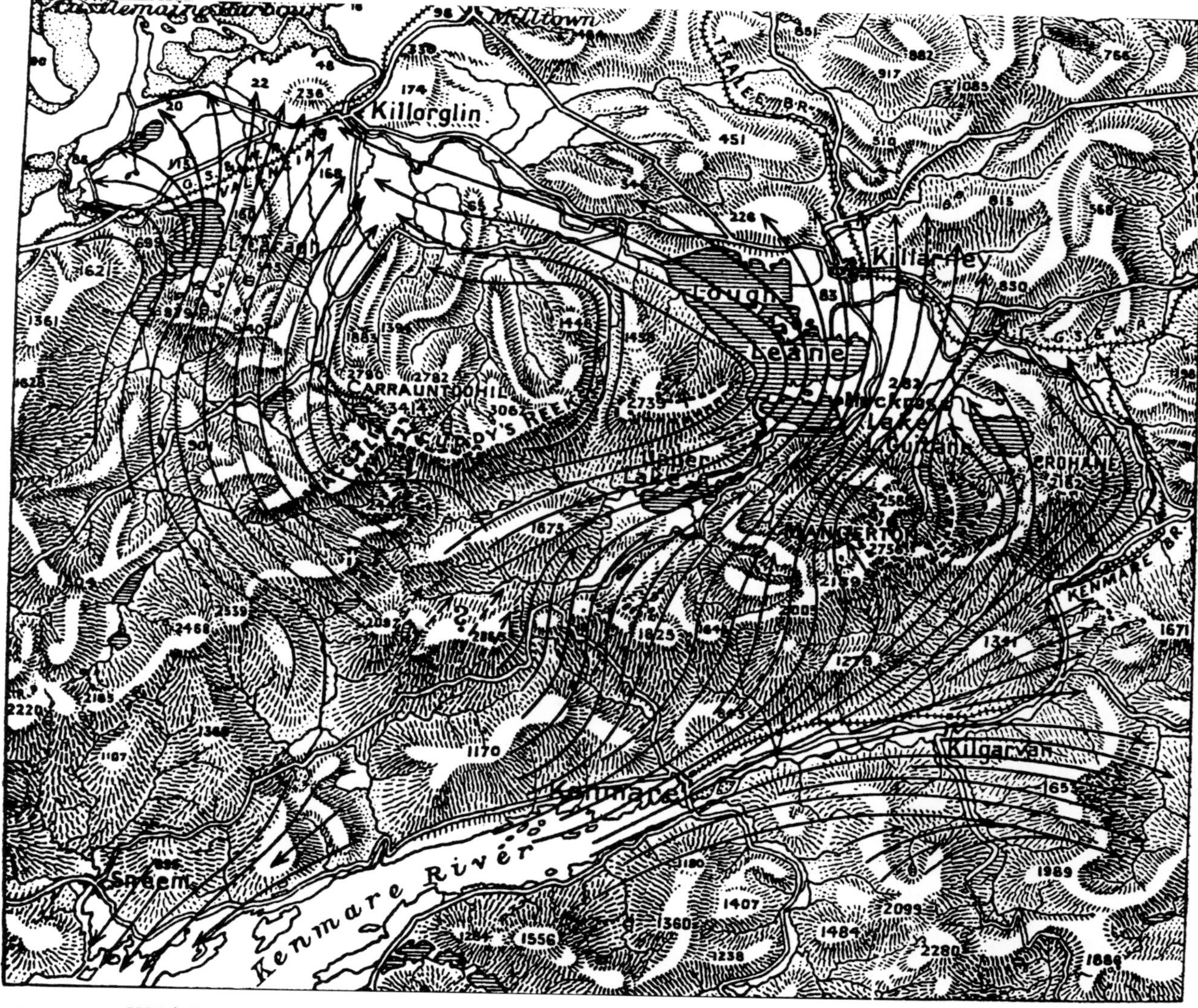

FIGURE 8.15. *Wright's map of the glacial directions of flow in the Killarney and Kenmare region based upon his field-observations between 1911 and 1913. The map featured in the memoir on the Killarney and Kenmare region published in 1927.*

Pleistocene geology and to be held in Ireland during July 1915. The conference was to be sponsored by the Survey; its Dublin venue was to be the Royal College of Science; it was hoped that up to twenty of the world's most eminent Pleistocene geologists would attend; and the members were to spend their time in the field-examination of significant sites rather than in the lecture-theatre listening to formal papers. By April 1914 W. M. Davis had already intimated his desire to attend and on 24 June 1914, just four days before the assassination of Archduke Ferdinand in Sarajevo, the proposal received the approval of the Department of Agriculture and Technical Instruction. The invitations to attend the conference should have been despatched over the ensuing weeks, but the fast-changing international situation put paid to the entire project. If the conference had taken place, its programme would have included one novel element. There was to be a visit to Deansgrange cemetery to pay homage at the grave of Maxwell Henry Close 'as a token of respect to that pioneer in glacial observation'. There was no suggestion of any similar vigil being mounted outside 5 Raglan Road, the former Dublin home of the Hull family!

But for Wright 1914 was by no means an entirely bleak year. There were two happy events. First, it was the year of his marriage in London to Mabel Crawford MacDowell, one of Cole's former students at the Royal College of Science. Soon after her marriage she was deploying her talents in the Survey interest through study of fossils from the Leinster Coalfield, a subject upon which she eventually published in the *Proceedings of the Royal Irish Academy*. Second, and of more importance in the present context, is the fact that the early summer of 1914 saw the publication of the book which won for Wright his international reputation. The publisher involved was Macmillan. The price of the volume was seventeen shillings. The weight of the

FIGURE 8.16. *The only known photograph of the interior of a Survey officer's field-quarters: the cottage at Castlecomer used by Wright while investigating the Leinster Coalfield during the summer of 1914. He had been married only a few weeks earlier, and Mrs Wright is reading a newspaper, doubtless to learn of the latest momentous events taking place upon the continent of Europe.* (Photograph by the kindness of Barbara, Lady Dainton.)

five-hundred page tome was three pounds - a weight which evoked mild complaint from the reviewer in the *Geological Magazine*. The front cover of the book was decorated with a gold-engraved mammoth. And the title of the work was *The Quaternary Ice Age*.

The volume offered its readers an invaluable and engaging conspectus of the events of the Quaternary as they were then understood. The chapters range in content from a discussion of the major types of glacier and the varieties of glacial drift, to accounts of Quaternary fauna, the glaciation of the Alps, and the Quaternary lakes of the American West. His Chapter XVIII, 'The Isostatic Theory of the Quaternary Oscillations of Sea-Level', was highly original, and his Chapter XVI, 'Raised Beaches and Submerged Forests of the British Isles', was especially esteemed by British readers.

Wright informs us that the preparation of the volume extended over many years. That we may freely accept. Almost every page of the work reveals its author as possessed of a far-ranging command of an immense international literature. Indeed, the book poses for us two mute questions. First, how did so committed a field-geologist find the time for so deep a library study of the literature? Second, on which library collection did he chiefly lean? Can he really have relied upon the Survey's own library in Hume Street? In October 1886 Hull had received a sharp rebuke from Archibald Geikie for having permitted the publication of a catalogue of that library. Not only was Geikie critical of Hull's slapdash editing of the catalogue, but he felt that the publication of a catalogue merely revealed to the world the inadequacy of the Survey's literary holding. Perhaps by Wright's day things were somewhat improved.

Wright's book represents the new age in Quaternary studies. Nothing upon its pages will induce palpitations in even the most susceptible of modern Quaternary geologists. The Marine Submergence Theory has gone and the Land Ice Theory reigns supreme. The till is recognised as the

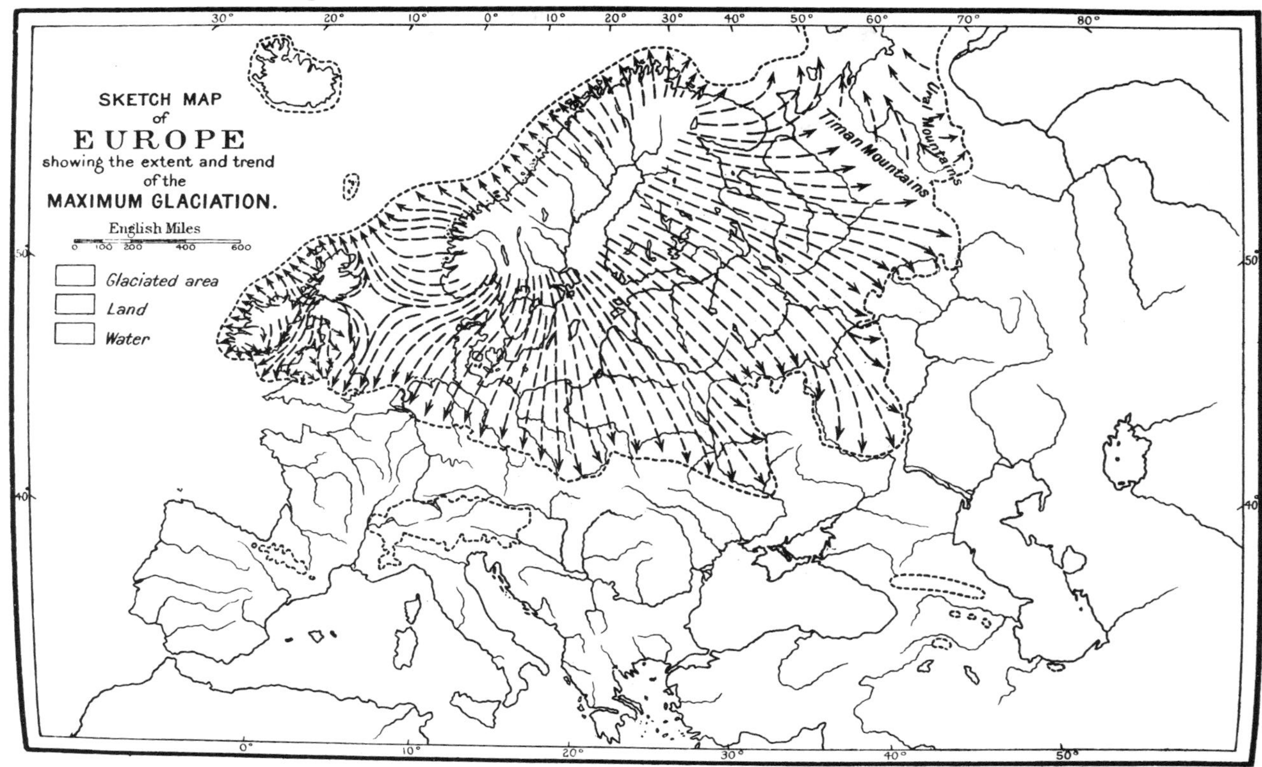

FIGURE 8.17. *Plate XIII from the first edition (1914) of Wright's* Quaternary Ice Age. *In the original the glaciated areas (Iceland, Faeroe Islands, northern Europe, Pyrenees, Alps, and Caucasian mountains) are coloured in green, while the land is yellow and the sea is blue. The map depicts the modern shorelines, but Wright fully understood that the Quaternary had seen considerable changes in the relative levels of land and sea. The volume carries the dedication 'To the memory of T.F. Jamieson of Ellon originator of the Isostatic Theory of the Quaternary oscillations of sea-level'.*

moraine of former glaciers. The shelly gravels are accepted as ice-dredged deposits. The stratified drifts are ascribed a glaciofluvial origin. The eskers are viewed as the channel deposits of former ice-confined streams. And the kames, so widespread in the Irish Midlands, are correctly interpreted as deltas built into ice-ponded lakes. In one respect only does Wright inspire a slight raising of our eyebrows. Many of his contemporaries already suspected that the Quaternary Ice Age had witnessed a complex series of events consisting of several glacial episodes separated from each other by clear interglacial periods during which more temperate conditions had prevailed. But Wright remained agnostic about most of the deposits which had been claimed as interglacial sites. He conceded that ice-fronts had been subject to periodic fluctuation. He expressed his admiration for Albrecht Penck's studies of the glacial history of the Alps. He introduced his readers to Penck's interpretation of the Alps as the scene of four glaciations named by Penck as the Günz, the Mindel, the Riss, and the Würm. The following is nonetheless Wright's considered judgement upon the subject of interglacial sites:

> We must, however, as Mr. Lamplugh has long maintained, get back to solid ground in this matter before it is possible to make any real advance. There have been altogether too many speculations and too many loose correlations from place to place in dealing with this problem. We are bound to take our stand on the comparatively simple monoglacial hypothesis until we can prove at least one interglacial period. It will then be time enough to proceed to consider further possibilities.

Lamplugh remained a convinced monoglacialist down to his death in 1926. I wonder whether, in the pages of Wright's *Quaternary Ice Age*, we are seeing the persistent influence of the man who led the novice Wright over the drifts of the Howth peninsula back in 1901.

After the completion of the Killarney and Kenmare drift survey, Wright was to have undertaken a similar survey of the Waterford region. But wartime duties intervened, and then in 1921 there came his decision to sever his link with the Irish Survey. Thirty years ago there was current in Hume Street a story that Wright became disillusioned with Ireland after finding himself caught up in some incident during the so called Anglo-Irish War. But Lady Dainton knows nothing

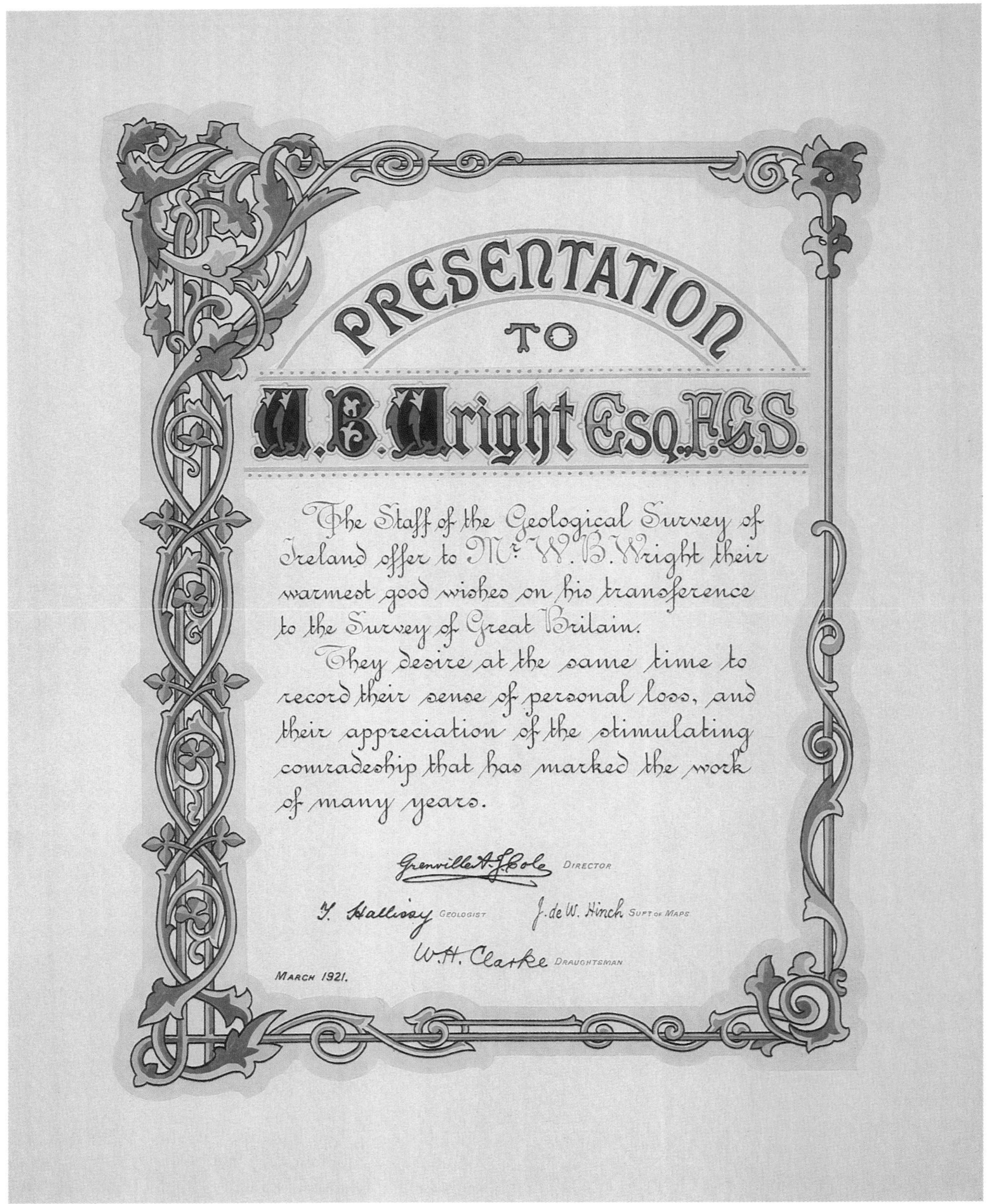

PRESENTATION TO

W. B. Wright Esq. F.G.S.

The Staff of the Geological Survey of Ireland offer to Mr W. B. Wright their warmest good wishes on his transference to the Survey of Great Britain.

They desire at the same time to record their sense of personal loss, and their appreciation of the stimulating comradeship that has marked the work of many years.

Grenville A. J. Cole DIRECTOR

T. Hallissy GEOLOGIST J. de W. Hinch SUPT OF MAPS

W. H. Clarke DRAUGHTSMAN

MARCH 1921.

PLATE X. *W. B. Wright's testimonial presented to him by his Dublin colleagues in March 1921 on the occasion of his departure to join the Geological Survey in Britain. The original is in the possession of Wright's daughter, Barbara, Lady Dainton, who has kindly allowed this reproduction. The size of the original is 42 x 34.5 centimetres.*

of her father's entanglement in any such event during The Troubles, and we are left to explain what happened simply in terms of the evidence preserved within the Survey's archives. There the story appears with stark simplicity. After some months of exploratory discussion, (Sir) John Smith Flett, the Director of the British Survey, offered Wright the post of District Geologist in charge of the Geological Survey's new regional office in Manchester. He was to have special responsibility for the South Lancashire Coalfield. Wright accepted the offer. Flett apologised to Cole for enticing away his best geologist. Cole deplored what had happened as a grievous blow to the cause of Irish geology (Plate X).

These are the simple facts, but behind Wright's decision there must surely lurk some hidden causal factor. Of itself the Manchester offer hardly looks sufficiently enticing to draw Wright away from Hume Street. There he had *de facto* responsibility for the entire Irish Survey. Cole was in poor health following his severe illness late in 1919 and Wright was the clear heir presumptive. As the Senior Geologist in Ireland, Wright already held a post equal in status of that of a District Geologist in Britain. There admittedly was a slight salary differential. As a result of a recent salary increase in Britain the scale for a District Geologist now rose to £650 per annum whereas in Ireland the Senior Geologist's salary was still only £600 per annum. Did that £50 perhaps make all the difference or had his encounter with Darrell Figgis and Sinn Féin's Commission of Inquiry into the Resources and Industries of Ireland (see p.149) convinced Wright that the Ireland then emerging was not for him? We shall probably never know. A little tailpiece has to be added to this story of Wright's departure from Ireland. Without any actual mention of Wright's name, Figgis referred to the matter in the Dáil on 16 November 1922 as evidence that the new Ireland would have to increase the salaries of its scientists if it was to retain their services.

Wright received no further promotions within the British Survey. He remained District Geologist in Cottonopolis until his retirement from the Geological Survey in 1938. He never again made any detailed Pleistocene field-studies comparable to those which he made in the Killarney and Kenmare region on the eve on World War I. But that is not to imply that he lost interest in the story enshrined within the drifts. In 1934 his *Quaternary Ice Age* passed out of print and he set about the task of preparing a second edition for publication in 1937. That second edition remained a standard text down to my own undergraduate years during the early 1950s. Wright must have worked at the revision as he sat in his office at 270 Oxford Road where the Geological Survey had its Manchester headquarters during the 1930s. Outside, university students hurried to their classes in treeless Lime Grove. Across the street the black edifice of the church of the Holy Name stood as a gaunt memorial to the local atmospheric pollution. Along Oxford Road red and cream tramcars numbered 41 and 45 rattled their way out to Platt Lane, Ashburne Hall, Fallowfield, and Didsbury. It was all a far cry from the screeching gulls wheeling above the 'pre-glacial' platform at Howe's Strand in County Cork and from the graceful green curvature of the moraines down below Kate Kearney's cottage in County Kerry.

During September 1936, Wright, accompanied by his wife and teenaged daughter, attended the Third International Quaternary Association Congress, held in Vienna. Of that occasion his daughter today carries two particular memories. First, she recollects a post-conference excursion to the Pasterze glacier on the Gross Glockner. For thirty-four years her father had been writing on the subject of the glaciers of the Pleistocene but not until that 1936 visit to the Hohe Tauern did he first make contact with an actual glacier. The modest salary of a Survey Officer - and his family responsibilities - had never allowed him to indulge in the kind of glacial excursion of which he must so often have dreamed. Second, his daughter remembers the deference with which her father was received by the assembled European geologists meeting under their Honorary President, Albrecht Penck. For the first time she became aware that her father was a man possessed of an international reputation. That reputation was grounded upon his authorship of a book which for forty years was the standard work in its field. On its title page the first edition of the volume carries beneath the author's name the simple inscription 'Of the Geological Survey of Ireland'.

Cole was entirely correct. Wright's departure for England was indeed a serious matter for Irish geology in general and for Irish Quaternary studies in particular. But that event was by no means the end of the Survey's delving of the Irish drifts. The Survey continued both to explore Ireland's superficial mantle and to decipher the story which it seemed to tell. Early in the 1920s the mapping of the superficial deposits of the Liffey basin was undertaken in connection with the proposed hydro-electricity scheme at Pollaphuca on the border between counties Kildare and Wicklow. A drift version of the relevant one-inch Sheet 120 (Naas) was far advanced before the plan for its publication, with an accompanying memoir, finally fizzled out around 1936 (see p.158). One of those involved in this mapping project was Farrington who had just joined the Survey, from University College Cork, during December 1921. While engaged in the

FIGURE 8.18. *Mittagsschläfchen. Wright while attending the Third International Quaternary Association Congress in Vienna during September 1936.* (Photograph by the kindness of Frank Mitchell.)

survey, he came close to sharing the fate of Foot and W.B. Leonard, the two Survey Officers who had died by drowning. He fell into the Ballydonnell Brook with a heavy, rock-laden rucksack upon his back and he told me that he extracted himself from the water only with the greatest of difficulty. It was nonetheless this Survey assignment among the Leinster drifts which gave to Farrington's life its particular scientific orientation. He went on to become one of the most respected students of the Irish Pleistocene, but his outstanding reputation in this field was achieved after he left the Survey in 1928 to become the Resident Secretary at the Royal Irish Academy.

Another Survey officer who followed in Wright's footsteps was Mike O'Meara. Born near Roscrea, the son of a farmer, O'Meara graduated from University College Dublin and then worked as a county council engineer before joining the Survey in 1935. Here he eventually became Assistant Director, but the bibliographer will search largely in vain for geological publications bearing Mike's name. He was a shy and self-effacing individual with no ambition to see himself emblazoned in print. Over the years he nonetheless attained a deep personal knowledge of Ireland's Quaternary deposits and that knowledge was made freely available to anybody who was able to overcome Mike's initial reticence. In his later years, Mike came to enjoy a close scientific relationship with a Survey colleague who mirrored his own interest in the Irish Quaternary. That colleague now becomes the final

FIGURE 8.19. *The International Geographical Union party at Muckross, 19 July 1964. Francis Synge is seated on the extreme left. The party was just about to depart for Dublin at the conclusion of the excursion, and hence the unexpected sartorial elegance. Our splendid C.I.E. driver, a great character named Con Murphy, stands eighth from the left. In front of Con sits Tony Orme, and the author is seated next to Francis.*

Survey officer to receive mention in the present chapter. He was Francis Millington Synge.

Francis was a grandnephew of the playwright John Millington Synge and a relation by marriage of Tony Farrington. The careers followed by Wright and Synge display strange similarities. They were both graduates in science from the University of Dublin. They both in later years returned to their *alma mater* to receive the degree of Sc.D., although in neither case was the degree conferred *honoris causa*. They both resigned from the Survey and then they both decided to return to Hume Street after an absence of six years. They both held posts outside Ireland in England and Scotland. They both married ladies possessed of strong geographical interests. They both found Pleistocene shorelines to be especially fascinating. They both achieved international acclaim, with their reputation standing particularly high in Scandinavia. And, sadly, they both died within only a few months of retiring from their respective Geological Survey posts.

Francis was a remarkable personality. Legion are the stories told of him reflecting his single-minded devotion to Quaternary geology. Like Sir Richard Griffith, that 'Father of Irish Geology', Francis would often travel by night in order to avoid the loss of a day in the field. I well remember his delight at the discovery that if he spent a vacation in Iceland he would be able to leave Hume Street at 17.00 on a Friday, fly to Glasgow and thence to Reykjavik, so as to be at work in a real glacial environment soon after breakfast on the Saturday morning. Sometimes he would travel from Dublin to the west of Ireland via Belfast so that he might spend the small-hours discussing some abstruse problem of Pleistocene chronology with a Northern geologist. For Francis, days in the field were rarely punctuated by leisurely alfresco luncheons; if sustenance was called for, then a hunk of cheese devoured while examining a gravel-pit was quite sufficient. A tale is told of his driving his car down on to a beach so that after nightfall he might continue to work a coastal section by the illumination of his car's headlamps. The raconteur's final detail that Francis returned from the Pleistocene to the present only as the headlamps disappeared beneath the waters of a flood-tide is, I suspect, merely an apocryphal embellishment.

Francis first joined the Survey in 1957 but he resigned in 1963, disillusioned because of the Survey's failure to achieve any programme for the publication of maps and memoirs. The next six years he spent in academic posts in Belfast, Leicester, and Aberdeen, but following the revivification of the Survey under Dr Williams, Francis in 1969 returned to Dublin to take charge of the Survey's new Quaternary Division. Over the decades Francis explored the drifts in many a corner of Ireland, either on behalf of the Survey or as a task arising from his personal research programme. As a graduate student he devised a clever interpretation of the glacial deposits around Trim in County Meath. As an academic in Belfast he painstakingly surveyed the post-glacial shorelines of northern County Donegal in the company of his colleague, Nicholas Stephens. As a Survey officer he experimented with one-inch drift mapping in County Mayo and he spent several years mapping the drifts of County Limerick in order to provide a geological basis for a study of the county's soils. This drift map of the county was published by the National Soil Survey of Ireland in 1966 at a scale of half an inch to the mile (1:126,720).

Francis died as recently as 1 October 1983 and it would be neither timely nor appropriate to attempt here an assessment of the immense contribution which he made to our understanding of Quaternary events both in Ireland and overseas. Instead I will conclude this chapter with a simple personal story, which, in a tenuous way, serves to link Francis Synge to W.B. Wright, the greatest of his Survey predecessors.

In July 1964 the International Geographical Congress convened in London, and associated field-excursions were arranged throughout these islands. It fell to Francis, Tony Orme of University College Dublin, and myself to lead a party of geomorphologists through Leinster and Munster on an excursion entitled 'The Physique of the south of Ireland'. Much of the 16th July we spent working from a base in Kinsale and examining Wright and Muff's 'pre-glacial' platform on a day of glorious sunshine. The next day we had to shift our base from Kinsale to Muckross, which lies in the heart of Wright's Killarney and Kenmare region. On the first leg of the journey, from Kinsale to Cork City, I told Francis of a little incident which had occurred to me during the previous summer. In a Cork secondhand-bookshop, located upon the very banks of the Lee, I had purchased a mint copy of the first edition of Wright's *Quaternary Ice Age*. It was in such pristine condition that it still retained an immaculate dust-wrapper, and the volume gave every appearance of having emerged from some publisher's warehouse rather than from the library of some deceased geologist. An expression of pained concern spread over Francis's face. He explained to me that he desperately wanted a copy of Wright's first edition to call his own. The next pause upon our excursion was to be at Gouganebarra Lake, but there was no moving on from Cork until Francis had visited my bookshop to see if a second copy of Wright might be sitting somewhere upon the shelves. Sadly, my little tale is devoid of joyous ending. As our coach rolled into Muckross that evening, over the moraines mapped by Wright on the eve of World War I, Francis was still without his personal copy of Wright's masterpiece.

CHAPTER NINE

THE MYSTERY AT CAPPOQUIN

> We have now to mention one of the most curious features in the physical geography of the south of Ireland.
>
> J. Beete Jukes in the Memoir to one-inch sheets 176 and 177, published in 1861.

The reach of the Munster Blackwater between Cappoquin and the sea at Youghal used to be hailed by Victorian guide-books as 'the Irish Rhine'. During the early 1860s a little wooden-hulled paddle-steamer - the *Daisy* - plied that section of the river on behalf of the Cork and Youghal Railway Company. I wonder. Did Joseph Beete Jukes ever tread the decks of the *Daisy*? I hope that he did because I like to picture him there one hot afternoon during the summer of 1861.

In my imagination, Jukes comes over the *Daisy's* brow, drops his hammer and knapsack upon one of her thwarts, shakes out a large Cambridge blue, white-spotted kerchief, and with it wipes the perspiration from his weather-beaten face. He moves across to the *Daisy's* gunwale and leans over to watch a shoal of fish in the shallows beneath. The engineman stokes his furnace and the safety-valve blows. Ropes are cast off. The paddles begin to churn grey water into a white froth. People wave. The repeated splash, splash, splash, from the paddle-boxes sends a pair of herons lazily skyward. The *Daisy* glides downstream past the Italianate seat of the Musgraves at Tourin and that of the de Decies rock-perched at Dromana. Jukes pulls at his pipe. He is in contemplative mood. He observes the landscape closely as the little vessel - she is but 23 metres in length - presents him with a varied succession of open vistas and hill-squeezed gorges. He is wrestling with a geological problem - a problem which literally must now engulf him were it not for the skill built into the *Daisy* by her North Shields shipwrights.

In all probability we will never know whether Jukes really did make such a journey aboard the *Daisy*. But there are two associated facts in which we may have complete confidence. First, if one afternoon the *Daisy* did convey Jukes downstream to Youghal, then that experience for the moment failed to inspire Jukes with a solution to the problem which taxed him. Second, when Jukes did finally solve his problem, his solution had such far reaching implications that it brought international fame to the waters once thrashed by the *Daisy's* Geordie paddles. As a result, over the decades, geological pilgrims have come to Cappoquin from far and wide. They have stood hard by the quay where the *Daisy* used to berth, but they have not come in remembrance of a tiny specimen of Victorian marine engineering. Rather have they come to pay their homage to a great Victorian geologist who here began the formulation of a group of concepts of the highest importance to any earth-scientist. Upon a summer's afternoon the *Daisy* must have made a pretty picture as she lay at Cappoquin, her graceful lines reflected in the waters of that tranquil river. It is Jukes's far more robust reflections upon those same waters which were to bring 'the Irish Rhine' to the attention of geologists the world over.

Cappoquin lies close to the centre of one-inch Sheet 177 (Lismore). The geology of the sheet was mapped by Andrew Wyley before he resigned from the Survey in January 1855 upon his appointment as Government Geologist to Cape Colony. The sheet was published early in 1858 (not in October 1857 as its marginal information claims), being one of the 23 one-inch sheets issued that year. In December 1855 Murchison circulated his directive indicating that henceforth every one-inch sheet was to be accompanied by an explanatory memoir. By that date it was the Breede, rather than the Blackwater, which was holding Wyley's attention, so the preparation of a memoir to Sheet 177 became Jukes's responsibility. He was engaged upon the task during 1861 and he then may have wished to refresh his memory as to the character of the rocks and the topography around Cappoquin. Therein lies my justification for supposing Jukes that summer to have been a passenger aboard the *Daisy* for one of her runs between Cappoquin and Youghal.

It was while he was preparing the memoir to Sheet 177 that Jukes first became fully alive to the intriguing mystery which at Cappoquin stares us in the face. That mystery concerns the River Blackwater itself, and underpinning the mystery there lies one simple fact of physical geography: structurally much of Munster is rather like a sheet of corrugated roofing material. Long, west to east trending troughs are separated from each other by equally long, narrow ridges possessed of similar orientation. For the greater part of its length the Blackwater flows down one of those troughs in Munster's corrugated surface.

FIGURE 9.1. *A northward prospect over the valley of the River Blackwater below Cappoquin. The photograph was taken from the ridge developed upon the Watergrasshill Anticline, and it shows the river cutting through the ridge on the Dromana Forest Anticline and then flowing across the lowland developed on the Rathcormack Syncline. In the far distance are the Knockmealdown Mountains.* (Photograph by the author.)

The Blackwater originates in the uplands around Rathmore in County Kerry. From there it flows eastwards for a distance of more than one hundred kilometres, past Banteer, Mallow, Fermoy, and Lismore, until it arrives at Cappoquin. Throughout the greater part of this distance the river occupies a well defined synclinal valley where ancient Hercynian earthmovements have produced a long, narrow downfold in the local strata. Today that valley is floored by a synclinal outlier of Carboniferous rocks which the Survey's maps have for long differentiated into the Lower Limestone Shales at the base and then the Carboniferous Limestone above (see Plate XI). To the north and the south, this long west to east trending valley is overlooked - abruptly overlooked - by uplands developed upon the anticlinal belts of tough Old Red Sandstone which were arched upwards by the same Hercynian earthmovements. To the north of the synclinal valley the anticlines form the Ballyhoura and Knockmealdown Mountains, while to the south the anticlines form the Boggeragh and Nagles mountains.

At Cappoquin the Blackwater has arrived within 18 kilometres of the sea at Dungarvan. The Carboniferous-floored synclinal valley, which the river has been traversing above Cappoquin, is continued eastwards to Dungarvan without any interruption. Structurally the character of the syncline above Cappoquin is identical to the character of the syncline below Cappoquin. Both above and below Cappoquin the syncline is floored with the same relatively weak Carboniferous strata. Despite the presence of some superficial drifts atop the Carboniferous strata, the surface of the eastward extension of the valley only locally rises more than 24 metres higher than the level of the Blackwater at Cappoquin. Below Cappoquin, as above Cappoquin, the syncline is overlooked by the same brooding uplands developed in anticlinal Old Red Sandstone. It all looks so simple. At Cappoquin the fate of the Blackwater seems to be predetermined. It must surely persist in its eastward course and then empty itself into the waters of Dungarvan Harbour. Amazingly, this the river fails to do. At Cappoquin the Blackwater swings through a right-angle, heads southward for the Old Red Sandstone hills, breaks out of its synclinal valley and makes for the sea at Youghal. The Blackwater behaves like a prisoner who, after long acceptance of his confinement, suddenly decides to escape over the prison wall upon the very eve of his release. The course taken by the river from Cappoquin to Youghal is actually slightly longer than would be the far more reasonable course from Cappoquin to Dungarvan. But this is only a small point. What really leaves us bemused is the structural complexity of the river's preferred course compared with the structural simplicity of the course which the river rejects.

Between Cappoquin and Dungarvan the river would face no significant geological obstacle; between Cappoquin and Youghal the river has to cross no less than four Old Red Sandstone anticlines, each of them carrying a ridge of hills possessed of a crest-line standing at least 100 metres above the level of the Blackwater at Cappoquin. Around Cappoquin the river is traversing the Dungarvan Syncline. From there its southward course takes the river successively across the Dromana Forest Anticline, the Rathcormack Syncline, the Watergrasshill Anticline, the Clashmore Syncline, the Clashmore Anticline, the Ardmore Syncline, and the Youghal Anticline. It is a remarkable performance and it is this slicing across successive Old Red Sandstone anticlines and Carboniferous-floored synclines which gives to the river below Cappoquin that alternation of picturesque gorges and more open vistas which once earned this reach of the river its title as 'the Irish Rhine'. Surely Jukes would have seized the opportunity of joining the *Daisy* in the making of so remarkable a geological transect. Perhaps it was as the *Daisy* entered the gorge in the Dromana Forest Anticline that there dawned upon Jukes an observation which he was later to put into print: in the gorge a dam only twelve metres in height would be entirely adequate to confine the Blackwater to the Dungarvan Syncline and to send it off on its way down to the sea at Dungarvan Harbour.

The existence of a mystery at Cappoquin is manifest to anybody who stands upon the bridge in the town and from there looks down upon the right-angled bend in the Blackwater. Should that observer have in hand a map of the region, then the

FIGURE 9.2. *The gorge of the River Blackwater where it transects the sandstone ridge developed on the Dromana Forest Anticline. The Knockmealdown Mountains are in the distance to the north.* (Photograph by the author.)

FIGURE 9.3. *Looking eastwards from the bridge at Cappoquin and over the River Blackwater as it swings from an eastward direction of flow into a southward direction.* (Photograph by the author.)

nature of the mystery will be driven home with even greater force. Anyone seeking to solve the mystery has to grapple with two underlying problems. First, what processes have brought into being that broad valley which is developed upon the Carboniferous strata of the Dungarvan Syncline both above and below Cappoquin and, as a concomitant, what processes have left that valley overlooked to the north and to the south by steeply-flanked Old Red Sandstone uplands? Second, at Cappoquin why does the Blackwater turn southward to follow a difficult course to the sea at Youghal across the 'grain' of the country when it could have remained within the Dungarvan Syncline and taken a far simpler 'grain accordant' course down to the sea at Dungarvan? These two questions clearly fascinated Jukes. But to be aware of the mystery of Cappoquin was by no means the same thing as being able to solve the mystery. Very understandably Jukes was perplexed. When his combined memoir for sheets 176 and 177 was published in 1861 he offered the following understatement in confession of his bafflement.

> It is not very easy to assign an adequate cause for the formation of this deep transverse glen between Cappoquin and Youghal.

The mystery at Cappoquin involves us with that branch of the earth sciences which is concerned with an understanding of landforms - with that branch of the earth sciences today known as geomorphology. When Jukes first came to Cappoquin geologists interested in the earth's topography were explaining landforms in terms of the operation of one or another of three sets of terrestrial forces. Of these forces, one set was seen as operating inside the earth's body just as cancers or goitres develop within the human frame. The other two sets of forces were seen as external to the earth and operating upon the terrestrial skin much as the file of the chiropodist or the hands of the masseuse play upon the human epidermis. I will here parade these three sets of telluric forces in the descending order of their popularity among the British and Irish geologists of the 1850s.

The first and most frequently invoked forces were the external forces of marine erosion. As we saw in the previous chapter, during the middle decades of the nineteenth century most geologists within these islands subscribed to belief in a recent submergence of the world's land masses. It therefore seemed entirely logical to regard the continental landforms as having been shaped by the marine processes active during this submergence. Surely every square centimetre of our present land masses must have come under the influence of wave action as the lands slipped beneath the sea and as they again arose from their bath. Had our valleys not been excavated by powerful marine currents and were our inland cliffs not striking testimony to the former activity of mighty ocean waves? That was certainly the opinion of De La Beche. He explained the steep western face of the Blackstairs Mountains in County Carlow in terms of powerful Atlantic breakers once having rolled in from the west.

The second most popular set of forces was that set of forces internal to the earth - the forces of earthmovement. Many geologists interpreted the earth's topography as being a result of seismic events. Plateaux, hills, and mountains were areas where crustal blocks had been heaved upwards, broad vales were crustal sags, and gorges and ravines were actual gaping crustal fissures. Such geologists saw the earth's face as wrinkled, pimpled, swollen and chapped. Here, for example, is Murchison writing as late as October 1864.

> In common with what I hold to be the opinion of by far the greater number of practical geologists, I believe that most of the valleys in mountain-chains owe their first traces not only to fractures, but often to great and rapid convolutions, or foldings of the strata, which have left depressions where sharp synclinal lines or narrow troughs have been formed between up-raised masses of rock.

The third set of forces are again forces external to the earth - the forces of subaerial denudation. Surely rocks exposed to the elements will weather just as similarly placed monuments of human construction so patently weather. Surely fast-flowing streams will excavate their beds just as overspilling water from an ill-tended rain-butt will carve a channel across the adjacent ground. During the years around 1800 two famed Edinburgh scholars, James Hutton and John Playfair, had strenuously urged that the great majority of landforms were explicable in terms of processes no more dramatic than the every-day action of rain and rivers. The two Scotsmen reasoned that such processes - the fluvial processes - might seem to be insignificant, but they were actually capable of effecting vast transformations provided they were seen as having acted through aeons of time.

This fluvialistic interpretation of topography had found little favour among British and Irish geologists during the first half of the nineteenth century. The issue had come to focus upon that most fundamental of all landforms, the river valley. Were rivers really capable of excavating valleys? It became a geological version of the chicken and the egg debate. Which came first, the river or its valley?

If Hutton and Playfair were right, then it of course followed that valleys are the creation of their rivers rather than rivers being the creation of their valleys. But against this interpretation there had to be raised several telling objections. One of these objections was so frequently employed and with such damning effect that in 1969 I gave it its own identity by terming it the Limnological Objection, limnology being the scientific study of lakes. It is an objection which for a moment must hold our attention.

In mountainous regions such as the Alps, many of the rivers have upon their courses long, narrow lakes. Such lakes serve as natural settling-basins. Very little of the debris which the incoming river brings into the lake is carried on downstream by the departing outlet river. Now if the valley upstream of such a lake really has been excavated by its river, then it follows that the volume of sediment in the lake should be roughly equal to the volume of the valley upstream of the lake. There should be a kind of see-saw effect with upstream denudation being balanced by downstream lacustrine sedimentation. But in the overwhelming majority of cases there exists no such balance. The volume of the sediment present in the lakes is quite insignificant as compared with the volume of the valley upstream. Indeed, the point may be made even more strongly. The volume of the valley upstream of the lake is commonly vastly greater than the volume of the entire lake basin, so had the valley really been excavated by its river, it follows that there must have been produced sediment sufficient to fill the lake many times over. Yet the lakes are still there. This is the Limnological Objection. Hutton and Playfair must have been mistaken.

There we have in outline the three geomorphic theories of landscape development which Jukes carried in his intellectual baggage when first he arrived at Cappoquin. Were any of the theories able to account for the character of the terrain traversed by the Blackwater? Were any of the theories able to elucidate the mystery at Cappoquin?

Jukes believed in the reality of a recent marine transgression, but he doubted the ability of the marine erosion theory to shed light upon the behaviour of the Blackwater at Cappoquin. How could the same suite of marine processes be held responsible on the one hand for the narrow north to south gorges on the river between Cappoquin and Youghal, and on the other hand for the broad west to east valley developed on the rocks of the Dungarvan Syncline. The theory which related

FIGURE 9.4. *In the Burren of County Clare. A limestone pavement on the seaward face of the Burren Plateau to the south of Black Head.* (Photograph by the author.)

valley formation to seismic convulsions he dismissed out of hand. Murchison, the Survey's Director, might entertain such whimsies, but Jukes was far too perceptive a field-geologist to follow his chief into such absurdity. His detailed six-inch field-mapping in Ireland had satisfied Jukes that valleys were not to be regarded as stress-related ruptures. Valleys were clearly erosional in origin. But any attempt to explain the contrasted styles of valley around Cappoquin in terms of the fluvial processes must instantly run up against the insuperable obstacle represented by the Limnological Objection. To renounce Murchison's cataclysmic interpretation of valleys in favour of a fluvialistic interpretation would seem to be flying from one lunacy to another.

At Cappoquin Jukes in the summer of 1861 faced an impasse. Try, as he undoubtedly did, he could find no adequate explanation for the behaviour of the Blackwater. It was this failure which he had to confess before the readers of the memoir to sheets 176 and 177 when it was published during that year. The mystery at Cappoquin remained unsolved. And the river itself just continued its lazy progression around that tantalizing right-angled bend. Like a larger and more famed river elsewhere, the Blackwater

> He don't say nothin',
> But he must know somethin',
> He just keeps rollin',
> He keeps on rollin' along.

There now occurred two events of importance within the present context. One of these events took place in Ireland and involved Jukes himself. The other took place in Switzerland and involved Jukes's close friend Ramsay, who was then Local Director of the Survey in England and Wales.

By 1861, the Irish Survey had pushed its mapping northward into County Clare, and during the summer of that year Jukes went to Clare to inspect Foot's progress in the country depicted upon sheets 114 (Ballyvaghan), 122 (Hags Head) and 123 (Ennistimon) . These three sheets encompass the most remarkable topography to be seen anywhere in Ireland. They depict the region known as the Burren. Lying immediately southward of Galway Bay, the Burren is a plateau developed in very gently dipping Carboniferous Limestone. Its uniqueness

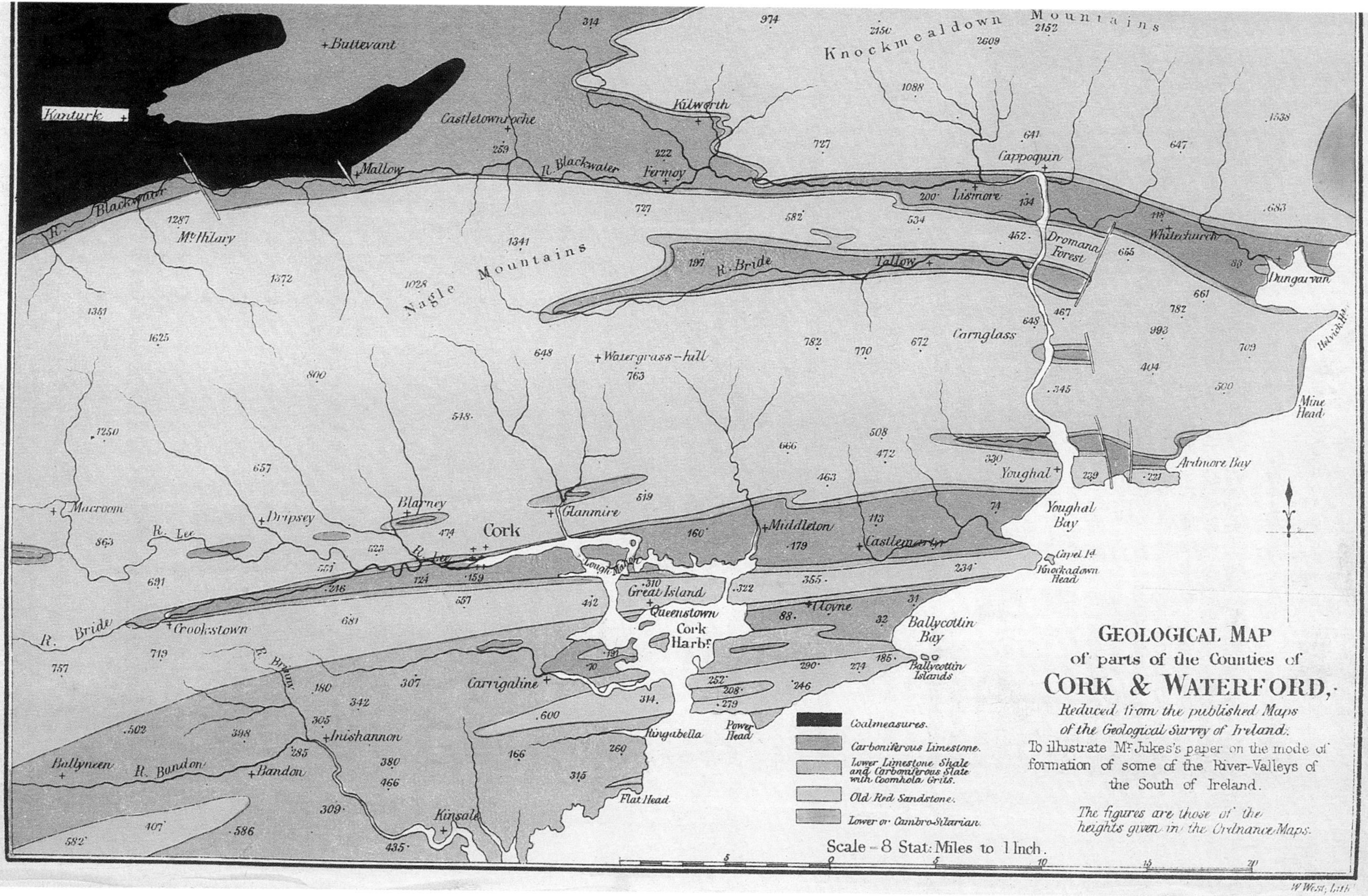

PLATE XI. *The geological map which accompanied Beete Jukes's paper on the rivers of the south of Ireland published in 1862 in the* Quarterly Journal *of the Geological Society of London. The map is here reproduced at about the same scale as the original.*

among the regions of Ireland arises from the presence of a magnificent display of what the modern geomorphologist terms karstic or glacio-karstic phenomena. It is a region of weird, grey, primaeval-looking landscapes. Here the earth's flesh has been peeled away to reveal the underlying rocky skeleton. Here Nature washes that skeleton in acid solutions. Here the earth is being trephined. Vast expanses of bare rock form limestone pavements rising tier upon tier like the steps of some Cyclopean stairway. And those pavements each constitute miniature geomorphic worlds of their own. There chemical weathering has converted the gigantic limestone treads into wildernesses of flat-topped clints separated from each other by the joint-aligned fissures of leg-breaking grykes. Strewn across the pavements are innumerable sharp-cornered residuals, the last surviving crumbs of limestone beds higher in the succession than those which are forming the clints of the modern landscape. As Foot wrote of those residuals in his memoir to the three Burren sheets:

> ...every block is obviously grooved and furrowed by the rain, and looks as if it were melting away.

Jukes was profoundly impressed by what he saw in the Burren. His mind was stimulated. The region afforded him with an object lesson in the ability of rainwater to fret and destroy the most widely distributed of all Ireland's rocks. If rainwater played so obvious a part in the shaping of the Burren, then what might rainwater have done to the limestones elsewhere in Ireland? The road to Ballyvaghan was for Jukes the first stage of the journey down the road to Damascus. As he tramped the Burren pavements with Foot at his side during the summer of 1861 he began to move towards the thoroughgoing fluvialism advocated long before by Hutton and Playfair. He was soon at work extrapolating the lessons of the Burren into the other limestone regions of Ireland and preaching his new faith with all the fervour of the recent convert. In October 1862 Jukes was the President of the Geology Section of the British Association for the Advancement of Science at its meeting in Cambridge, and in his presidential address he confessed that since the previous year's meeting in Manchester, during September 1861, he had

> ...been compelled to arrive at the conclusion that the great limestone plain of the centre of Ireland had lost a thickness of 300 or 400 feet at least, by the mere action of the rain that had fallen upon it.

His experience in the Burren had certainly given Jukes an insight into the fate which awaited the exposed Irish limestones, but that is not to say that the Burren led him to an instant understanding of the fluvial origin of river valleys. The force of the Limnological Objection remained undiminished by any of the topographical features which he there saw developed upon the Clare limestones. Indeed, the presence within the Burren of many a well developed but riverless a valley might easily have encouraged Jukes towards a belief that valleys exist quite independently of rivers. That such did not happen was a result of events well outside the Burren and far beyond Erin's shores. It was a result of the impact which the glacial landscapes of Switzerland had upon the scientific imagination of Andrew Crombie Ramsay, Jukes's friend and Survey colleague in England.

It all began with Ramsay's honeymoon spent in Switzerland during the summer of 1852. Never before had he seen landscapes comparable to those of the Alps, and he tells us that at his first glimpse of their majestic forms, 'he opened his eyes so wide that he feared they would never close again'. On 7th August, while crossing the Lake of Lucerne, he caught his first sight of a glacier as it glinted in sunlight high up on the north face of Uri-Rotstock. In his diary he noted: 'It was an event in our lives'. Thereafter he was a frequent visitor to the Alps, and gradually summer by summer, he was led to the conclusion that glaciers are among the most powerful of Nature's agents of erosion. For long it had been recognised that glaciers are capable of polishing, striating and plucking the rock surfaces over which they pass, but Ramsay was beginning to suspect that glaciers possess the potential for adding to the landscape features vastly larger than such geomorphic minutiae. In particular, he was beginning to suspect that the swollen glaciers of the Pleistocene Ice Age had in some way been capable of excavating the rock-basins which today contain the lakes ornamenting so many of our highland regions. He clearly had little idea as to exactly how the former glaciers had performed their work as basin-forming gouges, but he noted that there was far too close a correlation between regions of former glaciation and modern rock-basins for the relationship to be dismissed as mere fortuitous coincidence.

Characteristically Ramsay allowed his views to mature gradually. Not until 1859, in an essay written for the Alpine Club, did he first make public reference to his theory that many a modern lake owes its basin to glacial scour. He developed his theme more fully in a paper which he read to the Geological Society of London on 5 March 1862. It was a paper with an expansive title: 'On the glacial origin of certain lakes in Switzerland, the Black Forest, Great Britain, Sweden, North America, and elsewhere'. In the paper he argued that lake basins in a region such as the Alps are not structural features associated with synclines, nor are they areas of crustal subsidence or fissuring. Having disposed of such earlier explanations, he went on to urge his conclusion that the rock-basins of formerly glaciated regions must be ice-excavated.. They result from the ability of a glacier to scallop its bed. They are embellishments which glaciers have added to the floor of valleys, the valleys themselves being essentially of pre-glacial origin.

This was all very novel. We now know that Ramsay was correct, but many of his contemporaries dismissed his thesis as absurd. How could so weak and unstable a substance as glacier-ice ever have eroded some of the toughest rocks in the world? Ramsay certainly encountered powerful opposition. He was himself convinced that the Geological Society of London would never have published his paper had he not enjoyed a degree of privilege as the society's newly elected President. But a few geologists - some of them men of real stature - did rally to Ramsay's support. Among these men were Charles Darwin, Archibald Geikie, Edward Hull, Thomas Henry Huxley and John Tyndall. And there is one other of Ramsay's disciples who has to be mentioned - Jukes.

Jukes was evidently not present in Burlington House to hear Ramsay's paper delivered to the London society on 5 March 1862. Not until it appeared in the society's *Quarterly Journal* during August 1862 did Jukes have the opportunity of studying the paper. However, it is hardly likely that Jukes remained ignorant of Ramsay's thoughts on rock-basins until as late as August 1862. The two men were close friends and regular correspondents and, even if Jukes did not hear the paper read at Burlington House, he must surely have learned of the general gist of the paper well before the end of March 1862. Jukes must instantly have recognised that this was no ordinary, run-of-the-mill contribution to the structure of their science. Ramsay's thesis was possessed of wide ramifications.

Initially Ramsay seems not to have appreciated the full geomorphic implications of his glacial-erosion theory of rock-basins. He was perhaps standing a little too close to his beloved glaciers to escape their dazzle and to see clearly his theory in its widest context. Jukes faced no such a problem. In Dublin he was somewhat removed from the clash and thrust of the intellectual sword-play which now surrounded Ramsay's theory. From his Irish vantage point he saw what Ramsay had really achieved. If Ramsay was correct - and Jukes was convinced that he was - then it followed that Ramsay had pushed aside the Limnological Objection to fluvialism just as a glacier might push a boulder from its path. If the rock-basins which contain so many of our modern lakes are of recent glacial origin, then it follows that such basins hold no significance for the debate over fluvialism. They should never have been dragged into court to testify against fluvialism. Such basins were younger than their enclosing valleys; they were merely glacial details added to landscapes which were essentially of pre-glacial origin. The basins had not even been in existence when the valleys further upstream had been excavated. The modest amounts of sediment within the basins could not be enlisted to prove that the valleys upstream were of non-fluvial origin. The modest amounts of sediment indicated nothing more than the recent formation of the basins themselves. The Limnological Objection was dead.

Three important cards had now come into Jukes's hand. First, around 1860 he had become aware of the existence of a major geomorphic problem at Cappoquin. Second, in 1861 his experience of the Burren had convinced him of the power of Nature's weathering processes. Third, early in 1862 he perceived that Ramsay had eliminated the once formidable Limnological Objection to fluvialism.

These three cards lay upon Jukes's desk during the winter to 1861-62. As ever he was busy. He was preparing the memoir to accompany Sheet 194 (Bandon). As he studied that sheet a puzzling fact was brought home to him. The River Bandon emulates the River Blackwater. It flows eastwards along the 'grain' of Munster's Hercynian structures, but instead of persisting in its eastward course down to the sea at Cork Harbour, the river swings to the south at Inishannon and cuts across the 'grain' to enter the sea at Kinsale Harbour. He must have looked up from his map. He must have stroked his beard. He must have pondered. He must have remembered the three cards. Then, in an instant, a solution was upon him. To give employment to one of his favourite words, he had just spiflicated the mystery at Cappoquin. But he soon realised he had done much more than solve a local geomorphic problem. He had placed himself in such a vantage point that he was now able to sketch a geomorphic history of the whole of the south of Ireland. I am told that in the hands of an experienced cracksman a bent wire will serve to open many a treasure-chest. In Jukes's imaginative mind a bent river served to open the chest containing some of Nature's Irish geohistorical secrets. It was time to play his three cards as a winning hand.

On 28 April 1862 Jukes wrote to Murchison. He requested of his Director permission to present a paper to the Geological Society of London on the subject of the rivers of the south of Ireland. Approval was granted, but the first airing of Jukes's paper was in Dublin rather than in London. The members of the Geological Society of Dublin foregathered in the Museum Building of Trinity College on 14 May 1862 for one of their monthly meetings. I suspect (on no very good evidence) that the proceedings took place in what was once lecture room number 5 on the ground floor of the building on its southern side, a room which today serves us as a practical laboratory for the college's Department of Geography. The Society's President, Samuel Haughton, was certainly in the chair, and Jukes's paper was the chief item upon that evening's agenda.

At the time of the paper's presentation, the Museum Building was but five years old. Its architects were Sir Thomas Deane and Benjamin Woodward, and while the building was under construction the two men received a commission to design a structure of similar function for the University of Oxford. Today their Oxford Museum contains a plaque commemorating the fact that within one of the building's rooms there on the 30 June 1860 took place that famed encounter between Bishop Samuel Wilberforce and T.H.Huxley on the subject of organic evolution. Sadly, the Dublin building contains no such plaque commemorative of the reading of Jukes's paper. It is, perhaps, a lacuna which should be remedied. Admittedly, the Dublin occasion, unlike that in Oxford, was not the scene of high excitement with cheers, jeers and a fainting lady, but Jukes's paper is arguably the most important paper ever to have been prepared by a geologist at work in Ireland. Its only rival for that position of eminence is surely the paper on seismic shock-waves which Robert Mallet read to the Royal Irish Academy on 9 February 1846.

A week after the reading of Jukes's paper, the Council of the Geological Society of Dublin, on 21 May 1862, recommended the paper's publication. But in the event there appeared in the Society's journal nothing more than an abstract of the paper and Haughton's presidential review of the main thrust of the paper. During that year the never very affluent Society (in 1862 it had only 176 members) had to spend the unusually large sum of £70 upon publication and it was explained that the Society simply could not afford the cost of the coloured map and diagrams necessary to render Jukes's paper comprehensible. That Irish impecuniosity proved to be a blessing in disguise. Jukes took his paper over to London and on 18 June 1862 (I wonder did he note that it was the anniversary of the battle of Waterloo?), with Ramsay in the chair, he presented his paper before the Geological Society of London. The paper was accepted for publication in the London society's *Quarterly Journal,* and through the pages of that highly respected organ the paper received a far wider circulation than it would ever have achieved had it been published in the less prestigious journal emanating from Dublin.

A present-day reader of Jukes's paper could be excused for declaring it to be unexceptional. To anyone not versed in the geological literature of the mid-nineteenth century the paper might indeed appear trite and diffuse. Certainly any modern academic referee invited to assess the paper's fitness for publication would be likely to offer some fairly rigorous criticisms. But the paper must be judged by the standards of 1862 and not by those of our own day. And the opinion of his contemporaries is clear enough. They considered his paper to be startling in its originality and breathtaking in its vision.

At the core of Jukes's thesis there lay his simple appraisal of the nature of the River Blackwater. Jukes saw the river as a composite entity. It consists, he urged, of two segments of entirely different age and character. The north to south reach of the river between Cappoquin and Youghal is the surviving portion of a large and ancient southward-flowing river. That river originated long before the topography of the south of Ireland had been reduced to its present form and level, and during that reduction this venerable river has become dismembered and has all but disappeared. Of it there today remains little more than the reach between Cappoquin and the sea at Youghal. The eastward flowing reach of the river above Cappoquin, Jukes argued, is a younger, right-bank tributary of the ancient southward-flowing river. During the general lowering of the topography, this tributary developed along the west-to-east 'grain' of the country so that the branch is today far longer than the withered trunk onto which it has been grafted. For Jukes the Blackwater was a little like some ancient cathedral. The east front is the remains of a venerable Romanesque structure but the nave is nineteenth-century neo-Gothic.

Once he arrived at this appreciation of the nature of the Blackwater, the way was open for Jukes to develop a synoptic geohistory for the south of Ireland. He suggested that during Carboniferous times the entire region had lain beneath the waters of the Carboniferous sea. In that marine environment there had formed first a thick and expansive sheet of Carboniferous Limestone and then an equally thick and expansive mantle of Coal Measure strata. Jukes summarised this aspect of his thesis in the following words:

> I am, in fact, unable to escape the conviction that at the close of the Carboniferous Period one great plain of Coal-measures extended horizontally over all Ireland, with the exception perhaps of the loftier peaks of Connemara, Donegal, Down, and Wicklow, even if any parts of those mountains remained uncovered by the highest Coal-measure beds.

Next, post-Carboniferous earthmovements folded these strata into the gentle corrugations which today characterise the rocks over so much of southern Ireland. During or soon after the folding there occurred an uplift which converted the Carboniferous sea-floor into dry land, but as they emerged, the Carboniferous strata came under the influence of wave-erosion. This marine attack planed away all the ridges and valleys produced by the earthmovements and brought into being a southward-dipping plain of marine erosion bevelled across the gently folded beds. Upon this surface, as it gradually emerged from the sea, there were generated a number of rivers which flowed southwards towards the gradually receding shoreline. It was a fragment of one of these ancient rivers, Jukes believed, which survived to this day to form the southward-flowing reach of the Blackwater below Cappoquin.

Jukes conceded that Ireland had recently been drowned beneath the chilly waters of the Glacial Submergence, but he understood that event to have been an experience of brief duration. He believed that throughout the greater part of post-Carboniferous time the south of Ireland had remained dry land and that during this interval the modern Irish landscape had been shaped almost exclusively by the slow action of the fluvial processes. Atmospheric humidity had caused rocks to decay. Raindrops had made their impact. Soil had crept downslope. Rivers had rasped down their beds. Slowly the Coal Measures had been peeled away until they remained only in the few outliers which today are scattered over the surface of Ireland like the final vestiges of a winter's melting snowfall. With their protective mantle of Coal Measures gone, the underlying Carboniferous Limestone was attacked by vigorous chemical weathering, just as Jukes had sensed the Burren to be under modern chemical attack during his visit in 1861. So effective was this weathering that in places the Carboniferous strata were pierced to reveal the underlying Old Red Sandstone. Where this happened the tough Sandstone was left to form uplands while the less resistant Lower Limestone Shales and the Carboniferous Limestone weathered away to form lowlands. In this manner, Jukes suggested, there came into being the Carboniferous-floored synclinal valleys of Munster, each of them overlooked by ridges of hills and mountains developed upon anticlines in the Old Red Sandstone.

Jukes maintained that as the fluvial processes so etched out the west-to-east 'grain' of Munster, the ancient southward-flowing rivers were largely dismembered as differential denudation produced across their paths this pattern of west-to-east trending uplands and vales. The ancient rivers could no more maintain their southward direction of flow than rainwater could be expected to flow over a tin roof normal to its corrugations. Only in very special circumstances did a portion of one of the ancient rivers manage to persist in its southward progression across the developing anticlinal uplands. As differential denudation developed its variegated topography, new 'grain-accordant' rivers were born in the vales, and for Jukes the right-angled bend in the Blackwater at Cappoquin was simply the point at which the waters of an eastward-flowing 'grain-accordant' tributary entered one of the few surviving fragments of a southward-flowing river. In Jukes's estimation the Blackwater below Cappoquin was one of Ireland's oldest rivers. To embark in the *Daisy* for an excursion down river to Youghal was to follow the course of a river which was possessed of Palaeozoic ancestry.

The evidence of the Blackwater having led Jukes to formulate a geohistory for the south of Ireland, he completed his logical cycle by enlisting his new geohistorical theory in explanation of other features of the southern Irish drainage pattern. The Bandon and the Lee, he noted, belong to the same genetic class of river as the Blackwater. They are each rivers of a composite nature. The reach of the Bandon below Inishannon was literally descended from one of Ireland's ancient southward-flowing rivers, while the Bandon above Inishannon is a rather younger 'grain-accordant' tributary. Likewise, in the case of the Lee, the river consists of an ancient north-to-south reach, which has now been flooded to form Cork Harbour, and a younger west-to-east reach draining the vale developed upon the Carboniferous strata of the Cork Syncline.

Five other major rivers of the south of Ireland also attracted Jukes's attention and became incorporated into his comprehensive geohistorical explanation. Those five rivers are the Slaney, the Barrow, the Nore, the Suir, and the Shannon. He recognised that in their courses each of these five rivers displays a strange anomaly. For the greater part of their lengths they each flow sluggishly over the plains of the Irish Midlands, but in their lower reaches all five rivers move into upland regions and they reach the sea only after passing through tracts of hills and mountains developed upon some of Ireland's oldest and toughest rocks. In their own ways the five rivers all thus emulate the behaviour of the Blackwater.

The Slaney wanders over the rolling country around Tullow and then crosses the axis of the Leinster Mountains in a constricted reach between Kildavin and Bunclody. The Barrow moves slowly over the Carboniferous Limestone country around Athy, Carlow and Leighlinbridge before traversing the Leinster Granite at Graiguenamanagh in a gorge excavated between the Blackstairs Mountains and Brandon Hill. The Nore gently waters the Carboniferous Limestone plains around Kilkenny and Bennettsbridge before escaping to the sea through a picturesque valley carved through the uplands between Thomastown and New Ross. The Suir, in counties Tipperary, Kilkenny and Waterford, similarly follows a lowland developed upon the weak Carboniferous Limestone and then crosses onto much tougher Lower Palaeozoic rocks in order to join the sea in Waterford Harbour.

Of the five rivers it is the Shannon, Ireland's longest river, which displays the most dramatic anomaly. For more than 200 kilometres the river flows lethargically over the Carboniferous Limestone plain of the Midlands and in places its waters expand to form such features as Lough Ree and Lough Derg. From that latter lake it would be reasonable to expect the waters to overspill down the limestone-floored corridor which leads from Scarriff Bay, past Tuamgraney and down to salt-water near to Shannon Airport. But in reality the river disregards that course. Instead, the Shannon leaves Lough Derg at Killaloe by means of a narrow passage excavated across an inlier developed in the tough Old Red Sandstone and the scarcely less resistant Silurian slates. To the west the Slieve Bernagh massif towers 500 metres above the level of the Shannon at Killaloe and to the east the Arra Mountains similarly rise 420 metres above the level of the overspilling waters. As Jukes observed, a dam 50 or 60 metres tall at Killaloe would be entirely sufficient to divert the Shannon away from Killaloe and into some fresh outlet.

Jukes had his interpretation for the anomalous behaviour of these five rivers. All of them, he explained, were modern representatives of the ancient southward-flowing rivers. Their ancestors were initiated upon the plain of marine erosion bevelled across the Coal Measures at the time of Ireland's late-Carboniferous emergence from the sea. As the fluvial processes gradually reduced the surface of Ireland, the rivers found themselves flowing at successively lower levels and over geological structures completely different to those exposed at the time the rivers were initiated. The five rivers were thus interpreted as being possessed of much the same history as that of the reach of the Blackwater below Cappoquin. They were all like the flat-dwelling, do-it-yourself electrician who falls through his floor and finds himself dungareed in bed with the negligéed girl in the apartment beneath.

Jukes's paper possesses significance at two levels. On the one hand, it possesses a local significance as a pioneering contribution towards our understanding of the evolution of Ireland's physique. On the other hand, it possesses an international significance as a seminal contribution to that science now known to us as geomorphology.

Locally, Jukes's paper was highly innovative. Irish geology had never before seen anything like it. Jukes had found within the Irish landscape a problem such as no earlier geologist had discerned and to that problem he had offered a solution which was both profoundly imaginative and enormously stimulating. Of course, that is not to suggest that his contemporaries immediately embraced his thesis. Indeed, there was some disagreement. The disputatious G. H. Kinahan, for example, argued during the 1870s that the course of the Blackwater below Cappoquin must have been determined by the presence of a crustal fissure because he claimed that 'in Ireland, in general, the rivers are due to the valleys, not the valleys to the rivers'.

In 1878 Edward Hull suggested that the Blackwater could only have been diverted out of the Dungarvan Syncline by the presence of some physical barrier between Cappoquin and Dungarvan. The same idea was favoured by Henry Carvill Lewis, the astute American geologist who came to Ireland in 1885 and 1886 to study glacial deposits (see p.219). In his notebook for 1886 he suggested that the barrier between Cappoquin and Dungarvan might have been either a moraine or the ice of an actual glacier, and that the present course of the Blackwater must be accounted as an example of the glacial diversion of drainage. This idea was developed by James Porter of Bandon in a lecture he delivered to the Cork Naturalists' Field Club on 15 May 1902 and in a paper which he read on 15 September in the same year to Section E (Geography) of the British Association for the Advancement of Science when it assembled in Belfast. Porter confidently asserted that the north to south reaches of the Blackwater, the Lee, and the Bandon must all have been excavated by waters overspilling from ice-dammed lakes.

When the Geological Survey was mapping the drifts of the Cork region during the field-season of 1903, Lamplugh took the opportunity to check each of these alternative explanations against the field evidence presented by the drowned north to south reach of the Lee in Cork Harbour. His verdict was decisive. The idea of glacial interference could be dismissed. In all probability Jukes had been correct. The presence of Wright and Muff's 'pre-glacial' rock-platform (see p.223) around the shores of Cork Harbour seemed to afford conclusive proof that the north to south reach of the Lee had existed well before the onset of the Ice Age. That reach of the river was no child of the glacial episode. Today our deeper insight into the complexity of the Pleistocene might cause us to be slightly more cautious, but to Lamplugh it seemed clear that the north to south reach of the Lee must have been fully formed before the icebergs began to drift in from the south and before the glacial snouts nosed in from the north and the west.

From Lamplugh in 1903 down to 1975 Jukes's solution to the mystery at Cappoquin passed virtually without question. True, there were some slight modifications to Jukes's theory. It came to be accepted, for example, that the southward-flowing Irish rivers had originated not during the late Palaeozoic and upon a plain of marine erosion cut in the Coal Measures, but, rather, upon a newly emerged late-Mesozoic sedimentary surface carpeted with Cretaceous chalk. In this form Jukes's theory was for seventy years part of Irish geological orthodoxy. Among the many distinguished students of Irish geology who made their obeisance to Jukes by accepting his theory were Kilroe in 1907, Cole in 1919 and 1920, Cole and Hallissy in 1924, and John Kaye Charlesworth in 1953 and 1963. Not until 1975 was the long unchallenged reign of Jukes's theory brought to a close. In that year a rival contender for scientific favour entered the lists through the pages of *Irish Geography*. We today have available two alternative solutions to the mystery at Cappoquin.

This is not the place to discuss the details of the 1975 challenge. It suffices to say that I was then one of the pair of authors who were bold enough to attempt a toppling of Jukes's long-established theory. Whether we succeeded in our effort is , of course, for others to judge. But what I do claim is that, having grappled with the mystery at Cappoquin, I feel particularly well qualified to appreciate the highly developed powers of scientific analysis and reasoning which are revealed in Jukes's paper of 1862. Nothing which we wrote in 1975 is to be taken as in any way diminishing my regard for Jukes as one of the finest geologists of his day. When he addressed the Geological Society of Dublin on 14 May 1862 he enormously expanded our knowledge of Ireland's geohistory. The words which he spoke have ever since continued to reverberate throughout the entire Irish geological community. The walls of Trinity College's Museum Building - itself a masterpiece by Deane and Woodward - that May evening looked down on the unveiling of a truly remarkable Irish geological masterpiece.

There are many human creations which locally are declared to be shining masterpieces but which lose much of their lustre once they are transposed into a wider and international context. Not so Jukes's paper of 1862. As its context is enlarged the paper merely assumes a fresh significance. In Ireland the paper is hailed as a pioneer contribution towards our understanding of the making of the Irish landscape. Internationally the paper is acclaimed as a vital step towards the formulation of some of the fundamental truths relating to the evolution of the earth's surface.

In 1954 William David Thornbury of the Department of Geology in Indiana University published a textbook of geomorphology which was extensively used throughout the world. Within that work Chapter Two is devoted to the presentation of what the author saw as the ten fundamental concepts of basic modern geomorphology. The first four of these concepts might have been derived directly from Jukes's paper. Could Jukes in some way have been made aware of that fact, then he obviously would have glowed with satisfaction, but I suspect he hardly would have been surprised. The very first sentence of his paper reveals that he was fully alive to the broader international implications of his Irish study.

> The determination of the method by which the surface of the land has been carved out of subjacent rock into its present form is a geological problem which has not yet been solved, except in a very general way.

In a postscript to his paper he specifically suggested that the lessons which he had learned in the south of Ireland should now be brought to bear upon other specified regions of the earth's surface. He mentioned the Avon Gorge at Bristol, the incised valley of the Wye in Herefordshire, the Weald of Kent, the right-angled bend in the course of the Rhône at Martigny in Switzerland, and the valley of the upper Rhine above Lake Constance as features which should all now be re-examined through a lens of Munster manufacture.

What were these far-reaching conclusions to which Jukes had been led while involved with the mystery at Cappoquin?

First, he had come to appreciate that - as evinced in the Burren - the slow-acting, little-by-little, fluvial processes are possessed of a potential entirely adequate to account for the formation of the majority of the landforms which we see around us. There was just no need to invoke mighty seismic convulsions or the power of breakers and currents during some supposed marine submergence. The sole assumption which was necessary was the supposition that the fluvial processes must have operated through a span of time enormous in its immensity and, to employ Jukes's own words, 'vast beyond all human effort at conception'. I quote again from Jukes's paper.

> ...I think it reasonable to suppose that the mode of action in the production of river-valleys, which I have here endeavoured to establish, will ultimately be found applicable to all river-valleys in all parts of the world. Atmospheric denudation or degradation will then have to be taken into account as one of the most important geological agencies in the production of the "form of ground" on all the dry lands of the globe.

Second, he had grasped the fact that the world's topography is a result of protracted circumdenudation. The landscapes which surround us are merely a residue. Most of the mountains, hills, and plateaux of the modern world are just the lineaments which have thus far survived Nature's winnowing process.

> The present surface of the ground, where it differs from the original surface of deposition of the immediately subjacent rock, is in all cases the direct result of denudation, either atmospheric or marine, the internal

> forces of disturbance having only an indirect effect upon it, and having ceased to act long before the present surface was formed.

Third, he perceived that during the evolution of a landscape, differential denudation will etch out the character of a region's geological structure. The tougher rocks will be left to form uplands while the weaker rocks will be reduced to form linear vales or extensive lowlands.

> The denudation will of course act upon the rocks unequally, in accordance with the inequalities in their chemical composition or physical structure, and will of course produce a form of ground in accordance with these inequalities.

Finally, he recognised that in any region it may be possible to discern two classes of river. On the one hand there may be rivers which follow courses that are discordant in relation to the local geological structures. These are Jukes's 'transverse streams' or 'lateral streams' and, as we have seen, he related such rivers to ancient streams initiated upon the slopes of some pristine surface which stood well above the level of the present topography. On the other hand, there may be rivers which are concordant in relation to the local geological structures. These are Jukes's 'longitudinal streams' developed as differential denudation picked out a region's lines of geological weakness.

> I may also be allowed to ask whether it will not turn out to be a general law in all mountain-ranges in the world, that the lateral valleys are the first formed, running directly from the crests of the ranges down the steep slopes of the mountains, while the longitudinal valleys are of subsequent origin, gradually produced by atmospheric action on the softer and more easily eroded beds that strike along the chains.

In his paper Jukes admitted that many of his readers were likely to blench at some of the concepts which he was advancing.

> ...I am fully aware that it will have rather a startling effect on some persons' minds, to be called on to believe that mere rain and other atmospheric influences can have washed away a thickness of some hundreds of feet of rock from off the surface of a whole country.

His paper did most certainly stimulate a major British debate upon the subject of the landscape-shaping efficacy of the fluvial processes. Jukes's fear did prove only too securely grounded: there were indeed many geologists who refused to stomach his fluvialism. But he did win some influential converts, among them being his British Survey colleagues Ramsay and Archibald Geikie. They were both excited by the new vistas which Jukes had placed before them, and that excitement comes bubbling out of a letter which Ramsay wrote to Geikie on 15 May 1864.

> Have you brooded patiently for six months without ceasing over that passage at the end of Jukes's memoir on the Irish rivers, in which he discusses the valley of the Rhone above the Lake of Geneva? It is admirable and true and by'r lakins! he never saw the location!

Ramsay employed some of Jukes's concepts in the course of six lectures for working-men which he delivered in London's Museum of Practical Geology during January and February 1863. Those lectures became the basis for Ramsay's very successful *Physical Geology and Geography of Great Britain* (six editions between 1863 and 1894), and in the second edition of the work (1864) Ramsay took up Jukes's suggestion relating to the Weald by applying to that region all the lessons taught by the southern Irish rivers. In this manner, Jukes played his part in helping to elevate the Weald to its eventual status of being one of the world's classical geomorphic regions. A scientific circle was thus closed. Ramsay's paper on the glacial excavation of lake-basins had removed the Limnological Objection and cleared the way for Jukes's espousal of the fluvial doctrine. Now Jukes's fluvialistic interpretation of the south of Ireland was allowing Ramsay to view the English landscape with fresh eyes.

Archibald Geikie had in 1861 begun to collect material for a book devoted to the geohistory of his native Scotland. He, too , was soon looking at landscapes through the moist optics of the fluvialist. His book, entitled *The Scenery of Scotland viewed in Connexion with its Physical Geology*, was first published in 1865 (later editions in 1887 and 1901) and it is an admirable regional application of the fluvial doctrine. Geikie admitted that while developing his theme he found valuable inspiration in the writings of James Hutton, John Playfair, and Ramsay himself, but it was to Jukes that Geikie paid this very special tribute.

> Although I have long held the belief of Hutton, that our valleys are mainly the work of atmospheric waste, the history of the process of their excavation was but dimly understood by me until the appearance of the admirable paper by my colleague, Mr. J.B. Jukes on the River-Valleys of the South of Ireland.

I must mention one other early and notable convert to Jukes's theory. He is today the best remembered scientist of his age: Charles Darwin. In 1867 Darwin wrote from Down House to James Croll in Edinburgh.

> I was formerly a great believer in the power of the sea in denudation, and this was perhaps natural, as most of my geological work was done near sea-coasts and on islands. But it is a consolation to me to reflect that as soon as I read Mr. Whittaker's [sic] paper on the escarpments of England and Ramsay and Jukes' papers, I gave up in my own mind the case.

That Jukes influenced Darwin is thus beyond question, but there is another aspect of the relationship which I wish to mention. Was this relationship reciprocal? In solving the mystery at Cappoquin was Jukes influenced by Darwin?

Darwin's book *On the Origin of Species by Means of Natural Selection* was published on 24 November 1859. Jukes must have read the work soon thereafter because he discusses its message in the second edition of his own *Student's Manual of Geology* published during the spring of 1862. He was thus digesting Darwin's ideas at the identical moment as he was also in toils over the mystery at Cappoquin. In the *Origin* Darwin suggested that within the organic world a multitude of minute changes among successive members of one species might eventually result in the emergence of an organism belonging to a completely new species. Jukes in his 1862 paper was advocating a similar evolutionary view of Ireland's topography. He explained the conversion of his postulated, high-standing plain of marine erosion into the modern, low-lying Irish landscape, as being the impressive result of the summation of countless mutations, which in themselves were individually of little importance. A tiny chemical reaction occurs here, a sand-grain is washed from over there, on yonder hill-side bare earth is exposed when a gale uproots a tree and, hey presto, we eventually find ourselves with a new species of Irish terrain.

Such evolutionary thinking in geomorphology was hardly original to Jukes, but his adoption of a little-by-little fluvialism may well have been encouraged by his encounter with Darwin's concept of organic evolution. That, however, is perhaps far from being the limit of Darwin's influence upon Jukes. I suspect that there are two other respects in which we may see Darwin mirrored in Jukes's 1862 paper.

First, the full title of Darwin's work was *On the Origin of Species by Means of Natural Selection, or the Preservation of Favoured Races in the Struggle for Life.* Is this not what Jukes was likewise attempting within his own field of study? Was he not demonstrating that geomorphology displays its own version of the struggle for life? In the geomorphic struggle for life are the favoured races not tougher rocks and are they not preserved in comparison with the less favoured races represented by the weaker rocks? Did Jukes perhaps see the removal of the Coal Measures from the greater part of Ireland as equivalent to the near extinction of a biological species? Was the presence in Munster of Carboniferous vales overlooked by Old Red Sandstone uplands not a geomorphic example of what Herbert Spencer was to term 'survival of the fittest'?

Was Jukes's interpretation of the drainage system of Munster not itself the story of a struggle for dominance involving two species of river? On the one hand, there were the southward flowing transverse rivers which, with the passage of time, became increasingly ill-adapted to their environment. These rivers had formed in response to the existence of a wave-cut surface developed in the homogeneous Coal Measures. But denudation soon caused the disappearance of that surface, and as the Carboniferous strata were peeled away, the ancient rivers found themselves entirely out of harmony with a new environment which was diversified by outcrops of tough pre-Carboniferous rocks. On the other hand, there were the eastward-flowing longitudinal rivers which had developed in response to the creation of the new geological environment and which had brought about the progressive elimination of almost the entire drainage system. Was the map which accompanied Jukes's paper - the map here reproduced as Plate XI - not a truly remarkable cartographic illustration of the principle of the survival of the fittest?

Second, Chapter Thirteen of the *Origin* contains a discussion of the vestigial organs to be found in certain plants and animals. In plants with separate sexes, for instance, there are rudimentary pistils in certain male flowers, some snakes have vestigial legs, and flightless birds possess wings. Evolution has left for us a blazed trail, but Darwin observed

> ...that an organ rendered, during changed habits of life, useless or injurious for one purpose, might easily be modified and used for another purpose.

Is that not the light in which Jukes viewed the Blackwater, the Lee, and the Bandon? Were the north to south reaches of these three rivers not the vestigial relics of transverse rivers? Had those vestigial relics not now been 'modified and used for another purpose'?

It is more than thirty years since I first entered into print on the subject of Jukes's paper of 1862, but it was only yesterday (19 April 1994) that it dawned upon me that there might be a link between Darwin's *Origin* and Jukes's essay. I had been woefully slow in seeing the light. Interestingly, my moment of eureka came as I tramped the limestone pavements of the Burren where, during the summer of 1861, Jukes had first appreciated the potential of subaerial denudation. Jukes had gone to the Burren to inspect Foot's work; I was in the Burren to take the photograph which appears herein on page 242.

The fundamental principles embodied within Jukes's paper today lie at the very heart of modern geomorphology. What Jukes termed transverse rivers are now termed consequent rivers; what he termed longitudinal rivers are now termed subsequent rivers; and the sequence of events which he offered in explanation of the discordances within the southern Irish drainage is now termed drainage superimposition. The man who took these three concepts from Jukes's paper and then built them into the fabric of geomorphology was the great American geologist William Morris Davis. It was from the passage by Jukes which I have quoted on page 250 that Davis actually derived his term 'subsequent' for any river which has developed its course along some line of geological weakness. During his 1911 pilgrimage around the classic geomorphic sites of Europe, Davis, accompanied by Cole, went to pay his respects to Jukes by standing on the bridge at Cappoquin. In Dublin, the very next day, Davis prolonged his tribute by going to a library - presumably to the library in Hume Street - to read again Jukes's great paper.

This chapter opened with the *Daisy* paddling her way down the Blackwater and through the lush green landscapes of County Waterford. I close the chapter amidst landscapes of a completely different character. I close the chapter in North America in the state of Utah. There, to the south of Hanksville and to the west of the Dirty Devil River, the landscape is certainly not lush and it might appropriately be described as any colour save green. It is a desert. It is a tract of country dominated by the remote peaks of the Henry Mountains. To earth-scientists those mountains are familiar because in 1877 they were the subject of a renowned monograph written by the eminent United States geologist Grove Karl Gilbert. In that monograph Gilbert announced that he had named one of the eminences 'Jukes Butte' in honour of that geologist's contribution to our understanding of the origin of landforms.

Jukes's gravestone in St Mary's churchyard at Selly Oak, near Birmingham, was evidently carved from the local Triassic sandstone. Today the gravestone is toppled and weathered beyond identification. In that fact there is perhaps something strangely appropriate, but his memorial among the Cretaceous sandstones of the American West will prove rather more durable. There Jukes Butte will long survive to evoke memories of a brilliant Director of the Geological Survey of Ireland who in 1862 offered a solution to the mystery which he had found beneath the bridge at Cappoquin.

Postscript. On 14 July 1994 I once again found myself gazing over the parapet of the bridge at Cappoquin. Immediately below the bridge there now stands the club house of the Cappoquin Rowing Club. I noted that the house had recently been repainted. I also noted that the house now proudly bears the inscription 'Founded 1862'. What an odd coincidence!

CHAPTER TEN

CASED COLLECTIONS

All fossils, rock-specimens, and minerals collected during the progress of the Geological Survey are to be regarded as the property of the Survey.

Grenville Cole in the Geological Survey of Ireland's *Regulations,* 1 January 1914.

A laden dray belonging to one of the Irish railway companies turns down St Stephen's Green East. To vigorous shouts of 'Whoa!' it comes to rest outside the Museum of Irish Industry. The carthorse whinnies and then micturates. A black iron bit is champed between yellow equine teeth. The carter lays aside his reins and climbs down. He unloads a heavy cask. Assisted by the house-porter he carries the box down the steps into the area of number 51, through the basement door, and into the space reserved for the reception of goods consigned to the Museum. Outside, as they pushed their burden across the pavement, Augusta Jukes had held aside her crinoline so as to allow the two men space in which to manoeuvre the cask across her path. She had just descended the eleven steps from the Museum's hall-door. She had been up in her husband's office on the first floor. She went up to ask Beete for a half-sovereign because she has seen a pair of embroidered shoes at Switzer's in Grafton Street. She proposes to buy them to wear at the St Patrick's ball next Monday evening. The year is 1867.

I cannot be certain that Mrs Jukes really did buy a new pair of shoes for the St Patrick's ball of 1867, that she really did visit number 51 in search of replenishment for her purse, or that she really did patronise Switzer's emporium at the corner of Grafton Street and Wicklow Street. But the other little incidents of my vignette must actually have occurred. Indeed, there must have been many occasions upon which the sounds of an impatient dray-horse outside number 51 were matched by the sounds of human labour as heavy casks were unloaded and then carried down those basement steps. The casks contained the latest specimens collected by the officers of the Geological Survey and now sent up to Dublin for further examination or for display in the Museum. Sometimes they were perhaps minerals from Avoca assembled by Jukes himself and then consigned to the Survey via the Dublin, Wicklow and Wexford Railway through Harcourt Street station. Sometimes they were perhaps fossils from County Tipperary collected by Wynne and then despatched to the Survey over the Great Southern and Western Railway via its headquarters at Kingsbridge station. Sometimes they were perhaps samples of Connemara Marble knocked from some rain-lashed quarry-face by Kinahan's hammer and then forwarded to the Survey by way of the Midland Great Western Railway and its terminus at Broadstone station.

Howsoever they may have arrived, number 51 was soon the repository for an enormous collection of rocks, minerals, and fossils. Indeed, the volume of the geological material coming into his new Museum evidently gave some concern to Sir Robert Kane, the Museum's Director. It was on 7 October 1846 that Kane informed De La Beche of his readiness to receive the Survey into its new home in St Stephen's Green, but shortly thereafter Kane wrote to Oldham asking him to refrain from the placing of heavy specimens in the Survey's upper rooms. He evidently doubted the ability of Georgian joists to support the weight of blocks of Carboniferous Limestone.

Within the Museum the rocks were brought together as a convenient illustration of the varied types of geological material from which the Irish landscape has been compounded. There were examples of Old Red Sandstone conglomerate up from Kerry, slabs of slate brought over from Killaloe, and specimens of anthracite from Massford Old Colliery down Castlecomer way. From northern Ireland there were black basaltic columns torn from the Giant's Causeway, there were lumps of white chalk from Garron Point, and there were blocks of grey Kieselguhr from Toomebridge. And then there were the Irish granites. By peering into a few glazed cases - by sliding open a few museum drawers - it was possible to compare samples of the granites of Galway or Wicklow with those of Donegal, Mayo, or Mourne. The Survey's collection of rocks afforded a remarkable conspectus of Ireland's geology. There, in the Museum of Irish Industry, the public had access to a microcosm of Ireland's rocky skeleton. The Survey's one-inch sheets, Jukes's small-scale map of 1867, and Hull's similar map of 1878 all depicted the spatial distribution of the Irish rocks; in the Survey's section of the Museum of Irish Industry it was possible to see, to feel, and, in the case of the Kieselguhr, perhaps even to taste, actual specimens of the rocks which upon the maps appeared as nothing more substantial than

FIGURE 10.1. *Sir Robert Kane (1809-1890), author of* The Industrial Resources of Ireland *(1844), and the Director of the Museum of Irish Industry. Reproduced from T. S. Wheeler* et alia, The Natural Resources of Ireland *(Royal Dublin Society, 1944). The illustration is derived from a pastel portrait by George Francis Mulvany (1809-1869), the first Director of the National Gallery of Ireland.*

a wash of ultramarine, a band of magenta, or a splash of vermilion.

Similarly, the officers of the Survey collected good mineral specimens so that both their fellow geologists and the general public might have tangible evidence of the wide range of crystal forms to be discovered amidst Ireland's rocks. There was perhaps beryl from Boylagh, calcite from Carlow, galena from Glendalough, or sphalerite from Silvermines. But apart from their educational significance within the museum, minerals were worthy of collection and display for quite another reason. They possess a strong aesthetic appeal. Minerals are among the most beautiful of Nature's creations. From the ancient mystics of yore to the modern advocates of crystal therapy, the members of our species have commonly found a strange fascination lurking within the form of crystalline minerals. A cluster of sparkling quartz crystals or a mass of chalco-pyrite are capable of evoking human emotions of a type and intensity very different from those aroused by the sight of a piece of sandstone or the perusal of a block of granite.

The assembly of an instructive and decorative collection of Irish rocks and minerals was fundamentally a public service which the Survey rendered for the benefit of the members of their own profession and for that of the Irish public at large. Where the collection of fossils was concerned the motives of the Survey's officers were very different. The Survey's officers collected fossils because those fossils were essential to their own geological investigations. To return from the field laden with rock-samples, or carrying some choice mineral specimens, were two little luxuries in which Survey Officers indulged either in the interest of their science or for the education of the Irish people. To return to number 51 bearing a cask of carefully wrapped and located fossils was a vital part of a Survey officer's normal duties. People - a matron from Mullingar or a major of the 88th just returned from the Crimea - would doubtless be fascinated by the worm tracks in a slab of the Liscannor Flags or by the crinoids in a piece of Fermanagh limestone, but the Survey's officers were not really collecting fossils for the amusement and edification of the populace. They were collecting fossils because geology without fossils is like chess without a chess-board.

Different and distinctive plants and animals have existed at discrete moments within the history of our earth. At the time of their death some of those plants and animals became entombed within the sedimentary rocks then being formed, and today we discover the fossilised remains of those ancient life-forms within many of the rocks surrounding us. Since about 1800 it has been recognised that certain fossils characterise certain strata, and for the geologist fossils have thus come to hold a vital significance. On the one hand, the presence of similar fossil-assemblages within two rock formations allows those formations to be correlated even though they may lie in widely separated localities. On the other hand, since fossils vary through time, their discovery allows the geologist to arrange the strata of a region into a chronological sequence. Fossils are to the geologist what coins or shards of differing styles of pottery are to the archaeologist. The geologist who lights upon some fossil which is new to science is expected to describe and figure the fossil in the palaeontological literature. Such a new fossil by this means is elevated to the status of being a type-specimen, and as such, other geologists will wish to examine it in order to compare its form with that possessed by other fossils of their own finding. A type-specimen sets the standard by which other similar fossils are judged.

Because fossils possess such importance for geology, their collection has always for the Survey been a matter of high priority. The Victorian one-inch sheet-memoirs each contained a section devoted to palaeontology, or, more correctly, they each contained such a section provided the sometimes recalcitrant Baily could be persuaded to perform his duties expeditiously. Similarly, the Survey's fossil collection soon became replete with Irish type-specimens which, through illustrations, were familiar to palaeontologists the world over. Never has the Survey employed a specialist rock or mineral collector, but from 1845 down to 1901 the staff of the Survey always contained at least one man holding the post of Fossil Collector. Four of those Fossil Collectors were regarded as particularly successful in their skilled but arduous task, the four, with the dates of their tenure of the post, being James Flanagan (1845 - 1859), Charles Galvan (1855 - 1870), Alexander McHenry (1861 - 1877), and Richard Clark (1877 - 1901).

A certain pathos surrounds Flanagan; he is one of the Survey men who died, as it were, on active service. During the summer of 1858 he was taken ill while collecting at the famed Kiltorcan site in County Kilkenny. He was then lodging in a house belonging to one Richard Ruith in nearby Ballyhale, and for many months he lay there tended by Bridget Ruith, a daughter of the house. He ceased to communicate with the Survey, and on 5 April 1859 Du Noyer was sent down to Ballyhale to see what had happened to the man who for a quarter of a centuary had been his colleague upon either the Ordnance Survey or the Geological Survey. The next day Du Noyer reported to Jukes that Flanagan was clearly not destined to remain in the world for very long, and that during their meeting the veteran fossilist had expressed a strong desire to see again his chief. Jukes wrote to Murchison explaining that 'poor Old Flanagan has picked up his last fossil and is about to carry his hammer to another world', and he asked the Director to tell Portlock that his onetime Ordnance Survey Fossil Collector was about to quit this life.

Jukes himself took the first train down to Ballyhale on 7 April, and he went down again on 14 April, only to discover upon arrival that the event anticipated had actually occurred. Flanagan had expired at 5 a.m. that very morning. Jukes remained at Ballyhale in order to attend the funeral on 16 April, and from the graveside he then went to the Ruith's house to go through the deceased's effects in the presence of the Ruiths and the local sergeant of the Royal Irish Constabulary. The late Fossil Collector had clearly led a simple existence. His effects consisted of little more than letters and papers, some clothes, a few books, a pistol, and a gold watch and chain described by Jukes as being 'of very inferior workmanship and material'. Why Flanagan possessed a pistol I just cannot say, but where his books are concerned I do like to think that one of them may have been *The Old Red Sandstone* written by Hugh Miller, the Scots former stone-mason who became a best-selling geological author. Miller too possessed a pistol. Surrounded by his fossils, he used the gun to terminate his own life on Christmas Eve in 1856.

FIGURE 10.2. *A portrait of James Flanagan sketched by Du Noyer for presentation to Sir Roderick Murchison. Flanagan, 'a very intelligent civil assistant' with the Ordnance Survey of Ireland, was Portlock's fossil collector, and Fossil Collector with the Geological Survey of Ireland from 1845 until his death on 14 April 1859. He was, on 28 March 1845, the first member of staff to be offered a post with the new Survey after Henry James himself. The sketch was taken at Ferriters Cove, County Kerry, on 9 September 1856, twelve days after Murchison had left Dingle. The original drawing is in the archives of the British Geological Survey and it is here reproduced by kind permission of the British Survey.*

As a result of the activities of its Geologists and Fossil Collectors, the Survey rapidly amassed a large collection of rocks, minerals, and fossils. In May 1864 Jukes told the Select Committee on the Dublin scientific institutions that in the Survey's section of the Museum of Irish Industry he then had on public view more than one thousand rock-specimens, 11,821 Irish fossils, and 5,598 British fossils. In addition, the Survey's cabinets contained between eight and ten thousand further fossils which could be made available to the serious student of Irish palaeontology.

Not all of this material was of the Survey's own gathering. In October 1845, for example, the

FIGURE 10.3. *Alexander McHenry (1843-1919). The son of a policeman from Ballyvoy, County Antrim, and the longest serving member of staff in the history of the Survey. McHenry, Symes, and Wilkinson would appear to have shared a certain facial similarity, and the reader might be excused for concluding that one gentleman has been featured twice, if not three times, in figures 3.14, 5.3, and 10.3. Each of the figures does, nevertheless, come quite independently from impeccable sources among the present-day relatives of the three officers. The photograph of McHenry is reproduced, by courtesy of the National Museum of Ireland, from an original in the archives of the Museum's Geological Section.*

Survey took over the Irish natural history collections which had been assembled earlier during the course of the Ordnance Survey's abortive memoir project (see p.9). Exactly how much of this material eventually arrived in St Stephen's Green is unclear, but James - and later Oldham - may well have felt overwhelmed by the scale of the 'instant museum' which they had inherited. An inventory made in 1843 reveals that the Ordnance Survey's collections then contained no less than 1900 minerals, 4,824 fossils, 70 boxes of unidentified fossils, 16 boxes of soils, and 13,580 named non-fossiliferous specimens with their geographical place of origin carefully marked upon six-inch maps. Within this vast collection of Ordnance Survey material the most important items were the specimens collected during the progress of Portlock's survey of mid-Ulster between 1830 and 1843 (see p.11). Indeed, many of the fossils which now came under the Survey's control were the type-specimens which Du Noyer had figured for Portlock's great memoir of 1843 on the geology of County Londonderry and its surrounding regions.

The British geological material arrived in the Museum because from 1845 onwards there was a regular exchange of specimens between the Irish Survey and its counterpart in England and Wales. Similar exchanges took place between Dublin and Edinburgh following the formal establishment of the Geological Survey of Scotland in 1867. Other specimens came from further afield. During his years in the East, for example, Oldham arranged for some Indian specimens to be despatched to St Stephen's Green, and sometime before 1862 the Museum purchased a set of European igneous and metamorphic rocks from Dr A. Krantz of Bonn.

Within 51 St Stephen's Green the official position was that the geologists retained responsibility for all the geological specimens which were in active use by the Survey, but once any specimen was no longer required for Survey purposes, it was supposed to be handed over to the Museum of Irish Industry for its fate to be decided. In reality what seems to have happened is that rocks and fossils were generally regarded as falling permanently within the ambit of the Survey, while minerals were viewed as the prerogative of the Museum. So far as a visitor to the Museum was concerned, there was no tangible evidence of such a dichotomy. No galleries were visibly designated as belonging to the Survey. It was simply - and literally - that the Museum authorities held the keys to the mineral cabinets, while the Survey held the keys to the cabinets containing the rocks and the fossils.

When the reconstruction of number 51 was completed during 1854, the offices and laboratories of the Survey and the museum were installed at the front of the house, while the large and newly-constructed lecture-theatre was located at the rear of the building. Upon two levels between the offices and the lecture-theatre there lay the galleries of the Museum. Four long galleries (the Upper and Lower North and South galleries) paralleled the newly-developed long-axis of the building, and at the western end two shorter galleries (the Upper and Lower Cross galleries) paralleled the Museum's street-frontage along St Stephen's Green.

The three lower galleries were all given over to the display of varied materials which - except for coal - were of inorganic origin. The Lower Cross Gallery contained building stones, decorative marbles, roofing slates, specimens of clays, and examples of the substances employed in cement manufacture. The Lower South Gallery housed the minerals - in 1862 Kane claimed that this display was confined to the minerals 'that have practical uses' - and the various metallic ores. The manner in which the different ores were processed was illustrated, and artefacts were offered in demonstration of the uses to which the metals might be put. One third of this gallery seems to have been devoted to the cases containing the Survey's collection of rocks. Here Jukes adopted a simple generic classification which involved the placing together of all the granites, all the felstones, all the sandstones, all the clays, and so on. In 1866 the geological collection became the subject of a published 128-page catalogue prepared by Jukes himself. The Lower North Gallery was largely reserved for the presentation of coal, coal-mining, iron-ore, and iron smelting, but a part of the gallery was dedicated to sand and its uses in glass manufacture, and to clays and their use in pottery. The gallery contained a collection of Wedgwood ware and of Irish-made pottery.

Towards the eastern end of the building, adjacent to the lecture-theatre, access to the upper galleries was obtained via a handsome staircase illuminated by stained-glass windows which were themselves intended to illustrate the craftsman's use of natural materials. The three upper galleries were dedicated to an exposition of the role which organic substances play in our lives. There were, for example, displays demonstrating all the stages in the cotton, jute, linen, and woollen industries. There was an explanation of the manufacture of soap and candles. There was a section devoted to the Irish fishing industry, with specimens of all the fish native to Irish waters, examples of the fisherman's gear, and a collection of models of typical Irish fishing-boats.

The entire Upper South Gallery was allocated to the Survey for the exhibition and storage of its fossil collection. Here Jukes wisely adopted a stratigraphical arrangement so that there might be seen together examples of the Irish Silurian fossils, specimens of the fossil-forms characteristic of the Carboniferous Limestone, samples of the ammonites and gastropods from the Jurassic of Ulster, and a representative selection of the fossils from the shelly drifts of the Dublin region. Sadly, no catalogue of the collection was ever published, but within the Museum there were two groups of fossils which must surely have shared joint pride of place (see Plate XII).

First, there were the strange fucoid forms which had been found within the Cambrian rocks at Bray Head in County Wicklow and in similar rocks at a few other localities. Originally discovered by Oldham in 1840, they were in 1848 named *Oldhamia* in his honour, and at the time the Museum of Irish Industry opened its doors to the public, *Oldhamia* was the world's oldest known fossil. Nobody could then decide whether the fossil represented the remains of a plant or of an animal, and it was therefore classed as a zoophyte which places it in the same category as the sponges and the

FIGURE 10.4. *Edward Forbes (1815-1854), Palaeontologist to the Geological Survey of England and Wales as from 1844, and, after 1 April 1845, Palaeontologist to the Geological Survey of the United Kingdom. Reproduced from the frontispiece to George Wilson and Archibald Geikie,* Memoir of Edward Forbes, F.R.S. *(1861).*

sea-anemones. The debate about the fossil's true nature has continued on down to the present day.

Second, there were the magnificent plant remains from the Upper Devonian beds at Kiltorcan in County Kilkenny. They had been discovered by Flanagan in 1851 (see p.48), and most notable among them was a beautiful fern-like plant possessed of fronds about a metre in length (*Archaeopteris hibernica* (Forbes) Dawson 1861). Because of their size and splendour, these fossils had attracted much attention from both palaeontologists and the general public. We may therefore be confident that Jukes will have wished to give them a place of prominence among the display of the Upper Palaeozoic fossils. The Kiltorcan fossils certainly caught the eye of two distinguished German geologists from Breslau - Arnold von Lasaulx and Ferdinand Roemer - when they visited the Museum in August 1876. It was, incidentally, while collecting further Kiltorcan fossils, that Flanagan was smitten by his mortal illness during the summer of 1858.

The Survey's officers were themselves responsible for the identification and arrangement of all the Survey's rocks destined for a place in the Museum galleries. All the minerals were determined and arranged in collaboration with William Kirby Sullivan, the chemist to the Museum of Irish Industry. But the fossils presented more complex problems. They demanded a high level of specialised palaeontological expertise. From 1845 until his appointment to the Edinburgh chair of natural history in 1854, the Irish fossils were one of the many responsibilities of Edward Forbes, De La Beche's London-based Palaeontologist. As we noted earlier (p.23), Forbes was one of the finest naturalists of his day, but he was also a man who was evidently possessed of a remarkable personal charisma. The British scientific community was severely shaken by his death on 18 November 1854 at the early age of thirty-nine and only a few weeks after his assumption of the Edinburgh chair. On 21 November Jukes was just completing a letter to Ramsay when the sad tidings arrived from Auld Reekie.

> 3 p.m. I have received the news. God help us!

Forbes's widow soon married William Charles Yelverton (later the fourth Viscount Avonmore), and in her new status she speedily found herself involved in a celebrated marital case possessed of considerable Irish dimensions. Eventually the House of Lords had to adjudicate on the issue of whether or not she really was Yelverton's wife.

From 1845 down to 1853 Forbes visited Dublin regularly to identify the Survey's fossils and to arrange them in the Museum. Some years he made two trips across the Irish Sea. One such year was 1847. Then he paid a spring visit to Ireland and he returned at the close of the year to continue his work and to join the Oldham family in its Yuletide festivities. We must hope that he enjoyed his Christmas. Ireland, of course, was then in the grip of the Famine, and during his spring visit that year he had added the following sorrowful postscript to a letter sent from the Museum on 1 April.

> I am in a land of misery and tears at present, hence the dull tone of this short note.

A warm relationship existed between Forbes and Oldham, and Oldham was best man at Forbes's wedding at Lymington, in Hampshire, on 31 August 1848. One good turn is deserving of another. It was at a meeting of the Geological Society of Dublin on 15 November 1848 that the newly-married Forbes proposed that the fossils which Oldham had discovered at Bray Head eight years earlier should henceforth be known as *Oldhamia*.

Forbes paid his last visit to Dublin early in November 1853, and the following words from Jukes's pen convey his memory of that stay of ten days' duration.

> Although the fossils were then in a complete chaos, and the gallery cases only just finished, yet such was the easiness and quickness with which he worked, that he had arranged every specimen with his own hands, and all were in their places, with descriptive cards, before the end of a week.

Jukes's comment that the cases which were to receive the fossils had only just been completed in November 1853 is of some interest. It suggests that the Survey's palaeontological display in the recently constructed Upper South Gallery cannot have been fully opened to the public much before the close of 1853. Such an opening was a little too late to catch the attention of the 1,156,212 people who from May to October of that year had flocked to Leinster Lawn in order to visit the Great Industrial Exhibition located there in an Irish version of England's Crystal Palace.

The Museum of Irish Industry obviously could never hope to match the attendance figures achieved at the Great Industrial Exhibition, but nonetheless the Museum clearly did excite a good deal of public interest. Taking 1859 as a typical year, we find that the Museum was then open on weekdays from 11 a.m. to 4 p.m. and on certain weekday-evenings - usually evenings when classes were being held in the lecture-theatre - from 7 p.m. to 9.30 p.m. During that year the Museum received 22,997 daytime visitors and 13,660 evening visitors. It was clearly an institution enjoying some popularity. Two years earlier the English naturalist William Samuel Symonds, the Rector of Pendock in Worcestershire, visited the Museum and recorded his memory of the occasion as follows.

> The Museum of Irish Industry is a credit to Dublin, and to the gentlemen connected with that institution. It is a most instructive collection of the manufactures, the raw materials, the geology, and the mineralogy of Ireland. The stranger-geologist and naturalist wants to see Irish fossils and minerals; and here, thanks to the labours of the Geological Surveyors, he can do so without being, in any way, incommoded by boats, harps, South Sea canoes, Chinese slippers, and cobwebs.

Forbes's successor as Palaeontologist to the Geological Survey of Great Britain and Ireland was John William Salter, who had been Forbes's assistant since 1846. He was a strange and prickly individual, and De La Beche was not entirely happy about his appointment to the vacancy. That Salter knew his fossils - especially his trilobites - is beyond question, but he suffered from sudden changes of mood which left his colleagues perplexed and uneasy. During the 1850s he became victim to prolonged bouts of depression, and during the 1860s he degenerated into fits of actual insanity. One of his physicians interestingly suggested that some of Salter's problems may have arisen from the suppression of sexual desires within the frame of a man possessed of 'strong animal passion'. Be that as it may, Salter certainly took his own life. On Monday 2 August 1869 he was drowned after jumping into the Thames from a steamer bound from Margate to London. I presume it to be merely a coincidence that Jukes had died in his Dublin

PLATE XII. *Three classic Irish fossils from the Survey's collections. Upper left:* Oldhamia radiata *from Bray Head in County Wicklow (true size). Upper right:* Anodonta jukesii *(now* Archanodon jukesi *(Forbes 1853), this specimen having been collected by James Flanagan at Kiltorcan between 1851 and 1853 (one third of true size). Lower right:* Paleopteris hibernica *from Kiltorcan (one quarter of true size). These three fossils were kindly selected for photography by Dr Matthew Parkes.*

lunatic asylum just four days before Salter plunged into the waters off Thames Haven.

Salter clearly shirked his Irish responsibilities. He was in Ireland during the summer of 1856 to join Griffith, Murchison, and the Irish Survey party in the Dingle Peninsula of County Kerry, but that excursion was the end of his association with Jukes and his men. Perhaps Salter had been disgusted by the Irish weather (it had been extremely wet in Dingle and Murchison had been in ill humour after failing to find waterproof clothing in Limerick). Perhaps Salter disliked the Museum of Irish Industry (displaying his usual anti-Irish prejudice Murchison had that summer noted in his diary that most of the galleries of the Museum presented the 'industry of the world to instruct the benighted sons of Erin'). Perhaps Salter found Jukes intolerable (the two men had already crossed swords back in 1851). Salter certainly now claimed that he was already overburdened with English work, that it was unreasonable to expect him to make regular visits to Dublin, and that the demands of his other duties rendered it impossible for him to perform his Irish duties to that standard which he normally strove to attain. In October 1856 he made a unilateral declaration of independence; he no longer regarded himself as having any Irish palaeontological responsibilities.

This news threw Jukes into a fit of despair. On 28 October 1856 he sent to Murchison a frantic plea for help. He explained that in the basement of number 51 there were 22 large boxes of fossils opened but with their contents unexamined, and eight unopened casks containing the fossils collected during the 1856 field-season. Upstairs, in Jukes's office and in the Survey's workroom, there were seventy large drawers and 106 small drawers, all of them crammed with fossils awaiting study and determination. Jukes begged of Murchison. *Please* , could the Irish Survey be granted its own full-time specialist in palaeontology? Murchison was clearly sympathetic to this request, and a kindly fate played into his hands. On 12 November 1856 Willson announced that he was resigning from the Survey in order to join Oldham in Calcutta. Here was Murchison's opportunity. He decided that instead of filling the Irish vacancy through direct recruitment, he would redeploy one of his existing officers. He would send William Hellier Baily from London to Dublin. Baily, a nephew of the noted sculptor Edward Hodges Baily, was an experienced palaeontologist. He had been a curator in Bristol Museum, he had worked under Forbes and Thomas Henry Huxley in the British Survey's London museum first in Craig's Court and then in Jermyn Street, and he arrived in Dublin in July 1857 bearing the title Geologist (Acting Palaeontologist).

FIGURE 10.5. *John William Salter (1820-1869), successor to Edward Forbes as Palaeontologist to the Geological Survey of the United Kingdom. Salter renounced his Irish duties as from October 1856. Reproduced from a plate in Archibald Geikie,* Memoir of Sir Andrew Crombie Ramsay *(1895)*

For the next thirty years Baily was responsible for the identification of the thousands of fossils annually collected by the Survey, for their arrangement in the cabinets of the Museum's Upper South Gallery, and for the preparation of the palaeontological section of each of the one-inch-sheet memoirs. His was a crucial task, but throughout his Irish years he remained dissatisfied with the status being accorded to him. He wanted the title 'Palaeontologist in Ireland', coupled, of course, with an appropriately enhanced salary. In this ambition he was strongly supported first by Jukes and then by Hull, but London repeatedly refused to sanction Baily's promotion to such an unprecedented rank. When he died in Rathmines in August 1888, after a lingering illness, his standing was still merely that of Senior Geologist (Acting Palaeontologist).

Jukes viewed London's refusal to promote Baily as a slight upon both the Dublin Museum and the entire Irish Survey. He adverted to the matter in the most vigorous and undiplomatic of terms in the memoir to one-inch sheets 187 (Cork), 195 (Queenstown), and 196 (Ballycotton) published in 1864. But while Jukes strenuously supported Baily's claims to advancement, it is all too clear that Baily repeatedly proved himself to be a very difficult colleague. Jukes might perhaps have handled him with greater tact, but in their frequent altercations it was almost invariably Baily who was in the wrong.

There is some indication that at least in his later years the Acting Palaeontologist was over addicted to the bottle, and in alcohol we may have a partial explanation for the fact that so often he had to be reprimanded for the dereliction of his duties. It greatly distressed the tidy-minded Jukes when several one-inch sheet-memoirs had to be published without their fossil-list simply because Baily had failed to meet his deadlines.

One typical fracas between Jukes and Baily took place in August 1861. Baily, who was always short of money, invited Jukes to perjure himself by certifying that Baily had completed a set of fossil-drawings which were to serve as illustrations for some lectures which Jukes was about to deliver in the Museum of Irish Industry. In reality the drawings were still unfinished, but Baily explained that he needed the fee involved so that he might attend that year's British Association meeting in Manchester where he proposed to present a paper. Jukes very properly refused to sign the certificate in question, and at this Baily blazed into a fit of fury. On 27 August Jukes wrote to Murchison complaining that Baily was refusing to perform his duties satisfactorily and protesting that Baily had been 'grossly insolent, and finally set me at complete defiance'. He had commanded that Jukes should never again address him save in the course of duty, and Jukes, not unreasonably, now informed Murchison that he could no longer tolerate Baily's behaviour. In consequence Murchison suspended Baily from his duties as from 2 September for 'gross insolence and insubordination', and he was threatened with dismissal should such behaviour recur.

The 2 September was just two days before the British Association meeting opened in Manchester. Baily had found the money necessary to get himself to Cottonopolis and Jukes was there too. Baily's paper turned out to be one devoted to the palaeontology of the Irish Silurian strata, and we may only wonder what happened in the Geology Section's meeting chamber in the Manchester Royal Institution when Baily was confronted by that year's President of the Section. The President was Murchison himself. Perhaps soothing Mancunian oil was poured upon troubled Hibernian waters. Certainly the culprit eventually apologised to Jukes, and Baily was reinstated in his office in late October. There nevertheless lingers a strong suspicion that under Baily's control the Survey's palaeontological collection may have been rather less well tended than Jukes - and later Hull - might have wished.

The man responsible for the concept underlying the Museum of Irish Industry was, of course, Sir Robert Kane. In that Museum he had given to his native land a most valuable institution. One may only wish that modern Ireland contained a comparable establishment where Irish people - both young and old - might first learn about the range of their island's resources and then see how those resources were to be exploited in the national interest. In our own day there has been endless talk of the development of some modern counterpart to the Museum of Irish Industry, but we have lacked a Kane with which to beat our fantasies into structural form. For twenty years the Museum at 51 St Stephen's Green stood as the remarkable creation of a remarkable Irishman. In the second half of the twentieth century our history books bulge with accounts of the achievements of such nineteenth-century Irishmen as Daniel O'Connell, Michael Davitt, and Charles Stewart Parnell, but there are few of us who today remember the enormous contributions made to Irish life by the likes of Kane, Sir Richard Griffith, or William Dargan. Such men deserve better of us.

That said, it has to be admitted that at the Museum of Irish Industry relations between Kane and the Survey were often somewhat strained. The root of the problem was that Kane and the Survey were the reluctant victims of an arranged marriage. The Museum and the Survey were striving to achieve ends which were not entirely reconcilable, yet the two bodies had been forced into cohabitation at number 51.

The establishment located at number 51 had been founded in 1845 as an institution entitled the Dublin Museum of Economic Geology. It was intended to be an Irish equivalent to De La Beche's Museum of Economic Geology founded in 1835 at Craig's Court in London. The Dublin Museum was to be an adjunct to the Geological Survey of Ireland just as the London Museum was an adjunct to the Geological Survey of England and Wales. Initially, in January 1845, the proposal was that Kane's appointment would be as chemist to the Irish Survey and as curator of its Museum. In this dual capacity he was to be responsible to De La Beche as the Director of the Geological Survey of Great Britain and Ireland.

From the outset Kane clearly had other ideas. He was very much the man of the moment. His widely acclaimed work *The Industrial Resources of Ireland* had been published in 1844, and it achieved a second edition during the following year. Somebody somewhere now began a pulling of governmental strings. By March 1845, Lord Lincoln, the First Commissioner of Her Majesty's Woods, Forests, Land Revenues, Works and Buildings, had decided to forget about the duality of chemist and curator. Instead, he offered Kane the post of Director of the Dublin Museum of Economic Geology, and he made it abundantly clear that the Museum was no longer to be regarded as the exclusive preserve of the Geological Survey.

> I propose that the Repository should be divided into two portions, the one to be attached to and considered as in the custody of the director in chief of the survey, the other exclusively as your own.

In view of this changed conception of the Museum, it was now understood that as the Museum's Director, Kane would be responsible directly to the First Commissioner rather than to De La Beche. Number 51 was to be like a ship with two captains.

Kane had escaped from the Survey's ambit; he was soon to make use of his new-found freedom. In rural Ireland the potato blight was on the rampage and starving people were flocking to the soup-kitchens. It was a moment of crisis. Kane was convinced that the nation needed something more than a museum specialising merely in economic geology. Such a museum might be highly appropriate in England, but Ireland was a special case. Ireland needed a museum where people could be shown more than just the native rocks, minerals, and fossils. Ireland needed a museum where people could be introduced to every facet of the Irish natural environment - where people could be led to a realisation of Ireland's potential through an examination of all aspects of the nation's economic life. Kane clearly found support for his view within official circles. The upshot was that he was permitted to re-orientate his Museum. He suggested that the Museum might be restyled 'the Industrial Museum for Ireland'. But Lord Morpeth, the new First Commissioner, had other ideas. He preferred the name 'Museum of Irish Industry', and in 1847 that was the new title bestowed upon the still unopened institution which De La Beche had thought was going to feature within his own administrative empire as the Dublin Museum of Economic Geology.

This change in the character of the Museum discomfited the Survey. If geology was not to be at the heart of the new museum - if the display of rocks, minerals, and fossils was not to be its prime purpose - then what was the Survey doing housed in number 51? Why was the Survey not accommodated elsewhere? What affinity did Oldham, Jukes, and the Survey's other officers have with Kane's displays devoted to Irish fishing-boats and flax-growing, or to the cabinets containing the Italo-Grecian and Etruscan vases so liberally deposited in the Museum by Lord Talbot de Malahide?

For his part Kane must have resented the fact that in order to satisfy the Survey he had to devote the whole of one of his four largest galleries to an exposition of Irish palaeontology. Forbes might be a fine palaeontologist, but was he not upstairs in the Upper South Gallery fiddling with his brachiopods while outside the Museum's walls Ireland was crying in anguish? Surely the national interest decreed that some more pertinent role should be found for the Upper South Gallery. At such a moment of crisis, was another geological display really a national priority? Dublin already had extensive geological collections on view both in Trinity College and at the Royal Dublin Society. As recently as 1844 the latter collection had been richly augmented by the gift of large numbers of Silurian and Carboniferous fossils from the cabinets of Richard Griffith. Had the Museum of Irish Industry no loftier objective than the replication of collections already extant elsewhere in Dublin?

Kane was a strenuous advocate of the importance of applied science, but when Jukes arrived in number 51, Kane found himself in association with a man possessed of a rather different approach to science. Jukes repeatedly emphasised that he saw the work of the Survey as first and foremost an exercise in pure science. When, on 21 December 1866, and in the presence of the Lord Lieutenant (the Marquis of Abercorn), Jukes delivered a lecture in the Museum descriptive of the activities of the Survey, these were among the first words that he spoke.

> But I should be false to my own convictions if I did not rate intellectual gain at a far higher value than any material profit, and did not put the scientific results of the Survey of the Heavens and the Earth, carried on by the Royal Observatories, and Her Majesty's Geological Survey, far before their practical application to navigation and mining.

Clearly, Kane and Jukes were likely to entertain different notions about the manner in which the Survey should use its allocated share of the Museum's space.

There was also an incipient problem looming over future competition for space. Kane may well have viewed the Survey as some kind of malignant growth which shortly would choke its own Museum apartments and then begin to spread along the corridors and to burst through its confining walls into neighbouring chambers. Again, it must have been fossils which looked like becoming the crux of the difficulty. Each year the Survey was adding thousands of fossils to its collection. In 1857, for instance, 5,616 fossils were added to the cabinets, and in 1863 the collection was increased by the arrival of 2,588 fossils. On 31 May 1864, when Jukes gave evidence before the Select Committee on the Dublin scientific institutions, he was specifically asked whether the Survey's palaeontological collection was likely to grow in the future. His reply was surely sufficient to give Kane the quivers.

> Yes, greatly. There are many large districts of Ireland at present unexamined, which are known to be rich in fossils of a different kind to those which we have examined, and therefore we shall require a considerable augmentation of space, if we are to have an adequate representation of the geological structure of the different parts of Ireland.

On 9 November 1852 Dublin was shaken by an earth-tremor. After the arrival of the Survey in number 51 during November 1846 the house was regularly shaken by lesser tremors as Kane and the Survey developed their respective sections of the Museum in accordance with their conflicting ideals. The apportionment of the Ordnance Survey's former natural history collection between Kane and the Survey caused problems in the autumn of 1846. On 21 December that year De La Beche wrote to Ramsay.

> That fine fellow Oldham is getting sadly bothered by Kane and his requirements. There has been a sad rumpus about transferring some old Ordnance collections to Kane, collections, by the way, of which he (Kane) hath no earthly or heavenly knowledge whatever.

Five days later De La Beche again penned a note to Ramsay.

> Touching Muzzy [Museum] matters, it would be better not in any way to allude to the Museum in Dublin - the arrangements connected with which have been a blunder - or mistake, which ever you like.

Kane's insistence that the Survey should collect soil-samples for use in the Museum was a constant source of friction during the years between 1847 and 1852 (see p.37). Something of the atmosphere prevailing in number 51 during those years is conveyed by the following passage in a letter from Oldham to De La Beche and dated 4 June 1849.

> Sir R. Kane had the Lord Lieutenant here on Saturday and never said one word to me about it, though I saw him that forenoon, and never once brought him near to our part of the house. This is the friendly way he acts towards us.

By the 1860s Kane and Jukes would appear to have settled into a state of peaceful coexistence at number 51. But there still lurked beneath the surface old differences of emphasis between Kane's applied science and Jukes's pure science. This became evident in 1862 when there was appointed a Treasury Commission charged with the task of examining the relative roles of the Royal Dublin Society and the Museum of Irish Industry. The Commissioners pointed out to Kane that the Survey's section of the Museum was 'arranged without reference to industrial uses', and he was asked whether the section might, with advantage, be removed from number 51 and then amalgamated with the Museum of the Royal Dublin Society. 'Yes', replied Kane.

That Treasury Commission was clearly expected to make recommendations which would effect financial economies, and among its suggestions there are two holding of significance in the present context. First, it was suggested that the Museum of Irish Industry should be closed and that all the collections save for those belonging to the Geological Survey should be subsumed into the museum of the Royal Dublin Society, thus creating a 'National Irish Museum'. Second, it was proposed that all the Survey collections should be removed from number 51 and transferred to the new building then under construction for the National Gallery of Ireland. Neither of these proposals was ever implemented, and the second of them today looks somewhat bizarre. Behind that second proposal there lurks an odd little story.

During the middle years of the nineteenth century, Dublin lacked any adequate public library. The nearest thing to a true public library was Marsh's Library at St Patrick's cathedral, but that library's book-stock was deficient in modern literature, and its building was in a poor state of repair. With the approval of Archbishop Richard Whately, it was therefore proposed to remove the library from St Patrick's and to re-locate it within a specially designed, self-contained library section of the new National Gallery building upon Leinster Lawn. The foundation-stone of the new building was laid on 29 January 1859, and it was intended that within its chambers the books from Marsh's would constitute the nucleus of a centrally-located public library. In the event, Marsh's Library never left St Patrick's, and by the autumn of 1862 it was evident that some other use would have to be found for the accommodation originally designed for Marsh's at the National Gallery site. It was this accommodation which the Treasury Commission proposed should now be allocated to the Geological Survey as a home for its museum. Exactly what was to happen to the remainder of the Survey's facilities the Commission nowhere made clear.

Jukes never appeared before the Treasury Commission of 1862. While the commissioners were taking their evidence in Dublin between 2 and 9 October, Jukes was away in Cambridge presiding over Section C of the British Association. Two years later both Jukes and Murchison did appear before the Select Committee on the scientific institutions of Dublin. There the proposal for moving the Survey's museum from number 51 to the National Gallery again surfaced. Jukes was asked whether he had inspected the Gallery rooms which might be available for the Survey's use. He had. He was asked whether he regarded the rooms as affording sufficient space for a Survey museum. They did not. They were too small. They were adequate for the storage of the specimens in boxes but not for their proper presentation in display cases. Murchison said much the same thing as Jukes. He had not actually seen the National Gallery building (he had evidently not visited Ireland since 1857), but he indicated his understanding that the rooms being offered to the

FIGURE 10.6. *Dublin's complex of buildings lying between Kildare Street and Merrion Square, and intended for cultural purposes. Kildare Street lies in the foreground, and in plan the complex of buildings forms a letter* **H**. *The northern (left-hand) elements within the complex are the National Library of Ireland (1890) and the National Gallery of Ireland (1864). The southern elements are the National Museum of Ireland (1890) and the Natural History Museum (1857). The cross member, parallel to Kildare Street, is Leinster House (1745). The Curved Gallery linking Leinster House to the Natural History Museum is hidden from view behind the National Museum building. The illustration makes clear how the unity of the site was destroyed when Leinster House was in 1924 purchased by the state as a meeting-place for the Oireachtas. A version of the drawing was published in the report of the Dublin meeting of the Museums Association held during June 1894.*

Survey lacked the fenestration appropriate to the quarters of a geological museum.

That was the last heard of the National Gallery proposal. Neither the volumes from Marsh's Library, nor the fossils from number 51, were ever destined to lie in proximity to works by Brueghel, El Greco, Monet, or Rubens. Change was nevertheless in the air. In August 1867, at the stroke of an administrative pen, the Museum of Irish Industry was transformed into the Royal College of Science for Ireland, a teaching institution dedicated to the advancement of applied science. Whatever their former differences of approach, Jukes was shocked at the treatment being meted out to Kane. On 14 March 1867 Jukes wrote to his sister.

> The Department of Science and Art is a great deal worse than any Fenian insurrection. They coolly suppress the office of director of our museum, dismiss Sir R. Kane, and propose to govern us through a secretary, one of their science inspectors.

Such was the general outcry that Kane was shortly re-instated in number 51 as the permanent Dean of the new college, but not for long did Kane and the Survey remain lodged together. The house was now the home not of a museum, but of an educational establishment, and the presence there of the Survey was more anomalous than ever. Quite apart from that, the expansion of the Survey's establishment after 1867 (see p.64) made it impossible for the Survey to remain any longer in number 51. So it was that shortly after Jukes's death in July 1869, the Survey's possessions began to be removed from number 51 and to be taken around the corner to the Survey's fine new headquarters at 14 Hume Street.

The Survey was delighted with its new abode, but in one respect Hume Street was thoroughly unsatisfactory. Number 14 contained no chamber suitable for the public display of the Survey's collections. Presumably some of the more important fossils were carted over to Hume Street, but the bulk of the Survey's geological collections remained in number 51 where they became a part of the educational equipment of the Royal College of Science. The Survey remained responsible for its collections within the Royal College, but the move to Hume Street brought about an unfortunate divorce of the Survey officers from the collected materials of their trade.

Presumably Baily went regularly over to number 51 to tend his fossils, and Hull certainly conducted visitors around the corner from Hume Street so that they might inspect the Survey's collections. But every museum curator knows what happens to museum collections which are not in receipt of frequent close attention. Dust gathers, reference numbers fall from specimens, items become misplaced, captions become illegible as ink fades, and cards bearing titles become yellow and curled. Admittedly, evidence bearing upon the subject is not to hand, but such must surely have been the fate of the Survey's collections during the twenty years which followed the removal of the Survey's officers to their new home in Hume Street.

On the afternoon of Friday 10 April 1885 the sounds of a military band drifted across Dublin's Merrion Square. The band was that of the Duke of Cornwall's Light Infantry. They were playing upon Leinster Lawn. There eight thousand guests are said to have been gathered. I presume that Dr and Mrs Hull were present. Perhaps they had with them some of their six children. It was a royal and festive occasion. The Prince of Wales was about to lay the foundation-stone of the new Dublin Museum of Science and Art. The customary vacuous speeches were made (for once the Prince failed to refer to 'my lamented father'), the stone was laid, and the Prince and his Princess left for the Royal University of Ireland where they were each the recipient of a doctorate *honoris causa,* he in laws and she in music.

The story of the new museum-building initiated that April afternoon goes back to the year 1877. Then, after prolonged discussions and complex negotiations, it had been decided that the museum -collections of the Royal Dublin Society should be handed over to the state, that they should be combined with certain other museum-collections located in Dublin, and that all these collections should together constitute a new institution to be know as the Dublin Museum of Science and Art. The Survey's collections were included within this reorganisation. It was resolved that all the Survey's cabinets in the Royal College of Science should be cleared and that all the materials therein contained should be removed to the new Museum.

The Dublin Museum of Science and Art (in 1908 it was restyled the National Museum of Science and Art) was built immediately to the southwest of Leinster House, along Kildare Street, and upon a site formerly occupied by the Royal Dublin Society's Agricultural Hall (see Fig. 10.6). The contractors - James and William Beckett, William being Samuel Beckett's grandfather - handed the completed building over to the Department of Science and Art on 4 November 1889, and the splendid new Museum was opened by the Lord Lieutenant (the Earl of Zetland) on 29 August 1890.

The removal of the Survey's collections from number 51 St Stephen's Green, and their transportation to the new Museum, commenced during July 1890. The Geological Survey itself was then being scaled down following the completion of the last few sheets of the one-inch map (see p.100). Before their retirement one of the last Survey duties of the likes of Hull, Kinahan, Cruise, Mitchell, and Wynne may well have been to pay a final visit to the old Upper South Gallery of what once had been the Museum of Irish Industry. There they perhaps assisted in the emptying of cases which had been installed in the gallery almost forty years earlier under Kane's direction. Kane had died on 16 February 1890. Now there were again on the move specimens which had been collected under the hammers of Flanagan or Galvan, which had been determined by the skill of Baily or Forbes, and which had been arranged through the patience of Jukes or Oldham. Each specimen now had to be assessed and its fate decided. Many a specimen unwanted by the Survey was presented to the Royal College of Science where, presumably, all such specimens were left to await the arrival of Grenville Cole as the successor to Hull in the College's chair of geology. The specimens being kept by the Survey all had to be wrapped, boxed, taken down to the street, and then carted past the west end of Hume Street, around the corner of 'The Green', in front of the Shelbourne Hotel, and along Kildare Street. By November 1890 almost all the specimens being retained by the Survey had made their quarter-mile journey and were securely lodged within their new home.

At the Museum of Science and Art, the Survey's collections were accorded a position of some prominence. Exhibits such as textiles, arms and armour, glass, and furniture were all accommodated up at first-floor level, and a collection illustrative of economic botany was banished to the second storey. But not so the Survey's collections. They were placed on the ground-floor in galleries immediately adjacent to the museum's Central Court. Initially the bulk of the Survey's collections were intended for galleries 1.E and 2.E (now closed to the public as a part of the Museum's office and library accommodation), and at least a part of the collections may have been so located on the day of the museum's opening in August 1890. But almost immediately it was decided to interchange the Survey's collections in galleries 1.E and 2.E with the Museum's mineral collection located next door in Gallery 3.E. This was carried out during 1891, and the interchange brought the Survey's collections into one of the Museum's largest galleries. Even before this move, Gallery 3.E had contained some of the Survey's specimens arranged in wall-cabinets, but now, in 1891, the Survey's collections were unified and laid before the public in a splendid setting. Nolan, McHenry, Clark, and the other Survey men must have been well pleased. Readers unfamiliar with the architecture of our National Museum may gauge something of the relative importance of Gallery 3.E from the fact that, at a later date in the Museum's history, this was the gallery selected as accommodation for a display devoted to the 1916 Rising and the Anglo-Irish War, while today (1995) the gallery is home to an exhibit entitled 'The Road to Independence'.

Although so prominent a feature of the museum, the Survey's collections remained entirely under Survey control, and there was always one officer who was designated as 'officer in charge of the collections'. McHenry was the first officer to hold that title; he was assigned responsibility for the Survey's collections when he finally attained the rank of Geologist on 1 September 1890. In July of the following year McHenry handed his Museum duties over to the newly-appointed Watts, who was arriving in Dublin fresh from his experiences as a lecturer with the University of Cambridge Extension Programme. In the Museum, first McHenry and then Watts both had the assistance of Clark, the former Fossil Collector, although it was made clear that Clark's new Museum role as Assistant Curator did not preclude his being sent off to collect in the field as the need might arise. Indeed, he must still have spent a good deal of time in the field. When the Survey's collections were being arranged in the Museum it became clear that there were a number of gaps in the coverage, and these had to be remedied by further collection carried out between 1890 and 1894. It should also be remembered that Clark was heavily involved in the revision of the Lower Palaeozoic rocks which engaged the Survey's attention throughout the 1890s (see p.105).

That the Museum should have bestowed such prominence upon a geological collection which was not even under the Museum's control might, in retrospect, evoke some surprise. The explanation perhaps lies in the character of the man who from 1883 until 1895 was the Director of the Museum. He was Valentine Ball, one of the three remarkable sons of Robert Ball, the onetime Director of the museums in Trinity College Dublin. All three sons became professors within their father's college, one became a knight, one a baronet, and the third - Valentine - a Companion of the Bath. But it is the fact that Valentine Ball was himself a geologist which presently holds significance for us.

After reading the undergraduate course in Trinity College Dublin, Valentine Ball had in 1864 left for the East to join the Geological Survey of India under Thomas Oldham. There he established for himself a substantial geological reputation, his particular métier being within the area of economic geology. In 1881 he returned home and was appointed professor of geology and mineralogy in his alma mater. (It is interesting to note that among the seven candidates for the chair there were three other geologists who have featured in my story: Kinahan, Sollas, and Teall.) Ball's tenure of the chair was of brief duration. He once admitted that 'the management of a museum of wide range had been,

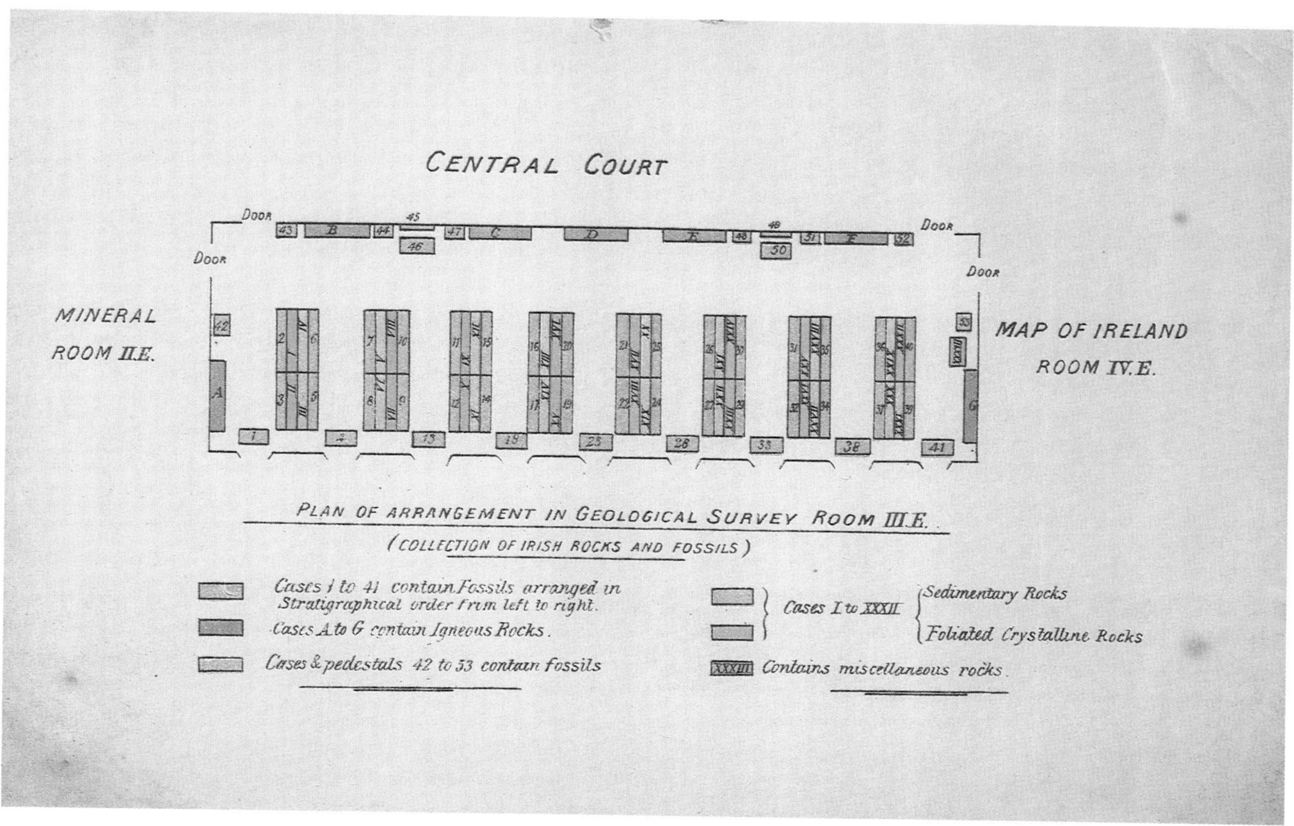

PLATE XIII. *The Geological Survey of Ireland in the Dublin Museum of Science and Art.*
The upper illustration shows the arrangement of the Survey's display in Gallery 3.E soon after the opening of the Museum in 1890.
(Reproduced from the guide to the collections written by McHenry and Watts and published in 1895.)
The lower illustration is one of the panels which perhaps first decorated a wall in Gallery 4.E when it housed the relief model of Ireland. The panel was then presumably relocated in the Curved Gallery. The panel survives in the archives of the Survey.

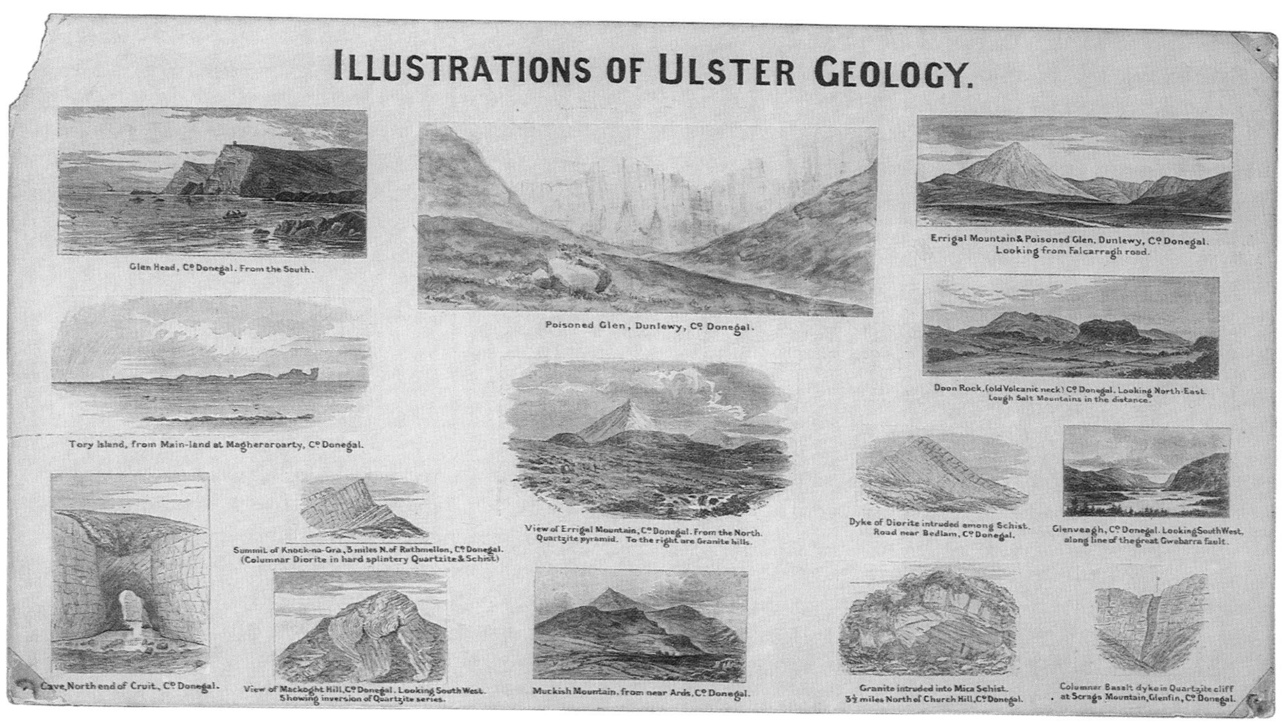

I may say, the dream of my life', and when in 1883 there fell vacant the office of Director of the Dublin Museum of Science and Art, Ball was delighted to be offered the appointment. In 1890, when the officers of the Geological Survey arrived in Kildare Street with their collections, they found a kindred spirit seated in the Director's office within the new Museum. Ball was one of the local geological community. He was a past-President of the Royal Geological Society of Ireland, and, at a more domestic level, he during the 1880s had been a close neighbour of Edward Hull in Dublin's Raglan Road. The Balls resided at number 1 while the Hulls lived at number 5.

The Survey's exhibit in Gallery 3.E was designed to illustrate the geology of Ireland by means of specimens, sections, maps, drawings, and photographs. There were 53 cases of fossils, mostly arranged so that a visitor moving through the gallery in a northward direction would encounter each of the typical life-forms in their true stratigraphical sequence (see Plate XIII). Upon entering the gallery from the Central Court, for example, the visitor was confronted by Case 1 containing possible organic forms from some of the most ancient rocks of County Donegal. At the opposite end of the gallery the final major case - Case 40 - facing the exit into Gallery 4.E, contained such Quaternary items as marine shells from the glacial drifts of Leinster, leaves and hazel-nuts from a peat-bog in King's County, and worked-flints from Larne in County Antrim. The richness and importance of the Survey's fossil collection was revealed by the presence within the gallery of more than sixty type and figured specimens.

The Survey's rocks were displayed with a geographical arrangement based upon the four Irish provinces. Specimens of all the igneous rocks were placed in seven large wall-cases lettered from A and B (Leinster) to G (Munster). Within each set of cases there came first the province's plutonic rocks, if any, then the intrusive rocks which had originated at shallow depths in the crust, and finally there were offered specimens of any volcanic rocks formed by actual extrusion over the surface of the earth. The sedimentary rocks and the 'foliated crystalline' (metamorphic) rocks were displayed in 32 cases arranged in nine bays, each bay being carefully planned so as to afford a chronological conspectus of the bedded rocks occurring within any given province. In the second bay, for instance, the visitor was surrounded by the sedimentary rocks of Leinster, in the third bay by the metamorphic rocks of Leinster, in the fourth bay by the sedimentary rocks of Connaught, and so on.

Around the walls of the gallery there were displayed illustrative materials such as one-inch geological maps, horizontal and vertical sections, drawings, and photographs. Some of the drawings were the work of Baily, McHenry and even Archibald Geikie, but most of them bore testimony to the now long-extinguished artistic talents of Du Noyer. Among the photographs there was a set of plates presented to the Survey by some members of the Belfast Naturalists' Field Club and featuring examples of the work of that noted Belfast photographer Robert John Welch.

After the summer of 1895, and for the expenditure of nine pence, the serious student of Irish geology was able to enter Gallery 3.E bearing a comprehensive, 156-page guide to the Survey's museum display. The title page of the guide bears the names of McHenry and Watts, but it was Watts who actually wrote the work. He had continued his preparation of the guide following his transfer to the British Survey in 1893, and under his influence the guide developed into what Cole hailed in the *Irish Naturalist* for November 1895 as 'a work of reference which will be welcome to all geologists in our islands'.

We must now leave Gallery 3.E by way of that exit located just across the aisle from Case 40 and its Quaternary fossils. Through the doorway there today wafts the aroma of Bewley's coffee and the sound of plates being deposited upon plastic trays. Nowadays the doorway opens into the Museum Café. But during the 1890s that place of modern refreshment was still exhibition Gallery 4.E. The gallery then contained another geological display in which the Survey had a strong involvement. The story of that exhibit goes back to the 1880s and begins in the Model Schools of the Commissioners for National Education at Tyrone House in Marlborough Street, Dublin.

In Marlborough Street during the 1880s there was a teacher who seems to have possessed strong geographical instincts. His name was T.W. Conway, and he was later to become a fellow of the Royal Geographical Society. Around 1887 a group of Marlborough Street pupils, working under his direction, constructed a plaster relief model of Ireland. Perhaps it was their way of celebrating the Queen's Golden Jubilee. It was certainly a most impressive achievement. The horizontal scale of the model was one inch to one mile (1:63,360) and the vertical scale was exaggerated - perhaps over exaggerated - by a factor of eleven. In size the model must have measured in excess of seven metres from north to south and five metres from east to west. Carrauntoohil, the highest peak in Ireland, must in the model have risen 18 centimetres above the level of the sea in nearby Dingle Bay.

A copy of this model was in 1888 made for the Museum of Science and Art, and this second version was immediately coloured geologically under the supervision of McHenry acting on behalf of the

Survey. (In 1907-8 the model was re-coloured under Hallissy's supervision, presumably so as to represent the Survey's recent revision of the Lower Palaeozoic strata.) The result can only have been both a spectacular exhibit and a graphic illustration of the geological bones underlying Ireland's superficial anatomy. The model lay centrally within Gallery 4.E, and around Mr Conway's creation there were arranged photographs illustrating the actual appearance of the topographic features which his model could only render in plaster. Nobody alive today will be able to remember seeing the relief-model in its original position in Gallery 4.E, but there are still those who recollect being captivated by the model as it lay in a later and less prominent Museum location. Indeed, the model became one of the favourite sights of the Museum, and for it Cole eventually wrote a special Museum memoir which was first published in 1909 with a second edition in 1920. The model itself survived until 1961 when its useful life was deemed to be at an end. Mr Conway's Ireland was then demolished by men armed with hammers.

During the early 1890s four of the Museum's most accessible galleries were devoted to the earth sciences. In E.1 and E.2 lay the Museum's minerals, some of them being specimens from the famed Leskean Collection purchased by the (Royal) Dublin Society in 1792, in E.3 were amassed the Survey's collections, and in E.4 the relief model of Ireland was the centrepiece to a varied group of geological exhibits. I earlier expressed regret that modern Dublin possesses nothing to match Kane's imaginative creation at the Museum of Irish Industry. Similar sentiments must fill the mind of any earth-scientist who reflects upon the rich geological experience which in the early 1890s awaited visitors to the eastern ground-floor galleries of the new Dublin Museum of Science and Art. We have no means of knowing how many people entered those particular galleries, but the Museum as a whole clearly achieved some popularity. In 1893, for example, it was visited by 367,645 people. The Museum was open, free of charge, every weekday of the year save for Good Friday and Christmas Day, and every alternate Sunday afternoon. Never before had the Geological Survey been afforded so splendid an opportunity of making contact with the people of Ireland.

The Survey's exhibit in Gallery 3.E was designed by none other than Sir Archibald Geikie himself. It was observed in Chapter Four that between 1890 and 1901 Geikie was the *de facto* Director of the Geological Survey of Ireland (p.108). As we remember the splendid Survey display which once occupied Gallery 3.E, we must again conclude that Geikie took very seriously his Irish responsibilities.

But even Geikie had to admit that the exhibit in 3.E suffered from one serious defect. Parts of the gallery were gloomy. Its illumination was poor. Cole raised the matter in the *Irish Naturalist* for November 1895, Ball accepted the criticism, Geikie conceded the existence of a problem, and there were complaints from the visiting public. It seems that the gallery's eastward-facing fenestration was inadequate and the problem was exacerbated in 1894 when the Royal Dublin Society began to build for itself a new lecture-theatre immediately outside the windows of 3.E. Electric lighting was installed throughout the museum in 1890-91 but this evidently did little to diminish the problem.

The Director of the Museum discussed the difficulty with Geikie and McHenry during July 1896, and there emerged the proposal that the Survey should vacate Gallery 3.E and transfer its exhibit to the well-illuminated Curved or Quadrant Gallery. This gallery was a broad corridor which had been constructed in about 1857 to link Leinster House to the Royal Dublin Society's newly-constructed Natural History Museum on the southern side of Leinster Lawn. Geikie went to inspect the Curved Gallery during a visit to Dublin in October 1896, and he evidently considered the proffered accommodation to be satisfactory. It was agreed that the Survey would leave Gallery 3.E and re-establish itself in the Curved Gallery. The move took place during 1897, but while the location of the collection might have changed, its general arrangement remained the same. So, when a new edition of the guide to the exhibit was published in 1898, it was really just a reprint of the first edition of 1895.

The poor illumination of Gallery 3.E was undoubtedly the prime reason underlying the Survey's removal of its collections to the Curved Gallery. But there were two other factors involved. First, late in 1890 there arrived in the Museum the enormously rich collection of Irish antiquities belonging to the Royal Irish Academy. This event, coupled with a waxing nationalistic interest in Ireland's 'Golden Age', necessitated some re-ordering of the Museum's galleries. Second, Ball had died suddenly on 15 June 1895, thus removing from the Director's office the only geologist ever to have been its incumbent. Ball's successor was a former officer of the Royal Engineers - Lieutenant Colonel George Tindell Plunkett - and there is nothing to suggest that Plunkett shared Ball's sympathy for the earth sciences. The proposal to remove the Survey's collections from 3.E was in the air before Ball's death, but once Plunkett had taken over, the plan was speedily put into effect, and at much the same time the relief model was banished from 4.E and placed in the Museum Annex.

The removal of the Survey's collections to the Curved Gallery must to some extent have diminished their impact upon the Irish public. From their former home, just off the Central Court, the collections had been taken to a relatively secluded corner of the Museum's complex of buildings. It is difficult to believe that many but the geological aficionados will have taken the trouble to explore what, for the general public, was little more than a remote cul-de-sac branching out of the Natural History Museum. Nonetheless, the Survey initially was entirely happy with its new gallery. Twenty-five years were to elapse before there became clear the full consequences of the events of 1897. Could Geikie have seen the future revealed within one of the Survey's quartz crystals, he would surely never have agreed to the Survey's exchange of 3.E for the Curved Gallery.

In the Curved Gallery the Survey watched over its collections with devoted attention. The successive officers in charge of the collections in their new and arcuate home were (?) McHenry (1897-1902), Seymour (1902-1909), Hallissy (1909-1919), and Hinch (1919-1924). Under their care the displays were never allowed to degenerate into that state of fossilisation which so often creeps over a museum display and which had perhaps characterised the Survey's collections during their final years in St Stephen's Green. The officers now constantly made improvements; they regularly introduced fresh displays. In 1902, for instance, Seymour devised a new, albeit somewhat expensive, method of mounting rock-specimens, while there was added to the display an exhibit illustrative of the drift survey of the Dublin and Belfast districts. A few years later Hallissy compiled an exhibit devoted to soils. Around 1910 there was put on show some of the material raised by the *Helga* and described in Cole and Crook's memoir. In the aftermath of World War I the exhibit underwent a complete refurbishment and new items were introduced to give the display the slightly more economic slant appropriate to a Survey which was about to publish a map and memoir devoted to Ireland's economic minerals.

The Survey's efforts were widely praised. Teall thought highly of the display when he made a visit of inspection about 1903. At around the same time the Director of the Science and Art Museum wrote, with a verbal clumsiness perhaps forgivable in a man who for forty years had been a soldier of the Queen:

> It would be impossible to find any collection of rock specimens exhibited better than, it may probably be said as well as, these now are in Dublin.

Almost twenty years later, after the post-1918 refurbishment, the Visitors to the National Museum shared Plunkett's, sentiments.

> The Geological Section - especially that part of it connected with the Irish Geological Survey, is very creditable. The rock-specimens are particularly well displayed, and the excellent policy has been adopted of severely limiting the number of representative specimens while increasing their quality. Too often the student finds himself bewildered with large numbers of specimens when a very few picked ones would give him all he requires. There are some excellent new exhibits of economic importance in the Survey Department, such as those on Diatomaceous Earths, the results of the Magnetic Survey of the Ballard and Ballycapple iron ore deposits, and the exhibits of felspars.

Sir Archibald Geikie was in Dublin during April 1920. He was then in his eighty-fifth year, but he remained remarkably vigorous, and he had now returned to Dublin as the Chairman of a Royal Commission on the University of Dublin. The Commission held its meetings within Trinity College, but surely Geikie will have found the time to slip away from Trinity and over to the Museum to visit again the Curved Gallery. He had known the Survey's collections in the Museum of Irish Industry in the days of Jukes and Hull. He had seen them in Gallery 3.E in the days when Nolan had been his lieutenant over in Hume Street. He had seen them here in the Curved Gallery during his own final visits to Ireland as the Survey's Director-General. Now, as he strolled along the gallery there perhaps flooded in upon him the memories of a lifetime's association with Irish geology. Here were rock-specimens collected by the volcanic Kinahan and by 'Mac', that delightful field-companion who had died in Ballsbridge just twelve months earlier. There were type fossils named after departed Irish Survey colleagues: *Actinocrinus wynnei; Anodonta jukesii; Lunulicardium footi; Orthis bailyana.* On the walls there were maps compiled by Cruise, Egan, and Hardman, and drawings, too, in Du Noyer's distinctive style. There were even sketches made by Geikie himself.

But perhaps Geikie's Museum visit was one tinged with sadness. Here was a great geologist taking his leave both of Irish geology and of the Irish Survey. Fine classicist that he was, he knew it only too well.

> Nulla herba aut vis mortis tela frangit.

His only son had died in tragic circumstances in 1910, his youngest daughter had died in 1915, and his wife had died in 1916. He must have recognised his own remaining years as numbered. As he surveyed the collections in the Curved Gallery - collections still arranged according to the scheme which he had devised thirty years earlier - he doubtless viewed the display as one other personal memorial which he would shortly be leaving to posterity at the close of his long life's work. He was deceived. He and the exhibition in the Curved

Gallery were destined to die in the very same year - 1924. But the styles of their deaths were utterly different. Geikie died peacefully at his home in Haslemere at the heart of the English Weald. The display in the Curved Gallery died a violent death in the midst of political turmoil.

It was in June 1922 that Michael Collins, acting on behalf of the Provisional Government, asked to be shown over the Royal Dublin Society's headquarters at Leinster House. Shortly thereafter the Society was invited to release its commodious lecture-theatre for use by Dáil Éireann as an assembly chamber. The Society saw no option but to acquiesce. The Dáil did not actually convene in the lecture-theatre until 9 September 1922, but by the end of the previous June the Provisional Government was already in occupation of various apartments in and around Leinster House. For the Royal Dublin Society it was to prove the thin end of the wedge. Initially, the political presence was supposed to be temporary, but the Society must have sensed the direction of the wind when it learned in 1923 that the government proposed to erect upon Leinster Lawn a memorial to the deceased Arthur Griffith and the assassinated Michael Collins. By the time the memorial was unveiled on 13 August 1923 the government was in occupation of the greater part of Leinster House, and during the following year, the Society, under some duress, sold its home of over one hundred years to the state for the sum of £68,000.

Major repercussions followed from this political development at the heart of what hitherto had been a complex of buildings dedicated to Athene. The politicians brought in their train problems which never had been associated with the archaeologists, botanists, and stratigraphers who formerly had been among the denizens of the site. Rarely do numismatists, mycologists, or palynologists fall victim to the assassin's bullet, but the same is hardly true of government ministers - particularly during a civil war. Just such a war was tearing Ireland asunder during the summer of 1922. Forces opposed to the Anglo-Irish Treaty had in April occupied the Four Courts and several other Dublin buildings, and the authorities recognised that a similar seizure of the buildings around Leinster House would pose a serious threat both to personal security and national stability. On 28 June 1922 the entire National Museum was therefore declared to be closed until further notice. That was the very day upon which the forces of the Provisional Government launched their successful attack to recover the Four Courts. Some two months later it was also decided that the new (1911) buildings of the Royal College of Science, adjacent to the Museum, would not be opening for the session of 1922-23, and it was this closure which forced Cole to conduct some of his College classes at 14 Hume Street (see p.150).

The Civil War dragged on into 1923, but only slowly was something approaching normality restored to the buildings in the vicinity of Leinster House. Not until 2 June 1924 was the Natural History Museum reopened to the public, but anybody who that day entered the Museum intent upon inspection of the Survey's collections in the Curved Gallery was doomed to disappointment. The door to the Curved Gallery was locked. That gallery was no longer a part of the Museum. It had been requisitioned by the government. It was being partitioned to create offices for clerical assistants attached to the Dáil. The Survey had been evicted.

Sometime during 1924 - that was the year of Cole's death - the Survey was simply told to clear its collections from the Curved Gallery, and it was given very little time - perhaps only two weeks - in which to comply with the order. Two men were sent over from Hume Street to execute the task, one of the men presumably being Hinch, the officer then in charge of the collections. Case by case they removed the collections, wrapped the specimens, labelled each as best the limited time allowed, and then deposited the little parcels into the boxes provided. What then happened to all the material is not entirely clear. It seems that the showcases in which the collections had lain were put into the basement of 34 Molesworth Street, which was used by the Museum as a store. The illustrative material evidently went over to Hume Street, as, seemingly, did the boxed specimens, and for the next fifty years those specimens, or at least the great majority of them, lay neglected in the Survey's damp Hume Street basement.

In a way this entire sad episode was strangely ironic. In 1924 the Survey's collections were in the Curved Gallery largely because thirty years earlier the Royal Dublin Society's new lecture-theatre had cast a physical shadow across the collections as they lay in Gallery 3.E. Now, in 1924, the collections had been ejected from the Curved Gallery because a figurative shadow had fallen across them as a result of their proximity to the Dáil forgathered within the body of that same lecture-theatre.

The Visitors to the National Museum were shocked by the treatment inflicted upon the Survey's collections. In 1926 they observed that 'it is difficult to speak of it in restrained manner', and they reminded the authorities responsible that the Survey's collections represented a considerable investment of public money. They suggested that the assembly of the collections could hardly have cost less than £30,000. On 10 July 1929 the collections formed the subject of a question in the Dáil, and the Minister of Education (John Marcus O'Sullivan) responded by expressing the hope that the collections would shortly be removed from storage and returned to public display. But it may be that O'Sullivan's time-scale was that of Clio rather than that familiar to ordinary mortals; he was the professor of history in University College Dublin. Certainly nothing was done about the collections.

There was no room to display the collections in Hume Street, the Survey had no curatorial expertise, and the shrivelled size of the Survey left the officers with no time to devote to what once had been an esteemed Museum display. On 7 July 1937 Hallissy made the problem of the collections the subject of a three-page letter addressed to the Department of Industry and Commerce. Hallissy urged his case with vigour - and with a dash of chauvinism.

> It can be claimed for our Collections that they are of considerable economic, cultural, and National importance; and as such they surely deserve to be allotted space in the National Museum in preference to all foreign exhibits, no matter how interesting.

But by no means did he neglect the international ramifications of the problem. He explained that palaeontologists from around the world were regularly approaching the Survey seeking access to the type-specimens within the collections. All such requests, he observed, have to be refused 'on the absurd grounds' that the collections were in store and unavailable. Hallissy asked his Department to raise the issue with the Minister of Education as a matter of urgency. And there we have revealed another facet of the problem. Since 1 April 1928 the Survey and the Museum had lain in different areas of ministerial responsibility. The Survey was under Industry and Commerce, whereas the Museum had remained under Education. Hallissy got nowhere.

Hallissy's highlighting of the broader aspects of the problem was entirely justified. Like a great work of art, type-specimens are part of an international heritage. In their own way, they are international treasures. The global community of geology certainly deplored the treatment being inflicted upon the Survey's collections. The Eighteenth International Geological Congress was scheduled to be held in London during the summer of 1940, and those organising the event were concerned that any conference delegates who chose to visit Ireland would have no access to the Survey's collections. Two British Survey officers - Edward Battersby Bailey and Cyril James Stubblefield - were therefore deputed to enter into discussion with the Irish authorities on the whole subject of the Irish national geological collections. Again the efforts were fruitless, and in the event the 1940 congress had to be cancelled. I hasten to add that the cancellation was no result of Irish recalcitrance; the cancellation occurred because, come the summer of 1940, London was more concerned with Messerschmitts and Spitfires than with Mesozoics and spilites. Bailey was out with the Home Guard and Stubblefield was doubtless fire-watching over the roofs of South Kensington.

The cancelled conference was rescheduled to be held in London during 1948, and again there arose the question of the displaced Irish geological collections. This time the matter was raised by the Visitors to the National Museum in their report for 1946-47. They pointed out that at least 120 of the delegates attending the conference would be coming to Ireland, and they asked for some material to be brought out of storage to create both an interesting display and a good impression. Their plea fell upon deaf ears.

Far from improving, things would seem to have been getting worse. On 4 November 1947, Bishopp reported that the Survey's material was 'chaotic, and appears to have suffered much damage through the decay or destruction of labels'. A few months later, O'Meara went down into the Hume Street cellars to examine more closely the wreck of the Survey's former Museum exhibit. He reported that the material relating to the Twenty-Six Counties was lying in 65 boxes 'while another 13 boxes contain Museum stores'. His report, dated 31 March 1948, certainly conveys some impression both of the haste with which the Curved Gallery must have been cleared in 1924, and of the subsequent neglect of the collections as they lay in what once had been the kitchen of number 14.

It was not only geological visitors who were incommoded by the disappearance of the Survey's collections into the cellars of Hume Street. As Hallissy pointed out in his letter of July 1937, the Survey's officers needed access to the fossil collections in order adequately to perform their duties. An embarrassing situation arose within this area during 1947. The British Geological Survey had just established a branch office in Northern Ireland (from 1921 until April 1947 Northern Ireland was devoid of any geological survey) and as one of its first projects the new office embarked upon a drilling programme in the Dungannon Coalfield of County Tyrone. The officers responsible for the drilling approached Hume Street with an urgent request. Could they please see the fossils collected in the region by Hardman and described by Baily in the memoir to one-inch Sheet 35 (Dungannon), published in 1877. The fossils were needed to shed light upon the local stratigraphy. Now it so happened that the Dublin Survey also wanted to see the fossils since they had relevance to a search that was being made for coal at Carrickmacross in County Monaghan. But the fossils were 'in store' and thus irretrievable from amidst the chaos in the Hume Street cellars. James Phemister of the British Survey came over to Dublin to see the situation for himself, and the upshot was a generous offer to lend to Hume Street the services of a British Survey palaeontologist, with an assistant, for between one and two months while there was conducted a search for the Hardman material.

Similar work continued under Mr Murrogh O Brien, although now without any British input. From 1953 onwards some of the boxes in the cellars were opened and the contents taken upstairs to be arranged in drawers. This, however, was only a fitful activity, undertaken as other duties allowed. It was not until after appointment of Dr Dave Naylor to the Survey as Principal Geologist in 1976 that a serious attempt was made to recover and reorganise the collections. It was all a part of the post-1967 revival of the Survey. The damp and dusty boxes were taken from the Hume Street cellars which for fifty years had been their home. They were carried up into the hallway, past the chipped plaster bust of Jukes, and out through the front door. They were again to be set in motion through the streets of Dublin. This time there awaited them no railway-company drays such as those which used to bring the latest specimens to the door of the Museum of Irish Industry, nor was there a departmental handcart such as that which took the duplicate six-inch sheets to their place of safety in 1921 and 1923. Now the Survey had its own fleet of transport. After the cellars had been cleared of their burdensome containers, Dr Jean Archer went down to see what remained. She found a Du Noyer painting of the Giant's Causeway stuck to the cellar floor by mould. Presumably the painting had once graced the walls of the Curved Gallery. Happily it still survives in the Survey's archives. Its life was saved by the skill of conservators at the National Gallery.

From Hume Street the boxes were taken to 'Jacob's Factory', to 4 Kildare Street, and, later, to Baggot Bridge House. In those locations there was space for the opening of the boxes, for the examination and sorting of the contents, and for the arrangement of those contents within newly acquired steel cabinets. It was work carried out under the immediate supervision of Dave Naylor who thus, after a fifty-year hiatus, found himself to be Hinch's *de facto* successor as the Survey's officer in charge of collections. Other experts were brought in to work upon the collections on a part-time basis, and eventually the collections were all reunited within the fine modern storage facilities located down in the basement of the new building at Beggars Bush. There the work continues under the direction of Dr Andrew Sleeman and with the financial support of the National Heritage Council. A consultant palaeontologist - Dr Matthew Parkes - has been engaged, and work is presently in train upon the establishment for the collection of a sophisticated computer database. It is hoped to complete the curation and computerisation of the Survey's palaeontological collections by the close of 1995, and it is intended to publish a catalogue of all the type, figured, and cited specimens.

All this curatorial work carried out on the Survey's collections over the last twenty years is perhaps of little direct interest to the general public. Not many people propose to spend several weeks working through tray upon tray of graptolites taken from the rocks at Grangegeeth in County Meath or from the Slieve Bernagh. The moistening of such specimens with a touch of alcohol and their examination beneath a microscope is unlikely ever to match the popularity of a dram of the hard stuff and a good evening's crack. The form of a fossil holds far less popular interest than that of a horse, and the number of a graptolite's stipes will never receive that attention which we bestow upon the number of a champion's strokes as he plays the eighteenth at Killarney. The studies which are now in progress around the Survey's collections are of the highest significance for Irish geology, and they are by no means devoid of international ramifications. But for the non-geologist it is perhaps all rather puzzling. Fossils are an acquired taste and few but palaeontologists have developed the appropriate palate.

The revitalised Survey has nevertheless in recent years been doing something else with its collections - something which is readily comprehensible by us all. It has put some of the material from its collections on public display for the first time since the Survey was so rudely expelled from the Curved Gallery in 1924.

When the Beggars Bush building was being designed, care was taken to ensure that it included a sizeable exhibition hall. That hall is today named the Ganly Gallery in honour of Patrick Ganly who for long lived nearby in Bath Avenue and who did much of the field-work for Richard Griffith's quarter-inch geological map of Ireland first published in 1839. In the gallery, on the afternoon of 16 December 1986, Dr Cyril Williams declared open the Survey's new exhibition entitled 'Down to Earth'. Devised by Dr Jean Archer, the exhibition seeks to present a picture of the geological resources of Ireland, to trace the geological history of the island, and to lay before the public actual specimens of Irish rocks, minerals, and fossils. The Ganly Gallery thus today contains an exhibit possessing much the same objectives as those which, one hundred years ago, were in the mind of Archibald Geikie as he planned the exhibit destined for Gallery 3.E of the new Dublin Museum of Science and Art.

'Down to Earth' has been a great success. Since 1986 it has received many thousands of visitors, and the Survey must be particularly gratified by the response to the exhibition within the educational community. Teachers from all around the country have regularly brought parties of their pupils to visit the display, and it has served as a splendid shop-window both for the science of geology and for the Survey itself. As in all carefully tended exhibitions, the material comprising 'Down to Earth' is changed from time to time. During September 1994 a group of Carboniferous fossils was removed from its basement storage-cabinet and added to the exhibition display. I am given to understand that those very fossils may well first have been exhibited to the Irish public in the Upper South Gallery of the newly-opened Museum of Irish Industry. Siobhan from the convent school and Patrick from the Christian Brothers will have no understanding of such things, but those of us who do know something of the story of the Survey's cased collections will look at those fossils and think - think of their being collected, perhaps by poor old Flanagan, and then of their first being arranged for display by the dextrous hands of Forbes 'in a land of misery and tears'. Each of those specimens is not only a piece of geological history; each of them is also a piece of the history of the Survey itself.

CHAPTER ELEVEN

REACHING OUT

> Lastly, allow me to hope that my Lectures in Wexford may have raised an interest in your own mind, as well as in the minds of some others, in the wonderful and absorbing science of Geology, and that the subject may not be allowed altogether to drop out of your recollection.
>
> J. Beete Jukes in a letter dated at Wexford on 23 January 1854 and published five days later in the Wexford *Guardian*.

As usual, the venue was the House of the Royal Irish Academy at 19 Dawson Street, Dublin. It was 1987, and seated around the table of the Academy's imposing Council Room were the members of the Irish National Committee for Geology. A portrait of Sir Robert Kane watched over the proceedings. Some of Ireland's leading modern earth-scientists were present. Ralph Horne was representing the Survey. Under discussion was the programme for an event to be called 'Irish Geology Week' which the Committee had decided to hold during the September of the following year. Somebody made a suggestion. 'Why don't we hire a suitably large mechanical excavator - a JCB - build around it the form of a full-sized *Tyrannosaurus rex*, and then despatch our mechanical beast to cruise the highways of Ireland?' It was never a very serious proposal, and it was certainly never acted upon. Clearly, there would have been a host of concomitant problems. But what a public impact our dinosaur would have made! Just think of the shoppers' heads turning as our monster moved along St Patrick's Street in Cork. Just imagine an *Irish Times* front-page photograph of our beast poised over W.B. Yeats's grave at Drumcliff with an effectively primordial Benbulbin in the background.

That sort of publicity is what Irish Geology Week was all about. The Press Launch for the Week took place - with appropriate refreshments - in the Ganly Gallery at Beggars Bush on the morning of 16 February 1988. The Week itself was that of 9-17 September 1988, and during the Week there were staged a multitude of geological events. There were exhibitions, field-excursions, and city walks to examine the character of building stones. There were open-days at drilling-sites and visits to quarries and mines. Participants were even invited to go looking for flakes of gold in a prospector's pan, or to sprout wings in order to study geology in its broader aspects through airborne windows. That February morning in the Ganly Gallery the then chairman of the Irish National Committee for Geology, Professor Tony Wright of Queen's University Belfast, explained the objectives of the Week. They were to focus public attention upon the earth's crust as a fundamental element within our environment, to remind people of the practical and financial importance of rocks, minerals, and fossils, and to demonstrate to everybody the absorbing fascination of the science of geology.

Professor Wright made his points in telling fashion, but, truth to tell, there really was nothing new in the gospel which he preached. Irish Geology Week itself might be a novel medium, but the message which it carried was just as old as the Irish geological community. For almost two hundred years Irish geologists have constantly sought to remind the public both of the economic importance of their science and of its high intellectual value. In 1833 one of the earliest acts of the newly-founded Geological Society of Dublin was to organise the delivery of a course of public lectures on geology (the course was given by William Francis Ainsworth, a cousin of the novelist William Harrison Ainsworth), and Irish Geology Week 1988 was just another venture in the same tradition. It was an effort - a most successful effort - to place geology squarely and prominently before the Irish public.

Events such as the Geological Society of Dublin's lecture-course in 1833 and the Irish Geology Week of 1988 might appropriately be regarded as missionary activities conducted on behalf of the Irish geological community. The members of the community, like geologists the world over, are commonly enthusiastic about their science. Geology is for them a shared philosophy of the natural world rather than just a means of earning a living. Their enthusiasm - their philosophy - they wish to communicate to others. They want the non-geological public to understand. They wish to curry public favour. They desire to win converts. Politicians seek our support by means of the door-to-door canvass. Evangelists pray for conversions at mass rallies. The armed services - and the universities - stimulate their recruiting by the holding of open-days. And geologists strive to arouse interest in their science through the medium of events such as Ainsworth's course of public lectures in 1833 and Irish Geology Week 1988.

The officers of the Survey have invariably taken a leading role in all this missionary activity on behalf of geology. Perhaps that was only to be expected. Since the foundation of the Survey in 1845, its officers have invariably constituted the largest single corporate group within the Irish geological community. As the state-funded, 'established church of geology' the Survey has enjoyed peculiarly favourable opportunities to proselytise on behalf of the science. The historian who reviews the Survey on the occasion of its bicentenary in the year 2045 will doubtless be able to tell of the Survey having conducted geological missions through TV programmes, through video-cassettes, through computer games, and through other media as yet undreamed of. But, as we look back over the history of the Survey from our present temporal standpoint, we can see that, apart from its officially assigned duty of providing the Irish public with geological maps and memoirs, the officers of the Survey have also reached out to that same public in four other ways. Those four other media I term the static display, the theatre discourse, the field exposition, and the non-official publication. A parade of these four types of activity among the Survey's officers constitutes the theme of the remainder of this chapter.

Of the static display I need write little. It formed the subject of the previous chapter. It takes us back into the world of museums and showcases. In the Museum of Irish Industry, in the National Museum of Science and Art, and in the Ganly Gallery at Beggars Bush, the Survey has laid out some of its rocks, minerals, fossils, and other materials in an effort first to attract the attention of the Irish public and second to give to that public some insight into the enthralling story which the earth sciences have to tell. The exhibits are left to speak for themselves and they would seem to have spoken with eloquence. As we have seen, both Colonel Plunkett and the Museum's Visitors were most impressed by the message which the Survey had encapsulated within its exhibit in the Curved Gallery (p.270). There are still a few able to remember being thrilled in the Museum Annexe at the sight of the relief model of Ireland coloured under the direction first of McHenry and then of Hallissy (see p.268). Today similar success is surely indicated by the fact that some teachers return to the Ganly Gallery year after year, bringing with them fresh parties of pupils come to learn the lessons of the Down to Earth exhibition. Who knows? Perhaps Siobhan from that convent school or Patrick from the Christian Brothers will one day themselves become a Survey officer as a result of a road to Damascus experience beneath the bright lights of the Ganly Gallery.

The second of the missionary media - the theatre discourse - involves the Survey officer in the actual preaching of the geological gospel to some assembled congregation. It sees the presentation of the geological message through the spoken word and within some formal pedagogic setting. The Survey has possessed a number of officers who were both experienced and talented in this particular form of communication. Four Local Directors and Directors have actually held regular teaching appointments concurrently with their Survey posts. There were those within the geological profession who regarded such a combination of classroom and Survey duties as highly desirable and likely to result in a valuable cross-fertilisation between the theory of academe and the practice of the Survey.

Oldham was the professor of geology in Trinity College Dublin throughout his tenure of the Survey's local directorship between 1846 and 1850. He was required to deliver a course of at least twelve lectures during each of the College's three annual terms. Foot, Hull, and H.B. Medlicott were three future Survey officers who began their geological careers in Oldham's classes. Hull tells us that before joining Oldham's class he knew nothing of geology, and his fellow students warned him that it was the most difficult subject on the course. He therefore approached the class with some apprehension lest geology 'might prove beyond my powers of mind'. But Oldham speedily laid the young man's fears to rest.

> His lectures were illustrated by diagrams and specimens, and were delivered with a lucidity and attractiveness which engaged my interest and attention, so that as the subject was developed from time to time my interest increased; and to my surprise I discovered it opened out a physical history of the world far exceeding in wonder and beauty my highest conceptions.

Hull was a son of the cloth, and until he sat at Oldham's feet his knowledge of earth-history had been limited to the opening chapters of *Genesis*. Now all was changed.

> ... the geological history revealed by the study of the earth's crust and its fossil contents opened up a vast field of enquiry hitherto undreamed of by me; and I found geology to be the subject which above all the others taught in the course captivated my mind and responded to my reason.

In a very literal sense, Oldham had won a convert for geology.

When Jukes was in 1850 appointed to succeed Oldham as Local Director he hoped that he would also be succeeding Oldham in the Trinity chair. His credentials for the post were certainly impeccable, and his powerful application was supported by four heavyweight referees: Charles Darwin, Roderick Murchison, Andrew Ramsay, and Adam Sedgwick. He had played four aces, and to improve his chances still further he even indulged in a little cosmetic 'surgery'. He was well-known for his bushy black beard, but his Survey friends advised him that 'the Irish paddies' would never fill a chair with a man whose face was so decorated. Jukes was to cross to Ireland on 29 November 1850 to assume his new Survey post, and the previous evening two of his colleagues - Ramsay and Alfred Richard Cecil Selwyn - joined the still bearded Jukes in Holyhead to give him an appropriate sendoff. Great was the amusement in the hotel the following morning when Jukes appeared clean-shaven having finally been persuaded to 'offer up my beard as a sacrifice to the Infernal Deities, to propitiate their favour'. But it was all to no avail. On 21 January 1851 the Board of Trinity College made its choice. Five votes went to the internal candidate, the Carlow-born Samuel Haughton, and only three votes went to Jukes. Over at 51 St Stephen's Green, Jukes's visage was rapidly restored to its barbate normality.

For the moment Jukes was denied the opportunity of regular encounter with the receptive minds of students, but that is not to say that he was temporarily struck dumb. Far from it. On 30 June 1852 he spoke with great effect to one of the most unusual audiences he ever can have encountered. It consisted largely of young men who intended shortly to leave England bound for the Australian gold-fields.

During 1851 gold had been found first at Bathurst in New South Wales, and then at Ballarat in Victoria, and there ensued the usual hectic gold-rush. At the newly-opened Museum of Practical Geology, in London's Jermyn Street, it was resolved to do something to cater for the needs of those British hopefuls who planned shortly to depart for the diggings. A course of six lectures was therefore devised around the theme of gold. A ticket for the course cost three shillings, and the lectures were scheduled for evening delivery because it was felt that the clientele was likely to consist of artisans who would be in employment during normal working hours. Between 1842 and 1845 Jukes had seen a great deal of Australia while he was with H.M.S. *Fly*, and he was now asked to deliver the first lecture in the Jermyn Street course.

Jukes's discourse was entitled 'The Geology of Australia, with especial reference to the Gold Regions', and some three hundred would-be gold-miners came to hear him. According to the press reports, the lecture was much appreciated, and Jukes's graphic descriptions evoked frequent bursts of applause. As always in his lectures, he made effective use of maps and diagrams; he introduced his auditors to some of the basic principles of geology; and he described the telltale indications to which the prospector must ever be alert. But on one subject he refused to be drawn. He wisely declined to speculate as to the actual richness and extent of Australia's auriferous regions. And, for those who might eventually be forced to admit that they had failed in their efforts to strike it rich, he had some words of consolation. In the phrases of one press report of the lecture:

> He stated that he was well acquainted with Australia; and his conviction was, irrespective of the gold discoveries, that for the enterprising and the energetic there was a better chance of gaining competence and wealth in Australia than in any other part of the world.

What he evidently failed to reveal was that just three years earlier he had declined to transfer himself to this land of abundant opportunity. He had then rejected the offered post of Geological Surveyor to New South Wales.

Back in Dublin the lecture-theatre in the rear portion of the Museum of Irish Industry was evidently not completed until 1854, and only then did the departure of the contractor's men allow there to be implemented a proposal which had lain dormant for several years. The principle of self-improvement through education was fast becoming a leitmotif for the age, and its high-priest, in the shape of Samuel Smiles, was shortly to don his robes. It was in 1855 that he completed the manuscript for his enormously influential *Self-Help*, where the opening words present the aphorism 'Heaven helps those who help themselves'. The government, in tune with this prevailing spirit and acting through the newly-constituted Department of Science and Art, in 1854 resolved to graft on to Kane's Museum a new educational establishment cumbrously styled the Government School of Science Applied to Mining and the Arts attached to the Museum of Irish Industry. Initially four chairs were established for the so-called Dublin Science and Art Professors - chairs in geology, natural history, natural philosophy, and theoretical and practical chemistry - and the first of the new lecture-courses were offered during the session of 1854-55.

Jukes was appointed to this new chair of geology, and he thus in 1854 achieved that pedagogical opportunity which in 1851 had been denied to him within Trinity College. He was pleased to have received the appointment, not only because as a professor his annual salary was augmented by £200, but because he was one of those who saw advantage in the integration of Survey with academic duties. As he explained to the Select Committee of 1864:

> I find that since I have been lecturing in the museum at Stephen's Green, I am better able to direct the operations in the field, because one requires to systematise one's knowledge, and to make it definite in order to lecture.

As a Department of Science and Art professor, Jukes was expected to deliver annually some fifty-four lectures. Twenty-four of these were elementary lectures delivered either in the afternoon, in the Royal Dublin Society's lecture-theatre, or in the evening, in the Museum of Irish Industry. These lectures were termed the 'Popular Lectures', and they were open to the public without charge. The remaining thirty lectures constituted a coherent course delivered in the evening in the Museum of Irish Industry. These were termed the 'Systematic Lectures', and a fee was demanded of those wishing to join the classes.

Jukes's Popular Lectures normally consisted of classes in either geology or physical geography, and during his first ten years as a professor, the average attendance at these of his lectures varied from 410 people in 1854-55 to 121 people in 1861-62. In the afternoons, at the Royal Dublin Society, the audiences consisted largely of members of the society and their families, of clergy, and of ladies intending to become governesses. In the evenings, at the Museum of Irish Industry it is said that about seventy per cent of each audience consisted of individuals drawn from the artisan classes.

But although both the afternoon and the evening attendances were large, Jukes was far from happy about the character of his audiences. People were mostly there not out of interest in science, but simply because the lectures were seen as a gratuitous diversion. At the Royal Dublin Society the members placed their children in the front seats where their behaviour became a disruptive nuisance; at the Museum of Irish Industry people just drifted in off the street because the bright gas-lamps looked inviting upon a chill winter's evening. People came looking for entertainment rather than for instruction and, as Jukes expressed it, the tone of the lectures had to be debased *ad captandum vulgus.* He was convinced that the audience at most of his Popular Lectures would have preferred to see the rostrum occupied by a juggler! In consequence Jukes was opposed to the principle of free public lectures. Before the Select Committee of 1864 he pleaded that everybody attending a Popular Lecture should be required to pay six pence as an earnest of their serious intent.

The Systematic Lectures were quite another story. They constituted a comprehensive course intended to satisfy the needs of dedicated students of geology. As evening lectures they were available to men - and to women - who might be otherwise employed during the earlier hours of the day. Here Jukes's sole complaint was that thirty lectures in geology hardly afforded him with adequate time in which fully to explore so comprehensive a subject in all its ramifications. There is to hand clear proof of the success of Jukes's Systematic Lectures. Five of those who joined his classes went on to become officers of the Irish Survey: Cruise, W.B. Leonard, McHenry, Nolan, and Wynne.

These lectures associated with the Dublin School of Science Applied to Mining and the Arts over the years allowed Jukes to preach his geological message to many hundreds of the city's inhabitants, but his lecturing was by no means confined to the Irish metropolis. From time to time his voice was to be heard reverberating in halls in many another part of the country. He was there to deliver courses in geology on behalf of the Department of Science and Art's Committee of Lectures.

The Committee of Lectures (Sir Richard Griffith and Sir Robert Kane were among its eight members) was responsible for the organisation of the educational programme at the Royal Dublin Society and the Museum of Irish Industry, but it was also charged with the duty of disbursing monies from a parliamentary grant made to allow the delivery of courses of science lectures in provincial towns throughout Ireland. This was an exercise in the taking of science out to the people of small-town Ireland; it was another exercise in providing the opportunity for self-help.

Each year the Committee of Lectures announced through the press that it was ready to receive applications from local groups wishing to make themselves responsible for the organisation of lecture-courses in subjects such as agricultural botany, electricity and magnetism, physical or palaeontological geology, heat and the steam-engine, hydrostatics, or optics and acoustics. Applications were received at the committee's office in Dublin Castle, the relative merits of the submissions were considered, decisions were made, and lecturers were allocated to the selected courses and venues. The lecturers were drawn from a panel of distinguished Irish-resident scientists, among their number being Charles Alexander Cameron, public analyst to the city of Dublin, Edmund William Davy of the Royal Dublin Society, Robert Harkness of Queen's College Cork, William Henry Harvey of Trinity College Dublin, William King of Queen's College Galway, William Kirby Sullivan of the Department of Science and Art, and Charles Wyville Thomson of Queen's College Belfast. The Survey's two representatives upon the panel were Jukes and Baily.

The provincial lectures were normally delivered during the period from April to November, and a typical course consisted of at least nine hour-long lectures given every other weekday over a period of three weeks, the lecturer being required to remain at the urban venue throughout the period of his course. On average between one hundred and two hundred students enrolled for each course, and the students came from backgrounds such as small-shopkeepers, members of mechanics' institutes, and supporters of literary and philosophical societies, although at some centres the courses were by no means disregarded by the gentry. In order to stimulate diligence, students attending classes were encouraged to present themselves at an examination held following the conclusion of their course, and at those examinations excellence was rewarded with Department of Science and Art medals and book-prizes. Those proposing to take the examinations received further tuition from their teacher on those days when he was not lecturing, and the teacher was also expected to give such students advice about suitable course-related reading.

A typical year in the programme of provincial lectures was 1857. That year the Committee of Lectures arranged for courses to be delivered in the following twelve towns, the Ulster bias of that year's offering being quite characteristic: Ballymena, Carlingford, Carlow, Drogheda, Dungannon, Enniskillen, Kilrush, Londonderry, Omagh, Portlaw, Sligo, and Strabane. Neither Jukes nor Baily was involved in lecture courses every year, and Jukes clearly sought to integrate his provincial lecturing duties with his Survey programme of field inspection. In 1857, for example, he gave a course of geological lectures in Carlow between 5 October and 20 October, and the local one-inch sheet - Sheet 137 (Carlow) - was published during the following year. In Carlow his lectures drew an average attendance of only seventy students, and a mere seven students appeared at the examination on 21 October. The identities of the four prize-winners among the seven are nonetheless interesting. They were, first, Jeanie Franklin (medal), second, Isabella Thornton, third, Constantina Thornton, and fourth, Thomas Richardson junior. The presence of a strong female component within Jukes's 1857 Carlow prize-list is by no mean atypical of Department of Science and Art prize-lists as a whole, but, oddly, only one future Survey officer appears to have emerged from the provincial lecture courses; Hugh Leonard, then aged seventeen, attended Baily's lectures in Drogheda during 1858. There thirty-three candidates presented themselves for examination and Leonard took the second prize.

During the middle decades of the nineteenth century, geology was a science very much in the public eye. For the Victorians geology was the cynosure among the sciences just as is genetics in the late twentieth century. There is another parallel between the two sciences. Today, among the sciences, it is the discoveries of the geneticist which torment us with many a moral problem; in Victorian times it was the achievements of the geologist which seemed to be raising the crucial moral dilemmas. Employing his novel techniques, the geologist was then beginning to probe the secrets of earth-history, but in so doing, he was trespassing - trespassing into territory which had for long been the preserve of revealed religion and the First Book of Moses. Part of the excitement which attracted audiences to the lectures of Jukes and Baily, in both Dublin and the provincial towns, may well have arisen from the fact that in some quarters geology was viewed as a rather disreputable science. It had all the appeal which attaches to anything deemed to be slightly risqué.

In January 1854 Jukes must have been reminded of the controversial nature of his science. He had gone down to Wexford to deliver a course of geological lectures similar to those which he was later to offer in other Irish towns as a professor of the Department of Science and Art. The Wexford *Guardian* promptly took him to task over his lectures. It was claimed that he had deviated from a literal interpretation of *Genesis,* that he had failed to attribute due geological significance to the Noachian Deluge, and that he was guilty of a display of that arrogance which the *Guardian's* editor held to be all too common among scientists. In the pages of that newspaper there ensued a brief and most courteously conducted debate over the validity of the views which Jukes had been propounding. His course of lectures had clearly made its impact along the banks of the Slaney.

The programme of provincial lectures was terminated in 1867 when the Museum of Irish Industry and the Dublin School of Science Applied to Mining and the Arts were fused within the fresh corpus of the Royal College of Science for Ireland. Jukes carried his chair into the new institution. He thus retained the opportunity of delivering regular geological discourses, and he launched his first course within the Royal College - a course of seventy-five lectures in geology - on 19 November 1867. During the following session - the session of 1868-69 - Jukes's increasing ill-health forced his frequent resort to the use of a locum tenens at the lectern. For such assistance he normally turned either to Baily or to Alphonse Gages, the Librarian and Museum Curator at the Royal College of Science. One or other of those two gentlemen probably had to complete Jukes's course that year because his wife and two physicians had the professor committed to Hampstead House on 8 May 1869 (see p.70).

Following Jukes's death in July 1869, Hull succeeded to the chair of geology within the Royal College and he combined his occupation of the chair with his Survey directorship down to his retirement in 1890. In Hull's day there were never more than a mere handful of students reading geology at the College, but Hull's first class of students was nevertheless the seed-bed whence there came three future Survey officers; Hardman, Kilroe, and Mitchell all graduated as associates of the College in 1870. It is also interesting to note that, later in the 1870s, Hull's class contained Gerrard A. Kinahan, the son of George Henry Kinahan. We may only wonder what Kinahan senior perhaps thought of his son being under the tutelage of the arch enemy! While the numbers attending Hull's classes were only small, his College duties were by no means merely nominal. During the session of 1887-88, for instance, he met with his class from 11 a.m. until noon on Tuesdays and Thursdays for two terms of the year, and from 11 a.m. until noon on Saturdays for one term, the Saturdays of the second term being devoted to geological field-excursions.

Following Hull's retirement in 1890, the link between the Survey and the chair of geology within the Royal College of Science was temporarily broken. For the next fifteen years the Survey was denied any regular opportunity of bringing geology to the attention of Irish students through the medium of lecture delivery. Visually, by means of its publications and its Museum displays, the Survey remained in close contact with its public; verbally, the Survey largely fell silent when Hull packed his lecture-notes and then quitted Dublin bound for London. Not until 1905 was a Survey voice again regularly to be heard in the lecture-theatre. In that year the link between the Survey and the Royal College of Science for Ireland was re-established when Cole, Hull's successor in the College's chair of geology, was given the additional appointment of part-time Survey Director. The Survey thus recovered its voice in the halls of academe; there was restored that duality which had existed within the Survey during the days of Oldham, of Jukes, and of Hull.

One afternoon during the summer of 1983 I visited a nursing-home in the Dublin suburb of Rathgar to talk with a nonagenarian - with a Miss Mildred Alice Latimer. She had graduated in the onetime Royal University of Ireland in 1908, and by 1983 she was perhaps the last survivor of those able to remember Cole in his heyday during the years before 1914. Despite her age - she was then in her ninety-fifth year - I found that she remembered Cole extremely well. His diminutive form, so small, she observed, that in lectures at the Royal College of Science his audience could scarcely find him when he retired behind the demonstration bench. Like a ventriloquist's doll, I suggested. She smiled. She spoke of his sparkling eyes. She recollected his passionate enthusiasm for the earth sciences. She talked of his lucid eloquence. And she lapsed into thoughtful silence after telling me of the near hypnotic spell which he was capable of casting upon an audience. It was almost as though that spell retained its power even after the lapse of seven decades.

Mildred Latimer died on 15 May 1984. She was my sole human link with a man who was generally esteemed to be one of the finest public lecturers of his generation. Certainly the Survey could have found for itself, and for the cause of geology generally, no more effective a verbal champion than Grenville Cole. On 8 July 1911, when the recently-crowned King George V declared open the magnificent new buildings of the Royal College of Science (now Government Buildings) in Dublin's Upper Merrion Street, the Survey must have anticipated a continuing fruitful relationship between the College and Hume Street. Five of Cole's former students in the College - Thomas Haigh, W.D. Haigh, Hallissy, Seymour, and Valentine - had all found work with the Survey during the years before Ypres became a shambles, and two other of Cole's former students married into the Survey: Blanche Vernon (Mrs Cole) and Mabel Crawford MacDowell (Mrs Wright).

It is an impressive fact that during the fifty years following the establishment of the Royal College of Science in 1867, the Survey gave employment to eleven geologists who had cut their scientific teeth in the College classes of Jukes, Hull, or Cole. During that same interval only three young geologists went to the Survey from Trinity College Dublin, and of those three, two (Egan and Traill) joined the Survey in 1868 at the very beginning of the fifty-year period. As the royal party drove off into Merrion Square that Saturday afternoon in July 1911, Cole doubtless remained within the College again to survey his new facilities with pride and satisfaction. He may well have regarded them as a fine modern nursery where there would be nurtured many more generations of Survey officers. If those really were his sentiments, then he was sadly deluded. The relationship between Hume Street and the lecture-theatres of the Royal College of Science was near to its end.

In the entire one-hundred-and-fifty-year story of the Survey there is one year which stands apart from all the others. Without any doubt it was the Survey's blackest year. It was a year of calamity. It was 1924. That year Cole's death removed the Survey's only remaining officer possessed of an international standing. That year death finally silenced the regular prelections of a Survey voice within the lecture-theatre. That year it became clear that the Royal College of Science, closed for security reasons in 1922, was unlikely ever to reopen its doors. That year the Survey, for the first time ever, found itself devoid of even an acting Director. That year the Survey was transferred from beneath the useful wing of the Department of Agriculture and Technical Instruction and then stuffed beneath the feathers of a Department of Education which was to prove a flightless bird in the Survey interest. That year the Survey's collections were loaded into boxes and then banished from the Curved Gallery of the National Museum. After 1924 the Survey had to live in a different world.

Today, within the medical profession, many a senior figure holds a university chair alongside a hospital appointment. Such a situation is entirely analogous to that pertaining for the Survey's Director or Local Director down to that watershed year of 1924. But today all is changed. Such duality of appointment for Survey officers is a thing of the past. The mind boggles at the thought of a modern Survey Director having to excuse himself from a ministerial gathering in order to dash off to some campus where he has to deliver his usual Thursday afternoon lecture in course 309! Indeed, I imagine that such a combination of Survey and academic posts would fall foul of the modern civil-service contract of employment. That, however, is not to imply that our modern Survey officers are denied the opportunity of presenting their science to the public within the context of the theatre discourse. Far from it. In Beggars Bush the Survey has even equipped itself with its very own little auditorium.

Today, as throughout the history of the Survey, officers will seize whatever opportunities may arise for the verbal exposition of their science. Over the decades there must have been innumerable such occasions. On 7 May 1973, when Bob Aldwell spoke about groundwater to a Galway and Mayo regional development group, he was treading in the footsteps left by Jukes when he spoke about quarrying at the Museum of Irish Industry on 20 November 1854. On 5 March 1987, when Jean Archer introduced the 'Down to Earth' exhibition to a party of schoolteachers gathered in the Ganly Gallery, her seminar was another contribution towards that tradition which Lamplugh had been building on 14 January 1902 when he spoke in the Natural History Museum on boulders and shells from the glacial drifts.

The third medium employed by the geological missionary I termed the field exposition. Here the geologist conducts a group of interested observers out beyond the lecture-theatre and into the real world of Nature itself. Here the members of such a group are shown rocks as they actually exist. Further than that, our geologist demonstrates how, in skilled hands, those rocks can be milked to yield a generous, rich, and perhaps even addictive, potation of geohistory. In some blasted quarry-face the exposed and gently-folded strata are woven into a tale of gigantic earthmovements. Along some wave-washed coast a sombre black band of rock serves to inspire an account of onetime fiery red volcanoes. On some exposed hill-top built in slate the presence of a massive granite boulder stimulates an awe-inspiring saga of a land once held in the icy grip of immense glaciers. In the case of the field exposition actual geological phenomena thus became the highly tangible texts around which the geological preacher seeks to build a compelling sermon.

Such open-air sermons are surely by far the most effective means of arousing and developing public interest in the earth sciences. Over the decades Survey officers must have delivered countless thousands of such sermons to a multitude of varied audiences. I propose to offer an account of just one such a Survey field exposition. It stands here as exemplar for all the others. I choose this one illustration because it is an early specimen of the genre, because it involves one of the largest (only one larger is known to me) groups ever taken into the field by Survey officers, and because the two officers concerned are, I do confess, two of my favourite Survey characters. But in one respect, this field exposition is far from being typical It was a disaster.

In 1857, for the eight days beginning on Wednesday 29 August, the British Association for the Advancement of Science held its annual meeting in Dublin. Jukes and Du Noyer announced that on the Thursday following the conclusion of the meeting they would lead a party of the Association's members to study the geology of Lambay Island, lying off the County Dublin coast. The party, limited in number to two hundred, was to assemble at Amiens Street station in time to leave for Howth on the special 9.30 a.m. train kindly provided by the Dublin and Drogheda Railway Company. At Howth the party was to transfer immediately to a steamer generously made available by Messrs Palgrave, and aboard this vessel the excursionists would be carried across to the island. There the event's handbill held out the promise of Lower Silurian slates, conglomerates, highly fossiliferous limestones, intrusive and contemporaneous greenstones and porphyries, and a patch of unconformable Old Red Sandstone. As if this was not already a surfeit of geological riches, the excursionists were also offered a seaborne inspection both of Irelands Eye and of the coastal geology of County Dublin around Rush and Loughshinny. Refreshments would be available aboard the steamer 'at a reasonable rate', and the return train for Dublin would leave Howth at 6.0 p.m. 'precisely'. A ticket for the excursion cost two shillings.

That is what was supposed to happen. What really did happen is revealed by a press-cutting inserted in the scrapbook maintined by Jukes's aunt,

Jane Jukes. That scrapbook now lies before me as I write.

Almost two hundred ladies and gentlemen gathered at Amiens Street and boarded the train for Howth. The sky was sullen and rain began to fall as they travelled out through Killester and Raheny. When they arrived in Howth a strong north wind was blowing and a high sea was running. The pelting rain and the sound of the breakers crashing against the pier revealed some to be faint-hearts. They turned tail and took the next train back to Dublin. But the majority persevered. With Jukes at their head, they proceeded to the end of the pier only there to discover that Messrs Palgrave had let them down. There was no steamer either present or in sight. They resolved to wait. Eventually, a smudge on the horizon became a corkscrewing steamer at the harbour entrance, but the sight of her gyrations was sufficient to convince the assembled multitude that a visit to Lambay was somewhat less compelling than it had seemed only two hours earlier. Experienced deep-water sailor that he was, Jukes announced, amidst laughter, that discretion was the better part of valour and that he proposed to abandon the attempt to reach Lambay. Instead he offered the party 'a jolly walk over Howth and down to the Baily lighthouse'. And that is how the remainder of the day was spent by Jukes, Du Noyer, and almost one hundred and fifty rather damp excursionists. There was also one gentleman from the press. He would appear to have been both devoted to his duties and impressed by the mood of the occasion. The very next day the following of his words appeared in his newspaper.

> Nevertheless, there were amongst the party enough of true sons of science provided with hammers and - what is somewhat more essential - intelligent and informed minds, and enough of eagerly listening auditors to the way-side discussions to fulfil the announcement of the programme in the spirit, if not in the letter, and to defeat the untoward churlishness of the September weather.

Through their static displays, their theatre discourses, and their field expositions, the officers of the Survey, over fifteen decades, must have brought their science to the notice of hundreds of thousands of people. But the overwhelming majority of those people were drawn from the local Irish community. They were the people of Booterstown who had climbed the staircase in the Museum of Irish Industry, or the people from Drumcondra who made their way along the Curved Gallery. They were the citizens of Carlow who had enrolled for Jukes's course of provincial lectures, or the inhabitants of Kingstown who were registered students in Cole's classes at the Royal College of Science. They were the members of the Dublin Naturalists' Field Club who went to Sligo with Seymour in July 1901, or the members of the Irish Geological Association who, led by Synge, toured the glacial deposits of County Meath on 30 October 1960.

All the while, over the horizon, there lay a vast international throng which was never going to be touched by Irish Survey officers arranging museum exhibits, giving lectures down in Carlow, or conducting field-excursions over in Sligo. There was then only one means whereby the Irish Survey officers could bring themselves, their investigations, and the entire field of Irish geology before a wide international audience. That means was through the medium of publication. Non-official publication is thus my fourth form of missionary activity employed by Irish Survey officers.

The publication of maps and memoirs is an important part of the normal duties of any Survey officer. Such official publications emanating from the Irish Survey will clearly serve to attract attention both to Irish geology and to Irish geologists. The frequency with which such publications are pumped into the international circulatory system of science is indicative of what I earlier termed the Survey's official pulse rate (p.164). The story of that particular pulse rate is the message which throbs through the heart of the first seven chapters of this volume. As we have seen, over much of its history the Survey has displayed a vigorous official pulse rate, even if there have been some periods during the twentieth century when that pulse rate was so enfeebled that some ill-informed overseas consultant might have been tempted to certify the Survey as dead. On the subject of the Survey's official pulse rate I will here write nothing further.

As I explained earlier (p.164), an institution such as the Survey may display a second pulse rate which, while similar in character to the official pulse rate, is yet different in origin. This second pulse rate is the one which here concerns me. It is the private pulse rate. It is the pulse rate which measures the frequency with which the individual members of a Survey feel moved to publish work of their own volition and for their own private satisfaction. It is the pulse rate which indicates the strength of an officer's desire to persist with scientific activity on beyond the limits required by the call of professional duty. Turn to *Hardwicke's Science - Gossip* for April 1872 and there you will find the first of several essays by Kinahan entitled 'Sketches in the West of Ireland'. Writing those essays was no part of his official duties. He wrote them because it pleased him so to do. He wrote them because he wished to communicate to others his own enthusiasm for geology and his own love for the Irish scene. He was adopting the habit of the geological missionary and employing the medium of non-official publication to further his end. Unconsciously he was also

FIGURE 11.1. *'Cleavage in grey slate. Ringabella Bay, Co. Cork'. Plate XVII in Jukes's* Popular Physical Geology *of 1853. This is one of the twenty plates which illustrate the volume, all of them being derived from sketches made by Du Noyer. In the actual volume each plate is a 'double-tinted' lithograph. Note the hammer and Survey map-case in the left foreground.*

contributing to a maintenance of the Survey's private pulse rate.

In this cynical age of ours I will, I know, be reminded that the motives of any missionary are neither pure nor simple. That I willingly concede. I am sure that the geological missionaries within the ranks of the Survey experienced a variety of motivations aside from the desire to arouse in others a passion for the earth sciences. There were creative instincts to be satisfied. There were contemporary reputations to be established. There were do-it-yourself literary mausolea to be erected. There was even money to be earned. I will make no effort to disentangle these varied motives. I will simply observe that during the first eighty years of its existence, the Survey displayed a vigorous private pulse rate as a counterpart to the Survey's equally vigorous official pulse rate. Out of St Stephen's Green, and then out of Hume Street, there came a torrent of scientific papers, pamphlets, small-scale maps, and books, all of them being the purely voluntary offerings of Survey officers both to their international scientific community and to the non-geological world at large. It was a torrent which flowed from the sparkling spring of private motivation rather than out of the turbid pool of public duty.

Between 1845 and the demise of the Royal Geological Society of Ireland in 1890, Survey officers published some 130 papers in the journal of their local Irish geological society. How many papers Survey officers may have published in other home and overseas journals I just cannot say. The total must run into thousands. I happen to have upon my desk at the moment my copy of the London-based *Geological Magazine* for 1865. I see that it contains two papers by Irish Survey officers - by Baily and Kinahan - and a total of seven informative letters written by Jukes, Foot, and Kinahan. The contents of the volume will serve to emphasise that within the Irish Survey there was to be heard much scratching of pens upon paper. Sometimes that scratching was that of a mapping pen. In 1852, 1867, and 1878, three Survey officers - first Du Noyer, then Jukes, and finally Hull - all published their own small-scale geological maps of Ireland. The copy of Jukes's 1867 map which I acquired from a London dealer in 1978 serves as a further reminder that there was nothing insular about the Victorian Survey. The map is dissected, mounted upon linen, and folded into a slip-case, the spine of which bears the manuscript title 'Carta Geologica d'Irlanda di Beete Jukes'.

A few of the several thousand non-official scientific papers and pamphlets originating within the Survey have already received specific individual mention in the earlier chapters of the present volume. The small-scale maps of Ireland by Jukes and Hull were alluded to in their appropriate places in Chapter Three. What has so far escaped our attention is the part played by Survey-generated book-literature in the maintenance for the Survey of a lively private pulse rate. The production of a substantial book - literature written by Survey officers is one of the most remarkable aspects of the entire Survey story.

In 1846 M'Coy collaborated with Richard Griffith and J.W. Salter in the publication of a volume devoted to the Silurian fossils of Ireland. Griffith's preface to the volume is dated 29 April 1846, and, while there is no certainty that the volume was actually published before M'Coy effected his diplomatic retreat from the Survey on 30 September 1846 (see p.33) he had clearly worked upon the volume during his brief spell of Survey employment. M'Coy thus set a pattern of private authorship which was to be emulated by many a later Survey officer. Over the eighty years following the establishment of the Survey the remarkable total of thirty-four earth-science books came from nine different Survey officers. These thirty-four books were either new works written during an officer's Survey service, or fresh editions of works originally written before an officer joined the Irish Survey. It was a phenomenal outpouring of volumes and it must have played a significant part in earning for the Survey the international reputation which it then enjoyed.

Aside from M'Coy, Jukes was the first Irish Survey officer to launch a book upon the waters of international geology. In 1853 he completed a volume entitled *Popular Physical Geology* for publication in the 'Popular Natural History' series issued by Messrs Reeve and Company of Covent Garden, London. The book is dedicated to Sir Henry De La Beche, and is illustrated with twenty handsome 'double-tinted' lithographs prepared from drawings by Du Noyer. The objective of the book - a book described by the reviewer (Hugh Miller?) in the *Witness* as a work of 'great life and freshness' - was to bring the elements of physical geology to the notice of the general public, and the volume was a first sign that Jukes, in 51 St Stephen's Green, was taking very seriously his duties as an international pedagogue and geological missionary. Over the next ten years two other highly successful educational works came from his pen. One of these was an elementary textbook of geology intended for use by 'young persons of fourteen or fifteen years of age and upwards'. Perhaps in writing this work Jukes had in mind the more serious of the students who were attending his courses of Popular Lectures at the Royal Dublin Society and the Museum of Irish Industry. The second of the two educational works was a more substantial treatise. It was Jukes's *Student's Manual of Geology*.

The *Student's Manual* originated with Thomas Stewart Traill, the editor of the *Encyclopaedia Britannica*. Traill invited Edward Forbes to write the entry on geology for the new, eighth edition of the encyclopaedia, and early in 1854 Forbes asked Jukes to collaborate with him in the task. It was understood that the authors would expand their essay to book length in order to create a new text for publication by Messrs Adam and Charles Black of Edinburgh who were the owners of the *Encyclopaedia Britannica*. Jukes and Forbes discussed their collaboration when they met in Liverpool at the British Association meeting held there during September 1854, but Forbes's death two months later left Jukes to complete alone both the encyclopaedia essay and the book. He worked at his task, as he explained, 'in the intervals of other occupations, on wet days in country inns, in railway carriages, in remote parts of the country', but his encyclopaedia entry was not finished in time for it to take its place in the volume containing the initial letter 'G'. The essay eventually appeared in 1856 under the initial letter 'M' as 'Mineralogical Science', and the book which grew out of the entry was published during the following year as the *Student's Manual*. The volume is dedicated to the memory of Forbes by 'one of the many who will never cease to regret his loss and cherish his remembrance'.

In our own day of supposedly accelerated desk-top publishing it is sobering to discover the speed with which a work might pass through the press at a time when a mouse was yet merely a 'tim'rous beastie' which nibbled a compositor's lunch-time sandwich. Jukes was still writing his book on 5 November 1857, because on that day he penned to Ramsay a letter containing the following passage.

> That confounded book of mine hangs over me like an incubus. I am now at work at an alphabetical list of all genera, with a reference to every page in which each is mentioned. I begin it at six o'clock, A.M. It is an awful task, and has already taken me a month, and not near the end.

Nonetheless, Jukes had the completed, published volume, bound by John Gray of Edinburgh, in his hands before the Christmas of that same year, 1857. I know that because I have just removed from its shelf my own copy of the first edition of Jukes's *Student's Manual*. In Jukes's hand upon the flyleaf there is the inscription;

Georgina Augusta Jukes
from her afftn husband
The Author
Dec 24th 1857

I suspect that Augusta took little interest in her Christmas present that year. Even today, almost one hundred and forty years later, the volume is still in a near-mint condition.

The *Student's Manual* was well received by reviewers and public alike. It entered upon a second edition in 1862, by which time the work had swollen to a portly 764 pages, which, the reviewer for *The Critic* observed, rendered the tome 'too thick to be pocketed and carried about by any one less athletic than its author'. Sadly, by the date of that second edition's appearance, the days of Jukes's athletic reputation were numbered, and when a third edition of the *Student's Manual* was called for, an ailing Jukes had to invite the assistance of Archibald Geikie. It was Geikie who saw that third edition into print in 1872, when he paid his own tribute to Jukes's volume as 'one of the best Manuals in our language'. The Irish Survey had given birth to a work which, in its own day, was compared to the famed *Manual of Elementary Geology* by Sir Charles Lyell.

Not all the volumes originating within the Survey achieved the same eminence as that accorded to Jukes's *Student's Manual*. Indeed, among the thirty-four books written by Survey officers, there are two which were more likely to earn for their authors condemnation rather than commendation. The first of these two books was a strange little work by Kelly entitled *Notes upon the Errors of Geology* and published in 1864. It was an old man's aberration. In the book, Kelly outlined a new theory of the earth of his own devising, and then he sought to show how his theory was to be reconciled with the six days of the hexaemeron. In character it was a sadly dated little work; the less said of it here the better. Jukes must have been pleased to note that on the title-page Kelly described himself just as 'Vice-President of the Royal Geological Society of Ireland'. There is no mention of his association with the Survey.

The second dubious volume was equally anachronistic. It is Kinahan's *Valleys and their Relation to Fissures, Fractures, and Faults* of 1875. It seems that Kinahan and Warren had planned to write this work together, and that Kinahan continued with the task alone after Warren's death (seemingly from tuberculosis) in November 1872. The book was intended as a contribution to the debate over the origin of the earth's topography. Was it the result of earthmovements? Was it the result of marine action during recent submergence? Or was it the result of the long-continued action of the fluvial processes? By 1875, and thanks in no small part to Jukes's paper of 1862 on the rivers of southern Ireland (see Chapter Nine), the issue had largely been decided in favour of the fluvial processes. But Kinahan obstinately clung to the view that valleys were essentially crustal shrinkage fissures, and he now sought to prove his point by drawing upon his vast Irish field experience In fairness to him, it has to be observed that he was by no means unique in his adherence to such an outmoded view, and between 1872 and 1874 a vigorous opponent of fluvialism had actually held the presidency of the Geological Society of London. That President was the eighth Duke of Argyll who had contemptuously dismissed fluvialism as 'the gutter theory'. It was to the Duke that Kinahan dedicated his book on valleys.

When Hull arrived in the Irish Survey during May 1869 he already had to his credit a book generally recognised to be the most significant work in its field. It was a volume devoted to the coalfields of the world. Coal was then the focus of enormous public interest. The black diamonds being won from the bowels of the earth by miners' brawn were the basis of Britain's industrial prosperity. Even the sails of the ships ruling the waves on behalf of Britannia were now being blackened by the smoke of best steam-coal being burned in John Penn's Greenwich-built boilers. In the 1850s it was estimated that annual world production of coal amounted to 96, 737, 547 tons. Of this total 65, 887, 900 tons came out of British and Irish mines. How long would British and Irish coal-seams be able to sustain such massive exploitation? Was Britain rapidly digging away the very foundations upon which there rested the national wellbeing?

These were questions to which Hull had addressed himself, and the result was his *Coal-Fields of Great Britain*, first published early in 1861, and a work in such demand that it passed into a second edition during that same year. Hull felt able to offer the public some comfort. He concluded that if the workable limit of coal was set at a depth of 4000 feet (1130 metres), and if it was assumed that sixty million tons of coal were to be mined annually, then Britain had coal reserves sufficient to endure for a thousand years.

The coal question remained highly topical. Jukes, and then Hull, were both members of a Royal Commission which investigated the subject between 1866 and 1871 under the chairmanship of the Duke of Argyll, and, to satisfy the persistent public interest in the problem, Hull produced a third edition of his book in 1873 and a fourth edition in 1881. It was thus out of the Director's office in Hume Street that there came the standard work devoted to one of the major national issues of the second half of the nineteenth century.

Sir Richard Griffith often expressed the hope that one day he would be able to find the time necessary for the writing of a book-length study of the geology of Ireland. His magnificent quarter-inch (1:253, 440) geological map of Ireland was published in 1839, but he died in 1878 never having completed the full-scale memoir which was to have been the map's accompaniment. By the time that Griffith was laid to rest in Dublin's Mount Jerome cemetery, the other parts of the then United Kingdom all possessed their geological interpretations. Archibald Geikie's *Scenery of Scotland viewed in connexion with its Physical Geology* dated from 1865, and Ramsay's *Physical Geology and Geography of Great Britain* reached its fifth edition in the year of Griffith's death. But for Ireland there was nothing quite comparable.

Clearly, it was only a matter of time before somebody sought to remedy this Irish lacuna. An obvious temporal stimulant to action was the fact that during the summer of 1878 large numbers of scientific visitors would be coming to Ireland to attend the British Association for the Advancement of Science meeting which was scheduled to be held in Dublin during the August of that year. It was equally obvious that when the lacuna was finally filled, the author responsible was likely to be a Survey officer. What was not so obvious was that two Survey officers were simultaneously, yet independently, going to feel moved into print on the subject of the geology of their native island. That was nevertheless what happened. When, during the late summer of 1878, visiting members of the British Association went to the Dublin bookshop of Messrs Hodges, Foster, and Figgis enquiring for something relating to the geology of Ireland, there were three recent publications available for their examination. First, there was Hull's geological map of Ireland (scale 1:506, 880, see p. 81) in two sheets, priced at 25 shillings for the pair. Second, there was *The Physical Geology & Geography of Ireland* by Hull, priced at seven shillings. Third, there was a *Manual of the Geology of Ireland* by Kinahan, priced, presumably, at somewhere around twelve shillings. All three items had been published that very year, 1878.

We are told that Hull and Kinahan worked at their respective books entirely in ignorance of what the other was doing. We are asked to believe that parturition had reached a very advanced stage before the two men discovered that they were each pregnant of a volume devoted to Irish geology. That may well be true, bearing in mind the strained relationship existing between Kinahan and his Director, but since, in his writing, Kinahan had recruited the assistance of Baily, Egan, McHenry, and Traill, it is difficult to believe that rumour can have failed to drift down from the upper floors of Hume Street and in through the keyhole of the Director's office. Perhaps that declaration of ignorance of the other man's literary doings was just a cover story. Perhaps in reality both men knew exactly what the other was up to . Perhaps neither man was prepared to leave the exposition of Irish geology exclusively to the other. Perhaps it was no accident that during 1878 two books devoted to the geology of Ireland appeared within just a few months of each other.

Hull's book appeared first, bearing a dedication to the third Earl of Enniskillen, the owner of that most renowned of Irish private palaeontological collections. But the Earl can never have seen Hull's book; by 1878 he inhabited a black world of blindness. Kinahan dedicated his volume to Griffith, but again the dedicatee probably never saw the volume. In Griffith's case the cause was not blindness, but death. On 1 August 1878 the work was clearly still in press because Kinahan was then able to add to his preface a postscript alluding to the recent death of Thomas Oldham. Griffith himself died on 22 September 1878, only seven weeks after Kinahan penned his postscript.

A consideration of the finely balanced relative merits of the two volumes I will leave to others. On 27 February 1879, Kinahan's reviewer in *Nature* suggested that Hull's book was more suited to the general reader, while Kinahan's would be best for the professional geologist. With that verdict there is little need to quarrel. What I may assert with confidence is that had I stood in the Grafton Street premises of Messrs Hodges, Foster, and Figgis in the autumn of 1878, with Hull in one hand and Kinahan in the other, I would, despite its higher price, have opted to buy Kinahan. It is the larger of the two volumes (464 pages as against 307), it contains a folded geological map of Ireland (hand-coloured by McHenry) at a scale of 1:1, 710, 720 as compared with Hull's frontispiece map at half that scale, it has the more attractive illustrations (some of them by Mrs Kinahan), and its front cover is decorated with a fine vignette of the Fastnet Rock based upon a drawing by Wyley. Kinahan would certainly have proved the better financial investment. Today copies of his book are difficult to find, whereas at every Irish bookfair there seems to be offered for sale at least one copy of Hull in either its first edition or the second edition of 1891.

All true Irish men and women enjoy a story in which somebody hoodwinks the authorities. If those authorities should happen to be the British government, then so much the better. It is just such a tale that it would seem I now have to tell. To some extent the actual details can only be surmise, but I suspect that readers will be left with little doubt as to the veracity of the interpretation which I place upon the events now to be unfolded.

Under the terms of the Dublin Science and Art Museum Act of 1877, the Royal Dublin Society

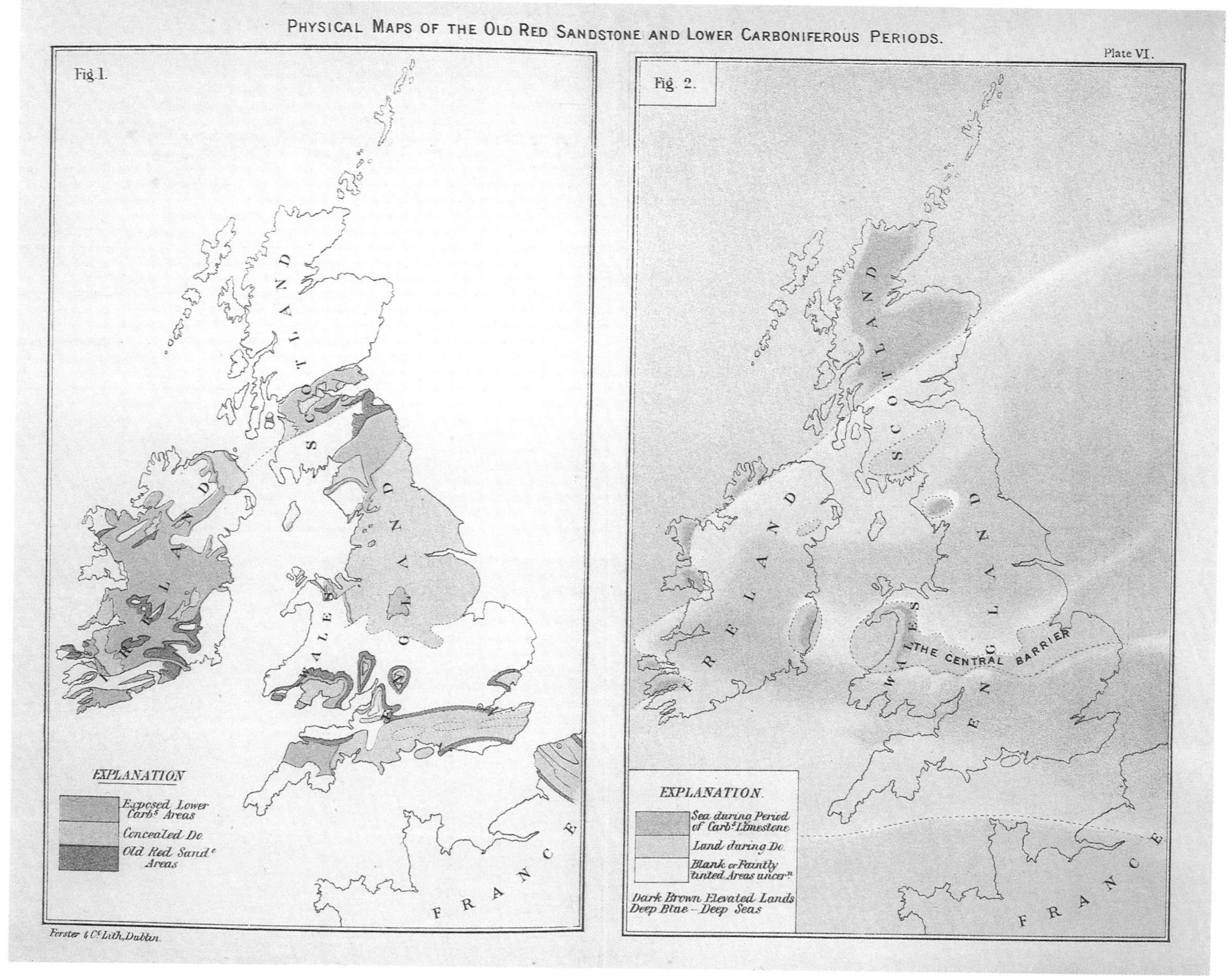

PLATE XIV. *Edward Hull's conception of the geography of Old Red Sandstone times and of the Lower Carboniferous. Two of the palaeogeographical maps from his* Contributions to the Physical History of the British Isles *published in 1882.*

agreed, *inter alia,* to hand over its library and museum collections to the government. As a part of its side of the bargain, the government agreed that for a period of five years it would finance the publication of the Society's two scientific journals - the *Scientific Proceedings* and the *Scientific Transactions* - to a standard equal to that displayed by the publications of the Royal Society of London. The result was that the Society's principal journal - the *Scientific Transactions* - achieved a quality of production unequalled by any Irish scientific periodical either before or since.

Now Hull had for some time been nursing a pet project. He wanted to publish for the British Isles what today would be termed a palaeogeographical atlas. The atlas was to consist of a series of maps illustrating the distribution of land and sea within the region at different stages in its geological evolution. But Hull was stymied by the expenses involved. His atlas required twenty-seven colour-printed maps and involved the preparation of sixty-two lithographic stones. Very understandably, publishers advised him that the resultant costs would be prohibitive. But then somebody had a brainwave. Why not prepare the atlas, offer it to the Royal Dublin Society for publication in the *Scientific Transactions,* and let the government pay for the preparation of all the maps under the terms of the 1877 agreement? The atlas would appear as a paper within the *Scientific Transactions*, and, once made, all the chromo-lithographic stones could be handed over to a commercial publisher who would then proceed to the publication of the atlas in conventional book form. Thus the government would unwittingly be dipping into its coffers to finance Hull's private palaeogeographical ambitions.

This is precisely the plan which was put into effect. Hull submitted his atlas to the Royal Dublin Society as a paper and it was published in the Society's *Scientific Transactions* during November 1882. As soon as the Dublin printers (Messrs Alexander Thom and Company) had finished with the sixty-two lithographic stones, they were handed over to Messrs Edward Stanford and Company in London. That firm then published the atlas in full book form in 1882, and almost contemporaneously with the appearance of the *Scientific Transactions* paper back in Dublin. The title of the atlas in the book version is *Contributions to the Physical History of the British Isles* (Plate XIV).

The map is an utterly merciless medium. It denies to its compiler all opportunity of disguising uncertainty behind fine phrases. Instead, it demands an infinity of decisions which then have to be displayed for all to see in the clinical form of a cartographer's lines. Before Hull's essaying of the task, there had been no attempt at the compilation of a palaeogeographical atlas of the British Isles. In view of the rigorous demands of the medium, and of the sketchiness of so much of the geological evidence, a wiser man than Hull might have reined his ambition. As with Hull's post-1878 revision of the geological mapping in Munster, it was a case of a fool rushing in where an angel would have feared to tread. A reviewer in *Nature* on 31 May 1883 suggested that it was 'an evil hour' for Hull's reputation when the Royal Dublin Society agreed to arrange the finance necessary for the preparation of his maps. Certainly some of the maps are seriously flawed, but, that aside, Hull in his volume of 1882 had laid the foundation for a completely new genre of geological literature. Yet another significant innovation had emerged from the Geological Survey of Ireland. Interestingly, Hull's concept of a palaeogeographical atlas was seized upon by Jukes's nephew, Alfred John Jukes-Brown (he had assumed his late uncle's name upon his own twenty-first birthday in 1872), and developed between 1888 and 1911 in the three editions of his book *The Building of the British Isles.*

I have made no attempt to tell the tale of each and every one of the thirty-four books which came out of the Survey during the first eighty years of its existence. The purist will doubtless insist that the next work which I do mention is not really a book at all. It certainly possesses a peculiar publication history. It is a volume from Kinahan's pen and devoted to the economic geology of Ireland.

Kinahan clearly possessed an encyclopaedic knowledge of those Irish rocks and minerals which hold economic significance. Now in March 1889, when Geikie wrote his confidential report upon the officers of the Irish Survey, he expressed the opinion that Kinahan was close to the end of his life. In reality, Kinahan survived for a further nineteen years, to die, aged 78, in 1908. But it may be that during the 1880s Kinahan himself had reason for feeling that his life was approaching its close. That is perhaps why he then resolved to have preserved in permanent form all his accumulated knowledge of Ireland's economic geology.

Between 24 March 1886 and 18 January 1888 Kinahan presented at joint meetings of the Royal Dublin Society and the Royal Geological Society of Ireland a total of nine papers descriptive of the economic geology of Ireland. The papers were published in volumes 5 and 6 (New Series) of the *Scientific Proceedings of the Royal Dublin Society*, and then, after the addition of 8 pages of preliminaries, the insertion of a few supplementary paragraphs, and the preparation of an index, the whole was reprinted by the Royal Geological Society of Ireland as the three parts which together form volume 8 of that society's *Journal.* Of those three parts, the first (1887) is devoted to metallic mining, the second (1887) is devoted to marbles, limestones, and arenaceous rocks, and the third (1889) is devoted to slates, clays, granites, igneous rocks, and metamorphic rocks. The coverage is detailed and comprehensive, but there is one glaring omission: there is no section devoted to peat as an economic resource. This Kinahan deeply regretted, but he explained that it was an omission forced upon him by the fact that the necessary surveys had never been made.

On our library shelves the volume combining the three parts of volume 8 of the *Journal of the Royal Geological Society of Ireland* commonly stands apart from the other seven volumes comprising the run of that journal. Libraries not in possession of a run of the journal have been at pains to secure a copy of volume 8. The spine of the volume is likely to display the title *Economic Geology of Ireland* and the name of the work's author, surely the most remarkable Survey officer of all time. In his preface to the volume, Kinahan listed some of the groups of people which he hoped would find his work to be of value. He named landed proprietors, trustees, speculators, land-agents, mining-agents, miners, engineers, architects, builders, quarrymen, masons, and bricklayers. His hopes have been amply fulfilled. For one hundred years Kinahan's *Economic Geology* has remained a valued vade mecum for all Irish economic geologists. It proved invaluable to Cole as he prepared the Survey's 1922 map and memoir on minerals of economic importance (see p.147); it remains invaluable today as a fine inventory of Ireland's geological resources. On 21 May 1889 Samuel Haughton wrote to Kinahan congratulating him upon the publication of the final part of his book. I leave Haughton's words to close my brief review of Kinahan's achievement. Those words serve as a reminder of the political background to Kinahan's study and of the exaggerated claims which some nationalists were making on behalf of Ireland's mineral wealth.

> Your book will not satisfy those who wish to believe that Ireland possesses Mineral Resources equal to those of any other country; but it will be a useful guide to those who confine their speculations to matters of fact.

Kinahan's *Economic Geology* was both the last publication ever to be issued by the Royal Geological Society of Ireland and the final book to come from the Survey during the nineteenth century. Survey pens remained active under the regime of Nolan and then under that of Lamplugh, but during those years between 1890 and 1905 no Survey officer felt moved to quicken the Survey's private pulse rate through the injection of a book into geology's international circulatory system. After the surgery of April 1905 things were different. Between 1905 and 1924 commercial publishing houses issued no less than thirteen works written by Survey officers. A minor literary avalanche was then rolling out of Hume Street. One of the volumes published during those years - Wright's *Quaternary Ice Age* of 1914 - became the international classic which has already engaged out attention (see p.229). The other twelve works all originated within the lively and fertile mind of Grenville Cole.

Cole was a prolific author. He pumped papers, reviews, essays, and books into the world of science with just the same vigour as he pumped air into the pneumatic tyres of the bicycles which he so loved to ride. When he arrived in Hume Street he was wearing the mortarboard of a professor in the Royal College of Science, and, since he had to combine the duties of Director and professor, that mortarboard remained upon Cole's Hume Street desk throughout his occupation of the Director's chair. He was thus a geologist fully experienced in the universal academic tradition of scholarly publication. But he had also encountered a second and more local influence which was likely to infuse a man with literary ambitions.

Ever since his arrival in Ireland in 1890, Cole had been a member of that lively group of Dublin scientists which, in the 1890s at least, used to meet each afternoon in the tea-rooms kept by the Misses Gardiner at numbers 1 and 2 Leinster Street. There the scientists talked of their research, of their forthcoming publications, and of their scientific dreams, all the while, we are told, consuming vast quantities of buttered toast. Among the members of this group of scientists, publication was second nature. Nobody exemplified this point better than the group's most eminent botanist, the famed Robert Lloyd Praeger.

Cole was one of the best-known geological authors of his day. Two of the twelve books dating from his Survey years were clearly intended chiefly for an Irish readership, but the remainder are all works directed at a readership spread throughout the English-speaking world. Such is the size of the full corpus of literature bearing Cole's name that any adequate discussion of it here is out of the question. I propose simply to allow the titles of six important books dating from his Survey years to speak for themselves. They will suffice to indicate something of the nature of the missionary campaign which Cole was conducting from his twin citadels of the Survey and the Royal College of Science and on behalf of the science to which he had devoted his life. The dates are the years in which a work was published *de novo* or in which there appeared a fresh edition of a work. *Aids in Practical Geology,* Cole's widely praised and most successful work, was first published in 1891, the year following his arrival in Ireland.

Aids in Practical Geology (1906; 1909; 1918)
The Changeful Earth: an Introduction to the Record of the Rocks (1911)
Rocks and their Origins (1912: 1922)
Outlines of Mineralogy for Geological Students (1913)
The Growth of Europe (1914)
Common Stones: Unconventional Essays in Geology (1921)

Shortly before the outbreak of war in 1914, Cole completed a stratigraphical account of the geology of Ireland. It was to form part of a volume devoted to the stratigraphy of the British Isles, the volume being prepared for issue by a German publisher. The work finally appeared in 1917 with Heidelberg as its place of publication. After the war the London publishing house of Messrs Thomas Murby and Company acquired the rights to the work and it was decided to produce a new edition in two volumes, one volume being devoted to Great Britain and the other to Ireland. By the time this decision was taken, Cole was in poor health and he therefore asked Hallissy to assist him in the preparation of the Irish volume.

The two authors must have completed their work upon the book around the time of Cole's first stroke, in March 1924, and the book was published some six months after Cole's death. For thirty years the volume remained the standard work on the geology of Ireland. It offers a concise summary of the Irish stratigraphical sequence, each chronological section of the work being supported by a valuable bibliography. Thousands of students must have acquired their knowledge of Irish geology by devouring the pages of the book. I certainly did so myself.

Cole and Hallissy, as the volume was always affectionately termed, is only a slim volume. Its final page is numbered 82. At the foot of that page the publishers should have emulated their predecessors of an earlier age by having the printers insert the word FINIS. That final page was not only the end of another Survey book - it was also the end of another Survey tradition.

During the seventy years which have elapsed since the publication of Cole and Hallissy, not one Survey officer has turned aside from his or her official duties in order to become the parent of a privately conceived geological volume. Between 1845 and 1924 that remarkable total of thirty-four earth-science books flowed from the Survey. Since 1924 the literary stream has been completely dry. Survey officers still reach out to the public through museum displays, through lectures, and through field-excursions. Survey officers today maintain for the Survey a healthy private pulse rate through the publication of geological papers in the world's scientific journals. But the hand which once reached out to the public through a non-official book-literature has been withered and dead these last seventy years.

Perhaps since 1924 the missionary fervour of our Survey officers has been somewhat cooled. Perhaps our Survey officers have recognised that official eyebrows might today be raised at public servants who conducted missionary campaigns on behalf of their favourite science through the publication of tomes likely to yield private financial gain. Perhaps our Survey officers are now just too busy to be able to think of emulating such of their predecessors as Jukes, Hull, Kinahan, or Cole. I do not know. What I do know is that the Survey's literary tradition described in the latter part of this chapter now has to be declared extinct. It died with the publication of Cole and Hallissy. Perhaps my reader will already have noted the year in which that final work appeared. It was the year which I have already singled out as the blackest year in the Survey's history. It was 1924.

CHAPTER TWELVE

THE SURVEY SURVEYED

> It is obvious that the physical toil and intellectual labour required by the Survey can only be undertaken by men whose bodily and mental abilities are above the average. No amount of either, or both, of those qualities, however, will fit a man for our work unless he have that natural instinct for it which will induce him, like Professor Ramsay, and myself, and many other officers of the Survey, knowingly to abandon all hope of wealth, all love of ease, and all ambition of advancement in life, in order to devote his whole energies, thoughts and aspirations to the pursuit of Geology.
>
> J. Beete Jukes in the published notes to a lecture delivered before the Lord Lieutenant at the Museum of Irish Industry on 21 December 1866. (Reproduced here with due apology to all the women who have given devoted service to the Survey over the years which have elapsed since Mary Connaughten's appointment as a Temporary Professional Assistant during the summer of 1917.)

I move aside a stack of papers and draw the old-style dial-telephone towards me. It's a Dublin number I propose to call. No need for the directory. I know the number well. My finger sets the dial spinning. 0-1-6-7-0-7-4-4-4. The slowness of the contraption taxes my patience. I listen to the ringing tone at the other end. As I wait I doodle in pencil upon my notepad. They are slow to answer today. Must be busy. My pencil has almost finished shading the side of a third perspective cube before the ringing ceases. A slight pause and then a friendly female voice responds to my call. 'Geological Survey', she says employing a slightly quizzical intonation. Momentarily I hesitate. My mind has drifted away. I look down at my three doodled cubes. It occurs to me that each might represent half a century in the life of the institution I have just called. But really, what is this institution? What is this Geological Survey to which I am now linked through the wizardry of modern telecommunications? 'Geological Survey', repeats the female voice at the other end of the line. There is now a strong inquisitorial tone to her voice. She brings me back to earth. 'The Director, please', I say. She swings into her well-drilled patter. 'Who shall I say's calling?' I explain and am put through. We discuss our business. The call ends. I return my receiver to its cradle. And there upon my notepad are the three doodled cubes. They remind me of my question. What is the Geological Survey? Undisturbed by any distant female voices I am left alone with my question.

As I reflect upon my question there comes to mind the poem called *The Blind Men and the Elephant* written by John Godfrey Saxe, the nineteenth-century American humorist. The following is the first stanza of that poem.

> It was six men of Indostan
> To learning much inclined,
> Who went to see the Elephant
> (Though all of them were blind),
> That each by observation
> Might satisfy his mind.

The poem then describes the blind men's differing experiences of the elephant. One who handled its trunk announced that an elephant was like a snake. One who felt its tusk claimed an elephant to be like a spear. One who explored a leg declared an elephant to be like a tree. One who took hold of an ear protested the elephant to be like a fan. One who ran his hands over its flanks proclaimed an elephant to be like a wall. And one who grasped the tail exclaimed that an elephant was like a piece of rope. A similar poem might be written about the Geological Survey. That institution is different things to different people. It all depends upon whether, as it were, the individual has encountered the proboscis of the Survey, its ivory, its limbs, its auricle, its thorax, or its caudal, wherever that may be.

What is the Geological Survey? 'It's a large, red-brick building', says a thirsty man who espies a wall-plaque as he hurries past Beggars Bush towards his pint of porter in nearby Ryan's. 'It's a museum', says

Siobhan as she explores the displays in the Ganly Gallery under the watchful eye of Sister Concepta. 'It seems to be a remarkable storehouse of geological information', says Chuck, a mining geologist from Miami. 'That's not *the* Miami', he explains, 'mine's Miami Arizona'. He flew in yesterday for his first visit to Ireland, and he's just spent the morning bent over six-inch field-sheets in the Public Office. He has a hunch - mental and metallic not physical and deforming - but he wouldn't wish me to reveal the location of the ground in which he's interested. 'It's an advisory service', say two men as they descend the steps of the Survey. Oddly, they both share the name of Ó Cathaoir. One of them is a county engineer who has been in the Survey seeking information about the geology likely to be encountered during the construction of a new section of motorway. The other is a farmer up from County Wexford who has been enquiring whether there is any chance of his finding water if he drills up at the top end of his haggard.

What is the Geological Survey? 'C'est l'institut national which fabri -, err, makes ze cartes géologiques for Irlande', says a petite Renault-driving visitor who has the Survey's 1:750,000 map of Ireland beside her in the front of the car and several boxes of our Carboniferous fossils in the back. I take care to read her number-plate as she speeds off in the direction of Rosslare. I see the number 34. 'That's Hérault', I say to myself. 'She's probably something to do with the university at Montpellier. Wonder what she thought of an Irish summer?' 'Geological Survey? Just another of our innumerable little headaches', laughs the neatly-suited gentleman over in the Department of Finance. 'Know it well. I see it there in the estimates every year. We find the money to keep it going. I'm never very clear about what the Survey actually does. I've certainly never been there. I did economics in college. Never was much good at science. But I'm sure what the Survey does must be of national importance. Otherwise it wouldn't be getting almost two million a year, would it?'

What is the Geological Survey? I'm back in Beggars Bush and in the Survey's Tea Room. I put my question to a girl I've never seen before. 'Don't ask me', she responds, 'I'm only a Clerical Assistant and I'd never heard of the Survey myself until last Wednesday morning. I'd been in the Department of ——— for seven months and the supervisor told me I'd been transferred here. So I'm only learning. But nowadays there isn't much difference between one government office and another. They seem a nice bunch here, but I'd rather have a job on the north side of the river. You see, I live up in Finglas'.

There we have seven perspectives upon the character of the Survey 'elephant'. All of them are of course true. The Survey *is* housed in a large red-brick building. In the Ganly Gallery it *does* contain a geological museum. It *is* indeed a rich storehouse of geological information. It most certainly *does* serve as an advisory body. It *does* issue geological maps. It *is* an item in the annual national budget. It *is* another government institution providing employment for men and women skilled in the operation of sophisticated modern office hardware. It is many other things too; the Survey 'elephant' is a remarkably varied creature.

Being an academic myself, there is certainly one other attribute of the 'elephant' which I consider just *has* to be mentioned. The Survey is a centre for geological research. Its officers play their part in the maintenance of the healthy pulse rate which today characterises the Irish earth-science community as a whole. Survey officers publish their research findings in scientific journals which circulate throughout the world, and those officers thus pay the intellectual dues which entitle them to membership of the international geological community. The standing of individual officers, of the Survey itself, of Irish geology, and, indeed, of Ireland, are all enhanced in the eyes of the geological world by the publication and wide circulation of significant geological research emanating from within the walls of Beggars Bush.

One of the first elephants ever to be the subject of a scientific dissection was a showman's elephant which died in a Dublin fire on 17 June 1681. The carcass was acquired by Alan Mullen (or Molines), a medical graduate of Trinity College Dublin, and the account of his dissection of the animal was published in London during 1692. My Survey 'elephant' is no carcass - far from it! - but if I make it the subject of a vivisection, I know exactly what I will find when I arrive at the heart of the creature. I slice through the tough hide of that red-brick building. I remove the fine museum tusks. I gently push aside all the publications forming its circulatory system. I lift out the lungs which have allowed its trumpetings to be heard throughout the land for a century and a half. I pull away the stomach where the incoming budget is digested. I pin back the muscles which impart to the organism that strength which makes it the focus for an entire work-force. And there, at last, we see what lies at the very heart of the creature. Its heart is a vast, pulsating, throbbing mass of information about the geology of Ireland. Chuck from Miami, Arizona, hit the nail squarely on its head. The Survey is multi-faceted, but at its core it is really neither more nor less than a storehouse containing an immense and ever-growing body of information relating to the rocks, minerals, fossils, landforms, and geological resources of Ireland. It has been said that elephants never forget. It is the task of the Survey to ensure that facts about the geology of

Ireland, once discovered, are never allowed to become forgotten.

A great library - the British Library in London or the Library of Congress in Washington - preserves upon its shelves the accumulated wisdom of the ages recorded in either manuscript or printed form. The Survey has undertaken a similar, albeit narrower and far more specialised a task, as one of its two great duties. It seeks to preserve from the past, to make available today, and to hand on to the future, all our accumulated wisdom relating to the geology of the national territory. In its maps, in its publications, in its library, in its specimen cabinets, in its photographic collections, in its computer disks and tapes, and, by no means least, in the minds of its officers, the Survey at Beggars Bush encapsulates on one small site the geology of the entire Republic of Ireland. That encapsulation the Survey strives to make available to all those, both at home and overseas, who are in need of geological information or geological advice relating to this tiny portion of the terrestrial crust.

The second great duty of the Survey is to ensure that this vast body of information relating to the geology of Ireland never itself becomes fossilised. The corpus of data must constantly be augmented, reassessed, and modified in the light of new information arriving from sources such as the mineral exploration companies, the drillers of water-wells, the university departments of geology, and, of course, from the field investigations conducted by the Survey itself. The Survey strives to ensure not only that geological information is available upon enquiry, but also that the geological information incorporates the latest discoveries and the most modern interpretations.

It was that great geologist, Jukes, who first clearly enunciated the view that, as one of its basic objectives, the Survey must become what, in the terminology of a later age, we would today term a national geological data-base. Could Jukes return to Beggars Bush to be introduced to some of the Survey's modern methods of geological information storage, then I am sure that his eyes would open just as wide as did the eyes of Ramsay when first he saw a glacier. In one of the upstairs offices he would be puzzled to learn that the two officers studying patterns on the screen of a VDU were seeking a fresh interpretation of the mineralised country around Silvermines in County Tipperary. Down in the basement fire-proof store a look of blank incomprehension would greet our announcement that a few reels of tape carried the results of an aeromagnetic survey made by lifting instruments high into the air over the Irish Midlands.

But Jukes would find himself completely at home with one aspect of the Survey's modern multifaceted data-base. His noble head would nod in profound approval as he was shown the duplicate copies of the six-inch field-sheets lying in their boxes in the Public Office. Perhaps he would remind us that on St Valentine's day in 1855, after an excellent and convivial Geological Society of Dublin dinner at Jude's Royal Hotel in Grafton Street, he had devoted much of his final presidential address before the Society to an exposition of his personal views on the philosophy which should underlie the work of a sound national geological survey. He there had emphasised that detailed six-inch field-mapping must lie at the very core of a survey's activities, and that the resultant field-sheets must be preserved for all time as 'a great public document of reference'. He would doubtless be gratified to learn that each succeeding generation within the Survey has viewed the six-inch field-sheets in precisely that light. They are simply invaluable, and in view of their importance, their security has frequently been of concern to the Survey. They were placed in Milners' Patent Fire-Resisting safes in May 1891; they were removed to a place of safety during the War of Independence in 1921 and again during the Civil War in 1923; and in 1982 they were all photographed in order to bestow upon them a still greater hope of immortality. Those field-maps, many of them bearing the annotations of several generations of Survey officers, are still in daily use by Survey officers and by other inquirers come to Beggars Bush in search of the answer to some problem in Irish geology. The six-inch field-sheets remain a very strong currency within the Survey's data-bank.

A great and ancient cathedral is likely to display features originating at many differing periods in history. The nave, as in Our Lady of Chartres, may date from 1194; the south transept and the tower may be early thirteenth century; the Lady Chapel and the Chapter House may date from around 1400; the choir screen may be Victorian, and the reredos may be modern. It is much the same with the Survey's data-base; it is an amalgam of material belonging to different periods. The six-inch field-sheets - the 'nave' of the Survey - date back to 1845. The twin spires of the one-inch maps and memoirs are mid- to late- Victorian. The foundations of the Survey's drift mapping were laid in 1901 with Lamplugh as the architect. The damp side-chapel dedicated to groundwater began to be built by Duffy in 1950 after the introduction of the Department of Agriculture's scheme of grants for the installation of piped domestic water-supplies in farm-dwellings. The 'reredos' of the aeromagnetic survey was completed in 1981. And the screen - the VDU screen - made its appearance in the Survey during the 1980s as the Survey choir sang an anthem praising the manner in which computerisation would be of benefit to the officers in their daily devotions, and to everybody else arriving in the Survey to confess their geological needs.

There is one other respect in which the Survey's geological data-base may be likened to a great cathedral: the cathedral and the data-base are both human creations built in satisfaction of human needs. The great cathedrals of Europe were each raised by a highly skilled labour-force composed of stonemasons, carpenters, glaziers, artists, and the like. The Survey's data-base has been assembled by a far less complex, but no less skilled, labour-force drawn from just one profession - from the profession associated with the science of geology. In the Survey's earlier years the geologists of course received regular assistance from their Fossil Collectors, and more recently a whole band of Executive Officers, cartographers, technicians, Clerical Officers, and Paperkeepers has been drafted into the Survey to provide the geologists with the support they require. But ultimately, the creation and maintenance of the Survey's geological data-base is, and always has been, the responsibility of the Survey's geologists alone.

Where the great cathedrals are concerned, we commonly know little or nothing about the individual craftsmen who actually raised and embellished those glorious structures. At Wells, for example, what was the name of the stonemason (or were there several of them?) who was so obsessed by dental decay that he carved eleven faces distorted by the pangs of toothache? We shall probably never know. Where the Survey is concerned, there is no such problem. We know the identities of every one of the Survey officers who has contributed to the construction of the Survey's data-base. For most of them we possess a great deal of biographical information (see Appendix II). It is in the company of these geologists that I propose to spend the pages remaining to me within the main body of this volume. If I introduce the earlier officers of the Survey more frequently than I introduce their more modern successors, then I trust that my reader will understand. It seems far more appropriate to write freely of the men who served with James, Oldham, Jukes, Hull, Nolan, Lamplugh, Cole, Hallissy, or Bishopp, than it would be to write freely of those who served with Mr Murrogh O Brien or with Dr Cyril Williams, or those who continue to serve with Dr Peadar McArdle.

Between the foundation of the Survey in 1845, and its removal from Hume street to Beggars Bush in 1984, a total of 101 geologists served as full-time officers of the Survey. To this total there surely has to be added the figure of Grenville Cole. He was only a part-time Director, but it would be absurd to omit him from the Survey's geological roll. It is this small body of only 102 geologists which has been chiefly responsible for the creation of Ireland's entire national geological data-base. Of the 102, sixty-two have been Irish by birth, and only six have been women. The three longest serving officers have been McHenry with forty-seven years (but this includes his sixteen years as a Fossil Collector before his appointment as a Temporary Assistant Geologist), Cunningham with forty-three years, and O'Meara with forty years. By the celebration of the Survey's sesquicentennial in 1995 no less than thirty-seven of the former or currently-serving officers will each have been with the Survey for twenty years or more.

Why, over the decades, did 102 men and women choose to accept employment as officers of the Survey? Presumably to that question each of the 102 individuals would have their own distinctive answer. I am nevertheless sure that through all the answers there would run a single common thread. Each of the individuals must in some manner have discovered the fascination of geology, and in consequence they wished to devote their working lives to the pursuit of the science. I suspect that every one of the 102 individuals would to some extent have shared the sentiments expressed by Jukes when he spoke the concluding words of the passage reproduced at the head of this chapter. It is important to remember that down to the second half of the twentieth century there were very few openings for those wishing to develop for themselves such careers in geology. Academic posts in the science were few and far between, and geological posts in industry were virtually non-existent. Throughout the world the prospect of a post with one of the national geological surveys was the principal hope for all those men who aspired to a career in the earth sciences. For the women who shared such an aspiration to a geological career, there was of course, little real hope at all.

A post with the Irish Survey was thus a plum to be reached for with eagerness. But once in hand the fruit was often discovered to be blemished and somewhat sour to the palate. Henry James, the Survey's first Local Director, resigned after only one year in office because he found

> ... that my position on the Geological Survey of Ireland is not such as I had reason to believe it would be when I undertook the duties of Local Director.

Peirce Hoskins found himself in a similar predicament. He was a school master in Kinsale when he decided to quit his classroom in order to become a Survey Fossil Collector. He joined the Survey on 1 October 1854 and he resigned during the following January because 'my present situation does not answer my expectations'. Even as recently as the years between 1954 and 1981 seven officers were appointed who stayed with the Survey only sufficiently long to amass between them a combined service of merely 123 months, or an average of rather less than eighteen months apiece.

It is an odd fact that the Survey's records are far more informative about the reasons for the resignations of James and Hoskins in the mid-nineteenth century, than they are about the reasons underlying resignations during the period since 1950. At all periods many factors - some of them purely personal - have doubtless conspired to cause officers to resign their appointments, but taking a broad historical perspective we may see two groups of reasons why a Survey post may have been discovered to possess serious drawbacks. The first group consists of the drawbacks which arose from the contractual conditions of an officer's employment, and the second group consists of the drawbacks which arose from the environmental conditions in which Survey officers had to perform their duties.

On the contractual side there were problems over salaries, promotion, and pension entitlement. Until recent decades, Survey salaries were decidedly parsimonious in view of the skills demanded, the responsibilities entailed, and the rigorous conditions under which the work often had to be executed. When he arrived in Dublin, Jukes's annual salary as the Local Director was £300. This compares unfavourably, for example, with the £400 per annum being paid to the gentleman in charge of the Royal Navy's victualling yard at Cork. Jukes must have looked with envious eyes upon the annual pension of £1,500 which Sir Richard Griffith was shortly to receive as the retired Chairman of the Board of Works and the former Commissioner of the Valuation. As for the Provost of Trinity College Dublin, his income was in 1853 estimated to be around £3,500 a year. By 1876 the Irish Director's salary was on a scale of £400 by increments of £25 to a maximum of £600, but as late as 1905, when Cole became the Survey's part-time Director, his new Survey duties brought him a salary increase of only a derisory £100. Further, it was made clear to him that this sum was not going to be taken into account for the purposes of his pension.

The scales of remuneration for the more junior members of staff were, of course, related to the salary-scale of their chief, and many of the juniors clearly had difficulty in making ends meet. On 25 November 1872 a memorial signed by every member of the Survey save for Hull and Warren (he died that very day) was submitted to the authorities asking for a new salary and wage structure. They claimed that the Survey had been treated less favourably than other branches of the civil service during the financial adjustments which had been made to meet a recent sharp rise in the cost of living. On the subject of wages there survives a poignant letter addressed to Jukes on 29 January 1863 by Galvan, the Fossil Collector. He explains that he cannot support himself, his wife, and a child upon his income of six shillings per day (his scale was three shillings per day increasing by six pence per diem per annum to the maximum of six shillings per day), that he would like to open a shop to eke out his Survey wages, but that his frequent changes of field-station entirely precluded his entering retail trade. In particular, it was the cost of accommodation in the field which proved to be so draining upon pockets at all levels within the Survey. The words which follow were addressed to Ramsay by Jukes writing at Monkstown, County Cork, on 22 July 1851.

> As to money, by Jove, sir, this country is awful! It may be cheap to live in if you can settle down anywhere; but for travellers like us, I assure you it is at least as expensive as England, without half the comfort. They all look upon me as a government officer and fair game, and they naturally, without previous concert, combine together to impose on us.

Seventy years later Duffy and Farrington still faced exactly the same problem. They were likely to find themselves out of pocket whenever their duties took them into the field. As we have seen (p.155), this was one of the factors which in 1928 resulted in the Survey losing Farrington's services.

Officers had little opportunity of improving their financial position either through a promotion at home in Ireland or through advancement into the British Survey. I strongly suspect that around 1880 Hull had hopes that he might be translated to Jermyn Street as Director-General in succession to Ramsay. But I doubt whether anybody else can have seen him as presenting a serious challenge to the obvious candidature of Archibald Geikie, the talented Director of the Scottish Survey. A few Irish officers were transferred to the British Survey at various times, but W.B. Wright, in 1921, was the only Irish officer ever really to be promoted out of Ireland and into the British Survey.

Since the foundation of the Irish Survey, its senior post has fallen vacant on eleven occasions, but on eight of those occasions the post - rightly or wrongly - has been awarded to a candidate from outside the Irish Survey. Kinahan was furious at being passed over in 1869. It will be remembered that in 1906 Seymour protested that if the directorship of the Survey and the chair of geology in the Royal College of Science for Ireland were henceforth going to be linked, then it followed that Irish Survey officers were likely for ever more to find themselves debarred from the senior post in Hume Street (p.128). I myself have a recollection of being told in 1965 that the conditions for the appointment of the new Director were being framed expressly with the objective of precluding the candidature of Cunningham, because it was felt that the new chief should come from a tribe which prowled lands outside Hume Street.

At more junior levels within the Survey, the lack of internal opportunities for promotion was for many decades a matter for bitter grievance. The justification for this grievance is well illustrated by the events which followed the 1867 authorisation of the expansion of the Survey. Over the next ten years, thirteen officers were recruited. All of them entered possessing geological qualifications, and all save one (McHenry) had passed the appropriate civil service examination. But they were all required to join the Survey as lowly Temporary Assistant Geologists without any security of tenure and without any pension rights. By 1890 only three of these thirteen officers - Nolan, Warren, and Wilkinson - had secured promotion to the permanent and pensionable grade of Geologist, and Wilkinson had been promoted to that grade only because Warren had died. The remaining ten officers had either died (two officers), resigned (three officers), or soldiered on as Temporary Assistant Geologists (five officers). Cruise served from 1867 until his retirement in 1890 as a Temporary Assistant Geologist; Egan served similarly from 1868 until 1890; and even Hardman, the discoverer of Western Australian gold, had still not attained the rank of Geologist when he was struck down by typhoid in April 1887. It is perhaps small wonder that at the time of his death he was making arrangements for a permanent return to the antipodes.

The case of Baily will also be remembered. For thirty years he tried to secure promotion. On 4 November 1871 he addressed the Lords of the Committee of Council on Education pointing out that his international palaeontological reputation had been sufficient to earn him honorary membership of scientific institutions in Dresden, Liège, Strasbourg, and elsewhere, but at home he was still denied a palaeontological grade of District Surveyor's standing. He died seventeen years later still trying to whisper the same plea into stone-deaf official ears.

Dissatisfaction with the career structure offered by the Geological Survey was by no means confined to Ireland. Exactly the same problem existed within the British Survey, and it was one of the issues which the Wharton Committee of 1900 was asked to review. But in the Irish Survey the problem lingered on for many years. Between 1922 and 1929 Hallissy found it difficult to secure for Duffy and Farrington their promised promotion from the grade of Temporary Geologist to that of Geologist (see p.155). The able and deeply conscientious Cunningham served from 1930 until 1955 in the Survey's most junior permanent grade of Geologist, and the no less efficient O'Meara served similarly in that same grade from 1935 until 1964. Today the situation within the Survey is much improved. I trust I will break no confidences if I record hearing that when the directorship was being filled in 1992 six candidates were interviewed for the post. They were all of them serving Irish Survey officers. Kinahan would have been pleased; Seymour would have been delighted.

On the subject of the pension problems faced by Survey officers little further needs to be said because the issue is so closely related to the problems of promotion already discussed. It will suffice to mention just one case in illustration of the problem, although I must admit that my example is hardly typical. It is the most extreme case of them all. It concerns McHenry. He became enthused with a passion for geology after attending one of Jukes's courses at the Museum of Irish Industry. In 1861 he became the Survey's Fossil Collector in succession to Flanagan, and from 1869 until 1877 he worked alongside Baily as Acting Assistant Palaeontologist. In 1877, at the insistence of his Survey colleagues, he was appointed to the grade of Temporary Assistant Geologist, and in 1890 he was promoted to the rank of Geologist. For forty-seven years 'Mac' gave devoted service to the Survey, but when he retired in October 1908 it was discovered that his pension entitlement dated only from 1890. No benefits accrued to him from the first twenty-nine years of his service. Happily, bureaucracy for once was sympathetic and special arrangements were made for 'Mac' in view of his long period of meritorious service.

The second set of drawbacks inherent in an Irish Survey career - the environmental drawbacks - are broadly divisible into four categories: the Irish weather; poor field accommodation; occupational hazards; and the frequently disturbed political state of the country.

The Irish, of course, talk incessantly of their weather, and even the most ardent of Hibernophiles has to concede that the Irish climate commonly does little to ensure the bodily comfort of the field-geologist. Upon innumerable occasions Survey officers must have stood beneath weeping nimbus skies, their faces washed by rain, drops tickling down their nose and dripping onto pencils which refused to record observations because the notebook was become a damp pulp of blotting paper. Upon innumerable days Survey officers must have peeked cautiously into a map-case lest the gale roaring in off the Atlantic should rip the field-sheet from their hands. Here I write with feeling. One March day long ago just such a gale made off with one of my own sheets as I toiled around the slopes of Mangerton in County Kerry. Upon innumerable January mornings Survey officers must repeatedly have thrown their arms about themselves in an effort to restore life to frozen fingers. Having only partially succeeded, an ill-aimed hammer-blow brings a pale thumb into contact with a sharp rock. Red blood on white snow tells its little tale. And as the thumb thaws the pain arrives.

Today's Survey officers are perhaps more independent of the elements than were their predecessors. They travel out to their ground in a vehicle where knobs may be twiddled to create for the driver a mobile microclimate. In winter the modern officers don thermal nether garments, in summer they sport little sun-hats inscribed 'Made in Korea', and at all seasons they have the protection of sophisticated anoraks designed to keep the rain at a distance. But the officers of the nineteenth century had to meet the natural elements virtually upon their own terms. During the primary mapping of Ireland, officers were commonly out in the field at all times of the year. They normally travelled on foot, sometimes they hired a horse, and longer journeys they made aboard an outside car. Weatherproof clothing was being made (J.C. Cording of London's Strand manufactured 'Dreadnought coats warranted to resist the effects of any climate') but during the wet August of 1856 Murchison was unable to find any such garments on sale in Limerick. Normally Survey officers seem to have been content to take to the field attired in what are best described as 'country tweeds'. They must often have been as wet as frogs.

In many a Survey annual report the Local Director or the Director explains that a bad summer had seriously interfered with the year's field-programme. Inclement conditions also adversely affected the lives of individual officers. O'Kelly became a bronchial asthmatic after spending the damp winter of 1858-59 mapping the Slieveardagh Coalfield. His problems there developed brought him close to the end of his field career. He had to take six months' sick-leave so that he might pass the winter of 1863-64 at Malaga, and in October 1866 he was happy to succeed Kelly in the indoor post of custodian of the Survey's office. One winter (it was probably that of 1866-67) Kinahan and his family were living in the old police barracks at Recess in County Galway when heavy falls of snow cut them off from the outside world for almost three weeks. Kinahan had to take to the moors with his gun in order to keep filled the family cooking-pot. Early in the 1870s Wilkinson and some of his colleagues went out to the County Mayo island of Inishturk intending to map the island's geology in no more than two days. But a great storm blew up. They were marooned for a week with little food and in a ruinous house which shook alarmingly at every gust of wind. Between 1876 and 1882 the Kinahans lived at Avoca while the local mapping was under revision. Kinahan claimed that conditions in the deeply incised Vale of Avoca were so damp that the excessive humidity had been a major factor contributing to the death of one of their children. A little farther south, and somewhat later in time, O'Meara's health is said to have been permanently damaged by his supervision of the all-weather, day-and-night drilling at Castlecomer between 1959 and 1963 (see p.180). He certainly had to hand over his responsibilities for the work to Dilys Jones.

I revert to the days of Jukes for my final words illustrative of the problems which Survey officers faced under the influence of the Irish weather. This is Jukes writing from Castlebar, County Mayo, on 29 April 1867.

> This morning there is a howling wind and pelting rain, and I have to do thirty miles of this country on an outside car, with only a dirty ill-kept public-house, that calls itself a hotel, at the end of it. Such is my country life in Ireland, and I have now been a month at that work .... I shall be heartily glad when I can escape with a pension....

Jukes's reference to that 'ill-kept public-house' leads me to the second of the environmental drawbacks in the life of a Survey officer - to the problem of inadequate field accommodation. Before the 1960s development of Ireland as a significant tourist destination, it was commonly extremely difficult for a field-scientist to find accommodation within the area which was to be the subject of examination. Here, again, is Jukes writing, this time in a letter to Murchison dated 3 February 1863

> It is often impossible to get any lodgings at all in small towns or large villages, or any where else over considerable districts notwithstanding the numerous houses, the inhabitants of which would be supposed from experience in all other countries to be quite ready to let them. The prices asked for very indifferent accommodation are often exorbitant to a ridiculous extent.

During the nineteenth century it was normal for a Survey officer to rent a house at some convenient location within his ground and then to reside there until the local mapping was completed. This was how the Kinahans came to be living at Recess during that unusually cold winter in the 1860s. Between 1872 and 1876 the family lived in the town of Wexford, from 1876 until 1882 they were at Avoca, and then, after 1882, they were in County Donegal, first at Letterkenny and then at Rathmelton. It was, incidentally, a persistent complaint within the Survey that there was no removal allowance to cover expenses incurred in the removal of a family's possessions from one field-station to another. In 1867 Du Noyer tried to establish a claim under this head, but he was refused, and Murchison reminded him that every officer had to accept the fact that he 'is an ubiquitous observer, who is not to be stationed permanently in any one place'.

Here, in passing, I must allude to one of the less reputable facets of the Survey's story. Certain geologists developed the habit of leaving behind them a trail of unpaid bills as they moved on from one field-station to another. On 27 July 1875 Hull issued to all his officers a memorandum deploring such behaviour and threatening dismissal to any officer who disgraced the Survey in so reprehensible a manner. The practice nevertheless seems to have persisted and many are the letters of rebuke that Hull addressed to Cruise because of his failure to satisfy a variety of creditors.

Sometimes the accommodation rented by officers was decidedly primitive. In 1856, after his first - and last - reasonably complete Irish tour of inspection, Murchison noted, with a characteristic dash of chauvinism.

> Jukes is a fine energetic fellow, and I made the acquaintance of all his men (inspecting their work), who are really good hard-working youths, who can stand a life no Englishman would tolerate ....

The deterioration of O'Kelly's health at Slieveardagh during the winter of 1858-59 was attributed to his having 'lived for weeks in houses very little better than sheds, into which the wind and rain freely entered'. Late in December 1874 (the month should be noted) Symes went out to inspect W.B. Leonard's work at Belmullet, and there he discovered that Leonard, without any permission or notification, had been absent from his station for six weeks. W.B. Leonard was proving to be a very unsatisfactory officer, but he offered illness as the excuse for his absence, the illness having been caused, he claimed, by the poor accommodation which was all he had been able to find in that remote corner of Ireland. Perhaps he told the truth. By April 1876 W.B. Leonard had transferred himself to a new field-station at Glenamoy, just a few kilometres to the east of Belmullet. His work was again inspected, this time by Kinahan, and on 7 April 1876 Kinahan wrote as follows to Hull.

> It seems to me that Mr Leonard has shown considerable zeal for the public service, by locating himself and family, as I found him, in a miserable hovel with a clay floor, that he might be near his work.

But where W.B. Leonard was concerned Kinahan may not have been an entirely impartial observer because Kinahan's sister, Katherine Stuart Kinahan, was to marry W.B. Leonard's brother Hugh on 24 October 1876. W.B. Leonard was not present at the wedding. He was dead. He was drowned while bathing at Belmullet on 23 August 1876, leaving a widow and four young children.

Sometimes, in remote districts, the geologists obtained the use of shooting-lodges, and during the summer of 1875 they were allowed accommodation in the coastguard station at Ballycastle, County Mayo. It was from there that they mapped most of the wild country between Broad Haven and Killala Bay. In order to allow them to cope with regions which were devoid of any kind of accommodation, the Survey in January 1872 spent £25 upon a tent of size sufficient to sleep four men. Interesting social problems arose when Wilkinson had to use the tent while mapping in the Cuilcagh Hills on the borders of counties Cavan and Fermanagh. Wilkinson, the son of an army officer, saw himself as a social cut above his colleagues, and on 22 April 1876 he wrote to Hull protesting that it was quite impossible for him to share the tent with his servant! Did Wilkinson *really* take to the field accompanied by a valet?

In 1884 the Survey purchased from the Royal Irish Constabulary a pre-fabricated hut for use in the field. The hut was erected first at Malin More at the far western end of the Slieve League Peninsula of County Donegal. There it served as a field-base during the summer of 1884, and there it survived the winter of 1884-85. In March 1885 the hut was dismantled and removed to Fintown, County Donegal, to be re-erected upon a plot of land just behind the post-office. There the hut ended its brief association with the Survey. It was severely damaged by storms during the winter of 1885-86, and on 18 March 1886 the local Royal Irish Constabulary sergeant reported the structure to be beyond repair. After some hard bargaining the ruin and its contents were sold to the Fintown postmaster for £8 in May 1886. But that was by no means the end of the caravanserai life-style of the Survey's officers. In the summer of 1895, for example, Kilroe went off to revise the mapping around Westport, County Mayo, taking with him the Survey's canteen, bedstead, and mattress, together with one of the Survey's two pillows.

The modern Survey did for some years possess two caravans, but nowhere in Beggars Bush have I ever seen canteens, bedsteads, mattresses, or pillows. Today's Survey officers live in a completely different world from that of their nineteenth-century forebears. When today's officers take to the field they are likely to find awaiting them a multitude of Irish Tourist Board-approved bed-and-breakfast establishments, well-appointed 'Hidden Ireland' guest-houses, and hotels displaying A.A. signs emblazoned with almost as many stars as feature upon the Australian flag. After a hard day's work in the field a modern Survey officer may - just very occasionally - sit down to dinner in a Egon Ronay recommended restaurant.

The third set of environmental drawbacks faced by the Survey officer consists of the occupational hazards unique to the officer's own profession.

Geologists, like sailors, often have to ply their skills in localities which are inherently dangerous. In their search for an understanding of the character of the earth's surface they have to resort to those places where wounds have been inflicted upon the terrestrial skin either by Nature's own turmoil or by the activities of the human race. Those wounds, in common with all wounds, are unsafe lacerations. There the geologist, like the single-handed yachtsman, commonly has to face entirely alone whatever threats may arise.

The geologist examining a coastal cliff may fall, break a limb, and be overtaken by a flood tide. The geologist working a riverine section may slip upon a water-washed surface and be swept away by the current. The geologist exploring exposures in the face of a quarry or gravel-pit may become the victim of a rock-fall. Geologists measuring the dip of the strata exposed within a railway-cutting may be so engrossed by their task that they fail to notice the approach of the express which delivers a mortal injury.

While he was on railway-section duty in 1847 and 1848, Du Noyer must have become aware of the threat posed by the 'iron horse', but no Irish Survey officer has ever been killed by a train. (The great Charles Thomas Clough of the Scottish Survey, who features in the group on page 226, was killed in 1916 by a group of loose-shunted wagons.) The Irish Survey has nevertheless experienced its fair share of all the other types of accident just adumbrated. Hugh Leonard was the victim of a serious fall while examining a cliff near Ballycastle, County Mayo, during 1875, and in 1881 his injuries led to his retirement from the Survey as unfit for further duty. By 1889 something had happened to Symes which rendered him, in Archibald Geikie's words, 'physically incapacitated for mapping where cliffs and precipitous sections require to be examined'. During the drift survey of the Limerick region in 1904 Kilroe was involved in two serious accidents, the precise nature of which is nowhere made clear, and during the mapping of the drifts on one-inch Sheet 120 (Naas) in the 1920s, Farrington fell into the Ballydonnell Brook and was almost drowned under the weight of his specimen-filled rucksack. To all these incidents there has to be added the fact that in 1901 Egan died of injuries sustained in a car accident while travelling with the Director-General and McHenry on a tour of inspection in County Wicklow (see p.108)

After such a recital of disaster it comes as a relief to be able to report that the most recent major accident involving a Survey officer resulted in nothing more serious than a fractured femur. Unfortunate it most certainly was, but it was an event hardly likely to have fatal consequences. Oddly - fortunately - it happened not in some remote mountain fastness, but at the docks in the heart of Galway city. Mr Raymond Keary fell one night as he was repairing on board the *Lough Beltra* during one of her programmes of offshore investigation in 1985.

The fourth and final set of environmental drawbacks bearing upon the life of a Survey officer arises from the fact that Ireland has often been in a disturbed political condition. Survey officers are seen as officials associated with whatever government may be in power in Dublin, and locally in rural Ireland the writ of that government has not always been acceptable. In consequence, it is all too easy for a Survey officer in the field to be regarded by the local populace as a government spy and informer. Why else would this stranger be tramping the countryside carrying maps and making notes? As a result, over the decades, many a Survey officer has felt their personal security to be threatened.

During the Fenian unrest of the 1860s, Galvan, the Fossil Collector, reported that he felt unsafe in the country around Castlecomer to which he had been sent. Jukes therefore wrote as follows to a local officer of the Royal Irish Constabulary.

> He writes me that he is looked upon by the people as a spy on the Fenians and seems in dread of ill treatment by the peasantry. May I ask you to be so good as to tell me whether in your opinion there is really any danger in his traversing the country alone?

In Dublin in 1867 a rumour went around to the effect that certain government officials were to be assassinated. Jukes heard the rumour and on 14 March he felt inspired to include an Irish bull in one of his letters.

> As to what is to take place next Sunday, no one knows; but the military authorities firmly believe there is much work in store for them. There is a strong rumour that we are all to get up murdered next Monday morning....

Kinahan was clearly much exercised by the problem of his personal security, and among the *Kinahan Papers* in the Royal Irish Academy there are licences granting him permission to carry a six-chambered revolver within certain of the Irish counties. But Kinahan clearly felt the need for enhanced fire-power because during the winter of 1880-81 he tried to persuade the Survey to buy for him a Winchester repeating rifle! And this was more than three years before he paid a visit to the North American West.

Hull includes in his autobiography a chapter entitled 'The Irish "Reign of Terror" ', and he was himself caught up in a potentially ugly situation during 1882. For the weekend of 5 to 8 May that year he stayed at the Great Southern Hotel in Killarney. On the Sunday morning some of the guests were assembled in the hotel's drawing-room prior to leaving for church, when there burst into the room an excited messenger bearing the news that the previous evening Lord Frederick Cavendish and Thomas Henry Burke had been murdered in the Phoenix Park, Dublin. A deep sense of shock and foreboding descended upon the entire company. The next day Hull joined the Dublin train, and just before its departure from Killarney there came into his first-class compartment a distraught-looking gentleman who seated himself, produced a revolver, and began to look around in a manner indicative of deep fear. Hull shortly discovered that his new travelling companion was the agent for one of the County Kerry estates and he had just learned that an attempt was to be made upon his life. That life he was clearly determined to sell dearly, perhaps taking with him into the next world the Director of the Geological Survey of Ireland. Little more than a year later, Hull, with Kitchener at his side, was to face the threat of Arab ambush in the Wadi Araba. Perhaps being a Survey officer in Ireland during the Land War was as good a preparation as any.

In the spring of 1884 Archibald Geikie visited the southwest of Ireland to inspect the revision mapping of the region carried out according to Hull's misguided reinterpretation devised in 1878 (see p.81). Geikie had with him McHenry, his favourite travelling companion, and one evening, as the two geologists drove down towards Bantry, their jarvey was at pains to point out the site of every recent murder or attempted murder. But 'Mac' had his own tales to tell. Throughout their tour he regaled Geikie with umpteen graphic accounts of the experiences through which he and several of his colleagues had gone during the period of the recent outrages. When Geikie observed that it was a happy thing that the more peaceful state of the country now made it unnecessary for Survey officers to carry weapons, 'Mac' offered no response. Geikie was puzzled. 'Do you mean that you still carry a gun?', he enquired in some surprise. 'Indeed I do', responded 'Mac', 'for you never know what's going to happen'. With that he withdrew a revolver from beneath his coat.

Forty years later the Survey's field-programme was severely curtailed during the War of Independence (1919-21) and the Civil War (1922-23) because of the risks which Survey officers would have had to face in many parts of Ireland. In his annual report for 1921-22 Cole specifically states that the disturbed state of the country had prevented almost all field-investigation, and it will be remembered that during 1921 Cole failed to attract C.A. Matley to Ireland as a Temporary Professional Assistant because Mrs Matley was concerned about her husband's safety (see p.150).

In more recent years Ireland's modern troubles inhibited Survey work in parts of the five Border counties during the 1970s and 1980s. There is a Survey story - apocryphal I am sure - of two Survey officers who did go to examine some exposures just to the south of the Border. They had scarcely arrived upon their ground when a helicopter appeared in the sky overhead and the pair soon found themselves surrounded by soldiers pointing automatic rifles. 'Are you subversives?' demanded the senior military gentleman in a tone of high authority. Then his tone changed to one of supercilious condescension as he framed a second question. 'Or would you just be geologists?'

But it is not only in the Border counties that the modern Survey officer may encounter difficulties associated with Ireland's most recent troubles. I offer here a purely hypothetical case. A Survey officer is working a piece of remote ground somewhere in Munster. In a clearing within a forest the officer comes upon ten armed men wearing combat jackets and Balaclava helmets. They are obviously relaxing after the completion of some exercise. What should the officer do? I leave my reader to deliberate upon the several possible answers to my question.

I have outlined many drawbacks inherent in the life of a Survey officer, and I come now to one of the most remarkable statistics in my entire story. At first sight the life of a Survey officer might seem to offer a healthy, out-of-door existence, but, so far as the nineteenth century is concerned, the facts are hardly supportive of such a rosy perspective. The influence of some of the environmental drawbacks just discussed must evidently be taken very seriously. During the nineteenth century a total of forty-four officers and Fossil Collectors worked for the Survey. Of these no less than twelve died either while still in service or soon after a premature retirement caused by injuries received while engaged upon Survey work. Two of the twelve deaths were caused by drowning and these can hardly be blamed upon the exigencies of Survey life. Foot, for example, met his end in Lough Key in 1867 while trying to rescue some skaters who had fallen through the ice, and W.B. Leonard, as we have seen, was drowned in 1876 while bathing at Belmullet. Leaving aside Foot and W.B. Leonard, we are still left with ten nineteenth-century Survey men who never lived to enter upon a normal retirement. Those ten constitute almost twenty-three per cent of the Survey's nineteenth-century field-staff and that would seem to be a remarkably high proportion. It would be interesting to know how this Survey figure might compare with an equivalent statistic for, say, the Valuation Office or the Ordnance Survey in Ireland. All I am able to confirm is that an officer was evidently somewhat safer with the Survey in Ireland than with Oldham's Geological Survey of India. Of the six Irish officers who between 1850 and 1862 resigned to join Oldham in

Calcutta, two - J.S. Kennedy and Willson - died prematurely while still carrying their hammers.

Since the death of Egan in 1901, only four officers have died while still in service, these four being Cole (1924), McCluskey (1963), and the Survey's two First World War casualties, Valentine (1916), and H.T. Kennedy (1917). Reading through the archives of the Survey for the twentieth century one is nevertheless impressed by the numerous references to ill health among the officers. Before the 1950s absence from duty through sickness would seem to have been a far more common occurrence than I suspect it to be today. When Duffy was taken ill in the field in June 1942 his sick-leave became so protracted that he was reduced to half-pay, and even the very fabric of Hume Street would seem to have become contaminated by disease. From Bishopp's Survey daybook we learn that on 26 October 1942 it was necessary for the office of Miss M.T. Murray, the Survey's long-serving typist and librarian, to undergo a course of fumigation!

Over the last few pages I have presented a somewhat gloomy picture of Survey life. I have depicted sickly, underpaid, promotion-starved officers working in dangerous places under sullen skies and sometimes surrounded by elements representative of a hostile populace. All this is true, but such collied details form merely the image engraved upon the reverse of the Survey medallion. Upon the obverse of the medallion there is to be discovered a most handsome design supported by a wealth of carefully executed embellishment. It is now time to turn the medallion over - to proceed from the somewhat dismal reverse to the far more cheerful obverse.

Looking at the obverse my first point has to be that a post with the Survey has ever been a means of converting a private fascination into a professional career. Officers such as Oldham, Jukes, Kinahan, Hull, Lamplugh, Wright, Cole, Cunningham, Synge, and many another, were all geologists to the core. They were men who were passionately involved with their science. They had dedicated their lives to geology. As Survey officers they must have been delighted at their good fortune. They were actually being paid to indulge in those activities which were their heart's desire. What they craved for was an opportunity to commune with rocks in the field. As Survey officers this private craving was transformed into a happy public duty.

That there really did occur within the Survey a fusing of private desire with public responsibility is nicely demonstrated if we examine the activities of several Survey officers during the periods of their annual leave. In many cases that leave took the form of a busman's holiday. Having spent the year at grips with problems of Irish geology, come their annual leave, it was by no means unusual for officers to go off in search of yet further geological experiences outside the confines of their professional bailiwick. While on sick-leave following his accident at Kenmare in 1864, Jukes made a study of the rocks around Coblenz. In 1866 Foot spent his vacation - his last vacation, as it transpired - geologising in Norway. Symes went to see the ancient volcanoes of Auvergne during 1870, and Hull followed him thither in 1880. Nolan explored the Siebengebirge and the Lower Eifel during the September of 1875. After the 1884 meeting of the British Association for the Advancement of Science at Montreal, Kinahan evidently joined an excursion of two weeks' duration along the Canadian Pacific Railway and into the Rocky Mountains to the then railhead lying just westward of the Kicking Horse Pass. In 1908 Kilroe spent part of his vacation inspecting the German bauxite deposits near Giessen that he might the better understand the Interbasaltic Horizon of northeastern Ireland. Throughout their Survey careers, first Wright and then Synge lost no opportunity of spending their leave studying their beloved Quaternary deposits within some fresh environment.

A post with the Survey certainly offered the deep satisfaction of a career in geology, but at a different level a life with the Survey must have offered innumerable other satisfying and pleasurable experiences. There was the fulfilment which Clark must have felt when he found fossils in the hitherto barren Lower Palaeozoic rocks of one-inch Sheet 58 (Monaghan) (see p.105). There was the delight of lazing in the heather atop Croghan Mountain on a hot July day as there shimmered that glorious northward panorama extending from the Vale of Arklow, through Lugnaquillia to the Castlecomer Plateau and the Blackstairs Mountains. There was the thrill which Wilkinson experienced when for five minutes a magnificent golden eagle preened itself within ten feet of him on a mist-shrouded Ben Gorm in County Mayo. There was the pleasure of walking alongside a barefoot colleen one summer's evening as she drove homeward two sheep from the great August fair at Borris, County Carlow. There was the excitement of sitting beside a winter's turf-fire listening to tales of the Indian Mutiny - of Cawnpore and Lucknow - told by a onetime soldier of the Connaught Rangers as tearfully he fingered the treasured Mutiny medal which he had just removed from an alcove over the hearth. Once the medal's ribbon had been white and scarlet; now it is black with the peat-dust of decades.

There was humour too. The antics of Edward Forbes were famed throughout the Survey and presumably he reduced the Irish staff to peals of laughter whenever he joined them in the field.

Here, for example, is one account of Forbes the contortionist.

> Separating his feet, he could sit down between them, and then twisting his arms through his legs, bring his knees over his shoulders. In this position he walked upon his hands, with his face peeping comically from between his legs, like some of the elvish forms that he loved so much to design.

The lighter side of Irish Survey life is also revealed in a letter which Ramsay penned on 29 September 1872. He had just been at Warrenpoint, County Down, inspecting Traill's work, but it was more than Traill's skill as a geologist which came under examination. The Director-General wrote of his young officer:

> He looks something like what I did when I joined the Survey, only he is much handsomer, sings a great dealt better, but cannot jump so high.

One officer even had a tale to tell of his encounter with the supernatural. It was Wilkinson. He always aspired to live in some modest style, and during the final stages of the mapping of County Donegal in the 1880s he found himself field accommodation at the dilapidated Doe Castle, near Creeslough. One November night, around the witching hour, Wilkinson was reading by the light of a candle and a roaring fire when Shot, his faithful retriever, suddenly became terror-stricken, evidently convinced that there was something evil in the adjacent room, the castle's disused dining-hall. Wilkinson seized a poker and threw open the intervening door. The candle and the fire-light filled the chamber with long shadows. Old paper hung from the damp walls in great festoons. A bat fluttered. There was nobody there, and yet.... Shot cowered beneath a table, and Wilkinson felt some presence. They were being watched. On three nights they had the same eerie experience. Wilkinson heard a tale of a woman who had been murdered in the castle and whose ghost now walked its floors. He felt uneasy. He resolved to vacate the castle. Wilkinson, Shot, and Maggie, his (Protestant) maid, all removed themselves to a cottage in Dunfanaghy.

And then there was the little episode of the poteen and the royal ferns. Again we have to rely upon Wilkinson's reminiscences. Around 1870 some officers - Wilkinson among them - rented as their field-station a house located at Dernasliggaun upon the southern shores of Killary Harbour in County Galway. One night, when the officers were asleep, there came loud raps upon one of the windows. Investigation revealed the cause of the disturbance to be the local purveyor of poteen who was down from the hills with a churn of his fiery spirit for sale. He was admitted, and the Survey men decanted the precious liquid into whatever bottles they could find, paid their visitor ten shillings, and sent him off home with a hunk of bread and a piece of meat. The following morning the geologists went down to the Killary for their customary swim, but upon their return they were horrified to see that the district was being combed by a detachment from the Royal Irish Constabulary. While his companions kept cave, Wilkinson removed the incriminating bottles from the house, dug a hole, buried all the evidence, and topped off his handiwork with a fine clump of royal fern (*Osmunda regalis*). When the constables arrived they were most admiring of his horticultural activities. They even told him where he might find some more ferns for his garden. But of poteen there was spoken not a word. The Survey officers learned with some relief that the constables were in the district bent merely upon the task of collecting the regular agricultural returns!

The incidents just described may each be trivial, but they do nonetheless contribute to our understanding of the Survey. The vignette of a troubled Wilkinson quitting a haunted castle, or of his hasty interment of the officers' poteen, are revealing of the men who stand behind the maps and memoirs. Then, as now, the Survey was more than just a catalogue of publications, a building stocked with geological information, and a couple of lines in the annual national budget. The Survey was - the Survey is - an institutional context wherein there has laboured - wherein there continues to labour - a community of real, searching, smiling, striding, shopping, sleeping people. They have, over the decades, gathered in the tea-room to welcome some newly-appointed officer. They have together enjoyed a companionship in science. They have admired each others' prowess with the hammer in the field, and have sought to emulate each others' skill with the pen in the office. They have toasted departing colleagues during evenings of farewell joviality. They have stood beside open graves and carried wreaths inscribed 'In Memory, from Survey Friends'. And, in just one notorious case, their personal passions became so inflamed as to generate that notorious Victorian feud between the Director and the geologist who should have been his chief aide. The historian of the Survey, like any historian, is really concerned with people. I may only hope that readers who have followed me through the preceding chapters will by now have come to feel themselves as being upon reasonably intimate terms with some of the leading figures in the Survey's story.

And, of course, that story goes on. Within our modern society Survey men and Survey women are continuing to advance our knowledge of Ireland's geology and seeking to make that knowledge available to all who have need of it, both at home and overseas. That bearded and surpliced chorister, who assists in the filling of St Patrick's cathedral with noble and welling sound, is a Survey officer. Tomorrow he will be back among his maps and his fossils. That lady in the maroon Ford Escort waiting to turn right at the traffic-lights in Northumberland Road is a Survey officer. Yesterday she was out on the production platform for the Kinsale Head Gas Field; today she is impatient to reach her office where she has to complete the photographic exhibition which the Survey is shortly mounting at a Dublin venue. That unusually tall gentleman who at Blackrock has just joined the morning commuters aboard a DART train is a Survey officer. Through Booterstown, Sydney Parade, and Sandymount he sits engrossed in some official-looking papers. Normally he leaves the train at Lansdowne Road for the short walk over to Beggars Bush; this morning he goes on to Pearse Station because he has to represent the Survey at some meeting in a government department.

Singing in choirs; trays of fossils; visits to production platforms; photographic exhibitions; commuting on DART; and discussions at conference tables. But what of the Survey's modern face-to-face contact with the actual rocks of Ireland? In this age of the remote sensing of our environment and of computer data-bases, the Survey officers of today are far more likely to be found in their Beggars Bush offices than amidst the drumlins of Cavan or the Reeks of Kerry. That Survey 'butterfly', flitting across the countryside from exposure to exposure, is by no means extinct, but such a 'butterfly' is much less common a sight than formerly. Certainly far gone are those days when Survey officers and their families resided in some tract of country, perhaps for years on end, until its mapping was finally completed. I am sure that the officers of those distant days - Du Noyer, Kinahan, or Foot - would be puzzled by the life-style of their modern counterparts. I am by no means certain that the officers of a rather later generation - Kilroe, Wright, or Cunningham - would be all that much more understanding.

But I have no intention of parting from my reader in the choir of St Patrick's, at some Dublin traffic-lights, aboard a DART train, around the conference table, or before a Beggars Bush VDU. The Geological Survey of Ireland is all about the rocks of Ireland. I propose to spend my final paragraphs out among those rocks, surrounded by magnificent scenery, and upon a glorious September afternoon. We are going on a little journey.

We are travelling northward from Galway bound for Louisburgh in County Mayo. It's a day of near sub-tropical heat - a day we will remember for years to come.. We've just paused at Eddie Hamilton's shop in Leenaun for some cans of refreshment and a couple of bars of chocolate. Now we head onwards past the Sheep and Wool Museum opened by President Mary Robinson on 15 July 1993, past the much-photographed falls of the Erriff at Aasleagh, around the head of the Killary, and on up the Bundorragha. There a young German couple driving a BMW have paused to admire the view and to exercise their Leica. We exchange the waves of joyous souls. We hasten on past the centre belonging to Delphi Adventure Holidays and then we swing right over Delphi Bridge. Just over the bridge, on the left-hand side of the road, and squeezed between the road and the clear waters of a languid Bundorragha, the county engineer has left for us a tiny patch of surfaced ground just large enough to contain one parked vehicle. Today a vehicle sits there - a vehicle we know so well that its presence here brings a smile to our faces. It's a cream-coloured van. Upon its side is the inscription 'Geological Survey of Ireland'. Of course, we stop.

There's nobody around. We try the van's doors. They're locked. We peer through the windows. Above the dashboard there lies a clinometer, a copy of the Ordnance Survey's half-inch Sheet 10, two official, brown, harp-bearing envelopes, a half-empty tube of Rowntree's fruit pastilles, and the skins of several oranges. Down on the grubby floor is a muddy pair of wellies together with several dirty grey field-socks. The passenger seat is littered with odds and ends. I note there a plastic envelope containing air-photographs, a copy of the memoir to one-inch sheets 83 and 84, and some very dog-eared papers which it eventually dawns upon me are photocopies of six-inch field-sheets. Atop all this there lies a pot of Nivea, a recently opened pack of Band-aid, and an Oral-B toothbrush still in its sealed container. It looks like somebody has been visiting a pharmacy. In the back of the van we catch a glimpse of a cardboard box which once safely transported bottles of Heinz tomato ketchup to some supermarket, but which is now evidently full of rock-samples. We have met the modern Survey in the field, but we see no clue as to the identity of the officer whose duty has brought him - or is it her? - to so idyllic a spot upon so perfect a day.

We turn away from the van to gaze westward out over the magnificent panorama spread before us. Invisible insects fill the warm air with their incessant buzzing. The azure sky contains just one wispy cloud back towards the Killary. A fish jumps and plops back into the Bundorragha. A seemingly irate female voice drifts up the valley from the Adventure centre. In the background Mweelrea looks superb, its rugged grey and purple form shaking itself free of the alluvium and peat of its lowland mantle. High up on the mountain the cliffs of its two great corries seem to quiver in the heat. I know that in each of those corries there nestles a secluded tarn. Who knows? Perhaps our Survey geologist is up there right now enjoying a refreshing dip after some sweaty hammering. A car travelling north over the bridge and along the road beside us stimulates our speedy mental descent from the Mweelrea basins. It's the Germans again in their BMW. We're old friends now. Again we exchange waves.

As the Germans disappear down the road towards Dhulough Pass, my thoughts turn to the past. The little bridge by which we stand carries a tablet explaining that the structure was originally built in 1823 by the Scots engineer William Bald. I happen to know that while he was hereabouts he tried to understand the local geology in those far-off days before anybody had even thought of the Geological Survey of Ireland. Later, and for the Survey, this was Wilkinson's ground. He had wanted to be a soldier, like his father. Instead, he found himself sent here to County Mayo to wrestle with conglomerates rather than with Chinese at Peking, with slates rather than with Sikhs in the Punjab. Ben Gorm lies just behind us and it was near its peak that he had his close encounter with that golden eagle sometime in the years around 1870. Perhaps among those photocopies in the van there are reproductions of some of his actual field-sheets. Kinahan was here too. On 8 May 1871 he wrote to Hull offering a reward of £1 to the first officer able to find a fossil in the local rocks of what was then being termed 'the Doolough Series'. The one-inch sheet of the region - Sheet 84 - was published in 1874, and its accompanying memoir, combined with that for one-inch Sheet 83, appeared two years later bearing the names of Kinahan, Hugh Leonard, Nolan, Symes, and Wilkinson. Now, in the 1990s, my peering through the van's windows has revealed that a modern officer has thought it useful to bring that ancient memoir west from Beggars Bush and back into the country which it describes. A compliment, indeed, for the officers of yesteryear.

Southward down this road in the spring of 1889 there came Archibald Geikie as he sought to relate the geology of the Scottish Highlands to that of northwestern Ireland. With him he then had Peach of the Scottish Survey, Hyland, the Irish Survey's most recent recruit, and, of course, the invaluable 'Mac'. Kilroe came here around 1900 during his revision of the Lower Palaeozoic rocks of Ireland. His revised mapping around Mweelrea was not regarded as sufficiently detailed to justify the publication of a fresh edition of Sheet 84, but some of his revisions did feature in Geikie's drift map of Ireland (1906) and in the paper which Kilroe himself read to the Royal Irish Academy on 24 June 1907. Then there came the calamity of World War I followed by the Survey's long period of enforced paralysis. Like the golden eagle, the Survey officer became extinct on Mweelrea. For more than half a century the Survey resigned the region to hammers other than its own. It was 1962 before the Survey returned to this ground. It was a return led by Francis Synge. In that year he came here to map the glacial drifts in his own inimitable style, and the moraine which trails across the valley beside the Adventure centre is one of the features which Francis then explored.

Since 1962 many a Survey officer has been here. Dr Michael Max (with T.J. Kelly) remapped much of this ground during the 1970s, and just a few kilometres to the north Mr Deepak Inamdar (again with T.J. Kelly) made that geophysical study of the Corvock Granite which is described in the 1979-80 issue of the Survey's own *Bulletin*. Now the presence of this parked van indicates that somewhere out beyond that spongy peat, or perhaps behind us on Wilkinson's Ben Gorm, a still more modern Survey officer is here at grips with some of Ireland's oldest and most fascinating rocks.

Shall we write for the absent officer a little message in the grime on the side of the van? I think not. Such a childish act would in some way seem to desecrate so perfect a scene and to trivialise the memory of those bygone geologists who so recently have filled our thoughts. We will just continue on our way to Louisburgh expressing the silent hope that the Survey officer out there is relishing so memorable a day, and that he or she will this evening return to the van tired but satisfied, to use one of Jukes's favourite phrases, that geological problems have been spiflicated.

We were supposed to have been in Louisburgh half an hour ago. Another piece of Eddie Hamilton's now melting chocolate, back onto the road, and off we go. The journey takes us on past Fin Lough, past Delphi Lodge, and over Glenummera Bridge. Just beyond the bridge we note that a tiny harbour by the side of Doo Lough contains three good-looking clinker-built boats. In one of them there sits a finely attired tweedy gentleman. His ample cap is pulled low to shade his eyes in the glaring lacustrine sunlight. He is giving close attention to some detail of one of his unusually long fishing-rods. He never even raises his head in acknowledgement of our transit. We drive on. We pass a roadside memorial to the local victims of the Famine, and the site where some recent exploration geologist has discovered a workable gold deposit. A few minutes more and we come to a halt outside Durkan's grocery in the main street of Louisburgh. I lock the car and am just pocketing the key when a thought flashes into my mind. Back down the road. Doo Lough. That tweedy gentleman in the boat at Glenummera Bridge. Did he not look remarkably like the photograph of Sidney Wilkinson? Do modern fishermen really use rods like those we saw? I wonder. I just wonder.

APPENDIX I

CHRONOLOGY OF EVENTS IN THE HISTORY OF THE GEOLOGICAL SURVEY OF IRELAND 1845 – 1992

1845	April 1	The Geological Survey of Ireland comes into existence as a part of the new Geological Survey of the United Kingdom. Ultimate control of the Survey rests with the First Commissioner of Her Majesty's Woods, Forests, Land Revenues, Works and Buildings. The Director of the Survey is Sir Henry De La Beche and his Local Director in Dublin is Captain Henry James, Royal Engineers. The office of the Survey is in the Custom House, Dublin.
	May 22	De La Beche directs James to break ground in southeastern Ireland.
	October 28	Botanical, geological, and zoological materials collected by the Ordnance Survey are handed over to the Geological Survey.
1846	April 16	Sir Robert Kane asks James to collect soil-samples.
	July 4	James ceases to be Local Director and Thomas Oldham takes over.
	September 24	The First Commissioner directs the Survey to begin the collection of soil-samples.
	October 7	Kane reports to De La Beche that 51 St Stephen's Green is ready to receive the Survey.
1847	April	Oldham presents sheets of sections to the Lord Lieutenant.
	June 9	G.V. Du Noyer appointed to investigate railway geology.
1848	July 26	The county map of Wicklow is published, the Survey's first published map.
1850	November 30	Oldham ceases to be Local Director and is succeeded by J.B. Jukes.
1851	May	County maps of Dublin and Wexford are published, the last of the series of county geological maps.
	Summer	James Flanagan's discovery of the richly fossiliferous upper Old Red Sandstone beds at Kiltorcan, County Kilkenny.
1853	January	Kane and Jukes agree that the collection of soil-samples should cease.
	April 1	The new Department of Science and Art assumes responsibility for the Geological Survey, under the Board of Trade and then, after 25 February 1856, under the Lords of the Committee of Privy Council on Education.
1854	August 24	De La Beche, Jukes, and A.C. Ramsay at Glengarriff discuss the future of the Geological Survey in Scotland.
		Jukes appointed to the chair in the Dublin School of Science Applied to Mining and the Arts.
1855	April 13	Death of De La Beche.
	May 5	Sir Roderick Murchison becomes Director.
	December 1	Murchison directs that every one-inch sheet is to have its accompanying memoir.

1856	December	Publication of the first eight one-inch quarter sheets (Sheets 36 and 41, in 1858 renumbered sheets 120, 121, 129, 130 138, 139, 148, and 149).
1858	July 28	Publication of the first one-inch sheet memoir (Sheet 45 S.E., later Sheet 166).
1860	April	Publication of the first four of the New Series longitudinal sections.
1862	May 14	Jukes reads his paper on the southern Irish rivers to the Geological Society of Dublin.
1864	March	The Survey receives the Portlock Collection of books from Mrs Portlock.
	July 27	Jukes's accident at Kenmare.
1867	April 1	The expansion of the Survey comes into effect. Murchison becomes Director-General and Jukes becomes Director.
	July 1	Publication of 'Jukes's Geological Map of Ireland'.
1869	May 6	Edward Hull arrives in Dublin to take charge of the Survey during Jukes's illness.
	July 29	Death of Jukes.
	October 16	Hull appointed Director.
1870	March	The Survey's headquarters is transferred from 51 St Stephen's Green to 14 Hume Street.
1871	October 22	Death of Murchison.
1872	March 15	Ramsay becomes Director-General.
1873		Decision taken to use the 'hill edition' as the base-map for all future one-inch geological sheets.
1874	October	Publication of one-inch Sheet 28, the first sheet on a hachured base-map.
1878	March 30	Publication of 'Hull's Geological Map of Ireland'.
1879-81		McHenry revises the mapping of the south of Ireland under Hull's direction.
1880	May	Hull and Symes visit the Northwest Highlands of Scotland.
1881	May 26	Hull announces his discovery of Laurentian rocks in County Donegal.
	August 9	Ramsay instructs officers that future field-mapping is to be on the one-inch rather than the six-inch scale.
	December 31	Retirement of Sir Andrew Ramsay from the post of Director-General.
1882	January 1	Archibald Geikie becomes Director-General.
1887	October	Primary geological mapping of Ireland completed near Rathmelton, County Donegal.
1888	June 4-24	Kilroe, Kinahan, McHenry, Nolan, and Wilkinson visit the Northwest Highlands of Scotland.
1890	April 1	Symes and Wilkinson transferred to the Geological Survey of Scotland. Cruise, Kinahan, Mitchell, and Wynne all retire.
	August 29	The Dublin Museum of Science and Art is opened with galleries devoted to the Survey's collections.

	September 30	Hull retires from the directorship.
	October 1	Nolan takes over the Survey as Senior Geologist in Charge.
	November 21	Publication of Sheet 10, the final sheet of the one-inch geological map.
1892	April 1	The final one-inch sheet memoir is published, it being for sheets 22, 23, 30, & 31 (in part).
1894	December	Publication of Sheet 35, the final sheet in the series of longitudinal sections.
1897		Survey collections removed from the main museum building to the Curved Gallery.
1900	September 24	The Wharton Committee reports.
1901	March 1	Retirement of Sir Archibald Geikie from the post of Director-General. Jethro J.H. Teall becomes Director (not Director-General) of the Geological Survey of the United Kingdom.
	April 30	Retirement of Nolan from the post of Senior Geologist in Charge.
	May 1	G.W. Lamplugh takes charge of the Survey as District Geologist.
	May to November	Drift survey of the Dublin region.
1902		Drift survey of the Belfast region.
1903		Drift survey of the Cork region.
1904		Drift survey of the Limerick region.
1905	April 1	The Survey is transferred from the Geological Survey of the United Kingdom to the Department of Agriculture and Technical Instruction for Ireland. Lamplugh finally returns to England. G.A.J. Cole becomes the Director of the Survey.
1905-6		Drift survey of the Londonderry region.
1906		Soil survey at Ballyhaise, County Cavan.
		Geikie's *Map showing the surface geology of Ireland* is published.
1907-9		Survey of the Interbasaltic Horizon.
1907	Autumn	Publication of J.R. Kilroe's *Soil-Geology of Ireland.*
c.1908		Soil laboratory fitted out in 14 Hume Street.
1908	April 23	Clare Island Survey launched.
1911-13		W.B. Wright's survey of the Killarney and Kenmare region.
1914	March	Publication of Sheet 11, the first sheet of the new quarter-inch geological map of Ireland.
	Summer	The Survey accepts one student for its new course in field-mapping.
	July 15 to August 31	The Dublin Civic Exhibition.
1916	June (to 1919)	The Survey's fertilizer experiments.
1917		Publication of the six-inch drift map of the Dublin region (Sheet 18).
1918	December 17	Drilling commences at Washing Bay, County Tyrone.
1921	June	Duplicate set of six-inch maps removed to a place of safety. (Returned January 1922).

1922	June 28	National Museum declared closed because of security problems at Leinster House.
1923	January	Duplicate set of six-inch maps again removed to a place of safety. (Returned December 1923.)
	July 18	Geological materials relating to Northern Ireland handed over to the new Six County government.
1924	April 20	Death of Cole. Timothy Hallissy stands in as the acting head of the Survey.
		Survey told to remove its collections from the Curved Gallery in the National Museum of Science and Art.
	June 2	The Survey is transferred from the Department of Agriculture and Technical Instruction to the Department of Education.
1928	April 1	Survey transferred from the Department of Education to the Department of Industry and Commerce (after 1977 Industry, Commerce and Energy).
		Publication of the 'one to a million' geological map of Ireland.
	August 9	Hallissy appointed Director.
1939	November 7	Hallissy retires as Director. T.J. Duffy takes over the administration of the Survey.
1940	December 24	D.W. Bishopp takes over as Director.
1941	November 7	Thomas Murphy seconded to the Survey from the Emergency Scientific Research Bureau to undertake geophysical studies.
1943		Publication of the first of three Emergency period pamphlets.
1949		Two maps of vertical magnetic intensity published.[1]
1950	September 12	Bishopp resigns from the directorship and Duffy again takes over responsibility.
1952	June 16	Mr Murrogh O Brien becomes Director.
1953	Summer	Scheme introduced for the employment of Temporary Field Officers.
	August to December	Drilling at Abbeytown, County Sligo.
	December (to late 1954)	Drilling at Murvey, County Galway.
1956	June 19 to 27	Cunningham works in the Tynagh region in County Galway.
1959	March (to January 1963)	Drilling on the Castlecomer Coalfield.
1960	July (to September 1962)	Drilling on the Connaught Coalfield.
1962		Publication of the 1:750,000 geological map of Ireland.
1964	February 29	Mr Murrogh O Brien resigns as Director. Mark Cunningham takes over the administration of the Survey.
1967	March	Dr Cyril Williams arrives in Ireland to assume office as Director.
	September 5	Dr Williams submits to the Minister a memorandum entitled *Proposals for the Reorganisation of the Irish Geological Survey.*
1970	November	Publication of the first number of the Geological Survey of Ireland *Bulletin.*

1973-77		Survey organises the first Irish nationwide vertical aerial photographic survey.
1974		Construction commences of the new Survey headquarters at Beggars Bush.
1979-81		Aeromagnetic Survey of the Irish Midlands employing E.E.C. funding.
1980		The Survey is transferred to the Department of Energy.
1981		The Survey's Department becomes the Department of Industry and Energy.
1982	February (to late 1986)	Review of the Survey's activities carried out by a group under the chairmanship of Mr Sean Fitzgerald of the Department of Energy.
1983		Initiation of the release of previously confidential exploration company reports held by the Survey for surrendered ground.
1984		The Survey's Department reverts to being the Department of Energy.
	May	The Survey moves its headquarters from 14 Hume Street to Beggars Bush.
1985		The Cunningham Family establish the Cunningham Awards in memory of Mark Cunningham, the awards being administered by the Survey.
1986	December 16	'Down to Earth' exhibition opened at Beggars Bush.
1987	November 6	Dr Cyril Williams retires as Director.
	November 9	Dr Ralph Horne takes over the administration of the Survey.
1988		Publication of the first nine sheets of a proposed 1:25,000 Bedrock Geological Map of Ireland.
1990	December 20	The Minister for Energy (Mr Robert Molloy) launches a management review of the Survey to be undertaken by a group under the chairmanship of Mr Thomas Reeves.
1992	January 31	The management review is completed.
		Publication of the *Bulletin* suspended.
	February 28	Dr Peadar McArdle appointed Director.
		Following upon the management review, five sections are established within the Survey: Bedrock Mapping; Quaternary and Geotechnical; Goundwater; Minerals; Marine.
	April	Minerals Exploration and Development Division established within the Department of Transport, Energy and Communications but outside the Survey. Four Survey officers transferred to the new body.
	September	Publication of Sheet 6 (North Mayo), with its accompanying memoir, the first sheet of the 1:100,000 Bedrock Geological Map of Ireland.

APPENDIX II

STAFF LIST FOR THE GEOLOGICAL SURVEY OF IRELAND 1845 - 1992

This selective list has been compiled by the author from a wide variety of sources, including personal information kindly provided by present members of the Survey. Limitations of space and lack of information precluded any attempt at a totally comprehensive listing. The focus of this list is on professional and technical staff of the Survey, many of whom are, of course, referred to in an historical context within the main body of the text.

The cited literary sources relating to the Survey officers are intended merely to be indicative rather than exhaustive.

The universities and other institutions mentioned are those in which the various individuals have studied.

The following are the abbreviations employed within the list.

ALLIB.	Austin Allibone, *A Critical Dictionary of English Literature and British and American Authors*, Philadelphia, 1899.
ANDREW	Biographical notes in C.J. Andrew, R.W.A. Crowe, S. Finlay, W.H. Pennell, and J.F. Pyne (editors), *Geology and Genesis of Mineral Deposits in Ireland*, Irish Association for Economic Geology, 1986, pp.xvi + 710.
b.	born.
d.	died.
DAB	*Dictionary of Australian Biography.*
DIAS	Dublin Institute for Advanced Studies.
DNB	*Dictionary of National Biography.*
DSB	*Dictionary of Scientific Biography.*
ESH	*Earth Sciences History.*
GM	*Geological Magazine.*
GS	Geological Survey.
GSGB	Geological Survey of Great Britain.
GSI	Geological Survey of Ireland.
GSIB	*Geological Survey of Ireland Bulletin.*
GSL	Geological Society of London.
GSS	Geological Survey of Scotland.
ICS	Imperial College of Science.
IG	*Irish Geography.*
IN	*Irish Naturalist.*
INJ	*Irish Naturalists' Journal.*
JG	*Journal of Glaciology.*
JRGSI	*Journal of the Royal Geological Society of Ireland.*
JRSAI	*Journal of the Royal Society of Antiquaries of Ireland.*
MII	Museum of Irish Industry.
MM	*Mineralogical Magazine.*
MPMLPS	*Memoirs and Proceedings of the Manchester Literary and Philosophical Society.*
N	*Nature.*
ONFRS	*Obituary Notices of Fellows of the Royal Society.*
P & P2	Charles Mollan, William Davis, Brendan Finucane (editors), *More People and Places in Irish Science and Technology*, Royal Irish Academy, 1990, pp.108.
PGA	*Proceedings of the Geologists' Association.*
PGSL	*Proceedings of the Geological Society of London.*
PRIA	*Proceedings of the Royal Irish Academy.*
PRS	*Proceedings of the Royal Society.*
QCB	Queen's College Belfast.
QCC	Queen's College Cork.
QJGS	*Quarterly Journal of the Geological Society of London.*
QUB	Queen's University Belfast.
RCSI	Royal College of Science for Ireland.
RGSI	*Records of the Geological Survey of India.*
RIA	Royal Irish Academy.

RSM Royal School of Mines.

RUI Royal University of Ireland.

SARJ William A.S. Sarjeant, *Geologists and the History of Geology: An International Bibliography from the Origins to 1978*, London and Basingstoke, 1980.

SIN Robert Lloyd Praeger, *Some Irish Naturalists: A Biographical Note-book*, Dundalk, 1949, pp. 208.

TCD Trinity College Dublin.

TGSSA *Transactions of the Geological Society of South Africa.*

TIBG *Transactions of the Institute of British Geographers.*

U University.

UC University College.

UCD University College Dublin.

UCG University College Galway.

UCL University College London.

WW *Who's Who.*

PERSONNEL

ALDWELL, CHRISTOPHER ROBIN
b. Liverpool 10.02.1938.
TCD.
Geologist 30.09.1960; Senior Geologist 24.07.1970; Principal Geologist 30.07.1979.

ARCHER, JEAN BARBARA
b. Dublin 04.04.1947.
TCD; UCG.
Geologist 01.07.1976; part time 31.03.1989.

ATTLEY, PETER
b. Dublin 1961.
Cartographer 09.03.1981; Left on career break 28.02.1986 and did not return.

BAILY, WILLIAM HELLIER
b. Bristol 07.07.1819.
Assistant Curator Bristol Museum 1837-44.
Draughtsman GSGB 1844; Assistant Geologist GSGB for museum work 1845; Assistant Naturalist GSGB 1854.
Geologist (Acting Palaeontologist) GSI 07.1857; Senior Geologist (Acting Palaeontologist).
d. Rathmines, Dublin, 06.08.1888.
QJGS (Proceedings) 45, 1889, p.39; *GM* dec. 3, 5, 1888, pp. 431 & 575; *N* 38, 1888, p. 396; *SIN*; ALLIB; SARJ.

BARNES, EILEEN E.
Worked part-time on the Survey's collections in the National Museum during 1920 and thereafter as an occasional draughtsman down to c 1938.

BARRAGRY, JOAN (Mrs Brück)
b. Dublin 27.05.1946.
Mapping Draughtsman 09.10.1967; Resigned 21.04.1971.

BELL, ANDREW M.
b. Liverpool 23.04.1950.
Sheffield U.
Worked for 3 years with GSS.
Geologist 15.01.1979; Resigned 16.09.1983.
ANDREW p. 701.

BISHOPP, DOUGLAS WALLACE
b. Lee, Kent, 14.08.1900.
RSM; ICS.
Mining geologist in Africa and North America; Staff of the Rhodesian Museum; Geological Survey of British Guiana.
Director GSI 24.12.1940; Resigned 12.09.1950.
Geological Survey of Cyprus 1950-53; Other appointments in Africa.
d. Compton Abbas, Dorset, 01.03.1977.
GSL *Annual Report 1977*, p. 28; SARJ; *Tonbridge School Register* (entrants of 1914).

BLAKELY, JOHN
b. 21.12.1841.
General Assistant, House Keeper, and Hall Porter 1888; Retired 31.10.1912.

BOLAND, MAEVE ALISON (Mrs Hitzman)
b. Kilkenny 02.02.1955.
TCD.
Geologist 10.11.1986.

BROWNE, ALAN
Geologist 30.11.1964; Resigned 04.06.1965.

BRÜCK, PETER MICHAEL
b. Cambridge 22.03.1940.
Edinburgh U; UCD.
Temporary Geologist 01.11.1968; Geologist 03.02.1969; Senior Geologist 25.02.1974; Resigned 31.08.1979.
Professor of Geology in UCC.

BURKE, J.J.
Draughtsman c 1912-19.

BYRNE, MARGARET (Mrs Wright)
Mapping Draughtsman 08.1971; Resigned 06.01.1977.

CARTER (née Gormley), MARY JOSEPHINE
b. Dublin 06.09.1955.
TCD.
Project geologist.
Geologist GSI 03.11.1980.

CLARK, RICHARD
b. 16.06.1853.
Temporary Fossil Collector 23.06.1877; Fossil Collector 1878; Assistant Curator of Collections 08.01.1891; Temporary Assistant Geologist and Superintendent of Maps 1901; Geologist 01.04.1901; Retired 16.06.1918.
d. Rathgar, Dublin, 29.10.1933.
Irish Press, 31 October 1933.

CLARKE, W.H.
b. 27.07.1857.
Worked in Ordnance Survey.
Occasional draughtsman in GSI from 16.02.1920 until c 1926.
d. ?

COLE, GRENVILLE ARTHUR JAMES
b. London 21.10.1859.
RSM.

Professor of Geology RCSI 1890-1924.
Director GSI 01.04.1905.
d. Carrickmines, Co. Dublin, 20.04.1924.
WW; *PRS* series B, 100, p. iv; *QJGS* (Proceedings) 81, 1925, p.lxvi; *GM* 61, 1924, p. 285; *PGA* 36, 1925, p.190; *N* 113, 1924, p. 649; *MM* 20, 1924, p. 257; *IN* 33, 1924, p. 57; *GSIB* 4(2), 1989, p. 151; *SIN*; SARJ; *The Times,* 22 April 1924; *Irish Times,* 21 April 1924.

CONNAUGHTON, PADRAIG
b. Dublin 07.03.1952.
Mapping Draughtsman 09.03.1970; Cartographer 31.12.1979; Senior Cartographer 03.11.1980; Assistant Superintendent, Cartography Unit, 21.01.1981; Superintendent 11.07.1989.

COSGROVE, FRANK
Mapping Draughtsman c 1970.

CREIGHTON, JAMES RONALD
b. Antrim town 03.04.1948.
QUB.
Geologist 01.08.1975.

CRILLY, KEVIN
b. Lurgan 1948.
Drilling Unit 08.1975.

CRUISE, RICHARD JOSEPH
b. Moynalty, Co. Meath, 16.06.1842.
MII.
Analytical Chemist, Silvermines, Co. Tipperary.
Temporary Assistant Geologist 09.08.1867; Retired 31.08.1890.
d. Rathmines, Dublin, 24.10.1895.

CUNNINGHAM, MARK ANTHONY
b. Rushestown, Co. Galway, 17.04.1908.
UCG.
Geologist 01.08.1930; Senior Geologist 01.04.1955; responsible for administration of GSI 1964-67; Assistant Director 16.07.1970; Retired 16.07.1973.
d. Dublin 06.10.1980.
GSIB 3(I), 1981, p. iii.

DALY, DONAL
b. Tullamore 02.09.1952.
UCG; Birmingham U.
Geologist 18.09.1978; Senior Geologist 13.04.1992.

DALY, EUGENE PAUL
b. Dublin 12.09.1947.
UCD; TCD; N. Carolina State U.
Assistant Geologist 09.06.1971; Geologist 14.07.1975.

DE LA BECHE, SIR HENRY THOMAS
b. London 10.02.1796.
Director GS 01.04.1845.
d. London 13.04.1855.

DEVITT, GERARD C.
Senior Technician 04.09.1972; Resigned c 1975.

DHONAU, NICHOLAS BEN
b. Sheringham, Norfolk, 10.06.1943.
Cambridge U.
Geologist 03.03.1969; Senior Geologist 24.11.1976; Transferred to Exploration & Mining Division in Department of Transport, Energy and Communications 04.1992.

DONNELLAN, TERASA
b. 14.10.1960.
Cartographer 05.10.1987; Resigned 11.11.1988.

DONOVAN, ARCHIE
b. Tipperary town 10.02.1956.
Cartographer 05.10.1987.

DOOLEY, JOHN
b. London 05.08.1954.
Mapping Draughtsman 24.05.1976; Cartographer 11.02.1980; Senior Cartographer 06.07.1989; Assistant Superintendent, Cartography Unit, 22.02.1990.

DOWNING, DERMOD TIMOTHY
b. Dublin 02.10.1932.
TCD.
Geologist 15.01.1959; Resigned 31.03.1964.
ANDREW p. 702.

DUFFIN, WILLIAM E. L'ESTRANGE
b. Co. Down c 1844.
TCD.
Parliamentary work in connection with railways and public works.
Temporary Assistant Geologist 19.05.1871; Resigned 14.02.1874.
Became a County Surveyor.
d. post 1912.

DUFFY, JOHN
b. 08.03.1930.
Paperkeeper 29.08.1969; Printer of GSI publications 1970-88; Early retirement 09.12.1988.

DUFFY, THOMAS JOHN
b. Enniskeen, Co. Monaghan, c. 1895.
RCSI.
In the army 1915-19.
Temporary Geologist 20.12.1921; Geologist 24.03.1929; Senior Geologist 05.1941; Senior Geologist in Charge 1950-52; Retired 31.03.1955.
d. ?

DU NOYER, GEORGE VICTOR
b. Dublin 1817.
Ordnance Survey staff 1834 - 42; Schoolmaster.
Special Service with GSI 09.06.1847; Temporary Assistant Geologist 30.09.1848; Assistant Geologist 04.1849; District Surveyor 01.04.1867.
d. Antrim town 03.01.1869.
PRIA 10, 1866-69, p. 413; *GM* 6, 1869, p.93; *JRSAI* 123, 1993, p. 102; *SIN*; SARJ; *P & P2*, p. 32; National Gallery of Ireland, *George Victor Du Noyer 1817-1869: Hidden Landscapes*, Dublin 1995, pp.88.

EDE, DAVID P.
UC Swansea.
Geologist 03.11.1975; Resigned 31.03.1977.

EDWARDS, LEWIS
Geologist 08.09.1845; Dismissed 18.10.1845.

EGAN, FREDERICK WILLIAM
b. Dublin 31.07.1836.
TCD.
Work on Great Southern and Western Railway.
Temporary Assistant Geologist 05.1868; Geologist 01.09.1890.
d. Dublin 06.01.1901.
GM dec 4,8, 1901, p. 95; *IN* 10, 1901, p. 47; SARJ.

ELLIS, M.
See FEGAN, M.

FARRELL, DECLAN
Mapping Draughtsman 07.01.1974; Resigned 20.06.1977.

FARRELL, LORETO PHILOMENA CATHERINE
b. Harlockstown, Co. Meath, 09.01.1950.
UCD.
Assistant Geologist 22.11.1971; Geologist 1981; Transferred to Exploration & Mining Division in Department of Transport, Energy and Communications 04.1992.

FARRINGTON, ANTHONY
b. Cork 09.1893.
UCC; Camborne School of Mines.
Temporary Geologist 20.12.1921; Resigned 15.03.1928.
Assistant and Resident Secretary RIA 1928-61.
d. Bray, Co. Wicklow, 23.02.1973.
RIA *Annual Report* 1972 - 73, p. 3; *TIBG* 62, 1974, p. 155; *IG* 4, 1963, p. 311, and 6, 1973, p. 637; *SIN*; *P & P2*, p. 64.

FEGAN (née ELLIS), MARY
Technician 1971; Senior Technician c 1980; Resigned 1987.

FLANAGAN, JAMES
Ordnance Survey Staff.
Fossil Collector GSI 24.05.1845.
d. Ballyhale, Co. Kilkenny, 14.04.1859.

FLEGG, AUBREY MARTIN
b. Dublin 23.05.1938.
TCD; Leicester U.
Temporary Geologist 19.06.1968; Geologist 21.02.1969; Senior Geologist 23.09.1980.

FOOT, FREDERICK JAMES
b. 1830.
TCD.
Assistant Geologist 01.08.1854; Geologist 01.04.1862.
Drowned in Lough Key while attempting to save life 17.01.1867.
JRGSI 1, 1867, p. 268; *GM* 4, 1867, pp. 95 and 132; *SIN*; SARJ.

FORBES, EDWARD
b. Douglas, Isle of Man, 12.02.1815.
Palaeontologist GS 10.1844; Resigned 05.1854.
d. Edinburgh 18.11.1854.

FRENCH, GERRY
b. Dublin 1960.
Cartographer 25.11.1991.

GALVAN, CHARLES
Laboratory Porter in MII 1851-55.
Fossil Collector & General Assistant 16.01.1855.
d. 25.07.1870.

GARDINER, PIERS RICHARD ROCHFORT
b. Murree, India (now Pakistan), 17.06.1940.
London U; TCD.
Geologist 19.09.1966; Senior Geologist 14.08.1973; Principal Geologist 26.01.1982; Transferred to Exploration & Mining Division in Department of Transport, Energy and Communications 04.1992.

GAVIN, MARTIN WILLIAM
b. 26.07.1849.
Worked at Ordnance Survey 1865 - 1902.
Draughtsman to GSI 19.01.1903.
d. post 1914.

GEIKIE, SIR ARCHIBALD
b. Edinburgh 28.12.1835.
Director-General 01.01.1882; Retired 01.03.1901.
d. Haslemere 10.11.1924.

GEOGHEGAN, MICHAEL A.
b. 28.05.1953.
UCG.
Assistant Geologist 05.02.1979; Geologist 02.04.1980; Resigned 23.02.1990.

GIBLIN, MAUREEN B.
Draughtsman 28.07.1952; Resigned 14.06.1957.

GOLDEN, BRENDAN
Mapping Draughtsman 08.04.1974; Resigned 31.03.1976.

GORMLEY, M.J.
See CARTER, M.J.

HAIGH, THOMAS
b. Blarney 31.08.1886.
RCSI; UCD.
Schoolmaster in Cork.
Temporary Professional Assistant 1913-14.

HAIGH, WILLIAM D.
b. Blarney 31.08.1886.
RCSI.
Temporary Professional Assistant 1909-12.

HALLISSY, TIMOTHY
b. Blarney 11.1869.
RCSI; QCC; RUI.
Temporary Professional Assistant 1905; Geologist 26.10.1908; Senior Geologist 01.04.1921; Director 09.08.1928; Retired 07.11.1939.
d. Terenure, Dublin, 13.07.1958.
SIN.

HAND, EDDIE
b. Dublin 11.11.1957.
Mapping Draughtsman 07.1976; Cartographer 11.02.1980; Senior Cartographer 06.07.1989.

HARDMAN, EDWARD TOWNLEY
b. Drogheda 06.04.1845.
RCSI.
Temporary Assistant Geologist 15.07.1870; Special Colonial Duty in Western Australia 1883-85.
d. Dublin 30.04.1887.
DAB; *GM* dec 3, 4, 1887, p. 334; *N* 36, 1887 p. 62; SARJ; *ESH* 5, 1986, p. 33.

HIGGS (née MATHESON), BETTIE
b. Gateshead 15.02.1950.
Sheffield U.
Geologist 01.11.1978; Resigned 14.01.1981; Returned part-time 07.1981 to 1986.

HIGGS, KENNETH THOMAS
b. Birmingham 19.09.1949.
Sheffield U.
Geologist 14.07.1975; left on career break 01.09.1986; Resigned 07.07.1991.

HINCH, JOHN DE WITT
b. Dublin 1875.
Served in National Library of Ireland 1890-1919.
Superintendent of Maps and Collections GSI 1919; Geologist 23.09.1921; Retired 15.04.1930.
d. Blackrock, Co. Dublin, 16.12.1931.
INJ 5, 1935, p. 212; *SIN*; SARJ.

HORNE, RALPH ROSS
b. Aberdeen 05.09.1940.
Aberdeen U; Birmingham U.
Geologist 03.03.1969; Principal Geologist 25.09.1978; Assistant Director 02.12.1981; responsible for administration of GSI 09.11.1987 to 27.02.1992.

HOSKINS, PEIRCE
Schoolmaster.
Fossil Collector & General Assistant 01.10.1854; Resigned 01.1855.

HULL, EDWARD
b. Antrim town 21.05.1829.
TCD.
Assistant Geologist GSGB 1850; Geologist 1859; District Surveyor GSS 1867.
Temporary Director GSI 28.04.1869; Director 16.10.1869; Retired 30.09.1890.
d. London 18.10.1917.
WW; PRS 90, 1919, p. xxviii; *QJGS* (Proceedings) 74, 1918, p.liv; *GM.* dec 6,4, 1917, p. 553; *IN* 27, 1918, p. 17; *SIN;* ALLIB; SARJ; *Irish Times*, 20 October 1917; Hull, E., *Reminiscences of a Strenuous Life*, London 1910, pp. iv + 120 + iv.

HURLEY, D.
Geochemical Analyst c1948-50.

HYLAND, JOHN SHEARSON
b. Liverpool 1866.
UC Liverpool; Leipzig U; TCD.
Petrologist 1888, Assistant Geologist 01.09.1890; Resigned 1891.
d. Elmina, West Africa, 19.04.1898.
QJGS (Proceedings) 55, 1899, p.lxii; *IN* 7, 1898, p. 153.

INAMDAR, DEEPAK DAHYABHAI
b. Gujarat, India, 22.05.1941.
Baroda U; Glasgow U.
Geologist 01.09.1969; Senior Geologist 25.05.1977.

JAMES, (SIR) HENRY
b. in Cornwall 1803.
Royal Engineers 1825; Ordnance Survey 1827.
Local Director GSI 01.04.1845; Resigned 03.07.1846.
Superintendent of Works, Portsmouth Dockyard 1846-50; Superintendent of Ordnance Survey Edinburgh Office 1850-54; Director-General of Ordnance Survey 1854-75.
d. Southampton 14.06.1877.
DNB; QJGS (Proceedings) 34, 1878, p. 34; ALLIB.

JAMES, TREVOR EVANS
Geologist GSGB 14.05.1840; Transferred to Ireland 21.06.1845; Transferred back to Britain 30.09.1845.
d. in Australia.

JONES, DILYS PENELOPE LINDSEY
b. Manchester 22.06.1929.
Manchester U.
Geologist 01.09.1951; Resigned 31.07.1963.

JONES, KEITH D.
Geologist 07.12.1964; Resigned 17.02.1965.

JUKES, JOSEPH BEETE
b. Summerhill, near Birmingham, 10.10.1811.
Cambridge U.
Geological Surveyor Newfoundland 1839-40; Naturalist H.M.S. *Fly* 1842-46; GSGB 1846-50
Local-Director GSI 30.11.1850; Director GSI 01.04.1867.
d. Dublin 29.07.1869.
DNB; DSB; DAB; QJGS (Proceedings) 26, 1870, p. xxxii; *GM* 6, 1869, p. 430; *SIN*; ALLIB; SARJ; Browne, Cara Amelia (editor), *Letters and Extracts from the Addresses and Occasional Writings of J. Beete Jukes*, London 1871, pp. xx+ 596.

KEARY, RAYMOND
b. Woodford, Co. Galway, 18.08.1937.
UCD; UCG.
Lecturer in UCG.
Senior Geologist 01.09.1975.

KEENAN, JIM
Mapping Draughtsman 04.05.1967; Resigned 12.01.1972; Cartographer 13.10.1980; Assistant Superintendent, Cartography Unit, 13.10.1980; Resigned 02.01.1981.

KELLY, CATRIONA
b. 02.10.1962.
Cartographer 22.04.1981; Resigned 15.07.1982.

ELLY, JOHN
b. Borrisokane, Co. Tipperary, 1791.
Personal Assistant to Richard Griffith 1814-53.
Assistant Geologist in charge of the office GSI 01.07.1856; Resigned 20.10.1866.
d. 05 or 06.1869.
ALLIB.

KENNEDY, BRENDA M.
Draughtsman 07.01.1957; Resigned ?

KENNEDY, HORAS TRISTRAM
b. London 1889.
Cambridge U.
Geologist 30.06.1913.
Killed in action near Ypres 06.06.1917.
GM dec. 6, 4, 1917, p. 335; SARJ.

KENNEDY, JOHN STUDDERT
b. c 1832.
TCD.
General Office Assistant 01.11.1853; Resigned 1854.
Geological Survey of India 1855-56.
d. India 02.1856.

KEOGH, NOEL
b. 10.12.1959.
Cartographer 05.10.1987.
d. 15.09.1989.

KILROE, JAMES ROBINSON
b. 27.03. 1848.
RCSI.
Science teacher.
Temporary Assistant Geologist 25.06.1874; Geologist 01.09.1890; Retired 28.06.1913.
d. at Dawlish, Devon, 24.03.1927.
SIN; SARJ.

KINAHAN, GEORGE HENRY
b. Dublin 19.12.1829.
TCD.
Worked as an engineer on the Boyne Viaduct.
Temporary Assistant Geologist 21.08.1854; Geologist ?; Senior Geologist 23.03.1861; District Surveyor 01.03.1869; Retired 31.08.1890.
d. Clontarf 05.12.1908.
DNB; *GM* dec 5, 6, 1909, p. 142; *IN* 18, 1909, p. 29; *SIN*; ALLIB; SARJ.

KINSELLA, MICHEÁL
b. Birr 18.12.1962.
Cartographer 27.04.1981.

LAMPLUGH, GEORGE WILLIAM
b. Driffield, Yorkshire, 08.04.1859.
Worked in commerce.
Assistant Geologist GSGB 1892; District Geologist in Charge GSI 01.05.1901; Returned to GSGB 17.10.1904; Assistant Director for England and Wales 1914; Retired 1920.
d. 09.10.1926.
WW; *GM* dec 6, 5, 1918, p. 337 and 64, 1927, p. 91; *PGA* 38, 1927, p. 243; SARJ; *JG* 6 (44), 1966, p. 307.

LEESON, EDWARD
Fossil Collector 28.11.1870; Dismissed 16.10.1881.

LEONARD, HUGH
b. Drogheda 1841.
MII.
Temporary Assistant Geologist 07.08.1867; Retired as unfit for further duty 1881.
d. Blackrock, Co. Dublin, 16.02.1909.
GM dec 5, 6, 1909, p. 191.

LEONARD, WILLIAM BENJAMIN
b. Drogheda c 1850.
MII.
Temporary Assistant Geologist 06.08.1867.
Drowned while bathing at Belmullet 23.08.1876.

LITTLETON, MARGARET M.
Temporary Draughtsman 03.10.1955. Resigned 21.10.1956.

LONG, CHARLES BARRY
b. Upminster, Essex, 02.10.1938.
Bristol U; UCG.
Geologist 21.05.1975.

LYNCH, THERESE
Mapping Draughtsman 24.05.1976; Resigned 08.02.1980.

McARDLE, PEADAR
b. Dublin 06.11.1945.
UCD.
Geological Survey of Malawi 1970-73; Mining Geologist, Silvermines, Co. Tipperary, 1973-75. Geologist GSI 01.07.1975; Senior Geologist 23.07.1982; Director 28.02.1992.
ANDREW p. 704.

McATEER, ANTHONY D.
b. 30.12.1955.
Geologist 26.05.1980; Transferred to Petroleum Affairs Division 20.08.1980.

McCARNEY, M.
See MARINI, M.

McCARTHY, HONORA
Mapping Draughtsman 06.02.1961; Resigned 31.03.1967.

McCLUSKEY, JAMES ANTHONY GERRARD
b. c 1903.
UCD.
Engineer in Ireland 1925; Assistant Geologist, Phoenix Oil & Transport Co., Ploesti,
Romania 1925-27; Engineering Inspector, Shannon Power Scheme 1928-30.
Geologist GSI 30.01.1930; Assistant Economic Geologist, Mines & Minerals Section, Department of Industry & Commerce 28.04.1934; Acting Economic Geologist, Mines & Minerals Section 06.1938; Assistant Economic Geologist GSI 29.01.1941; Senior Geologist 18.12.1945.
d. Dublin 08.02.1963.

McCORMACK, C. A.
Draughtsman 02.02.1943; Resigned ?

McCORMACK, NOILEEN
Trainee Technician 19.07.1971; Technician c 1972-76.

M'COY, (SIR) FREDERICK
b. Dublin 1823? 1817?
Worked as a palaeontologist in Dublin.
Assistant Geologist 24.05.1845; Resigned 30.09.1846.
Assistant to Adam Sedgwick, Cambridge U; Professor QCB 1849-54;
Professor Melbourne U 1854-99.
d. Melbourne 16.05.1899.
DNB; DAB; WW; QJGS (Proceedings) 56, 1900, p. lix; *GM* dec 4, 6, 1899, p. 283; *IN* 8, 1899, p. 197; *SIN*; SARJ.

MACDERMOT, CONOR VICTOR
b. Bognor Regis, Sussex, 16.05.45.
TCD.
Geologist (unestablished) 26.10.1970; Geologist 25.02.1974; Senior Geologist 16.10.1985.

McDONNELL, CHRISTOPHER DANIEL
b. Dublin 10.1944.
Worked for 11 years in UCD.
Senior Technician 02.10.1972.

McEVOY, HARRY
b. Fermoy 29.10.1932.
UCG.
Worked with Dublin Corporation and then with the Land Commission.
Engineer Grade I GSI 04.09.1988.

McGUIRE, HELEN
Mapping Draughtsman 04.02.1974; Resigned 31.03.1976.

McHENRY, ALEXANDER
b. Ballyvoy, Co. Antrim, 24.10.1843.
MII.
Fossil Collector 12.01.1861; Acting Assistant Palaeontologist 1869-77;
Temporary Assistant Geologist 22.03.1877; Geologist 01.09.1890; Retired 24.10.1908.
d. Dublin 19.04.1919.
QJGS (Proceedings) 76, 1920, p.lx; *GM* dec 6, 6, 1919, p. 336; *IN* 28, 1919, p. 102; *SIN*; SARJ.

McINTYRE, THOMAS
b. Co. Offaly 1952.
Trainee Technician 09.10.1972; Technician 1973; Senior Technician 1985.

McLAUGHLIN, J.J.
A Land Commission draughtsman for many years.
Temporary Draughtsman GSI 01.04.1954 until c 1956.

McMONAGLE, EDDIE
b. Carrick-on-Shannon 02.08.1961.
Cartographer 04.05.1981.

MARINI (née McCARNEY), MARIE
b. 23.03.1961.
Cartographer 10.02.1980; Left on career break 06.1987; Returned 06.1993.

MAX, MICHAEL DAVID
b. Madison, Wisconsin, 29.05.1942.
Wisconsin U; Wyoming U; TCD.
Geologist 15.08.1969; Senior Geologist 23.09.1980; Left on career break 16.08.1985; Resigned 16.08.1990.
ANDREW p.704.

MEDLICOTT, HENRY BENEDICT
b. Loughrea 03.08.1829.
TCD.
General Assistant 01.10.1851; Transferred to GSGB as Assistant Geologist 01.10.1853; Resigned 1853.
Geological Survey of India 1854 & 1862-1887;
Superintendent (Director after 1885) Geological Survey of India 1876-87.
d. Clifton, Bristol, 06.04.1905.
DNB; WW; QJGS (Proceedings) 62, 1906, p.lx; *GM* dec 5, 2, 1905, p.240; *N* 71, 1905, p.612;
RGSI 32, 1905, p.233; ALLIB.

MEDLICOTT, JOSEPH G.
b. Loughrea c 1825.
TCD.
General Assistant 10.1846; Resigned 30.09.1851.
Geological Survey of India 1851-62.
d. 1866.

MEDLICOTT, SAMUEL
b. c 1832.
TCD.
Assistant Geologist 01.09.1854; Resigned 30.06.1856.
Commissioned in the Militia. Later a clergyman.
d. prior to 1905.

MITCHELL, WILLIAM FANCOURT
b. 1845.
RCSI.
Apprentice at Vulcan Foundry, Newton-le-Willows, Lancashire.
Temporary Assistant Geologist 10.02.1875. Retired 31.08.1890.
Worked in Valuation Office and as a tutor in geology.
d. ?

MOONEY, DENIS
Temporary General Assistant 04.1857; General Assistant 07.1857; House Keeper & Hall Porter, 14 Hume Street, 01.05.1870.
d. Dublin 31.05.1888.

MOORE-LEWY, GEORG
b. Wechterswinkel, Germany, 20.05.1922.
Berlin U; TCD.
Senior Geologist 01.05.1970; Retired 24.05.1987.

MORRIS, JOHN HENRY
b. Queen Camel, Somerset, 22.01.1948.
TCD; Waterloo U.
Mine geologist in Canada.
Geologist 01.09.1980; Principal Geologist 03.04.1992.
ANDREW p.704.

MUFF, HERBERT BRANTWOOD
b. Ilkley, Yorkshire, 27.08.1879.
Cambridge U.
GSS 1901-10. Service with GSI 1902 & 1903 and in British East Africa 1905-6; Changed his name to Maufe 1909.
Director of the Geological Survey of Southern Rhodesia 1910-35.
d. London 08.05.1946.
WW; QJGS (Proceedings) 103, 1947, p.lvi; *SIN*; SARJ.

MULHOLAND, PETER
Mapping Draughtsman 20.09.1971; Resigned 09.1972.

MURCHISON, SIR RODERICK IMPEY
b. Tarradale, Easter Ross, 19.02.1792.
Director 05.05.1855; Director-General 01.04.1867.
d. London 22.10.1871.

MURPHY, GERARD J.
Geologist 25.01.1954; Resigned 30.11.1956.

MURPHY, SIOBHAIN
b. 01.10.1962.
Cartographer 09.03.1981; Resigned c 1985.

MURPHY, THOMAS
Fossil Collector 1845; dismissed 31.05.1846.

MURPHY, THOMAS
b. Bootle, Lancashire, 17.10.1917.
UCD.
Geophysicist (Temporary) 30.06.1945 to 30.01.1946.
Senior Professor in DIAS.

MURRAY, JOHN CLIVE
b. Dublin 1944.
Worked for ten years in UCD.
Senior Technician 31.05.1971.

MURRAY, M.T.
Typist and then Typist & Librarian c 1922-42.

NAYLOR, DAVID
b. Cleckheaton, Yorkshire, 31.07.1935.
Leeds U; TCD.
Petroleum geologist and Lecturer in TCD.
Principal Geologist 02.01.1976; Assistant Director 20.04.1978; Resigned 31.08.1981.

NOLAN, JOSEPH
b. Queen's Co. 1841.
MII.
Temporary Assistant Geologist 03.08.1867; Geologist 26.04.1883; Senior Geologist 01.09.1890; Senior Geologist in Charge 30.09.1890; Retired 30.04.1901.
d. Clontarf 20.04.1902.
GM dec 4, 9, 1902, p. 288; SARJ.

O BRIEN, MURROGH VERE
b. Parteen, Co. Clare, 15.12.1919.
TCD, ICS & RSM.
Mining geologist.
Director 16.06.1952; Resigned 29.02.1964.
General Manager of Tara Exploration & Development Co. Ltd.

O'BRIEN, RICHARD
b. Roscrea 1941.
Drilling Unit 1988.

O'CONNOR, M.P.
Draughtsman 01.10.1951; Resigned 15.03.1952.

O'CONNOR, PATRICK OLIVER JAMES
b. Ennis 03.04.1947.
UCD; Utrecht U.
Geochemist Leeds U.
Geologist 17.06.1975; Senior Geologist 13.04.1992.
ANDREW p.704.

O'DALY, GERALDINE
Mapping Draughtsman 12.12.1973; Resigned 31.03.1976.

O'KELLY, JOSEPH
b. Dublin 1832.
TCD.
Worked in the Valuation Office.
Assistant Geologist 13.11.1854; Senior Geologist 01.04.1863.
d. Dublin 13.04.1883.
GM dec 2, 10, 1883, p. 288; SARJ.

OLDHAM, THOMAS
b. Dublin 04.05.1816.
TCD; Edinburgh U.
Ordnance Survey of Ireland 1838-43; Curator to the Geological Society of Dublin 1843-44;
Professor of Geology TCD 1845-50.
Local Director 04.07.1846; Resigned 30.11.1850.
Superintendent Geological Survey of India 1851 - 1876.
d. Rugby 17.07.1878.
DNB; DSB; JRGSI 5, 1879, p. 132; *QJGS* (Proceedings) 35, 1879, p.46; *GM* dec 2, 5, 1878, p. 382; *SIN*; ALLIB; SARJ.

O'MEARA, MICHAEL FRANCIS
b. near Roscrea 06.12.1912.
UCD.

Worked in county engineer's office, first in Kilkenny & then in Tipperary (N.R.).
Geologist 06.07.1935; Senior Geologist 16.04.1964; Assistant Director 14.08.1973;
Retired 01.03.1978.
d. Dublin 15.06.1986.
GSIB 3(4), 1985-86, p. 350.

O'NEILL, VALERIE
b. 05.04.1960.
Worked in the Ordnance Survey.
Cartographer 05.10.1987; Transferred back to the Ordnance Survey 20.12.1991.

OPPENHEIM, MICHAEL J.
Senior Geologist 17.05.1971; Resigned 30.09.1976.

PENNY, JAMES
General Assistant in charge of GSI office 1845; Resigned 10.1846 to become office keeper in MII.
d. before 08.1865.

PYNE, JOHN FRANCIS
b. Dublin 25.02.1947.
UCD; TCD.
Assistant Geologist 11.10.1971; Geologist 08.07.1975; Senior Geologist 13.04.1992; Transferred to Exploration & Mining Division in Department of Transport, Energy and Communications 04.1992.
ANDREW p.705.

RAMSAY, SIR ANDREW CROMBIE
b. Glasgow 31.01.1814.
Director-General 16.03.1872; Retired 31.12.1881.
d. Beaumaris 09.12.1891.

REEVES, THOMAS
b. Mullingar 29.08.1946.
UCD; TCD.
Temporary Geologist 01.11.1968; Geologist 04.02.1969; Transferred out of GSI 15.10.1978.

REILLY, THOMAS ALEXANDER
b. 18.04.1938.
TCD; London U.
Mining geologist in Africa.
Temporary Geologist 22.07.1968; Geologist 25.02.1974; Senior Geologist 15.07.1977; Principal Geologist 23.09.1980; Retired 31.12.1988.
ANDREW p.705.

RIDDIHOUGH, ROBIN P.
Senior Geologist 25.09.1972; Resigned 30.09.1974.

ROBINSON, KEITH WARREN
b. Harrow-on-the Hill, Middlesex, 06.12.1942.
TCD; Oxford U; DIAS.
Geologist 01.09.1970; Senior Geologist 09.04.1975; Principal Geologist 12.02.1979; Seconded to Petroleum Affairs Division as from 03.1977; Resigned from GSI 24.01.1980.

SALTER, JOHN WILLIAM
b. 15.12.1820.
Assistant Palaeontologist GS 1846; Palaeontologist 1854-63.
d. London 02.08.1869.

SCANLON (née MURPHY), ANNE
b. Dublin 17.10.1962.
Cartographer 09.03.1981.

SEYMOUR, HENRY JOSEPH
b. Co. Cork 05.06.1873.
RCSI; QCB; RUI.
Temporary Assistant Geologist 25.04.1898; Geologist 01.04.1901; Resigned 01.11.1909.
Professor of Geology UCD, 1909-47.
d. Dublin 28.01.1954.
WW; SIN; University Review 1, 1954, p. 66.

SHANNON, PATRICK M
b. New Ross 07.04.1952.
UCD.
Geologist 02.10.1978; Transferred to Petroleum Affairs Division 04.1979.

SLEEMAN, ANDREW GORDON
b. Bovey Tracey, Devon, 19.05.1947.
Liverpool U; TCD.
Geologist 16.06.1975.

SMYTH, (SIR) WARINGTON WILKINSON
b. Naples 26.08.1817.
Cambridge U.
Mining Geologist GS 1845-51.
d. London 19.06.1890.

SOLLAS, WILLIAM JOHNSON
b. Birmingham 30.05.1849.
Cambridge U; RSM.
Professor of Geology & Zoology UC Bristol 1879-83;
Professor of Geology & Mineralogy TCD, 1883-97.
Temporary Assistant Geologist 1893-97.
Professor of Geology, Oxford U 1897-1936.
d. Oxford 20.10.1936.
DNB; WW; PGA 48, 1937, p. 110; *N* 138, 1936, p. 959; *QJGS* (Proceedings) 93, 1937, p. cix; *SIN*; *ONFRS* 2, 1938, p. 265; ALLIB; SARJ.

STANLEY, GERARD ANTHONY
b. Dublin 30.04.1955.
UCD; Acadia U. (Nova Scotia); Camborne School of Mines.
Geologist 23.07.1984; Left on career break 18.07.1988; Returned 1993.

SYMES, RICHARD GLASCOTT
b. Kingstown, Co. Dublin, 08.05.1840.
TCD.
Worked in Great Southern & Western Railway Works at Inchicore.
Assistant Geologist 08.04.1863; Geologist 1869; Transferred to GSS 01.04.1890; Retired 1900.
d. Monkstown, Co. Dublin, 27.07.1906.
GM dec 5, 3, 1906, p. 432; *IN* 15, 1906, p.249; SARJ.

SYNGE, FRANCIS MILLINGTON
b. Dublin 26.05.1923.
TCD; Oslo U.
Aberdeen U 1949-57.
Geologist GSI 10.01.1957; Resigned 10.08.1963.
In QUB, Leicester U, Aberdeen U.
Senior Geologist, Head of Quaternary Division, 01.05.1969; Retired 01.05.1983.
d. Dublin 01.10.1983.
PGA 96, 1985, p. 189; *IG* 16, 1983, p. 126; *GSIB* 3(3), 1984, p.229.

TEALL, (SIR) JETHRO JUSTINIAN HARRIS
b. Northleach, Gloucestershire, 05.01.1849.
Director 01.03.1901; Retired 05.01.1914.
d. Dulwich 02.07.1924.

TRAILL, WILLIAM ACHESON
b. Bushmills c 1844.
TCD.
Temporary Assistant Geologist 04.1868; Resigned 08.1880.

Managing Director of Giant's Causeway Electric Tramway 1883-1933.
d. Portstewart 06.07.1933.
Belfast News Letter, 7 July 1933.

VALENTINE, ROBERT LEPPER
b. Enniskillen 16.04.1890.
RCSI.
Geologist 11.11.1914 while serving in the army.
Died of wounds, Loos, 30.04.1916.
IN 25,1916, p. 98; *Irish Times*, 16 May 1916; SARJ.

VAN LUNSEN, HENDRIKUS A.
Utrecht U.
Geologist 23.10.1969; Resigned 19.12.1975.

WADDELL, D.
Technician c 1971-72.

WALSH, AMOS JOSEPH
Worked with National Soil Survey, Ordnance Survey, and Tara Mines.
Superintendent, Cartography Unit, 01.06.1973. Retired 28.10.1988.

WARREN, JAMES LILEY
b. 1844.
TCD.
Temporary Assistant Geologist 30.07.1867; Geologist 23.03.1870.
d. Dublin 25.11.1872.

WARREN, WILLIAM PATRICK
b. Dalkey, Co. Dublin, 22.06.1948.
UCD.
Assistant Geologist 22.11.1971; Geologist 08.07.1975; Senior Geologist 13.04.1992.

WATTS, WILLIAM WHITEHEAD
b. Shropshire 07.06.1860.
Cambridge U.
Cambridge U Extension Lecturer.
Temporary Assistant Geologist (Petrologist) 10.07.1891; Transferred to GSGB 1893.
Assistant Professor Mason College, Birmingham, and Professor at ICS and RSM.
d. 30.07.1947.
DNB; WW; GM dec 6, 2, 1915, p. 481; *SIN*; *ONFRS* 6, 1948, p. 263; SARJ.

WEAFER, RAYMOND PAUL
b. Dublin 26.06.1951.
Mapping Draughtsman 21.01.1971; Cartographer 31.12.1979; Senior Cartographer 21.10.1980.

WILKINSON, JEAN MARGARET
b. Batley, Yorkshire, 19.10.1937.
Manchester U.
Geologist 04.02.1959; Resigned 16.12.1959.

WILKINSON, SIDNEY BERDOE NEAL
b. Montreal 05.04.1849.
Temporary Assistant Geologist 01.08.1867; Geologist 1872; Transferred to GSS 1890; Returned to GSI as Senior Geologist 01.04.1905; Retired 05.04.1914.
d. Derry 28.06.1928.
Wilkinson, S.B.N., *Reminiscences of Sport in Ireland*, Salisbury 1987, pp. xxvi + 226.

WILLIAMS, CYRIL EDWARD
b. Durban, Natal, 09.11.1922.
Capetown U.
Military Service; contract mapping for the GS of South Africa; Geologist in Uganda, Mauritius, New Hebrides; Director, Geological Survey of Uganda 1963-67.
Director GSI 03.1967; Retired 06.11.1987.

WILLSON, WALTER LINDSAY
Worked for Ordnance Survey for 5 years.
Assistant Geologist 24.06.1845; Resigned 12.11.1856.
Geological Survey of India 1857-78.
d. Calcutta 27.03.1878.
JRGSI 5, 1879, p. 133.

WRIGHT, GEOFFREY RICHARD
b. Thornton-Cleveleys, Lancashire, 09.01.1945.
ICS; UCL.
Company engineering geologist and hydrogeologist.
Senior Geologist GSI 14.10.1975; Left on career break with the Ministry of Water Resources, Sultanate of Oman, 14.07.1988; Returned 02.08.1994.

WRIGHT, WILLIAM BOURKE
b. Dublin 24.09.1876.
TCD.
Geologist 12.04.1901; Transferred to GSGB 09.1904; Returned to GSI 01.07.1910;
Senior Geologist 06.04.1914; Returned to GSGB as District Geologist 01.04.1921;
Retired 31.10.1938.
d. Prestbury, Cheshire, 11.10.1939.
MPMLPS 1938-39, p. viii; *QJGS*(Proceedings) 96, 1940, p. lxxiii; *N* 144, 1939, p. 775; *INJ* 7, 1940, p. 250; *SIN*; SARJ.

WYLEY, ANDREW
b. Belfast c 1820.
Schoolmaster.
Geologist 07.10.1845; Resigned 31.01.1855.
Government Geologist to Cape Colony 1855-59.
d. post 1885.
TGSSA annexure to vol. 39, 1936, p. 50.

WYNNE, ARTHUR BEAVOR
b. Sligo 10.1835.
MII.
Worked in Valuation Office.
Assistant Geologist 01.04.1855; Resigned 30.09.1862.
Geological Survey of India 1862-83.
Rejoined GSI as Resident Geologist 24.08.1883; Retired 31.08.1890.
d. Veytaux, Switzerland, 22.12.1906.
QJGS(Proceedings) 64, 1908, p. lxii; *GM* dec 5, 5, 1908, p. 143; *SIN*; SARJ.

YOUNG, DAVID G.G.
b. 01.10.1941.
Senior Geologist 27.09.1978; Resigned 16.05.1981.

HISTORICAL SOURCES AND OTHER WORKS REFERRED TO IN THE TEXT

I. MANUSCRIPT SOURCES, TYPESCRIPTS, ETC.

BRITISH GEOLOGICAL SURVEY, the archives of the Survey in the Survey's Library at Keyworth, Nottingham.

CUNNINGHAM, MARK A., *The Cunningham Papers*, being a collection of diaries for every year from 1930 to 1964, together with a collection of Survey correspondence from 1930 to 1946. In the Survey's archives.

____________________ *Some traditions and early memories of G.S.I.*, a 2-page typescript in the Survey's archives.

____________________ *Summary of service in Geological Survey*, a 3-page typescript in the Survey's archives.

DE LA BECHE, HENRY T., *The De La Beche Papers* in the Department of Geology, the National Museum of Wales, Cardiff.

DU NOYER, GEORGE V., Five volumes of sketches (pencil, pen and ink, and watercolour) of landscapes, fossils, etc., in the archives of the Survey, together with various unbound watercolours.

____________________ Various paintings in the Geological Section, the National Museum of Ireland.

____________________ Eleven volumes of drawings and watercolours in the Royal Irish Academy.

____________________ Thirteen notebooks and twelve volumes of drawings in the Royal Society of Antiquaries of Ireland.

FARRINGTON, ANTHONY, *The Farrington Papers* in the archives of the Survey, but mostly dating from after his resignation from the Survey in 1928.

GEIKIE, ARCHIBALD, *Confidential report on the Geological Survey, 5 March 1889*, Public Record Office London DSIR 9/71.

____________________ *The Geikie Papers* in the University Library, Edinburgh.

GEOLOGICAL SURVEY OF IRELAND, the Geological Survey of Ireland archives. A partial listing of the archives is available within the Survey.

HUNTING GEOLOGY AND GEOPHYSICS LTD, *Airborne magnetometer survey,* N.D. [c. 1982], an 8-page report in the archives of the Survey.

JAMES, HENRY, *The Sir Henry James Papers* in the Library of the Royal Society of London.

KINAHAN, GEORGE H., *The Kinahan Papers* in the Library of the Royal Irish Academy, Dublin.

LARCOM, THOMAS A., *The Larcom Papers* in the National Library of Ireland.

M'COY, FREDERICK, *The M'Coy Correspondence* in the Mitchell Library, Sydney.

____________________ *The M'Coy Papers* in the National Museum of Victoria, Melbourne.

McHENRY, ALEXANDER, *The McHenry Collection* of maps and other items in the Geological Section, the National Museum of Ireland.

MURCHISON, RODERICK I., *The Murchison Papers* in the Geological Society of London.

MURPHY, THOMAS, AND CUNNINGHAM, MARK A., *Geophysical prospecting at Avoca, Co. Wicklow by self potential surveys and some resistivity measurement 1942-1944,* a typescript dating from c. 1954 and in the archives of the Geological Survey. The Survey also possesses various maps and notebooks related to this geophysical work during the Emergency.

O BRIEN, MURROGH V., Quarterly reports 1 April 1951 to 31 March 1955 in typescript.

O'MEARA, MICHAEL F., *Some reminiscences of a long stint in the Geological Survey of Ireland, 1935-78,* typescript in the Survey's archives, pp.27.

PHILLIPS, JOHN, *The Phillips Correspondence* in the Science Museum, Oxford.

RAMSAY, ANDREW C., *The Ramsay Papers* in the archives of the Imperial College of Science and Technology, London.

ROYAL GEOLOGICAL SOCIETY OF IRELAND, *The Royal Geological Society of Ireland Papers* in the Department of Geology, Trinity College Dublin.

SEDGWICK, ADAM, *The Sedgwick Papers* in the University Library, Cambridge.

WILLIAMS, CYRIL E., *Reorganisation of the Irish Geological Survey*, a memorandum to the Secretary, the Department of Industry and Commerce, dated 5 September 1967. A copy is in the Survey's archives.

II. BOOKS

ANDREW, COLIN J. *ET AL.*, *Geology and genesis of mineral deposits in Ireland*, Irish Association for Economic Geology, 1986, pp. xvi + 712.

ANDREWS, JOHN H., *A paper landscape: the Ordnance Survey in nineteenth-century Ireland*, Oxford 1975, pp. xxiv + 350.

ARDEN-CLOSE, CHARLES F., *The early years of the Ordnance Survey,* Newton Abbot 1969 (reprinted), pp. xxxvi + 164.

BAILEY, EDWARD B., *Geological Survey of Great Britain*, London 1952, pp. xii + 278.

BERRY, HENRY F., *A history of the Royal Dublin Society*, London 1915, pp. xvi + 460.

BOWEN, ELIZABETH, *The Shelbourne Hotel*, New York 1951, pp. vi + 240.

BROWN, ALASTAIR G. (editor), *Prospecting in areas of glaciated terrain. Ireland 1979. Excursion Handbook*, Irish Association for Economic Geology, 1979, pp. iv + 92.

________________ (editor), *Mineral exploration in Ireland: progress and developments 1971-1981,* Irish Association for Economic Geology, 1982, pp. 180.

BROWNE, CARA A. (editor), *Letters and extracts from the addresses and occasional writings of J. Beete Jukes, M.A. F.R.S. F.G.S.,* London 1871, pp. xx + 596.

BUTLER, ELENOR, *Structural geography of Ireland as part of the region of N.W. Europe*, Dublin N.D. [1924], pp. 98.

CHARLESWORTH, JOHN K., *The geology of Ireland: an introduction*, Edinburgh and London 1953, pp. xvi + 276.

________________ *Historical geology of Ireland*, Edinburgh and London 1963, pp. xxiv + 566.

COLBY, THOMAS F., *Ordnance Survey of the County of Londonderry. Volume the First. Memoir of the City and north western Liberties of Londonderry. Parish of Templemore.* Dublin 1837, pp. 11 + 336 + 16.

COLE, GRENVILLE A.J., *The gypsy road: a journey from Krakow to Coblentz*, London and New York 1894, pp. xiv + 168.

________________ *Aids in practical geology*, fifth edition, London 1906, pp. xvi + 431; sixth edition, London 1909, pp. xvi + 431; seventh edition, London 1918, pp. xvi + 431.

________________ *The changeful earth: an introduction to the record of the rocks*, London 1911, pp. x + 223.

________________ *Rocks and their origins,* Cambridge 1912, pp.viii + 176; second edition, Cambridge 1922, pp. viii + 176.

________________ *Outlines of mineralogy for geological students,* London 1913, pp. viii + 339.

________________ *The growth of Europe,* London 1914, pp. 256.

________________ *Ireland the outpost,* Oxford 1919, pp. 78.

________________ *Common stones: unconventional essays in geology,* London and New York 1921, pp.260.

________________ AND COLE, BLANCHE, *As we ride*, Royal City of Dublin Hospital 1902, pp. iii + 107.

________________ AND PRAEGER, ROBERT Ll. (editors), *Handbook to the city of Dublin and the surrounding district*, Dublin 1908, pp. viii + 442.

________________ AND HALLISSY, TIMOTHY, *Handbook of the geology of Ireland*, London 1924, pp. viii + 82.

COLLINS, GEORGE B., *Wildcats and shamrocks*, printed at North Newton, Kansas, U.S.A., for private circulation, 1976, pp. 102.

COYNE, WILLIAM P. (editor), *Ireland: industrial and agricultural. Handbook for the Irish pavilion. Glasgow International Exhibition, 1901*, Department of Agriculture and Technical Instruction for Ireland, Dublin 1901, pp. x +290.

________________ (editor), *Ireland: industrial and agricultural*, Department of Agriculture and Technical Instruction for Ireland, Dublin, Cork, Belfast 1902, pp. xii + 532.

CROKE, FIONNUALA (editor), *George Victor Du Noyer 1817-1869: hidden landscapes*, The National Gallery of Ireland 1995, pp. 88.

CROLL, JAMES, *Climate and time in their geological relations: a theory of secular changes of the earth's climate*, London, fourth edition 1890, pp. xviii + 578.

DARWIN, CHARLES ROBERT, *On the origin of species by means of natural selection, or the preservation of favoured races in the struggle for life*, London 1859, pp. x + 502.

DE COURCY, CATHERINE, *The foundation of the National Gallery of Ireland,* The National Gallery of Ireland 1985, pp. xii + 108.

DE LA BECHE, HENRY T., *The geological observer*, London 1851, pp. xxxii + 846.

EVANS, EMYR E. AND TURNER, BRIAN S., (editors), *Ireland's Eye: the photographs of Robert John Welch*, Belfast 1977, pp. iv + 196.

FIGGIS, DARRELL, *Recollections of the Irish War*, London 1927, pp. x + 310.

FLETT, JOHN S., *The first hundred years of the Geological Survey of Great Britain*, London 1937, pp. 280.

FRASER, ROBERT, *General view of the agriculture and mineralogy, present state and circumstances of the County Wicklow, with observations on the means of their improvement*, Dublin 1801, pp. xvi + 290.

GEIKIE, ARCHIBALD, *The scenery of Scotland viewed in connexion with its physical geology*, London and Cambridge 1865, pp. xvi + 360.

________________ *Life of Sir Roderick I. Murchison*, London 1875, in two volumes, pp. xiv + 388 and viii + 376.

________________ *Memoir of Sir Andrew Crombie Ramsay*, London 1895, pp. xii + 398.

________________ *A long life's work: an autobiography*, London 1924, pp. xii + 426.

GEIKIE, JAMES, *The Great Ice Age and its relation to the antiquity of man*, second edition, London 1877, pp. xxx + 624.

GILBERT, GROVE K., *Report on the geology of the Henry Mountains*, Department of the Interior, Washington 1877, pp. x + 160 + plates.

GORMAN, MICHAEL J., AND WOODWORTH, W. FITZGERALD, *The College of Science for Ireland: its origin and development, with notes on similar institutions in other countries, and a bibliography of the work published by the staff and students (1900-1923),* Dublin 1923, pp. 56.

GRIFFITH, RICHARD, *Geological and mining report on the Leinster Coal District*, Dublin 1814, pp. viii + xxiv + 136.

_________________ *Geological and mining survey of the Connaught Coal District in Ireland*, Dublin 1818, pp. viii + 108.

_________________ *Report on the metallic mines of the Province of Leinster in Ireland*, Dublin 1828, pp. 29.

_________________ *Geological and mining surveys of the Coal Districts of the counties of Tyrone and Antrim in Ireland*, Dublin 1829, pp. x + 78.

_________________, M'COY, FREDERICK, AND SALTER, JOHN W., *A synopsis of the Silurian fossils of Ireland*, Dublin 1846, pp. 72 + 5 plates.

[HERRIES] DAVIES, GORDON L., *The earth in decay: a history of British geomorphology 1578-1878*, London N.D. [1969], pp. xvi + 390.

_________________ *Sheets of many colours: the mapping of Ireland's rocks 1750-1890*, Royal Dublin Society 1983, pp. xiv + 242.

_________________ and MOLLAN, ROBERT C. (editors), *Richard Griffith 1784-1878*, Royal Dublin Society 1980, pp. vi + 222.

HOCTOR, DANIEL, *The Department's story - A history of the Department of Agriculture*, Institute of Public Administration, Dublin 1971, pp. xvi + 304.

HOLLAND, CHARLES H. (editor), *A geology of Ireland*, Edinburgh 1981, pp. viii + 336.

HULL, EDWARD, *The coal-fields of Great Britain: their history, structure, and duration*, London 1861, pp. xvi + 194; third edition, London 1873, pp. xxiii + 499; fourth edition, London 1881, pp. xviii + 556.

_________________ *The physical geology & geography of Ireland*, London 1878, pp. xvi + 292; second edition 1891, pp. xvi + 328.

_________________ *Contributions to the physical history of the British Isles*, London 1882, pp. xvi + 144 + 13 plates.

_________________ *Reminiscences of a strenuous life*, London 1910, pp. iv + 120 + iii.

HUTTON, JAMES, *Theory of the Earth, with proofs and illustrations*, Edinburgh 1795, in two volumes, pp. viii + 620 and viii + 568.

JAMES, KENNETH W., *"Damned nonsense!" - the geological career of the third Earl of Enniskillen*, Ulster Museum Publication no. 259, 1986, pp. 24.

JUKES, JOSEPH B. *ET AL*, *Lectures on gold for the instruction of emigrants about to proceed to Australia*, London 1852, pp. iv + 215.

_________________ *Popular physical geology*, London 1853, pp. xvi + 360.

_________________ *The student's manual of geology*, Edinburgh 1857, pp. xiv + 610; second edition, Edinburgh 1862, pp. xx + 764; third edition, edited by GEIKIE, ARCHIBALD, Edinburgh 1872, pp. xx + 778.

_________________ *The school manual of geology*, Edinburgh 1863, pp. xv + 362.

_________________ *Her Majesty's Geological Survey of the United Kingdom, and its connection with the Museum of Irish Industry in Dublin, and that of Practical Geology in London, an address*, Dublin 1867, pp. 34.

JUKES-BROWNE, ALFRED J., *The building of the British Isles: a study in geographical evolution*, London 1888, pp. xiii + 343.

KANE, ROBERT, *The industrial resources of Ireland*, Dublin 1844, pp. xii + 418; second edition, Dublin 1845, pp. xvi + 438.

KELLY, JOHN, *Notes upon the errors of geology illustrated by reference to facts observed in Ireland*, London 1864, pp. xvi + 300.

KINAHAN, GEORGE H., *Valleys and their relation to fissures, fractures, and faults*, London 1875, pp. xvi + 240.

_________________ *Manual of the geology of Ireland*, London 1878, pp. xx + 444.

KUHN, THOMAS S., *The structure of scientific revolutions*, second edition, Chicago 1970, pp. xii + 210.

LASAULX, ARNOLD VON, *Aus Irland: Reiseskizzen und Studien*, Bonn 1878, pp. viii + 240.

LEE, JOHN J., *Ireland 1912-1985: politics and society*, Cambridge University Press 1989, pp. xxii + 754.

LEWIS, HENRY C., *Papers and notes on the glacial geology of Great Britain and Ireland*, London 1894, pp. lxxxii + 470.

LYELL, CHARLES, *A manual of elementary geology*, fifth edition, London 1855, pp. xvi + 656.

McCARTNEY, PAUL J., (BASSETT, DOUGLAS A. editor), *Henry De La Beche: observations on an observer*, Cardiff 1977, pp. xiv + 78.

MEENAN, JAMES, AND CLARKE, DESMOND (editors), *RDS: the Royal Dublin Society 1731-1981*, Dublin 1981, pp. x + 288.

[MINERAL EXPLORATION], *Mineral exploration in Ireland*, Irish Association for Economic Geology, 1979, pp.viii + 92.

MOLLAN, CHARLES, *ET AL.* (editors), *Some people and places in Irish science and technology*, Royal Irish Academy, Dublin, 1985, pp. 108.

_________________ *Nostri Plena Laboris: an author index to the RDS scientific journals 1800-1985*, Royal Dublin Society 1987, pp. 120.

_________________ *More people and places in Irish science and technology*, Royal Irish Academy, Dublin, 1990, pp. 108.

NOLAN, JOSEPH, *The history and antiquities of Glendalough*, Dublin 1871, pp. 48.

NORTH, FREDERICK J., *Geological maps: their history and development with special reference to Wales*, Cardiff 1928, pp. vi + 134.

O'RIORDAN, COLM E., *The Natural History Museum, Dublin*, Stationery Office, Dublin, N.D. [1984], pp. 76.

PLAYFAIR, JOHN, *Illustrations of the Huttonian Theory of the Earth*, Edinburgh 1802, pp. xx + 528.

PLUNKETT, HORACE, *Ireland in the new century. Popular edition with an epilogue,* London 1905, pp. xx + 340.

PORTLOCK, JOSEPH E., *Report on the geology of the County of Londonderry, and of parts of Tyrone and Fermanagh*, Dublin 1843, pp. xxxii + 784.

_________________ *Memoir of the life of Major-General Colby*, London 1869, pp. xiv + 314.

PRAEGER, ROBERT Ll., *The way that I went: an Irishman in Ireland*, Dublin and London 1937, pp. xiv + 394.

__________________ *A populous solitude*, Dublin 1941, pp. x + 272.

__________________ *Some Irish naturalists: a biographical note-book*, Dundalk 1949, pp. 208.

RAMSAY, ANDREW C., *The physical geology and geography of Great Britain*, London 1863, pp. 146; second edition, London 1864, pp. viii + 199; fifth edition, London 1878, pp. xvi + 640.

RECESS COMMITTEE, *Report of the Recess Committee on the establishment of a Department of Agriculture and Industries for Ireland*, Dublin, Belfast, and London 1896 pp. iv + 420.

ROYAL DUBLIN SOCIETY, *Bi-centenary celebrations 1931: official handbook and catalogue of museum*, Royal Dublin Society 1931, pp. xxx + 116.

SAMPSON, GEORGE V., *Statistical survey of the County of Londonderry, with observations on the means of improvement*, Dublin 1802, pp. xxvi + 510 + 42.

SARJEANT, WILLIAM A.S., *Geologists and the history of geology: an international bibliography from the origins to 1978*, in five volumes, London and Basingstoke 1980.

[SCOULER, JOHN], *Memorandum of objects of geological interest in the vicinity of Dublin*, Dublin 1835, pp. 26.

SIMOENS, GUILLAUME, *The gold and the tin in the south east of Ireland*, Dublin 1921, pp. vi + 198.

STEINMANN, G., AND WILCKENS, O., (editors), *Handbuch der Regionalen Geologie*. III Band, 1 Abteilung, 'The British Isles', Heidelberg 1917, pp. 354.

THORNBURY, WILLIAM D., *Principles of geomorphology*, New York and London 1954, pp. x + 618.

TIGHE, WILLIAM, *Statistical observations relative to the County of Kilkenny, made in the years 1800 & 1801*, Dublin 1802, pp. xvi + 644 + 199.

TOWNSEND, HORATIO, *Statistical survey of the County of Cork, with observations on the means of improvement*, Dublin 1810, pp. xx + 749 + 96.

TUNNICLIFF, STEPHEN P., *A catalogue of the Lower Palaeozoic fossils in the collection of Major-General J.E. Portlock*, The Ulster Museum, Belfast, 1980, pp. 112.

TURNER, BRIAN S. *ET AL.*, *A list of the photographs in the R.J. Welch Collection in the Ulster Museum*, The Ulster Museum, in two volumes 1979 and 1983, pp. 110 and 36.

WEST, TIMOTHY T., *Horace Plunkett: co-operation and politics, an Irish biography*, Gerrards Cross, Bucks, and Washington D.C. 1986, pp. xviii + 288.

WHEELER, THOMAS S. *ET AL.*, *The natural resources of Ireland; a series of discourses delivered before the Royal Dublin Society in Commemoration of the centenary of the publication by the Society of Sir Robert Kane's "The Industrial Resources of Ireland"*, Dublin N.D. [1944], pp. 90.

WILKINSON, SIDNEY B.N., *Reminiscences of sport in Ireland*, reprinted Salisbury 1987, pp. xxviii + 226.

WILSON, GEORGE, AND GEIKIE, ARCHIBALD, *Memoir of Edward Forbes, F.R.S.*, Cambridge and London 1861, pp. xii + 590.

WILSON, HAROLD E., *Down to earth. One hundred and fifty years of the British Geological Survey*, Edinburgh and London 1985, pp. iv + 190.

WILSON, ROBERT B., *A history of the Geological Survey in Scotland*, Edinburgh 1977, pp. 24.

WOODWARD, HORACE B., *The history of the Geological Society of London*, London 1907, pp. xx + 336.

WRIGHT, WILLIAM B., *The Quaternary Ice Age*, London 1914, pp.xxiv + 464; second edition London 1937, pp. xxvi + 478.

WYSE JACKSON, PATRICK (editor), *In marble halls: geology in Trinity College Dublin*, Department of Geology, Trinity College Dublin 1994, pp. 136.

III. SURVEY AND OTHER OFFICIAL PUBLICATIONS

AERIAL PHOTOGRAPHY UNIT, *Aerial photography: information on the 1:30,000 aerial photographic survey of Ireland*, Geological Survey of Ireland, IC81/1, 1981, pp.12.

ARCHER, JEAN B., AND RYAN, PAUL D., (editors), *Geological guide to the Caledonides of Western Ireland*, Geological Survey of Ireland Guide Series 4, 1983, pp.62.

________________ (editor), *Directory of current research in Irish geology (1985-1986)*, Geological Survey of Ireland and the Irish National Committee for Geology, 1985, pp.iv + 78.

BALL, VALENTINE, *General guide to the Science and Art Museum, Dublin*, Dublin 1890, pp.56.

BISHOPP, DOUGLAS W., *A short review of Irish mineral resources*, Geological Survey of Ireland Emergency Period - Pamphlet No. 1, Dublin 1943, pp.20.

____________________ *Irish sources of lime and magnesia of high purity limestone, dolomite, and brucite-marble*, Geological Survey of Ireland Emergency Period-Pamphlet No.2, Dublin 1947, pp.52.

____________________ AND McCLUSKEY, JAMES A.G., *Sources of industrial silica in Ireland*, Geological Survey of Ireland Emergency Period-Pamphlet No.3, Dublin 1948, pp.48.

COLE, GRENVILLE A.J., *Description of the raised map of Ireland*, National Museum of Science and Art, Dublin 1909, pp.16. Second edition 1920.

____________________ AND CROOK, THOMAS, *On rock-specimens dredged from the floor of the Atlantic off the coast of Ireland, and their bearing on submarine geology*, Memoirs of the Geological Survey of Ireland, Dublin 1910, pp.iv + 36.

____________________ *ET AL.*, *The Interbasaltic Rocks (iron ores and bauxites) of north-east Ireland*, Memoirs of the Geological Survey of Ireland, Dublin 1912, pp.vi + 130.

__________________________ *The geology of Clare Island, County Mayo*, Memoirs of the Geological Survey of Ireland, Dublin 1914, pp.iv + 54.

____________________ *Memoir and map of localities of minerals of economic importance and metalliferous mines in Ireland*, Memoirs of the Geological Survey of Ireland. Mineral Resources, Dublin 1922, pp. 156. Reprinted 1956.

COMMISSION OF INQUIRY INTO THE RESOURCES AND INDUSTRIES OF IRELAND, *Memoir on the Coalfields of Ireland*, Vol.I. Text, Dublin 1921, pp.xii + 396; Vol.II Maps, Dublin 1921.

____

____________________ *Report on peat,* Dublin 1921, pp.ii + 112.

DALY, DONAL, AND WRIGHT, GEOFFREY, *Waste disposal sites,* Geological Survey of Ireland IC 82/1, 1982, pp.50.

DEPARTMENT OF AGRICULTURE AND TECHNICAL INSTRUCTION FOR IRELAND, General Reports of the Department 1900 to 1925.

____

____________________ *Geological Survey of Ireland. Regulations,* 1st January 1914, pp.18.

DEPARTMENT OF EDUCATION, *Report of the Department of Education for the school year of 1924-25 and the financial and administrative years 1924-25-26,* Dublin 1926.

DEPARTMENT OF SCIENCE AND ART, the reports published annually from 1854 onwards, and containing the reports of the Geological Survey, the Museum of Irish Industry, the Royal College of Science for Ireland, the Dublin Museum of Science and Art, and the Committee of Provincial Lectures in Ireland.

GEOLOGICAL SURVEY OF IRELAND, *Explanations to accompany Sheet 134 of the map of the Geological Survey of Ireland,* Dublin 1861, pp.46.

____________________ *Explanations to accompany sheets 176 and 177 of the maps of the Geological Survey of Ireland,* Dublin 1861, pp.30.

____________________ *Explanations to accompany sheets 194, 201, 202 of the maps of the Geological Survey of Ireland,* Dublin 1862, pp.28.

____________________ *Explanations to accompany sheets 114, 122, and 123 of the maps of the Geological Survey of Ireland,* Dublin 1863, pp.32.

____________________ *Explanation of sheets 187, 195, and 196, of the maps, and part of Sheet 5 of the sections, of the Geological Survey of Ireland,* Dublin 1864, pp.66.

____________________ *Explanation to accompany sheets 115 and 116 of the maps, and sheets 17 and 18 of the longitudinal sections,* Dublin 1865, pp.44.

____________________ *Explanations to accompany sheets 96, 97, 106, and 107 of the maps of the Geological Survey of Ireland,* Dublin 1867, pp.44.

____________________ *Explanatory memoir to accompany sheets 73 and 74 (in part) 83 and 84 of the maps of the Geological Survey of Ireland,* Dublin 1876, pp.84.

____________________ *Explanatory memoir to accompany Sheet 35 of the maps of the Geological Survey of Ireland,* Dublin 1877, pp.94.

____________________ *Instructions for the guidance of the officers of the Irish Branch of Her Majesty's Geological Survey of the United Kingdom,* Dublin 1876, pp.24.

____________________ *List of geological maps, sections, and explanations, published by the Irish Branch of the Geological Survey of the United Kingdom,* Dublin 1888, pp.4.

____________________ *List of memoirs, maps, sections, &c. published by the Geological Survey of Ireland,* pp.20. Copies exist dated 1906, 1910, 1915, 1923, 1930, 1938, and 1962.

____________________ Annual Reports have been issued for 1991 and each subsequent year.

____________________ *Publications list: summer 1991,* pp. 14.

____________________ *Publications and services,* April 1993, pp.42.

GEOLOGICAL SURVEY OF THE UNITED KINGDOM, *Summary of progress of the Geological Survey of the United Kingdom,* annually from 1897 onwards.

GOVERNMENT OF IRELAND, *Programme for economic expansion. Laid by the Government before each House of the Oireachtas, November 1958,* Pr4796, Stationery Office Dublin, pp.50.

HALLISSY, TIMOTHY, *Explanatory memoir to Sheet 58, illustrating parts of the counties of Armagh, Fermanagh, and Monaghan,* Memoirs of the Geological Survey of Ireland, second edition, Dublin 1914, pp.iv + 26.

____________________ *Barytes in Ireland,* Memoirs of the Geological Survey of Ireland, Dublin 1923, pp.vi + 82.

HIGGS, KENNETH, *ET AL., Stratigraphic and systematic palynology of the Tournaisian rocks of Ireland,* Geological Survey of Ireland Special Paper No.7, 1988, pp.94.

HORNE, RALPH R., *Geological guide to the Dingle Peninsula,* Geological Survey of Ireland Guide Series 1, 1976 pp.iv + 54.

____________________ AND GARDINER, PIERS R.R., *The Geological Survey of Ireland,* Geological Survey of Ireland IC2, 1970, pp.14.

HOUSE OF COMMONS PAPERS, *Geological Survey (Ireland),* 1845 (238), XLV, pp.7.

____________________ *Report from the Select Committee on scientific institutions (Dublin),* 1864 (495), xiii, pp.lvi + 468.

JUKES, JOSEPH B., *Inventory catalogue of the specimens illustrating the composition, structure, and other characters of the Irish, British, and foreign rocks, in the collection of the Industrial Museum of Ireland,* Dublin 1866, pp.vi + 122.

KANE, ROBERT, *General descriptive guide to the Museum of Irish Industry,* Dublin 1857, pp.114.

KILROE, JAMES R., *A description of the soil-geology of Ireland, based upon Geological Survey maps and records with notes on climate,* Department of Agriculture and Technical Instruction for Ireland, Dublin 1907, pp.300.

____________________ *The geological features and soils of the agricultural station of the Department of Agriculture at Ballyhaise, in the county of Cavan,* Memoirs of the Geological Survey of Ireland, Dublin 1910, pp.iv + 50.

LAMPLUGH, GEORGE W., *ET AL., The geology of the country around Dublin,* Memoirs of the Geological Survey of Ireland, Dublin 1903, pp.viii + 166.

____________________ *The geology of the country around Belfast,* Memoirs of the Geological Survey of Ireland, Dublin 1904, pp.viii + 166.

_______________ *The geology of the country around Cork and Cork Harbour,* Memoirs of the Geological Survey of Ireland, Dublin 1905, pp.viii + 136.

_______________ *The geology of the country around Limerick,* Memoirs of the Geological Survey of Ireland, Dublin 1907, pp.vi + 120.

McHENRY, ALEXANDER, AND WATTS, WILLIAM W., *Guide to the collections of rocks and fossils belonging to the Geological Survey of Ireland, arranged in Room III.E. of the Museum of Science and Art, Dublin,* Dublin 1895, pp.156.

_______________ *Guide to the collections of rocks and fossils belonging to the Geological Survey of Ireland, arranged in the Curved Gallery of the Museum of Science and Art, Dublin,* Dublin 1898, pp.156.

MAX, MICHAEL D., AND INAMDAR, DEEPAK D., *Detailed compilation magnetic map of Ireland and a summary of its deep geology,* Geological Survey of Ireland RS 83/1, 1983, pp.10.

MINISTER FOR INDUSTRY AND COMMERCE, *Science and Irish economic development,* in two volumes Pr8975 and Pr9093 N.D [1966], pp.xxx + 198 and vi + 246.

MUSEUM OF IRISH INDUSTRY, *Inventory catalogue of the specimens illustrating the nature, extent, and uses of the Irish, British, and foreign coal and peat fuel deposits, and the materials, processes, and products of the iron and steel manufactures, in the collection of the Industrial Museum of Ireland,* Dublin 1866, pp.42.

NATIONAL MUSEUM OF SCIENCE AND ART, the published reports of the Visitors.

NOLAN, JOSEPH, [Glacial features in County Wicklow] pp.153-155 in *Summary of progress of the Geological Survey of the United Kingdom for 1897,* Memoirs of the Geological Survey, London 1898, pp.176.

O'CONNOR, PATRICK J., *Report on a reconnaissance radiometric survey of the Irish Republic,* Geological Survey of Ireland RS 81/1, 1981, pp.26.

OIFIG THAIGHDE EOLAíOCHTA Ré NA PRáINNE: EMERGENCY SCIENTIFIC RESEARCH BUREAU, *Report,* Stationery Office, Dublin N.D. [1946], pp.96.

REID, CLEMENT, *The Pliocene deposits of Britain,* Memoirs of the Geological Survey of the United Kingdom, London 1890, pp.viii + 326.

ROYAL DUBLIN SOCIETY ETC., *Report upon the Royal Dublin Society, the Museum of Irish Industry, and the system of scientific instruction in Ireland,* report of the Treasury Commission, Dublin 1863, pp.126.

SCIENCE AND ART MUSEUM, Reports of the Director of the Science and Art Museum, Dublin, and of the Director of the National Museum of Science and Art.

SMYTH, WARINGTON W., On the mines of Wicklow and Wexford, *Records of the School of Mines and of Science Applied to the Arts* 1(3), 1853, pp.349-412.

VISSCHER, HENK, *The Permian and Triassic of the Kingscourt Outlier, Ireland,* Geological Survey of Ireland, Special Paper No.1, 1971, pp.vi + 114 + plates.

[WHARTON COMMITTEE] *Report of the committee on the Geological Survey and the Museum of Practical Geology,* 24 September 1900, pp.10. A copy is in the archives of the British Geological Survey.

WILKINSON, SIDNEY B., *The geology of the country around Londonderry,* Memoirs of the Geological Survey of Ireland, Dublin 1908, pp.viii + 106.

WOODWARD, HORACE B., *Soils and subsoils from a sanitary point of view, with especial reference to London and its neighbourhood,* Memoirs of the Geological Survey of England and Wales, second edition, London 1906, pp.vi + 82.

WRIGHT, WILLIAM B., AND MUFF, HERBERT B., Early-glacial raised shore, *Memoirs of the Geological Survey. Summary of Progress of the Geological Survey of the United Kingdom and Museum of Practical Geology*, 1903, pp.127 - 128.

_______________ *The geology of the Ballycastle Coalfield Co. Antrim,* Memoirs of the Geological Survey of Ireland, Dublin 1924, pp.viii + 188.

_______________ *ET AL., The geology of Killarney & Kenmare,* Memoirs of the Geological Survey of Ireland, Dublin 1927, pp.viii + 112.

IV. GEOLOGICAL MAPS OF IRELAND OTHER THAN OFFICIAL GEOLOGICAL SURVEY MAPS

1838, GRIFFITH, RICHARD, / GEOLOGICAL / MAP OF / IRELAND / to accompany the Report of the / RAILWAY COMMISSIONERS / 1837 /. Map V in the *Atlas to accompany 2[D] Report of the Railway Commissioners Ireland 1838.* Scale about one inch to ten miles (1:633,600). 63.2 x 79 centimetres. Hand coloured.

1839, GRIFFITH, RICHARD, / A GENERAL MAP / OF / IRELAND / to Accompany the Report / of the / RAILWAY COMMISSIONERS / shewing the / Principal Physical Features and Geological Structure / OF THE COUNTRY /. Dublin, Hodges and Smith, and London, James Gardner, first published May 1839. Scale one inch to four miles (1:253,440). In six sheets, each 73.7 x 60.5 centimetres. Hand coloured.

1852, DU NOYER, GEORGE VICTOR, / FRASER'S / Travelling Map of IRELAND / SHEWING ALL THE / TOWNS, LAKES, RIVERS, ROADS AND RAILWAYS /. The geology compiled from the maps of Griffith, Portlock, and the Geological Survey of Ireland, by G.V. Du Noyer 1852. The map exists with various later dates in the margin. Dublin, McGlashan and Gill. Scale one inch to ten miles (1:633,600). 56 x 72.5 centimetres. Hand coloured.

1853, GRIFFITH, RICHARD, / GEOLOGICAL MAP / OF / IRELAND / to accompany / THE INSTRUCTIONS TO VALUATORS / appointed under the 15th & 16th Vic. cap 63 /. Lithographed and printed in colour by Forster & Co., 2 Crow St, Dublin. August 1853. Scale about one inch to sixteen miles (1:1,013,760). 35.5 x 51.2 centimetres. Colour printed.

1867, JUKES, JOSEPH BEETE, / GEOLOGICAL MAP / OF / IRELAND /. London, Edward Stanford, and Dublin, Hodges and Smith, 1 July 1867. Scale one inch to 7.8 miles (1:494,208). 71.5 x 94.7 centimetres. Hand coloured.

1878, HULL, EDWARD, / GEOLOGICAL MAP OF / IRELAND / FOUNDED ON THE MAPS OF THE GEOLOGICAL SURVEY / OF SIR RICHARD GRIFFITH AND OF PROF[R]. J. BEETE JUKES /. London, Edward Stanford, 30 March 1878. Scale one inch to 7.8 miles (1:494,208). 71.5 x 94.7 centimetres. Hand coloured.

1906, GEIKIE, ARCHIBALD, / MAP SHOWING THE / SURFACE GEOLOGY OF / IRELAND / REDUCED CHIEFLY FROM THE / ORDNANCE AND GEOLOGICAL SURVEYS /. The Edinburgh Geographical Institute. N.D. [1906]. Scale one inch to ten miles (1:633,600). 56 x 74 centimetres. Colour printed.

V. ESSAYS AND PAPERS

ANON., Museum of Irish Industry, *Dublin University Magazine* 42, no.248, August 1853, pp.230-244.

_______ Geological surveys: their objects and utility, *Dublin University Magazine* 46, no.276, December 1855, pp.679-685.

_______ Denudation in the Geological Survey, *Irish Naturalist* 13(10), 1904, p.231.

_______ The Department of Industry and Commerce, *Administration* 9(2), 1961, pp.120-148.

ARCHER, J.B., Patrick Ganly: geologist, *Irish Naturalists' Journal* 20(4), 1980, pp.142-148.

___________ AND HERRIES DAVIES, G.L., Geological field-sheets from County Galway by Patrick Ganly (1809? - 1899), *Journal of Earth Sciences Royal Dublin Society* 4(2), 1982, pp.167-179.

___________ *Adieu* Hume Street: a retrospective view of the Geological Survey of Ireland, *Geological Survey of Ireland Bulletin* 3(3), 1984, pp.159-170.

___________ Science loners: the *Journal of the Geological Society of Dublin* and its successors, pp.49-68 in HAYLEY, BARBARA, and McKAY, ENDA, (editors), *Three hundred years of Irish periodicals,* Dublin 1987, pp.146.

___________ Geological artistry: the drawings and watercolours of George Victor Du Noyer in the archives of the Geological Survey of Ireland, pp.133-144 in DALSIMER, ADELE M., (editor), *Visualizing Ireland, national identity and the pictorial tradition*, Boston 1993, pp.vi + 232.

BAILY, W.H., Palaeontological remarks upon the Silurian rocks of Ireland, *Report of the British Association for the Advancement of Science, Manchester 1861,* part 2, p.108.

___________ On fossils obtained at Kiltorkan quarry, Co. Kilkenny, *Report of the British Association for the Advancement of Science, Exeter 1869,* part 1, pp.73-75.

BALL, V., The museums of Dublin, pp.21-62 in HOWARTH, ELIJAH, and PLATNAUER, HENRY M., *Museums Association: report and proceedings with the papers read at the fifth annual general meeting, held in Dublin, June 26 to 29, 1894,* Sheffield and York, 1895, pp.260.

BANNON, M.J., The making of Irish geography, III: Patrick Geddes and the emergence of modern town planning in Dublin, *Irish Geography* 11, 1978, pp.141-148.

BAYLISS, R.A., The travels of Joseph Beete Jukes, F.R.S., *Notes and Records of the Royal Society of London* 32(2), 1978, pp.201-212.

BISHOPP, D.W., The occurrence of nickel and magnetite in some Irish serpentines, in conjunction with a magnetic survey, *Scientific Proceedings of the Royal Dublin Society* N.S.24(14), 1946, pp.125-133.

_____________ Some upper and lower limits of the Devonian System in Ireland, with proposed corrections to maps, *Proceedings of the Royal Irish Academy* 53(3), 1950, pp.25-32.

BOUD, R.C., The early development of British geological maps, *Imago Mundi* 27, 1975, pp.73-96.

BYRNE, K.R., The Royal Dublin Society and the advancement of popular science in Ireland, 1731-1860, *History of Education* 15(2), 1986, pp.63-79.

[CLARE ISLAND SURVEY], Proposed survey of Clare Island, *Irish Naturalist* 17(6), 1908, p.128.

CLARKE, D., Dublin Society's statistical surveys, *An Leabharlann* 15(2), 1957, pp.47-54.

COFFEY, P., George Victor Du Noyer (1817-1869), *Sheetlines* (The Charles Close Society), no.35, 1993, pp.14-26.

___________ George Victor Du Noyer (1817-1869). Artist, geologist and antiquary, *Journal of the Royal Society of Antiquaries of Ireland* 123, 1993, pp.102-119.

COLBY, T.F. An address delivered at the sixth annual meeting of the Geological Society of Dublin, Dublin 1837, pp.22.

COLE, G.A.J., The geologist at the luncheon-table, *Irish Naturalist* 4(2), 1895, pp.41-44.

___________ Early geological mapping in Ireland, *Irish Naturalist* 10(1), 1901, pp.10-11.

___________ AND CROOK, T., On rock specimens dredged from the floor of the Atlantic off the west coast of Ireland in 1901, Appendix IX to Part 2 of the *Report on the sea and inland fisheries of Ireland for 1901,* Department of Agriculture and Technical Instruction for Ireland, pp.9.

___________ The Geological Survey of Ireland, *Department of Agriculture and Technical Instruction for Ireland Journal* 5(4), 1905, pp.619-629.

___________ The red zone in the Basaltic Series of the County of Antrim, *Geological Magazine* N.S. dec 5, 5(8), 1908, pp.341-344.

___________ Probable Cretaceous and Cainozoic outliers off the coast of Co. Kerry, *Geological Magazine* N.S. dec 5, 5(10), 1908, pp.463-464.

___________ Glacial features in Spitsbergen in relation to Irish geology, *Proceeding of the Royal Irish Academy* 29B(3), 1911, pp.191-208.

COLHOUN, E.A., Early discoverers xxix. Early record and interpretation of ice-wedge pseudomorph in County Londonderry, Northern Ireland, by J.R. Kilroe, *Journal of Glaciology* 9, no.57, 1970, pp.391-392.

COLLINS, T., Praeger in the West: naturalists and antiquarians in Connemara and the islands 1894-1914, *Journal of the Galway Archaeological and Historical Society* 45, 1993, pp.124-154.

CROLL, J., The boulder-clay of Caithness a product of land-ice, *Geological Magazine* 7(5), 1870, pp.209-214; 7(6), 1870, pp.271-278.

[CROOK, T.,], obituary notice: Mr. Thomas Crook, O.B.E., *Nature* 139, 1937, p.141.

D'ARCY, F., Mandarins and mechanics: the Irish provincial science lecture system 1836-1866, pp.24 within *University of Ulster, Symposium: the history of technology, science, and society 1750-1914,* no pagination, pp.544, September 1989.

DAVIS, W.M., A geographical pilgrimage from Ireland to Italy, *Annals of the Association of American Geographers*, 2, 1912, pp.73-100.

DU NOYER, G.V., On the evidence of glacial action over the south of Ireland during the Drift Period, *The Geologist* 5(7), 1862, pp.241-254.

EYLES, V.A., The first national geological survey, *Geological Magazine* 87(5), 1950, pp.373-382.

FARRINGTON, A., AND MITCHELL, G.F., Some glacial features between Pollaphuca and Baltinglass, Co. Wicklow, *Irish Geography* 6(5), 1973, pp.543-560.

FINCH, T.F., AND RYAN P., Soils of Co. Limerick, *Soil Survey Bulletin* No.16, National Soil Survey of Ireland, N.D. [1966], pp.xii + 200.

[FLETCHER, G.], The Civic Exhibition, Dublin, 1914, *Department of Agriculture and Technical Instruction for Ireland Journal* 14(4), 1914, pp.731-733.

FOOT, F.J., Meteorological journal kept at Ennistimon and Ballyvaughan, County of Clare, during the year 1861, *Journal of the Royal Dublin Society* 3, 1860-62, pp.327-341.

_________ On the botanical peculiarities of the Burren District, County of Clare, *Proceedings of the Royal Irish Academy* 8, 1861-64, p.136.

_________ Notes on a storm which occurred on Thursday, October 29, 1863, at Ballinasloe, about 150 feet above the sea, *Proceedings of the Royal Irish Academy* 8, 1861-64, pp.405-406.

_________ Notes on a tour in Norway in the summer of 1866, *Journal of the Royal Dublin Society* 5, 1870, pp.96-114.

_________ On the distribution of plants in Burren, County of Clare, *Transactions of the Royal Irish Academy* 24, 1871, pp.143-160.

FORBES, E., On Oldhamia, a new genus of Silurian fossils, *Journal of the Geological Society of Dublin* 4(1), 1848, p.20.

__________ On fossils of the Yellow Sandstone of the south of Ireland, *Report of the British Association for the Advancement of Science, Belfast 1852,* part 2, p.43.

FOX, C.S., Presidential address [the story of the Geological Survey of India], *Transactions of the Mining and Geological Institute of India* 31(1), 1936, pp.13-37.

GARDINER, M.J., The National Soil Survey, *Irish Geography* 4(6), 1963, pp.442-453.

GEIKIE, A., Recent researches into the origin and age of the Highlands of Scotland and the west of Ireland, *Proceedings of the Royal Institution of Great Britain* 12, 1889, pp.528-546.

GEOGHEGAN, H.C., A plea for Irish mines and minerals, under an Irish Board, and for preparation of a mining survey, *Journal of the Statistical and Social Inquiry Society of Ireland* 12(88), 1908, pp.141-161.

[GEOLOGICAL SURVEY], Geological Survey of Ireland, *Geological Magazine* N.S. dec 5, 2(6), 1905, p.288.

GILLMOR, D.A., The revival of base metal mining in the Republic of Ireland, *Irish Geography* 5(3), 1966, pp.220-225.

GREGORY, J.W., The Irish eskers, *Philosophical Transactions of the Royal Society of London* Series B, 210, 1921, pp.115-151.

_____________ The glaciation of Ireland, *Geological Magazine* 58(3), 1921, pp.137-140.

GRIFFITH, R., On the geological map of Ireland, *Report of the British Association for the Advancement of Science, Dublin 1835,* part 2, pp.56-58.

HAIGH, W.D., A method for the estimation of hygroscopic moisture in soils, *Scientific Proceedings of the Royal Dublin Society* N.S. 14(40), 1915, pp.529-534.

HALLISSY, T., Irish soil maps, *Irish Naturalist* 17(11), 1908, p.242.

___________ Geology [of Clare Island], *Proceedings of the Royal Irish Academy* 31(7), 1914, pp.1-22.

___________ The Geological Survey. Review of its functions and work. Mineral development, *Irish Trade Journal,* August 1928, pp.135-136.

HAMILTON, C.W., On certain appearances of the surface of rocks in the neighbourhood of Bantry Bay. This paper was never published, but see *Journal of the Geological Society of Dublin* 3(1), 1844, pp.10-11; 4(2), 1849, p.186.

_______________ Address, *Journal of the Geological Society of Dublin* 3(2), 1845, pp.97-118.

_______________ Address, *Journal of the Geological Society of Dublin*, 3(3), 1846, pp.168-178.

[HERRIES] DAVIES, G.L., Joseph Beete Jukes and the rivers of southern Ireland - a century's retrospect, *Irish Geography* 4(4), 1962, pp.221-233.

_____________________ The Geological Society of Dublin and the Royal Geological Society of Ireland 1831-1890, *Hermathena* no.100, 1965, pp.66-76.

_____________________ The tour of the British Isles made by Louis Agassiz in 1840, *Annals of Science* 24(2), 1968, pp.131-146.

_____________________ The University of Dublin and two pioneers of English geology: William Smith and John Phillips, *Hermathena* no 109, 1969, pp.24-36.

_____________________ AND WHITTOW, J.B., A reconsideration of the drainage pattern of counties Cork and Waterford, *Irish Geography* 8, 1975, pp.24-41.

_____________________ The making of Irish geography, II: Grenville Arthur James Cole (1859-1924), *Irish Geography* 10, 1977, pp.90-94.

_____________________ Notes on the various issues of Sir Richard Griffith's quarter-inch geological map of Ireland, 1839-1855, *Imago Mundi* 29, 1977, pp.35-44.

_____________________ The earth sciences in Irish serial publications 1787-1977, *Journal of Earth Sciences Royal Dublin Society* 1(1), 1978, pp.1-23.

_____________________ The history of Irish geology, pp.303-315 in HOLLAND, CHARLES H. (editor), *A geology of Ireland,* Edinburgh 1981, pp.x + 336.

_____________________ Irish thought in science, pp.294-310 in KEARNEY, RICHARD, (editor), *The Irish mind: exploring intellectual traditions,* Dublin 1985, pp.366.

_____________________ Geology, pp.294-311 in HOLLAND, CHARLES H., (editor), *Trinity College Dublin and the idea of a university*, Dublin 1991, pp.384.

HOBSON, B., Report of an excursion to west Mayo and the Sligo district, *Proceedings of the Geologists' Association* 24(2), 1913, pp.78-86.

HORNER, A.A., Sir Robert Kane's land classification maps - a mid-nineteenth century cartographic initiative, *Irish Geography* 27(2), 1994, pp.107-121.

HULL, E., Additional observations on the drift-deposits and more recent gravels in the neighbourhood of Manchester, *Memoirs of the Literary and Philosophical Society of Manchester* Series 3, 2, 1865, pp.449-461.

________ On a section of the drift deposits in the banks of the Ribble, near Balderston Hall, *Proceedings of the Literary and Philosophical Society of Manchester* 6, 1866-67, pp.136-140.

________ Observations on the general relations of the drift deposits of Ireland to those of Great Britain, *Geological Magazine* 8(7), 1871, pp.294-299.

________ On the progress of the Geological Survey of Ireland, *Report of the British Association for the Advancement of Science, Belfast 1874,* part 2, p.83.

________ On the progress of the Geological Survey of Ireland, *Geographical Magazine* 1, 1874, p.309.

________ On the geological age of the rocks forming the southern highlands of Ireland, generally known as "The Dingle Beds" and "Glengariff Grits and Slates" (Jukes), *Quarterly Journal of the Geological Society of London* 35, 1879, pp.699-723.

________ Note on a new geological map of Ireland, *Journal of the Royal Geological Society of Ireland* 5(2), 1879, pp.104-105.

________ On the Laurentian beds of Donegal and of other parts of Ireland, *Report of the British Association for the Advancement of Science, York 1881,* p.609.

________ On the geological structure of the northern Highlands of Scotland, *Journal of the Royal Geological Society of Ireland* 6(1), 1881, pp.56-68.

________ On the origin and probable structure of the domite mountains of central France, *Journal of the Royal Geological Society of Ireland* 6(1), 1881, pp.93-97.

________ On a proposed Devono-Silurian formation, *Quarterly Journal of the Geological Society of London,* 38, 1882, pp.200-209.

________ On the Laurentian beds of Donegal and of other parts of Ireland, *Journal of the Royal Geological Society of Ireland* 6(2), 1882, pp.115-116.

________ On the Laurentian rocks of Donegal, and of other parts of Ireland, *Scientific Transactions of the Royal Dublin Society* Series II, 1(18), 1882, pp.243-256.

________ Palaeo-geological and geographical maps of the British Islands and the adjoining parts of the continent of Europe, *Scientific Proceedings of the Royal Dublin Society* Series II, 1(19), 1882, pp.257-296.

________ The Great Submergence, *The Glacialists' Magazine* 1(3), 1893, pp.61-66.

INAMDAR, D.D., AND KELLY, T.J., Geophysical study of the Corvock Granite, Co. Mayo, *Geological Survey of Ireland Bulletin* 2(4), 1979-80, pp.333-348.

IRISH ASSOCIATION FOR ECONOMIC GEOLOGY, *Annual Review - 1985*, pp.60.

IRISH BASE METALS LTD, *Tynagh: a case history of mining in Ireland,* [Dublin c.1971] pp.16.

JAMES, H., Note on the Tertiary deposits of the Co. Wexford, *Journal of the Geological Society of Dublin* 3(3), no.2, 1846, pp.195-197.

JARRELL, R.A., The Department of Science and Art and control of Irish science, 1853-1905, *Irish Historical Studies* 23(92), 1983, pp.330-347.

JUKES, J.B., Annual address, *Journal of the Geological Society of Dublin* 6(2), 1855, pp.252-283.

__________ Address to the Geological Section, *Report of the British Association for the Advancement of Science, Cambridge 1862,* part 2, pp.54-65.

__________ On the mode of formation of some of the river-valleys in the south or Ireland, *Quarterly Journal of the Geological Society of London* 18(4), 1862, pp.378-403.

__________ [On the river-valleys in the south of Ireland], *Journal of the Geological Society of Dublin* 10(1), 1863, pp.51-52 and 71-74.

__________ On the flint implements found in the gravels of St. Acheul, near Amiens, and their mode of occurrence, *Proceedings of the Royal Irish Academy* 8, 1861-64, pp.220-223.

__________ Atmospheric *v.* marine denudation, *Geological Magazine* 3(5), 1866, pp.232-235.

__________ Notes for a comparison between the rocks of the south-west of Ireland, and those of north Devon, and of Rhenish Prussia, *Journal of the Royal Geological Society of Ireland* 1(2), 1867, pp.103-138.

KELHAM, B.B., The Royal College of Science for Ireland (1867-1926), *Studies 56* (no.223), 1967, pp.297-309.

KELLY, T.J., AND MAX, M.D., The geology of the northern part of the Murrisk Trough, *Proceedings of the Royal Irish Academy* 79B(15), 1979, pp.191-206.

KILROE, J.R., Directions of ice-flow in the north of Ireland, as determined by the observations of the Geological Survey, *Quarterly Journal of the Geological Society of London* 44(4), 1888, pp.827-833.

____________ On directions of ice-flow in the north of Ireland as determined by the observations of the Geological Survey, *Scientific Proceedings of the Royal Dublin Society* N.S. 6 (22), 1888, pp.259-262.

____________ The distribution of drift in Ireland in its relation to agriculture, *Scientific Proceedings of the Royal Dublin Society* N.S. 8(52), 1897, pp.421-429.

____________ The river Shannon: its present course and geological history, *Proceedings of the Royal Irish Academy* 26B(8), 1907, pp.74-96.

____________ The Silurian and metamorphic rocks of Mayo and north Galway, *Proceedings of the Royal Irish Academy* 26B(10), 1907, pp.129-160.

____________ On the occurrence and origin of laterite and bauxite in the Vogelsberg, *Geological Magazine* N.S. dec 5, 5(12), 1908, pp.534-542.

[KILROE'S *SOIL-GEOLOGY OF IRELAND*] *Department of Agriculture and Technical Instruction for Ireland Journal* 1(4), 1901, pp.675-678.

KINAHAN, G.H., The eskers of the Central Plain of Ireland, *Journal of the Geological Society of Dublin* 10(2), 1864, pp.109-112, and *Dublin Quarterly Journal of Science* 4, 1864, pp.109-112.

__________ On crannoges in Lough Rea, *Proceedings of the Royal Irish Academy* 8, 1861-64, pp.412-427.

__________ On ferns observed in Iar, or West Connaught, and also in south-west Mayo, *Proceedings of the Natural History Society of Dublin* 6(1), 1871, pp.67-68.

__________ Middle gravels (?), Ireland, *Geological Magazine* 9(6), 1872, pp.265-268.

__________ Sketches in the west of Ireland, *Hardwicke's Science-Gossip* April 1872, pp.83-85, and various subsequent issues.

__________ On the Laurentian rocks in Ireland, *Report of the British Association for the Advancement of Science, York 1881,* pp.609-610.

__________ Economic geology of Ireland, *Journal of the Royal Geological Society of Ireland* 8, 1885-89, pp.x + 514.

__________ The recent Irish glaciers, *Irish Naturalist* 3(11), 1894, pp.236-240.

KIRWAN, R. A plan, for the introduction and establishment of the most advantageous management of mines in the Kingdom of Ireland, *Transactions of the Dublin Society* 1(1), 1799 (published 1800), 277-284; 2(2), 1801 (published 1802), pp.245-251.

LAMPLUGH, G.W., 'Calcrete', *Geological Magazine* N.S. dec.4, 9(12), 1902, p.575.

LLOYD, B., An address, *Journal of the Geological Society of Dublin* 1(1), 1833, pp.i-xviii.

LYBURN, E.St J., Mining and minerals in the Transvaal and Swaziland, *Scientific Proceedings of the Royal Dublin Society* N.S. 9(2), 1898, pp.12-21.

__________ Prospecting for gold in Co. Wicklow, and an examination of Irish rocks for gold and silver, *Scientific Proceedings of the Royal Dublin Society* N.S. 9(31), 1901, pp.422-435.

__________ A brief report on a survey of the mineral resources of Ireland, *Department of Agriculture and Technical Instruction for Ireland, Second General Report of the Department 1901-1902,* Dublin 1902, pp.144-145.

__________ Irish minerals and raw materials: opportunities for development, *Department of Agriculture and Technical Instruction for Ireland Journal* 16(4), 1916, pp.621-628.

McNAMARA, K.J., AND DODDS, F.S., The early history of palaeontology in Western Australia: 1791-1899, *Earth Sciences History* 5(1), 1986, pp.24-38.

MALLET, R., On the dynamics of earthquakes; being an attempt to reduce their observed phenomena to the known laws of wave motion in solids and fluids, *Transactions of the Royal Irish Academy* 21, 1848, part 1, pp.51-105.

MILLER, A.A., River development in southern Ireland, *Proceedings of the Royal Irish Academy* 45B(14), 1939, pp.321-354.

MONAGHAN, N.T., Geology in the National Museum of Ireland, *Geological Curator* 5 (7), 1989, pp.275-282.

MORRIS, J.H., Bedrock geological map production by the Geological Survey of Ireland, *Geological Survey of Ireland Bulletin* 4(3), 1990, pp.217-220.

__________ Bedrock geological map production by the Geological Survey of Ireland, *Irish Association for Economic Geology: Annual Review 1989*, pp.22-24.

MUFF, H.B., AND WRIGHT, W.B., On a preglacial or early glacial raised beach in County Cork, *Report of the British Association for the Advancement of Science, Southport 1903*, pp.657-659.

__________ On a preglacial or early glacial raised beach in County Cork, *Geological Magazine* N.S. dec 4, 10(11), 1903, pp.501-503.

MURCHISON, R.I., [On the origin of river valleys], *The Reader,* 22 October 1864.

NAYLOR, D., The Geological Survey of Ireland, *Irish Geography* 11, 1978, pp.155-160.

NELSON, E.C., Mapping plant distribution patterns: two pioneering examples from Ireland published in the 1860s, *Archives of Natural History* 20(3), 1993, pp.391-403.

NIMMO, A., On the application of the science of geology to the purposes of practical navigation, *Transactions of the Royal Irish Academy* 14, 1825, part 1, pp.39-50.

NOLAN, J., Notes of a geological tour through the Siebengebirge and the Lower Eifel, *Journal of the Royal Geological Society of Ireland* 4(3), 1876, pp.124-131.

__________ On the ancient volcanic district of Slieve Gullion, *Geological Magazine* N.S. dec. 2, 5, 1878, pp.445-449.

NORTH, F.J., Geology's debt to Henry Thomas De La Beche, *Endeavour* 3(9), 1944, pp.15-19.

O BRIEN, M.V., Phosphatic horizons in the Upper Carboniferous of Ireland, *Congrès Géologique International, Comptes Rendus de la Dix-Neuvième Session, Alger 1952,* Section xi, Fascicule xi, pp.135-143.

__________ Report on Ireland, pp.359-361 in GUZMÁN, E.J. (editor), *Symposium sobre yacimientos de petroles y gas, Tome V. Europa*, xx Congreso Geológico Internacional, Mexico 1956.

__________ The future of non-ferrous mining in Ireland, *Proceedings of a Symposium on the future of non-ferrous mining in Great Britain and Ireland, London, September 1958,* Institution of Mining and Metallurgy, pp.26.

OLDHAM, T., On the more recent geological deposits in Ireland, *Journal of the Geological Society of Dublin* 3(1), 1844, pp.61-71.

__________ Some further remarks on the more recent geological deposits in Ireland, *Journal of the Geological Society of Dublin* 3(2), 1845, pp.130-132.

__________ On the supposed existence of moraines in Glenmalur, Co. of Wicklow, *Journal of the Geological Society of Dublin* 3(3), 1846, pp.197-199; 3(4), 1847, pp.222-223: 4(2), 1849, pp.185-187.

__________ On the maps and sections of the County of Wicklow, published by the Geological Survey, *Journal of the Geological Society of Dublin* 4(1), 1848, p.20.

O'RIORDAN, C.E., Some notes on the dispersal of the Ordnance Survey of Ireland collections, *Geological Curator* 3(2&3), 1981, pp.126-129.

PARKES, M.A., *ET AL.*, Geological Survey of Ireland: National Heritage Council funded curation project of 19th century collection, *Geological Curator* 6(2), 1994, p.70.

PORTER, J., Geographical evolution in Cork, *Irish Naturalist* 11(7), 1902, pp.153-156.

__________ The Cork valleys, *Irish Naturalist* 11(11), 1902, p.286.

__________ On some features of the Cork river-valleys, *Report of the British Association for the Advancement of Science, Belfast 1902,* p.648.

PRAEGER, R.Ll., General introduction and narrative [of the Clare Island Survey], *Proceedings of the Royal Irish Academy* 31(1), 1915, pp.1-12.

QUIN, E.G., AND FREEMAN, T.W., Some Irish topographical terms, *Irish Geography* 1(4), 1947, pp.85-89.

RAMSAY, A.C., The old glaciers of Switzerland and North Wales, pp.400-470 in BALL, JOHN (editor), *Peaks, passes, glaciers. A series of excursions by members of the Alpine Club*, London 1859, pp.xvi + 520.

__________ On the glacial origin of certain lakes in Switzerland, the Black Forest, Great Britain, Sweden, North America, and elsewhere, *Quarterly Journal of the Geological Society of London* 18(3), 1862, pp.185-204.

ROEMER, F., Geological sketch of a visit to Ireland in August, 1876, *Geological Magazine* N.S. dec 2, 5, 1878, pp.54-62.

ROYAL COLLEGE OF SCIENCE FOR IRELAND, *Programme of the educational arrangements for the session 1887-88*, Dublin 1887, pp.26.

RUSKIN, J., Banded and brecciated concretions, *Geological Magazine* 6(12), 1869, pp.529-534.

SCANNELL, M.J.P., AND HOUSTON, C.I., George V. Du Noyer (1817-1869). A catalogue of plant paintings at the National Botanic Gardens, Glasnevin with aspects of his scientific life, *Journal of Life Sciences Royal Dublin Society* 2, 1980, pp.1-13.

SCHARFF, R.F., The Clare Island Survey, *Irish Naturalist* 24(10), 1915, pp.177-187.

[SCIENCE AND ART MUSEUM], The Science and Art Museum, Dublin, and the National Library of Ireland, *Nature* 42, 1890 pp.391-393.

SCOULER, J., Account of certain elevated hills of gravel, containing marine shells which occur in the county of Dublin, *Journal of the Geological Society of Dublin* 1(4), 1838, pp.266-276.

SECORD, J.A., John W. Salter: the rise and fall of a Victorian palaeontological career, pp.61-75 in WHEELER, ALWYNE, AND PRICE, JAMES H., (editors), *From Linnaeus to Darwin: commentaries on the history of biology and geology*, Society for the History of Natural History Special Publication 3, London 1985, pp.vi + 214.

SEYMOUR, H.J., The centenary of the first geological survey made in Ireland, *Economic Proceedings of the Royal Dublin Society* 3(17), 1944, pp.227-248.

SIMINGTON, R.C., AND FARRINGTON, A., A forgotten pioneer: Patrick Ganly, geologist, surveyor and civil engineer (1809-1899), *Journal of the Department of Agriculture Republic of Ireland* 46, 1949, pp.36-50.

__________ AND WHEELER, T.S., Sir Robert Kane's soil survey of Ireland: the record of a failure, *Studies* 34, 1945, pp.539-551; *Journal of the Department of Agriculture (Ireland)* 44, 1947, pp.15-28.

SLEEMAN, A.G., The palaeontological collections of the Geological Survey of Ireland, *Geological Curator* 5(7), 1989, pp.283-291.

SOLLAS, W.J., On pitch glaciers or poissiers, *Report of the British Association for the Advancement of Science, Ipswich 1895*, pp.680-681.

__________ An experiment to illustrate the mode of flow of a viscous fluid, *Quarterly Journal of the Geological Society of London* 51, 1895, pp.361-368.

__________ On pitch glaciers or poissiers *Geological Magazine* N.S. dec.4, 2(12), 1895, pp.566-567.

__________ A map to show the distribution of eskers in Ireland, *Transactions of the Royal Dublin Society* Series II, 5(13), 1896, pp.785-822.

STEPHENS, N., AND SYNGE, F.M., Late-Pleistocene shorelines and drift limits in north Donegal, *Proceedings of the Royal Irish Academy* 64B(9), 1965, pp.131-154.

STEWART, D., *The report of Donald Stewart, Itinerant Mineralogist to the Dublin Society*, Dublin 1800, pp.142. The report is also included in *Transactions of the Dublin Society* 1(2), 1799 (published 1800).

STODDART, D.R., Joseph Beete Jukes, the 'Cambridge Connection', and the theory of reef development in Australia in the nineteenth century, *Earth Sciences History* 7(2), 1988, pp.99-110.

SYMES, R.G., On the "Geology and extinct volcanoes of Clermont, Auvergne", *Journal of the Royal Geological Society of Ireland* 3(1), 1871, pp.16-23.

SYMONDS, W.S., Notes of a geologist in Ireland during August and September, 1857, *The Geologist* 1(7&8), 1858, pp.292-296; 330-335.

SYNGE, F.M., The glacial deposits around Trim, Co. Meath, *Proceedings of the Royal Irish Academy* 53B (10), 1950,, pp.99-110.

__________ The glaciation of west Mayo, *Irish Geography* 5(5), 1968, pp.372-386.

TEALL, J.J.H., The drift map of the Dublin area, *Irish Naturalist* 11(11), 1902, pp.274-275.

TOPLEY, W., Report upon national geological surveys: Part I., Europe, *Report of the British Association for the Advancement of Science, Montreal 1884*, pp.221-237.

WHEELER, T.S., Sir Robert Kane: life and work, *Studies* 33, 1944, pp.158-168 and pp.316-330.

__________ Life and work of William K. Sullivan, *Studies* 34, 1945, pp.21-36.

WHITE, H.B., History of the Science and Art Institutions, Dublin, *Department of Agriculture and Technical Instruction for Ireland Journal* 12(1), 1911, pp.117-144.

__________ History of the Science and Art Institutions, Dublin, *Museum Bulletin. National Museum of Science and Art, Dublin* 1(4), 1911, pp.7-34 and 2, 1912, pp.41-44.

WRIGHT, M.C., Limnestheria: a new conchostracan genus from the Kilkenny Coal-Measures, *Proceedings of the Royal Irish Academy* 35B (10), 1920, pp.187-204.

WRIGHT, W.B., Some results of glacial drainage round Montpelier Hill, Co. Dublin, *Scientific Proceeding of the Royal Dublin Society* N.S. 9(48), 1902, pp.575-582.

__________ The glacial origin of Glendoo, *Irish Naturalist* 9(4), 1902, pp.96-102.

______________ AND MUFF, H.B., The pre-glacial raised beach of the south coast of Ireland, *Scientific Proceedings of the Royal Dublin Society* N.S., 10(2), 1904, pp.250-324.

______________________________ The pre-glacial raised beach of the south coast of Ireland, *Irish Naturalist* 13(12), 1904, pp.291-294.

______________ On a preglacial shoreline in the Western Isles of Scotland, *Geological Magazine* N.S., dec 5, 8(3), 1911, pp.97-109.

______________ On the occurrence of submerged forests in certain inland lakes in Donegal, *Geological Magazine* N.S. dec.5, 9(3), 1912, pp.115-120.

______________ The drumlin topography of south Donegal, *Geological Magazine* N.S. dec 5, 9(4), 1912, pp.153-159.

______________ On the Lower Carboniferous succession at Bundoran in south Donegal, *Proceedings of the Geologists' Association* 24(2), 1913, pp.70-77.

______________ An analysis of the Palaeozoic floor of north-east Ireland, with predictions as to concealed coal-fields, *Scientific Proceedings of the Royal Dublin Society* N.S. (45), 1919, pp.629-650.

______________ Minor periodicity in glacial retreat, *Proceedings of the Royal Irish Academy* 35B (6), 1920, pp.93-105.

______________ Age and origin of the Lough Neagh Clays, *Quarterly Journal of the Geological Society of London* 80(4), 1924, pp.468-488.

WYSE JACKSON, P.N., On rocks and bicycles: a biobibliography of Grenville Arthur James Cole (1859-1924) fifth director of the Geological Survey of Ireland, *Geological Survey of Ireland Bulletin* 4(2), 1989, pp.151-163.

INDEX